# The Gentry in England and Wales, 1500–1700

Felicity Heal

and

Clive Holmes

First published 1994 by
THE MACMILLAN PRESS LTD
Houndmills, Basingstoke, Hampshire RG21 2XS
and London
Companies and representatives
throughout the world

ISBN 0–333–52728–3 hardcover
ISBN 0–333–52729–1 paperback

A catalogue record for this book is available
from the British Library.

Copy-edited and typeset by Povey–Edmondson
Okehampton and Rochdale, England

Printed in China

For Bridget, Mike and Phil

# Contents

# Preface and Acknowledgements

This is a volume about the experience of being a gentleman or gentlewoman in early modern England and Wales. It is concerned with mental worlds and expressive gestures; with authority and claims to rulership; and with the ways in which power was employed in this culture. It traces changes of attitude, values and behaviour over a critical period of political and ideological upheaval, when the centralising Tudor monarchy, the Reformation and the débâcle of the Civil War forced the landed élite to engagement and action. In these profound changes the gentry were both agents and victims: they responded to initiative from the political centre, but also held sufficient power to influence and manipulate outcomes.

Studies of the Stuart gentry, in particular, have been overwhelmingly influenced by the desire to locate this key social grouping within the matrix of 'the causes of the Civil War'. The great debate upon the 'rise of the gentry', though largely dormant since the early 1970s, continues to remind historians of the seductive attractions of an interpretation, first mooted by James Harington in the 1650s, that emphasises that social and political aspirations destabilised the English polity and that the gentry in the House of Commons were the prime culprits. Rather more recent studies of the county communities 'in peace and war' also explicitly focus on the power of the gentry, though here historiographical opinion is divided between those who see ideological fractionalism as providing some of the key momentum for war, and those who believe that most communities were bent on isolationist localism. These debates will inevitably play some part in the chapters that follow. It is, however, important to emphasise at the outset that we are not preoccupied with offering yet another explanation for why the Civil War was fought (or why it should not have been contested). Our choice of periodisation is here intended to be significant. Century dates are, of course, a mere convenience, but they can subvert the early modernist's instinct to analyse the long century from 1530 to

1660: from Reformation to Revolution, as one of the county studies puts it. Instead we hope to offer an analysis which links the world of clientage and lordship of late fifteenth-century England to that of the Tudors, and to conclude chronologically in an environment that had ceased to be dominated by the experience of Civil War.

The historian of the sixteenth-century gentry now has the benefit of a decade of impressive publication on the landed élite of the late medieval period. Lordship, patronage and service have been scrutinised at the county and regional level by a generation of historians inspired by the example of Bruce McFarlane. Few comparable studies exist for the Tudor decades: indeed the first half of the sixteenth century might now be designated as the 'dark age' of gentry scholarship, despite the work of Smith on Yorkshire and MacCulloch on Suffolk. Nevertheless, the artificiality, for many purposes, of the late medieval/early modern divide means that it is possible to draw upon the earlier local studies for these decades as well. Thereafter the density of material, both primary and secondary, increases in a remarkable manner, and the rich regional historiography for the early Stuart years offers the possibility of effective synthetic interpretation. Post-Restoration studies have developed in a rather different direction, concentrating upon broad investigations of the whole aristocracy over some *longue durée*, though regional examples remain represented in works such as that of Jenkins on Glamorgan.

Our emphasis on regional studies is very deliberate. Only through an understanding of the gentry in their own *pays*, in the environment in which they logically exercised authority, can we approach a broader interpretation of their social and political significance. But, as one of us has already argued in print, gentry identity transcended the localities. A major part of the story of the English and Welsh élite in these two centuries is that of growing integration into a national culture. Through education, increased mobility and urbanisation, and especially through the intensified attraction of London, gentlemen were reconstructed in ways that distinguished them sharply from their late medieval predecessors. And new political identities demanded engagement in national decision-making, even if loyalties continued to be constructed partially from localist concerns.

We have benefited from discussions with a number of colleagues during the evolution of this volume. Particular thanks are due to members of the Institute of Historical Research's early modern seminar, which has heard both of us on different aspects of this text, and offered valuable ideas and comment. A number of our theories have been tried out on successive generations of undergraduates working on the Oxford optional subject, Nobility and Gentry in England, 1560 to 1680. Both they and colleagues teaching the course have helped to shape our argument. Richard Cust, John Ferris, Perry Gauci, Christopher Haigh, Ann Hughes, Paul Hunneyball, Vivienne Larminie, Diarmaid MacCulloch, Robin Priestley and Alison Wall have offered valuable suggestions at various points in the production of this text. John Morrill read the entire text and provided an extremely helpful commentary. But our greatest debt, which will be very apparent in our citations, is to those writers of books, theses and articles on gentry history, especially on the history of particular counties, without which a work of synthesis of this kind would not be possible. Both of us have had the advantage of sabbatical leave from our college and university posts to complete the volume, and of research grants which have greatly facilitated archival work.

We have received every assistance from many libraries, local history societies, and archives. We would like to acknowledge the help of the following repositories, where we have used books and manuscripts extensively: the Public Record Office: the British Library; the National Library of Wales; the Bodleian Library, Oxford; Cambridge University Library; Nottingham University Library; the Record Offices of Cornwall, Dorset, the Isle of Wight, Kent, Lincolnshire, Northamptonshire, Somerset, Staffordshire, and the West Riding of Yorkshire; and the Yorkshire Archaeological Society, Leeds. Dr J. E. J. Altham kindly arranged for us to see the Altham papers, now in private hands.

Photographs are an integral part of the text: images as well as words were a major part of the self-expression of the gentry and we have endeavoured to use them as an alternative means to communicate their values. We are grateful for help in providing them, especially to Mr A. F. Kersting, on whose architectural photographs we have drawn extensively, and to Mr Edward Johnson, who accompanied us around a number of churches to take those not otherwise available. This would not have been possible if a variety of incumbents and churchwardens had not been helpful in making access easy: since churches now almost invariably have to be locked for security reasons, this can no longer be taken for granted. Bridget Heal and Alison Eastwood provided valuable research assistance.

One of the most satisfying and exciting aspects of this project has been its status as a joint venture. The discerning reader may find within the text slight inconsistencies that indicate areas where we are still not wholly agreed on matters of interpretation. But in general we have hammered out a mutually acceptable and, we hope, a lively and coherent approach. We have dedicated this book to our children who have been audience to, participants in, and arbiters of, many of the dinner-table discussions that have formed the work.

FELICITY HEAL
CLIVE HOLMES

# List of Illustrations

# Introduction

## GENTRY VALUES: SOME PERCEPTIONS

Read and record rare Edmund Fetiplace
A knight right worthy of his rank and race
Whose prudent maneage in two happie raignes
Whose publique service and whose private paines
Whose zeale to God, and towards ill severitie,
Whose temperance, whose iustice, whose sinceritie
Whose native myldnes towards great and small
Whose faith and love to frends, wife, children all
In life and death made him beloved and deer
To God and menn and ever famous heer
Blessed in soule, in bodie, goods and name
In plenteous plants by a most vertuous dame
Who with his heire as to his worth still debtor
Built him this tomb, but in her heart a better.

*Tomb of Sir Edmund Fettiplace, d.1613, Swinbrook, Oxfordshire*

In the rural parish churches of England and Wales lie some hundreds of men like Sir Edmund Fettiplace: marmorealised gentlemen stiffly paraded to the public view, often accompanied by their equally rigid wives and small trails of offspring. Although their knightly predecessors were sometimes commemorated in stone, and their eighteenth- and nineteenth-century successors hung their formal tablets on church walls, it is the gentlemen of Tudor and Stuart England who most assertively demand our attention. If no other evidence had survived about the social structure of early modern England, the tombs would inform us that these men claimed power and influence in their communities and displayed that power proudly in a public context.

Sir Edmund's tomb, however, endeavours more than the representation of influence. The ponderous elegy identifies at least some of the distinctive qualities a gentleman might be expected to possess: justice, temperance, mercy and zeal as a public figure; faith, domestic affection and good household care as a private man. The

1. Tomb of Sir Edmund Fettiplace, d. 1613, and ancestors, Swinbrook Church, Oxfordshire

categorisation is interesting: it depends upon stereotypes ultimately deriving from classical definitions of the cardinal virtues, but it also conveys specifically the vision of gentility that Sir Edmund's family wishes to preserve. Here was a man, they claim, whose public service and religious zeal were defining features of his experience; whose 'rank and race' was legitimated by his actions.

Elegies upon tombs inevitably reflect well and generously upon their subjects. The converse is true of the other form of record most distinctively associated with the gentry, those legal documents produced by the intense litigiousness of the landed classes in early modern England. In legal disputes the gentry reveal themselves unflatteringly as men in avid pursuit of private gain. But, coincidentally, they often offer historians the opportunity to disinter attitudes and behaviours only glimpsed in other forms of evidence. No one case or gentleman can confidently be displayed as paradigmatic. However, occasionally a rich seam of material illuminates far more than the individual participants. This is the situation with Sir Thomas Posthumous Hoby, a gentleman descended from a famous family of learned courtier-knights, who in 1596 married an heiress from the North Riding of Yorkshire, Margaret Dakins. Hoby is an unprepossessing protagonist for any tale – a 'spindle shanked' knight, to quote one of his enemies – whose status as a younger son, carpet-bagging landowner and zealous Puritan seems to have squeezed from him most generous and friendly impulses. His wisest action was his pursuit of Margaret, whom he married as her third husband: her deep Puritan commitments matched his, and, though the diary that she kept refers very formally to her spouse, there does seem to have existed between them a bond of affection and loyalty.[1]

The Hoby household at Hackness was deprived of children, but was otherwise a microcosm of the godly Protestant commonwealth, dominated by prayer and meditation. Lady Hoby lived a cycle of devotion, guided by her chaplain Mr Rhodes; Sir Thomas participated whenever he was at home, and servants and dependants were also expected to conform to the godly discipline. Puritan zeal set the Hobys at odds, however, with many of their neighbours, in an area where Catholicism was still of great influence among the élite. In such an environment, the devotions performed in an important household like that at Hackness became a public challenge to local tradition. Sir Thomas made this explicit by linking his godliness to his attempts to achieve political status within the North Riding. His court connections quickly secured him a place on the bench after his marriage: indeed within a few years he was serving as a justice of the peace in all three regions of Yorkshire, 'a thing', another of his enemies asserted, 'very unusuall and rarely knowne in those parts'. It was far more difficult to translate this success into local power, and Hoby sought to do so by a combination of zealous efficiency and dependence on central authority. He wrested the Liberty of Whitby Strand from the local Cholmley family, reminding his superiors that the North Yorkshire coast was an ideal landing place for seminary priests. By the turn of the century he had firmly lodged in political minds his role as a defender of godly religion. When Hoby was absent, noted one member of the Council of the North in 1599 'the people are wholy defected from religion xx myles along the coste'.[2]

All this had been achieved at the cost of considerable local conflict. Sir Thomas was already an experienced and determined litigant by the time that he brought into Star Chamber in 1600 the action that reveals much about his values and those of his peers. The Cholmleys understandably resented his behaviour and, more seriously, he had alienated the powerful Eure family, hitherto the principal leaders of North Riding society. In 1600 the younger members of the two families hit upon a curious mode of revenge. They invited themselves to the Hoby home at Hackness, on the pretext that they had been hunting in nearby Pickering Forest and were benighted. Once in the house they began, with great deliberation it would seem, to subvert its godly order; playing cards, singing and drinking heavily. They may have engaged in blasphemous counter-ritual while the servants were at prayer, though it is equally possible they were simply roaring drunk by this time and full of bawdy talk. Next morning they were still riotous, overturning tables, breaking the odd window-pane, damaging a newly laid driveway and insulting their hosts. Mr Rhodes, fortunately absent, was a particular target: Sir William Eure was said to have threatened that 'he woold have gelded him' given the opportunity.[3]

Sir Thomas apparently felt himself bound by traditional ideals of hospitality, and unable to evict his guests until they reached the stage of insulting Lady Hoby. Thereafter his wounded sense of honour was given full rein. He appealed first to the Council of the North and directly to his cousin Sir Robert Cecil in London. When neither provided him with full satisfaction he turned to Star Chamber, thus providing himself with the opportunity to parade his grievances before the Privy Council. The formal complaint was that the young gentlemen had been riotous, thus both disturbing Sir Thomas and threatening the public peace. The substance of Hoby's case, pursued vigorously through detailed interrogatories, was that in impugning a gentleman's honour within his household, that microcosm of the commonwealth, the guests were also impugning public honour. This was affirmed, in his view, by the failure of Lord Eure, as President of the Council of the North, to bind the offending parties to the peace. Instead he claimed that Eure had talked of duels, and said that he must 'know that menn hadd not swordes onelie to weare, but sometimes to drawe them to defende theire reputacions'.[4]

It would be easy to present Sir Thomas's litigation as a clash between old and new systems and values, between authority, law and religious obedience as defined at the centre and more anarchic, even neo-feudal, behaviours among the northern élite. There would be some truth in this reading: it is, as already suggested, the one that Hoby himself employed when communicating with the Council. But in practice much of the interest of the dispute for an understanding of the gentry lies in the way in which both plaintiff and defendants utilised a mixture of ideas in the service of their local position. Sir Thomas was clear that in order to exercise power he needed to subscribe to essentially the same honour values as his opponents. The fact that, according to his enemies, he 'came over the water with his coch and three horses butt all scante worth sixpence' made such identification all the more urgent. He was as eager to assert that he gave his unwanted guests hospitality 'answerable unto their several birthes and callinges' as to criticise them for appearing unbidden. Moreover, while he was dismayed by the partiality of the Council of the North, Hoby for a time apparently thought it wise to submit to its informal arbitration, sealing a temporary friendship by coming 'in kindnes and good neighborhood' to visit the Eures. The Eures in their turn were careful to appeal to the sensitivities of the Council not only by denying the perversion of local and regional justice, but by minimising the role of those whom Hoby contemptuously called 'the[ir] kinsfolks, and allyes, servants, reteynors, followers and especiall friends'[5]

Sir Thomas Hoby achieved his victory: the unwanted guests were reproved in the very public forum of Star Chamber. But the pattern of feud was not broken, and bitter dispute with the Cholmleys, Hilyards, Constables and other local families continued. No doubt the rioters also achieved part of their purpose: in a society in which the gentry still depended heavily on a culture of honour, a public shaming of the Hackness kind was not readily forgotten. In his national dealings with godly divines like Laurence Chaderton and

William Gouge, Hoby could present himself with much conviction as a leader of lay Puritanism. In the north he was always viewed with more suspicion: some observers like Sir William Brereton praised him as 'the most understanding, able and industrious justice of peace in this kingdome'. More thought of him as a meddlesome prig, a disturber of the peace whose vendettas subverted proper royal government in the North Riding. And these many enemies always had at their disposal the story of the ritual humiliation of 'little Sir Thomas' who strutted in his 'greate britches'.[6]

The story of Sir Thomas Hoby and his enemies focuses many of the issues and ideas to which this study is addressed. His social position, and the political advantages he derived from it, allowed him to wield great local influence and maintain himself in the face of considerable hostility. He deployed his knowledge of law, as well as of the late Elizabethan Court, to advance his interests, and he possessed a religious ideology that was held passionately and that presumably gave him a dualistic view of the world that sustained him in his local battles. He represented in North Yorkshire the new and intrusive – a new faith, a metropolitan perspective, an intensified adherence to the bureaucratic apparatus of government. He challenged older networks and affinities constructed to maintain control by the established families. In some senses, Sir Thomas appears as one of R. H. Tawney's 'rising' gentry, while his opponents, like the Cholmleys, fit the model of Trevor-Roper's 'mere' gentry. But, as we have already suggested, the case of Sir Thomas indicates that things are not exactly as they seem. His aspirations, if we except religion, were not fundamentally different from those of his rivals: he sought local power, employing his connections as an appropriate lever to acquire it. The Eures and Cholmleys, meanwhile, were equally likely to seek metropolitan intervention in their quarrels, to use the leverage of the law and the Council to achieve their ends. In much of the ensuing volume we shall pursue the tension between the powerful desire for continuity and stability that characterised the landed élite, and their ability to adapt to the changes of two profoundly disturbing centuries.[7]

## WHO WERE THE GENTRY?

Although the unique and particular case can serve to illuminate behaviour, it is also necessary to establish general parameters in any study of a social group. Who were the gentry? Contemporaries offered a variety of answers to this deceptively simple question. 'What a gentleman is', wrote Selden, ''tis difficult with us to define, in other countries he is known by his privileges, in Westminster Hall he is one that is reputed one, in the Court of Honour he that hath arms'. Most commentators started, as do most historians, from the affirmation that all non-noble landowners with some claim to exercise lordship or jurisdiction were unquestionably gentlemen. 'Authority', remarked Sir William Temple, 'is much observed to follow land'. The ability to live on the land without manual labour, to 'live idly' as William Harrison put it more perjoratively, might be a further defining characteristic at a time when manorial and local jurisdictional structures were in decline. But such formulations, it would have been acknowledged, were neither necessary nor sufficient for the drawing of a boundary around the social group. In 1500 the claim to gentility based upon land was still, in its lower reaches, somewhat fragile. Historians of the fifteenth century have shown that lesser landowners had only gradually been able to sustain a claim to status against crown and noble perceptions that stressed office and service as the key route to honour. Although this ceased to be a major problem under the Tudors, when local estimations of standing were more readily accepted by the heralds as a test of the right to bear arms, there were always ambiguities at the margin. Among the parish élites claims of an individual to status had to be validated by gestures of gentility and supported by the readings of the local community. In 1638 a plaintiff before the High Court of Chivalry was said to be no gentleman because he worked in husbandry and 'in the parish rates and other writings he is only written Richard Inckpen without the addition of gentleman to his name'.[8]

If land, lordship and local acknowledgement were the key determinants of gentle status, there is still the problem of those groups who claimed gentility without these attributes. The most important of these were the professionals, crown servants and lawyers, doctors, teachers and academics and, especially after the Reformation, the married clergy. Here we have Harrison's famous and clear statement that all these, except perhaps the last, were accounted and taken for gentlemen because of the liberal nature of their employment. We may be tempted to regard this as a consequence of the social mobility of Elizabethan England, but at least some of these groups, especially officials and lawyers, had had little difficulty in claiming gentle status a century or more before. However, there are throughout this period subtle distinctions to be drawn within this growing band of professionals. Their status was scarcely seen as homogeneous: parish clergy and teachers in particular existed in an uncomfortable limbo, partly because of lay attitudes to the Church after the Reformation, partly because few were able to confirm their standing through access to land. At the other extreme, barristers often came from propertied families, made significant fortunes and strengthened their status claims by land purchase. Gregory King's categorisation of the élite at the end of the seventeenth century underlines these contrasts effectively: sergeants at law and deans of cathedrals were placed beneath the knights but above the esquires, barristers were ranked with the esquires, all other clergy, and the lesser members of the other professions, were separated into their own hierarchies.[9]

Even greater ambiguities surround the merchants and urban oligarchies. Harrison, despite his catholic definitions of status, did not contemplate including the urban élites, mainly because of the means by which they generated wealth. The London aldermen were usually accorded armigerous status without question, and there was always some interest in accepting high ranking townsmen as part of the honour community, not least because younger sons of landed families were so often apprenticed to merchants. The permeability of the urban–rural divide makes formal categorisation difficult. The career of Denis Bond, esquire, Mayor of radical Dorchester in the 1630s, is exemplary. His family held an estate on the Isle of Purbeck, though his father John only gained outright possession of it in 1616. John was four times Mayor of Weymouth, then spent his last years in the country. Denis, his heir, never lived on the Isle, and leased out the property after his father's death, yet proudly asserted his pedigree before the heralds in 1623 as that of Bond of Lutton. Two important points emerge from this example: firstly that it was not difficult for men whose wealth and power remained largely mercantile to claim gentle status; secondly that the full affirmation of this standing was still dependent on access to office and landed territory. Without property, James Harrington warned, money would 'lightly come, lightly go'. However, the full growth of what Everitt has labelled the 'pseudo-gentry', dependent on urban forms of wealth but in mores and style indistinguishable from their rural neighbours, was delayed until after the Restoration. By the end of the seventeenth century social observers like Celia Fiennes and

Daniel Defoe recognised that urban prosperity was producing a large corpus of families who could legitimately claim gentility. Celia Fiennes found Shrewsbury full of an 'abundance of people of quality', while for Defoe Exeter was 'full of gentry and good company'.[10]

Flexible definitions of gentility were a necessary feature of the rather mobile society of early modern England. Though lineage was always desirable, some standing could be constructed out of wealth and consolidated by the holding of acres: 'first riches, and then honour, for it is lightly found . . . and reputation is measured by the acre' said Thomas Adams in the early seventeenth century. Sir Thomas Smith, in his analysis of gentle status that followed closely upon Harrison, remarked that without the solid basis of property and wealth underpinning his claims a would-be gentleman 'will beare a bigger saile than he is able to maintaine'. Wealth was for Smith the main guarantee of social position. Status was also articulated by the holding of office: for by a humanist extension of the old idea that lordship was a necessary part of gentility came the assertion that it must be an essential attribute of the new forms of governorship, as a justice of the peace (JP) or other local official.[11]

It is scarcely surprising that these adaptable models did not command universal approbation. Humanists and reformers, who sought to revivify the old idea that 'true nobility is made by virtue rather than a long pedigree', recognised the importance of service to the commonwealth as a test of standing, but were ambiguous about the dominance of wealth. Others feared the whole concept of mobility. For them blood lineage and the ability to exercise martial skills remained the foundation of true nobility. The heraldic writers were predictable exponents of these last views: John Ferne, in his *Blazon of Gentrie* (1586), deferred to humanist sentiment upon virtue, but directed his argument to 'the gentlemen of blood'. Merchants, he urged, must be excluded from the privileges of gentle status except 'there concurreth also some notable collaterall desert to his countrye, arising from some branch of the Cardinall vertues'. Edward Chamberlayn in the early editions of his *Angliae Notitia* (1669 to 1692) denounced the habit of putting younger sons to apprenticeship as 'a perfect servitude . . . [bearing] the marks of slavery' wholly unworthy of a landed class. Ferne, following his fellow herald Robert Glover, also thought that the élite should be divided along traditional lines: esquires, often by this period accepted as the wealthier members of the landed élite, should be hereditary figures

– eldest sons of peers or knights – or senior office-holders such as sheriffs and escheators. These restrictive views of the social order were understandably popular with those who had a vested interest in ancient blood, and tended to be reiterated most vigorously at times of crisis. The Civil War and Restoration, in particular, produced a rich harvest of conservative theorists who blamed the political trauma they had experienced on excessive social mobility, and on the corrosive effects of wealth upon good order. Yet practice in gentry communities usually seems closer to Smith than to Ferne, or rather it was flexible in incorporating those elements of contemporary theory that best suited local circumstance. The Hoby case suggests that a man who offended communal definitions of proper gentility could be assailed as an upstart despite his perfectly valid claims to high family status and coat armour. Richard Gough, writing of local Shropshire families at the end of the seventeenth century, underlines the centrality of behaviour as a means of gaining social acknowledgement. The Harris family of Boreatton and the Edwards of Greet were both of lowly origin, both rose to baronetcies in the first half of the seventeenth century. The latter family 'make no great figure in town or country', but were accepted for their generally good behaviour; the former were resented because their head was a 'proud imperious person', loved by neither gentry nor commoners, who called him 'a buck of the second head'.[12]

With such a diversity of possible criteria serving to define the gentleman, it is hardly surprising that the task of evaluating the total size of the group is well-nigh impossible. Contemporary understandings change somewhat over our two centuries, and there are moreover no forms of record-keeping that are sufficiently standardised or consistent to offer appropriate norms. Tax records, the most promising source, are useful for comparisons over shorter periods – the subsidy, for example, has much value for the reigns of Henry VIII and early Elizabeth. Heraldic visitations, superficially the most relevant for the gentry, are, as we shall argue below, of very limited utility after the Restoration and of variable quality before that date. County studies by historians employing a wide range of sources are undoubtedly of most assistance in minimising these interpretative difficulties, but their chronological as well as their geographical range is usually limited. Those existing on the margins of gentility inevitably remain elusive: a recent study of four Lancashire parishes, for example, found only 3 gentlemen listed in the 1585 Protestant Association oath, but 37 in the slightly later freeholders' books. A careful study of gentry housing in three Norfolk regions concludes that often it was only the most minor stylistic variations that singled out these houses from others of the 'great rebuilding' period. Moreover, circumstance altered definition: taxation by status, as in the poll ratings of 1641 and 1691, was likely to change the attitude of those making grandiloquent claims to rank. 'It were worth any wise man's laughter', reported a Cheshire correspondent in 1641, 'to see how these apple esquires that gloried in the title do now assume humility and a lower style.' In 1691 only two individuals were taxed as gentlemen in the whole of Merioneth and Caernarfonshire although, as it was noted in Parliament, the counties appeared to have their proper complement of high sheriff, two MPs and eight JPs apiece.[13]

Precision is impossible: the general pattern of change is much easier to determine. The sixteenth century witnessed a growth in the total number of families claiming gentle status, a growth that outstripped general population increase in the same period. Since status and public office were so closely linked, the extension in royal administration was added to the dissolution of the monasteries and the expansion of the land market to increase the number of armigerous families. Conservative figures for Yorkshire, all based on heraldic visitations, show 557 armigerous families in 1558, 641 in 1603 and 679 in 1642. For Warwickshire, figures calculated on a similar basis by separate studies give 155 families in 1500, 288 in 1642. A more extreme suggestion is that Somerset gentry numbers quadrupuled between 1502 and 1623, without any significant shift in the criteria defining gentility in that region. As a percentage of the population, figures of this kind seem to have ranged at the turn of the sixteenth century from under 1 per cent for Yorkshire to more than 3 per cent for Lancashire. In the seventeenth century the story is less consistently one of growth: it has been argued, on the basis of tax returns, that the Lancashire gentry actually declined in numbers from 763 to 662, while for Huntingdonshire the small gentry community identified by the heraldic visitations apparently contracted from 60 families to 53 between 1613 and 1684. The troubles of the mid-century, the fall in farming profits from the 1670s and the relatively heavy incidence of taxation in the 1690s, all placed pressure on smaller landowners and contributed to consolidation or decline in gentry numbers.[14]

It would, however, be surprising, given the growing flexibility of social categorisation, and the diversity of routes by which gentility might be acquired, if these seventeenth-century figures told the whole story. National estimates have been treated with intense suspicion by recent historians, but in all their crudeness they give a powerful aggregate image of increase. In 1524, at the time of the subsidy assessments, there may have been approximately 200 knightly families, and 4,000–5,000 lesser esquires and gentlemen. Wilson in 1600 gives figures of 500 knights and 16,000 esquires and gentlemen; King at the end of the century 780 baronets, 620 knights, 3,000 to 3,500 esquires and between 12,000 and 20,000 gentlemen. Wilson's figures are certainly inflated, and those of King obviously range very widely, but even savage deflation of both would leave intact the argument for expanding numbers, perhaps multiplying four times over while the population at large rather more than doubled.[15]

Landholding and wealth are perhaps more interesting issues than mere numbers. Estimating aggregate acres under gentry control inevitably involves building 'guestimates' upon one another, and is complicated by the fact that estate size did not correlate neatly with social status. This means that great landowners, including peers and the richest gentry, are separated from lesser landowners, who may include non-gentlemen as well as substantial knights and esquires. The estimates can best be made in 1436, when there was a national income tax assessment and again in 1688 from Gregory King's figures. The percentage of land in the hands of the greater landowners may have stayed broadly the same between these dates, at between 15 and 20 per cent, but the property of the lesser owners rose, from about 25 per cent, at the earlier date to 45 or 50 per cent at the end of the seventeenth century. The clear losers in this transfer were the Crown and the Church, which between them retained only 5 to 10 per cent of cultivable acreage.

Another rough estimate, that at the accession of Elizabeth the knights may have held as much as 8 per cent of the cultivated territory of the realm, is revealing of their power if we recall that they were less than 10 per cent of the gentry population. Rather more precise insight into the gentry's access to power may be found in Everitt's estimates for Kentish families in 1640. There baronets, knights, and other gentlemen held approximately 32 per cent of the county's wealth, as compared to only 5 per cent in the hands of the peerage.[16]

Another important component of gentry political and social influence is their geographical distribution. Some counties were more obtrusively gentrified than others, and even within counties there are marked differences created by medieval patterns of ownership and by land type. Stone and Stone suggested that a very crude index of gentry spread in the later seventeenth century might be produced by expressing the number of large houses – with twenty or more hearths listed in the hearth tax – as a proportion of a county's acreage. This generates figures such as an index of five, for Surrey, the most densely gentrified county, and 393 for Pembrokeshire, which had scarcely any great houses. Even as a crude indicator these figures present difficulty; Welsh gentlemen, for example, were not short of lineage pride, or a willingness to display the authority of an élite: they simply lacked cash for grand building. It is more satisfactory to look closely at county studies which have examined the distribution of resident gentry. These produce some striking results: MacCulloch, for example, shows that in Suffolk, where there was a large gentry population, uneven distribution meant that 58 per cent of communities still had no resident gentleman in the early years of Elizabeth's reign. A century later Glamorgan had gentlemen of some kind in each parish, but with an extraordinarily strong concentration of power towards the coastal plain where all the greater estates of the county were located. By the second half of the period lesser gentry might congregate several families to a parish in favoured areas: the Ealing census of 1599 lists seven gentlemen; Gough's village of Myddle had ten gentlemen in the last years of the seventeenth century. This distribution of the landed élite has resonances far beyond their own ranks: political control and social organisation were profoundly influenced by the presence or absence of a resident squirearchy.[17]

Thus far our crude calculations of numbers, control of land and geographical diffusion seem to represent a justification of the old thesis of the rise of the gentry. But the story is more complex than this suggests. In particular, the broadening of the social group occurred within a relatively fixed hierarchical structure of power and wealth. The three status categories of knights, esquires and gentlemen, afforced at the top after 1611 by the newly created baronets, remained rather sharply separated in patterns of landholding and median wealth. By the early Tudor period wealth had become a major criterion for the creation of knights: Smith argued that they were now elevated 'according to their substance and riches . . . most commonly according to the yearly revenue of their lands'. Feodary surveys for the 1520s confirm this pattern: in a group of 185 surveys studied by Dr Cornwall, knights had a median income from land of £204 per annum, esquires £80 and gentlemen £17. It is worth noting that the knights in their turn were sharply divided from the peers, whose median income at the same date was between £800 and £900. Although the serendipidous process by which various monarchs promoted men to the rank of knight changed the correlation between wealth and status somewhat, there was still a proximity between the two on the eve of the Civil War. Then 73 of the Yorkshire families studied by Cliffe, using sequestration and composition records, had incomes of over £1,000 per annum, and most were of knightly status; 238 had revenues of less than £100, and none were knights. Yorkshire knights had an average income of £1,097, lesser gentlemen £270. At the same date Kentish knights had an average income of £873, while lesser squires and gentlemen had only £270. Stone calculates that in 1641 the mean net income of the peerage was over £5,000.[18]

While these aggregate figures suggest that many of the élite survived the century of price rise successfully, they also underline the sharp contrasts of wealth within the landed hierarchy. If we add regional differences to those of status group the contrasts become acute. It has been estimated that in the 1540s it was possible to maintain a claim to gentle status in Caernarfonshire on as little as £3 per annum from land. A century later this would clearly have been an impossibility, but Welsh gentlemen still survived on revenues that would have been unthinkable in southern England. Major-General Berry remarked to Secretary Thurlow in the 1650s: 'I find by experience, that the gentlemen of Wales have more honour than inheritance; and you will sooner find 50 men of 50l *per annum* than five of an hundred'. The proverb retailed by Celia Fiennes 'a Yeoman of Kent with one year's Rent could buy out the Gentlemen of Wales . . . and a Lord of the North Country', is an exaggeration, but one that contains some kernel of truth. On the eve of the Civil War it was still possible to make an effective claim to gentry status in Cheshire and Shropshire with revenues of £50 per annum or occasionally less. But even where slightly greater wealth was needed to sustain status it is important to recognise that the effect of the expansion of gentry numbers was to leave a large total of individuals near the bottom of the pyramid. Our aggregate figures for land ownership and wealth suggest that estates must have become smaller in the century preceding the Civil War, and the struggle to achieve gentility at the margins more intense.[19]

Contemporaries acknowledged the significance of a correlation of wealth and status, and roughly equated knights, esquires and gentlemen to upper, middling and lesser gentlemen. In terms of authority the first group was identified as the county élite, dominating the magistracy and high office, and usually possessing economic interests that extended beyond a limited locality. Since an average landed estate for a knight in 1524 was approximately 6,000 acres, these interests might well transcend county as well as manorial boundaries. Most of the senior gentry whom we shall encounter in this study had a firm locus of power in one principal seat, but manipulated property far more widely to advance their economic interests. The esquires were still formally those who had a duty to administer justice for the Crown, but were also accorded status because of wealth and ancient descent. In Cumberland and Westmorland, for example, half the esquires of 1600 headed families that had been established before 1536: a far higher proportion than the ordinary gentlemen. A 'mere' gentleman was less likely to hold public office, and far more likely to have economic interests confined to one manor or parish. Most historians of the county communities have found that the three-tier model serves as a valuable, if crude, analytical tool for the separation of groups within the broad ranks of the gentry.[20]

The evidence of wealth, land and office-holding seems to point to a lack of identity between the various ranks of the gentry. We need, however, to consider why it was possible for contemporaries to embrace these diverse individuals within one linguistic category; a category that retained much of its relevance through two centuries of social upheaval. An obvious possibility is that it was clearly separated from those above and below, peers on the one hand and yeomen on the other. Perhaps the most common argument advanced against the notion of the gentry as an integrated group is that no such demarcation can be established at the upper end of the social spectrum. The peerage might possess distinction of title, but their behaviour, values and even wealth differed little from that of the greater gentry. Contemporary analysts like Sir Thomas Smith lend some support to this latter view by associating the 'greater' and 'lesser' nobles under the broad categorisation of 'those who rule'. We should probably accept that neither peers nor gentlemen could have been seen as part of social classes, with the antagonism that inevitably implies in Marxist analysis. Their structure as status groups means that rigidity in classification was matched by easy boundary fluidity and low inter-group aggression. The creations of the early Stuart period, the Irish and Scottish peerages and the baronetcies, at least in their first years, existed upon the status boundary. But a deep awareness of hierarchy did ensure that difference was maintained conceptually and was regarded as defining social behaviour. Sir William Holles was reluctant to marry his daughter to an earl for he did not 'like to stand with . . . cap in . . . hand to [his] son in law'. He preferred 'an honest gentleman with whome I may have friendship and conversation.' The gentlemen of Norfolk who paid court to the dukes of Norfolk at Kenninghall each Christmas, or those of Lancashire who greeted the earls of Derby at the borders of the county on their return to their home territory, were expressing an equally powerful sense of distinction. Secondly, peers and gentlemen only associated in certain contexts: many counties, in much of our period, for example, managed their political affairs without a resident magnate. Court nobles and court gentlemen no doubt shared closer identities than many, but even they were likely to be differentiated by role and scale of interest. It may well be that the shared values of landownership and the desire for political control transcended these contrasts, but they were present and were invoked by contemporaries to explain more than the central political division between peers and commoners.[21]

The lower boundary is at once easier and more complex to define: the important issue here is that contemporaries, even in 1700, acknowledged that an important division existed. Gregory King's description of gentlemen and 'reputed gentlemen' evokes both the relevance and the awkwardness of the social category. Gentlemen were bound together partly by a recognition that they distinguished themselves in a variety of fundamental ways from those 'beneath' them. Smith summed the matter up with his usual concision: 'a gentleman must go like a gentleman, a yeoman like a yeoman, and a rascall like a rascall'. As we have seen, the reality was more complex because individuals at the margin of gentility could define themselves, and be defined by others, as belonging to the higher status group or not according to circumstance. These gentlemen/yeomen had, in Morrill's words, to add together a certain 'score' of the characteristics of the gentleman before the criteria of contemporaries were met. But the difficulty of placing individuals, and the almost total fluidity of marginal classifications does not mean that this boundary was not real.[22]

Definition in comparison to others provides, however, only rather weak arguments for gentry homogeneity. Much of the time the parochial gentry must have existed in very different social worlds from the county élites. Nevertheless in key areas such as family identity and kinship no absolute hierarchical division can be made meaningful. Friendship, marriage, education, regional sentiment, and longevity of settlement all blurred the formal status categories established to demarcate elements within the gentry. Moreover, there existed 'a landed interest' long before the phrase itself became current in the eighteenth century. Land and the need to secure its descent produced a commonalty of political and legal beliefs: lordship, still in some measure inherent in land, encouraged similar views on authority.

All these material connections are necessary manifestations of some form of group identity. But they do not seem sufficient without the addition of the less tangible quality of gentility. 'Prithee, son,' says the newly gentrified Old Shepherd in *The Winter's Tale*, 'we must be gentle now we are gentlemen'. Of course he has no chance of assuming the true mantle of gentility and becomes one of the endless victims of the playwrights' desire to satirise social aspiration. Yet the ethical code to which he appeals surely underpins the homogeneity of the gentry. In the hands of the humanists that code was a demanding combination of virtue, learning and good birth. Richard Brathwait, a Caroline author of tracts on gentility, described the code as issuing in virtuous action which was the *essential* fruit of good birth. The frontispieces to his *English Gentleman* and *English Gentlewoman* embody the 'Englishing' of this humanist ideal. The gentleman stands planted with his feet firmly on his land, with his hope in heaven: his rearing, service to the commonwealth, godly behaviour and cultivated leisure all express the principle of virtue. The lady plays, predictably, a less public role, in which the cultivation of private spirituality, prudence, wisdom and sexual integrity predominate.

Yet despite the intense efforts of such conduct writers and of religious reformers to establish elaborated patterns of gentle behaviour, the basic cultural identities that bound the élite together were probably less demanding. They might be summed up as adherence to a code of honour, and a willingness to display appropriate 'port and countenance'. These qualities could readily be demonstrated in those environments that brought the gentry into routine contact with one another: the household, the hunting field,

2. Frontispiece from Richard Brathwait, *The English Gentleman* (1630)

the parish church, quarter sessions and assizes. Acceptance by others that one was part of the honour community was, as the Hoby case suggests, a major concern of the gentleman. Even when, towards the end of our period, that community began to weaken and to be replaced by a notion of polite society, the preoccupation

3. Frontispiece from Richard Brathwait, *The English Gentlewoman* (1631)

with drawing social boundaries, and locating oneself firmly within them, remained. At the risk of tautology we therefore must conclude that the gentry were that body of men and women whose gentility was acknowledged by others.[23]

# 1

# Lineage

In his 'Advice to his Descendants' Sir John Oglander asked,

> Wouldest thou feign see me, being dead so many years since? I will give thee my own character. Conceive thou sawest an aged, somewhat corpulent, man of middle stature, with a white beard and somewhat big mustachios, riding in black or some sad-coloured clothes from West Nunwell up to the West Downs, and so over all the Downs to take the air . . . and to see there his fatting cattle, on a handsome middling black stone-horse, his hair grey and his complexion very sanguine.

This wry verbal portrait in its easy, pastoral setting contrasts markedly with the more public image that Oglander chose to erect in Brading Church. The military and 'medieval' effigy that Sir John designed for himself is stiffly formal, pompous in its anachronism. Yet from Oglander's various reflections in his notebooks and journals we can begin to comprehend this alternative, apparently incongruous, self-presentation.

Sir John took great pride in his ancient descent. Of his family, he wrote:

> The de Oglanders are as ancient as any family in the Isle of Wight. They came in with the Conqueror out of Normandy . . . And there have not wanted knights also to this family, but I confess they were of better esteem the first hundred years immediately after the Conquest than they have been since. Yet this is their comfort – that they have have not only matched and given wives to most of the ancient families of the Island, but that the name is still extant in a lineal descent from father to son, which I wish may long continue.

And again, more directly in his 'Advice to his Descendants',

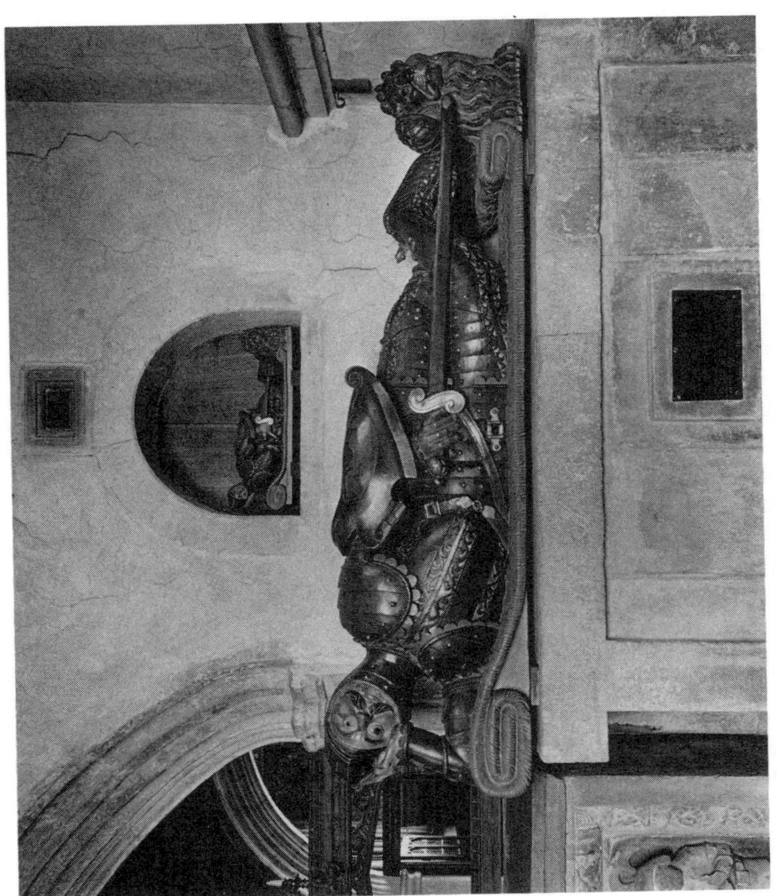

4. Effigy of Sir John Oglander, d. 1655, Brading Church, Isle of Wight

> We have kept this spot of ground this five hundred years from father to son, and I pray God thou beest not the last, nor see that scattered which so many have taken care to gain for thee.

Yet Sir John's jottings embody more than a superficial vanity in his Norman 'de Oglander' ancestors. His sentiments are both deeper and more troubled. It is the antiquity of his family *and* the continuity of its possession of their Nunwell estate which Oglander emphasises. *Lineage*, the conjunction of blood and tenure, defines and legitimises individual status. Oglander's contemporary, the Worcestershire gentleman William Higford, advising his grandson in the 1650s, wrote in a similar vein. Having invoked the great Socratic injunction, 'Know thyself', Higford turned immediately to the legal documents that detailed his family's ancient possession of their estate; these deeds were both 'the very nerves and sinews of your estate', and displayed how 'your ancestors'. . . blood runneth in your veins'. The individual is seen as standing at the apex of a double helix intertwining land and blood. Lineage also creates a web both of privileges and of duties. The latter are to friends, neighbours, tenants, servants – but pre-eminently to the lineage itself. Higford warns his grandson 'every acre of land you sell you lose so much gentile blood' and enjoins 'take notice you are but a trustee for others'. Oglander also insists that the key responsibility is to the continuation of the lineage, or 'house' as he calls it, of which the current holder of the estate is representative and beneficiary.

> Be sure, whatsoever misfortune befalls thee, sell not thy land, which was with much care and pain provided and kept for thee and hath continued so many ages in thy name. Rather feed on bread and water than be the confusion of thy house . . . Observe this above all.

Behind the boasts in lineage apparent in their writings and in Oglander's tomb, both he and Higford display an uneasy awareness of the fragility of the family–land conjunction; heirs must be warned against becoming 'the confusion of thy house'. Both men's apprehension was undoubtedly a product of the Interregnum. Higford's work is shot through with a nostalgia for a vanished era of Elizabethan splendour, recalling the glorious Queen 'with a train of ladies like stars in the firmament'. Oglander referred bitterly to his own imprisonment and dismissal from office during the Civil War, to the 'affronts and disgraces put upon me' when he and the rest of the Wight gentry 'lived in slavery and submission to the unruly, base multitude'. In Yorkshire, Oglander wrote, a hundred families of the ancient gentry were ruined by the war, 'so that none of them could appear again as gentlemen . . . and so many base men, by the other's loss and slaughter, made gentlemen'. The tenuous nature of the hold of gentry families upon their lands and their social power was more acutely apparent in the 1640s and 50s, and this may explain both commentators' particular emphases. Yet the phenomenon was recognised before the peculiar circumstances of the Civil War and its aftermath. Oglander knew it from his antiquarian researches into the history of the Isle of Wight.

> Great Rookelie of Rookeley . . . one of the Antientist Gentlemen and of the best estate in owre Islande. There were many knyghtes of the name, butt for want of Issue male to proppe it up, that greate house fell and in the fall divers gott shares on whom the lawe threwe itt. There's only one left now in the Island of that name, but havinge his share in these fortunes, hath lost also his Gentillitie.

Again, writing of owners of Quarr Abbey and its estates after the Henrician dissolution of the monasteries,

> Then came Sir Richard Milles, who sold it for nothing to Sir Thomas Fleming, Lord Chief Justice of the King's Bench, whose father was a merchant in Newport and the most miserable of men. . . So now you may see how this great abbey of Quarr . . . is come to the posterity of a merchant of Newport. *O tempora, O Mores!* Such is the inconstancy of Fortune, which, by the aid of her servant Time, pulleth down great things and setteth up poor things.

For Oglander gentle status and the prerogatives that it enjoyed are pre-eminently a product of lineage, of an ancient family's long possession of ancestral lands. And yet that relationship was fragile. Ancient families decayed; 'base men' succeeded to their estates. 'Such is the inconstancy of Fortune.' This tension, so apparent in Oglander's writings, between a status that was legitimised by antiquity of blood and estate and the observed facts of social change, is a theme that we will pursue more generally.[1]

## 1.1 LINEAGE CONCEPTS OF STATUS: PRACTICAL CONSTRAINTS

A definition of status that turned on the antiquity and continuity of a man's family always sat uneasily with hard demographic realities. Sir Adrian Scrope's statement, that he lived on in his children, was a rarer boast than we might imagine. At the close of the fifteenth century a landowner stood only a 70 per cent chance of having a son or a grandson as his legal heir. This figure is similar to that obtaining at the turn of the thirteenth century, though it had fallen far lower, almost to 50 per cent, in the half-century of high infant mortality following the Black Death of the mid-fourteenth century. In the seventeenth century the chance rose slightly, to nearly 75 per cent, but this still implied a high turnover rate among the landed classes. Between 1611 and 1623 King James granted the hereditary title of baronet to 203 leading gentry families. By 1700, 28 per cent of the titles had died out through the total failure of male heirs of the original grantee; in only 34 per cent could a family show a direct father to son lineal descent from the first baronet to the possessor of the title in 1700. Local studies reveal a similar general phenomenon, though with significant local and chronological variations. In Nottinghamshire 13 of the 45 knightly families resident in 1325 had failed in the male line by 1400, and a further eighteen failed in the next century; in Yorkshire nearly a fifth of the gentry families residing in the county between the accession of Elizabeth and the outbreak of the Civil War died out in the male line by 1642; a 'strange fatality' afflicted the Glamorgan gentry in the century after 1670, and 19 of the 31 great estates changed owners through the failure of male heirs.[2]

Genetic misfortune was an enduring element in the experience of gentry families, which cruelly mocked the boasted antiquity of their houses. Indeed, some of the most elaborate statements of pride in lineage were made by those whose families teetered at the edge of the abyss of oblivion. William Holcott, who willed that wherever he might die his heart was to be buried at Buckland, Berkshire, erected an inscription 'Hereby lineally resteth to rise againe the bodies of', and followed it with his own name and those of twelve Holcotts back to 1292. William died childless in 1575, leaving the loved ancestral estate to his sister's son – who quickly sold up to a Londoner. Gabriel Poyntz in 1606 erected wall monuments in the church of North Ockendon, Essex to himself, to his son who had

5. Detail of panel on monument to Sir Adrian Scrope, d. 1623, South Cockerington Church, Lincolnshire

predeceased him, and, on a smaller scale, to each of his six ancestors back to the fourteenth-century progenitor of the family in the parish; next year he was succeeded by his daughter's son. Sir George St Paul's boast on his Snarford, Lincolnshire tomb, 'the ninth heire male by linealle discent that hath possessed this house and manor', rang hollow, for he was childless. Poyntz and St Paul desperately sought by artifice to shore up their ancient lineage against malignant nature. Sir George left a considerable proportion of his estate to a Yorkshire gentleman who shared his name, but who was of the most remote, if any, kinship to him; Gabriel Poyntz insisted that the inheritor of his Ockendon estate should adopt the family name – Sir James Maurice *alias* Poyntz.[3]

Family continuity was most at risk from genetic chance, but estates could also be lost by the incompetence or misfortune of the occupier – hence the solemn injunctions of Oglander and Higford to their heirs. Many family histories and memoirs retailed horror stories of the black sheep who had risked the ruin of their lineage by personal irresponsibility. Gervase Holles, celebrating the greatness achieved by the branch of the family that sprang from Sir William Holles of Houghton, Nottinghamshire, could set as a counterpoint the rapid fall of the branch of the family stemming from Sir William's equally well-endowed elder brother, Sir Thomas. The latter was 'by his lavishnes and improvidence the ruine both of himselfe and his posterity', and his great-grandson, in consequence, was 'forced to beg his bread in the streetes of London amongst other poore children'; 'wee shall hardly finde . . . a greater example of Fortune's mutability'. Sir Christopher Guise trembled as he related the the excesses of his wastrel ancestor, Anselm Guise, a Henrician courtier, 'vaynly and wickedly spending his estate in luxury,' whose lusts were still the subject of Gloucestershire ballads over a century later 'to the terror of others and a warning to avoyd Courts and courtiers'. Sir Christopher was particularly appalled by Anselm's attempt to dispose of the family's estates to his bastard progeny, yet, as his grandson noted in his continuation of the family history, Sir Christopher himself, in his dotage, jeopardised the lineage by marrying a woman who had previously been his mistress and by leaving 'many estates of great value to her and her son'.[4]

Didactic family histories were supplemented by the efforts of lawyers, seeking, as we shall see, to devise estate settlements designed to secure family property against the improvidence of any individual. Yet financial difficulties, stemming from personal inadequacies or from a variety of material misfortunes, could ruin a family and displace it from its lands and concomitant status. In Yorkshire 9 per cent of the gentry families resident in the county between 1558 and 1642 slipped from the local élite when the burden of debt compelled the sale of their property. Most of those displaced left the county to pursue opportunities elsewhere; a few sad ghosts lingered on as tenants of those who had bought them out, as beneficiaries of the charity of their kin, or, like John Pudsey, once lord of the manor of Arnforth in Craven, as parish paupers.[5]

New families filled the shoes of those that died out or sold up. The vigorous land market of the century after 1540, swelled by the vast estates released by the Crown, particularly after the Dissolution of the Monasteries, provided opportunities for those who sought to invest in land and to secure the status that pertained to its possession. All the studies that have been undertaken of the social structures of particular counties display the presence of significant numbers of newcomers either to the area or to the ranks of the gentry, although again there are wide local variations in the density of parvenus: new families emerging after 1500 formed 61 per cent of those claiming gentle status in Yorkshire in 1642; 64 per cent in Lancashire; 80 per cent in Dorset; 83 per cent in Lincolnshire; 93 per cent in Warwickshire. If we confine our study of family antiquity solely to the greater gentry who formed the various county élites it appears that these were a more established group in most counties, though, again, there are wide regional variations. In 1642, 72 per cent of the greater gentry families in Lancashire could trace their families' possession of estates in the county into the medieval period; only 10 per cent of the Hertfordshire gentry could make a similar boast. These are the extremes; in most of the counties that have been studied – Leicestershire, Lincolnshire, Norfolk, Suffolk, Sussex, Warwickshire – the families that could claim medieval settlement represented about a third of the élite on the eve of the Civil War.[6]

Blood, lineage, house: these legitimised gentle status and the privileges that appertained to it upon which Oglander and Higford dwelt with such attention. And yet the sixteenth and seventeenth centuries were marked by a buoyant land market and an associated fluidity of social rank. Ancient families died out in the male line, or failed financially; their places in the status hierarchy were taken by those who acquired their lands, or those sold off by the Crown. This anomaly between the traditional conception of gentle status as a product of antique lineage and the social realities of an influx of new families was further emphasised by the uncertainties, disagreements, even feuds, that wracked the group ostensibly bearing professional responsibility for the maintenance of the formal status hierarchy in a pristine condition, the heralds.

In a Commission of 1530, Henry VIII had asserted both his own prerogative as the fountain of honour and his consequent controlling interest in the maintenace of the status hierarchy. He delegated this authority to the heralds, charging them to police the use of arms, but to permit their assumption by 'men of good honest reputacyon . . . not issued of vyle blood', for 'service doon to us', provided they had 'possessions and riches hable to maynteyne' their new honours. From this Commission stemmed the heralds' rights to make grants of arms, and to conduct visitations in the localities to ensure that coats of arms, and, after the Royal Commission of 1558, titles 'of honour and dignity as Esquire, Gentilman, or other', were not being usurped by those with no right to them. Most counties were visited by the heralds on average once every forty years from 1530 until 1686, after which date the practice ceased when William III refused to issue the requisite commissions. Such visitations maintained some check on improprieties. Claimants to arms were instructed to bring pedigrees and other proofs of their families' ancient use of arms to be scrutinised by the heralds. They might respite a claimant until better evidence could be provided; at the most extreme, they could refuse to accept a claim to gentility or to arms, and, in a manner designed to secure maximum public humiliation of the offender, forbid his use of them. Yet the visitation process was seriously flawed. The heralds were more concerned to secure a recognition of their authority, and thus the fees of those who appeared before them, than to undertake any serious defence of social distinctions. Squabbles among the heralds, usually concerning their respective authorities and perquisites, were frequent from 1530 to the Civil War, and the mutual denunciations among the professionals only fed public disdain for their incompetence or carelessness. In the course of a vitriolic dispute in 1616, Ralph Brooke, York Herald, tricked the Garter King of Arms, Segar, into granting, for a fee of 22 shillings, a magnificent coat of arms to the common hangman. Other well-publicised incidents suggested the heralds' venality and their readiness to defer to political pressure. In 1623 the gentry of Shropshire protested that the newly made baronet, Sir Thomas Harris, lacked the pedigree upon which the King had insisted when he established the order. Harris's grandfather was *not* an armigerous gentleman, but a Condover yeoman; his son had flourished as a mercer of Shrewsbury. Thomas, second son of this provincial tradesman, was a successful lawyer with a dubious reputation locally for 'usury, cunning and crafty dealing' as a property speculator. But Harris, whose heir had married one of the Duke of Buckingham's numerous relatives, was a client of the favourite, and, to the mortification of the Shropshire gentlemen, his specious pedigree and armigerous status were triumphantly upheld by a chorus of compliant heralds.[7]

Contemplating the apparent erosion of the traditional conception of hierarchy in the face of unprecedented social mobility and, as a corollary, the disarray among its professional guardians, some commentators argued for a frank recognition of a new ideal of status. Blood and lineage were irrelevancies, incapable of surviving long after the erosion of their material base. It was, simply, *wealth* that generated the goods, the leisure, and thus the reputation upon which a man's standing depended. This view, as we have seen, was expressed in its most stark form by Sir Thomas Smith, Elizabeth's Secretary of State, in 1583. For Smith, a man of substance who chose to live as a gentlemen, 'shall be called master . . . and shall be taken for a gentleman'. Such a man could equally easily acquire the trappings of gentility, for, Smith noted, with a cutting jibe at the practice of the heralds, gentlemen

> be made good cheape in England . . . a King of Heraulds shal also give him for mony armes newly made and invented, the title whereof shall pretende to have beene found by the said Herauld in perusing . . . olde registers, where his auncestors in times past had bin recorded to beare the same.

Smith accepts social mobility; families 'many times fail' and new stock replaces them. Nor does he see any harm to the commonwealth in the parvenu's desire to acquire the traditional symbols of status.[8]

A few Elizabethan writers concurred with Smith's analysis. The Staffordshire gentleman-antiquary, Erdeswick, agreed that 'new risings', 'a man that is but of mean parentage and riseth by commendable means', deserved to be honoured for their own deserts, not by the invention by perjured and venal heralds of spurious 'fables of their ancestors'. Most commentators, however, responded to Smith's sharp realism with a yet fiercer insistence on the traditional qualifications. Sir John Ferne, who found *De Republica Anglorum* so repellent that he chose to doubt its attributed authorship – 'falsely christened' with the name of the 'grave and wise' Smith – sneered that if wealth was the criterion for gentle status, then 'Pyrats and theeves, bankers and brothels, with the lyke, shall challenge nobility'. Ferne's *The Blazon of Gentry*, of 1586, obsessively reiterates the traditional conceptions of lineage. Christ was 'a Gentleman of blood, according to his humanity . . . and might if he had esteemed of the vayne glorye of the worlde . . . have borne coat-armour'; the Apostles, too, were 'Gentlemen of Blood'. Ferne seeks to uphold a strict apartheid between 'the shining and franke estate of gentlenesse' and 'churles broode', reserving educational opportunities for the former. Miscegination represents a fearful 'disparagement' to a gentry family, 'it is the unequall coupling in yoke of the clean oxe and the uncleane asse', and the issue of so perverse a union is 'but halfe noble, nay but halfe a man'.[9]

## 1.2 ALTERNATIVE VIEWS: HUMANISTS AND PURITANS

In the dispute between Smith and Ferne, the majority of the gentry, at least up to the Civil War, preferred the traditional arguments of the latter. Their preference emerges directly in their own attempts to create the 'fables of their ancestors' that troubled Erdeswick. Indirectly it appears in the pragmatic modifications to the radical redefinitions of status and of a properly organised social hierarchy that were mooted in the sixteenth century. We will examine these ideological shifts first.

Two intensely subversive challenges to traditional concepts of status had been propounded in the early sixteenth century. First, humanists argued that virtue, honed by appropriate education and placed at the service of the state, was the only justification for claims to status. Some radicals among them, like Sir Thomas More, who in the *Utopia* uses the word *generosus* only in a perjorative sense, voiced contempt for the conventional canons of gentility. Second, Protestant divines emphasised godliness, not lineage, as the true determinant of worth. These alternative views did not replace or directly subvert more traditional emphases, though their long-term effects may have been corrosive. The radical restatements were, in some measure, incorporated in modified forms into the older legitimising conceptions of blood and lineage, creating an unstable theoretical system, but one that the majority of the gentry found, for all its contradictions, usable and sustaining.[10]

Fifteenth-century commentators on gentility, while emphasising the importance of blood and descent in their definitions, also argued that service – both military and in public administration – were the activities that justified the leisure and privileges that the gentry enjoyed. They also recognised that moral virtue should be associated with gentle status and that the latter could be lost by the manifestly vicious. Sixteenth-century writers followed their medieval predecessors both in stressing the centrality of lineage, and in their discussion of service and virtue. Yet they could also embody the ideals of humanist critics of traditional concepts of status by redefining virtue in Christian-Ciceronian terms, by de-emphasising military service, and by encouraging the acquisition of the education that was essential to a gentleman's function as counsellor and local governor. So Ferne, for all his snobbery, borrows much from the humanists: he deeply approves of higher education, and recognises that it fits a man for service of the commonwealth, the proper calling of the gentry. Ferne is also prepared to allow that gentility can be acquired by a man who has performed 'some notable . . . desert to his countrye, arising from some branch of the Cardinall vertues'. Virtue is a necessary element of gentility, and those that lack it, though of ancient lineage and possessions, 'gentry of stock only', are 'but a shadow, or rather a painture of nobility'. At the beginning of the reign of Charles I, Francis Markham took a similarly ecumenical line. He praised ancient lineage, 'blood' that 'sends out an issue of Honor even to Infinite Generations,' yet recognised that 'good Qualities and good Vertues', the products of 'good Education', might lead to men being 'advanced into places in the Commonwealth' and thus to gentility by the king. Radical humanists had sought to challenge the conventions governing status in early sixteenth-century England. They were successful to the extent that the provision of a formal education for the development of the virtues and, more practically, to fit a man for civic service, was emphasised by later commentators and by the gentry themselves, who, as we shall see, increasingly attended the universities and the Inns of Court in this period and sought public office. Yet these new concerns were combined with the restatement of traditional views on the centrality of blood to gentle status – an amalgam neatly dissected by Shakespeare in the discussions of Shallow and Slender concerning the former's honour.[11]

Protestant emphasis on an alternative conception of the status hierarchy based on grace proved equally plastic in the face of the gentry's continued obsession with lineage. It might be dismissed or marginalised by those who were not manifestly godly. Sir Edward Dering glanced politely at the doctrine, 'heere is a tearme beyond all ascentes of climing degrees, to be the Sonnes of God': 'but', he continued suavely, 'we must not forget that . . . descent of bloud even among men and abstracted from this high advance is a blessing', and he proceeded to set out his own inventive history of the pre-Conquest Derings. Thomas Lyte of Lytescary, Somerset, piously denied that his genealogical interests stemmed from 'any ostentation of birth or kindred', quoting Job on the vanity of worldly ambition – but he wrote two extensive pedigrees of his family, and filled the hall and chapel of his mansion with armorial glass representing his family connections, particularly emphasising alliances with those families of 'honour and worship'.[12]

Perhaps more significant are the compromises made by the divines themselves in accommodating traditional pride in lineage within their alternative formulation. The funeral sermons of Puritan gentlemen may argue that 'It is nothing to be born a Gentleman, it is all in all to live and die a good Christian', or that 'a Saint hath the richest coat [of arms]', but few divines could resist the opportunity to detail the ancient lineage of their patrons, even as they announced its irrelevance. So Thomas Froysell stressed Sir Robert Harley's 'descent' which 'eleveated [him] above the rate of ordinary men', while insisting that he was a man 'whose veins Free Grace had filled with nobler blood'. William Hinde argued that it was *not* John Bruen's 'birth and bloud to be so worshipfully descended, nor his gentry and dignity, to be so honourably allyed', that made him worthy of remembrance. Yet the minister saw the Bruen family, antique itself, and 'allyed to many of the most ancient and worshipfull houses' of the region, as beneficiary of a providential blessing on the godly, and he gloated over local families, obviously less deserving of divine favour, that had 'had their posterity swept away as dung, and their names overwhelmed with the ruines of their houses'. The ambivalence of the Puritan ministers reflected the traditionalist concerns of their patrons. Most shared the interests of their less godly counterparts in genealogy and in heraldic display. For example, the marriage negotiations between Simonds D'Ewes and Anne Clopton were largely conducted within the canons of godly discourse: D'Ewes noted that his prospective bride was 'verie religiouslie educated', while her grandmother, Lady Anne Barnardiston, praised 'the good begininge of grace' that she saw in him. Yet D'Ewes also revelled in the antiquity of his wife's family which linked him 'either nearlie or moore remotely to . . . all the ancient nobilitie of England'. Equally, Lady Barnardiston pressed D'Ewes to acquire a knighthood; such 'litle additions,' she wrote delicately, might gain him 'further respecte amonkst her kindred'. Sir Francis Hastings, who strove 'to live his life in such a way that he might testify that he had been numbered among God's elect', nevertheless decorated his manor house at North Cadbury, Somerset with a wealth of stained glass designed to glorify his family both by showing its antiquity and by particularly emphasising its, often slight, connections with a number of illustrious persons. In this latter respect the attitude of the Puritan Hastings, expressed iconographically, exactly replicates that of the Yorkshire recusant, Thomas Meynell, who boasted that, although his mother had brought little land to the family, 'I had by hir fyve worthie Cote Armors and as many Crestes', and carefully listed the *eminent* families to which he was allied in his *Book of Evidences*.[13]

Humanists and Calvinist intellectuals might, in abstract, question the gentry's claim to status based on lineage, on 'blood' and 'house'. Yet their ideas were tamed, and, purged of their radical critique, were incorporated into or made compatible with the traditional framework of legitimation preferred by their gentry patrons. Godly gentlemen, like D'Ewes, 'ever accounted it a great outward blessing to be well descended, it being in the gift only of God and nature to bestow it'. Families who had risen by service to the prince preferred to acquire medieval ancestry rather than stress their humanist credentials, the 'commendable means' whereby they were elevated. So the Mildmays conveniently forgot their yeoman progenitor who kept a stall in Chelmsford market and in 1583 received heraldic blessing for a pedigree displaying their thirteenth-century origins and connections with 'dyvers noble Erles, Barons and other great personages of this land'. As a group the gentry agreed with Sir John Wynn of Gwydir, 'a great temporal blessing it is, and a great heart's ease to a man to find that he is well descended and a greater grief it is for upstarts and gentlemen of the first head to look back unto their descents, being base.' In consequence they vigorously endeavoured to discover a usable lineage, 'to intrude themselves into the masks of Antiquity'.[14]

## 1.3 THE MANIPULATION OF LINEAGE

In the sixteenth century the 'counterfeit' genealogies of which Erdeswick complained might involve the most elaborate fantasy and naked fraud. The Wellesbourne family of Hughenden, Buckinghamshire descended from a Wycombe clothier enriched in the early fifteenth century, went to unusual trouble to assert antique descent. They offered Wellesbourne de Montfort, a previously unrecorded son, or, in an alternative version of their genealogy, an illegitimate brother, of the notorious Earl Simon, as the progenitor of their lineage at Hughenden. They sought to validate this claim by fictitious deeds and forgeries of medieval seals, by appropriating a genuine fourteenth-century tomb in the local church upon which they had their coat of arms carved, and by constructing a series of crude marmoreal effigies purporting to be those of their knightly ancestors of the thirteenth and fifteenth centuries. Few families went to quite such lengths in their pursuit of status. Some sustained the mythic accounts of their family's longevity with forged documents; 'medieval' deeds, as in the case of the Lambert family, or, less sophisticated, 'medieval' narrative or verse genealogies. The Smiths of Cressing Temple, smallholders in western Essex in the fifteenth century but enriched by legal practice, office, and a succession of fortunate marriages in the sixteenth, were, by 1590, claiming descent from a 'belsire ycleped Sir Michael Carrington', standard-bearer to Richard the Lionheart, on the strength of a conveniently discovered family history. This explained that a Carrington, whose support of Richard II had rendered him obnoxious to the Lancastrian dynasty, took the name Smith so 'he mowten by thilke name everye wheren voyden suspecte and perill when he mowten comen into England'. The Staunton and Wodehouse families relied on 'medieval' verse narratives to bolster their claims to antiquity; the Churchills, as part of an elaborate claim to descent from a companion of the Conqueror, produced a 'contemporary' epitaph in English verse to their twelfth-century ancestor; having described his valiant death in battle, the poet continues in Ye Olde Englysshe as absurd as that of the Carrington narrative

> And nigh thik Place, a tyny Ville
> Now standeth and there is
> Me clypeth it right sooth Cherchile
> After his name, I wiss.

But such blatant forgeries were scarcely necessary. Most families relied merely on family tradition to uphold the speculative genealogies and heraldic achievements that they displayed as ostentatious demonstrations of their lineage. Family chapels and funeral monuments most visibly embodied family pretensions. At Lydiard Tregoze, Wiltshire, Sir John St John deployed all the resources of artistry to flaunt his lineage: statuary; a painted tryptich of his family and its ancestry and matches; stained glass, in which, with a complacency that is breathtaking, a panel of armorial glass indicating the descent of the Tregoze manor to the St Johns is flanked by figures of St John the Evangelist and St John the Baptist. Such shrines were, naturally, a favoured environment for the public statement of questionable genealogical claims. Sir Richard Hyde boasted in an inscription painted on the chancel wall at Sutton Courtenay Church, Berkshire, of his direct descent from a family whose estate was 'bestowed upon the first advancer thereof for his vertue and valour, by Canutus the first Danish King, who by conquest obteyned this kingdome in the year of our lord — [sic]'; the key detail obviously eluded Hyde's scholarship. At Blickling, Norfolk, the late-Elizabethan tomb of Sir Edward Clere recites the names of ten ancestors with accompanying heraldic shields; the first nine of these, beginning with a 'Clere Monte, assistant to William Duke of Normandy' are spurious.[15]

The exterior and interior decoration of gentry houses could equally embody family pride and the attendant genealogical fantasies. In 1633 Lady Abigail Sherard rebuilt the fifteenth-century wing of Stapleford Hall, Leicestershire, and incorporated a series of statues in niches on the façade designed to illustrate 'the fine pedigree of the Sherards and their matches'; William the Conqueror and Gilbert de Clare figure prominently among these worthies. Antiquaries and heralds lovingly record the armorial glass that glowed in the halls, parlours, and dining rooms of gentry houses. Sir John Ferrers painted the parlour at Tamworth Castle with shields exhibiting a pedigree, badly garbled in the earlier generations, back to the Norman Conquest, and his claim to distant affinity with David, King of Scots, from 'whom descendeth King James our Soveraigne'. Many families acquired vast parchment rolls detailing their pedigrees. The production of these became the growth area for the heraldic industry from the late sixteenth century. Decorated with miniature paintings of coats of arms, copies of seals and deeds, and portraits of mythical ancestors

– including Noah seated in a tiny ark in the case of the Popham family – scrolls were thought appropriate for room decoration and could be of vast extent and complexity. The 1632 pedigree roll of Sir Thomas Shirley, nearly 12 feet wide and 30 feet long, is probably the largest, but its size is almost rivalled by some of the productions, like that of the Mostyns which commences 'Adam, son of God', that embody the high pretensions of the Welsh gentry.[16]

It has been suggested that the lively interest of the country gentry in antiquarian studies resulted, by the seventeenth century, in an enhanced sophistication that forced the abandonment of the more spectacular products of the luxuriant imaginations of Tudor genealogists. This seems an optimistic conclusion. Few Jacobean or Caroline antiquarians were ready to deploy their well-honed critical skills upon an analysis of their own pedigrees. The careful chronicler of the Rookwood family, who warned of the 'so many counterfett' genealogies in circulation and of the need for the proper analysis of medieval evidence, could still solemnly record the family's tradition that their coat of arms – six chess rooks – was given to the first of the family 'for his excellente skyll in this exercyse . . . playeinge with the Conqueror at his firste entery into this lande'. And in several cases, as with Sir Edward Dering, the learning of the scholar-gentleman merely produced an impressive apparatus designed to enhance the plausibility of the fictitious family descent. Dering, like many seventeenth-century gentlemen, was deeply dissatisfied with the pedigree constructed for his immediate predecessors. His grandfather, 'uncareless' in these matters, had employed 'a pettyfogger in heraldry and . . . armoriall designs' to produce a family tree and heraldic achievement; he was clearly content with the product, which took Dering ancestry back to the fourteenth century, and he employed the invented heraldic coat on his seal and in armorial glass. Sir Edward was not so easily satisfied, and he shared the fashionable ambition of many of the Caroline élite to allege a *pre*-Conquest origin for their families. In this period Sir Kenelm Digby, who could boast a genuine thirteenth-century pedigree, employed a number of experts at a cost, it was alleged, of £1,200, to devise a genealogy running from one Aelmar, 'Anglicus-Saxonicus', while the Temples of Stowe, Buckinghamshire, a family that rose from obscurity in the late fifteenth century and to great wealth only with the Reformation, claimed the Saxon earls of Mercia as their progenitors, as well as the impressive but quite fabulous arms attributed to them. Sir Edward Dering was a little less pretentious in his claims; his researches, an odd mix of serious analysis of Domesday Book and pure invention, discovered a mythic Saxon thane killed at Hastings: Dering, son of Sired. Sir Edward alleged that the deeds and charters that could prove his descent from this 'Kentish valiant' had been purloined by the journeyman-genealogist so regrettably employed by his grandfather, but copies were available, and these mendacious productions were supplemented by tampering with genuine historical documents. On the strength of these fictions Sir Edward employed a motto in ungrammatical old English, and used a simpler, more pristine coat of arms than that devised by his grandfather's hired antiquary. To validate this coat, Dering had the font in Pluckley Church re-cut to incorporate his preferred arms, and laid a series of skilfully forged family brasses, ostensibly from the late medieval period, in the chancel. John Philipot, Somerset Herald from 1624, was a first-class antiquary, a student and friend of the great Camden. He placed his considerable learning, and a pliant scholarly conscience, at the disposal of the Kentish and Sussex gentry, and a series of prestigious pedigrees for such families as Finch and Pelham flowed from his pen; these are remarkable for his quite deliberate tampering with the records – taking a genuine medieval document, and replacing the names in it with those required for his genealogical purposes.[17]

Historical studies did not, of themselves, create a critical sensibility that was intrinsically hostile to the gorgeous products of the pedigree-makers. Yet by mid-century a more detached attitude to lineage claims does emerge among the antiquaries, and is apparent in a number of contemporary family histories. Sir Christopher Guise, having noted the heralds' account of the family's origin (descended from a brother of the Duke of Guise who was a companion of William the Conqueror), wrote 'soe sayes my escotition, the truth of which I will nott discusse, but follow more certayne lights'; he then reviewed the deeds among his muniments that indicated the family's tenure of their Gloucestershire estates from the late thirteenth century. Gervase Holles rehearsed the claim of his clan to shadowy medieval eminence with a nice balance of family piety and scholarly doubt, but ultimately abandoned the pedigree, acknowledging that the real 'foundation and groundworke for that greatnes our family is now arrived at' must be attributed to a Tudor lord mayor of London.[18]

## 1.4 POST-1660: LINEAGE – A WANING OBSESSION?

Such realism is not restricted to those with antiquarian interests: it is symptomatic of a more general shift of attitude among the gentry after 1660. The emphasis on lineage as a central element in claims to status was no longer so intense, and the elaborate genealogical fictions of the pre-Civil War period were not so relentlessly publicised. This is apparent both in the tepid response to the heralds' visitations after 1660, and in changes in the design of marmoreal effigies in the later seventeenth century.

Despite standards of preparation and organisation, particularly of those visitations in which Sir William Dugdale was involved, that were far higher than those of the pre-Civil War heralds, the gentry did not flock to secure official confirmation of their claims to status with any alacrity after the Restoration. When Sir Edward Bysshe, Clarenceaux King of Arms, visited Oxfordshire in 1669, it was reported that 'Many look'd on this matter as a trick to get money', and the local gentry failed to attend Bysshe because of a more pressing social engagement – a horse-race at Brackley. Only 25 per cent of those required to appear for the visitation of Northamptonshire and Rutland in 1681 answered the summons, and barely half of this small group entered a pedigree before the heralds. In the next year, visiting Warwickshire, Dugdale's own county, the heralds were treated more respectfully, with half of the group summoned responding. But even this visitation recorded a mere 105 pedigrees, as against the 256 taken by the heralds in its 1619 predecessor. The visitations were abandoned after the Glorious Revolution, yet, as Philip Styles has argued, 'the system had lost much of its old vitality' by the 1680s and 'must eventually have died out' for social reasons independent of William III's refusal to grant the authorising commission.[19]

Late seventeenth-century tombs might still embody genealogical fictions. Elizabeth Grimes, 'an inferiour servant of a very mean capacity', who married Lord Coventry 'in his declin'd old age', and then, substantially endowed by her doting husband, secured an equally brilliant second match to Thomas Savage, Esquire, of Elmley Castle, Worcestershire, thought it worth while to claim descent from an armigerous and loyal Norfolk family – though in fact the daughter of 'a mean person', a London turner. She had this specious claim validated by the heralds, and then engraved with 'false arms' on her first husband's tomb, to the fury of his heir. But the characteristics of sixteenth- and early seventeenth-century monuments that emphasise lineage as an essential element of status were gradually abandoned. The effigy of the deceased arrayed in armour, as favoured by Sir John Oglander, disappeared. Roman drapes or contemporary clothes were displayed where full-length marmoreal representations were employed, but these were far rarer. The architectural or cartouche wall tablet became the common monumental form, and where an effigy was used, the portrait bust was favoured. The employment of the monument as a family record, a visible pedigree with the effigies of the children marked by name-labels amd armorial cartouches indicating their marriages, ceases. The form had been favoured by the Royley family, the Burton-on-Trent monumental masons and their clients in the later sixteenth century; examples can be found up to 1640, such as the tomb of Sir William Sandys of Miserden, Gloucestershire, of that year, but die out during the Civil War. Heraldic display became simpler, and the multiplied painted shields of sixteenth-century tombs gave place to classical motifs, cherubs and allegorical figures. The extended genealogical epitaph was displaced by an encomium, usually in Latin, stressing the deceased's moral virtues.[20]

The changed attitudes to lineage and status among the gentry, apparent in their cool response to the opportunities for gaining formal recognition of their claims by the heralds, and in the changing taste in funerary monuments, was also expressed more freely by writers on the social order, even those who approached questions of status from a heraldic viewpoint. Sir Thomas Smith's emphasis on wealth as the essential foundation of claims to status, that had been lashed by Ferne, dominates discussions after 1660. Even Sylvanus Morgan, for all his luxuriant armorial fantasies, could acknowledge Smith's premise: so, having discussed Adam's heraldic shield, Morgan lapsed into verse,

> it is Industry that gains us Riches,
> And Riches gains us Honour, Coat and Briches.
> Virtue and Learning, and Honest Parents, can
> With Spade and Spindle, make a GENTLEMAN.

Morgan's friend, Edward Waterhouse, frankly accepted the reality of social mobility. Ancient families decay, *probably*, but not necessarily, as a consequence of divine justice which, to punish their wickedness, 'razes their posterity and glory out of honourable record'. Their places in the hierarchy are taken by new families, enriched by law, or learning, or trade, 'which in the income of them are equivalent to Landed Mannors, and by exchange purchases them'. Waterhouse piously hopes that wealth is honestly acquired, and insists that a family's longevity will depend on the moral standing of its founder, but he recognises that money buys favour and thus honour; 'ill title' transmutes easily into 'solid estates'.[21]

Such works reflect, rather than generate, the less intense concern for lineage among the gentry in the late seventeenth century. The fact of social mobility was finally recognised and Smith's views could be incorporated without embarrassment even in the pieties of family history: Gervase Holles insisted that he 'would not scrape a chimney sweeper out of my pedigree', and castigated those whose refused to acknowledge 'those honest ancestors whose industry prepared the way to our better condition'. In the early eighteenth century coats of arms were thought to provide appropriate decoration for coaches, servants' liveries and plate. But there is far less sense that their employment entails a vital claim to status based on lineage; rather the use of heraldic symbols becomes a matter of taste. Edward Peyto, rebuilding his mansion at Chesterton, Warwickshire in the Palladian style in 1658, consigned the dazzling array of armorial glass commissioned by his ancestors and solemnly discussed and illustrated by Dugdale, to the dustbin. Sir Edward Turnour, ordered by the bishop to repair the dilapidated family chapel at Little Wratting, Suffolk instructed the incumbent to have it demolished. Some few individuals maintained an active interest in family genealogy and heraldry, and asserted antique lineage and elaborate pedigrees: Edward Dryden of Canons Ashby, Northamptonshire, inscribed under the garish family coat of arms that dominated his drawing room of 1710, 'Ancient as the Druids', and consciously employed mock-medieval motifs in his refurbishment of the house. But such interests were viewed as eccentric and became, as in Vanburgh's play *Aesop* [1697] with its comic Welsh genealogist who begins his pedigree with Noah 'for brevity's sake', the butt of the wits.[22]

The changed attitude of the gentry to social mobility and to lineage may have owed something to the growing popularity and sophistication of one branch of antiquarian studies. Social mobility was drawn forcibly to the attention of the gentry by the researches of those of their number who studied local topography and manorial histories. William Lambarde, whose 1576 *Perambulation of*

*Kent* represented the model for such undertakings until the publication of Dugdale's more thorough study of Warwickshire 80 years later, concluded that 'the Gentlemen be not heere (throughout) of so auncient stocks as else where, especially in the parts neerer to London'. Habington, the historian of Worcestershire, had begun his study deliberately to disprove the offensive suggestion that his county could boast few ancient families. His researches did not consistently sustain his original assumption, and his work is punctuated by a series of moralistic reflections, akin to Oglander's lucubrations, on the inconstancy of 'fortune's rowleing wheele'. At Clifton, 'to showe that eavery wordly thinge must have his period', the ancient family of that name are now extinguished; at Norton, 'to shewe that nothinge in thys Worlde is stable, but all subiect to mutability, hathe lately expyred the possessyon of the auntient family of Gowre'. By the end of the century, Sir Robert Atkyns, writing the history of Gloucestershire, for all his political conservatism, took it for granted that 'very few families continue to flourish above three generations, therefore there are few families above a hundred years standing'. The gentry could hardly read such works without a bleak recognition of the fragility of the lineage–land connection. In 1670 Sir Simon Degge borrowed a manuscript copy of Sampson Erdeswick's turn-of-the-century *Survey* of Staffordshire from a fellow gentleman. He was appalled to realise that since the completion of Erdeswick's study 'one half . . . of the lands in Staffordshire have changed their Owners'. Sir Robert Chernocke made a similarly gloomy calculation, of 'the gentlemen of quality that have sold their estates and are quite gone' for his native Bedfordshire.[23]

The rise and fall of landed families was a major social phenomenon of the sixteenth and seventeenth centuries in England. Families failed through genetic misfortune or personal incompetence; men newly enriched through trade, or law or royal favour purchased their estates, and the extensive lands made available by the Crown, and replaced them in the status hierarchy. Moralists and social commentators in the sixteenth century had recognised this process, but it is not until the late seventeenth century that such opinions become commonplace. Prior to that period the gentry, apparently in incongruous defiance of social realities, sought to maintain a status order based on 'blood' or 'house', and to justify their own position within it by emphasising, often by elaborate fictions, the antiquity of their own families. This insistence, by encouraging an ever more sophisticated examination of family and local history, may have carried the seeds of its own decay. Antiquarian scholarship was ultimately both subversive of the inventions of the Tudor genealogists, and, in the works of the topographers, clearly displayed, in Oglander's words, 'the inconstancy of Fortune, which by the aid of her servant, Time, pulleth down great things'.

Yet an explanation of changing attitudes to status that sees the Tudor emphasis on lineage toppling under the weight of its own internal contradictions in the mid-seventeenth century hardly carries complete conviction. A complex amalgam of other factors was involved. The Civil War was certainly one of these: the stark fact of mutability was inescapable. For Edward Waterhouse the execution of Charles I was the prime example of the malevolence of fortune, which was reinforced by considering the fates of the Royalist gentry. Gentlemen, Waterhouse concluded, 'whose greatness is variable, whose blood is capable of taint, whose wealth is casual, whose power is servile to unthought, unheard of accidents', *must* recognise the fluidity of their state.[24] And yet while the Civil War compelled the reassessment of traditional assumptions, it also ushered in a period in which the land–lineage bond became more secure. Genetic misfortune could still blast a family's hopes, yet the cooling of the economy after the inflationary spiral in the century before 1640 and the development of better credit mechanisms at mid-century meant that the financial ruin that had thrust the Tresham family from Rushton in the early seventeenth century receded as a prospect. Discussion of these changes in the economic climate will be postponed to the following chapters. Yet some of the associated legal developments must be discussed here, and they present a very significant paradox. The insistence on blood and house that we have analysed occurred in a period when a family's hold on its estates was most fragile, least well-defended legally.

## 1.5 INHERITANCE AND DESCENT: LEGAL CHANGES

By the fifteenth century a substantial amount of land in England was held in *entail*. The current occupier of the land had only a life interest in the estate; he could not sell it or will it away from the class of heirs – usually the heirs male of the original grantee – nominated when the entail had been established. A gentleman whose lands were held by virtue of an entail, and who had no son, would be obliged to contemplate 'his' lands going at his death to a distant kinsman, leaving his own daughters with nothing. This straitjacket was resented by some landowners, and their efforts to recover a freedom of disposition were successful in the courts in the late fifteenth century. The ability to break an entail gave a landowner power to dispose of his estate according to his own priorities, not those of some distant ancestor, and this freedom was reinforced by legislation, particularly the Statute of Wills, under Henry VIII. The current head of a family could now sell his estate, or will significant parts of it to his younger children or to his wife; the succession of his male heir, even of his eldest son, to the family estates was no longer guaranteed.[25]

The existence of a legal power did not mean that it was universally exercised. Some gentlemen scrupulously sought to recognise the claims of their family and name upon their estates. The childless Gervase Newton proposed to make his nephew his heir, despite a long-standing coolness with his brother, Sir John, out of a concern 'to support the name' – though his offer was in part an exercise in one-upmanship, after he had learned of Sir John's intention to sell off part of the main family estate. A more significant recognition of the claims of the lineage occured within the Altham family, in very adverse circumstances. In 1607 Thomas Altham, a Catholic, willed that his estate, in default of direct male heirs, should go to 'hym that shall dwell and mayntayne the hous of Markhall in Essex bearing the name of Altham'. In 1640 his son, James, a childless widower, prepared to dispose the estate in accordance with his father's instruction. It was to descend to his Protestant cousins 'to maintaine our Name in my father's mancion dwelling house'. Though James Altham solicited prayers for his cousins' conversion to 'the holy Romane Catholicke religion', it is clear in this case that family ties outweighed confessional division.[26]

The Altham case also shows an aspect of freedom of disposition of which contemporary gentlemen would have approved. Markhall should have come to Thomas Altham, but he had been disinherited by his father, 'much displeased with him for changing his religion', upon his conversion to Catholicism. Patriarchal authority could also be used to protect the family estate from the likely depredations of a demonstrably feckless heir. The eldest son of Sir Richard Bulkeley of Beaumaris was 'a very wild and unthriftie man . . . proud, a great hunter of women . . . given to all extravagancies'. He was finally disinherited, and Sir Richard's grandson named as heir, when murder was added to his already extensive and lurid catalogue of vices.[27]

Yet the freedom enjoyed by the current occupier of the estate was not always employed in ways that would be regarded as socially responsible nor with much concern for the claims of the lineage. Anselm, black sheep of the Guise family, had used his power of disposition to alienate fifteen manors and other 'goodly things' to fund his debaucheries, and his attempt to disinherit his brother and transfer what remained of the family estate to his bastards was only narrowly circumvented. Other family histories told of senile, doting or henpecked husbands who provided lavish endowments for their second wives or their children, to the disinheritance of the main line. John Smyth of Nibley, noting a series of disinheritances in the hundred of Berkeley, Gloucestershire, reflected darkly 'such power have younge wives over old husbands'. Sir James Thynne claimed that his stepmother had poisoned his relationship with his father, Sir Thomas; that she had driven him and his brothers from Longleat; that she had refused him permission to visit the old man during his illness. Worst, she had persuaded Sir Thomas to give her and his half-brother the bulk of his personal property, and a larger share of the lands than Sir James himself had received.[28]

Other families could also retail cautionary tales concerning the damage that stemmed from the legal situation which gave a power of disposition to the current head of a family, tales that were perhaps more troubling in that they did not turn on the feckless indifference of an Anselm Guise or the uxorious compliance of a Sir Thomas Thynne. Sir John Rodney of Stoke Rodney, Somerset had divided the family estates between his sons, upset, so the family tradition went, by his heir's bullying his younger brother. Both branches of the family held their estates in entail; if the elder branch of the family at Stoke Rodney had no male heirs, then the estate was to go to the younger branch, established at Conglesbury, and vice versa. In 1588 Sir John Rodney of Conglesbury, then 40 years old and with no sons, broke the entail; piqued by this indifference to the claims of the house, his cousin of Stoke, Sir George, a much younger man, reciprocated by breaking the entail on his lands. Two years later Sir John's wife bore him a son, but Sir George died childless; he left a will attempting to re-establish the terms of the entail that he had broken in spite, but this was poorly drafted and was challenged on a number of legal technicalities. Sir George's estate became enmired in a morass of litigation between the heirs general, Sir George's sisters, and the heir male, Sir John of Conglesbury. The suits were eventually compromised, and Sir John acquired the ancestral mansion – but only at the cost of a draining burden of debt, undertaken to pay the substantial legal costs and to buy out the interests of the other claimants.[29]

Sir George Rodney's momentary vindictiveness cost his family dear: so too did Sir Robert Strode's love for his daughter. Sir Robert held the family estates at Parnham, Dorset by an entail that would have brought them, as he had no son, to his brother, John, an eminent lawyer. Sir Robert was persuaded by a very distant kinsman, William Strode of Newnham, Devon that he could both splendidly provide for his only child, Katharine, and keep Parnham in the Strode name, by marrying the girl to William's son, Richard: the coupling of Parnham and Newnham 'would make a great and famous house'. This proved a tempting prospect: the entail was broken, and the marriage arranged, though the children were, respectively, 10 and 12 years old. But then things went badly awry. Katharine had three daughters, then died. Sir Robert, his fond hope that Parnham would 'continewe in . . . [his] both name and blud' shattered, sought to resurrect the terms of the original entail in favour of his brother. But he found that Sir William had 'much over reached him' in the drafting of the new settlement. Sir Robert's death in 1616 ushered in two decades of venomous lawsuits between his brother and his son-in-law concerning the ownership of Parnham.[30]

A father might suppose that, despite the freedom accorded by the legal changes at the beginning of the period, *he* retained a keen awareness of his responsibilities to the family; he might even appreciate the opportunities presented to discipline his children by the threat of disinheritance. Yet dared he trust his sons with the same powers, powers that could lead to the dissipation of the patrimony? The emphasis that fathers placed on the duties of the individual to the family in their letters of advice suggest that they felt insecure on this point. So too do their attempts from the late sixteenth century to circumvent the law's approval of freedom of disposition, to devise new forms of estate settlement that would reimpose, at least on their heirs, limitations akin to those that had existed under the medieval entail. A series of experiments were attempted only to fail in the courts before, in the late seventeenth century, conveyancers devised and the judges approved the *strict settlement*. Under its terms the current tenant of an estate could neither alienate it during his lifetime nor deprive his children of inheritances that were established in the negotiations for his marriage between his father and the family of the bride. The device was not foolproof. It could be circumvented in particular demographic circumstances. But the patrimony was a good deal safer under its regime after 1680 than had been the case for the previous two centuries. The individual's control over disposition and testation was fettered: the spectre of Anselm Guise – alienating his lands, endowing his bastards – faded.

And yet while the strict settlement resembled the medieval entail in form, substantively its terms differed from those that had been usual in the earlier period. In particular, those gentlemen settling their estates in the late seventeenth century tended to prefer, in the event of the failure of direct male heirs, the claims of heiresses rather than of collateral males. The plot of Jane Austen's *Pride and Prejudice* hinges on an almost inconceivable determination under a strict settlement: the estate to the repellent Rev. Mr Collins; nothing for the Bennett girls. In a letter of 1680, written upon the death of his only son, John Ferrers articulated the dominant attitude. He was, he wrote, 'deprived of the chiefest motive to desire the continuence of my name', and though he wished others of his clan luck, he saw no need to settle his estates to ensure the continuity of the land–lineage bond in the house of Ferrers, 'by collateral wayes'.[31] Estates were secured by the strict settlement for the nuclear family; the claims of the wider lineage on the patrimony were neglected. This raises another possibility concerning the complex of factors that led to the waning emphasis on lineage as the *sine qua non* of status in the late seventeenth century: that it may be related to changed attitudes to the family. An increased emphasis on the primacy of affective relations within the nuclear family eroded a sense of responsibility to groups, though linked by name and blood, beyond its confines.

The conceptual framework that linked gentility with ancient blood and lineage survived the challenges posed by humanist and Puritan critics in the sixteenth centuries. Families asserted their claims to gentle status by emphasising their lineage in a number of public contexts: by lavish heraldic display on their buildings and in the interior decoration of their mansions; by the heraldic and military motifs and the genealogical assertions graven on their marmoreal effigies; in pious works of family history. Yet after 1660 such displays became more restrained and the emphasis on antiquity and lineage as an essential aspect of gentility waned. This shift was associated with the growing sophistication of historical investigation that, while it had begun in family piety and the desire to discover an impressive lineage, became increasingly critical of the dubious products of earlier, more naive investigation. Exuberant fantasies that had passed muster in the sixteenth cetury could not survive an increasingly scholarly scrutiny. County histories revealed the inescapable fact of social mobility – a point driven home, as it was to Sir John Oglander, by the experiences of the Civil War. And yet the waning emphasis on blood and house cannot be explained purely in terms of a keener historical awareness. The apparently incongruous facts, that lineage was emphasised when the economic survival of families seemed most tenuous and when the movement of 'new men' into country estates was rapid, and that interest waned as greater stability was achieved, deserve further discussion. Equally, the hypothesis that an increased emphasis on affective relations within the nuclear family may have led to an erosion of concern for the claims of the lineage must be considered. These paradoxes and problems will be addressed in the next chapters, on the family life of the gentry, and on their economic fortunes.

# 2

# The Family

'Woo be to the and thy house for there is nothing in thy house butt blasfemy, wickednes, hoor hunting, dronkenes, myschief and all naughtines, happie are they that never came to yt'. Thus Lady Margaret Stanhope harangued her husband Sir Thomas, perambulating the courtyard of Shelford, Nottinghamshire, on a bitter winter's day in the 1580s. She had already, according to her husband, so far forgotten the norms of a patriarchal society as to seize from his hands the rod with which he threatened to beat her, broken it, and then torn off his ruff and part of his beard. Having thrown a candlestick and joint stool at him she left the house in fury, only to return four hours later swearing and cursing when the servants would not allow her entry. After breaking a window she finally gained admittance by demolishing a plaster wall! Next day, locked in the parlour by her irate husband, she appeared at the window screaming to passers-by that he intended to murder her. Thereafter the quarrelling pair sought the intervention of 'friends' and two local JPs arranged an informal separation.

Sir Thomas's story of bitter marriage breakdown is long and complex and, though we hear only one voice, we can read from it a variety of possible reasons for the disintegration of the family. Stanhope's own pugnacity must have been partially to blame: he was at odds not only with his wife, but also at various times with his heir John, and his younger son Edward. He denounced John for his 'misorders and lewd demanors', eventually accumulating a series of scriptural texts on the obedience children owed their parents at a time when his son was already an adult and married. Edward must have been slightly younger, still studying at the Inns of Court, when Sir Thomas threatened him with whipping, and when he was scorned, organised one of the servants to hold him while he beat him over the shoulders. It was this last incident that provoked Lady Stanhope's violent reaction. The father's complaints against the sons were that they gamed and gambled, Edward actually demeaning himself to beg from retainers who were visiting the Stanhope house for the Christmas season; that they did not obey his commands, and particularly that John had refused to be ruled by him in the matter of marriage. The latter's 'wilfulness' led his father to withhold part of the land he intended to pass to his heir, including the Shelford estate which was placed in lease for 60 years for Margaret and her younger children. As a consequence, John seems to have supported his father's enemies in some of the endless litigation in which the latter was engaged. Sir Thomas's local reputation also suggests that there were grounds for his wife's complaints: railing rhymes circulated in the marketplace denounced him as 'whoremonger' and 'thy beast lyvynge' and accused him of the attempted rape of his daughter-in-law. Lady Stanhope's own contribution to this unhappy menage seems to have been an understandable desire to celebrate 'singing all the day long to the lute' whenever Sir Thomas was lying sick. The bitterness outlived the warring couple, for some years later Margaret as widow is to be found petitioning Lord Chancellor Egerton about her 'miserable condition' since her husband's death, her eldest son by now having, she claimed, become as hostile as his father.[1]

If life in the Stanhope household was beset by bitter drama, that of Sir Hugh Cholmley was remembered for its sustained pleasure and positive purpose. Sir Hugh wrote to his sons 'to embalm [their mother's] . . . great virtues and perfections . . .' and more generally in praise of 'those preceding deserving women, mothers of families' from whom he was descended. Although his text lapses from this worthy aspiration to focus upon women, his account of his wife and their household resonates with affection. In their early years together they lived either in London with her father, the great antiquary Sir William Twysden, or in the gatehouse of the family's home in Whitby where '[we] loved much and joyed in one another'. In adversity they worked together, his wife negotiating the first part of his composition for royalism when he was in exile in France. In prosperity they ran a lively household in which Elizabeth trained up her children and had daughters of many of the local gentry in her service. Husband and wife even shared intellectual interests, for Lady Cholmley's 'chief delight was in her book' and she was 'well versed in history'. When her daughter Ann wished to marry a Gloucestershire gentleman, and Cholmley had reservations about the distance, Elizabeth gave voice to an uncommon sentiment for the period: 'she knew her daughter would be happy with him, and cared not into what country he carried her'. In April 1655 Elizabeth died in the south, and was buried in Kent at the Twysden home of

East Peckham. When Sir Hugh in his turn died he 'declined the being interred in his own country among his ancestors, and chose to be laid here beside her'. [2]

Marriages have always differed in intensity and affection, and the documents through which the historian can gain some insight into these intimacies are equally variable. The litigious conflicts that condition our readings of 'bad' gentry families, and the memoirs or diaries that guide us towards visions of domestic happiness, are not easy to juxtapose. They hardly offer tidy mirror images of relationships, since their purposes are so patently different. Conflict among the Stanhopes when their children were grown may well conceal earlier amity, and Sir Hugh had every incentive to portray Elizabeth as typologically ideal in the encomium constructed for his children. Nevertheless, the problems of the sources should not prevent us from assessing some of the inwardness of these households. They, and many similar examples, reveal both intense contrasts between families, and certain shared experiences and assumptions which served to condition the varied behaviour of the men, women and children who composed the nuclear unit.

## 2.1 IDEALS AND IMAGES

The early modern family existed as the primary focus of reproduction, consumption and socialisation. To the principal duties of ensuring biological survival and economic security were added moral obligations to rear children with the proper religious and social identity. The growing body of advice literature best exemplified by Gouge's *Of Domesticall Duties* (1622) only formalised assumptions about those identities. In these basic concerns the gentry cannot readily be differentiated from their superiors or inferiors within the social hierarchy. The capricious vagaries of biological fortune were equally cruel: the Royalist Sir John Gibson had fifteen children but by the time he was imprisoned in Durham Castle for his part in the Civil War was praying for 'my only hopes a Boye'. In extreme contrast a gentleman like George Owen, the Pembrokeshire antiquary, could be confronted with the need to provide for more than twenty survivors, though in this case admittedly seven of them were illegitimate. In matters of socialisation and moral training it is possible to discover some distinctive patterns of gentry behaviour, but once again the general concern for the schooling of the next generation in proper ethical and religious values was general to the society.[3]

The defining characteristics of the landed family lie rather in its obsession with the continuity of the lineage through the provision of a male heir and the transmission of property in a way that provided both for the survival of the family in the long term and its success in each generation. These elements have been examined in the preceding chapter; here we are concerned with their consequences for the individuals who composed the nuclear unit. Almost all the life choices of the gentry were referenced to these preponderant structural imperatives. This becomes obvious if we look at just three routine social scenarios. The situation of younger sons was dominated by the pattern of primogeniture: its effects upon them were not necessarily wholly negative, as we shall see below, but their position within the family was central to their life experience. Remarriage, either by men or women, was one of the most fraught problems for the gentry family: its emotional consequences were not ignored by contemporaries, but the principal issue was one of economic interest and long-term protection of children. A gentry jest in late seventeenth-century Norfolk referred to a widower as undesirable because he was so 'sonne burn't'. Finally, attitudes to women within the family were often determined by the demands of the group as a whole: constraints upon the choice of marriage partner, pressures in relation to remarriage, and powerful ideological emphasis upon a narrow gender identity, all referred back to a certain perception of familial need.[4]

While property and the proper management of wealth were focal for the gentry family, they also served the broader objective of the maintenance of political influence and social hegemony. As Sir John Lowther observed 'without [wealth] . . . nobilitie or gentilitie is a vaine and contemptible tytle hear in England'. But, he might have added, wealth opened the way to power: to alliance and influence in the localities and perhaps even in central politics. Thus heavy obligations lay upon the head of a gentry house and his wife to sustain appropriate 'port and countenance' in the face of their peers. Strategies had to be evolved for maximising the economic and biological potential of the family: problems, such as too many adult daughters or surviving dowagers, had to be managed with prudence and foresight. Above all, the family needed to display a collective identity: breakdown of the kind experienced by the Stanhopes was damaging to the individuals, but also, if carried too far, threatened the success of the nuclear unit, and even of the long-term dynastic survival of the house. The Willoughbys of Wollaton provide exemplary warning of what could happen: profound conflict between Sir Francis and his lady from the 1570s onwards led first to intense divisions within their household, secondly to hostility between them and their children and threats of disinheritance, thirdly to lavish spending which in part resulted from their ill-ordered establishment. The family did survive, but only in much reduced circumstances, and as a consequence of a stable and prudent marriage between the heiress Bridget and her cousin Sir Percival. The Bulkeleys of Beaumaris came even nearer to disaster, with three generations of traumatic marriages, fraught with accusations of adultery and poisoning and a mid-Stuart generation in which the heir was killed in a duel. They recovered, to emerge triumphantly in the House of Lords, but more by good fortune than any sound personal judgement. It is small wonder that advice to future heads of house by gentry fathers so often requires them to combine the qualities of Moses, Solomon and Job:

> Be nott (my sunn) as a lyon in thyne howse, but to thy famely be as a father: To thy wife be loving, pacient and cumfortable: To thy children, be thou milde and provident, And not provoking them: To thy Servants be sober, be circumspect, be just, especially favoring the good and dilligent, And removing . . . the Evill and negligent. [5]

To counter the vagaries of fortune therefore the gentry family depended heavily upon the personality and abilities of its head. His, or her, task, though fraught with difficulty, was at least underpinned by theoretical models of behaviour to which reference could be made in times of stress. The essence of those models remained the same throughout our period. The family was primarily conceived as a nuclear unit composed of parents and children, owing duties of varying strength and significance to a wider kin, especially to the grandparental generation and siblings. These last obligations were not necessarily culturally binding: in a moment of exasperation with his brother in 1636 Henry Oxinden could insist 'I doe not desire any more company in my house then my wife, children and servants', though he took in his brother as an act of kindness while he recovered from illness. Sir John Oglander expressed a view that seems widely held in the seventeenth century: 'having a loving wife, thou needest no more company than her and thy children'. Servants were integral to the household, and defined as part of the family, though here the second half of the seventeenth century witnessed a sharpening divide between the biological family and the rest of the domestic unit. Within the nuclear family roles were clearly delineated: wife as subordinate to husband, children as dependent on the will of both. Three major cultural influences served to modify this simple hierarchical model during these two centuries: Renaissance humanist thought, the Reformation and the ideological upheavals associated with the Civil War. The impact of these three on both theory and on daily behaviour has been the subject of vigorous debate among historians of the family. It would be foolish to deny that constructs did change – wife beating, for example, became less generally accepted; bastards, once readily acknowledged, became a greater embarrassment, and the double standard of sexual behaviour was at least subjected to some serious questioning. Yet the essential structures, and even some of the views on the affections that should sustain them, seem to have remained remarkably invariant.[6]

The expressive views that the gentry themselves chose to offer about the family can be extracted from a variety of literary sources. These have all the evidential problems commonly suggested by historians: they are biased in time – in favour of the seventeenth century – in social category – towards the upper end of the élite – and in gender – towards men. In addition they are often self-conscious constructs acutely attuned to audience and built with all the artifice of a trained mind. This is not to negate their utility, merely to encourage constant critical alertness in reading them, However, this is an area of social perception in which the visual is as powerful as the verbal, and survives more continuously, and it may be wise to begin there, rather than with the written word.

Throughout these two centuries some families – many families with sufficient means – chose to represent themselves collectively in death on the memorial brass, in stained glass or on the tomb chest. There are significant changes over time: while the reigns of Elizabeth, James and Charles are replete with infants and older children kneeling on their parents' tombs, proportionately fewer from the early sixteenth century include this motif, and it almost vanishes after the Restoration. The pre-1550 tombs that include children, such as that of Oliver Oglander at Brading, Isle of Wight, often have some of the distinctive quality that the group painting of the More family has in another medium. They are experiments in a

6. Panel of tomb of Oglander family *c.* 1530, Brading Church, Isle of Wight

relatively new cultural form. In the seventeenth century, however, it seems that a shift of aesthetic sensibility has taken place: children are represented, but in collective portraits in life, rather than the memorialised family at the death of its head. When children continue to be portrayed in tomb architecture they sometimes display the affectionate informality which was beginning to permeate pictures as well, as do the living and dead children on the tomb of Thomas Read, esquire, in Bardwell Church, Suffolk.

Funeral monuments of the family have the advantage of certain abiding characteristics that indicate more than the aesthetic choices of the sculptors. Husbands and wives are usually accorded equal treatment, as they had been on combined monuments since the

7. Panel from monument to Thomas Read, esquire, d. 1652, Bardwell Church, Suffolk

8. Tomb of Richard Bluett, esquire, d. 1614, and wife, Holcombe Rogus Church, Devon

Middle Ages, though occasionally a husband might lean on an elbow above his wife in a moderate gesture of patriarchal superiority, as in the Bluett tomb at Holcombe Rogus, Devon. Children were always subordinate, often performing the cultural functions previously given to bedesmen. There was, however, an increasing tendency to discriminate between them, at least to differentiate the living from the dead, and to add dead babes to the collectivity. Eldest sons might be separated by size or position from their siblings, but such a stress on primogeniture was by no means universal. Above all, there was almost invariably a sharp division by gender, often expressed by daughters kneeling behind wives, sons behind husbands. It was numbers, sex and assigned role that mattered; the nuclear family displayed in its collective strength, linked to the wider kin by its armorial displays. Thomas Fuller's story of the armorial glass erected by the wife of Sir Lewis Pollard in the church of Bishop's Nympton, Devon, in the 1530s charmingly evokes this pride in fecundity and in the dynastic nuclear family:

> the Lady, glassing the window in her husband's absence at the Term in London, caused one child more then she then had to be set up, presuming (having had one and twenty already, and usually conceiving at her Husband's coming home) she should have another child, which, inserted in expectance, came to passe accordingly.[7]

Tomb evidence would suggest that the nuclear family was of central importance to the Tudor and Stuart gentry and was at the heart of their broader concept of lineage. Celebration sometimes mingled with grief, as in the Elmley Castle monument to the Savages, in which four living sons kneel at the feet of their mother and father, and she cradles a surviving 'darling little daughter' in her arms. All this, Lady Catherine tells us, was done in token of her great love for her husband. The tomb could become an icon of unity and of the social identity of the family that transcended death. Portraits could also focus upon the mortality but integrity of the family unit, the famous examples being David des Granges's Saltonstall family and John Souch's Sir Thomas Aston at the deathbed of his wife. The latter's double representation of the natural and social body of Magdalene Aston, integrates the living and dead, although in this case in a powerful image of mourning which suggests the uncertainty of the family's future.[8]

9. Men of the Curson family *c.* 1527, stained glass window, Waterperry Church, Oxfordshire

10. Women of the Curson family *c.* 1527, stained glass window, Waterperry Church, Oxfordshire

11. John Souch, 'Sir Thomas Aston at the Deathbed of his Wife' 1635–6

It is more difficult to 'read' familial identity through portraits of the living. Here the primary focus throughout these centuries was on individual representation. Family portraiture, a subject sorely in need of more serious research, seems to have always been a minority taste, perhaps because of cost, but also because the need to display the family as a living unit does not seem to have been so generally experienced. When informal group portraiture began to make serious headway under Flemish and Dutch influence in the mid-seventeenth century, it was as likely to involve groups of unrelated adults, or sets of children on their own, as the nuclear unit. Paintings such as that of the third Sir Thomas Lucy and his family, are rare before 1700.

12. Cornelius Johnson attrib., 'The Family of Sir Thomas Lucy III', *c.* 1628

Prescriptive writers articulated the image that Sir Thomas chose to display visually. 'A private household of family', said Lady Mildmay, '(which may resemble a whole commonwealth) consist[s] of the master and mistress, the husband and the wife, children and servants, all of one mind in love, fear and obedience, being all well chosen, instructed and governed with true judgement'. What this meant in practice varied significantly both in time and with the particular preoccupations of the observer. For John Stuteville, writing under the perturbing conditions of the Commonwealth, it was a 'bulwarke against that Sea of Democracy, . . . to keepe theire descents pure and untainted from that Mungril breed, which would faigne mixe with them'. This is extreme: rather more commonly the family was seen as an opportunity to sustain and perpetuate a specific religious ideology: the godly Puritan family, whose defenders were so vociferous, or the Catholic household, whose advocates were understandably less noisy. Few proceeded to the other extreme of explaining the family purely as an economic unit operating for the accretion of wealth and power to its members, though the advice literature is full of the language of acquisition decently veiled as concern for prudential management. '[I] am resolved', said the elder Sir John Lowther, 'in a fair prudent way to husband our fortunes, and direct my children and their children with some benificence'. Christopher Wandesford, who carefully circumvented many of the material issues that agitated gentry writers, nevertheless stressed the virtues of using marriage as the means of enhancing the family estates 'that you give cause to be registered hereafter in the list of them who have enlarged their patrimonial Possessions'.[9]

## 2.2 MARRIAGE

Since the gentry family had to bear so complex a social charge, the moment of its formation was, to quote one of the Verney family, 'the weightiest business' a father and mother could undertake. Fathers of large families directed much of their energy to negotiation for suitable matches, and mothers, though less prominent in the records, often played key roles in calculating the acceptability of proposals. The outlines of marriage strategy are not difficult to discern. The transmission of wealth and property was crucial, the demands of primogeniture always making it difficult to resolve how much should be set aside for younger offspring. Political and social alliances were usefully cemented by marriage, perhaps most frequently those made within a particular locality. In a patriarchal society there was scant expectation that relationships would be formed by the young people concerned, although it is widely agreed that younger sons always had considerable freedom, and that the intensity of parental control tended to diminish somewhat over time. Negotiations for the construction of a marriage frequently foundered on material, less often on ideological or social, grounds and there was often little that the young could do to reverse parental opposition. The intervention of third parties was commonplace, and one of the most important functions of the wider kin network was to propose and vet suitable candidates for marriage. Two elements of change should be noted: firstly religious compatibility obviously became increasingly significant as a criterion for marriage; secondly, as London grew as a centre of gentry sociability, so it provided access to a national marriage market for those who had previously depended on the locality or kin-connection.[10]

The apparent 'facts' of gentry marriage have also been solemnly calculated in numerous local studies. Table 2:1 is the summary provided by Blackwood on endogamy in ten counties on the eve of the Civil War, with figures added from more recent studies on Warwickshire and Worcestershire. In the last two counties a striking percentage of gentry heads of families married not just outside the county, but beyond the contiguous group of counties, 24 per cent in each case. These calculations, however, are fraught with difficulty. Apart from the problem of comparing like with like, crude county figures disguise both the detail of geographical choice of marriage partners, and contrasts within the ranks of the gentry. Where more careful breakdown has been attempted it usually indicates, unsurprisingly, that lesser gentlemen tended to marry within their own neighbourhoods, while the magistracy and greater gentry

Table 2.1 *The Marriage Alliances of the Gentry in Twelve Counties, c.1642*[a]

| *County* | *No. of marriages* | *% within county* |
|---|---|---|
| Lancashire | 450 | 71.2 |
| Cheshire [b] | 371 | 65.0 |
| Cumberland & Westmorland | 120 | 62.5 |
| Dorset | 280 | 49.5 |
| Kent [c] | 170 | 82.0 |
| Essex [d] | 263 | 43.3 |
| Hertfordshire | 123 | 37.4 |
| Norfolk | 282 | 71.6 |
| Suffolk | 329 | 69.0 |
| Warwickshire [e] | 152 | 43.0 |
| Worcestershire | | 44.0 |

*Notes* [a] Blackwood, *Lancashire*, p.26.
[b] The Cheshire figure includes all marriages contracted by major families.
[c] The Kent figure excludes baronets and knights.
[d] The four eastern counties also exclude baronets and knights.
[e] Hughes, *Warwickshire*, pp. 39–40, where the Worcestershire figures are also cited.

were more variable in their preferences. The Suffolk magistracy, for example, showed an inclination for local marriage identical with that of the gentry cohort as a whole in the reign of Elizabeth: 60 per cent were allied in their own half of the county, but a larger group of the greater gentry looked to London or beyond for their brides – 22 per cent as compared with the general figure of 15 per cent. Figures like these suggest the use of broad networks for a substantial minority: an extended kin no doubt provided one such structure; shared national education or the sociable environment of London were obvious alternatives.[11]

The objectives of the pursuit of alliance were economic stability, or preferably advantage, combined with secure status and personal affection. 'I had but two great temporal blessings to beg of God Almighty' wrote Sir Edward Turnor to his daughter in 1685, 'to dispose of your brother and yourself in marriage as might make you both and myself most pleased and happy therein'. Many, if not most, parents were conscious of the value of active enthusiasm from their offspring, but were also alarmed by the perils of blind affection. 'I woold not for wealth', said Sir John Oglander to his beloved George, 'bynd your affection to an ill face [but] my advise was that vadinge Bewtie myght not blynd your better Iudgement'. Marriage could not, for the heir, be simply a personal matter for 'on your hapye Mariadge Depended your owne good and the welfare of your Brothers and Sisters'. Women were often the focus of similar anxieties, since their supposed temperamental weaknesses – impetuosity, sensuality and lack of reason – were seen to make them peculiarly susceptible to the passions. Oglander was only one of several fathers who offered the brutal advice, taken originally from William Cecil 'Marry thy daughters in time lest they marry themselves'. When Mary Throckmorton was offered an alliance with a Mr Hungerford her grandfather urged her to accept, since young women who preferred 'theyr owne fansye grownded upon no reasonable censure . . . [often] heaped upon themselves a contynuall repentaunce all theyr lyffe'.[12]

Since most surviving evidence about marriage arrangements among the gentry derives from the legal settlements that accompanied them, we cannot quantify the calculus of interest and emotion that marked gentry alliances. There were certainly many parents for whom direct financial interest took precedence over all else. Sir Edward Dering II recorded in 1680 that he was making great efforts 'to get a good wife for Charles, that being the best way of settlement I can think of, he being too old to take up any profession'. This is unusually direct: it was more common to make these cynical observations of the marriages of others, like Sir Edward Dering's observation to his wife in 1634 'Sir Sackville Cerow is married to £5000 and one Mrs. Manners'. Or Oglander on John Lisle's wife:

> Neither well-proportioned, fair nor wise:
> All these defects four thousand pounds supplies.

All that can usually be observed is the hard bargaining and care invested in such arrangements. In a full archive, like that of the Gage family of Sussex, one can trace agreements generation on generation, rising in financial value, and legal complexity, but essentially similar. The proper relationship between portion, lands settled on the couple, and the ultimate value of the jointure, was the main consideration, supplemented by smaller problems like the costs of the wedding, and place of residence of the nuptial pair.[13]

Non-monetary calculations, such as the social and political desirability of the alliance, must also have weighed very heavily with many parents. So, increasingly, did religious compatibility. Sir Thomas Coningsby, negotiating with Sir Robert Harley who wished to marry his daughter, believed or at least claimed that 'loufe and good neayghteborwhod [sic]' were the most valuable consequence of the match for the parents, and that for the couple 'maryage is a heavy and spyrytuall thinge'. Of course, as Harley's father pointed out to him, much of this was mere cover for a reluctance to advance enough cash, and the negotiations in this case failed. However, many of the same issues were revived when Sir Robert finally married his third and famous wife, Brilliana Conway, and here his father was so eager to secure a successful and godly alliance that he accepted a lower dowry than might have been anticipated and settled his main estate of Brampton Bryan on the couple for life.[14]

Despite the burden of cultural expectation and parental calculation there remained, of course, men and women who did 'marry themselves', either in outright opposition to parents, or by wearing down their elders until permission was reluctantly granted. The complete rebels were sometimes cut off without money or forgiveness – in an extreme example Peter Coryton, the eldest son of a Cornish family, was alleged to have murdered his father when the latter threatened to disinherit him because of his desire to marry a Mr Wray's daughter. Richard Bagot vowed that his eloping daughter Margaret should make him 'rule his purse, which shall make me better hable to helpe the rest'. More often the evidence suggests a calculated risk, and a justified expectation that there would be some subsequent accommodation. William Lowther, a younger son who married without consent, was threatened with the loss of his landed inheritance by his father, but a few years later was restored to grace and described as 'very diligent'. Jane Baynham, who made the mistake of 'hastely and unknowen' marrying the man who was supposedly matchmaker for her intended spouse, distressed her widowed mother more because there had been no proper financial negotiations than because she intended to reject her choice. Sir Charles Cornwallis deeply disapproved of the 'unadvised' marriage of his granddaughter but 'sithence the stone cast out of hand cannot be recalled . .' he offered her support in her new life. Anne Townshend, who had married John Spelman against her family's wishes, also pleaded her cause to her grandfather Sir Nathaniel Bacon, who 'gave her some comfort such as I thought good'. Her jointure was eventually settled and friendly relations between the two Norfolk familes restored. The patient might well envy the impetuous who succeeded in manipulating their elders: Gervase Holles's mother waited seven years for grudging parental 'permission' rather than consent, and the witty endurance of Dorothy Osborne while she was courted by William Temple produced one of the great letter series of the seventeenth century. 'I find', she famously remarked, 'I want courage to marry where I do not like'. [15]

Perhaps the most immediate access to the complexities of gentry marriage can be gained by studying the fortunes of one family over several generations. The Wynns of Gwydir corresponded on every conceivable matter, but nothing occupied their writing time more fully than the need to organise marriages. Most of our information derives from the generation of Sir John and his children between the 1570s and the 1640s, but this can be supplemented with examples from the next two generations in the post-Civil War period. The Wynns were upwardly mobile, and suffered from the general financial embarrassments of the Welsh gentry, so sentiment might be expected to yield to economic need in their negotiations, though the story is not quite so simple. Young John succeeded in achieving a good marriage, negotiated by his father and uncle, with one of the daughters of Sir William Gerard, chancellor of Ireland. Yet, in his enthusiasm for the match, he and his father apparently left loopholes in the marriage settlement: four years later he gloomily described himself as leading a miserable life because the 'jars' between his father and Gerard had left him impoverished. This experience, plus other complications which his father had had in placing his children, led John to be cautious about his own offspring. An early proposal from a local ally for a marriage for one of his daughters drew the response that he wished to wait until they were of 'ripe years' and the sonorous reflection that 'good wyll grownded on fyrme frindshipp breedeth (with gods plesure) alliance and not allwies maredges good will'.[16]

Although John extricated himself from this particular request, he did permit his daughters to marry young, and in ways that cemented his alliances among the North Welsh gentry. Bess married John Bodvel, as far as we know in an arranged match and one that turned out unhappily: Mary married Roger Mostyn, a very suitable match between two of the most powerful families in the shire, but one which Roger later claimed he made himself in the teeth of his father's opposition. This match proved very happy, despite continuing friction between the two Mostyns, friction in which Wynn aided and abetted his son-in-law.[17]

But these arrangements for daughters were as nothing in comparison to John's grand visions for his heir of the same name. Here local identities yielded to an ambition to play the national marriage market, as evidence of the power and success of the family. Negotiations began as early as 1597, when a younger daughter of the Knightley family was proposed. However, it was not until the younger John was at Lincoln's Inn in 1604, and able to orchestrate part of the negotiations himself, that the hunt began in earnest. Eligible ladies were discussed *ad nauseam* in correspondence between father and son, the tone suggesting that the son was as ambitious as the father, and did not need the latter's occasional warning against ill-advised matrimony. The issue of estate was always uppermost in their thoughts, but the younger John, because he was in contact with several of the ladies, inevitably formed firm likes and dislikes. In the case of Solicitor-General Fleming's daughter Wynn's London agent sounded warning notes 'It is most certen that there is mutuall great love betwen them. I would it hadd not bene soe upon suche incertain groundes'. Fleming indeed failed to meet Wynn's high expectations of portion, and so John was returned brusquely to his study. Among other candidates were the daughters of Sir Baptist Hicks, (the Welsh gentry did not despise city wealth) but this grounded on Lady Hicks's reservations about the godliness of the Welsh and on Sir Baptist's concern not to marry his daughter 'where he might have no comfort of her'. By this time John, junior, and the two London-based uncles who were assisting him, were thoroughly irritated by Wynn's greed for a large portion when he would only offer limited jointure. The saga continued, with possible matches dying and falling by the wayside, until at the end of 1606 John finally married the daughter of Lady Eleanor Cave who had first been proposed two years earlier. And after all this calculation and thought the marriage treaty again proved inadequate and the marriage itself perhaps the most unhappy of any made by a Wynn in this period.[18]

The whole experience of the younger John's marriage bred some revulsion in the family, and encouraged a temporary change of outlook. When Roger Mostyn was looking for a match for his heir Sir John (as he now was) wrote in passion that he would sooner marry his son to a country woman of 'plaen honest breedynge' with £2,000, than to a Londoner with twice as much. And after the death of his elder brother, Richard Wynn, now the heir, insisted that, although he would not marry without his father's consent, he would rather take someone he found desirable with less portion, remembering his brother's unfortunate match. The problem for Sir John was that good intentions did not produce the portion he found necessary for the support of his estate, and 1615 was almost as fraught a year of marriage negotiation as 1604 had been. Richard, at Court, was soon complaining that his countrymen told him Sir John proposed to sell him to the highest bidder and he was prevented from marrying the daughter of Sir John Trevor because of this greed. Another attractive candidate, the daughter of Sir Henry Baynton, was lost because her father died leaving her without sufficient portion, but after another year of uncertainty Richard found an apparently desirable wife in the daughter of Sir Francis Darcy. An interesting sidelight on this last case is that one of Sir John's agents used his contacts among the Welsh servants in the Darcy household to gain a 'character reference' on the young woman. Another is that the Darcys put strong, and effective, pressure on Richard not to take their daughter permanently to Wales: even after the death of his father he retained his prime residence in Middlesex.[19]

The younger Wynn sons had the obverse of the heirs' problems: too little attention and support from their father instead of too much. Owen, Henry and William eventually married, but after many traumas: Owen secured the niece of Bishop Williams on rather unfavourable terms, but probably only gained her at all because there was a chance he would inherit since Richard was still (and remained) childless. In terms of happiness and domestic calm, however, these younger sons fared well, and Grace Wynn, the niece the bishop, proved an unduly worthy partner for the rather feeble Owen.[20]

Sir John Wynn was obviously a formidable, ambitious and greedy father. Yet he was not without his moments of guilt about the consequences of his actions, and he was largely sustained by the belief that he was endeavouring the best for his house. Later in the century personal preference apparently played a greater part in such negotiations. We know most about the efforts of Lady Grace as a widow to secure a proper match for her granddaughter Mary, who was orphaned and made heiress to the Gwydir estates in the 1670s. There was no doubt that a marriage such as this should still be arranged, and there were suitors and matchmakers in abundance, but Lady Grace apparently determined that Mary should not be 'disposed of' until she could choose for herself. This did not prevent her grandmother seizing rapidly on some slight indications of affection to pursue an alliance with Sir Thomas Middleton of Chirk, desirable because of the proximity of his estates. That alliance foundered on the usual problems of proper terms and Mary eventually married far away from her own country, into the Bertie family of Lincolnshire, though we have no means of knowing if her own preference determined the outcome.[21]

The Wynn family's attitudes to marriage negotiations, while in no sense exhaustive, illuminate a number of the issues that moved the early modern gentry. An adequate economic return on any relationship was essential, not only because of the security of the next generation, but because a marriage portion was often needed to fund the expenditure of the current generation, especially to provide portions for other children. Exogamy, marriage outside the region or kin group, facilitated by the residence of the younger Wynns in London, was of particular social and political utility for the heir of a 'rising' house, and might also be a means for younger brothers to escape the financial constraints imposed by the transmission of the estate to the eldest son, though it must be said that the family were here singularly unsuccessful in the pursuit of 'good investments'. On the other hand, endogamy could strengthen local alliances: for, as Sir John observed of his daughters, they were well-beloved in his neighbourhood, and a 'great comfort' and 'the strength of my house'. Affection, as well as alliance, may have encouraged gentlemen to marry their daughters at home: Southerners certainly seem to have hesitated before committing a child to the remote fastnesses of Wales, and Richard was deracinated partly as a consequence of his marriage. As for love, it was assumed as a product of marriage where there was no pre-existing aversion to the partner. Sir John's own marriage proved warmly companionate, and the marital difficulties of his eldest son and younger daughter therefore genuinely seem to have shocked him. The depth and range of the Gwydir correspondence suggests that neither parents nor children saw any necessary tension between marriage for advancement and marriage for companionate affection, though the children were predictably more alert to the dangers of allowing financial considerations to be wholly dominant.

Once a marriage was finally made, the parents, kin and matchmakers who had been so active in its construction played a less prominent, though by no means negligible, part. Perhaps the most significant functions of parents were to secure the terms of the settlement itself, and often to provide accommodation for the young couple for a period of time before they established an independent household. The importance of discharging adequately the settlement cannot be overemphasised: although marital disharmony might be the consequence of any sort of incompatibility, its origins most often lay in conflicts about property, usually emanating from some failure of settlement. One of the most spectacular breakdowns of the Elizabethan years, that between Sir Francis Willoughby and his wife Elizabeth Littelton, originated in Sir John Littelton's inability to pay the full sum of £1,500 promised as her portion. Edmund Brudenell of Deene in Northamptonshire began a vitriolic dispute with his wife Agnes when the indulgent settlement made on her by her father was challenged by her uncle as heir male. Much of the marital and interfamilial litigation in the central courts of Tudor and Stuart England derived from the deficiencies of settlements, or the failure of one or other party to discharge them fully.[22]

The need to provide residence for the newly married couple was sometimes a consequence of the financial arrangements for the payment of the portion, and the commensurate provision of income.

It was frequently inconvenient for a new household to be established immediately at marriage, and the marriage settlement therefore made provision for co-residence or tabling in one or other parental household. No firm conventions appear to have governed the choice of establishment, or the length of time allotted, which could be as short as a few months or as long as three years. The balance of examples, however, suggests that new husbands more frequently moved to be with their parents-in-law than wives with theirs. The motives were mainly financial, but we may also discern interesting social consequences. When young gentry brides remained in their parental home it no doubt provided them with a continuity of experience in housekeeping and perhaps in the initial rearing of a child. That such training was deliberately intended is suggested by the Wynns, who took Margaret Cave into their household to learn Welsh and housewifery, while Henry's wife was there later 'for breedynge'. Nathaniel Bacon persuaded his mother to take in his young bride, Anne Gresham, on the grounds that she needed further training and that her indulgent parents were not the most appropriate people to provide it. The parental home may also have been seen as the best environment for learning the proper disciplines of marriage: when Elizabeth Willoughby rebelled against her husband's authority his sister suggested that they should return to Sir John Littelton's roof 'till such time as she should have lost her wilfullness'. Unusual circumstances, especially those of Civil War or major financial hardship, might prolong this extended household arrangement: Alice Thornton resided principally with her mother for eight years during the Interregnum, and John Newdigate II was supported by his father-in-law for the extraordinary period of nine years.[23]

When the arrangement was a stable one it could have interesting effects in bonding families, and constructing firm kin identities across more than one generation. A notable case is that of Sir Hugh Cholmley, who resided with his Twysden in-laws for much of the 1620s and came to identify with his learned father-in-law more strongly than with his own family. The younger Sir Edward Dering had much the same experience in the later 1640s, though without any loss of connection with his own family. There are numerous examples in gentry correspondence of close business relationships, obviously based on mutual trust, between fathers and sons-in-law, and it is at least possible that many of these were constructed from co-residence early in marriage. This was certainly the case in the

Newdigate family where the Fitton clan became the heart of John and Anne's social and business network. But co-residence was also liable to reveal the weaknesses of kin relationships, and the difficulties of transfer between families. There were disputes about the proper number of servants to be retained, about the length of stay and about standing within the household. In the case of John and Anne Spelman neither parent was prepared to face the costs, and Anne was forced to plead with her mother for houseroom. Sir Edward Aston, who was compelled to reside with his Lucy in-laws complained 'no man living would have endured with patience that hard usage I had there'. If a marriage began badly the habit of co-residence made it even more difficult for a daughter to detach herself from the parental home. Anne Aston exploited the forceful presence of her mother Joyce Lucy to extract concessions from her husband: 'Truly', her husband complained, 'my lady Lucy herself is the cause of my wife's discontent'. A more pathetic case was that of Thomas Congreve's daughter, Isabel, who was only with the greatest difficulty, and much support from her siblings, moved from Staffordshire to her husband's home near Welshpool, and returned to the parental roof at every available opportunity.[24]

Even when parents assisted the married pair with proper financial provision and suitable initial support, marriage was a hazardous undertaking. Temperament, the nature of expectations and changing external circumstances all contributed to the success or failure of the enterprise. It is in the nature of the surviving records, and perhaps of the privacy of the lives we are trying to investigate, that it is easier to generalise about failure and difficulty than about success: only when crisis threatened did men and women normally talk about their domestic experiences explicitly. There does, however, seem to be ample evidence from the correspondence and memoirs of the Elizabethan period onwards to justify Houlbrooke's assertion that 'married love clearly existed in practice and was highly valued as an ideal'. The practice can most routinely be observed in the correspondence of spouses separated by business, the ideal in memoirs and epitaphs. The weight of surviving correspondence between gentry spouses is interestingly skewed to the years between the 1580s and the Civil War: no accidental pattern, since these are the decades of intensifying focus upon London, the law courts and the social season, when it was less automatic that wives would accompany their husbands to the city than after the Restoration. Then inevitably the Civil War itself drove couples apart, and constrained them to express feeling at far remove. Characteristic of these offerings is the letter of 1606 from Jane Maurice to her 'dear and loving husband' Sir William. She informs him that she is in good health 'and so longe as you are in health all is welle to my mynde'. Her letter has only a little minor business included, and she only begs that her spouse write as often as he can 'and that will comfort my hart God knowes'. Women were perhaps more commonly expressive of emotion than men, but equal warmth from husbands is not difficult to find. Sir Edward Dering wrote of a letter sent him by his wife Unton that its 'Argent and Sable', the colours of her arms, 'is farr more sweete and pretious unto me then all ye Argent and Gules in the worlde, except that in thy cheeke'. Jonathan Rashleigh, in exile in 1646, wrote to his Mary 'thy kind letters doe much comfort my sad troubles, that all are well and in health is a great happiness to thy overburthened friend'. Even the crusty Sir John Wynn wrote to his wife from London 'I cannot be well yf yow be yll beynge the cardynall and cheefe prope and staye of my well fare'.[25]

Memorialisation seems to approximate most closely to some reality in the hands of writers like Cholmley, Slingsby and Holles. The last gives an account of his own wife deeply conditioned by the conventions of affectionate piety – 'envy never lodged in her', 'devout and pious she was in private', 'of so few words and those few to so much sense that in neither shee discovered woman' – yet the power of his love for his wife also echoes through his pages. He was so happy in marriage that he would willingly have buried himself in retirement, and after Dorothy's death he was scarcely able to move out of doors for three months. Many gentry husbands expressed grief and devastation of this order at the death of their spouses. Herbert Aston, for example, gives an account of his wife's deathbed that combines highly conventionalised Catholic piety, with a powerful immediacy. Katherine reassures him that he will survive without her 'I leave you ten for me, and Con [her eldest daughter] will quickly be a huswife, which I never was'. On the night she dies Herbert conveys his mental state in vivid terms:

> Whosever saw me then, much more my calmness by her all night but most of all my surviving such a loss, may conclude my love to her had little of passion, then I hope the more of truth, both then and ever. Indeed my strange quiet and resignation then, is more

> my owne wonder than it can be anyes, it was so contrary to what I felt, so beyond any I ever owned. . .

The mourning epitaphs of later Tudor and Stuart England articulate some of these griefs through all the formality of their language.[26]

Stable marriages, marked by at least a measure of companionability and affection, were sustained in part by the cultural constructs so often praised after death. Women displayed themselves as modest, obedient and pious, men as solicitous for the collective good of the family and naturally wise in the exercise of authority. Since much educational effort was directed to the assimilation of these roles resourceful gentlemen and women could employ these gender categories as a means of conflict avoidance, and as a method of unifying spouses in the face of servants and the external world. The rich correspondence between Sir Ralph Verney and his wife Mary after the Civil War reveals precisely this deployment of gender models to sustain a relationship that was both affective and effective. Sir Ralph retained his patriarchical authority by issuing minute instructions on all matters of business, especially when Lady Verney was pleading their cause before the Committee for Compounding. Mary ostentatiously deferred to his judgement: in July 1647, for example, she wrote to Sir Ralph in exile 'tis onely because you bid me doe itt, that I trouble you with my silly advise'. In practice, like many wives, she employed the language of gender deference while having to make critical decisions for herself. This worked both because of an innate acceptance of basic roles, and because of powerful sentiment between the spouses. Mary, after lengthy separation, wrote 'I cannot be any longer from you therefore I am resolved to stand or fall with you': earlier Sir Ralph had written in similar terms 'the grief of our fatal separation is not to be expressed'.[27]

One explanation for 'bad' marriages is therefore presumably a failure by one or both partners to perform according to cultural norms. This is a complaint most often directed at the wife in a gentry relationship, both because husbands tended to have more command of the mechanisms of grievance and because the normative demands upon the woman were in any case more intense. The most serious charge that could be made was that of adultery: Marmaduke Langdale, for example, accused his wife of fornication with his servant 'Pedro the Blackamoor', though the story of his own behaviour that emerges from the court case suggests that the accusations were designed to cover his own aberrant activities. In the Bulkeley family of Beaumaris, Angelsey, there were spectacular accusations of adultery in two generations, the first involving Agnes, wife of the second Sir Richard, who was accused in 1572 of poisoning her husband after twice having been suspected of illicit relationships. When such behaviour could be proved it offered, of course, the possibility of action for judicial separation through the spiritual courts. Even if the full breach was not made, a denial of paternity might lead to the disinheritance of the children of a wife suspected of adultery. Sir George Hervey disinherited his children in the early sixteenth century on the grounds that his wife was 'very light of her conversation'. In litigation about the breakdown of marriage it was routine to make reference to a woman's 'immodest and unseemly behaviour' towards other men. Some, of course, deserved the charge, like the Shropshire gentlewoman who deserted her husband to follow a royalist captain, only to find him already married: she was taken back by her spouse, but only after the payment of a second marriage portion.[28]

The survival of a double standard of sexual behaviour, and the ability to lead a public and mobile life may have enabled some men in tense relationships to escape direct conflict with their wives. But those very freedoms were often the cause, or at least contributors to, marital instability and breakdown. Prudent women might endeavour, as did Sir Richard Cholmley's second wife, to 'bear and connive at Sir Richard's amorous courses', but even she was only able to do so by avoiding co-habitation. Spectacular lechers like Gilbert Littelton or Anthony Bourne understandably found little welcome from their wives. Gilbert Littelton, head of one of the most senior gentry families of Worcestershire, abandoned his wife and '[did] betake himself to live in bad sorte with divers lewde and infamous women'. Anthony, the son of Queen Mary's Secretary of State, apparently married Elizabeth Conway for financial reasons and proceeded to sell the land she had brought into the relationship. Explosive hostility between the pair focused on a Mrs Pagnam, with whom he chose to live for much of the time. Although a variety of third parties, especially among Elizabeth's relatives, sought reconciliation between the two, there was a reluctant acceptance that Bourne's behaviour was intolerable and justified separation. It may have been adultery that also led to the breakdown between Sir James Scudamore of Holme Lacy, and Mary Baskerville, though her son Hannibal, whose narrative of his mother survives, is circumspect about such detail. A part of the tangled affairs of the Bulkeleys certainly turned on male infidelity: the fourth Sir Richard, who died in 1624, was a wild and 'unthriftie' man, who 'prov'd a great hunter of women' and whose wife seems to have returned the compliment with her own adultery.[29]

Other 'unwifely' behaviour also led to marital conflict. Scolding and undue assertiveness that it implied was perhaps the most important element here: the Stanhope case reveals Sir Thomas's accumulated resentment at his wife's aggression. Sir Thomas Aston claimed that the ferocious matriarchy of wife and mother-in-law were rendering his life miserable. Lady Elizabeth Fenton insisted that her stepmother Dame Margery Norris had made her father's life miserable with unwomanly behaviour and scolding, though Margery denied that there was more than the occasional 'unkindness' between them. One of the Cholmley ancestors, Francis, was 'overtopped and guided by his wife, which it is thought she did by witchcraft or some extraordinary means'. Verbal aggression and hostility by a wife were feared because they brought the family into public disrepute, as in a splendid brawl in the family of Lord Chief Justice Hobart in the early seventeenth century. His daughter-in-law Prudence was at odds both with her husband and his family: so much so that on one occasion his daughter Mary and his wife were moved to physical aggression. As Edward Hobart reported it to his brother 'my mother . . . ded begin to laye at Prudence with her stafe at the hale dore . . . We wente together scowldeinge to the kitchen dore . . . [where] Mary and she did buffett a while . . . she sweares we woulde have murthered her if company had not ben by'. In an extreme case, that of the Willoughby household, the brawling could reach the level of public scandal. The household was divided into warring factions, each bent on challenging the other's power. Such familial discord posed obvious threats to the 'natural' social order and was often firmly blamed on women. 'To discredit [your] husband', one of Willoughby's servants piously reminded his mistress, 'was to discredit [yourself] and posterity'.[30]

Much unhappiness was generated by forms of male authoritarianism. The assumed inequality between partners made it easy for abusive behaviour to flourish. Sir John Wynn was distressed by the brutality of Sir John Bodvel towards his younger daughter, and believed he would 'nott sease to vexe and abuse her untyll he kyll her', though he found it difficult to know how to restrain him, other than by keeping his daughter at home for a time in 1615. Mental cruelty was as difficult to handle as physical violence: Susan Verney described her sister Margaret's husband as a 'very humourous cross boy', who made his bride 'cry night and day'. This marriage did end in formal separation, after physical attacks on Margaret had occurred. One form of cruelty that may as have often been effect as cause of a bad marriage was the disappearance of the male spouse 'on his travels'. The younger Sir John Wynn, who was totally incompatible temperamentally with his wife, seems to have gone abroad mainly to escape his miseries. His brother-in-law Roger Mostyn advised that he should not be permitted to stay away too long, since his further absence would merely exacerbate the problem. Sir Matthew Arundell, who as a Catholic had his own motives for being abroad in the 1590s, had apparently abandoned his wife, who petitioned Robert Cecil for his return. In 1603 Lady Anne Townshend was greatly alarmed that her husband spoke of travelling abroad for seven years and leasing their main seat at Raynham: 'if there be no meanes made I may live this 7 yeares without eyther my children or maintenans, which is a lamentabell thing.'[31]

Other reasons for marital failure were legion: kin or servants might foster conflict for their own reasons, distance might simply isolate the elements of the family from one another, mental instability might spell disaster. But it is rare to find that at some point financial disputes or tensions did not play their part. Either contract arrangements failed to function, or a husband improperly exploited the property set aside for jointure, or indebtedness brought the whole family unit to collapse. When so many unions were contracted to stabilise the finances of an individual or his family the possibilities of disaster were ever present. At the very least the transfer of wealth could become a matter of cruel jest, as when Lord St John, having married a rich widow at the end of the 1560s, mocked her at his dinner table: 'your ladyship hath only paid for your place, wherefore if any can now make a penny more of you I would he had you.' Some wives would perhaps have envied her lot, since they were subjected to the more material traumas of indebtedness and poverty. Elizabeth Bourne's struggles to gain some maintenance from a wastrel husband occupy much of a British Library letter file, and Mrs Noye, one of a Cornish gentry family, was not untypical in pleading for some small part 'of that estate which her deere parentes with so manye yeres pasience . . . had contrebated to preserve'.[32]

There is no method of calculating what proportion of gentry marriages ended in breakdown. It is very unlikely to have been greater than the 10 per cent of peerage marriages which Stone identified as failing between 1570 and 1659. Stone also found a particular concentration of conflict in the last Elizabethan generation and under James I: this seems less evident for the gentry, where the spread of recorded crisis broadly mirrors that of the depth of general documentary evidence. It may have been harder for mere gentlemen to exploit such legal resources for separation as did exist, and the financial pressures to sustain marriage presumably increased as one moved further down the social order. Nevertheless, the tales of conflict and woe are sufficiently common to suggest that the ethical, moral and social constraints so carefully articulated and afforced in this period did not counterbalance the problems of poorly funded relationships, *mésalliances* or sheer incompatibility.

For the majority, however, the historian can merely observe that the family unit held together and formed the core of most social relationships. The rhyming Yorkshireman John Kaye suggests the essentially pragmatic basis of these arrangements:

My wife and I together mett
According to our parents will
Wedded we were at years sixtene
When neither of us had great skill
Yet dyd the Lord our wants fulfill
And sent us children, tenn and fyve
Wherof but tenn are now on lyve
Thes tenn and I doo yett remayne
To walke and wander too and froo
Here in this vale moost uncertayne,
Sometymes in wealth, somtymes in woo
As pleaceth Lord, yt must be soo

Wives, in this reading, were partners in the difficult management of household and resources. Christopher Wandesford told his heir that he would not have run his family successfully had not his wife 'never wasted six-pence in her life that she could creditably save'. Sir John Oglander praised his wife as 'no spender, [a woman who] never wore a silk gown but for her credit when she went abroad, and never to please herself. She was up every day before me and oversaw all the outhouses: she would not trust her maid with directions but would wet her shoes to see it done herself'.[33]

## 2.3 CHILDREN

It was the care and rearing of children that consumed most of the energy and resources of gentry marriages. Early rearing was physically, and usually emotionally, demanding, launching older children into the world a constant financial and organisational struggle. Infancy, once like domestic emotion largely *terra incognita* for historians, has been given sustained attention in recent years. Interest has focused largely on the social practice of wet-nursing, and on the degree of early bonding between parent and child. When observing the gentry it is easier to generalise with some confidence about the former than the latter issue. Wet-nursing seems to have remained the norm for the landed classes throughout the period, despite the powerful arguments from humanist and Protestant writers that maternal breastfeeding was desirable. There were some exceptions, who were felt worthy of especial comment: Anne Newdigate breastfed all five of her children, causing agitation to her friend and confidante Sir William Knollys who remarked 'I shuld like nothing that you play the nurse yf you wear my wife'. Thomas Congreve on the other hand accepted without particular remark his younger daughter Elizabeth who brought her nursing child with her to his Stretton home. Lucy Hutchinson was jealous of a younger sister suckled by her mother, and Alice Thornton fed two of her youngest children, both boys, presumably reflecting her anxiety to ensure the survival of an heir. The more common pattern was that that can be seen in the Bacon papers, where wet nurses were regularly employed for Roger and Anne Townshend, several of them identifiable as former servants within the household. Considerable care was often taken about the choice of nurses: even fathers and grandfathers played a part here. Sir John Conway recommended a nurse to his daughter-in-law, and Sir Robert Delaval, overjoyed at the birth of a grandson, offered extensive advice on the sort of woman who would produce proper milk. Despite our innate prejudices on this subject, it is difficult to equate wet-nursing with lack of care or even affection in early modern society.[34]

The problem of nursing is obviously connected to the contentious question of the strength of early bonding between parents and child.

Those who advocated maternal feeding saw it as much as a way of establishing affection as of securing the health of the child. Sir William Knollys, in the letter quoted above, acknowledges that breastfeeding 'argueth great love', but expresses the fear that if the child were subsequently lost 'yt would more greave you'. Was the premiss correct: did the general tendency not to breastfeed lead to a lower emotional engagement with the young child, and hence to that relative indifference to infant mortality of which Stone makes much? It is possible, of course, to cite examples and counter-examples: female diaries and memoirs, when they become available in the seventeenth century, predictably speak more often of grief at the loss of small children than their male counterparts. Alice Thornton gives moving accounts of the deaths even of her infant children. Nor should this be any surprise in a class which valued children so highly for the continuity of lineage, and wives in part for their ability to produce heirs. Mary Banks wished her cousin Joan well through the pains of childbirth with the prayer 'that at the last she may enjoy what then she will most desire to be the mother of a young sonne'. The matriarchal affection of Jane, Lady Bacon, for her infants and those of her descendants is suggested in the remarkable tomb at Culford in Suffolk on which she is surrounded by three generations of those of her family who died before they reached adolescence.

But the male diarists also display emotion for infants who survive to become recognisable personalities, and above all welcome the birth of children with enthusiasm. Richard Wilton of Topcroft Hall, Norfolk, kept a rather mundane notebook at the end of the sixteenth century, but the birth of each of his children was recorded in great detail, often accompanied by pious ejaculations that the Lord should make him worthy of such joys. Sir William Brownlow recorded in the family bible in the 1620s and 1630s mourning texts for his lost infants: even his last-born, George, who died at 10 months in 1642 was noted: 'I was at ease, but thou O God has broken mee a sunder and shaken me to pieces'. Special children – oldest sons above all – could generate powerful commitment, and equally intense grief even if they died before they had much passed infancy. By the mid-seventeenth century Sir Roger Burgoyne could embark upon full mourning for a lost one-year-old who was his heir.[35]

Yet in reacting against Stone's preoccupation with low affect in parent–child relationships, it would be foolish not to identify differences between the experience of the early modern family and

13. Detail of the tomb of Lady Jane Bacon, d. 1654, Culford Church, Suffolk

that of the post-industrial period. For the gentry wet-nursing did presumably diminish the intensity of early bonding. Large families created predictable pressures, even among the élite, which may have discouraged close identification with each individual child. The case of Sir Simonds D'Ewes, so often cited as an example of parental indifference, since he was reared by his grandparents and rarely saw his nuclear family, is unusual only in that he was the heir to the estates: younger children were readily handed to grandparents if circumstances so dictated. The appearance of a seventh or eighth son, or worse still daughter, must have been the cause for rather restrained celebration: Sir Patience Ward claimed that his Christian name was given because his father, a minor gentleman, 'did frequently say that if he had another son he would call him Patience'. William Blundell, another poor Northern squire, sounded bitter at the birth and death of a sixth daughter 'My wife has much disappointed my hopes in bringing forth a daughter, which, finding herself not so welcome in this world as a son, hath already made a discreet choice of a better'. However, he managed to turn his regret into a Catholic jest: 'I am now resolved to have none herafter but boys, goodly gallant boys for Bishops'. Marriage offers made, like that of Sir Francis Thornhagh to Sir Gervase Clifton for 'one of your daughters' suggest that even adult children could be perceived as rather undifferentiated. And cultural conditioning influenced parental behaviour: any form of spoiling, or 'cockering' as contemporaries called it, was regarded as dangerous indulgence. Sir Ralph Verney, who clearly loved his young Meg, said at her death that he 'had rather appeared to neglect her least our overfondness should spoil her'. Death was perforce as much the opportunity to reflect on the vanity of mortal hopes, as on the loving child who had departed. The funeral monuments to young children before the late seventeenth century are usually strongly in the *memento mori* tradition.[36]

As children moved from infancy to adulthood their roles in the structural and emotional life of the family were profoundly changed. Particularly intense bonds could clearly form between parents and any of their maturing children, but the logic of the latters' roles meant that some links would assume greater general importance than others, above all the relationship between the head of house and his heir. Upon the male heir devolved all the hopes and anxieties of the rest of the nuclear family, and his circumstances and personality, as already observed, did much to determine the fortunes of the whole. Immense care was often lavished upon his education and advancement: oldest sons were disproportionately represented among those who attended both the universities and the inns of court, and later in the seventeenth century were more frequently offered the luxury of the Grand Tour than their siblings. Attention was also given to social and political advancement: the marriage of the heir was critical, and there were often attempts, not always accepted by Tudor regimes, to place two generations on the local bench.[37]

In return fathers expected sons to devote themselves loyally to the interests that they defined as central for the family. The genre of 'Advice' literature, most often directed specifically to the heir, embodies the type of principles and problems that concerned the older generation. With due allowance for differences of time, personal attitude and religious belief, the advices could be summarised as advocating energetic defence of the material interests of the family; sound management of the estates; caution, but also generosity, in relations with tenants, kin, peers and friends; and marriage to a person of virtue but also appropriate fortune. These qualities the heir was already supposed to have learned and put into practice during childhood and adolescence. When relationships between father and son were warm, it was often because the latter discharged these expected roles: Ralph Verney steadily managing the family estates in the absence of his father Sir Edmund was a model son of this kind and was rewarded by deep paternal affection. 'You ar so good a sone that I see your father can do nothing without you', observed Lady Sussex. Model fathers inspired predictable loyalty in affectionate sons: Thomas Isham memorialised his 'deare and lovinge father' who was 'a patterne and an example to all . . . which lived abought him'. Intense expectations of the heir could generate profound grief if he died: Sir John Oglander's mourning for his George occupies many pages of his commonplace books. 'Oh George, my sonn George, thow weart to good for mee. All partes, Naturall and Artificiall did so abound in thee, that hadst thou lived thou hadst bene an honnour to thy family and Countrey.'[38]

Yet while familial pride, patriarchal values and concern for the lineage bound fathers and sons in intense relationships, they also provided substance for some of the most spectacular breakdowns within the nuclear unit. At the heart of most of these conflicts were tensions about wealth and inheritance, and they were usually expressed in bitter acrimony over indebtedness or marriage.

Quarrels about debts could merely be skirmishing between generations with different priorities: the younger Sir Henry Slingsby was reproved by his father for spending too much in London and York rather than being 'more liberalle in the countree, as a thinge in my opinion better sorting with your reputacion'. Serious indebtedness by oldest sons frequently reflected the frustration of an heir who had golden expectations but limited current resources. John Phelips, the heir to the Montacute estate in Somerset in the 1580s, was still existing under the shadow of an elderly father when he was in his fifties. By then he had experienced 30 years of indebtedness and was so mired in financial difficulty that his father took the extreme step of granting away the estate to his prosperous youngest son, Edward, in order to save the whole property from ruin. Then, of course, there were those who fell into debt simply through their own fecklessness. Francis Carew, for example, was forced in 1630 to flee abroad where he was, in his father's anxious view, exposed to the twin horrors of Jesuits and French fashion. He left at home a wife 'to good for so bad a husband' and a father who appears always to have been generous and who in honour had to settle his debts which were 'the greatest disgrace that ever befell me'. An improvident father could be an equal cause of intergenerational anxiety: Henry Slingsby the elder was advised by his steward to persuade his father to stay in London, where he could do little financial harm to the Yorkshire estate. In the bitter quarrel between Sir William Russell and his son observers were clear that the father was ruining the estate by 'destroying the brave timber trees . . . [and] abominable iniustice and folly'.[39]

Debt problems were often a chronic, rather than acute, source of tension. Disagreements about marriage, on the other hand, could erupt into familial relationships with explosive force. Richard Broughton complained in 1577 to Richard Bagot that he had not seen his father for three years, since the breakdown of a marriage proposal, which led to 'irrevocable cholerick speeches'. The same Richard was also the confidant of John Yonge, who moaned that his eldest son had married himself 'to his uter undowinge and nopence to me to helpe his brothers nor sesters'. Sir John Lowther II moved to disinherit his eldest son John after he made a second unsuitable marriage 'to the lessinge of our familie by devidinge it' and Sir Thomas Mostyn tried to remove part of Roger's inheritance because he believed that, by marrying a Wynn, the latter had sacrificed the interest of his family to that of a potential enemy.[40]

The remarriage of a father was more consistently threatening than the marital behaviour of the heir, because it involved property division and the further danger of a second family. Although most men merely provided the second wife with an appropriate life-interest in the estate, there are some spectacular examples of attempts to disinherit the rightful heir or pass virtually all control into the hands of a stepmother. Sir Robert Barker tried to make his son of the second marriage heir, causing great suits and a final division of the estate: though in this case the surprising outcome was that 'the two knights . . . now live lovingly like brothers'. Sir Edward Phelips's family were horrified by his overwhelming generosity to his second wife, when his first had never been given a proper settlement even for her lifetime. Sir Richard Manley remarried at 76 a woman whom his heir claimed had been his mistress for twenty years; and promptly this 'unkind stepmother' encouraged her husband to break all his agreements with his heir. Sir Nicholas Pointz was not actually disinherited, but he claimed that his father had so committed his estate to the family of his second marriage that he was left with little of his own. It was a familiar story: though the fact that it was so often told during the course of litigation between heirs and stepmothers suggests the need for caution. Heirs frequently contested the provisions made for widows, and were often only too willing to besmirch the good name of their father's choice. The charge that a stepmother was a 'gold digger' was the most predictable: Sir James Thynne, for example, lauded his mother's family, and the contribution she made to the patrimony, while insisting that his stepmother had had little or no portion. He also claimed that his eldest brother had died of chagrin when barred from the presence of his father.[41]

Some sons took their revenge by harassing a stepmother after their father's death: even in some cases 'unpersoning' her, like the second wife of Sir Edmund Wyndham, who was claimed not to be able to provide evidence of marriage, and who was eliminated from all the family geneaologies. In a family where tensions never caused so complete a breakdown the triangle between father, heir and stepmother was often an uneasy one. Lucy Hutchinson described how her husband could 'enjoy no delight' in his father's house when a second group of children was being reared there. Sir Edward and Unton Dering appear to have lavished affection on the children of their own union at the expense of the younger Edward, who was from a previous marriage. After his father's death, when considerable estates were left to the sons of the last match, and Unton was given control of the family seat of Surrenden Dering, litigation between the two was inevitable, though it never led to a total collapse of contact. It may have been at this stage that Edward formed the view expressed in his autobiography 'the first misfortune I had was the loss of [a] prudent and virtuous mother. The next was that of my Father marrying again.'[42]

The circumstances of second marriages indeed made it particularly difficult to reconcile father and heir because there was no natural mother to interpret between competitive males. Although we hear fewer female than male voices in these transactions, there is a general sense that mothers often could and did intervene to mitigate and arbitrate. In a major conflict between Edward Montagu and his father over property and the small income the former was allowed, it was his mother who pleaded for him. When a century later the Newton family were at odds about a settlement, it was Lady Mary who wrote in conciliatory tones to her son. In a more general sense women like Brilliana Harley, Anne Townshend and Elizabeth Smyth seem to have acted as the major contacts between adolescent sons and rather removed fathers. Women could gossip freely with their sons in a way that was less available to men: Elizabeth Smyth's affectionate letters to her son Thomas at Oxford mingle concern for his well-being with sharp comment on the strains of life with her depressive husband. Anne Townshend chattered happily of her son's health and of local news: though she sometimes inserted more serious advice into her correspondence, as when she prayed 'God put into your minde to bethink your selfe of a good wife'.[43]

Although mothers often appear to have played predictably warm roles towards their first-born sons, we should not assume that they therefore possessed fundamentally different standards from their spouses. Sir John Wynn, urging his son to honour his mother when he had gone, remarked that Lady Wynn was not apt to take offence 'except she be too muche wronged'. In widowhood, in particular, that sense of individual and familial honour often led women to reprimand their sons with some force. Agnes Throckmorton expressed to Robert her irritation that her motherly advice was neglected, although it sprang from love, and that he was making all the country say that in running horses 'that Papist hath so much monie that thaye run it awaye'. Andrew Archer's mother was even more anxious when her son's behaviour threatened the reputation of the family as good landlords: they must not, she said 'have the curse of the people'. Bridget Phelips, faced with conflicts about jointure and the division of property with her heavily indebted son, was swift to invoke the family's honour: 'as for my preserving your fathers Honor, I wish for yor owne, you weare as carefull therof in deeds as in words'. 'I am but mocked', she added, 'with the titel of honered Mother'. Many women found it difficult to control determined adolescents: Dorothy Bacon wrote of the son of her first marriage: 'I pray God he maye nooe more urdg my alowance to travell for I have vowed nevermore to grant it'.[44]

The structural and financial problems created by widowhood were likely to intensify these difficulties. When mothers of under-age heirs had the necessary ability to secure wardship, discipline their children and exercise responsibility for the estate, they could find it difficult to accept their later transition to subordinate status. Some, like Meriel Littelton, effectively continued to administer the family property for an absentee or negligent heir. Others, like Lady Bridget Kingsmill, simply refused to retreat gracefully: she was still besieging her son with unwanted estate advice in the 1650s, two decades after he had entered upon his majority. Widows whose sons were grown at the death of their fathers often found that the need to secure their jointure from the estate became a source of conflict. Sir Robert Phelips had anticipated Bridget's troubles with his heir and endeavoured to protect her in an unusual testamentary declaration, but this did not prevent several years of bitter negotiation with 'Ned'. And security of jointure could become entangled with the even more sensitive issue of remarriage. Although jointure in the form of land could not normally be alienated from the patrimony, most widows had the liberty to take their moveable wealth and annual profits into a second relationship. Acrimony between the generations was a likely outcome: for example, the bitter hostility between Sir Richard Bulkeley, his mother and her second husband Thomas Cheadle revolved initially around the heir's belief that Cheadle married to gain wealth and status at the expence of the Bulkeley dynasty. Mothers and sons rarely ended in such vitriolic accusations of poisoning and 'offence in the sight of heaven' as in this case, but remarriage undoubtedly strained existing loyalties and identities. A determined second husband could apply his intelligence to maximising the profit from his wife's jointure: an inept heir like Sir Francis Foljambe could rapidly convince himself that 'sinister and fraudulent practices' were involved. When the heir was still a minor such behaviour had to be borne, but it could erupt in later litigation, as when Francis Willoughby sued his stepfather in 1685 for waste of his mother's jointure, and probably in revenge for an unhappy childhood. Remarriage was common, though its incidence was diminishing: 37 per cent of the widows in a sample of wills from the Prerogative Court of Canterbury proved between 1500 to 1558 had been married at least twice; this corresponds to Hollingsworth's calculation that 36.8 per cent of the peerage remarried in the years 1550–74, a figure that fell to 20.0 per cent a century later. Yet it is difficult to find a memorialist who expresses any warmth on the subject of female remarriage. An exception is Sir John Reresby, but his comment on his mother is so guarded as to reinforce the generalisation: 'being then [when widowed] about thirty-four years of age and very hansome, soe that . . . her second marriage a few years after was the more excusable'. And Reresby's later diary entries reveal the expected hostility to his stepfather.[45]

Younger sons possessed one major advantage within the gentry family: that of gender. There was always the possibility, at least in the case of a second or third male child, that the inheritance might fall to them, or that familial wealth might be sufficiently great to launch them upon an independent career as cadet gentlemen. But the general view of historians has been that most younger sons were not so fortunate, and that the bitter complaints of that younger son Thomas Wilson embodies their shared experience. 'He [the heir] must have all, and all the rest that which the catt left on the malt heape'. Revisionism has now reached younger sons, and it has been pointed out that many enjoyed both close relationships with their parents, and a strong sense of familial loyalty that helped to transcend the structural problems of their position. There is certainly plenty of evidence of fathers, and mothers, who wished to see the family as a unit, in which all siblings had a share, and in which each was responsible for the other. The Wynns provide a rich vein of material on such interdependence: the older brothers were supposed to take care of the younger, especially when they moved to school or to London: the business of any part of the family was to be pursued by those best placed to undertake it and loyalty to siblings was enjoined. In his 'Advices' Sir John made a point of instructing his heir to 'cherishe and make muche of your brethren' who were to be brought together from time to time 'to Renew love amonge yow'. Thomas Butler, in his will of 1557, took the practical step of leaving money to his heir to provide a yearly dinner at which he and his two siblings could come together. The Congreve family also saw the interests of its individual members collectively: brothers protecting one another on first seeking employment in London and pursuing litigation to defend the rights of their young widowed sister. In the Hale family of Essex a younger brother, Rowland, consistently acted as the organiser of family business in London.[46]

The concern to deal justly with younger sons, but also to see them as part of a collective familial enterprise, was, the surviving sources suggest, widespread. There were perhaps few gentry fathers who managed this dual exercise as well as John Lowther, the first baronet of the Cumberland and Westmorland family. He had dissuaded his grandfather, who was in conflict with his father, from settling the estate on him 'out of my care that my brothers should be brought up like gentlemen'. When his own younger sons, Christopher and William, were of age they were trained in trade and became major figures in the family's extensive business enterprises. Although both were highly successful individual merchants they regarded their activities, at least in the years before their father's death in 1637, as bound into the general support of the kin group. Sir John Lowther was aware that this situation would not necessarily outlive him and, despite his earnest pleas for continuing co-operation, the brothers each went their own way, though apparently without rancour between them. The economic circumstances and ruthless business determination of the Lowthers make them a rather distinctive case, but it is possible to identify other 'family firms' like the Gawdys of Norfolk, who operated in a similar way in the more familiar marketplace of politics and patronage. Philip Gawdy, the invaluable agent to his brother Bassingbourne at the Elizabethan Court, constantly protected familial interests, though not without some wistful reflections on his sibling's 'farthyer fortunes'. Persuading brothers to collaborate for their mutual advantage was one of the best ways in which to fulfil what must have been a common parental desire, articulated by Anne Newdigate, to ensure that they should all have 'what their father had left them'.[47]

This careful collective management of resources might succeed in favourable cicumstances, and particularly when one or both parents survived to hold siblings together and nurture identity. But the plaints of younger brothers cannot simply be set aside because there are good examples of co-operation and loyalty. Their situation in a society directed to primogeniture was inherently uncomfortable and unstable, and only the most intelligent educational strategies and sensible allocation of resources, as well as general good will, could mitigate these structural disadvantages. Many fathers had neither the resources, nor the far-sightedness, to resolve their younger sons' problems: in 1668, for example, Edward Phelips's brother-in-law urged him to make a better settlement for his younger sons, despite his financial difficulties, since his current arrangement would only be tolerable if he lived long enough for the relevant property to increase in value. After a father had died no amount of earlier pious exhortation to mutuality and love would necessarily resolve the competing claims of siblings and the nuclear family of the heir. Sir John Wynn, for all his endeavours to incorporate his sons, never had enough revenue to prevent them from envying one another, and uttering loud, if intermittent complaints against their father's hard dealing. The children of Sir Percival Willoughby exemplify the tensions: Sir Percival himself was heavily indebted at various points in the mid-Jacobean period, and therefore not well placed to assist his children. Even so, he may be thought to have deserved better than his fourth and sixth sons: Henry was a lawyer, but constantly accumulated debts and beseiged his father with begging letters; Robert stole quantities of jewels and money from Sir Percival, claiming that he was allowed nothing on which to live. In this case the second son, Edward, was disproportionately favoured, since he was given an estate which shared with the main Willoughby lands rich mineral resources. Moreover one son, Percival, had the good sense to rescue himself from the collapse of the younger sons: he pressed successfully to be apprenticed to a physician, Dr Van Otter, saying that he believed he would thereby be happier than his brothers and that 'he believed that he could never stand in need of them, but he questioned not but they would stand in need of him'.[48]

Fear that they would be left without adequate maintenance sometimes drove younger sons to desparate measures: like Thomas Bulkeley, who was alleged in 1621 to have introduced an armed gang into the house where his father lay dying in order to preempt a will from which he believed himself excluded. Most problems arose, however, after the death of a father, when the eldest son became head of house and responsible for whatever portion had been allocated to his siblings. Then the duty to see the family as a whole might become increasingly irksome, and the applications for payments of annuities or portions intolerably burdensome. When Emanuel Altham, who had managed to waste much of his estate, assured his eldest brother that he would 'Remember the Vine I cam from' James might have been excused for wishing for a little amnesia: one of the other brothers remarked that money sent to Emanuel 'will bee soe much cast awaie hee not beeinge of a Capacity either to governe himselfe or what is his owne'. Some elder brothers endeavoured to restrain this type of profligacy by withholding monies properly due to their siblings: the Norcliffe brothers had to go to arbitration at least twice, since Sir Thomas was withholding a portion due William, who he claimed was 'wastefully given'. These conflicts no doubt looked very different from the perspective of the younger brother: Richard Swale spoke for many in complaining to his uncle that he did not know if his brother was 'fish or flesh', but he was assuredly a covetous gentleman. Even virtuous intentions by one side or the other could have divisive outcomes: Walter Montagu died in 1616 leaving lands in Chepstow for the poor, the support of a preacher and the residue to his younger brother Henry. However, the head of the Montagu house, Sir Henry, was firmly convinced that the lands should have returned to him in reversion and 'having receyved this disinherison' would not even attend the funeral.[49]

The girls in a family had very different experience and expectations from their brothers, although they shared the same ultimate dependence on its collective resources. Adult daughters often appear as constant burdens and obligations to their parents, whose energies were bent upon their 'proper bestowing'. Once a daughter was finally married, and her jointure arrangements secured, she was in some measure lost to her own kin, though, as we have seen, residential arrangements and particular affections might continue to bind her to her family of origin. Before she reached the stage of marriage a girl might possibly find it easier than her brothers to establish deep loyalties within the family. Although nursed in precisely the same manner, she was less likely to be sent out of the household for schooling, at least until adolescence, and by no means always even then. Autobiographies by women certainly suggest the depth of affection between mothers and daughters: Anne, Lady Halkett, Lucy Hutchinson, Anne Fanshawe and above all Alice Thornton all sing the praises of their mothers. Mary Baskerville delivered a delightful encomium to her mother Elizabeth Throckmorton, who was 'dear in her love to her children above other women'. In some of these cases, bitter disappointment with husbands and fathers seems to have intensified the loyalty between mother and daughter: Alice Thornton and Mary Baskerville had no particular reason to be enchanted by their spouses. But we should not allow the biographers to paint too roseate a picture: wives, as we have already seen, often supported the authority of husbands against children, and there are well-attested examples of conflict, as when Lady Cave dragged her offending daughter from the house by her hair for contracting a secret obligation to marry. There was no love lost between Bridget Willoughby and her mother, despite the attempts of the former to mediate between her warring parents. A younger Willoughby daughter, Winifred, was locked up for falling in love with Percival Willoughby's younger brother. Some tension may well have existed between mothers who believed in the proper performance of duty, in relation to marriage as well as much else, and daughters with other notions. Anne Townshend seems to have felt that her daughter's violent humour in loving John Spelman would shorten her life. Yet bonds between generations among the women probably proved more durable than most: the experience of childbirth in particular held mothers and daughters together; many mothers when their own period of child-rearing was past were eager assist at the endless lyings-in of the next generation.[50]

The relationships between fathers and mature daughters are less easy to characterise. The demands of gentry marriage strategy, added to the cultural effect of patriarchalism and generation difference, could construct this as one of the most authoritarian and distanced bonds within the nuclear family. A rebellious daughter who chose her own marriage partner, or otherwise separated herself from her parents, could legitimately be treated with cold anger, as was Margaret Mostyn who, having refused to accede to her father's wishes, spent most of the ensuing decade trying to be reconciled to him. 'My feare', she wrote to her eldest brother in 1685, 'is to indever his faver I might incres his displesour'. Even close relationships could be threatened by signs of female independence: Sir Henry Slingsby was deeply troubled by his daughter Ann who, in 1617, resided in York to be near godly preachers 'which they coule puretans'. Henry Oxinden, furious with his twelve-year-old daughter's refusal of a marriage alliance, told his wife to 'lett her know I shall never againe desire to see her face'. Most tragically of all, Holles's ancestor Peter Frescheville, forced himself to sustain a life-long vow never to see his beloved daughter Frances face to face after she married without his consent. The affection of daughters for fathers must often have been undermined by such patriarchalism: Elizabeth Isham, for example, submitted without public complaint to her father's refusal to continue marriage negotiations with the Dryden family in 1631, but her subsequent refusal to marry is presumably indicative of her feelings about the loss of a man with whom she had corresponded in most intimate terms.[51]

Yet if the difficulties of marriage negotiation or unusual demands for independence elicited the worst of patriarchal attitudes, obedient daughters could also establish some of the closest bonds across generations precisely because they did not threaten established cultural norms. Daughters were endlessly described as the 'comfort' of their parents, and, lest we should think of this as an exclusively authority-centred view, we have the evidence of women like Ann Fanshawe and Alice Thornton of love, as well as reverence, towards their fathers. Ann Lennard's charming letters to Sir John Oglander are suffused with affection: 'the great expression of your love', she wrote in 1646, 'makes me very often to weepe for joy', but she was grieved 'that you live so mallincolly a life'. The close bonding established from childhood onwards with daughters was sometimes revealed in marmoreal art. Henry Brook expressed the wish in his 1558 will that he be buried, not with his first wife, but with his beloved daughter and heiress Katherine. And in a moving memorial to several of his children (*c.*1580) Edmund Brudenell eulogised his tenth child Dorothy 'which lovingly lyved and dyed mylde' and added

> My body with thyne I desyre should lye
> When God hath appoynted me to dye.[52]

## 2.4 KIN

The nuclear family was the critical focus of the emotional and social experience of the English gentry. Yet kin were also of great significance: they were bound to the nuclear core by the perception of lineage, by mutual economic and political interest and even by ties of emotion. Lineage was both an exclusive and inclusive concept: it focused the family intensely upon the generational descent from father to eldest son, but it also bound together all those who possessed identity of name and blood. Both these elements can

14. Portrait of John Kaye, esquire, and his children (1567)

be seen in the primitive images of John Kaye and his wife: he stands surrounded by his nuclear family; she is framed by an endless list of their extended kin.

15. Portrait of Dorothy Kaye (1567)

Holles's *Memorials* exemplify a view of the family that is kin-based, perhaps because of his standing as a younger son of a cadet branch. In less accomplished hands this belief in the bonding of the lineage could descend into muddle: the biblical question 'who is my neighbour' was more often asked by gentleman in the form 'who is my kinsman', and some answers seemed almost as comprehensive as Christ's. Hannibal Baskerville's attempts to identify his kin over four generations trailed away into confusion as he pursued the descendants of second marriages by cousins already several times removed. Cousin spotting was then, as now, also a particularly favoured pastime for the Celts.[53]

In practice kin were those who shared social worlds or had mutual interests. The odd 'outsider' – the poverty-stricken Holles whom the Earl of Clare employed as a kitchen-hand for the sake of his blood, or female cousin left without means of support like Jane Clifford who reminded Sir Nicholas Carew of their 'long breding together' – might be given bare assistance. Elderly or temporarily homeless kin might be offered accommodation, subject to a financial agreement about the costs of 'tabling'. Sir William Wentworth advised that such kin should be well-regarded, yet 'of kinsfolks esteem the company of them most that be rich, honest and discreet and use them in your causes before others'. Few gentlemen would have been so direct: many in practice behaved in exactly this way. Blood and self-interest should construct a clan which would enhance the ability of its smaller components, the nuclear families, to face the outside world. Sir Charles Cornwallis expressed this powerfully when he instructed his grandson that 'blood and affinitie, being by their overt accons made knowne, doth yield unto them A great strength both in realitie and reputacion'. Kin groupings served their members in a remarkable range of ways: they offered patronage and the opportunity for advancement, marriage brokerage, arbitration in disputes, loans and bonds, protection of dependent orphans, help to the newly married, entertainment, accommodation and sociability. It is almost impossible to isolate one or other of these functions as most significant, or most widely employed, since the successful grouping was adaptable and attended to the needs of the individuals within it. To take just one example, a determined recusant like Richard Cholmeley of Brandsby turned automatically to his Hungate kin, who were also Catholic, for mutual protection in the face of persecution.[54]

If kin bonds were to work effectively they needed to be fostered by conscious effort, especially in the area of hospitality and social communication. Women were often seen as pivotal in these networks of contact, fostering visits and friendships and, particularly by the seventeenth century, linking kin by correspondence. The warm interchanges between Meriel Littelton and her aunt Meriel Knyvett held together a kin divided between Worcestershire and Norfolk, and in Kent it was largely the Twysden women who kept alive loyalties among their menfolk. It was therefore particularly important that wives should be willing to show an affection to their husband's kin as strong as that to their own family of origin. Several memorialists praised this balancing act by gentry wives: Sir John Lowther went further, and isolated as one of his wife Mary's crowning virtues that she was 'a lover of hir husbands friends and Kindred above hir owne'. Even this remark was not presumably intended to imply that Mary should have rejected her own kin, since one of the benefits of gentry marriage was conceived as being the extension of the web of affinity. For example, after Sir Roger Townshend married Mary Vere, parts of their Norfolk families which had had no previous social contact began to exchange visits. Sir John Tracey, a cousin of Lady Vere, began to visit Stiffkey and to sign himself to Sir Roger 'your affectionate kinsman'. Finally, a species of kinship could be constructed, or its special qualities enhanced, by the practice of godparenting. The arrival of Protestantism did little to subvert the belief in the significance of spiritual parenting, at least at this level of society, and those diarists who carefully recorded the birth of children rarely failed to give precise details of their sponsors. The abolition of godparenting under the Commonwealth was a source of particular grievance and distress to Anglican gentry like the Twysdens and Verneys who believed 'gossips' to be necessary to the spiritual and secular well-being of a child.[55]

Structural analysis of the nuclear family and its affines inevitably focuses our attention away from the experience of change. Two centuries are perhaps too short a span to expect evidence of profound upheaval in so fundamental a social construct: the balance of view among historians is that at least three, and possibly as much as five, centuries provide the appropriate *longue durée*. Nevertheless, it is perfectly possible to itemise a whole series of changes which did impinge on the experience of the gentry family under the Tudors and Stuarts. In no particular hierarchy of significance we might isolate greater mobility, especially that provided by the coach; access to London and other, later, centres of fashion; an expanding market in luxuries; literacy and cultural sophistication, particularly for women; humanist and Reformed ideas; and finally the establishment of the strict settlement and of more effective instruments of credit. The economic and social changes afforded the opportunity for greater security and intergenerational equity, linked with an expanding choice in marriage arrangements and some measure of individual flexibility. And cultural and ideological changes of these two centuries at the very least revolutionised the *forms* in which identity could be expressed.[56]

It seems less likely that core assumptions or relationships within the family were fundamentally altered. The high expectations of affect and intimacy for which MacFarlane and Houlbrooke have argued, surface intermittently throughout these centuries. The 40 per cent of the astrologer Napier's patients who brought troubles about love and family to him exemplify the contemporary conviction that marriage should be far more than an economic arrangement marked by suitably deferential domesticity. It is precisely because expectations were high, and there was a belief that marriage should produce the combination of security, affection and intimacy of which a memorialist like Cholmley spoke, that the records of family breakdown are so full of bitterness and intensity. In reacting against Stone's arguments for the 'restricted patriarchal nuclear family' with its limited bonding between individual members, historians have been tempted to eulogise domestic harmony. The records of contemporary litigation more than correct this impression: they suggest that all too often high expectations collided with, on the one hand financial and logistical demands which were integral to gentry marriages, on the other the usual emotional failures that bedevil any close personal regime. In Tudor and Stuart England these failures by men and women who were not mere private citizens, but the public leaders of an intensely hierarchical society, became the concern of the commonwealth. Conflict within families, lamented the moralists, presaged conflict within the state: rejection of patriarchal authority was the first stage in the rejection of the bonds of obedience. The gentry were expected through their marriages to uphold an image of patriarchal power and to engage in proper performance of the domestic roles assigned to them. Their public authority was partially legitimated by these private performances. Though these expectations were often disappointed in practice, their existence lent deep moral earnestness to the routines of domestic life.[57]

# 3

# Wealth: Income

## 3.1 INTRODUCTION: THE WEALTH OF THE GENTRY

Francis Harris was a knight, of an armigerous family of Southminster, Essex and allied to many of the leading county families. By the late 1620s he had sold the ancestral estate, and was living in a series of very temporary lodgings in London. In 1629 he had been reduced to pawning his doublet and hose, and was begging cast-off clothing, occasional hospitality and small sums from his country relatives. He repaid them by running errands in the city and forwarding news, and by seeking out suitable matches for younger cousins in the marriage market. He retained not only his gentry networks, but his sense of honour; in 1628 he fought in its defence – with the lamentable result that he broke his sword and could not afford to replace it. Sir Francis Harris, a threadbare gentleman, was an embarrassment to his relatives and an anomaly in terms of contemporary theories of gentility. So, too, were Eusebius Andrewes and Sir Popham Southcote. Andrewes, a prisoner in the Fleet for debt, insisted that he and his wife should be accorded the status and precedence due to his '21 descents'. The warden of the prison responded to his pretensions by loading him with chains, incarcerating him in less salubrious quarters, and seizing his books, his papers, and his precious pedigree. In 1638 Southcote was maintaining himself by acting as the enforcer for the soap monopolists in the south-western counties, and in that role he sought the assistance of the Exeter civic authorities to halt unlicensed manufacture. Not only was the mayor uncooperative, but he spurned Southcote's claims to status. 'It was a greete piece of matter to be a knight now,' the mayor sneered, 'Hee . . . was able to buy mee out of all I had, with all my Clowts: badd mee goe and swagger in my Country thatch ale-howses.'[1]

Wealth, in the opinion of heraldic purists like Ferne, could not create gentle status. The High Court of Chivalry, in its short and unpopular recandescence under Charles I, might find itself defending the 'Birth and Blood' of an impecunious London hack writer, who claimed distant kinship with Lord Aston, from the abuse offered him by a printer – 'base Knave and stinkeinge beggerly knave . . . not . . . worth a hundred pence'. But wise fathers, advising their sons, recognised how hollow were the lineage-based claims to status of men who lacked a landed income sufficient to maintain an appropriate lifestyle. Higford made the point with an elegant simile. Gentle status 'will be much impaired and in effect lost, neither can it be well preserved, without the preservation of your estate also. They are like two twins, inseparable, born together, and must live and die together.' Most gentlemen were content to adapt, paraphrase, or plagiarise Burghley's famous aphorism, as did Sir George Heneage: 'Gentility being nothing but ancient riches,' he wrote to his son, 'if the foundations do sink the building must necessarily follow.'[2]

In their 'Advices' and didactic family histories gentlemen emphasised that feckless irresponsibility could lead, if not to hopeless ruin, certainly to substantial embarrassment. The vicious Anselm, 'vaynly and wickedly spending his estate in luxury', carelessly abandoning his lands to his creditors and failing to follow up promises of royal favour, provided a horrible warning to future generations of the Guise family. The Foljambes had been ruined, opined the eighteenth-century heir to the fag-end of their once substantial estates, in part because Sir Francis, who inherited a landed income of £3,000 a year which was reduced by his death in 1640 to £1,000, combined a 'profuse temper' with 'small under-standinge by reason of his education to manage so great an estate'. Similar parables are retailed in law-suits, as heirs sought the courts' protection against the indifference or the incompetence of their predecessors. Henry Ayscough of Blyborough, Lincolnshire, was an 'inexperienced gentleman'. While he drank, wrestled and squabbled with his neighbours, his estate, inextricably enmired in a web of debt and lawsuits, was sold up. John Eyre of Hope, Derbyshire, was 'a weak and simple man, much given to drunkenness' – an easy prey for his aggressive relatives, the Eyres of Hassop. In 1613 the heirs of Francis Shirley of Staunton Harold, Leicestershire, who had died in 1571, complained that he 'did little or no wyse at all meddle in the government of his estate, other than with his horses, hounds and deere in his Parke . . . wherein he tooke greate delight.' Francis resigned the management of his lands to his wife, and she, in her 'womanish simplicitie', was 'overreached' by those in whom she trusted. In all these cases, with their uniform pattern of incompetence/debt/sale, there is a clear implication of moral failure, of irresponsibility. Guise, Eyre, Shirley: each was a wastrel who, like Ayscough, 'regarded more his pleasure than his profit'. But other histories, like that of Sir Edmund Harewell of Besford, Worcestershire, who 'fyrst consumed and last sould all', were less straightforward in their moral implications. Harewell was no rake. He was 'most ryche to God'; his 'wytt was extraordinary, his learninge above vulgar skollers, on the Benche a most sufficient Justyce, in commissyons most expert'. Harewell was a man 'eavery waye wise, but in guydinge his estate'. Contemplating this tragedy, gentlemen might well, with his friend, Habington, who reported it, 'wonder . . . to see suche a Pylot so to misgoverne'.[3]

Catastrophes like that of Harewell, so troubling to the moral perceptions of contemporaries, raise a broader question for the historian – whether the gentry of early modern England were obliged to wrestle with peculiar difficulties in relation to their finances? The sharp rise in prices that began in 1500 and continued until the mid-seventeenth century certainly posed a major challenge to all social groups. A crude 'cost of living' index displays a nearly six-fold rise between the decade 1500–9 and that of 1640–9. In 1650–9 the index displays its first fall in a century and a half, and for the next century, while fluctuating within a narrow band, it never achieves the level of the decade 1640–9. The gentry, then, were confronted by the potentially subversive consequences of rapid inflation from 1500 to 1650. The stagnation of prices thereafter, if less destructive, also demanded adjustments of economic expectations and of managerial technique.[4]

Confronted by the unprecedented effects of inflation, and with such exemplars of the fatal consequences of indifference to managerial concerns as Harewell before them, it is not surprising that the the relatives of neophyte landowners reiterated the benefits of knuckling down to the tedious but essential activities of accounting and management. Heirs were enjoined to 'looke upon your revenew', to 'seriously consider' their rentals, to become a 'great good husband', to live 'within your boundes', to 'order and understand your own estate', to 'take your own Accompts, and betimes inure yourself to examine how your Estate prospers'. In the 1570s Lord Keeper Bacon, fearing that 'your howse . . . suerly must fall and decaye without some good foresight in this matter', penned a solid lesson in basic book-keeping for his son-in-law, Sir Henry Wodehouse of Waxham, Norfolk, a young man already deeply in debt and selling land. Wodehouse *must* list the sums owed his creditors, the interest payments, the dates of foreclosure; he must calculate the sums owing to him, and devise a sensible strategy to cover the surplus of debt; he must 'establishe and proporcon your contynewall charg equall to your revennewe'.[5]

Much Polonian advice on finance and management took the form of Bacon's to Wodehouse: a notional double-entry book-keeping, with equal emphasis on income and expenditure. 'Look to your exports as well as your imports,' advised Higford, 'and so prevent growing mischiefs.' And yet Higford also indicates that while wealth was an essential element in gentility, its acquisition and its expenditure must also be in ways compatible with that status. His grandson was advised to maintain the 'glorious' family tradition, 'for bounty and for hospitality', and, equally, to uphold the ancestral paternalist concern for their tenants: 'let these men of bread, enjoy and eat the bread which they dearly labour for and earn.' The same point was made by Sir John Lowther in the privacy of his memorandum book. He noted, with an understandable complacency, his spectacular gains – £20,000 in a decade – and outlined the reasons for his success: 'providence and sparing of littles'; 'care and pains in good bargeins'; 'I saved yearly a good part and bargained with it with the best discretion I coulde'. Yet he added that he had not been niggardly, and had maintained 'our fashion with the best of our neighbours'. Nor had financial advance been achieved at the expense of 'the love and good reports of those with whome I delt'.[6]

Lowther's ruminations indicate a tension between the need for wealth to maintain status and the sense that the canons of gentility both demanded certain levels of expense and proscribed certain forms of moneymaking. In this and the next chapter we will examine this tension. We will organise the discussion around the division suggested by Lord Keeper Bacon, and deal with income and expenditure, with 'getting' and 'spending', separately. Most commentators, like Gervase Holles, believed that the income side of the equation was the more important. Holles, discussing the case of his grandfather, John Kingston, who was obliged to sell much of the substantial estate that he had inherited, acknowledged that Kingston had expensive tastes – 'rich apparell'; lavish hospitality; hunting; duels and affrays; a string of mistresses. Yet his prodigal expenditure was less fatal than his 'negligence . . . in managing his estate'. It was Kingston's failure to monitor and husband his income that 'hurt more than all the rest'. There were, as we shall see, countervailing examples: men whose assiduous attention to the maximisation of profit could not save their families from ruin. However, we will follow the weight of contemporary opinion and study income before analysing expenditure. And contemporary opinion, both nostalgic traditionalists, like William Higford, and the more realistic, like Sir George Heneage, assumed that the gentry income was and would be essentially derived from land.[7]

## 3.2 LAND

Writing in 1645, Sir Richard Weston of Sutton, Surrey, prefaced his account of Flemish agricultural techniques with an epistle to his sons, assuring them that the study of his tract would enable them to 'nobly augment your estates', and bask in the 'praise' that was accorded the man who left 'his Inheritance greater to his Successors than he received it from his Predecessors'. His optimism concerning the improvement of estates and the increase of landed income, as we shall see, was not universally shared. But, in abstract, economic trends, at least until the mid-seventeenth century, gave support to Weston's argument. In a period of inflation the gentry as landowners should have done well. An increase in the population of England from approximately 2.77 millions in 1540 to 5.28 millions in 1650 ensured that the prices of basic agricultural commodities rose most extensively – grains seven-fold between 1500 and 1650, other arable crops by 650 per cent. The gentry should have been able to exploit market opportunities by direct production on their estates, assisted by relatively cheap labour costs as wage-rates rose only three-fold to 1650. Their rents should have reflected the increased prices fetched by agricultural products.[8] But these expectations would be realised only if there were no barriers to the gentry's ability to take advantage of market forces as agricultural producers and rentiers. Personality was important here. As we have seen, it was a commonplace that a gentleman's indifference to basic managerial problems could be ruinous. But general cultural assumptions are also crucial. Did the behavioural characteristics that were associated with gentility *permit* landowners to exploit their holdings?

**Paternalism**

On her deathbed, Jane Mansell of Briton Ferry, Glamorgan, charged her son, 'as you shall answer before God', to treat his tenants 'well and conscionably and not to wrong or oppresse them in any way'. This solemn injunction against the exploitation of tenants was the general burden of the substantial sections that fathers, advising their sons, felt obliged to devote to their responsibilities as landlords. Even the misanthropic William Wentworth, whose 1604 advice displayed a bleak and wary attitude to all the social relationships in which a gentleman would find himself involved (including marriage), while remarking the 'fawninge and flatterie' of tenants who 'seldome love their landlorde in their hartes', felt sufficiently obliged by the conventions to insist that tenants should be used 'charitablie'.[9]

The landlord's paternalist obligation to his tenants was argued from a number of perspectives. Some fathers simply emphasised that a gentleman's reputation and standing depended upon the maintenance of good relations. 'Greive not thy tenants with exactions,' Sir Walter Mildmay advised his son, Sir Anthony, in 1570, 'live soe as thou mayest deserve good report.' In 1614 Sir Charles Cornwallis, advising his grandson, argued that exploitation was 'contrary to the nature of a gentelman'. Other gentry commentators affected an archaic language of quasi-feudal dependence. 'Be favourable, my son, to thy tenants. . . Prefer the children of thy ancient homagers,' advised Sir John Strode. Christopher Wandesford boasted that his management of his estate gained his tenants' 'affections for the Preservation of my House'.[10]

Perhaps the most common line taken in gentry advices was to emphasise that divine rewards and punishments, both for the individual and for his lineage, turned on the proper performance of a landlord's social responsibilities. 'Know you are but a steward and must make an accounte of the usage of your tenantes,' Sir Edward Montagu reminded his son in 1620, 'Be moderate in taking of fines and sparing in raysing of Rentes, that they may have cause both to pray and prayse God for you.' 'Oppress not thy tenants, but let them live comfortably of thy hands . . . that their soules may blesse thee and that it may go well with thy seed after thee,' Henry Tempest advised his son in 1648. 'Your ancestors have been moderate in their fines,' William Higford wrote in the 1650s, 'I trust God will bless you the better for it. . . To inclose, or not to suffer [your tenants] to renew their estates, whereby desolation shall ensue, draweth on a woe.' This was the line favoured by the clergy as they reflected on the social obligations of landlords. It was in these terms that the great preacher, Robert Sanderson, denounced the covetous landlord, 'racking the backs and grinding the faces of the poor'. Sanderson excoriated a series of practices of estate management that were utterly incompatible with Christian charity, corrosive of neighbourliness, and destructive of traditional society. Enclosure, 'pulling down houses and setting up hedges, unpeopling towns and creating beggars', headed the list. But 'engrossing' (the creation of large, market-oriented farms from a series of smallholdings), exorbitant and 'unconscionable' rent increases, and attempts to destroy the peasant's security of tenure, were equally malign. Gentlemen engaged in such rapacious aggrandisment of their estates were compared, unfavourably, with the tyrant Ahab in his dealings with Naboth. 'Many a petty lord of a hamlet with us would think himself disparaged in a treaty of enclosure to descend to such low capitulations with one of his poor neighbours as the great King of Israel then did.' And Sanderson turns sardonically upon the gentry, who, in defiance of all Christian obligations, 'Ahab-like, have killed and taken possession'. They may believe that they have 'nailed up . . . all the appurtenances, by fines and vouchers, and entails, as firm as law can make them', their legal advisers may be 'feed to peruse the instrument, and with exact severity to ponder . . . every clause and syllable therein'. Yet their subtle devices, designed to secure their ill-gotten territorial gains 'to thy child and his child, and his child's child for ever', are vain. God's curse upon Ahab is the inheritance of their lineage. 'In his son's days I will bring evil upon his house.'[11]

Most gentlemen who analysed their duties as landlords solemnly affirmed their social and moral responsibilities, often borrowing the language of Christian obligation and of divine sanctions employed by clerics like Sanderson. Yet the clear implication of the latter's denunciation was that a good number of landlords *were* exploiting their tenants ruthlessly. Were the solemn 'Advices' merely a lip-service to a prescriptive ideal, easily forgotten in the face of the opportunities for enrichment through exploitation and improvement? We catch some of the tension between social convention and market opportunity in a wistful remark of Sir John Hatcher in the course of an indignant denial that he had unconscionably exploited one of his Lincolnshire estates: he added that if he *had* done so, his rental from the land would have risen very substantially, from £13 to £100 p.a.[12]

But before discussing the tension further, we should examine the particular techniques and practices whereby a landlord like Hatcher might enhance the income from his estate, and the ways in which the employment of some of them might horrify a defender of the traditional conventions of paternalism like Sanderson.

## Techniques of Improvement

First, a working knowledge of the landed estate and an attention to the the detail of its management was, as fathers sought to impress upon their heirs, essential to financial success in a period of inflation. Sir Nicholas Bacon's injunction to his irresponsible son-in-law to 'understand your own estate' and to 'take your own accompts', made good sense. Bacon, who was investing the substantial profits of his legal office in building an extensive estate in East Anglia, practised what he preached. Lands were carefully surveyed, either before or immediately after their purchase, and their boundaries, their estimated value, the amount of stock upon them and their rents were recorded. All sources of profit, particularly rents, were strictly monitored, and every attempt was made to adjust the latter to rising land values. Modern policies of surveying, mapping, accountancy and record-keeping may have been more easily employed by a new purchaser, like Bacon, than by a family long-settled on its estates, and with a system of estate administration established in the earlier period of stagnant land values and rents. Yet the adjustment could be made. In 1541 John Littelton of Frankley, Worcestershire, came of age and took control of his family's estates, pieced together from the late fourteenth century. A concern for detail, most apparent in his meticulous audit of the accounts of his bailiffs, was a key element in his managerial style.[13]

Littelton also had to deal with another problem that did not confront a new purchaser like Bacon: his inheritance was substantial, but scattered. Littelton sought to consolidate his estates, selling outlying properties, and purchasing manors in the Frankley area. A similar problem faced Sir Thomas Tresham the elder of Rushton who inherited a widely dispersed estate, built up over the preceding century, in 1521. Seeking to develop an integrated block of territory in north-eastern Northamptonshire,

Tresham sold off outlying properties, and reinvested in lands in the neighbourhood of Rushton: the process was assisted by his service to Henry VIII and to Mary, which gave him the opportunity to buy a number of ex-monastic properties in the area and to lease adjacent Crown lands on very favourable terms.[14]

The creation of an integrated estate and a keener attention to its management did not necessarily threaten traditional values. Tresham senior proved a beneficent landlord to his tenants, granting long leases, confirming the inheritance of holdings, not attempting to raise rents. But this was unusual. Consolidation and a new managerial style were more normally a prelude to or associated with an attempt to enhance the owner's income from his estate at the expense of his tenants. Consider the case of Sir Thomas Knyvett of Ashwellthorpe, Norfolk. Knyvett inherited a group of manors in the north-west of the county in 1577. Their distance from the family's seat and the 'neglygence of officers' had resulted in very lax management; long leases, some for seventy years, had been granted, and the tenants claimed virtual rights of inheritance and fixed rents on the lord's demesne lands that had been anciently leased to them. Knyvett determined 'to have an eye unto my owne and that betyme'. He had the manors surveyed, and recovered the concealed demesnes and appurtenant rights into his own hands; short-term leases were granted, and rents raised. In twelve years, between 1578 and 1590, he doubled and in some cases trebled the income from this block of holdings. The Littelton estate rental virtually quadrupled in the last three decades of the sixteenth century, as John pursued a similar policy, permitting only tenancies at will on the demesne lands and negotiating their rents annually.[15]

Nor did the conservative attitude to tenurial relations displayed by Sir Thomas Tresham senior survive into the next generation. His grandson and namesake inherited in 1559, and by 1575, in addition to further consolidating the estate by purchases, was vigorously enhancing its revenue. The inheritable tenancies with their fixed rents were challenged, and, after successful litigation, were exchanged for short-term leases. Income from the tenants was pushed up substantially (five-fold at Great Houghton), despite the fact that Tresham was pursuing an alternative tactic to take advantage of market opportunities – direct production. Tresham refused to renew some leases and farmed the land himself, selling cattle, hogs, corn, cheeses, hops and timber in local markets and the metropolis. Rabbits, too, were a minor industry of the Rushton estate after a profitable contract for their sale had been negotiated with a London poulterer. But Tresham was pre-eminently a sheep farmer: the profits of this operation, about £1,500 in 1590, made up nearly half his income.[16]

The activities of progressive landlords like Tresham, Littelton or Knyvett raise two of the general concerns that so troubled Sanderson: the tenants' security of tenure and the enhancement – 'racking' – of their rents. In the stagnant economic conditions of the fifteenth century, few landlords had seen much benefit in direct production and had been content to receive a largely fixed income from their estates. In the sixteenth century, with prices rising and market opportunities multiplying, the landlord might find that the fullest exploitation of his lands was blocked by claims from his tenants that they enjoyed tenures, legitimised by custom, that gave the landlord only the right to fixed rents and to receive fines, also fixed by custom, when they alienated the farm or it passed to their heirs. Tenures that took this form were known to the lawyers as 'copyholds of inheritance' or, in the north of England, 'tenant right'. The courts upheld these tenures, but they hedged them with a multitude of restrictions. If the lord could prove that the land in question had once formed part of the manorial demesne, then the tenants' claims to copyholder status were worthless and he could farm the lands himself or transfer tenures to leasehold, with all its opportunities for the frequent renegotiation of rent in respect of market conditions. If he could prove that the copyholds had been customarily granted for a period of years or to named individuals for their lifetime, then, while rents might be fixed for uneconomically long periods, he could demand a substantial monetary payment – a 'fine' – when the copyhold term expired. Alternatively upon the expiry, he could 'sell' a new copyhold estate to the highest bidder. Here was a fertile source of landlord–tenant dispute. A successful assertion of copyhold status left the lord stuck on a stagnant income, and it was the tenants who benefited from the growing disparity between fixed rents and the inflated prices fetched by agricultural products. It was obviously in the interests of the tenants to assert that they held their lands by copyhold of inheritance, and for the lord to question this claim. This was the point of the surveys undertaken by progressive landlords, whether newcomers, like Sir Nicholas Bacon, or those, like Sir Thomas Knyvett, who had inherited estates neglected by their ancestors. A careful investigation of medieval records, like that undertaken by the great antiquarian and bibliophile, Sir Robert Cotton, and his son, Sir Thomas, on their newly acquired manor of Glatton, Huntingdonshire, might substantially increase the value of the property to the landlord. Their survey enabled the Cottons to reclaim demesne land embezzled by their tenants, and to defeat as a recent fabrication the assertion that 'customarily' the tenants' lands passed to their heirs.[17]

Where the tenants could prove that they held by copyhold of inheritance, then the lord's opportunities were severely circumscribed. The courts would not only uphold such tenures, but would protect the copyholders from the attempts by landlords desperate to improve their revenues to force the tenants to surrender such legal estates. A series of ingenious or nefarious schemes were checked by the courts in the Elizabethan period. Landlords like Robert Longe at Condover, Staffordshire, or Sir John Phillips at Walwyn's Castle, Pembrokeshire, had demanded exorbitant fines upon inheritance designed to prevent the heir from exercising his right. Landlords had enforced archaic manorial bye-laws strictly, and so claimed the forfeiture of the tenant's copyhold for a technical default – a subterfuge attempted by Sir John Danvers at Wigston Magna, Leicestershire, and Samuel Sandys at Ombersley, Worcestershire. They might, like Sir Edward Herbert at Loweswater, Cumberland, engage in a series of collusive 'sales' of an estate, and claim the traditional fine to the 'new' lord upon each fictitious change of ownership.[18]

A landlord confronted by a tenure, copyhold of inheritance, that was increasingly hedged about by the remedies available at Westminster that left him with few opportunities to enhance his landed income, could respond in a number of ways. If he needed immediate capital he might allow the copyholders to purchase their freeholds, as did the Danvers family at Wigston Magna, Leicestershire, after failing in their attempt to overthrow the custom of copyhold of inheritance. Or he might offer his tenants his acknowledgement of their status and an undisputed guarantee of their rents and fines subsequently in return for a cash payment. In 1635 the men of Threlkeld secured from Sir John Lowther a recognition of their 'tenant right' and a promise that fines would not exceed four times the ancient rents on their lands; it cost them £1,200; Sir John Talbot, after an unsuccessful attempt to raise the levels of fines in the previous decade, confirmed the custom of his manor of Ford, Shropshire, in 1608 in return for £1,880. In the 1650s and 60s there was a burst of enfranchisements or grants guaranteeing the customs by northern landlords, paying of debts generated by their Royalism in the Civil War. Conversely, if the landlord was prepared to invest in future improvement and enhanced income, he might attempt to buy up the estates of his copyholders, as did Sir John Littelton, Sir Thomas Rivet at Chippenham, Cambridgeshire, and Sir Ralph Verney at Claydon, Buckinghamshire, subsequently farming the lands himself or leasing them at rack-rents. The villagers of Aynho, Northamptonshire, experienced both processes: in 1611 Shakerley Marmion raised £2,000 by enfranchising eleven copyholders; his growing debts forced the sale of the estate in 1615, and the new landlord, Richard Cartwright, began to buy in the copyholds that survived his predecessor's sale.[19]

Not only did customary tenure prevent the landlord from increasing his income by adjusting his rents to take account of inflation, it also impeded any sustained attempt to improve the real profitability of the estate. The fullest advantage of market opportunities could be taken only on estates where the restrictions of the old system of open-field production had been abrogated. In all agricultural areas it was a commonplace that enclosed land, held in integrated farming units, was more valuable to its owner than was an estate where open-field husbandry survived, with its mix of scattered ploughlands in the arable fields and use-rights over the surrounding wastes. The source of the superior profitability of enclosed land varied over time and between agricultural regions. In the early sixteenth century, enclosure, particularly in the midland counties, was usually accompanied by the conversion of the lands to pasture for sheep farming. Those with money to invest in land sought to acquire estates either that were already largely enclosed and turned to pasture, or that could be so converted. Sir John Spencer who had flourished as a grazier on rented property in south-eastern Warwickshire, pursued the former tactic with his purchases of Wormleighton, Warwickshire, and Althorp Northamptonshire. In the same region, John Isham, enriched by trade and moneylending in London, manoeuvred in a whirl of purchases and exchanges, to consolidate his new holdings at Lamport, then to enclose and convert them to pasture.[20]

Between 1500–9 and 1590–9 wool prices trebled; in the same period grain prices increased five-fold. Yet even at the end of the century Sir Thomas Tresham the younger was still enclosing his Northamptonshire estates for pasture in order to accommodate his burgeoning flocks. In 1596 Sir Thomas converted his demesne lands at Haselbech, nearly a thousand acres, to grazing, and expelled the tenants who had previously leased it from him for arable production. As a result of this transformation, only two of the previously sixteen ploughs survived at Haselbech and 60 persons lost their livelihood. This process continued in the midlands or areas like the Lincolnshire uplands into the mid-seventeenth century. Sheepfarming, with its low labour costs – as Sir Thomas More noted, a single shepherd could displace the 'many hands' needed for tillage – might still be more profitable than grain production on poor soils or in areas where transportation costs were high. Yet by the early seventeenth century market forces ensured that much enclosure was being undertaken to establish efficient units of *arable* production, farms upon which the growing range of techniques of progressive husbandry could be employed.

Some gentlemen became devoted practitioners and enthusiastic proponents of technological advance. Sir Richard Weston experimented with new systems of rotation, and with new strains and new varieties of crops, seeking to improve fertility and thus output on the sandy soils of his estate. He worked with his neighbours to make the river Wey navigable and thus secure improved access to the London market; he answered local enquiries concerning his novel practices, and he circulated an account of his observations on Flemish husbandry. Few gentlemen could match Weston's crusading zeal, but many took the lead in local improvements: Sir Edward Lawrence introduced the flooding of water-meadows in the Piddle and Frome valleys in Dorset, as Rowland Vaughan had done in the Golden Valley; in the next generation other Herefordshire gentleman and clerics, including Sir James Scudamore, cooperated in the breeding of an improved cider apple; Cressy Dymock developed more efficient farm tools that were tested on his Wadsworth, Yorkshire estate. The interest of other gentlemen emerges, not in bold experiments, but in their careful reading and annotation of the growing numbers of works on husbandry, and in gradual, piecemeal improvement. In 1601 John Newdigate resolved to spend at least two hours a day in the study of husbandry; he certainly read Googe's popular translation *The Four Bookes of Husbandrie*, and his diary was filled with memoranda concerning crops and stock on his Arbury, Warwickshire, estate. Drayner Massingberd enclosed Ormsby, Lincolnshire, in 1648, but the new regime, based on convertible husbandry and the growing of sainfoin both on the demesne lands and those of his tenants, did not displace the older system before the mid-1670s.[21]

Enclosure was a prerequisite to the maximisation of the landlord's profit, whether the intention was to convert the land to pasture and establish a sheep-ranch, or to attempt a more productive arable exploitation deploying the latest technologies. Proponents of the latter, like Walter Blith of Allesley, Warwickshire, argued that new forms of husbandry did not produce the adverse social consequences, chiefly depopulation, associated with conversion of tillage to pasture. Blith and his circle recommended a husbandry that, while highly productive, was labour-intensive; land enclosed for arable would create *more* employment. They also argued that the essential process of enclosure could be undertaken equitably; multilateral agreements should be negotiated among all interested parties, disputes adjudicated by neutral referees, compensation provided for the poorer cottagers for the loss of use-rights. By the mid-seventeenth century, when Blith wrote, the gentry had already recognised the benefits of such enclosure by agreement, subsequently ratified by Chancery. To secure the agreement of their tenants to the enclosure, landlords offered various sweeteners: at Swinderby, Lincolnshire, Sir Henry Disney promised his tenants freehold interests in land previously copyhold; at Gretton, Northamptonshire, and Bromham, Wiltshire, the lords confirmed the manorial customs claimed by the tenants; long leases with low rents were offered at Ashby Magna, Leicestershire. Nor were the moral claims of the poor forgotten; at Clifton-on-Dunsmore, Warwickshire, enclosed by Sir Robert Whitney in the 1650s, an allotment of one and a half acres was made to each poor cottager.[22]

The expropriation and depopulation that attended Sir Thomas Tresham's 1590s enclosures at Rushton and Haselbach, his 'hard and extreme usage of his tenants and his countrymen', rendered him 'most odious in this country'. In 1607 his activities provoked a violent response from the injured peasantry, and, after the suppression of the rioters, government investigation and censure. The smooth machinery of enclosure by agreement as perfected by mid-seventeenth-century improving gentlemen and their lawyers attracted less unfavourable notice. And yet social conservatives, clergymen like Sanderson or scrupulous gentlemen like Edward Hussey, might still look askance at such enclosure. First, the ostensible agreement might have been obtained only by the landlord's employment of his social or political power. The naked oppression by a man like John Palmer, who told his West Angmering, Sussex, tenants that 'the kinges grace hath putt downe all the houses of monks, fryers and nunnes. . . Thierfore nowe is the tyme come that we gentilmen will pull downe the house of such poore knaves as ye be' or by George Barlow, who told the tenants of Narberth, Pembrokeshire, that he would 'crush and crack them like fleas', might still survive, concealed by the smooth phrases of an 'agreement' founded on blackmail, subterfuge and chicanery. So in Lincolnshire, Sanderson's own county, gentlemen might forget the promises designed to secure their tenants' compliance; Sir Henry Disney was slow to make good freehold estates to his ex-copyholders at Swinderby, while at Kirkby Laythorpe Sir William Carr used a legal technicality to deny the long leases that he had promised his tenants. Equally, those who refused to agree to a lord's enclosure scheme might be subjected to intense pressure. Sir Edward Carr and Sir Nicholas Sanderson commenced campaigns that combined assaults by hired thugs with lawsuits at Westminster against, respectively, a yeoman of Wilsford and a widow of Tetney who blocked their plans; both gentlemen used their powers as magistrates to have their opponents arrested on specious charges of trespass and riot. Sir Nicholas went one stage further: sitting on the bench at Caistor sessions when the poor woman sought redress, he solemnly assured his fellow justices that she was a witch.[23]

Even where an enclosure agreement was attained without undue pressure, and where its purpose was to practise the new arable husbandry, its social consequences might still prove destructive of traditional tenurial relations. Enclosure not only permitted experiment with new agricultural technology, but the development of farms of a more efficient size. Sir Henry Ayscough, questioned in the government's investigation of enclosure in 1608, firmly denied that the population of Blyborough, Lincolnshire, had been reduced by his enclosure. But he acknowledged that he had shut down a couple of smallholdings, consolidating their lands with those of his other farms to form larger units of production.[24] Changes of this kind – the engrossing denounced by Sanderson, 'joyning house to house and field to field' – did not force families from the village, but they did transform its social structure. Engrossing produced a small élite of substantial tenant farmers and a large pool of landless labourers.

## The Exploitation of Estates

For some gentlemen, whose estates were close to markets or good transport facilities, whose fields were already enclosed to form efficient farming units, whose leasing practices allowed the frequent renegotiation of rents, the maintenance of real income in a period of inflation was, as Professor Simpson has argued, a matter of prosaic management and few moral qualms. Yet for others a more activist managerial style – involving the abrogation of disadvantageous tenures; enclosure; engrossing; experiments with the new technologies – promised significant gain. Some gentlemen deliberately rejected such opportunities, and sought to uphold conventional assumptions about a lord's responsibilities to his dependants and the proper social order. Edward Hussey, lord of the manor of Caythorpe, Lincolnshire, rejected an enclosure scheme backed by the wealthier farmers with 'a prospect of improving their estates'. He believed that the project would be fatal to the cottagers and small farmers of the village, and he 'had a strong conceit' that enclosing gentry in the area had been punished by a series of providential judgements. Sir John Oglander, considering the vulnerability of the Isle of Wight to foreign attack, sought to strengthen its defences by increasing the number of tenants on his lands, refurbishing old and establishing new farms. 'No man,' he boasted, 'hath been a greater enemy against depopulation than myself.'[25] Yet Oglander's agricultural enterprises were, as he bitterly complained in 1632, not over-remunerative. Social responsibility, it seemed, did not pay immediate dividends, and the majority of the gentry, perhaps keenly aware of the dilemma that faced Oglander, appear to have been content with verbal affirmations of the traditional platitudes.

In some cases the disparity between prescription and practice is extraordinarily striking. In the preamble and exordium of the estate book that the Lincolnshire gentleman, Sir George Heneage, prepared, his son was reminded of the profound responsibilities that attach to lordship. The management of the estate must be 'to God's honour and glory'; 'use them which hereafter shall live under you conscionably, be upright and just in all your actions, and ever remember that sinne is the maine and efficient cause of the utter ruine and extirpation of families.' Yet in the body of the text Heneage coolly records a number of practices at which Sanderson would have trembled: a dubious but highly advantageous deal on the glebe and tithe in one property; enclosure; the engrossing of farms. Sir John Wynn solemnly advised his son in 1612, concerning an improvement scheme, 'to have god before you in all your accyons, howldyinge faythe in a good conscience . . . fleeyinge the cursse of the poore.' Yet in 1615 the Council of the Marches was appalled by accounts of Wynn's deployment of his authority as a JP and deputy lieutenant, including evicting families by force in the dead of night, to pressure the villagers of Penmaen and Llysvaen during a dispute over manorial rights. The humiliating censure inflicted on Wynn after this incident did little to modify his behaviour. In 1618 Sir John's relentless hounding of a tenant led the Bishop of Bangor to beg the Council that they 'would not suffer our great men thus to oppresse and tread over his Majesties poore subiects'. In 1627 Sir Robert Carr's steward, William Burton, discussed the renting of the Lincolnshire estates with his master. At Gosberton he thought the rent too high and proposed a reduction; the tenants would be better able to pay the new rents, but also 'they shall have cause to speake honourably of you for your kyndnesse towardes them'. He added that the rental of the estates in the vicinity of the Carr mansion at Sleaford could be raised, 'yet because your tenants . . . lie neere your chiefest house and wilbe alwaies readie at your call to do you service, it is hoped you will deale honourablie with them as all your Ancestors heretofore have done.' The sentiment is admirable, if conventional – yet utterly incongruous. The Carr family had an evil reputation locally as aggressive exploiters of their lands. Sir Robert's father had, it was claimed in 1611, enclosed 7,000 acres and shut down 20 working farms. He had broken the terms of the leases that he had made with his tenants; he had, with Burton as his agent, not scrupled to use his 'great revenues, power and authority' to crush those tenants who stood in the way of his nefarious schemes.[26]

The traditional ethic of paternalistic responsibility for their tenants was hammered into the gentry by clerics and by the precepts retailed in family 'Advices'. Yet the advantages of active, engaged estate management, of improvement, were also apparent and were equally stressed, as by Sir George Heneage, as essential to the maintenance of a family's status. The tension between these ideals was acute, but probably lessened towards the end of the seventeenth century. There are a number of reasons for the easing of landlord–tenant relations, and for a concomitant reassertion of paternalist values.

First, while managerial technique is ultimately a matter of individual aptitude and character, two groups of gentlemen were particularly prone to attempt the fullest exploitation of their estates: newcomers, and those experiencing pressing financial embarrassment. Both groups become less apparent in the social landscape of late seventeenth-century England.

Newcomers to an area, buying their way onto the land and untroubled by traditional ties to the local society, might seek an immediate return on their investment. When John Isham, a London merchant and moneylender, bought Lamport in conjunction with his brother, Robert, the parson of neighbouring Pytchley, the latter sought to prevent any enclosure or substantial increases of rent on the estate. After Robert's death, John, with scant sense of family piety, swiftly cut through the flimsy legal arrangements that his brother had set up in his will to defend the Lamport commoners, and began the enclosure, conversion to pasture, and depopulation of the community. At Condover, Staffordshire, another London mercer, Robert Longe, who purchased the estate in 1544, ruthlessly cut down timber, revived medieval dues, attempted to destroy the copyholds of inheritance by demanding prohibitive fines, and began a programme of enclosure.[27]

Manors previously held by the Crown or the Church, where lax management was the norm, were particularly susceptible to exploitation by their new landlords, though the latter faced the vigorous resistance of local communities used to independence. At the beginning of the seventeenth century, two sons of Archbishop Sandys of York, acquired such lands in, respectively, Worcestershire and the Isle of Ely. Both became locally infamous for their rapacity. Samuel Sandys acknowledged that he intended to exploit the manor of Ombersley 'for his best profit' even though this might lose him the good will of the tenants. He let his demesne lands 'to the very uttermost value', and sought both to secure the forfeitures of copyholds on technicalities, and to increase the revenue from the fines and dues from customary land. His brother, Miles, had purchased a number of fenland manors previously held by the bishop of Ely. Sandys, like other newcomers to this under-exploited area, had ambitious schemes for the enclosure and drainage of his lands. To silence the opposition of the tenantry he pursued a campaign of legal intimidation, based on the resurrection of antiquated manorial dues that included demands for labour services. His oppression of his Willingham villagers, fourteen of the 'gravest, auncientist and most harmlesse' of whom were imprisoned on trivial suits, was accompanied by a series of disputes with neighbouring landlords over engineering operations that frequently drained his lands at the expense of flooding theirs. One of the local gentry wrote nostalgically of a time of harmonious social relations on the Isle, 'before Sir Miles for our punishment planted himself in this countrie'.[28]

Not all parvenus exploited their purchases with the contempt for local values and personal reputation of the Sandys brothers; some very deliberately attempted to identify with traditional paternalist values. Sir Rowland Hill, a wealthy London merchant who purchased lands in his native Shropshire in the mid-sixteenth century, was a paragon among landlords: he 'never raysed rennts . . . he suffryd the child to inioy the fathers farme before all others, he was the frynd of the widowe and fatherles'. The Courteen family, at the apex of the mercantile and banking hierarchy of the city of London in the 1620s, acted 'more like parentes than landlordes to theyr tenauntes' on their newly purchased Worcestershire estates. Yet Habington, who reported their concern for the welfare of their dependants 'as I scarce eaver heardt he lyke', also remarked that it was particularly rare 'in suche as buy gentellmen out of theyre auncient . . . manors'. This was the popular perception: a Suffolk man, inciting revolt in 1569, encouraged his auditors to hang those 'rich churles' who were 'newe come uppe and be heardemen'; they had no quarrel with the 'gentlemen of old contynuance'.[29]

The second group tempted to undertake the fullest exploitation of their estates with little regard for the social cost were those gentlemen who found themselves in financial difficulties. The more importunate the creditors, the greater the temptation to conduct the equivalent of a smash and grab raid against one's tenants. Sir Pexall Brocas of Steventon, Hampshire, was a man whose grandiose ambition – to found Brocas College, Oxford – was hardly congruent with his vicious disputes with his son, scandalous life, and a heavily indebted estate entangled in litigation. Brocas's 'hard usage' of his tenants was legendary: demands for extortionate rents, and for loans that usually proved permanent, were backed by threats of vexatious lawsuits and the attentions of his thugs. Sir Roger Dallison, Master of the Ordnance to James I, was sued by the Crown for the recovery of over £13,000 that he had embezzled. Sir Roger, 'a cunning man', engaged in a series of desperate ploys to dodge the burden of debt that hung over him. These included extracting high fines for new leases from his Lincolnshire tenants; the leases proved worthless because of his creditors' claims against the estate, and 'many honest yeomen and farmers' were ruined by Dallison's 'fraud and cheat'. Less catastrophic financial crises than than those facing Brocas and Dallison might concentrate a gentleman's attention on estate-management. The extravagance of his Court-bred wife led John Frescheville to renegotiate the leases granted by 'his good father . . . at easy rates'. The endemic fiscal pressure on recusants ensured that a number of Catholic gentlemen, like Sir Thomas Tresham and Sir Thomas Gascoigne, won unenviable reputations as grasping landlords. Richard Cholmeley of Brandsby, Yorkshire, his tenants complained, 'would allow them nothing'; he was 'hard to them and every day at new covenants with them.'[30]

The less active land market after the Civil War, and the ready availability of cheaper and more secure mortgages ensured that the two groups among the gentry most likely to seek to exploit their tenantry prior to 1640 dwindled in the late seventeenth century. But these developments themselves were related to another important element in the easier landlord–tenant relations of this period: the stagnation of agricultural prices that followed the century and a half of inflation.

## The Later Seventeenth Century: Market Stagnation

Landowners had intermittently experienced problems with the collection of their rents during the period of inflation. In 1596–7, when war taxation and harvest failure coincided, Andrew Archer was barraged by requests for rent reductions and further time to pay arrears by the tenant of his Stratford-upon-Avon lands, 'it is as harde as hard may be and so harde that never a husbandman in England . . . can lyve,' he wrote. In 1623 Sir William Pelham of Brocklesby reported that as a consequence of a dearth of money and a slack market in Lincolnshire unemployed labourers were starving and his tenants were abandoning their farms. But such crises, occasioned by over-abundant or particularly bad harvests, or by wartime dislocations of the export trade and the money market, had been of relatively short duration. In general the landlord could anticipate the prospect of a rising income from direct production and from rents.[31]

The Civil War, involving the devastation of marauding armies and the dislocation of marketing systems in many areas, and high taxation universally, was a period of particular difficulty for landlords, even for those who were not liable to the penalties imposed on Royalists. Yet they might have regarded the problems – rent-arrears, requests for abatements, tenants abandoning their holdings – as temporary inconveniences, resembling the crises of the 1590s or the early 1620s. Such an attitude would have been reinforced by the high prices fetched by agricultural produce in the 1650s, by the significant increases in rents that landlords were able to extract in 1651 and 1652, and by the general upward trend in rents up to 1663. After 1664, however, landlords were forced to adjust to a new phenomenon – a long-term stagnation of agricultural prices. Indices of the prices fetched by all agricultural products show a fall of 4 per cent in the 1660s and 6 per cent in the 1670s from the prices that had appertained in the 1650s. Prices rose above 1650-levels only in the 1690s, by 6 per cent, but fell again in the next decade, and remained at or below 1650-levels into the 1740s. The capital value of land followed this trend until 1715, but then began a rapid rise that pre-dated the recovery of agricultural prices. With the exception of the 1690s, landlords found that they were unable to raise their income from their agricultural holdings, and were under pressure from their tenants to abate rents and to shorten leases. In certain periods – 1664–7, the last years of the 1670s – rents were 'ill paid', arrears grew rapidly, and landlords found themselves unable to lease out farms that were 'flung up by tenants for want of ability to pay'. The groans that punctuate the letters from distraught stewards and land agents to their masters witness to the extent of the agricultural depression. Landlords in the 1660s, while, with Sir Philip Constable, professing to do 'what is conscionable in these hard times', pressured tenants for arrears with talk of eviction and lawsuits. But there were serious checks on such behaviour, as tenants seem to have recognised by the next decade when they backed their demands for rent abatements with threats of abandoning their farms. Attempts to compel tenants to keep their contractual obligations might result in the deliberate neglect of the holding, as Sir John Lowther found at Whitehaven. Landlords knew that tenants were a scarce commodity, and that attempting to change them could be a difficult and expensive business; a man who was 'a good tenent and knows it too' was in a strong bargaining position. The gentry bewailed the irresponsibility and even –

incongruously – the 'disloyalty' of their tenants; but they granted the necessary abatements. When one of Sir Stephen Fox's Somerset farmers was at the point of surrendering his lease, the bailiff wrote urgently to his master, 'It will be a great loss to yor Honor to lose such a tenant.' Fox responded by offering the inducements necessary to persuade the farmer to continue. An alternative to granting abatements or finding new tenants was for the landlord to take farms into his own hands. Sir Ralph Verney preferred this course of action in the 1660s, but by the next decade he, with other landlords, was 'glad at any rates to get tenants'. As one of Verney's correspondents sardonically noted, a gentlemen, 'bred to nothing but to spend' his estate, was in no good position to commence direct production when markets were stagnant. Similar considerations limited the extent to which landlords could respond to the recession by capital investment, designed to develop larger units of production or to promote technological innovations on their estates.[32]

The gentry were not content merely to bemoan the decay of trade and the fall of rents and to tinker with the organisation of their own estates. Gathered in the House of Commons, they employed their legislative authority to establish a series of measures designed to protect their agricultural interests. After 1663 restrictions on the export of English grain were waived, and high duties imposed on imports; from 1672 bounties were awarded to those exporting grain. The interests of pastoral areas were also considered. In 1667, following limited interference in the trade in 1663, the importation of all Irish cattle was banned – a measure which advantaged the cattle-breeders of north and western England, but was less popular among the graziers of the south and east. In their legislation of 1663 'for the encouragement of trade', the Commons piously emphasised their concern for the public welfare, their endeavours to bring more land into production and to employ more people. The continuing depression of prices eroded this enthusiasm, and, as with the prohibition on the importation of Irish cattle, the Commons became a place of conflict for different interest groups within the agricultural sector. Large-scale improvement schemes, which required central authority, became a victim of these pressures. Attempts to gain legislative backing for drainage projects in Lincolnshire foundered on the hostility of those MPs with estates in the 'high country' adjacent to the fens, who feared that the superior productivity of improved land would yet further erode their declining rent-rolls. The new-found concern for the property rights of the indigenous peasantry sedulously expressed by the MPs in their rejection of these proposals may appear specious, but it too was an element in the easing of landlord–tenant relations in the later seventeenth century.[33]

The optimism of a Sir Richard Weston, the belief that the improvement of the ancestral estate would secure and enhance landed income, no longer typified gentry opinion in the late seventeenth century. Gentlemen bewailed waning market opportunities and falling rent-rolls. Yet such opinions had been intermittently expressed earlier, before the depression had gripped agriculture. Best known is Sir John Oglander's dispirited *cri de coeur*, penned in 1632 in 'his own blood':

> It is impossible for a mere country gentleman ever to grow rich or to raise his house. He must have some other vocation with his own inheritance, as to be a courtier, lawyer, merchant or some other vocation. If he hath no other vocation, let him get a ship and judiciously manage her, or buy some auditor's place or be a vice-admiral in his country. By only following the plough he may keep his word and be upright, but he will never increase his fortune.[34]

Obviously Oglander's jaundiced assumption that 'following the plough' condemned a man to honourable poverty was not generally acknowledged, and it would be easy to read it merely as the product of a bleak period of his life. In the summer of 1632 he was saddened by the departure of his feckless but much-loved son, George, to the continent on an educational tour, and by his wife's premonitions – soon to be vindicated – that the trip would end in disaster. But his comment does indicate the other activities that might prove lucrative to a gentry family. How far were such opportunities available to the gentry? Was Oglander correct in his assumption that these guaranteed wealth and, with it, the desired improvement in status?

Oglander's discussion embodies the traditional conception of a gentleman's landed estate as an agrarian unit. Yet this misses an important point. For many gentlemen it was the exploitation of the non-agricultural opportunities on their estates that freed them from dependence on 'following the plough'. These must be discussed before we move to the more speculative endeavours – the Court and the offices in its gift; the law; trade – that impressed Sir John.

## 3.3 ALTERNATIVE SOURCES OF INCOME

### Mining and Industry

Late in 1607 Sir John Wynn engaged in a flurry of correspondence concerning the possibility of mining mineral deposits in north Wales. His letters, a mixture of technical information, optimism, cupidity, and doubt – 'finding such uncertainty in alchemy, I durst never adventure such a work,' he wrote – nicely catch the hopes and the fears of those of the gentry who believed that untapped wealth lay beneath their lands ripe for their exploitation.[35]

Coal was the commonest mineral on their estates, and the gentry were aware that it promised significant income. John Smyth of Nibley, who loftily declared that husbandry was 'the only vocation wherein innocency remaineth', hired Coventry miners to prospect for coal on his estate. In 1603 Anne Newdigate was invited to London to witness the celebrations attending James I's entry and coronation; 'Ether come up now and se this bravey or close your eyes whillest you lyve,' her correspondent concluded urgently, 'And let Jak's colpitts pay for all.' Anne's husband, Sir John, worked five pits at the Griffe, Warwickshire at the beginning of the seventeenth century. Yet, as Sir John Newdigate was to learn, coalmining was a risky business. A gentleman seeking to develop mines on his property confronted serious technical problems, chiefly associated with mine drainage and often enhanced by deliberate sabotage by competitors, and had to manage an unruly labour force. He also risked potentially expensive conflict with neighbouring landowners over manorial boundaries and rights of way; with freeholders over mining rights in common and waste; with tenants over his rights to mine under their tenements. In the first two decades of the seventeenth century the vast, ramshackle schemes of the inventive but ludicrously optimistic Huntingdon Beaumont to develop the midland coalfields and to use the Trent and Humber to bring the product to the London market, led to over-capitalisation and over-production in the industry, particularly in this area. Beaumont was ruined, and many of the midland gentry, both his partners and his competitors, were seriously embarrassed. Midland collieries were still in difficulties in the 1640s, when it was said that Richard Knightley of Fawsley, Warwickshire, had lost £10,000 in his endeavour to develop the Bedworth mines. The Shropshire landowner, Sir John Weld, solemnly warned his son against speculation in coalmining; he was advised, 'not to be busy in searching for coals . . . not to be led away by colliers or miners or projectors, whose fair speech is but to get themselves money.' Not surprisingly, many Yorkshire gentlemen, both before and after the Civil War, preferred to lease out their coal-bearing lands to entrepreneurs who would bear the substantial risks of development.[36]

Weld's sober advice was not, however, invariably followed. Direct exploitation of coal was undoubtedly a gamble, but it still promised the chance of spectacular wealth. Wollaton House remained a magnificent monument to the wealth generated by the Willoughby family's mines. Substantial profits, while elusive, could still be made by the energetic and innovative in the seventeenth century. The elegant courtier, Sir William Slingsby, failed in his efforts to develop mines at Seaton Delaval, but his venture at Kippax was a success; the initial investment was considerable, but by 1623 profits had stood at £600 for several years, and £6,000 had been made since the accession of James. Another Yorkshire pit, at Baildon, brought in £80 per annum between 1620 and 1640, an income which was improved in the next decade by the initiative of Sir Richard Hawksworth, one of the co-owners, in sinking new 'deep' pits. Other gentlemen were similarly involved in developing mining techniques. Sir Thomas Gascoigne of Barnbow, Yorkshire, brought the same energy to his mining ventures that he gave to the improvement of his lands and to speculation in property and mortgages. He engaged in a series of experiments with pumps that permitted his miners to exploit deeper coal veins. Sir Roger Bradshaigh of the Haigh, Lancashire, was another gentleman, like Gascoigne of ancient ancestry, whose wide-ranging engagement in estate improvement included the technology of mining. In 1670 he completed the building of the Great Sough, a tunnel nearly a mile long which drained his and his neighbours' coal workings, 'for the good of my Posterity'. It was still functioning in 1945.[37]

The late sixteenth-century operations and profits of Sir Francis Willoughby were matched a century later by those of Sir Humphrey Mackworth of Neath, Glamorgan, or Sir John Lowther. In 1666 Lowther had sought to purchase all the coal-bearing lands within a mile of Whitehaven, Cumberland; by 1690 he controlled seams and rights-of-way within a five-mile radius of the town. Coal was brought down to Whitehaven, the harbour facilities of which Lowther had improved, by an expanding network of tramways.

The coal was then shipped to Dublin, where Lowther controlled an increasing percentage of a rapidly expanding market.[38]

A number of gentlemen also sought to benefit directly from the exploitation of other mineral deposits upon their estates. Like those involved in the coal industry, they were obliged to wrestle with a series of difficulties – technical and labour problems; the need to raise a substantial capital; poor transportation networks; fluctuating markets and recession; government intervention. Such problems could prove fatal to entrepreneurial initiative. Sir Solomon Swayle's lead-mining operations in Swaledale collapsed because transportation costs proved prohibitive, and the family was ruined. Sir John Wynn overcame his doubts and began lead-mining in 1620, but found himself unable to market his product profitably in the depression that gripped Europe in that decade. Sir William Clavell of Smedmore, Dorset, a man 'ingenious in diverse faculties', worked the alum deposits on his estate; his operation was compulsorily acquired by the those who had secured a monopoly of alum production from James I, who proceeded to ruin it. Sir William, 'who one Disaster dismayed not', then invested in glass production. Again his initiative fell foul of a monopolist and was closed down.[39]

Yet despite the difficulties metallurgy could be profitable. The rising fortunes of the Eyres of Hassop, Derbyshire, and the Brights of Carbrook, Yorkshire, both originally yeomen families, were underpinned by lead-mining. Rowland Eyre appeared as 'a man very covetous' to those who experienced his ruthless drive, his 'hard and unconscionable dealing' in his pursuit of mining rights. But Rowland was also experimenting with new mining and smelting techniques, and his expertise was acknowledged by the Crown whose officers frequently consulted him on matters concerning lead production. As with coalmining, aggressive newcomers were not uniquely qualified to exploit mineral resources. A number of well-established families also profited significantly through a mixture of luck and technical aptitude. Fortune smiled on Sir Thomas Pelham of Halland, Sussex. Despite the general decline of the Wealden industry, Pelham continued to invest in iron works, opening new forges on his estate in the late 1630s. His confidence paid dividends when the Civil War put a premium on munitions production: prices rocketed, and, between 1643 and 1645, Pelham received some £3,000 per annum from his furnaces and forges. Sir Francis Godolphin of Godolphin became a talented mining engineer whose skills played a major role in the adjustment of the Cornish tin industry to the challenge posed by the exhaustion of the surface workings. Godolphin, after consultation with German engineers, developed 'profitable conclusions of his own invention' that permitted deep mining into the lodes, a more expensive and hazardous process than the traditional tin-streaming. His 'labours and inventions', wrote his contemporary, Carew, not only enriched Godolphin himself but had been copied by other local gentlemen who had 'thereby gotten very great profit out of . . . works as they before had given over for unprofitable'.[40]

Engagement in the exploitation of the mineral deposits on their estates often led the gentry into ancillary activities that seemed yet more remote from the classic images that associated gentility with rural life or with leisure. Sir John Lowther experimented with the production of salt by boiling sea water at Whitehaven to employ poorer quality coal that it was uneconomic to transport; the Willoughbys' investment in a glass-works at Wollaton, the Lumleys in alum production at Hartlepool, Sir John Bradshaigh's in glass and pottery production, all had a similar purpose. Willoughby, like many coal-producers, was also directly involved in the carrying trade, owning a string of boats on the Trent. In other cases the gentry simply involved themselves in industries developing near their estates or sought to exploit local market opportunities. A number of West Riding gentlemen owned fulling mills. William Sheldon, the great Worcestershire sheep-master, invested in tapestry production both because it would be 'greatly beneficial to this commonwealth and a means to store great sums of money within this Realm', and to provide a ready market for his own wool. Thomas Archer and his son, Andrew, ran an iron mill near Stratford-on-Avon; sales were to traders and farmers of the area, but the annual profit [£200] represented about 10 per cent of the Archers' income.[41]

Tapping the mineral resources of their lands and developing ancillary industries was not the only non-agricultural use that the gentry could make of their estates. The possession of urban property or the ownership of manorial rights in towns or their environs could be exploited to produce a significant income. The profits derived from agriculture could be invested in the money market.

## Urban Development

In the late sixteenth century Sir Willoughby Hickman purchased the manor of Gainsborough from its lenient and non-resident lord, Lord

Burgh. Hickman engaged in the most aggressive reassertion of dormant manorial rights to tap the modest prosperity which the town was enjoying. He enclosed part of the common and sanctioned the erection of jerry-built cottages, so encouraging an influx of immigrants who became an immediate charge on the poor rate. He diverted revenues intended for the maintenance of the town's streets, church, and market to his own pocket. His most vigorous efforts went to cash in on the town's entrepôt function. He levied a tax on vessels carrying grain down the Trent; he extended the biennial fair, and encouraged 'the resort of the Londoners' who undersold local retailers; he increased the market tolls – by 1640 these, which Burgh had leased for £10 per annum, were valued at £250. Great Yarmouth, ostensibly better protected than Gainsborough by its ancient corporate status, was subject to a similar attempt to skim its trade-based prosperity by a neighbouring gentleman. Sir Robert Paston of Oxnead sought to develop his manor of Little Yarmouth, on the Suffolk bank of the river Yare, as a suburb that would enjoy all the the commercial privileges of the corporation, and he used his contacts in Parliament and at Court to secure the passage of the requisite legislation in 1665. Paston then employed the architect, Stephen Primatt, to plan his new town with extensive quays and a market area, a chapel, and, in stark contrast to Great Yarmouth, broad streets and substantial house-lots. A prospectus was issued, and agents appointed to encourage immigrants and speculative investment: Paston dreamed of an income of £2,000 a year from his project. However, the scheme never advanced beyond the drawing-board. The corporation of Great Yarmouth doggedly defended its privileges in a series of rearguard actions that exploited every legal inconsistency in the enabling legislation, while Paston's precarious financial position precluded him from personally investing in the development beyond the building of a quay.[42]

While relations between towns and those of the gentry who owned property within them were often tense, they were not always as parasitic as the activities of Hickman and Paston might suggest. The Ramsdens of Longley did much to encourage the growth of Huddersfield as an industrial and retailing centre, by establishing forges and mills, building houses, and securing market privileges; a similar role was played by the Litteltons of Frankley with respect to Stourbridge. Even the raffish Gilbert Littelton could claim that he had contributed to the town's economic growth by setting up 'dyverse meetings of gentlemen and others for cockfights and other pastimes'. His expanding mining operations and the concomitant growth of port facilities led Sir John Lowther to undertake a carefully planned expansion of Whitehaven, a classic company-town. Lowther himself financed the building of many of the houses 'to draw people thither'; he secured market privileges; he provided a new school, a church, a cockpit, a bowling green. The main street of Whitehaven – Lowther Street – was oriented to provide vistas of the family's mansion at Flatt Hall.[43]

**Moneylending**

The capital that John Isham, mercer and Merchant Adventurer of London, employed to purchase Lamport was in part acquired by moneylending. His grandson, Sir John, neatly inverted the process. Profits from his well-run estate were invested in the money market; between 1622 and 1640 the sum of £8,700 was loaned to eight local gentlemen on mortgages, and a steady income of £300–500 per annum realised. Yet Isham's involvement in moneylending would have been viewed uneasily by most commentators on status. Before the Civil War usury was fiercely condemned by many divines as in breach of divine law, and few theologians were prepared to give the practice unqualified approval. Many gentlemen shared their doubts. Sir Samuel Rolle, on his deathbed, took it 'as an especiall blessing that neither he nor his father nor his Grandfather (notwithstanding their many and great transactions in the world) had ever borrowed or lent upon usury'. Sir Simonds D'Ewes, while he recognised that usury was one of the 'controversial sins' like 'carding, dicing, mixed dancing', not universally subject to clerical denunciation, still 'thought it not lawful to . . . take use', and lent his money freely. Other gentlemen, who did not share the conscientious scruples of the godly, opposed usury as corrosive of ideals of friendship and neighbourliness. A gentleman should lend to needy friends and kinsmen freely, as did Sir Gervase Holles, who, from 'the great friendship he always bore' to Sir Percival Willoughby, loaned him £3,000; the same sentiment made Holles refuse to take 'severe courses' against Willoughby for repayment, and in consequence the bulk of the money was lost. Sir Robert Filmer, writing for his Kentish neighbours in the late 1620s, sought to demolish the argument of a scriptural prohibition against usury – but emphasised that he personally would never take interest on a loan.[44]

Yet some gentlemen, like Isham, were prepared to defy religious scruples and conventional assumptions regarding neighbourliness. They offered loans at the going rate, and they did very well out of it. Richard Hickson was heir to his grandfather, a substantial yeoman of Ropsley who died in 1591; Richard was described as 'gent.' in 1607, and, having served as Sheriff of Lincolnshire in 1621–2, thereafter became 'esquire'. Hickson's titular elevation reflected his growing landed estate in Kesteven, the product, basically, of aggressive estate management, the lending of agricultural profits on bonds and mortgages, and speculation in the estates that fell into his hands. In 1621 Hickson acquired the manor of Barkston, outbidding the eminent and long-established local worthy, Sir Edward Hussey, who coveted it; Barkston's owner was already deeply indebted to him, he offered more for the prize, and could guarantee immediate payment. Hickson's bequest of a clock at Gonerby 'that passengers may see the time of day', perhaps catches something of the drive and enterprise of this parvenu. But it was not just newcomers to gentry status or their immediate descendants who engaged in moneylending. Yorkshiremen borrowed money from Sir William Ingleby of Ripley, Sir Thomas Gascoigne of Barnbow, and Sir Ralph Maddison of Fonaby, Lincolnshire – whose interest in the money market extended to publication on abstruse matters of international currency manipulation. All three were representatives of long-settled families, and Gascoigne was a recusant who ended his days as a monk in Germany. Gascoigne and Maddison enjoyed unenviable reputations as aggressive creditors; Sir Ralph's 'hard, usurious and unconscionable' dealing in relation to loans was a subject of bitter complaint by his own son-in-law.[45]

By the mid-seventeenth century, with the development of a more extensive money market and with Chancery policing debtor–creditor relations, moneylending became neither as hazardous nor as suspect an activity as it had been a century earlier. A few gentlemen invested heavily in mortgages and bonds, usually loaning money to their neighbours; Sir John Bright was owed some £20,000 in 1682, and was the chief creditor in the West Riding of Yorkshire with loans to many of the leading families of the area – Jackson, Kaye, Rhodes, Smithson, Wentworth. Leviathans like Bright were exceptional; most gentry families would experience the money market in more modest transactions, with the rhythms of family life dictating their roles as borrowers or as lenders. Cash surpluses were invested when children were young; money was borrowed to raise portions for daughters' marriages. By the end of the seventeenth century investment diversified. Money was moved from the mortgage market into government bonds or the stocks of private enterprises, like the East India Company or the Bank of England. In the early eighteenth century both John Liddell-Bright and Sir Marmaduke Constable, heavily indebted, were obliged to sell property; in both cases the sales produced a surplus, which was then invested in a mix of mortgages, government funds, and stocks, including – typically, for two families that were pretty luckless in their fiscal dealings – stock in the South Sea company.[46]

## Trade and Shipping

Sir John Oglander advised his fellow 'mere' gentry to supplement the inadequate income provided by 'following the plough' by practising a vocation, including that of merchant. Most of the gentlemen who did become involved directly or indirectly in trade or finance did so, not, as Oglander implied, as an exogenous activity, but in an endeavour to exploit the non-agricultural potential of their estates – sinking mines, investing in facilities to process or transport their product, encouraging urban growth in the vicinity of their lands. There are a few examples of gentlemen whose involvement in industry or trade was not related intimately to the development of the potential of their own estates. Sir William Ashcombe, despite losing £500 as a young man backing a friend's schemes for a waterworks and for manufacturing silk stockings, remained fascinated by industrial and marketing projects throughout his life; for supplying London with oysters and alabaster; for producing bullets and gunpowder; for growing liquorice. He made little from any of these undertakings. Sir Edward Greville of Milcote, Warwickshire, was another 'projector', backing a new process to produce starch from bran. He secured monopoly rights from the Crown, but after four years the venture petered out as debts and unsold stock mounted. His later attempt to prospect for gold in Cardiganshire proved equally doomed.[47]

Neither does Oglander's advice to 'get a ship' seem to have guaranteed the wealth denied to those obliged to 'follow the plough'. Both Sir Thomas Sherley, jnr., of Wiston, Sussex, in 1602 and Sir John Wentworth of Gosfield, Essex, in the 1620s had ships, but in neither case was their management judicious. Sherley's raid on Spain, while 'not without great honor', produced but 'small profit'; his 'unprofitable voyage', like Wentworth's failed privateering venture later, led to ruin. Part of the problem was that these speculative ventures were often the desperate undertakings of men already in financial straits who lacked the capital, and, we may suspect from their previous undertakings, the application and aptitude to pursue them successfully. Sherley's father had been 'cast behindhand by hard fortune' through his involvement in the Elizabethan Court; both Greville and Wentworth were rakes and spendthrifts who swaggered on the margins of the Jacobean Court in a trail of debts and mortgages. Their experience raises further questions concerning Oglander's recipe for the advancement of the 'mere country gentleman'. Neither the vocation of merchant or that of courtier rescued Greville or Wentworth or enabled either to 'raise his house': quite the reverse.[48]

## The Court

Sir John Oglander's assertion that the vocation of a courtier, or possession of the offices to which Court-connection gave access is ironic. Sir John, appointed Deputy Governor of Portsmouth in 1620, sold the post in 1623. Although he had enhanced the profits of his place, Oglander decided to abandon it partly because of the high costs of entertainment that it involved, partly because he was obliged to 'neglect my own estate at home', which, in his absence, 'went to decay'. His reading of the Court experience of his father-in-law, Sir George More of Loseley, Surrey, was similarly negative. More received a series of minor Court preferments, but none answerable to his 'rare gifts of wit', his 'great abilities'; worse, their profits never outweighed the damage caused by the neglect of 'his own affairs' that was a by-product of his Court attendance. The death of Prince Henry blasted his hopes of appropriate preferment, and his services were repaid, particularly in the years of Buckingham's ascendancy, with 'specious promises instead of real performances'. Yet, despite these unhappy experiences, Oglander remained fascinated by the Court, by the possibilities for rapid advancement within it, and by the figure of Buckingham.[49]

The example of the Duke of Buckingham indicated the spectacular prizes available to the fortunate courtier. George Villiers was a younger son by a second marriage of a Leicestershire gentleman of ancient lineage but moderate means; his inheritance was an annuity of £50. In 1613 his exceptional good looks and a gloss of courtly elegance polished by a short stay in France brought him to the notice of James I. A decade later Villiers was a Duke, Lord Admiral of England, head of an extensive patronage empire, and enriched by the prodigal bounty of the doting king. 'You have filled a consuming purse, given me fair houses, [and] more land than I am worthy of to maintain both me and them,' he wrote gratefully to James. Yet few fathers, though they might share Oglander's envy or fascination, recommended their sons to attempt to emulate Buckingham's meteoric career. Most advised avoidance of the exhilarating but costly roulette of the Court.[50]

The legend of his wicked ancestor, the Henrician courtier Anselm Guise, recorded a century later by Sir Christopher, lost nothing in the telling, no doubt. Anselm, who 'did sufficiently partake of the disolute vices of that time and place . . . vaynly and wickedly spending his estate in luxury', failed to take 'any . . . advantage of the King's favour', and virtually ruined his ancient family. Yet reality, for some families, was not so remote from such parables. Sir John – nicknamed 'Lusty' – Pakington endeared himself to Elizabeth by his wit, his personal elegance and his athletic prowess. But, like Guise, he proved 'no good husband of opportunity' and his estate was sapped by Court attendance. Only a fortuitous marriage to a rich City widow, and retirement to rural Worcestershire saved him from ruin. Anthony Cooke was even less lucky. He inherited the family estates in Essex and Warwickshire, well-managed and bringing in an income from rents and direct production of some £2,000 a year, in 1579 at the age of twenty. In 1580, and for the next, catastrophic, five years, he graced the Court. He was particularly active in the lavishly ceremonious jousts and tournaments, and in pageants, and he attended the Queen on her progresses. He was one of the gilded entourage that accompanied the Earl of Derby in a trip to France in 1584 to invest Henry III with the Garter. Cooke also sought a reputation as 'the deere Chyld of the Muses' by patronising needy poets. But in this brilliant Court milieu, Cooke's 'charges be extreme, and there want not those to draw all that he hath from him'. He experienced outlawry for debt and a short spell of imprisonment in the Fleet; by 1585 he had been obliged to sell off piecemeal almost the whole of the Cooke estate, except the lands reserved as the jointures for his wife and his mother, for some £10,500. Cooke optimistically believed that 'carefull sparinge might recover superfluouse spendinge', but, though he abandoned the

Court, his extravagance remained untamed: a trip to Constantinople, with the intention of escaping his creditors, resulted only in a trail of new debts for, *inter alia*, an Arabian horse, jewellery, and a richly decorated gun. Creditors became importunate, and by 1591 Cooke was reduced to revising, to a far lower level, the provision originally made for his wife's jointure to release more of the family's estates to satisfy his creditors. When Anthony Cooke died in 1604 his son inherited his debts and five small manors in the vicinity of the family mansion at Havering, the flotsam of the holdings of what had been one of the five or six richest families in Essex in 1579.[51]

Cooke had been content to flourish in Elizabeth's brilliant Court at his own expense; he was never the recipient of royal bounty. The great debts of Sir Thomas Reresby of Thrybergh, Yorkshire, were similarly attributed to his 'following the Court without any other recompence then empty knighthood'. Sir Henry Bedingfield, of an old and loyal Catholic family, was promised 'great matters' by James II: he dissipated the best part of his wife's jointure on a London establishment and attendance at the Court, yet the promises proved 'but Court Holy Water' even before the Revolution finally dashed all dreams of preferment. Even the holders of profitable offices in the gift of the Crown might find that their tenure of these posts, hostage to factional struggles for control, was insecure, and that their expenses outran their perquisites. Sir Thomas Monson flourished in the first decade of James's reign, and he collected a string of offices – Master of the Armoury of the Tower, Steward of the Duchy of Lancaster, Master Falconer – with fees valued at £500 p.a. The fall of his Court patrons, the Howard family, his own tangential involvement in the great scandal of the murder of Sir Thomas Overbury in the Tower, and, finally, the attempt by his nephew, William Monson, to displace the newly risen Villiers in the King's affections – his Howard backers washed the young man's face 'every day with posset-curd' to improve his complexion – shattered his career. His Court service, never profitable, he whined, had left him 'impaired in his fortune, scorned and neglected'. He was still begging a grant from the Crown to recompense him for his 'service, sufferings, losse', in 1641. Edmund Wyndham of Kentford, Somerset, was encouraged by his ambitious wife to seek his fortune at Court. He sold lands valued at £1,000 to fund this venture, and, in return, secured minor offices, patents, newly drained lands in the fens, and a share in the infamous soap monopoly. All proved worthless when the Long Parliament began its session.[52]

Court life had a dangerous, addictive quality, particularly, as Wentworth suggested to the young Sir William Savile, for those who came to Court before they had 'Experience and Knowledge' of the management of their own estates. Gentlemen might be tempted to gamble away their patrimonies by the hope of securing the colossal prizes that attended royal favour. Some became so caught up in the glittering whirl of the Court that they plunged into the spendthrift excess that it encouraged without thought of securing a return or of the consequences for their estates. Yet some gentlemen retained perspective, avoided playing for the highest stakes or acquiring extravagant tastes, and managed to secure a modest prosperity by their Court involvement. Sir Thomas Cornwallis of Brome, Suffolk, one of the East Anglian gentry who rallied to support Mary in 1553, was rewarded with Court office; his devotion to Catholicism ended his official career in 1559 and he retired to his Suffolk estates. Yet his short connection with the Court proved a mildly profitable venture. It enabled him to acquire wardships, to purchase a number of royal manors and to secure favourable leases of others which continued to benefit his estate after his retirement. In Charles I's reign Sir Richard Wynn found a comfortable niche for himself at Court, first as groom of the Chamber to Prince Charles then as treasurer to Henrietta Maria. He met his wife through his Court contacts, made his home on her estate at Isleworth, prospered. A certain pliancy, that enabled him to abandon his first Court patron, Suffolk, shortly before his fall from favour, and his master at the outbreak of the Civil War when Wynn remained a member of the Long Parliament, ensured that he died rich in 1649.[53]

It was the extremes – the glittering prizes; the threat of disaster – and above all the fickleness of fortune at the 'slipper top' that mesmerised contemporaries and informed their comments on the Court. Individual instances can be found to illustrate this dualism, but we also find cases of effective survival and modest profit. It is impossible to isolate the typical experience, but the fate of a family that existed for much of our two hundred years near the heart of the political system may give a better sense of the balance of gain and loss from the holding of Court office and influence. The Haringtons were a complex family, with a variety of branches and one line, that of the famous Sir John, whose genealogy was somewhat questionable. The senior branch had exercised some influence in the medieval period, but had collapsed ignominiously in the fifteenth century, leaving the family settled at Exton in Rutland as the dominant line. The experience of the Exton Haringtons between the reign of Henry VIII and Charles can be baldly summarised thus: profit under Henry VIII, when Sir John was an esquire of the Royal Body and one of the treasurers to the army to Scotland; rural consolidation under Elizabeth when Sir James married a Sidney and built a new house; spectacular success under James when his son was made a baron, became guardian to Princess Elizabeth and *his* heir an intimate companion of Prince Henry; decline and collapse under Charles, the heir dying unmarried, a debt of £40,000 needing repayment and the extravagance of Lucy, Countess of Bedford, who inherited Exton, destroying what remained. The moral from this specific story seems to be that it was far easier to accumulate wealth through office early in the sixteenth century than to secure it and maintain a proper lifestyle under the early Stuarts.[54]

The cadet branches of the Haringtons did not experience quite so dramatic a rise and fall. John of Kelston, Somerset, gained influence because of his close personal loyalty to Thomas Seymour and subsequently to Princess Elizabeth. He experienced the vicissitudes of the mid-sixteenth century, but emerged on the victorious side, and was rewarded both by the Queen's affection and by the gift of a manor. With this he appeared content: it was perhaps the misfortune of his son, the Queen's 'witty godson' that he could never regard the Court as providing this combination of personal honour and modest support. At the end of the reign Sir John looked back bitterly on his experience: 'I have spent my time, my fortune, and almoste my honestie, to buy false hope, false friends, and shallow praise . . . this reckoning of a courtly minion.' The problem was that Sir John, although he had objectives in his haunting of the Court – the regaining of lands believed to be part of the Harington inheritance, office if it came his way – seems never to have focused firmly on these material issues. Instead he played the role of Renaissance courtier, delighting the Queen and charming his contemporaries, but 'had not my fortune been in *terra firma*, I might, even for my verses have danced barefoot with Clio and her schoolfellows until I did sweat'. Court reward was deeply uncertain, and Court habits could all too easily ruin even fortunes grounded in *terra firma*. A younger Harington who married into the Holles family was described by Gervase as bringing with her 'no portion but Court legacies: pride, passion and prodigalities'.[55]

Finally we may note that the mid-seventeenth century Haringtons all made sensible attempts to retrench the extravagance of their elders: they eschewed the Court, but politics still proved their downfall; James, the author of *Oceana* went mad after close imprisonment at the Restoration; his cousin, another James, was exiled for his role in the Protectorate; and John of Kelston, the son of Sir John, escaped trouble only by dying before Charles II returned. In a cost/benefit analysis the sufferings of the Harington clan might be thought to outweigh their rewards.[56]

**Law**

In 1623 Sir John Oglander abandoned the 'place' that gave him some access to the Court; nine years later he argued that the possession of such office was the only way by which a gentleman might 'raise his house'. His assertion that a legal career could prove similarly advantageous is equally paradoxical. A few months before he wrote in 1633, he had allowed his heir, George, to drop out of the Middle Temple when the boy complained that he was not enjoying his legal studies and that they did not suit his temperament, and to continue his education through continental travel. In abstract, Oglander's advice seems sound enough. By the seventeenth century almost every English county displayed examples of the law as a 'powerful economic and social escalator'. Magnificent houses like Blickling in Norfolk, Littlecote in Wiltshire, Montacute in Somerset, and Redgrave in Suffolk ostentatiously displayed the wealth that could accrue to a man through the practice of law and the attainment of legal office. Established families winced as they witnessed the land purchases of newly enriched lawyers. In James's reign the Earl of Lincoln complained that Richard Brownlow, Chief Prothonotary of the Common Pleas and a distinguished law reporter, was a 'villayne' who 'purchased land every day from under his nose and . . . would purchase Sempringham House if he were suffered'. A number of well-established families were saved from imminent ruin by the chance succession of a younger brother, trained in and enriched by the practice of the law. Sir John Strode and Richard Newdigate both had the resources and the competence to secure ancestral estates that were crumbling in the face of debt and obligations created by poorly designed family settlements.[57]

Gentlemen might envy the lawyers' wealth; they would encourage their younger sons to study law as a prospective career. Yet while, at least before 1650, they sent their heirs to the Inns of Court as part of their education, they did not expect them to practise law. Lawyers, like Henry Savile of Bradley, Yorkshire, or Sir James Whitelocke, who had established themselves on landed estates might encourage – faintly, in Whitelocke's case – their heirs to follow their footsteps to the bar, but such legal dynasties were not common. Landed gentlemen anticipated that their heirs' studies at the Inns might better equip them as landowners and local magistrates, to the 'profit . . . to your selfe and cuntry for which cause onely I maintaine you there to my greate charge', as Thomas Isham wrote to his son, John. The herald, Edward Waterhouse, writing of the Inns, put it nicely; 'the country gallant is here principled to his after improvement,' he wrote, 'he after becomes a luminary in the counterey firmament, an oracle of the justice bench, a worthy representative to Parliament.' This seems to have been Oglander's ambition for George: that the law might provide an additional, and lucrative, 'vocation' for the boy was never suggested.[58]

The reasons why the landed gentry avoided the profession of law may emerge in consideration of the experience of John Lowther. He was the heir of an ancient but financially embarrassed family. Sent to the Inner Temple by his father, he resolved to practise law, to 'make it a profession to preserve oure estate, whitch was then too like to fall to decaye'. Lowther was spectacularly successful in this ambition, and by 1627, ten years after his impoverished father's death, he could record complacently that he had 'bettered my estate . . . near £20,000'. Yet in his legal practice had brought in only £150 pre annum in this period, and Lowther complained that the work was excessively demanding – it 'requireth an whole man and all his time'. In 1623 he recorded his intention to cut back on his legal work, 'to perfect my sonnes Breading, to satisfie allsoe myself in my desier to know, and to advantage me in other things least in attending to it I loose as mutch or more otherwise'. Lowther resented the curtailment of his opportunities to undertake the accepted activities of the leisured gentry. He also recognised that his enrichment was largely achieved by his skilful management of his property. His legal knowledge was, he believed, of great benefit 'in the government of my oune estate and the understanding theirof'. It enabled him to conduct successful litigation securing the title to land jeopardised by his grandfather's improvident settlement. But legal practice did not explain Lowther's meteoric financial success: that was achieved by the astute exploitation of his ancestral estates.[59]

Although the last years of the seventeenth century saw the stagnation of the agricultural sector, clearly the century before the Civil War was one of significant opportunity for landowners. Prices rocketed, and market opportunities developed not only for the sale of grain and stock but for the development of metallurgical and industrial resources, and of urban property. Success in this economic milieu required hard work, an attention to detail, and a readiness to adjust to changing circumstances. In particular, traditional assumptions about the impropriety of a gentleman's direct engagement in commerce or usury, or the paternalist values assumed to govern landlord–tenant relations, had to be reconsidered. Newcomers, purchasing their estates with an eye to maximising their return, and not burdened by an antiquated machinery of estate administration, may have seen and developed market opportunities most swiftly. But families of most respectable lineage whose devotion to tradition appeared in their preference for the old religion, like the Gascoignes of Barnbow, were soon as deeply engaged as any parvenu in the fullest exploitation of their estates. The seductive opportunities for a gentleman to 'raise his house' by supplementing the income from his ancestral estate with 'some other vocation' were marginal and speculative. There were some dramatic success stories, but neither law, trade, nor the Court guaranteed that a man would 'grow rich'. And, as Oglander recognised, the time and energy required to cultivate such activities could lead to a fatal neglect of the estate. The income of the gentry remained firmly rooted in Harington's *terra firma*.

# 4

# Wealth: Spending

In the mid-seventeenth century the learned intellectual, Sir Justinian Isham, gave his attention, usually reserved for more profound and abstruse theological and scientific speculations, to questions of the economic well-being of his and other landed families. His unexceptional conclusions on financial failure followed the weight of opinion of the other gentry commentators that we have already noted. It was a man's neglect of the management of his lands and the improvement of their income that was the fatal flaw. While prodigality was often an accompaniment to such feckless indifference, few men who lost their estates could be said to have actually *spent* them. More careful historical investigation of the experience of some of his Northamptonshire neighbours might have given Isham pause before arguing that debt and land sales were a product, not of lavish spending, but of a more mundane neglect of the estate. Half a century before he wrote, while his grandfather was consolidating the Isham estates and the family's position in the county, the Treshams of Rushton had collapsed spectacularly. Yet Sir Thomas Tresham, who presided over the ruin of his ancient family, was a vigorous manager of his estates. By enclosure, direct production for the market, and the renegotiation of leases, Tresham raised the value of his lands considerably, to £3,500 in 1590. The motive for this energetic reorganisation was a heavy burden of debt, and despite all Tresham's business skills and the improved annual income that they generated, he could not erase it. Sir Thomas Tresham was a paragon of managerial efficiency, vitally engaged in profit maximisation, deeply concerned with the minutiae of rabbit sales – but he could not escape the web of debt that encompassed him.[1]

While Tresham is hardly a typical figure, a structured analysis of his indebtedness may provide a useful paradigm for a discussion of changing patterns of gentry expenditure in early modern England. Tresham's debts were generated, first, by his religious convictions: as a recusant Catholic he was liable for a series of draining payments to the Crown: second, by charges associated with the maintenance of his standing as a gentleman in the locality. Let us first examine these latter expenses, that were incumbent upon all those who sought to assert their gentle status, before turning to those costs that hit only a subset of the group as a consequence of their confessional or political choices. Not all mulcts by the state were discriminatory, and we will conclude with an examination of the burden of direct taxation upon the gentry as a whole.

## 1.1 HONOUR, STANDING AND REPUTATION

When, in 1608, Sir Charles Hussey of Honnington, Lincolnshire, was prosecuted in Star Chamber as an encloser and depopulator, he acknowledged that he had undertaken some reorganisation of his estate designed to enhance his income. He claimed that he had been obliged to do so because his revenue previously had been 'scarce able to mainetaine the port of this defendant's place and service in his countrey'. Hussey argued that his estate must uphold a lifestyle – the 'port' – commensurate with his standing as a gentleman and magistrate in the region. A similar concern exercised Sir Thomas Tresham, and increased his burgeoning debts. Tresham engaged in a series of elaborate building projects. Rothwell Market House was a statement of his concern for the good governance of his 'country' and his friendship with the local gentry; the triangular lodge at Rushton of his devotion to the Trinity. But these, with his rebuilding at Rushton and his new house at Lyveden, had the common design of emphasising his wealth and his standing. Gervase Holles, contemplating his debts generated by his new house at Grimsby, ruefully recalled Plutarch's comment that 'such as delighted to build, undid themselves without the help of any enemy'. Many gentlemen would have agreed, yet, as Wentworth insisted to Sir William Savile, a gentleman who inherited a house that was 'not suitable to your quality' must rebuild. 'We see an emulation in the structure of our houses,' noted Sir Henry Slingsby, and many gentlemen entered this extravagant competition. In Slingsby's Yorkshire, Sir Robert Savile and his son, Sir John, spent £30,000 on their vast mansion at Howley; the Stapletons' house at Carleton cost £4–5,000; Sir Stephen Proctor spent £3,000 on Fountain's Hall. Such expenses could be ruinous: Sir Francis Willoughby's estate never recovered from the £8,000 he invested in the elaborate house

16. The Triangular Lodge, Rushton, Northamptonshire, built by Sir Thomas Tresham, 1594

he commissioned from Robert Smythson, 'out of ostentation to show his riches,' at Wollaton, Nottinghamshire.[2]

Expenses could also be generated within the house by prodigal housekeeping. Tresham maintained a large entourage of 'gentlemen servitors' at Rushton, and gloried in the hospitality that he regarded as an essential family tradition. Lavish entertainment was provided for friends and neighbours, and for their followers 'to the number of twenty, forty, yea sometimes an hundred'. Frescheville Holles, though he received only a 'narrow' allowance during his father's lifetime, insisted that he must 'live according to his quality', a determination that resulted in a heavy burden of debt. Hospitality was a major aspect of this expensive concern for an appropriate lifestyle: Holles would 'never set down to meales unless he had some of his friends or neighbours with him, and in case they came not he would send for them'.[3]

Gervase Holles, who reports this story of his father, also offers cameos of his grandfathers, Sir Gervase Holles and John Kingston, both financially embarrassed, yet both determined to maintain their standing by appropriate behaviour and display without respect to expense. Lavish hospitality was only part of such behaviour. Both men delighted in their 'fielde pleasures' of hawking and hunting, and both shared a 'vanity to weare costly apparrell'. Though approaching his eightieth birthday, Sir Gervase was still prepared to pay £30 for the embroidery of a satin suit. Both men maintained a number of mistresses to their considerable cost: Kingston boasted that he had expended £1,000 to protect the reputation of the wife of the Town Clerk of Grimsby from scandal, 'yet he had layne with hir an hundred times'. Honour also demanded that local feuds should be maintained, but scuffles in the streets of Lincoln or Grimsby or at horse races could result in litigation that, in Kingston's case, 'cost his purse roundly'. Friends and relatives had to be supported with purse as well as with sword. Sir Gervase loaned money to his impoverished friend, Sir Percival Willoughby of Wollaton, and, when Willoughby defrauded him of the loan by a shabby cheat, he nobly refused to take legal action or 'to publish the infamy of a person he had loved infinitely'. Sir Thomas Tresham's attitude to Lord Vaux was similar: despite his own debts, Tresham sought to uphold the tottering estate of his brother-in-law. In consequence he threw away a good deal of money on costs associated with the dense litigation that surrounded Vaux's tangled affairs, and more by acting as a surety for loans upon which his kinsman subsequently defaulted.[4]

While much of the expense associated with 'port' was, as Holles implied when reviewing the actions of his attractive, wastrel grandfathers, a matter of individual temperament and whim, some patterns may be discerned. Broad changes in taste or behavioural conventions affected patterns of expenditure. Sir John Reresby attributed his great-grandfather's debts, in part, to his insistence on being attended by a great retinue, 'seldome going to church or from home without many followers in blew coats and badges'. By the late seventeenth century this kind of semi-military entourage, 'tall fellows', who in their liveries had largely existed to personate the power and status of their masters, was no longer fashionable. A coachman, a couple of footmen, and a page or two sufficed – with a commensurate saving of expense. An extravagantly lavish funeral had been an obligatory demonstration of status in the sixteenth century: by 1631 it was noted, regretfully, that 'funerals in any expensive way' were viewed as 'a fruitlesse vanitie' and had been abandoned even by 'noblemen and gentlemen of eminent ranke, office and qualitie'. The fashion for vast standing tombs with full-length effigies died out a little later; elegant, but cheaper, wall plaques replaced them. Cultivated taste shifted, and with it the expenses engendered by appropriate display.[5] But in two areas commentators remarked trends in gentry behaviour that involved them in an upward spiral of expense. These were the costs associated with the increased role of London in their social lives, and those necessary for the preferment of their children. Expenditures associated with both these social trends swelled Sir Thomas Tresham's burden of debt.

## London

The expenses of London life were felt by Sir Thomas Tresham in 1593 when he was obliged to pay off substantial debts contracted by his son, Francis, a troubled and extravagant young man who had settled in London and attached himself to the entourage of the Earl of Essex. Francis compounded his folly by involvement in the Earl's abortive rising in 1601 – and his father had to come up with at least £3,000 in fines and bribes. His escape on this occasion did not lead to any change in lifestyle, and in 1605 he was again 'much subject and in daunger for debts, by judgments, executions and outlaryes'. London living was still draining gentry purses in the early eighteenth century. Andrew Archer of Umberslade, Warwickshire, was a 'very prudent judicious person, no ways behind in the point of good husbandry'. Yet between 1714 and 1726 he accumulated debts of over £12,000; a significant part of this sum was associated with his family's residence in London whilst he was in Parliament as knight of the shire for Warwickshire. Speaker Onslow believed that many MPs in this period were, like Archer, 'ruining their estates in the luxury . . . of living in London, . . . a false grandeur for a country gentleman'. A few gentlemen professed to believe that living expenses concomitant on the need to maintain 'port' in the country might be saved by moving to London: experience, like that of Sir Edmund Harewell, mocked such hopes.[6]

Troubled by such examples, gentlemen, in their 'Advices' for sons and wards, pronounced solemn warnings of the exorbitant costs of London and of its traps and temptations for the unwary. 'Hate London, as to live there,' thundered Sir John Oglander. 'Dice and whores are the instrumental causes that bring many to beggary'. Thomas Isham cautioned his son about the 'coseners' who prowled the city, living by the 'spoile of such youthes as are unacquainted with there shiftes'. But it was not merely the youthful and inexperienced who succumbed to the seductive but expensive lure of London. In a neat inversion of the usual pattern, the Pembrokeshire knight, Sir Walter Rice of Newton, settled his estate upon his son who agreed to pay off his father's debts of nearly £2,500; bills from tradesmen in Westminster, Cheapside and Pettycoat Lane figured largely in this total. Middle-aged, serious men, like Sir John Newdigate, recognised the powerful pull exercised by London to the extent of reminding themselves, not just their heirs, of the costs associated with the city. In his copy of the Almanack for 1608 Sir John entered a list of 'London inconveniences': 'many vaine expenses' for travel, lodging and food; 'idleness'; 'many temptations'. Yet such jeremiads did not halt the growing involvement of the gentry in the expensive delights of city life, and by the early eighteenth century almost all the richest gentry even of distant Glamorgan were to be found in the capital for the season.[7]

## The Nuclear Family

Sir Roger Wilbraham approvingly recorded in his journal the opinion that a gentleman should organise his estate with a view to surviving those disasters that might be expected to befall him once in every decade. Four such 'casualties' were listed: lawsuits, building costs, service of the prince – and 'marrying a daughter'. In 1625 Sir Hardolph Wastneys had five marriagable daughters. This represented, argued the Earl of Clare who sought to have

Wastneys excused from the expensive office of sheriff, 'a disease in these goulden times worse then gowte or dropsy'. Sir Thomas Tresham had six daughters. Three were married during Sir Thomas's lifetime, at a cost of £6,800; this sum included the huge sum of £3,800, 'a portion seldom or never heard of for a knight', paid to Lord Morley upon the marriage of Elizabeth Tresham to his heir. Tresham's other three daughters were married after his death; their portions, totalling £5,400, were secured by trusts which severely curtailed the income from the estate available to their brother. Miss Finch has noted that Sir Thomas's liberality, given his debts, was 'a dangerous extravagance', but Sir Thomas was a victim of circumstances. First, of the social trend whereby the portion necessary to secure a good match for a daughter, a match that would reinforce a family's prestige, rose at a rate slightly greater than that of inflation in the sixteenth century and exceeded it dramatically in the seventeenth. This was a trend regretted by many commentators, like Sir William Temple, who noted the ruin of 'many estates by the necessity of giving great portions to daughters'. Second, Tresham was hostage to the demographic chance that left him with a cohort of six daughters for whom provision had to be made. Sir Thomas Tresham was not the only victim of these factors. Sir Thomas Temple's father, 'a frugal and provident gentleman', left him a plentiful estate, with a gross revenue of over £3,000 per annum in 1603; Sir Thomas himself, during his father's lifetime, had been described as 'a thriving man and a purchaser' of land. But Sir Thomas had a string of nine daughters, and his generous provision of about £2,000 in portion for each of them generated a tangle of debts.[8]

Demographic chance working within the framework established by social conventions and legal arrangement could affect a gentry family in other ways. The rise in portions was accompanied by a rise in the sums that fathers could demand in marriage negotiations for jointures, which were usually established by giving the widow a life-interest in part of the estate. In consequence long-lived widows could represent a substantial drain on a family's resources. The wide estates of the Foljambes of Walton, Derbyshire, were whittled away at the turn of the sixteenth century as the estate descended to a series of short-lived males, who, while they failed to produce direct heirs to succeed them, left widows of surprising longevity, rapacity and litigiousness. Sir John Reresby thought his father's debts and his sales of land and woods 'excusable', to be attributed not to 'ill husbandry' but to the 'narrowness of his then present fortune, ther being two great jointures out of his estate till about three years before he dyed'. Sir Anthony Chester inherited Chicheley, Buckinghamshire, in 1666, but he did not come into full possession of the family estates for another quarter of a century, upon the death of the last of three octogenarians, the widows of his uncle, father and grandfather. Others waited longer, and in vain. John Liddell-Bright inherited the bulk of his grandfather's estate, with a potential income of £2,300, in 1688. But jointures of £400 and £1,000 per annum had to be paid from the estate to the widows of, respectively, his uncle and his grandfather. His uncle's widow died 20 years later; his grandfather's widow, his fourth wife and 30 years his junior when he married her, proved even more resilient. In 1731 Liddell-Bright, who was badly in arrears with his payments of her jointure, noted wistfully that the old lady, though aged 79, 'has neither gout nor stone nor other distemper'. She proceeded to outlive him by two years, dying in 1737.[9]

A large number of sons could also represent a heavy burden on a family's estates. While the expenses of the upbringing and education of the eldest son would be met from the portion that his father would receive upon the boy's marriage, the costs of providing the wherewithall for younger sons – whether an annuity or landed endowment, or the training in a trade or profession – was not recoverable. As with the size of portions or of jointure provisions, the treatment of younger sons was not dictated entirely by social convention: love and favouritism could also be involved and might have very adverse financial consequences. The attempt to provide a substantial estate for a younger son, which was possible for very wealthy newcomers, like Sir Nicholas Bacon or Richard Brownlow, both eminent lawyers, could overstrain an established family's resources. Sir Thomas Temple's growing debts were, in the opinion of his friends, not contracted entirely by the need to provide portions for his over-abundant daughters, but by his desire to advance his favoured younger son, Sir John. Sir Thomas provided Sir John with land, livestock and money to the value of £10,000. The costs of this gift escalated when it was challenged in litigation by Sir Thomas's jealous elder son, Sir Peter, who claimed that his father had sold entailed land and broken existing family settlements to advantage Sir John at the expense of his inheritance. Relatives begged father and son to 'stop a public trial that can produce no other end than shame and dishonour', but the dispute ground through Chancery in dilatory and expensive proceedings for four years. The decline of the powerful Nottinghamshire family, Markham of Cotham, began when Sir John sought to endow his younger son, Thomas, at the expense of his legal heir, his grandson, Robert. The litigation that followed drained the purses and ruined the local 'estamations' of both men.[10]

Fecundity and longevity could drain an estate, so too could the chances of mortality. Until the Civil War most of the gentry possessed estates held technically in knight service of the Crown. Such estates were liable for wardship should their owner die when his heir was under age – a not infrequent occurrence. In Yorkshire at least 27 per cent of the 963 gentry families experienced a wardship between 1558 and 1642. Some luckless families were the victims of multiple minorities; Christopher Wandesford of Kirklington, Yorkshire, was the fifth heir in succession who inherited as a minor; in Somerset, the Portmans experienced a minority in 1612, and another only nine years later. Genetic misfortune of this kind was expensive: the Portmans paid out £2,300 in 1612, another £1,800 in 1621. Representatives of the ward's family usually managed to acquire the wardship, with its responsibility for the administration of the estate, and for the education, upbringing and marriage of the ward. They did so either by a direct payment of a fine to the Court of Wards, or by purchase usually at a higher rate when the wardship had been 'begged by some courtier' who had then received a grant of the Crown's interest. After 1611 a policy of normally making a direct grant to the ward's nearest relatives was instituted, lessening the risk of either the enforced marriage of the heir by a guardian or of lengthy haggling with a courtier grantee. But there was a *quid pro quo* for this reform: the Court of Wards began to demand higher fines from the guardians, based on more realistic evaluations of the income of the estate, a process that culminated in the 1630s. Under Elizabeth the fine rarely exceeded £100 for the wardship of a Yorkshire gentleman; under Charles one of the greater gentry families might have to pay £1,000: in Somerset the average fine increased from £107 in 1605–11 to £762 in 1635–41. In addition, there were a significant number of fees and *douceurs* that lined the pockets of the officers of the Court of Wards and which could, in the case of minor gentry families, represent a very considerable expense. Further loss might be occasioned by the inadequate supervision that the Court of Wards exercised over the activities of those to whom the wardship had been granted. Henry Calverley complained that his stepfather, who had control of the estate for the eleven years of Calverley's minority, had embezzled income and failed to provide proper accounts. The long minority of George Denton of Cardew had enabled his stepfather to grant a series of long leases on the estate to his own advantage. Sir John Harington, guardian of Sir Thomas Foljambe, married the boy at the age of 12 to his daughter, and then abused his position to entangle the estate in a morass of litigation and incumbrances designed to advantage his own family and defeat the claims of Sir Thomas's relatives.[11]

The statement in the Grand Remonstrance of 1641, that families had been 'weakened, and some ruined' through the malign influence of wardship, was a commonplace among gentry commentators. Their animus against what was increasingly a system of royal taxation, but one that fell so inequitably, according to demographic chance, is understandable. But they overemphasised its malign effects. Only 15 per cent of the Yorkshire families who fell into the clutches of the Court of Wards experienced financial difficulties that could, even partially, be attributed to the minority. Gentry hostility to wardship was responsible for the abolition of the Court of Wards by Parliament in 1646, and for the failure to revive it at the Restoration. The system that replaced it, whereby a panel of trustees nominated by the deceased parent administered the estate on behalf of the minor, and were subject to the scrutiny of Chancery in the execution of their responsibilities, was infinitely preferable. Indeed, a minority after 1660 could be extremely beneficial to a family. The trustees had to maintain the minor in appropriate style, but conspicuous expenditure could be curtailed, display muted, and, as on the estate of Richard Beaumont of Whitley, Yorkshire, between 1668 and 1676, revenue could be employed to repay debts, to meet charges for legacies and portions, and to purchase lands to develop the estate.[12]

If we discount the shift in the costs of minorities after 1642, it is easy to delineate an 'ideal' demographic regimen that would bring maximum economic advantage to a gentry family. Wives must die before their husbands, having borne few children, and with a preponderance of boys over girls. Should these circumstances be reversed, with long-lived dowagers or a multiplicity of daughters, debt or financial privation would result.

## 4.2 POLITICAL AND RELIGIOUS CHOICES

We have shown that claim to gentle status obliged a conformity to established norms of behaviour that necessarily entailed expense. All gentlemen were under some obligation to build and dress in the appropriate style, to educate their sons and to marry their daughters into the right families. But for some gentry families religious and political choices brought on additional financial burdens.

### Catholic Recusancy

Sir Thomas Tresham, convicted of recusancy in 1581, was thereafter liable for the statutory fine of £20 a month; in addition, a number of other mulcts were imposed upon him by the Privy Council for harbouring priests and for making a fraudulent conveyance of his lands to evade the fines. Between 1581 and 1605 Tresham paid nearly £8,000 in penalties associated with his Catholicism. Given that Tresham's income was of the order of £3,500 per annum, this was hardly ruinous, but, in conjunction with the other demands on his estate, it swelled the burden of debt. The irregular collection of the fines compounded Tresham's difficulties. Periods of governmental neglect were interspersed with high bills for arrears; a demand for nearly £1,000 in 1587, when the Council tightened its procedures against recusants generally, resulted in default and the concomitant seizure of the lands of his sureties. Thereafter Tresham's credit worthiness was tainted, and he was forced to borrow at high rates of interest, and to mortgage land as security for his loans.

Tresham made no secret of his recusancy, and the government responded by treating him with peculiar harshness. He was used as a hostage, seized and imprisoned on every occasion when the Privy Council was particularly troubled by the activities of foreign powers or domestic plotters. The penal legislation was enforced against his estate with a pertinacity that less ostentatious Catholics, or those in areas more remote from Council vigilance, did not experience: indeed, Tresham was one of only thirteen recusant gentlemen, ten of whom lived within 100 miles of London, upon whom the £20 a month was consistently levied. Recusant families might escape their liabilities by appealing to friends at Court, as did Sir Frederick Cornwallis in 1587; it cost him a lengthy stay in London, and the 'gifts and rewards' recorded in his accounts multiplied four-fold – but he escaped the fines. They developed complex schemes of trusts and fraudulent coveyances to conceal the ownership of their estates from the government and its informers. John Parham of Poyntington maintained a public appearance of Protestantism, but became legal adviser, trustee and moneylender to an extensive network of Catholics in the Yeovil region that included his own son. Thomas Pudsey played a similar role on behalf of Yorkshire recusants. Minor local officers might be bribed to show favour: in Allertonshire in 1596 the jury that ludicrously undervalued the lands of the Conyers and Meynell families had been empanelled by a Deputy-Sheriff noted as 'a dealer . . . in such causes for recusantes ease and profit'. Catholic gentlemen might rely on ties of neighbourhood and friendship with JPs or clergymen to protect them from investigation: at Pocklington sessions in 1615 various gentlemen escaped prosecution because of the readiness of some of the JPs to speak on their behalfs on the most tenuous grounds – the recusancy charge against Sir Henry Constable was rebutted by a magistrate who had once seen him visiting York Minster. The Timperleys were sheltered by the outright perjury of the Rector of Hintlesham, Suffolk. Village officers might be terrified into silence and connivance: when a grand-juryman denounced members of the Thimbleby family, whose village of Irnham was the major Catholic enclave in Lincolnshire, they responded with assaults and with a barrage of vexatious lawsuits.[13]

The ability of most recusant families to elude the full penalties of the legislation appears clearly in James's reign. The system was, in theory, stiffened after the Gunpowder Plot; more finable offences were created, and, more formidably, the Crown was given the right to sequester two-thirds of the landed property of recusant families – a penalty originally imposed in 1587 only on those who failed to pay their monthly fines. Yet the effect of this on the material situation of the Catholic gentry was not cataclysmic. Fraudulent conveyances, appeals on technicalities, and the connivance and patronage of the officers of the central government ensured that many estates were never sequestered. Most estates that were seized were grossly undervalued by local officials and jurors, and the Crown received only a pittance for its legal right to two-thirds – £63 from the lands of Sir Ralph Babthorpe of Osgodby, which actually produced £1,380 p.a.; barely £40 from the Vavasours' lands, which were worth nearly £2,000 a year. Even these trivial sums often went unpaid through the inefficiency of the local officers. Most recusant families, or their kinsmen or trustees, succeeded in gaining a lease of the sequestered property either from the Exchequer or from the courtiers to whom it had been granted. This process may have represented the most expensive aspect of the Jacobean system to the recusant community. Under Charles the system was altered again, and the draconian legislation, intended to force Catholics to conformity or to bleed them to extinction, provided merely the framework for a system of discriminatory taxation. The Crown sought to ensure that it received a greater proportion of the income from recusants' estates; it claimed only a third, but demanded a much more accurate survey of the lands and their value. In return, the family was permitted to take a long, 41-year, lease of the sequestered portion of the estate openly, and was freed from all other mulcts. The Crown was to benefit from recusancy, not its officers and courtiers through the web of fees, bribes and *douceurs* that had marked the jobbery of Jacobean proceedings. Influence was still effective in reducing the formal valuation or negotiating the annual composition rent, and there were wide variations between families in the percentage of income that was demanded in rent: Sir Philip Constable paid 18 per cent of the income from his Yorkshire and Lincolnshire lands; Sir Ralph Elleker only 8 per cent. The Crown never achieved the target figure of one-third, but Charles was receiving far more from the purses of his Catholic subjects than had been the case under James.[14]

In 1641 the Long Parliament fiercely denounced the Caroline practice whereby recusant fines were levied as a species of taxation, not with the intention of eviscerating the papists, and demanded a rigorous execution of the law. With the outbreak of war, the Parliamentarians were in a position to enforce their views in areas under their control, and, with the victories of their armies, gradually to impose them nationally. Those recusant gentlemen who had not otherwise compromised themselves by fighting in or voluntarily supporting the king's forces, were to suffer the full forfeiture of the statutory two-thirds of their estates, without remissions or leases back to them. The legislation was rigorously enforced. Complex and deliberately obfuscatory legal settlements, like that of the Thimbleby family, might continue to protect some part of the wealth of recusant families, while the prohibition against leasing estates back to Catholics proved to be an impossible requirement. But despite minor diversions from the legislation, the administrative machinery of the 1640s mulcted recusants at an unprecedentedly high rate. In the halcyon days of James I the Meynells of Kilvington, Yorkshire, had paid only £10 a year directly to the Crown; this was raised to £100 in the 1630s. In 1645, after a thorough survey had been undertaken by the local Parliamentary committees which valued the estates' net income at £400, Thomas Meynell was permitted to lease the sequestered two-thirds for £282; in 1649 the committees argued that the income of the estate had been improved to £650, and raised Meynell's rent to £420 per annum. Under the Protectorate, although Cromwell could not be persuaded to abrogate the system altogether, there was some relaxation of the fiscal demands on recusants. In Warwickshire the authorities accepted some very tenuous evidence of the Protestant conviction of the heirs of previously staunchly recusant families like the Throckmortons of Coughton, Warwickshire, and the sequestrations were lifted. In 1654 Anthony Meynell claimed, on a technicality, that his conviction for recusancy was invalid. The claim was upheld in London and the sequestration released; swiftly, before a new conviction could be obtained, Meynell conveyed the bulk of his estate to trustees. Meynell's adviser remarked that he had 'Rubbed up my ould experyence and skill' to devise this subterfuge, but it was only the tacit permission of a complacent government that effectively ended draining obligations under the penal laws for a number of families.[15]

Despite their expectations, Catholics were not formally released from the threat of recusancy fines at the Restoration. The government of Charles II intermittently saw some political advantage in taking an anti-Catholic stance, and would instruct the local authorities to present and convict recusants as a gesture of its concern. That process could then set in motion the Exchequer machinery for valuing and seizing lands. The threat was a troubling one to the recusant gentry, and obliged them to maintain the webs of legal fictions that protected their estates. Yet even in periods of ostensible government concern, as in 1674, recusants appear to have had little difficulty in escaping from sequestration. Roger Meynell was convicted in 1674; two years later his lands were valued – at £80, a tenth of their real worth – and provisional arrangements were made to lease the Crown's legal interest to family friends; next year a royal warrant halted further proceedings. Only between 1681 and 1685 does any money appear to have come into the Exchequer for recusancy fines. But the derisory sums raised, and a series of accusations of accounting irregularities by the central officers, suggests the ossification of the whole procedure.

After the Revolution of 1689, while the legislation that theoretically rendered Catholic estates precarious was never repealed – indeed was enhanced by enactments such as a 1700 Act denying to Catholics the right to purchase land, and allowing their Protestant next-of-kin to claim their inheritances – it was a dead letter. From 1693 the government took a new tack: the land tax was remodelled on a more accurate valuation, and Catholics were made liable to a double assessment. Some evasion was possible, but, while recusants seldom paid the double rate on all their lands, they were paying a higher proportion of income than their Protestant neighbours. And, in Anne's reign, when the land tax stood at 4 shillings in the pound, this represented a heavy burden.[16]

Throughout the period Catholic families experienced financial difficulties, became enmired in debt, and sold up. In the North Riding of Yorkshire the Lascelles were quite ruined by 1627; the Pudseys put Barforth on the market in 1660; in 1691 the Rokebys of Mortham sold their property. The rate of sales was, unsurprisingly, greatest in the immediate aftermath of the Civil War, when nine families sold up. Some figures suggest that financial embarrassment was suffered by a higher proportion of recusant than of Protestant gentry families: a disproportionate number of the gentry families in late Elizabethan Sussex and Surrey obliged to sell land were recusant; in early Stuart Yorkshire 51 per cent of recusant families, as against 34 per cent of their Protestant counterparts, were in financial difficulties. Yet, as was the case with Sir Thomas Tresham under Elizabeth, recusancy alone seldom led to ruin. Catholic squires who had no pre-existing burden of family debt, who avoided conspicuous consumption, and who knuckled down to efficient estate administration could, like the Gascoignes of Barbow, have sufficient surplus income to lend money, buy land, and acquire a minor title of nobility. Even in the very adverse circumstances of the late 1640s, the Meynell family, who had skilfully improved their estate in the 1630s, acquired a lease of the two-thirds of their estate seized for recusancy and considerably enhanced the income from their lands.[17]

## Royalism[18]

During and after the Civil War a large number of gentry families were subjected to the seizure of their estates of a kind that had been routinely if inefficiently imposed upon recusants since 1580. In the spring of 1643 both Parliament and the King ordered the seizure of the personal property and estate revenues of those who were supporting their enemies. The estates of Parliamentary supporters were gradually released from this thraldom with the advance of the victorious New Model, though their owners might have experienced considerable losses through Royalist occupation or raids: Sir William Armyne received nothing from his Osgodby, Lincolnshire, estate for three years when the cavaliers 'used it as if it had bin theire owne'; Sir Robert Harley's steward calculated that his master's losses from his Brampton Bryan, Herefordshire, estate totalled nearly £13,000 by 1646. But Armyne and Harley were MPs, well placed to solicit reparations for their losses upon the successful conclusion of the war. Many Royalist gentlemen in 1646 had similar tales of the plunder and devastation of their houses and lands. William Blundell of Crosby, Lancashire, was 'plundered to that extremity that the bread which my children eat was buried in the ground, thereby to preserve it for them from one meal to another.' In Staffordshire, Sir Richard Levenson claimed that goods worth £24,000 had been plundered, while damage to his mansion at Lilleshall and to other properties added a further £6,000 to his losses. Christopher Beresford's estate at Fulbeck, equidistant from the Paliamentarian garrison of Lincoln and the Royalists at Newark, was a waste from 1643 to 1646; in all, 7,000 men had been billeted in his house and, for this enforced hospitality, he had received a princely 31s.6d. Other Royalists had guaranteed substantial loans to finance the King's cause, and were pressed by their creditors. Unlike Armyne and Harley, the Royalists could expect no recompense for such losses and debts, and, worse, their estates remained under sequestration. This entailed the sale of their personal property, while the bulk of their rental income – after a one-fifth provision for the maintenance of their wives and families – was diverted into the Parliamentarian treasury.[19]

The situation changed in 1646, when Parliament began to permit Royalists to compound for their sequestered estates on a large scale; ultimately some 3,225 landowners throughout the country took advantage of this system. Apart from a small minority who were specifically disqualified, any Royalist who was prepared to take the Solemn League and Covenant might negotiate a composition. A survey of the estate, and of the settlements and debts charged against it, would be made by the local committee; they would also report on the extent of the Royalist's engagement in the war. From this information the London authorities would calculate an appropriate fine, which was expressed as a proportion of the capital value of the estate. A tiny cadre of aggressively active Royalists were fined at the highest rate, equal to eight years' annual income of their estates; most paid fines of two or three years' annual income. Once half the composition fine was paid over, the sequestration was lifted and the Royalist recovered his use of the estate. The latter was often in a poor condition: neither the local Parliamentary sequestrators nor their tenants, who could only lease for a year at a time, had had much interest in nurturing the estate.

A smaller group of 700 or so Royalists did not take advantage of the composition system, either because they could not raise the fine, or refused to take the required loyalty oaths to the usurping government, or because they were not permitted to do so: Catholics who had joined the royal armies or men who had rendered themselves particularly obnoxious to Parliament during the war and were exempted from pardon formed this latter category. Their lands remained under sequestration until 1651, when the Rump instituted a policy of the confiscation and sale of such estates. The primary object of the sales was, however, to raise money, not to punish the Royalists by total deprivation. The government made no effort to examine whether the nominal purchasers were, as was most frequently the case, acting as trustees for Royalist owners who were effectively repurchasing their own lands.

Sequestration; composition; sale: the financial consequences of Royalist commitment were experienced by a substantial group of gentlemen – perhaps one-third or more of the gentry of counties that were controlled by the king's forces for a significant part of the war or where, as in Kent, the Parliamentarian administrators were pertinacious in sniffing out 'delinquency'. Royalist gentlemen, whose estates were threatened with or which fell under sequestration, entered the shadowy world of chicanery and delay, of manoeuvre and wire-pulling, already known to their Catholic neighbours. Royalists could attempt to deny their delinquency. They could try to conceal their estates or to have them undervalued for purposes of composition or sale; they could inflate the payments – annuities, jointure, debt-charges – that burdened their lands. They could claim that legal settlements had been made prior to the outbreak of the war that vested title in trustees and gave them only a life-interest in the estate. These claims would be interrogated closely. The huge war-debt did not dispose the government, at

Westminster or at the county level, to generosity, and the war had created an army of local agents, paid in part by results, whose investigations were supplemented by those of venal informers. After a tedious process of negotiation, that generated further expenses in fees, for accommodation in London and the entertainment of 'sturdy, potent friends' there, for bribes, the Royalist would secure an order reinstating him in his property. Its execution could not, however, be guaranteed. Local administrators were often reluctant to terminate their control of and depredations upon sequestered lands, and further appeals to Westminster, with attendant delays and expense, were often required.[20]

After the Restoration, cavaliers harped on their extensive losses in the Royal cause. Clarendon, whose exile owed much to the anger of disappointed Royalists who believed that their services and losses had been insufficiently rewarded by his ministry, enshrined this view in his *History*: many Royalists, 'were compelled to sell half, that they might enjoy the other toward the support of their families'. Modern research has not confirmed these claims. Even in the most extreme case, where land was confiscated and sold, the bulk of it was acquired by nominees acting on behalf of its previous owners: in Yorkshire 67 per cent, in Lancashire 72 per cent, of property put on the market was immediately recovered by its owners. Even in the vicinity of London, where speculators were more active, 70 per cent of the property sold was eventually recovered; in the north the figure is well over 80 per cent. The prices the Royalists' trustees paid for the recovery of their properties, after all allowances had been made for claims of dower, entail and other reversionary interests with which the government was inundated, worked out to around six years' annual income for the bulk of estates. The process of compounding for the recovery of sequestered estates was cheaper. Despite the often formidable proportions of value demanded by the government, most Royalists in Northamptonshire secured their estates by paying less than two years' income as a fine, and some escaped with payment of less than one year's income. They succeeded in doing so by emphasising the reversionary interests upon their estates and the claims of creditors against them. They also got away with undervaluing their landed income significantly: in four cases where reasonable alternative estimates are available, estates were undervalued by 26 per cent to 41 per cent. Some of the northern Royalists were able to undervalue their estates by more than 50 per cent. 'Prepare a particular of your lands with as much art as you can and be sure to clog it with as much debt as you can,' a friend wrote to Sir Ralph Verney. Such 'art' would appear to have informed the accounting practice of the bulk of the Royalist gentry.[21]

Raising sums of money in the two-years' income range was well within the experience of the Royalist gentry; they had been obliged to mobilise such sums to advance their children. Sir Peter Osborne, having concealed 41 per cent of the real value of his Chicksands, Bedfordshire, estate, was fined £2,440; he was prepared to offer a portion of £4,000 with his daughter. Considering such cases, Sir John Habakkuk has concluded nicely that we can consider the fine as 'equivalent to an extra daughter or two'. The Royalist gentry had to borrow to acquire the capital to compound for sequestered, or to purchase confiscated, estates, but in most cases the monies were repaid out of income rather than by significant land sales. In some cases the penalties of Royalism appear to have represented a minor inconvenience; Sir Justinian Isham and Sir John Lowther took the fines in their stride and further extended their lands and business interests in the 1650s. Where substantial sales did occur, the family usually was burdened by heavy debts contracted *prior* to the Civil War. The Shireburns of Little Mitton, Lancashire, failed to repurchase the bulk of their confiscated estates in the 1650s, and in 1663 were forced to surrender their interest in the small proportion that they had recovered to their major creditor, a London goldsmith; but debts had weighed upon them long before the outbreak of war and had enforced land sales in the 1630s. The estates of the penurious Clarkes of Bidford, Warwickshire, who claimed to be 'great sufferers' in the Royalist cause, had been heavily mortgaged prior to 1642.[22]

For a few Royalists already in financial difficulties, the mulcts of the Civil War represented the last straw under which their already strained finances crumbled; others survived with a minimum of inconvenience. For the bulk of the Royalist gentry assiduous attention to estate administration designed to maximise revenue, and some sacrifices in the usual pattern of expenditure secured their families' survival. Cash might be raised by negotiating a good portion upon the marriage of an heir: Thomas Eyre's wife brought £4,000 to his father Rowland, almost all of which was immediately disbursed in part payment of the debt occasioned by the purchase, for nearly £15,000, of the family's confiscated estates. In the absence of such windfalls, sales of outlying estates, like those of Sir Philip Constable in Holderness, or selling freeholds to copyholders, might be undertaken. Attempts could also be made to enhance income, either by pressing tenants harder for rents and fines, or by agricultural improvement – though this might require the investment of scarce capital in enclosure and new technology. Sir Ralph Verney combined policies of sale and of improvement. Between 1648 and 1664 Sir Ralph sold all his outlying estates, which had produced about a third of his pre-war income; but at Middle Claydon, Buckinghamshire, he bought in copyholds and, at a cost of £1,000 enclosed some 500 acres, permitting a three-fold increase in rents. Such development of financial resources was time-consuming; Sir Thomas Peyton complained in the 1650s that all his time was unavoidably 'taken up with the business of farming.'[23]

Retrenchment also required the reconsideration of anticipated patterns of expenditure. Building projects and lavish display would be curtailed, or, if continued, other sacrifices made; Sir George Sondes finished his great mansion, designed by Inigo Jones, at Lees Court, but he remained a widower rather than burden his family with the jointure provision of a remarriage. Provision for younger children would be more meagre, and marital opportunities for daughters restricted. When in 1643 Sir John Oglander was faced with crippling fines, he feared that 'poore Brydgett should be undone'. Next year, at the nadir of his effort to avoid sequestration, Thomas Knyvett lamented that 'I shall have no means to do anything for poor Buss'. In a provisional settlement of 1638 Rowland Eyre projected an expenditure of £1,000 for the portion of each of his six daughters. Placing his older three daughters (one as a nun in Paris) in fact cost him £3,700, but then the effects of sequestration and repurchase began to bite; his fourth daughter lived at home, unmarried; the fifth and sixth girls were shipped off to a less prestigious, cheaper nunnery in Ghent. The fourth daughter married, at the age of 35, in 1671; the sixth, who had no religious vocation, in 1668, with a portion of £1,200. The Eyre family survived, but at some social and familial cost. A similar situation occurred in the Verney family. The courtier Sir Edmund had intended to endow each of his six daughters with £1,000, and had created a trust into which the profits of a minor piece of royal patronage that he enjoyed were sunk. This source dried up in 1642, with five of the girls still single. Sir Edmund's heir, Sir Ralph Verney, was saddled with a substantial debt from his father, and the estate, plundered and taxed by both sides during the war, was sequestered until 1647: thereafter Sir Ralph's sole concern was in clearing the obligations upon his inheritance. Sir Ralph refused to acknowledge any legal liabilities to provide dowries for his sisters, and the unfortunate young women, keenly aware that they 'grew in years' and were plain – 'not to all men's liking', not for 'many palates' – watched suitable matches shatter on Sir Ralph's intransigent refusal to provide any more than £60 annuities for them. They were eventually rushed into unsuitable marriages with men who were beneath them in social status. Habakkuk's observation on the composition fine as equivalent to 'an extra daughter or two' might not have amused the Verney sisters.[24]

Some historians have argued that the Civil War produced a major transfer of landed wealth that amounted to a social revolution. The Royalist gentry, impoverished before the war, were ruined by it. They were expropriated by the government, or foreclosed by their creditors, and their lands were acquired by newcomers, Parliamentarian supporters who were investing the profits of commerce or legal practice. Such views, based on the extravagant but suspect claims to losses in cavalier petitions to Charles II and the assumption that the agents who nominally acquired confiscated estates were the actual purchasers, cannot survive recent detailed research on particular families or localities in the Civil War. Indeed, the endurance of the great majority of the Royalist gentry despite the plunder, taxation and sequestration of the war years, and the composition fines and repurchases of the 1650s, suggests the intrinsic strength of the financial situation of the gentry as a whole by the mid-seventeenth century. Yet survival was only achieved at a cost. Servicing a debt created or enhanced by the war might require family sacrifices and circumscribed expectations for a generation beyond the Restoration.[25]

## 4.3 TAXATION

The jeremiads of the Royalists in the 1650s and 1660s concerning their financial losses were to be repeated by the landed gentry half a century later. The target of their complaint on this occasion was national taxation for the wars against Louis XIV, which, they insisted, fell upon land with a ferocity comparable to the depredations of the Parliamentarian administrators during the Civil War. In 1697 the Leicestershire commissioners for the land tax complained that a local JP had denounced them as 'sequestrators' and argued that the tax was simply another form of sequestration.[26] While taxation was hardly, unlike recusancy or royalism, a matter of personal choice, it does seem appropriate to examine it here.

By the late fifteenth century, unlike many of their continental counterparts, the English aristocracy and gentry had not acquired privileged exemption from national taxation. Direct taxation, voted in Parliament, fell on all landowners in this period, but it was no great burden: its incidence was irregular, and the money was raised on ossified quotas that bore little relation to current levels of wealth. However, the principle that the upper classes were subject to taxation was available for exploitation by the Tudor kings. And in 1513, Wolsey, seeking funds for his master's belligerent foreign policy, began to restructure the system of direct taxation. The new *subsidy*, a tax on income from land and the capital value of other forms of wealth, had some initial teething troubles in relation to rating, individual assessment and collection procedures, but its effectiveness as a fiscal device and the degree to which it bit on the taxpayers, is apparent in Parliament's reluctance to grant all that was demanded of it. In 1523 Wolsey had to retreat from an initial demand of a 20 per cent levy on landed income and, to further sweeten the deal with the gentry, agreed to abandon his crusade against enclosure for eighteen months.

The success of the subsidy, reaching its apogee in 1545 when Parliament voted a rate of 20 per cent on landed income and 12.5 per cent on capital value which brought in £196,000, was short-lived. Although the rate was fixed at this level in 1554, and although a crude price-index almost doubled between 1550 and 1630, the yield from each subsidy voted steadily fell, from £140,000 in 1559 to £55,000 in 1628.

The gentry in Parliament might vote subsidies; indeed, they increasingly voted multiple subsidies to accommodate their falling value – two subsidies were voted in 1589; four in 1601; six in 1628. But, as local commissioners the same men presided over the subversion of the system. Poorer taxpayers who died or moved were not replaced on the rolls, while the under-assessment of major landowners was a scandal denounced by the government and occasionally acknowledged by the gentry themselves. James Colbrand, a Sussex JP, argued that 'the rich were often rated . . . much too low, at not a fourtieth part of their wealth'. In his county the average assessment upon the leading families dropped from £61 in the 1540s to a derisory £14 in the 1620s. In the latter period, Sir

Thomas Pelham of Halland, with an income of over £2,000 a year, was rated at £50; for the twelve subsidies that Parliament voted in the the course of that decade he paid £100. In the periods of war – the 1590s, the 1620s – other forms of taxation fell upon landowners as the government scrabbled for money, often on the margins of legality. Yet Sir John Habakkuk's conclusion is still appropriate: from 1580 to 1630, the English gentry were 'grotesquely under-taxed'.[27]

This situation terminated with the Civil War. Charles I's ship-money experiment in the late 1630s, while leaving local officers to rate communities and individuals, had insisted on the payment a fixed amount from each of the English counties, based on a notional sense of their respective levels of wealth. This precedent was followed by the Long Parliament in 1641, and by both sides during the war. Taxes on land during the war years, even in areas insulated from the fighting or the marauding of garrisons, rocketed. On a number of estates in East Anglia in 1643–5 the various *assessments* devoured from a fifth to a third of rental values, while in January 1644 the Suffolk JPs calculated that direct and indirect taxation amounted to half every man's revenue. The end of the war brought some relief to landowners, but taxation on rental income still remained astronomically high by pre-war standards: on the Bedfordshire estates of the Gery family in the 1650s, taxes, while at only half the rate demanded between 1643–6, still syphoned 12.5 per cent of income.[28]

In the Commons in 1670 Sir John Duncombe expressed his hope that 'all ways will be tried before we come to Land-tax'; next year Sir Richard Temple believed that a new financial expedient 'will bury Land-Tax forever'. They voiced a favoured theme with members of the Cavalier Parliament. Yet despite their rooted antipathy to the Assessment, and the stagnation of agricultural incomes in this period, MPs found themselves reverting to the model of the Civil War period again and again in the various financial crises that punctuated the reign, when additional sums were required to supplement the settled revenue of the Crown.[29]

The point was driven home after the Glorious Revolution, when England, in securing the assistance of William III committed itself to a continental war against Louis XIV. The Commons might toy with a series of highly speculative fiscal experiments, and individual MPs would press the need to 'raise money without burdening Land'. But ultimately it was recognised that the only secure means of raising the millions required was either by a land tax or a general excise on all commodities, and the latter was objectionable to other, constitutional, concerns of the gentry. In consequence, MPs voted almost annually a series of land taxes to be rated at 20 per cent of rental income by local commissioners. These assessments were not universally paid at that rate. Despite attempts to secure a fairer division of the total burden among the counties, the aversion to this by MPs from the periphery was duplicated by the local commissioners in 1693 when reassessment was finally undertaken. In consequence Cornish, Welsh or Cumbrian gentlemen might escape with tax demands that represented only 5 per cent of their income from land. Yet in the lowland zone gentry accounts indicate both a payment close to the 20 per cent level, and the fact that, with agricultural prices falling, few landowners could transfer the tax to their tenants or afford to invest in techniques that might improve productivity and thus proportionally lessen the tax burden. The continuing high level of taxation became a central element in political polemic in this period. In 1702, as the country geared up for the renewal of the war, MPs were denounced as presiding over the destruction of 'all the landed gentlemen of England . . . already for the most part undone'. In 1749 a writer argued that the gentry were 'hastening to annihilation' under the continued burden of the tax.[30]

Debt had crushed Sir Thomas Tresham at the end of the sixteenth century. His manic activity – exploiting his tenants to a degree that provoked them to revolt, keeping at bay creditors whose penal bonds and mortgages could dismember his estate, endlessly seeking to renegotiate a series of short-term loans – could only postpone the final catastrophe, and his heir was obliged to sell Rushton to a London businessman. In the 1650s many Royalists were obliged to borrow heavily, and borrowing continued as a means to meet the tax demands of the 25 years of war at the end of the century: yet most gentry families, with some penny-pinching, some lowering of social expectations, survived. The extended genteel impoverishment of the recusant Constables of Everingham was more typical of the late seventeenth century than the crash of the Treshams. Sir Marmaduke Constable's Lincolnshire and Yorkshire estates brought in about £2,000 a year in the 1660s and 70s, yet of that sum £400 was disbursed in interest charges, and a further £900 in payments for those holding annuities or rent charges, the devices to which Constable had resorted to raise capital to repay his debts, largely occasioned by sequestration and repurchase in the Civil

War. In 1674 Sir Marmaduke leased the bulk of his estate to businessmen, who agreed to pay off the remaining debt over seven years, and, with an income of £150, went into semi-retirement. Debt still dogged his successor, Sir Philip. A considerable proportion of the income, declining in the face of occasional sales, high land-taxes (at the 40 per cent rate for recusants) and falling rents, was sucked into the charges associated with his mortgages, while a continued deficit enforced new borrowing. In 1697 Sir Philip was reduced to pawning his clothes; in 1706 he was unable to make the journey from London to Yorkshire for 'want of money'. But the Constables survived at Everingham. The disparate experience of Treshams and Constables raises the final issue that must be discussed in relation to gentry expenditure: the credit mechanisms available to them.[31]

## 4.4 BORROWING

In the sixteenth century, loans, perhaps interest-free, from family and friends were the first recourse for the necessitous gentleman. Securing large sums through such networks might prove impossible: the heavily indebted John Newdigate was fortunate in that his wife was the favourite niece of a wealthy bachelor who, 'out of his love' loaned £900 interest free, and on terms to repay the money when he 'could conveniently spare it'. If relatives were unable to oblige with the required sums, then gentlemen had little choice but to turn to professional lenders. Sir Simonds D'Ewes, who was persuaded that usury was sinful, had to employ the money market on occasions, where, 'not without much search and trouble', he found lenders prepared to 'purchase' annuities, so maintaining, if casuistically, his scrupulous refusal to pay interest. The need to secure large sums might lead gentlemen to turn to moneylenders and to pay interest; so might consideration of Lord Burghley's advice that it was preferable to borrow commercially from a stranger, 'where paying for it you shall hear no more of it', rather than from censorious kinsmen or friends.[32]

Commercial loans might be available in the localities, where some gentlemen were prepared to advance surplus capital at the going rates, but much business was transacted through London, where, after the 1571 legalisation of usury, credit facilities were publicly available. Although the 1571 Act brought down interest to 10 per cent from the black-market rate of 12–15 per cent that had previously prevailed, credit was still an expensive commodity at the end of the sixteenth century. Lenders were obsessed with securing themselves against the risks of their trade, and this made borrowing both expensive and potentially dangerous for those who sought their assistance. Moneylenders were seldom prepared to advance money for longer than six months; a borrower who needed long-term credit would find the negotiation of the renewal of the loan and the attendant legal costs a troublesome and expensive burden. The essentially short-term structure of the credit market also meant that an indebted landowner experiencing any kind of crisis would find his difficulties compounded by a stampede of nervous creditors demanding payment on their bonds and refusing to renew their loans. Sir Thomas Tresham had been able, early in the 1580s, to borrow as much as a £1,000 'upoon a bare byll of my hand'; in 1587, after he had been hit by the demand for the payment of the arrears of his recusancy fines, rumours of his difficulties swept through London, and he found himself unable to raise £100.

The difficulties faced by borrowers were enhanced by the legal device, the penal bond, by which most creditors defended their investments. In this the borrower acknowledged a debt of double the sum loaned him should he fail to pay principal and interest by a stipulated day. Some moneylenders were swift to take advantage of this windfall in the event of default. In 1593 Sir Thomas Tresham was denied the permission that he required as a recusant to travel to London, and in consequence was unable either to pay off or renegotiate loans that had fallen due; the 'merciless griping usurer' immediately threatened suit on the bond for the penal sum. An additional troublesome feature of the penal bond was that lenders often demanded collateral security from the borrowers' friends or relatives. An obligation to assist kinsmen or friends in difficulties to secure loans was recognised, but often had disastrous consequences. Tresham, who stood surety for his heavily indebted relative, Lord Vaux, found himself sued for £2,400 upon Vaux's failure to repay a loan originally of a mere £300. The constitutionally cautious Sir John Isham stood surety for several of his close relatives; in 1609 he received urgent warnings from his legal adviser that he stood in considerable risk in 'this . . . catchinge time' when one of them failed to pay. In such cases the sentiment that had originally led to the suretyship being undertaken was forgotten in the exchange of bitter recriminations. In 1604 Lord Sheffield censured the 'hard dealing' of Sir Henry Slingsby towards a relative, Robert Ryther.

Slingsby responded furiously to the charge; his father had stood surety for Ryther, and the latter's incompetence had led to substantial periods of demeaning imprisonment for the Slingsbys, father and son, and costs that had obliged them to sell lands. Not surprisingly, wise fathers advised their sons to avoid standing surety to back others' loans; 'he that hateth suretyship is sure', wrote Sir Edward Montagu.[33]

The money market of the late sixteenth century was characterised both by high interest rates, and by structures of borrowing that neglected long-term needs and that placed the borrower and his friends at considerable risk. It was this fearful system that William Higford remembered when he begged his grandson to avoid debt and borrowing at all costs: 'you may be swallowed up alive, and that house, wherein you your ancestors have been glorious for bounty and hospitality, may become the den of a merciless usurer'. Yet, when Higford wrote at the mid-century, a transformation had occurred that was critical to the survival of the Royalists in the face of demands for composition or repurchase. By the 1650s credit mechanisms were sufficiently well developed to accommodate the huge demand for loans, and credit appears to have been available to large-scale borrowers with good security thereafter, although government demands for loans in 1694–7 and 1708–11 temporarily reduced the sums available to landowners, and further enhanced gentry antipathy to the wars.[34]

This increase in the availability of credit was accompanied by a fall in interest rates; to 8 per cent in 1624, to 6 per cent in 1651, to 4 per cent by the 1680s. Not only were lenders charging less in interest but they were prepared to make long-term loans against the security of land in ways which were altogether less risky to the borrower. The mortgage of land had been available in the late sixteenth century as security for a loan, but penurious gentlemen only turned to it as a last resort: it was not until 1589 that Sir Thomas Tresham raised money by mortgage, and he did so only because his credit was so weak that he was unable to secure a loan by any other means. This was because mortgages, as Higford emphasised, carried a substantial risk of foreclosure. In a mortgage the borrower conveyed land to the creditor in fee simple, subject to the condition that if he paid the debt by a certain day then he could re-enter the estate. The terms of such conditional transfers were strictly construed in the common law courts: if the borrower failed to pay the stipulated sum by the set day then the creditor's title to the mortgaged lands vested. It was of no concern to the judges that the payment was only a day late or the land worth far more than the debt. The substantial injustices that could result from this strict interpretation, particularly when the law was exploited by chicanery, provoked the intervention of Chancery. By the late 1620s the Chancellor's readiness to relieve mortgagors in cases of hardship had transmuted into a general principle that protected the borrower and his heirs against forfeiture of his estate, provided that interest payments were maintained. Chancery's intervention made the mortgage a less precarious prospect than it had been in Tresham's day, and in the 1620s and 30s gentry borrowers – in Yorkshire; in south-west Wales – increasingly secured their loans on mortgages rather than bonds. Chancery's development of a novel legal principle in the 'equity of redemption' would have had little effect had it not been accompanied by a growing maturity and stability in the money market. Those with capital became less obsessed with fears of the risks involved in their trade, and, eschewing the windfall profits of forfeiture, were increasingly content with a steady return of 6 per cent or less secured against land.[35]

The development of a money market based on the mortgage of land was of enormous benefit to the gentry. A gentleman could borrow money against the security of his estates to pay a composition fine, or to raise portions for his daughters, or to build, or to invest in improvements. If debts were heavy then the mortgage facilities provided a breathing space, permitting retrenchment and the careful husbanding of resources gradually to pay off what was owed. By the eighteenth century the mortgage ensured that debt no longer threatened a family with catastrophic collapse and immediate extinction.

In 1683 Thomas Morgan of Tredegar, Glamorgan, attributed his extravagant expenditure on travel, clothes and gambling to his resolve 'to live according to my quality'. It was difficult to be a gentleman on the cheap at any time in our period. The swirling rhythms of fashion and changing expectations of gentle behaviour ensured that the elements in the bills contracted to guarantee reputation shifted their weight over the years. But there can be little doubt that the overall trend in the costs associated with gentility, with living 'according to my quality', was upward. The national culture and the metropolitan world in which the gentry participated by the end of the seventeenth century, while it might guarantee better access to credit, obliged a heavier outlay on marriage portions, education and items of conspicuous consumption. Increasing expenses, exacerbated by the significant rise in prices until the mid-seventeenth century, could be met, but only by adopting a more aggressive attitude to the exploitation of resources. Such a change raised questions concerning traditional assumptions about gentility. Was it fitting for a gentleman to concern himself with the technicalities of rabbit farming or mining technology, or to practice usury or to play the stock-market? In particular, was it right for him to treat his landed estate simply as an economic unit, and to profit from the opportunities provided by the buoyant market, though at the expense of the status or well-being of his tenants? To do so was to defy the traditional association of gentility with paternalism. As the rustic protagonist of a late sixteenth century work protests 'many are . . . cleaped gentill that deale full ungently with their tennants'.[36]

Paternalist values were never completely abandoned in the scramble for income; Sir Roger de Coverley treated his servants and tenants with 'a Mixture of the Father and the Master' and similar boasts were made by conservative gentlemen on their tombs into the eighteenth century. But they were often reduced to a series of symbolic gestures, like that of Sir John Reresby travelling back to Thrybergh from the sophisticated comforts of London and York each Christmas to preside over his tenants' feasts. In general, a transformation of attitude occurred that permitted landowners to exploit market opportunities. This was not without its social and political costs, however: traditions of tenant duty and deference were eroded. In the early sixteenth century the manorial tenants at Aynho had sworn oaths of fealty to their lord that emphasised reciprocal obligation: 'we be seche your worshippe to be good land lorde to us and . . . that we will lyve and dye at your fyet in Right and Trothe'. In 1642 the gentry found that tenants no longer felt under much obligation to 'live and die' with them. In September 1642 the Royalist Sir Ralph Hopton of Witham, Somerset, was besieged in Wells by local forces that included his tenantry 'unto his very gates'. William Davenport of Bramhall, Cheshire, sought the support of his tenants for the king; they unanimously refused, and some, 'not . . . caringe much for me', went off to enlist with the Parliamentarian forces. And yet as keen an observer as Selden did not attribute the end of a period when 'tenants would fight for their landlords' simply to economic pressure. Indeed, he sneered at those landlords who failed to extract the maximum profits from their estates – now mere 'vanity and folly'. For Selden the change in attitudes was less a product of the gradual shift in leasing policies than of the development of English political and administrative structures.[37] It is to those changes, and the gentry's role in them, that we will now turn.

# 5

# Administration

Gentlemen subject to the penalties enacted against Royalists in the Civil War faced an uncomfortable time. In their search for the most advantageous terms it was essential to solicit the patronage of power-brokers at Westminster and in the localities. While his wife attempted to fend off those 'those hard hearted people', the local committee, in Norfolk, Thomas Knyvett worked at Westminster to halt the sequestration threatened against his estate. He attempted to secure 'sturdy potent friends' in the Commons by mobilising a network of acquaintances and distant kinsmen – including the aged mother of John Hampden – to solicit the powerful on his behalf. He was assiduous in his attendance on the zealous Yarmouth lawyer-MP, Miles Corbett, who chaired the parliamentary committee investigating his case. Knyvett had to cringe, laugh at Corbett's jokes and tolerate his condescension: 'I bitt my lipp in anger,' he reported after one particularly humiliating interview, 'Oh, the miseryes that we are put upon to court these kind of people'. Lady Mary Verney, seeking to protect her husband's, Sir Ralph's, estate from seizure, also found the whole business exhausting and demoralising. The parliamentary administrators 'expect more waiting upon than ever the king did,' she wrote bitterly, 'and will give many promises and perform nothing'. It was not easy to grovel to men of lower status, to 'tradesmen committees', for those who had linked their status with public service and who were used to command.[1] It is to the gentry's involvement in local government, growing in intensity until shattered by the Civil War, that we will now turn.

In the period from the late-fifteenth to the early-eighteenth century the number of men appointed as Justices of the Peace, the key office of local administration in rural England, increased substantially, though at different rates in the various counties. Contemporary commentators suggested two basic reasons for the trend. First, they reasoned that the increasing number of tasks that Crown and Parliament imposed upon local administration required the appointment of ever more officers in the shires. In his handbook

Table 5.1 *The number of justices, omitting dignitaries, named on the commission of the peace for four sample counties*

| *County* | *Late 15th century* | *1562*[e] | *1636*[e] | *1702*[h] |
|---|---|---|---|---|
| Kent | 24–28[a] | 44 | 63 | 153 |
| Norfolk | 15[b] | 19 | 52 | 111 |
| Warwicks. | 8[c] | 16[f] | 22[g] | 57 |
| Yorks.: N. Riding | 11[d] | 17 | 39 | 75 |

[a] Average number of 'working' JPs in commissions issued 1500–1520, in M.L. Zell, 'Early Tudor JPs at work', *Archaeologia Cantiana*, 93 (1977) p. 126.
[b] Average number of local gentlemen in commission 1485–1500 in MacCulloch, *Suffolk*, pp. 395–7.
[c] Average number of local gentlemen in commission 1478–1500, in C. Carpenter, *Locality and Polity: a Study of Warwickshire Landed Society, 1401–1499* (Cambridge, 1992) p. 268.
[d] Number in 1489, in A.J. Pollard, *North-eastern England during the Wars of the Roses* (Oxford, 1990) p. 166.
[e] These figures (except Warwickshire) are from J. H. Gleason, *The Justices of the Peace in England, 1558–1640* (Oxford, 1969) pp. 86, 88.
[f] From *Calendar of Patent Rolls: Elizabeth, 1560–1563* (1948), p. 444.
[g] Hughes, *Warwickshire*, Appendix 1, p. 344.
[h] N. Landau, *The Justices of the Peace, 1679–1760* (Berkeley, 1984) Appendix A, pp. 367–72.

for the guidance of JPs, first published in 1582, William Lambarde noted that a century earlier the Lord Chief Justice had considered the JPs over-burdened; 'then how many justices (thinke you),' he continues wryly, 'may now suffise (without breaking theyr backes) to beare so manie, not loades, but Stacks of Statutes, that have since that time bene laide uppon them?' Lambarde was contemplating a period of particularly intense legislative intervention, much of it associated with the break with Rome and the need to police religious dissent, but the pace hardly slackened after 1585. In particular, further enactments in the late Elizabethan period designed to mitigate the social dislocation associated with population increase and the changing structure of the agricultural economy created a welter of new business for local magistrates. The increasing burden imposed by the administration of the Poor Law, tortuously shaped from the 1598 legislation by subsequent parliamentary, conciliar and judicial modifications, is apparent in the growing proportion of the manuals designed for the assistance of local justices dedicated to its explication.

As more business was deposited on local administration, so more justices were required to undertake it. But this equation was not the sole explanation of the increasing number of JPs in the counties offered by contemporaries. Lambarde emphasised not only 'the growing number of Statute lawes' to explain why the pool of JPs had 'increased to the overflowing of each shire', but the 'ambitious desire' of local gentlemen to secure the office.[2]

## 5.1 OFFICE AND STATUS

Lambarde raised an issue that troubled Elizabeth's government. William Cecil, seconded by a number of the Crown's law-officers, frequently expressed concern at the multiplication of magistrates, which, he argued, only enhanced the inefficiency of local administration. It did so by muddying the lines of communication between the centre and the localities, and by diluting the authority of the individual justice and eroding his sense of personal responsibility. These officials also questioned the motives of many of those who flocked to acquire the office. All too few, thought Lord Keeper Bacon in 1565, were concerned to 'maynteyne the common goode of theyre Countrye'. Some sought authority only to advance their private interests, 'as in overthrowinge an enemy or maynteyninge a frende'; others were wholly indolent, 'drones', concerned only 'to keepe the name and place of a Justyce . . . for reputation's sake'. In 1602 Lord Keeper Egerton added a third group to the litany of inadequacy. These were active justices, but busybodies, deliberately cultivating dissensions among their inferiors from 'an ambitious humour of gaining a Reputation among their neighbours. . . . That they may sit high on the Bench in the Quarter-Sessions'. The government recognised that the growing number of magistrates was as much a function of local demand as of the increased administrative burden. The gentry sought to secure an office that gave them opportunities for direct personal aggrandisment – 'overthrowinge an enemy or maynteyninge a frende' – and that enhanced their local prestige – 'that they may sit high on the Bench'.[3]

Magisterial office, then, reinforced gentle status. Shakespeare catches this point nicely in *The Merry Wives of Windsor*.

*Enter Justice Shallow, Master Slender, and Sir Hugh Evans*

Shallow. Sir Hugh, persuade me not. I will make a Star Chamber matter of it. If he were twenty Sir John Falstaffs, he shall not abuse Robert Shallow, Esquire.
Slender. In the county of Gloucester, Justice of Peace and Coram.
Shallow. Ay cousin Slender, and Custalorum.
Slender. Ay, and Ratulorum too; and a gentleman born, Master Parson, who writes himself 'Armigero' in any bill, warrant, quittance, or obligation: 'Armigero'.
Shallow. Ay, that I do, and have done any time these three hundred years.
Slender. All his successors gone before him hath done't, and all his ancestors that come after him may. They may give the dozen white luces in their coat.
Shallow. It is an old coat.[4]

The solemn discussion concerning Shallow's honour, so trampled by Falstaff, mingles references to the antiquity of the family and their armorial bearings with emphasis on Robert's standing as a Justice of the Peace. And not merely any justice – though the point has to be disentangled from the schoolboy Latin of these Gloucestershire worthies. Robert Shallow was *custos rotulorum*, the office held by a senior justice in each county with responsibility for the formal records of the magistracy and the staff of clerks that attended the sessions. The prestige of the office, and the patronage that it commanded meant that, from the early seventeenth century, it was usually granted to a local aristocrat. Shallow also takes pride that he is of the *quorum*. In late medieval England this was a group selected from among the general body of JPs whose greater experience or legal training meant that their presence was required at the sessions if serious matters were to be tried. Such a distinction brought honour with it: men boasted of being in the *quorum* – even, like Shallow, of being of the *coram* – on their tombs. Paradoxically, the pursuit of status through magistracy steadily eroded the honorific value of this prize. By 1636 a distinctive title once awarded to JPs particularly trusted by the Crown and in which Shallow rejoiced was promiscuously appended to four-fifths of the magistrates listed in the commission. An attempt was made in the immediate aftermath of the Restoration to revive membership of the *quorum* as an accolade, but it quickly fell victim, as earlier, to the pressure from magistrates eager to secure any additional element of prestige.[5]

The relationship between magisterial office and status ensured that the gentry manoeuvred to secure promotion to it, and, as vigorously, to deny it to their local rivals. The denunciations of the quality of the magistracy by Cecil and his colleagues suggest that the central government was only intermittently in full control of the process of the appointment and dismissal of JPs. This sense is reinforced by a study of the ways in which local men sought to advance their own and their friends' claims to office and to undermine the similar attempts of their rivals. Success depended not only upon appeals to the patronage of the obvious power-brokers – royal favourites, privy councillors, judges – but on appropriate application to the host of petty bureaucrats and clerks responsible for generating the formal documentation for the appointment of a magistrate. The unremitting attention of Philip Gawdy, a fringe figure in Elizabeth's Court, but a skilled navigator in its swirling currents of influence, was crucial to the success of the intrigues of his father and his brother to bolster their family'spre-eminence in south-west Norfolk. They sought to secure key local offices for themselves and to thwart the attempts of their neighbour, Thomas Lovell, to infringe their monopoly. This extended struggle demonstrates that, while the office of JP was crucial, the battle for status was fought out not merely in relation to appointment to and dismissal from that post. First, as with Robert Shallow, standing *within* the magisterial ranks was important; second, other offices in local administration became the focus of similar competition.[6]

In 1585 Lovell, to the horror of his enemies, was not only awarded the coveted post of JP, but had his name placed higher than that of Bassingbourne Gawdy, snr, in the commission of the peace. The machinations of the Gawdy family and their allies, who ensured that the Privy Council were apprised of his Catholic proclivities, secured Lovell's dismissal in 1587 and frustrated his attempts to regain a permanent place on the bench until 1599.

The issue of precedence within the commission did not arise on this latter occasion because his rival, now the younger Bassingbourne, had been knighted in 1597. In 1601 Lovell, after much importunity, also secured a knighthood; he immediately endeavoured to get his name once again placed above that of Sir Bassingbourne in the commission. Lovell's activities were shadowed by the attentive Philip Gawdy, and his skilled countermining thwarted the attempt. Clearly the place in which a justice's name appeared in the commission of the peace was a matter of critical significance for status: a Cambridgeshire magistrate dared to tamper with the document, erasing and interlining to get his name to a higher point on the list; a Hertfordshire JP invariably added a circled number to his signature on official warrants which indicated his position in the magisterial hierarchy. The precedence determined by the position of a man's name in the commission was no abstract issue, however. It entailed a public display of status, determining where – how 'high', to use Egerton's language – a man would sit in the public meetings of the bench. In 1615 the East Riding sessions were disrupted when a newly issued commission of the peace changed the usual order of precedence. After a good deal of elbowing, John Hotham, who believed that he had been particularly demeaned by the revised ordering, retired in dudgeon to the clerks' table and supplied a hostile commentary on the subsequent proceedings. In Herefordshire a similarly unseemly fracas occured at the sessions in 1589 as Sir Thomas Coningsby and Herbert Croft jostled for the higher place on the bench. In Wiltshire a scuffle broke out between two justices as each attempted to grab the official warrants that had to be validated to ensure that his signature would be in a higher place than that of his rival.[7]

Magistracy involved the very public and tangible display of fine gradations of status. Those successful in ousting rivals from the Bench often sought to enhance the consequent humiliation by withholding the new commissions until the court was in session and then obliging their victims to withdraw in a blaze of publicity. Sir Thomas Wentworth was the victim of such a 'disgrace in the publick Face of the county' in 1626. Sitting very high on the Bench, as *custos rotulorum* of the West Riding, Sir Thomas received 'even as I sit' the King's warrant for his dismissal that had been obtained by his local rival, Sir John Savile. The time and place was, he argued 'in sooth ill chosen, a stage ill prepared for venting such poor, vain, insulting humour'. But the bitterness and frustration that inform his response show just how effectively his enemies had orchestrated the dismissal to cause him the maximum of embarrassment. William Blythe attended the Kesteven Sessions in 1660 but was denied a place on the bench as a rival had bribed the Chancery clerks to forget to add his name in the commission. It was an intolerable affront to his dignity: 'I am asshamed to appeare any where with such a disgrace on me.'[8]

A place on the bench provided perhaps the most tangible demonstration of a gentleman's status. But honour and prestige also accrued from the exercise of other offices in the locality. The Gawdy family worked tirelessly to exclude Lovell not only from the magistracy, but from appointment to posts with temporary responsibility, such as the commission for the collection of parliamentary taxation, and from command in the militia. The latter was particularly important for the reinforcement of gentle status. It provided both a hierarchy of prestigious offices, with the administrative posts of Deputy Lieutenant and the regimental colonelcies as signal marks of governmental favour to those gentlemen of the highest local standing, and a tangential link to the chivalric elements still associated with gentility. Some gentlemen prior to the Civil War sought to emphasise the genuine military connotations of their status not only by being depicted in full armour (a commonplace in marmoreal effigies of the time) but clutching the batons that indicated their positions of command in the county militia regiments.

Appointment to such a post, as Underwit, the butt of Newcastle's comedy *The Country Captain*, gloated, was prestigious – certainly worth a little investment in the good will of the superior officers. Lord Burghley, when Lord Lieutenant of Hertfordshire, had to display considerable tact in a dispute concerning the appointment to a captaincy of a trained band company which divided his deputies; their prestige, as well as that of the competitors for the post, was at issue. Solomon-like, Burghley suggested splitting the company between the two aspirants. Once appointed, captains could dispute over precedence within their regiments, while dismissal from a post in the militia organisation was, as Sir William Thomas complained when removed from the Deputy Lieutenancy of Caernarfon, a personal affront, a 'disgrace'. Given the degree to which honour was associated with the militia, it is not surprising that when a group of passing revellers derided Richard Gardener as he drilled his company on Leatherhead meadow, the valiant captain was mortally offended; like Shallow, he made a Star Chamber matter of it.[9]

While local office was honourable, not all positions were assiduously sought. The post of High Sheriff was, in the words of Sir Simonds D'Ewes, 'an unwelcome preferment': the sheriff was tied to his county during his year of office, and was responsible for the activities of a staff who performed the basic legal and administrative routines of the office. Their incompetence or corruption, as Sir William Wentworth and John Rashleigh,

17. Monument to John Northcote, esquire, d. 1632, Newton St Cyres Church, Devon

respectively Sheriffs of Yorkshire and Cornwall, discovered, could land the sheriff in a morass of time-consuming appearances and costly litigation at Westminster. But even with competent subordinates, the office entailed expense – fees to bureaucrats at the centre; the entertainment of the local magistrates at the sessions, and, most chargeable, the honourable reception of visiting dignitaries, in particular the royal judges on their bi-annual visits for the assizes. Sir John Lowther, Sheriff of Cumberland in 1661, spent £600, buying a new coach, clothes and accoutrements for himself, liveries for his servants, and food and drink to entertain the judges. It was not easy to escape these charges. When William Farington, Sheriff of Lancashire in 1636, sought to pare some of the sumptuous provision traditionally made for the assizes, he felt the judges' displeasure: he was publicly rebuked and fined a total of £700 for a series of the most trivial technical mistakes in the performance of his office. Expenditure, then, was unavoidable. In consequence, many of those who learned that they were being considered for the post sought to mobilise the influence of friends and patrons to escape: Sir John Holles, whose help was invoked by his poor kinsman Sir Hardolph Wastneys, wrote pathetically to a host of the influential of the knight's poor estate, his debts, his five marriagable daughters, his diligent service as a JP.[10]

The ceremonial functions of the sheriff did, however, enable a man to make or enhance his local reputation and standing. Samuel Backhouse, sheriff of Berkshire in 1601, greeted the Queen upon her entry into the county 'exceedingly well horsed and attended' which 'won him commendation on all sides'. The escalating costs of the shrievalty were in part occasioned by each holder of the post's efforts to exceed his predecessor in such lavish display. A wealthy outsider settling in a county and seeking to signal his arrival among the élite, or a young man eager to claim the status traditionally enjoyed by his family, might see the shrievalty as an opportunity to make a mark. Major-General Berry's comment on a candidate for the shrievalty of Worcestershire in 1656 catches this aspect of the office nicely, if cynically: 'a riche clowne, that would be glad to be taken notice of'. In 1610 Sir John Wynn, who himself had sought to escape the office earlier, attempted to get his young son-in-law, John Bodvel, appointed sheriff. It was a 'public stage' on which he could gain reputation; Wynn was also angling for a knighthood for Bodvel, and the post of JP. By 1620, when Sir John Bodvel's local status was clearly established, the prospect that he might be chosen sheriff caused the usual trepidation and the Wynn family's Court connections were deployed to block the possibility.[11]

Sir John Wynn came to regret this last decision: it occasioned 'the greatest publike disgrace that ever I had in my tyme'. Parliament was summoned, and, in a vicious election, his son, Sir Richard, was defeated by the Wynn family's old rivals for supremacy in Caernarfonshire, the Gruffiths of Llyn, who were much assisted by a friendly sheriff. In 1626, Bishop Bayly, on this occasion in the faction-ridden politics of North Wales Wynn's ally, drew the moral. They must secure the office if they hoped to challenge the pretensions of the 'Llyn faction', given the sheriff's control over parliamentary elections – likely to be frequent in a period of war – and his power to pick jurymen in criminal and civil cases. It was essential 'that one of the WYNNES . . . stand in the face of the countrey to outface their adversaries'. It might be chargeable and onerous to be sheriff, but the office still held sufficient authority to recommend it to those eager to secure personal or factional advantage, like Sir Arthur Heveningham in Norfolk, in 1593 'the most importunate sutor to be shreife that ever was'. In counties split by gentry rivalries – Caernarfonshire or Cumberland in the Jacobean period; Norfolk in the last decades of the sixteenth century – there was serious competition for an office otherwise avoided.[12]

## 5.2 OFFICE AND LOCAL POWER

This brings us back to another issue raised in the jeremiads of the Crown's law officers concerning magistracy in general. They certainly objected to those who sought posts in local administration for motives of personal prestige. But they were perhaps more troubled by those who were indeed prepared to exercise their powers, but only to secure tangible personal benefits. 'A Justice of Peace,' an MP quipped in the Commons in 1601, 'is a living creature that for half a dozen of chickens will dispense with a whole dozen of penal statutes . . . These be the Basket-Justices.' The basket-justices, whose exercise of their authority had to be lubricated with appropriate *douceurs*, were a favoured butt of government denunciation and popular abuse. Yet, while a number of JPs were prosecuted in the Star Chamber for receiving gifts or taking bribes, more troubling to the government was the prospect that gentlemen might employ their authority to advance broader economic or political interests in the localities. Sir Thomas Throckmorton of Gloucestershire, Sir Nicholas Sanderson of Lincolnshire and Sir John Bale of Leicestershire all used their positions as justices to terrorise villagers with whom they were in dispute. Throckmorton, having failed in an attempt to indict one of his tenants for murder, deployed his power as a muster commissioner to impress the unfortunate man for service in Ireland. Bale had a substantial freeholder of Kibworth Harcourt who had offended his daughter sent to the House of Correction, where he was fettered and whipped. Sir John then suborned his tenants to testify against the man at the Assizes and sat on the bench to encourage these witnesses; only the most careful examination of the case by the judge secured the man's release. When a poor widow of Tetney, who stood in the way of an enclosure scheme devised by Sanderson, tried to sue his servants for an attack on her property, the knight, sitting on the bench at Caistor Sessions, 'did discountenance, check, disgrace, and threaten' her witnesses and levelled a charge of witchcraft against the woman herself.[13]

Other gentlemen used their official authority in property disputes with their equals or to protect their servants, friends and relations – particularly their recusant kinsmen and neighbours – from prosecution. The most spectacular abuses of power for private ends occurred in those counties that were split by the competition of substantial groupings among the gentry, as were, at the end of Elizabeth's reign, Herefordshire, Lincolnshire, Norfolk and Wiltshire. The official authority to command to keep the peace, to arrest and imprison suspects, to allow bail, all were powerful weapons, to be marshalled with libels, assaults and riots – even murder – in the conduct of these factional struggles. In feuds of this kind the private session was a favoured device, when magistrates of one faction assisted by a compliant sheriff, would secretly summon a court, impanel a jury of their dependents, and enter judgement against their rivals. So in 1604 two Lincolnshire JPs, allies of the Earl of Lincoln, summoned a private sessions, ostensibly to hear a trivial case but in fact to indict the followers of the Earl's enemy, Sir Edward Dymock, for riot and assault. Lincoln himself handpicked the jury, and selected a man with whom Dymock was engaged in litigation as its foreman. The plan, skilfully conceived, went wrong. Sir Edward was forewarned, and attended the special sessions with two JPs of his faction, plus his lawyers, his witnesses and a large group of armed servants. Predictably the sessions terminated in a brawl, with the rival magistrates hurling abuse and challenges across the court. As Chancellor Egerton complained in 1608, while the justices should use their authority to 'maintain peace . . . they rather make war.'[14]

The central authorities, aware that magisterial power could become a weapon of self-aggrandisment and the plaything of local faction, sought to punish abuse. From Wolsey's Chancellorship until 1640 magisterial deficiencies were heard in the Court of Star Chamber, where the Privy Council afforced by the judges formed the court. Conviction by that tribunal could involve a fine, solemn censure by the court, dismissal from office, and the additional humiliation of a public admission of guilt and apology in the locality. This last punishment was particularly feared. When Sir William Pope was ordered from the bench to the bar of the court at the Oxfordshire assizes to be harangued by the presiding judge, 'thear was great speaking an talking over all the countrye' of his humiliation. Sir Henry Winston, ordered to acknowledge his failings as a magistrate at the Gloucester assizes, responded that 'I desire rather to remain in prison than to receive open disgrace in my country.' While the government might dismiss, censure, humble incompetent or corrupt justices, they must have recognised, uneasily, that their sources of information concerning deficiencies were inadequate, even tainted. Failures in or abuse of office frequently came to the attention of the Council only as a spin-off from the local feuds among the gentry that the Council so deprecated. Winston had been engaged in a bitter struggle with Sir Thomas Throckmorton in Gloucestershire; both men denounced the other to Star Chamber, each providing an extensive catalogue of charges of the malaversion of authority; both were found guilty, dismissed and humiliated. But in localities where such conflicts did not occur the central authorities lacked adequate sources of information to police the local governors.[15]

## 5.3 AN IDEOLOGY OF PUBLIC SERVICE

The Crown's officers not only sought to punish the deficient, but, in a variety of ways, to educate the gentry to a proper sense of their magisterial responsibilities and to inculcate a sense of public duty in its appointees. The highly public censure of Star Chamber was one such means; so were Royal Proclamations or speeches by the law officers in Parliament. The model was provided by Cardinal Wolsey, who insisted that as many JPs as possible attend in Star Chamber annually to be 'newsworn'. There they were treated to a homily on their duties, occasionally to a lecture by the Chancellor himself – a practice continued by Audley in the 1530s. In Elizabeth's reign it became the usual practice for the Chancellor to address the judges of assize in a public forum also attended by those gentlemen who were visiting London. The speeches indicate the government's immediate law-enforcement priorities but also insist more generally on the duties of the JPs. The Chancellor's oration then provided themes and material for the judges themselves in their 'charges', ostensibly directed to the jurors, but before a wider audience of magistrates and inferior local officers assembled at the assizes in each county. In all these government pronouncements the same themes recur. The JPs are the local agents of a monarch whose zealous commitment to justice and beneficent rule they must emulate – 'to exercise Justice with a Herculean courage': the magistrates were to enforce, and were themselves answerable to the over arching structure of the common law – 'the best laws in the whole world'.[16]

The central government was assisted in its task of educating the local gentry magistrates by other commentators. The growing body of highly technical law for which they were responsible led to the production of a number of handbooks for the guidance of the JPs, the best by professional lawyers who also had considerable experience in local administration. Their utility is indicated by the number of editions that were produced: Lambarde's *Eirenarcha*, first issued in 1582, was reprinted 15 times by 1619; its replacement, Michael Dalton's *The Countrey Justice*, first appeared in 1618; it had reached its 14th reprinting by 1700. Two Devon justices, taking depositions in a murder case in 1603, found that neither had a Bible with him; of course, a copy of Lambarde's essential treatise was to hand so they swore the witnesses on that. These popular works were practical guides to the substantive law and to procedure: Dalton's revised discussion in 1630 of the appropriate way to handle a witchcraft accusation shaped the procedure until the end of the century. But they also provided general reflections on the duties of the magistrate that in many ways echoed the official line developed by the law officers. So Dalton, discussing legislation in which the JPs were enjoined to act at their discretion, noted, with profuse citation to Sir Edward Coke's writings, that this did not mean 'to doe according to our willes and privat affections,' rather 'to discerne, by the Right Line of Law . . . not by private opinion'.[17]

That magistracy was a solemn duty to be exercised for the public good was stressed by the professional commentators. That it was a duty peculiarly incumbent on the gentry was emphasised by the clergy, particularly in the sermons that were conventionally preached at the assizes. The ministers were quick to denounce the abuses of magistracy that had been emphasised by the central law officers: JPs 'that never sit on the Bench but for fashion'; the man who takes office 'onely . . . to hurt his enemies, profit his followers, to uphold his faction and partie'. More positively, they insisted, as did Robert Sanderson in a series of assize sermons preached in the east midlands, that public office was the proper 'calling' for a gentleman; it was that 'settled course of life, wherein mainly to employ a man's gifts and his time for his own and the common good'. A gentleman must not suppose that his elevated position, his 'birth, breeding, or estate', excused him from the general Christian obligation to 'labour in any vocation'. And the religious duty of magistracy obliged the gentleman justice not only to act 'with delight and zeal and cheerfulness', but to undertake law enforcement impartially and without self-interested ends. In Wales, the poets were quick to sense and to reinforce the emphasis on the duties of magistracy. Bardic eulogies no longer concentrated upon the martial virtues, but hymned the role of the gentleman as a conscientious magistrate, legally knowledgeable, and administering justice even-handedly.[18]

Some gentlemen justices obviously paid careful attention to the speeches, charges, handbooks, eulogies and sermons. In their commonplace books they reflected on magistracy as a duty and on the duties of magistracy. In various memoranda, Sir John Newdigate considered that the status he enjoyed, as a man who expected obedience and honour – 'to sit highest at the table . . . to be . . . worshipped with cappe and knee' – required a concomitant readiness for public 'imploiement' on his part'. As obedience is due to us, so is our study, our labour and industry, with virtuous example, due to them that be subject to our authority. 'The income and leisure that a gentleman enjoyed could only be justified if they were employed in reading and contemplation, the necessary preparations for magistracy. Other gentlemen kept notebooks in which they recorded decisions and the opinions of the professionals on the legal problems that might confront them in their local execution of the law. Henry Townshend, a Worcestershire JP, interleaved his copy of *The Compleat Justice* and wrote a series of notes on the text that were based on his wide reading in other legal works, on case decisions at the Assizes, and on private conversations with the judges over dinner at Worcester. Townshend was not merely concerned with technicalities; he also recorded the judges' pronouncements concerning the necessity of due process and legal uniformity, even though those opinions were not always complimentary to men like himself, amateurs – 'ignorant justices', as Chief Justice Hyde sneered in 1663 – who needed to be reminded that they were to uphold the law, not their own 'fancy and opinion'.[19]

Magistrates did not merely consign their thoughts on their duty to private notebooks. They often dilated upon them in public contexts. The JPs at quarter sessions followed the precedent set by the assizes, and used the 'charge' – the instructions given to the jurymen concerning their responsibilities – as an opportunity to engage in a more general reflection on the political order and the role of law and justice within it. The jurors were treated to 'carefully revised literary productions' on their duties to God, to the King, to the commonwealth, and to the locality. We may suspect that the dense citations from scripture, the fathers, the classics and legal commentators, and the frequently tedious verbosity of these efforts, may have meant little to their rustic audience. But these texts do speak to the gentry' s own sense of the role of magistracy, and, in particular, to their strong sense of the responsibility of public office. So in 1608 Sir John Newdigate warned a Warwickshire jury against partiality, and reminded each of them that he was 'the champion of justis, the patron of peace, the father of thy country and as it were as other god on earth.' Some 80 years later Hugh Hare, at Dorking Sessions, was insisting that his humble audience should play its role in the co-operative endeavour to enforce abstract justice: 'we are all concerned in our several stations to punish and repress these vices as Phineas did, without respect of persons.'[20]

Magistrates might use such rhetoric in their disputes with their fellows on the proper administration of justice, and not just in the formal platitudes with which they lectured their inferiors or decorated denunciations of their rivals to Star Chamber. Sir William Hall appealed to it as he sought the vindication of a poor woman, flogged at the orders of Sir Isaac and Sir John Sedley, though they had no legal grounds for their warrant. His pertinacity, his solid refusal to connive at their malfeasance, infuriated the Sedleys; 'there was a good constable spoyled when . . . Hall was made a Justice of the Peace,' sneered Sir John. In 1577 Lord Morley sought to protect one of his tenants who had got a girl pregnant; the couple would escape punishment, and a private financial settlement would guarantee the charges of mother and baby. The Hertfordshire JP, Thomas Leventhorpe, would have none of this cosy cover-up. The financial arrangement must be publicly acknowledged 'as the statute doth appoint', and the guilty pair whipped. Morley was horrified by this 'cruelty', but, undeterred by his threats, Leventhorpe insisted that 'the law of the prince and God's law upon which the prince' s law is grounded' must be obeyed.[21]

In the face of Leventhorpe' s probity Morley spat out a comment on the sanctimonious magistrate, with his array of punishments – whippings, mutilations – employed against the poor who were 'often times . . . more honest a great deal than the justices' who terrorised them. His language echoes a literary trope, most savagely developed in *King Lear*, of the pompous and insensitive magistrate, whose own failings and hypocrisies were cloaked in a heavy-handed administration of 'justice' that lacked all compassion. Jonson's Adam Overdo JP embodies this image: 'this is the special day for the detection of those foresaid enormities. Here is my black book for the purpose . . . On Junius Brutus! . . . in Justice' name, and the King's; and for the Commonwealth.' The employment of Overdo-like figures, men who could boast of themselves as 'the example of justice and the mirror of magistrates, the true top of formality and scourge of enormity', as part of the stock in trade of playwrights and wits, may further suggest the success of the attempts to educate local administrators in ideals of responsibility to national law and central directives. There were a sufficient number of zealous magistrates to form a recognisable type. But it also raises another issue: the zealous justice guyed in the theatre was very likely to be a Puritan.[22]

Divines of all theological persuasions emphasised that magistracy was a duty that a gentleman should undertake. However, Puritan ministers did give this doctrine a particular twist, arguing more insistently both that the failure to punish sin would draw a providential judgement upon England, and that magisterial authority should be employed for the protection of the godly and the advancement of godliness. So in 1621 at the Northampton

Assizes, Robert Bolton threatened 'the vengeance of God upon the face of this noble and famous kingdom' for its tolerance of sin. He was, however, less concerned with deficiencies in the administration of the traditional criminal law, than in the non-enforcement of moral regulations. He blasted the prophanation of the Sabbath; drunkenness – and any among the JPs who might be a 'secret supporter of any rotten alehouse'; those who derided 'faithfull ministers', and who persecuted 'God's people'. In 1629 he reiterated these themes, developing the argument that God empowered all governments and magistrates 'for the sakes and safety of the Saints alone'. Having defined their special sense of magisterial responsibility in their assize sermons, Puritan ministers privately encouraged the justices to follow their prescriptions. A minister, pressing Bassingbourne Gawdy to secure the promotion of a godly man to minor local office, concluded his missive, 'Sir, let the courage of godly Joshua be in you; bless your country with your constant obedience to your God, who ever bless you.' And in funeral sermons they praised their gentry patrons for their zealous activity in pursuit of these goals: Sir Edward Lewkenor of Suffolk, Sir Thomas Lucy of Warwickshire, Sir George StPaul of Lincolnshire, all were held up to emulation as models of godly magistracy. StPaul, according to John Chadwick was the 'bell-wether of the flock' of the Lincolnshire justices; as a JP, a Deputy Lieutenant, a subsidy commissioner he was dedicated to the service of the commonwealth, never avoiding any service, 'any paines or endeavours, though to the spending of his estate . . . to the wearying of his body and the empayringe of his health'. He patronised godly ministers, and used his magisterial authority to support their religious and social priorities.[23]

This is not merely the pious platitude of a particular genre, the funeral sermon. The correspondence and actions of some magistrates show that they internalised the concerns and the agenda of the godly ministry. So in 1629 Sir William Masham reflected on the bad weather that was ruining the barley harvest, and saw in it the hand of God indicating his anger at 'the spetiall sinne of our nation, which is drunkenness'. 'Justice against this sinne,' he continued portentously with appropriate scriptural citation, 'is the best expiation.' Accordingly he had used his magisterial authority to punish two alehouse-keepers and a number of their clients in one of the Essex villages near his house. His concerns had been shared by godly JPs since the reign of

Elizabeth. In 1575 four Puritan justices in north-east Norfolk co-operated in an effort to impose a strict moral discipline on the area. A more sustained effort to establish a godly regime occurred in Bury St Edmunds in the early 1580s. Encouraged by a faction within the town and by the Puritan ministers of the area, in 1579 three of the county JPs, Robert Ashfield, Sir John Higham and Sir Robert Jermyn, promulgated a series of ordinances for the government of Bury. In their regulations, the justices both arrogated to themselves an authority over ecclesiastical matters that were properly within the cognisance of the Bishop of Norwich – as he protested loudly – and also established a series of punishments for moral offences that had no basis in existing legislation. Fornicators and adulterers, for instance, were to be tied to a post for a day and a night in the marketplace, then whipped; women so offending were additionally to have their hair cut off. When, in 1583, the government through the justices of assize challenged this exercise of godly tyranny, the protests of the three signatories of the 1579 ordinance were supported by seven other active Suffolk justices.[24]

The intense Puritan emphasis upon magistracy has led some historians to suggest that godly gentlemen were peculiarly active in their ordinary roles as justices. Local studies suggest that this argument is overstated. The stereotype is valid in Cheshire, where, between 1625 and 1640, the 'austere Calvinist', Sir William Brereton, attended almost twice as many meetings of the sessions as any other justice. But elsewhere gentlemen with no obvious ties to the Puritan ministry – some, in Elizabeth's reign, with conservative sympathies – were equally assiduous in their attendance at assizes and quarter sessions, and in their out-of-sessions work. In Hertfordshire between 1580 and 1620, the Puritan Sir Rowland Lytton was a vigorous and committed justice; but his diligence did not match that of Sir Henry Cocke who had no such affiliation, and was rivalled by the involvement in magistracy of Andrew Grey and William Whyskyns, both of whom were accused of leaning to Catholicism. Neither in Warwickshire nor, more surprisingly, in Essex – that 'place of most life of religion in the land' – could Puritan gentlemen boast a monopoly of intense activity as local magistrates.[25]

In Tudor England the central government, while piling ever more responsibilities upon its local representatives, had many reservations about their efficiency. The gentry were berated for displaying greater concern for the titular honour of magistracy than for its duties, and for employing their authority with extreme partiality.

Exemplary prosecutions by 'the new law of Star Chamber' and deliberate dismissals forcefully reminded the local governors of their responsibilities. But the Crown lacked the resources to attempt any general purges of local officials: the balance of power in the counties remained essentially traditional and the government sought to persuade gentlemen that they had a vested interest in the promotion of good order as defined by the centre. The Crown and its ministers sought to inculcate a stronger sense of public duty by exhortations in Parliament, in the courts, at the assizes. In this task they were joined by lawyers and divines, though the engagement of the latter, many with an agenda of moral reform in advance of that of the government, created some tensions.

This barrage of propaganda was ultimately effective. By the 1630s there were still occasional horror stories of the ignorance or corruption of particular JPs, but the general record is one of compliance and efficiency. This is most apparent in the growing complexity, yet sophistication and professionalisation, of the system through which the justices executed the criminal and administrative law. The system developed partly in response to government pressure, partly out of the magistrates' perceptions of local conditions and needs. The Crown's law officers, both by exhortation and by the punishment of *ultra vires* acts by the JPs, emphasised the need for a regard for proper legal procedures in the administration of justice. In response, the local gentry sought to ensure that they acquired the necessary legal knowledge; sons were sent to the Inns of Court, though, like John Isham, to his father's 'greate charge', that they might afterwards 'profit' their 'cuntry'; they were exhorted not to waste their time when they got there; law books were willed, as by the assiduous justice, Sir Walter Covert, 'as standerds in my house to be and inure to the sole use and benefit of my next heir'. Legally trained themselves, the justices also employed an increasing number of professional lawyers to staff the local courts. We can see a similar process at work in the development of the 'petty sessions'. A variety of central directives from the later years of Elizabeth' s reign suggested that more formal meetings of the JPs for sub-units of the county would enhance administrative efficiency. These missives encouraged local experiment, and it was the expedient developed by the Northamptonshire justices, holding sessions every three weeks within each of their divisions, that the Privy Council recommended to all the counties in the 1631 Book of Orders.[26]

## 5.4 THE GENTRY AND TAXATION

The sense of public duty that increasingly informed local administration in the seventeenth century was slowest to develop in relation to direct taxation. The occasional, spectacular cases of fraud and log-rolling by individual gentry commissioners in their assessments were less troubling to government than the steady erosion of the value of a subsidy that we have already noted. From 1576 the Council sought to arrest the slide in yields and to crack down on the scandalous under-rating of the wealthier landowners. By 1594 JPs were being reminded that a landed income of £20 a year was a statutory requirement for a place on the bench, and were threatened with dismissal unless their assessment achieved this bare minimum. These efforts were unavailing and the erosion of values continued: in 1628 Charles I could complain that the £55,000 raised on each subsidy assessment was 'such a scanty proportion as is infinitely short, not only of our great occasions, but of the precedents of former subsidies'. The issue was intermittently considered in Parliament – so in 1628 a fixed assessment on all baronets was mooted – but this and all other reformist proposals were dropped. The government continued to press the local authorities: copies of the assessment figures of the mid-Elizabethan period were circulated and the commissioners instructed to explain the substantial shortfall from these; commissioners were instructed to send a copy of the sums that they assessed upon themselves directly to the Council. The threats of the 1590s were also repeated: magistrates rated at under £20 faced the 'daunger of the disgrace to be put out of theire Commission'. In most localities these instructions proved a dead letter, as on the Isle of Wight where only two JPs were rated above £12: 'wee feared not puttinge out of the commission', noted Sir John Oglander complacently on his copy of the Council's missive. The Lincolnshire commissioners were more forthright in calling the official bluff. They noted the 'great charges they undergo by their pains in his Majesty's several services', refused to enhance the rates on 'their small estates', and, in effect, dared the Council to dismiss them.[27]

The Restoration initially appeared to entail a reversion to pre-Civil War attitudes to direct taxation. Four subsidies in the traditional form were voted in 1663; each raised approximately the same, derisory, sum achieved in 1628, and Charles II was obliged to repeat his father's acid commentary of that year almost *verbatim*. In 1671 Parliament sought to refurbish the subsidy, establishing a comprehensively revised system designed to secure a realistic rating in the shires. The local commissioners proved less enthusiastic than their neighbours in the Commons, and less than half of the anticipated £750,000 was raised on their assessment. The yields from indirect taxation were also shaved by the manoeuvres of JPs designed to safeguard the interests of their localities. Magistrates were deeply reluctant to use their coercive powers to assist in the collection the excise and, particularly with the hearth tax, engaged in flagrant obstruction of the central officers. Sir John Reresby fought off hearth tax demands on behalf of the Sheffield cutlers for fifteen years; as he noted, his stance 'did not please the Court . . . but whatever I lost ther I gained in my country'. Attempts by the Crown to penalise such interference, as in 1675, were deeply resented in the Commons.[28]

And yet attitudes were changing. The Revolution committed the political nation to funding William III's ambitious foreign policy. The only serious alternative to a land tax was a general excise, and this was objectionable on fundamental constitutional grounds to a Parliament that had denounced the right of search in the hearth tax legislation as 'a badge of slavery upon the whole people'. Not only were the army of salaried officials petty inquisitors, prying into men's houses, but posts in the excise were a patronage resource for the government, and excisemen were suspected of interfering in local politics and elections. 'I am not for saving our lands to enslave our persons by excise,' thundered John Swynfen in 1690. So the Commons voted a series of unprecedentedly heavy taxes on land, and in 1693 sought to secure a rate of 4 shillings in the pound by a new assessment of local income. The commissioners, appointed from the local élite by Parliament, were, as we have seen, not uniformly enthusiastic in their response. In peripheral areas – Cornwall, Cumbria, Lancashire – the gentry, many unsympathetic to the Revolution of 1688, seized the opportunity provided by reassessment to enhance their already comparatively undertaxed status. One of their number, Sir Wilfred Lawson of Isell, Cumberland, was unique only in his honesty when he bequeathed £600 to Queen Anne 'in full recompense . . . for all such taxes as I ought, according to law, to have paid either to her or her predecessor'. But in lowland England the commissioners took their responsibilities seriously, and the new assessments were calculated at rates which entailed payment close to the 20 per cent of landed income demanded by the legislation. Thereafter, while there were some vigorous controversies *within* counties concerning the equity of the taxes on their various sub-divisions, the tax was paid regularly, producing nearly £2 million per annum in the war years. In all, £46 million was raised in the quarter-century from the Revolution to the Peace of Utrecht. And it was paid, as Colin Brooks has emphasised, 'year in and year out'. The English gentry, it seems, had finally extended their sense of public responsibility to the field of taxation.[29]

And yet the effective administrators of the land tax in the localities by the early eighteenth century were not drawn from the traditional ruling élite. MPs insisted that local commissioners should control the assessment and collection of the tax, and that the Commons, not the Crown, should nominate the commissioners. In consequence, the rolls were headed with the names of the greater gentry. But such men were seldom as apparent in the day-to-day administration of the tax: the work was done by a mix of clergymen, local lawyers and minor gentry.[30]

## 5.5 THE EIGHTEENTH CENTURY RETREAT FROM OFFICE

A dependence upon men of lesser status also emerged in the same period with respect to magistracy. The intensity of local administration and the complexity of its bureaucracy built on the seventeenth-century foundations. But the social profile of the bench shifted significantly. There are four salient features to this. First, there were more justices named in the commission of the peace than ever: the 1761 commissions for the five sample counties list more than twice as many men as those of 1702. Yet, second, despite this increase the proportion of the representatives of leading families of a county nominated as magistrates fell – sometimes slightly, as in Hertfordshire, occasionally cataclysmically, as in Northamptonshire. Third, a substantial and growing proportion of those nominated failed to take the oaths that permitted them to act. In a sample of seven counties, half of those nominated between 1706 and 1713 did not bother to take the oaths; the figure had risen to three-quarters between 1738 and 1760. Finally, in many areas the most diligent justices, as judged by their attendance at quarter sessions and their out-of-sessions work, tended to be drawn from groups other than the traditional ruling élite. In 1722 in Glamorgan 43 justices were nominated; of the 22 drawn from the gentry élite, only 6 bothered to take the oaths; 70 per cent of the lesser men did so, and the most active justices were all from this latter group, 'stewards or merchants, or else new gentry whose fathers had obtained gentle status through such careers'. The tempo of the withdrawal of the greater gentry from active involvement in magistracy was not uniform among the counties: it is apparent in the early 1680s in Lincolnshire; in the 1690s in Norfolk; it appears not to have occurred in eighteenth-century Kent. Mr Spectator, in 1711, could imagine Sir Roger de Coverley attending the Assizes, taking his place 'at the Head' of the bench, intervening in a trial, all 'to keep up his Credit in the Country'. But in this, as in so much else, the good knight was a somewhat antediluvian figure.[31]

The retreat of the greater gentry families from active magistracy in the early eighteenth century suggests that the possession and exercise of office was no longer a key element in definitions of gentility as it had been for Shallow. Other modes of display sufficed to validate status: as Stone and Stone have written, 'leisure to hunt, travel, and make lengthy visits to London' became more valued.[32] Why should this be?

In some measure changes in the tasks of magistracy and the institutional framework within which they acted may be responsible. In Elizabeth's reign Cecil frequently argued that the proliferation of lesser men in commission caused 'the better sort of justices' to 'be ashamed to sit with such companions as some of them be'. His suggestion of a magisterial Gresham's Law – justices of inferior status drive out men of standing – was repeated in the eighteenth century. What honour accrued to 'Gentlemen of any great Figure or Fortune' when associated in office with 'persons of small estates and mean education'? The government had to increase the number of justices to guarantee adequate coverage in the localities, but the swelling commissions and consequent appointment of lesser men only further discouraged the élite from service.

Equally, the growing formalisation and routinisation of the administrative law may have discouraged participation. Satirists from the sixteenth century on had portrayed magistrates – when not depicting them as zealous hypocrites – as pompous bumpkin dullards: Shallow, Clack, Sir Nicholas Treedle: 'He speaks words, but no matter, and therefore is in election to be of the peace and quorum.' Some gentlemen writhed in uneasy self-recognition. George Manners yearned for London society, and hoped he would not 'alwayes . . . live a poore base Justice, recreatinge myself in sending roges to the gallows'; Sir Charles Percy complained that he would soon be 'so dull that I shall be taken for . . . Justice Shallow' if he was obliged to stay much longer in rural Gloucestershire. By the eighteenth century the aspect of trivial routine in magisterial business, the circumscription of independence by an institutional framework and procedural rules, had been further enhanced. Squire Western's determination to imprison a servant for saucy language to his sister was halted by his pedantic clerk's insistence that it was contrary to law, and might embroil Western in further difficulties with his judicial superiors.[33]

Finally, the gentry élite became aware that the business of local government could be adequately conducted by their inferiors. It did not require their presence. This was a lesson they might have learned in the 1650s. The social quality of the bench fell dramatically in the course and aftermath of the war; authority devolved upon those who, while not lacking administrative experience before the war as high constables or grand jurors, could not have aspired to a place on the bench. Yet the institutional structure devised by central authorities and local gentlemen in the previous century functioned: bridges and roads were maintained, the supply of grain to markets guaranteed, the poor relieved, felons hung.[34] In 1660 the élite sought both the immediate recovery of their local power, and the opportunity to employ it against those who had triumphed over them in the war – particularly the dissenters. But by the 1690s the normal routines of local government came to hold fewer attractions for the gentry. Status could be displayed and reinforced in more enjoyable ways.

Yet reference to the Civil War should remind us that an explanation of the shifting relationship between status claims and the possession of local office cannot be based entirely on an analysis of changes in administrative conventions and powers. Changes in the *political* assumptions and experiences of the gentry were also involved.

# 6

# Politics

In 1633 John Abel, the King's carpenter, built a new timber-framed town hall for Leominster. The building is luxuriant in its carved decoration – a rich, if not wholly stylistically coherent, profusion of male and female busts, caryatids, monsters and lions, of fancy Ionic columns and heraldic shields, of pious texts. One of these inscriptions nicely raises the issue to be discussed in this chapter, of the political role and assumptions of the gentry. It reads, 'Like columnes do upprop the fabric of abuilding, so noble gentri dos support the honor of a Kingdom.'[1] A platitude, perhaps? But the dissolution of England into a Civil War which divided the gentry and smashed the monarchy within a decade of the erection of Leominster's new hall suggests that contemporary understandings of this sentiment were not unambiguous.

The Duke of Newcastle, writing in the bleak aftermath of war, defeat and exile, had a clear view of the supporting role which the gentry should have played in a well-organised state. In his discussion of the need to maintain order and ceremony and to 'keepe upp your Nobility & Gentery', he recalled an incident from the turn of the century that displayed the proper nature and exercise of political authority.[2] The passage is worth quoting in full:

> In my time, Gilbert, that great Earle of Shrewsbury whoe was a wise man, had a gentle soule, a Loyall, – at a St. Georges feaste, I have knowne Sir Georg booth a Cheshere knight And of six, or seaven, thousand pound, a yeare, weare my Lord of Shrewsburys blew Coate, on St. Georges Day, – as also Sir Vinsent Corbett, whose brother had 10,000 a year, & after the death of His brother, hee had 4 or 5000 a yeare, & hee wore my Lords blew Coate . . . butt the nexte day they satt both at my Lords table nexte to him, & nothing butt good Coosen Corbett, & good Coosen booth, & they were very wise in itt, for thus they did oblige my Lord, to bee their servant all the yeare After, with his power to serve them, both in Courte and westminster Hall, & to bee their solister, – agen my

18. The Old Town Hall, Leominster, Herefordshire, built 1653

> Lord had no busines in the Country, but they did itt for him, – & then the King had an Easey busines, for what soever busines his Majestie had in any County In England, or in all England, itt was but speaking to Shewsbury, or Darby, & such great men, itt was Done, with Ease & subilety . . . & what doth itt coste your Majestie, a blew Riban, a privey Counsellor shipp, or such offices as your Majestie cannot bestow better, then uppon such great men . . . then all their kindered, freinds, dependances, servants tenantes, are well pleased, & your Majestie safe

There is a good deal of romantic nostalgia in this account of the relationship that linked King James, the Earl of Shrewsbury and Sir George Booth. Shrewsbury did not invariably play the benign, paternal role that Newcastle attributed to him. The Earl's Yorkshire neighbour, Sir William Wentworth of Wentworth Woodhouse, found him an aggressive and mean-spirited bully. Wentworth, in his efforts to gratify the Earl, had loaned him money, permitted him hunting privileges over his land, allowed him to purchase an estate that Wentworth coveted, and appointed one of his clients as deputy sheriff: all these, and an ingratiating deference, had brought only further demands, suits, insults, threats, and substantial losses to Wentworth. Sir William wrote bitterly in the section of his advice to his son dealing with the nobility, 'itt is dangerouse to be familier with them, or to depend upon them, or to deale with or to trust them too muche.'[3] And yet, while Newcastle's account may be too rosy as history, it is powerful as ideology. He asserts a model of political authority in which the Crown, the nobility and the gentry co-operate in an organic hierarchy, symbiotically linked together to their mutual advantage. Royal mandates are enforced locally by the gentry because they are recommended to them by their lords; the magnates channel the flow of royal patronage into their localities which, reinforced by their own largesse to their gentry clients, lubricates the system.

Newcastle attributed the collapse of this form of government to the folly of James I in the last years of his reign, and to that of his son. Both neglected the ancient nobility, and allowed a narrowly based faction, a group of 'meane men' who lacked traditional local influence, who 'could not rayse A man', to 'Monopolise . . . totalye to Themselves' positions at Court and thus access to the Crown and its patronage. An inward-looking, narcissistic Court disaffiliated itself from the natural chain of authority; the traditional magnate power-brokers were despised because they were not 'a la mode', could not 'Dance a Sereban with castanetts of their fingers'; the machinery of government ground to a halt. This explanation has much to recommend it, particularly for the period of the Duke of Buckingham's supremacy, and has been developed by a number of modern historians. The Duke's predominance, his position as, in the words of the Venetian ambassador, 'the sole access to the Court, the sole means of favour, in fact one might say the King himself', was achieved by filling the Court with his relatives and clients, nonentities with small estates and little local standing, and displacing the great magnates. The latter, slighted and deprived of the central influence that had enabled them to advance the interests of their gentry clients and neighbours, had neither the inclination nor, perhaps, the authority to promote royal policies in the provinces.[4]

After the assassination of Buckingham, Charles very deliberately restructured his Court and government. Ostensibly, the status of the magnates and their traditional role in the relationship between centre and localities was powerfully re-affirmed. The profuse creation and sale of new titles abruptly ceased in 1629; royal Proclamations and the resurrected High Court of Chivalry were employed to protect the status hierarchy and the honour code; peers were invited in unprecedented numbers to advise the King as members of the Privy Council. In his Proclamations ordering the gentry to leave London and reside on their estates, Charles emphasised his commitment to the traditional, organic conception of local authority hymned by Newcastle. The resort of the gentry to the capital adversely affected local administration; but this was not seen as a mechanical activity, rather it was contextualised with the gentry's paternalist obligations, particularly to offer hospitality. An absentee gentry, the King insisted, left 'the poorer sort . . . not guided or governed, as they might bee in case those persons of qualitie and respect resided among them'. Yet, while Charles's rhetoric emphasised a conservative conception of the relationship between centre and localities, the actual operation of his government did not consistently embody these declared ideals. Real power at the centre of Court and Council devolved upon a narrow clique of yes-men. They possessed little local influence that might smooth the acceptance of royal policies in the provinces; indeed, they seemed to share the King's indifference to the popularity of his policies locally. Newcastle himself attempted to play an intermediary role in Derbyshire and Nottinghamshire during the 'Personal Rule'. He found it a deeply frustrating experience that explains his jaundiced views of Charles's regime that he expressed in 1658. He was given no voice in the creation of policy, his personal services went unacknowledged, he could do little to advance the interests of the locality at Westminster. He was simply a functionary, a conduit for the demands of a seemingly remote government. In 1630 he complained bitterly to Wentworth that his involvement in the rigorous enforcement of an unpopular policy, the knighthood fines, was losing him local respect. 'If your Lordship and I loose our Countries and have but little thankes above neither, wee have taken a great deal of paynes in vayne,' he wrote. Lord Castleton, promoting the same fiscal expedient in Lincolnshire, made a similarly bleak comment; 'my reward is the perpetuall losse of my countryes love'.[5]

Newcastle was obviously correct to emphasise the shift in relationships between the centre and the localities under James and Charles. His argument that they were uniquely responsible for the subversion of the organic political networks he praised is more dubious. At the turn of the sixteenth century, when, in Newcastle's opinion, Shrewsbury was the embodiment of a functioning system, others were already lamenting its decline. One voice in this chorus was that of Elizabeth's favourite, the Earl of Essex. From the mid-1580s Essex deliberately sought to build up powerful networks in the localities, particularly in Wales and in its border counties. In 1598 Susan Morgan complained to the Earl that his clients among the Carmarthenshire gentry, 'them that wears your honour's cloth in this country', were abusing the positions that they monopolised through his patronage. 'With their offices and brags they oppress all her Highness's poor subjects.' Yet Essex saw these endeavours as a last-ditch effort to re-create a social order that was seriously threatened by developments in Elizabethan government. He portrayed himself as the embattled defender of a traditional political community, a fraternity or caste defined by lineage, military virtue, and personal honour. He and his followers, 'the flower of the nobility and gentry of England' as he saw it, were were being ousted from their due authority by the pettyfogging bureaucrats and lawyers, 'base-born upstarts', of the *Regnum Cecilium* who dominated the Court and controlled the Queen. A new form of political authority, abstract and legalistic, had arisen; it was deeply subversive of personal and lineage allegiances and of the code of chivalric honour. Ironically, the failure of Essex's attempted rising might be thought to validate his diagnosis. In the localities, even in the Devereux strongholds in Wales, the networks so carefully fostered by Essex and his steward, Sir Gelli Meyrick, remained quiescent.[6]

Both Newcastle and Essex argued that the traditional norms of political culture had been subverted and displaced. Both attributed responsibility to the monarchy. Their views are hardly compatible, yet, in their emphasis upon the role of the Crown, both have much to recommend them. The transformation of political values is a complex and by no means unilinear process to which the policies of the Tudors were as important as those for which Newcastle excoriated their successors.

## 6.1 THE HONOUR COMMUNITY

We must not attribute a consistently anti-noble policy to the Tudor monarchs. The benefits of the chain of communication and authority delineated by Newcastle, the fact that a magnate could stabilise a region, were very apparent to them. The first two Tudor kings had been deeply suspicious of the authority wielded by the earls of Northumberland in the north-east and had sought to undermine Percy predominance in the region. But when Sir William Lisle of Felton, a client of the Percies and 'kyned and allied' of many of the border gentry, having fallen foul of the royal authorities, commenced a campaign of violence and terror as an outlaw, both the Sheriff of Northumberland and the King's Lieutenant of the Middle March proved powerless to check his activities. The Sheriff's own lands had been plundered by Lisle and his adherents; the Lieutenant cowered in Harbottle Castle, complaining that most of the local gentry refused to assist him against Lisle. Only when Wolsey restored the sixth Earl of Northumberland to the posts traditionally enjoyed by his family was Lisle persuaded to surrender. Sir William's original offence, which escalated into outlawry and treason, had sprung from a minor boundary squabble with a neighbouring gentleman. It was the kind of dispute that had flourished in Northumberland since the eclipse of the Percy family in 1489; the kind of dispute that a resident magnate would have been able to mediate. A similar situation occurred in East Anglia after the fall of the Duke of Norfolk in 1572. The Norfolk gentry were deprived of the monolithic presence, the autocrat, of their traditional political world. The community was shattered by a factitious competition for precedence and to discover and monopolise new routes to the patronage of the Crown.[7]

The Tudor monarchs destroyed a number of the magnates whom they distrusted. But they also sought, through often lavish grants of land and office, to build the local power of those of the aristocracy, some of their own creation, upon whose loyalty they could rely. After the execution of the Marquis of Exeter, the dominant magnate in south-western England, in 1538, Henry VIII created a substantial landed endowment for his servant, John, Lord Russell, from royal and monastic estates, clearly intending to fill the vacuum left by the fall of Exeter. The power of the Stanleys in the north-west, of the Talbots in the north and the Comptons in the south midlands, of the Herberts in south Wales, of the Howards in East Anglia; all had been consolidated and reinforced under – often, by – the early Tudor kings. In 1550 it was still possible to think of England as, in Dr Bernard's phrase, 'a confederation of noble fiefdoms'. Elizabeth continued to rely heavily upon the retinues of her peers to form the core of 'royal' armies to suppress insurrection or to defend the realm from invasion. The Queen's noble favourites, Leicester, and, as we have seen, Essex, developed their bases of territorial authority, reinforcing their inherited estates with royal grants, and building up a clientele among the local gentry by their distribution of royal patronage and access to royal favour.[8]

But, if the Tudors displayed no consistent hostility to aristocracy, they did seek to inculcate an attitude whereby, first, loyalty to the Crown took priority over other ties and, second, the Crown was seen as the ultimate guarantor of justice. This was necessary not only to prevent networks of local gentry from following their magnate 'good lords' into rebellion, but to ensure good government when magnates had been displaced. The eclipse of the Percies had not ensured royal authority in the north; rather, it had given free rein to men like Sir William Lisle, who, when asked 'have we not a God and a King to live under', responded with an oath 'there is nother King nor his officers that shall . . . have ado within the liberties of Felton'.[9]

The first two Tudor kings sought to achieve these ends by offering a direct and personal connection to important local gentlemen, the positions of esquire or knight of the body. This, by intruding royal power into the network of clientage and alliance, short-circuited the natural devolution of authority into the localities through a magnate intermediary. So in the north the Radcliffes of Derwentwater and Forsters of Adderstone, Northumberland, the Constables of Flamborough and Hothams of Scorborough, Yorkshire, the Curwens of Workington, Cumberland, were all families with traditional ties to the Percy family, holding either land or offices from them; another great Cumbrian gentry family, the Musgraves, were part of the clientele of the Lords Dacre. But between 1490 and 1520 leading members of all these families are found attached to the royal household. Some combined their royal posts with service to the magnates – Sir Edward Ratcliff was one of the fifth Earl of Northumberland's council; Sir John Hotham was a troop commander under him – but their posts as knights of the body to Henry VIII obviously muddied ties of allegiance. Henry VIII used the Court of Star Chamber, both directly and indirectly, to reinforce the principle of primary allegiance to the Crown. In 1519 Sir William Bulmer was prosecuted for wearing the livery of the Duke of Buckingham in the royal presence, though a sworn servant of the King. Star Chamber was also employed to discipline those of the nobility whose local authority the Crown distrusted. When Sir John Hotham and Sir Robert Constable, both ex-Percy dependents who had become knights of the body, fell foul of Northumberland, they appealed to Star Chamber, emphasising that the Earl's 'greate poure and myght in that countrie' gave them little prospect of securing local justice. Northumberland was forced to a humiliating submission. The power of the Crown was felt by the northern gentry communities directly; the intermedial authority of the area's traditional rulers was challenged. In 1537 the royal agent in the north-west explained the shifting pattern of local allegiances to Thomas Cromwell. 'In the late lord Dacre's time there was a cry "a Dacre, a Dacre" and afterwards "a Clifford, a Clifford". . . Now only "a King, a King".'[10]

The first two Tudor kings had challenged and eroded magnate clienteles by the direct and personal introduction of royal authority into the localities: gentlemen were bound to the monarch by intensely personal ties of allegiance, they experienced royal favour or displeasure very directly in patronage or punishment. Elizabeth lacked the resources either of supervision or reward to continue this policy effectively. Earlier prohibitions might be repeated and enforced, such as the order of 1595 that no retainer was to be appointed as a JP – an order much resented by the Earl of Essex: he was 'very loath to leave the name of Master to so manie honest gentlemen in Wales'. Noblemen who engaged in disputes with their gentry neighbours might discover, as did the Earl of Shrewsbury in his feud with Sir Thomas Stanhope of Shelford, Nottinghamshire, in 1593, that the Privy Council tended to favour his opponent. Lord Buckhurst told the Earl that the government was, on principle, reluctant to add to the power of the magnates and thought it 'both justice, equity and wisdome to take care that the weaker part be not put down by the mightier'. Yet the breakdown of a number of the shires, such as Norfolk, into feuding factions of local gentlemen competing for prestige and power, showed that the erosion of magnate networks left a vacuum that could be damaging to the effective government of the provinces. This the Crown endeavoured to fill by asserting and seeking to inculcate more abstract ideals of royal authority and of the duty of the gentry as local governors.

## 6.2 THE COMMONWEALTH

We have already examined the Elizabethan government's endeavours to educate the gentry on their specific legal and administrative responsibilities as local magistrates. We must now analyse the political content of these various official pronouncements. These take a number of forms: Proclamations, the charges of the judges at the county assizes, addresses to Parliament and in the Star Chamber. The series of elegant speeches delivered to MPs and JPs by Sir Nicholas Bacon, Lord Keeper 1559–1576, provides good examples of the central concerns of government rhetoric in this period. In his speeches Bacon invited his gentry audiences to join the Queen in a noble co-operative endeavour to ensure 'the good governance of the realm'. It was the duty of all subjects to endeavour to secure 'the preservacion of the common weale'. 'Private wealth's devise' was the target of all Bacon's speeches; it was one of 'the greatest adversayes that can be to unitie and concorde without which no common wealthe can longe endure and stande'. MPs and JPs were enjoined to set aside all narrowly personal interests, for these were invariably destructive of the common good. The gentry owed a duty to God, to the Queen, to 'your Contrie whose weale it concerneth universallye,' to act in Parliament or on the bench 'without respect of honour, rule or soveraignetie, profett, pleasure or ease . . . and without regarde of all other manner of private affection'. The assertion that subjects in general and the gentry in particular must seek to defend and advance the commonwealth was reinforced by the argument that the Queen did no less. Elizabeth, Bacon argued, dedicated her time, her energy, her resources to 'the preservacion of the common weale committed to her chardge'. The mutual involvement of the Queen and her subjects in furthering the common good was symbolically represented in Parliament. Bacon occasionally, particularly when requesting subsidies, went beyond this emphasis on mutuality to suggest that there was a reciprocal obligation between the Queen and her subjects. Elizabeth 'daylie doth employe her owne treasure . . . in the service of her realme'; she did not waste it in 'glorious tryumphes' or 'superfluous and sumptuous buildeinges of delighte': her subjects should recognise their consequent obligation to provide taxation. The theory of the commonwealth stressed the individual's duty to promote the common good, sacrificing personal considerations to that end. It emphasised that the monarch had a similar duty. Finally, Bacon argued that the rights and responsibilities of all within the commonwealth, including the Queen, were defined by a common law.[12]

These themes were not merely the stuff of government rhetoric. They were reinforced by the schooling of the gentry. Renaissance theorists had seen the service to the commonwealth as one of the chief goals of education, and their priorities were emphasised in the formal curricula of the grammar schools and the developing tutorial system of the universities. The spell at the Inns of Court that became an element of the education of many scions of gentry families developed some familiarity with language and substantive conventions of the common law. One of the key goals of the full gamut of education – university, Inns of Court, foreign travel – was, Wandesford informed his son, to instruct 'how to assist in the Government of Your Countrey'. Works that could reinforce and develop the lessons of youth were readily available from London or from provincial booksellers. The Kentish gentry had been praised for being 'acquainted with good letters' and 'trained in the knowledge of the lawes' in Elizabeth's reign, and by the 1630s there was a 'large and flourishing school of gentlemen scholars' within the shire. What this meant for local political culture appears in the events following the Maidstone Assizes early in 1637. The presiding judge had defended Charles's right to levy ship-money; after the conclusion of proceedings, according to Sir Roger

Twysden, the gentry got copies of the charge, 'retyred to their country houses', and reflected on the matter. They did so in the light of their extensive library holdings of law treatises, of works of political theory, and of chronicles and histories both of England and other polities.[13]

The Elizabethan government invited the gentry to participate actively in a co-operative endeavour, the advancement of the commonwealth. The gentry employed a similar language in their addresses to the lower ranks of society. William Lambarde's, charges to village officers and local juries contain a similar emphasis on the duty of all subjects to gear their efforts to upholding the common good, threatened by the 'sensuality', the 'unsatiable avarice and niggishness', of a minority of selfish individuals. That duty takes priority over all other ties to kinsmen, neighbours or landlords: in these 'common causes and public services' a jury of the 'honest and meaner sort' were exhorted in 1587 that they should not 'be afraid to join with God, her Majesty and the realm against any few . . . whatsoever'. As with Bacon, Lambarde suggests that the duty owed the Queen is reciprocal: a return for the benefits of Elizabeth's rule, not least that 'our country laws and liberties . . . are freely yielded unto us'. In the 1620s similar themes were employed in similar contexts. Sir Thomas Wentworth, addressing the subsidymen at Rotherham, depicted good government as 'a a most happy union twixt the King and his people' and argued that taxation was a return for the 'manifold blessings appropriated to this estate and commonwealthe' by the King. Sir Richard Grovesnor, in speeches at the sessions and to the freeholders at a county election, emphasised that lesser men, even 'the meanest of you', bore a responsibility for the good of the commonwealth. Men should do their duty as jurors or electors without fear of the powerful or affection for friends.[14]

The language of the commonwealth, vigorously promoted by the officers of Elizabeth's government in an effort to educate the gentry in their obligations, was, however, a two-edged sword. The rhetoric had been employed first in mid-fifteenth-century England by the opponents of the inept government of Henry VI, and it had retained a critical dimension in Henry VIII's reign. Late in Elizabeth's reign the government found itself being challenged from within the conventions of its favoured language. Lord Keeper Bacon had contrasted the public good of the commonwealth with the selfish and anti-social ends of individuals, and had portrayed the Queen as tireless in her efforts to uphold the former. What if individuals close to the Queen, within the Court, could be accused of self-aggrandisement? In 1571 some MPs spoke against royal grants to projectors whereby 'a fewe were enriched and the multitude impoverished'. This kind of attack multiplied in the last years of Elizabeth's reign, as the government, reeling under the fiscal burden of war, sought to find new, dubious sources of revenue that it – or its creditors, or favoured royal servants – might exploit. The response, in a period of high war taxation and economic crisis, was a predictable outcry against the depredations of projectors, monopolists and purveyors: an outcry that, with Bacon, contrasted private greed with the public good, but that suggested that the latter was being assailed by elements of the Court. The degree to which the rhetoric of the 'commonwealth' had been hijacked by critics of the Court appears in the debate on Monopolies in 1601. Nothing is 'more dangerous to the Commonwealth than the granting of these monopolies'; monopolists were 'bloodsuckers of the Commonwealth': a Commons committee discussing the issue was besieged by a group 'who said they were Commonwealth men' and who desired MPs to 'take compassion . . . they being spoiled, imprisoned and robbed by monopolists'.[15]

## 6.3 COURT AND COUNTRY

Elizabeth skilfully distanced herself from these attacks. She attributed the abuses in purveyance to a few rogue officers and an inefficient bureaucracy. She asserted that she had only issued monopolies that she believed to be 'good and beneficial to the subject in general', and that she had been misled by 'varlets and lewd persons'.[16] James, without the excuse of war, and with an increasing burden of debt that was largely the consequence of personal extravagance and a profligate Court, was less able to insulate himself from attacks on the shady figures who continued to prey on his subjects. In consequence, the rhetoric of the commonwealth was increasingly appropriated by critics of the Court, and with the Court as a whole as its target. A language that had been developed by the government in its endeavours to educate the gentry in their national responsibilities became a major plank in that political attitude we may describe as 'country' and that dominates gentry suspicions of the reigns of James I and his son.

The distinction between Court and country was employed by writers of the Tudor period. In contrasting the straightforward simplicity of life in the country with the artifice, novelty, dissimulation and extravagance of the courtier, as did Spenser, when he wrote of Calidore's resolution to

> set his rest amongst the rusticke sort
> Rather than hunt still after shadowes vaine
> Of courtly favour fed with light report
> Of every blast

they were employing a literary trope with impeccable classical antecedents. It may have appealed to the gentry, reading their Virgil at university, for that reason. For some, like Sir John Harington, it resonated with their own experience of the failure to acquire Court perquisites. Yet, while Elizabethan gentlemen warned their sons of the dangers of Court roulette, they did not perceive the Court as a political threat. By James's reign this was being done. The Court was the centre of not just of opulence, of vice, of sycophancy and of self-seeking, but of schemes deeply destructive of English law, government and religion. The country stood, not only for rustic virtues, but for the traditional ideals of the commonwealth and of common law – the very ideals that Elizabeth's ministers had found so lacking in the gentry and which they had sought to cultivate among them so assiduously. Government spokesmen resented the polarisation of language, and the imputation that came with it; in 1626 Sir George Goring, a client of the Duke of Buckingham's, 'tooke exception how the name of Courtyer was a woyrd of faccion, and how he thought that Courtyers were as honest men as any'. Yet they were obliged to recognise its powerful hold. Francis Bacon believed that a general attack on monopolies could be avoided in the 1621 Parliament if the government could plant a moderate reforming scheme with 'some grave and discreet gentlemen of the country, such as have least relation to the court' and get them to propose it to the Commons.[17]

The tendency to see politics in terms of a competition between Court and country, with the latter as the defender of traditional virtues, laws and government against an aggressive and unscrupulous Court, was enhanced by the dissemination of news among the gentry in the seventeenth century. While the Duke of Newcastle's belief that if there was a prohibition on newsletters rustic squires would quickly revert to the more traditional, and appropriate, topics of conversation, 'Hunting & Hawkeing, Boling, Cocking & such things', was naive, his sense of the importance of the accessibility of news in the localities in the undermining of the Stuart regime carries conviction.[18]

Sixteenth-century gentlemen had sought the latest news from London and the Court from their relatives, legal agents or business partners who were in the city. So Richard Bagot received a series of letters from his brother-in-law, an officer in the household of the Earl of Essex, concerning his master's local business, but also relaying the national and international news from 1577 to 1594. Such letters would then be passed around among local friends. Charles Percy, vegetating in the country, begged a London friend for more letters; a knowledge of events, however stale in London, 'will make mee passe for a very sufficient gentleman in Glocestreshire'. Family and business connections remained the major sources for the acquisition of news in the reigns of James and Charles, but were supplemented, for the richer gentry, by the efforts of semi-professional journalists who produced newsletters and 'separates', for example copies of parliamentary speeches. John Pory, whose clients included the Warwickshire gentlemen, Sir Thomas Lucy and Sir Thomas Puckering, was paid £20 a year for his newsletter by Sir John Scudamore of Herefordshire. Again, these products were circulated in the localities; William Davenport of Bramhall, Cheshire, copied separates that he had been loaned by his friends into his commonplace book. The tenor of the news that was being purveyed by these semi-professionals is key to the developing political ideology of the gentry. They presented politics in terms of conflict, and a conflict in which one of the competitors, the Court, was depicted very negatively. This is illustrated in the collection of separates transcribed by Davenport. He was a backwoods squire; penurious, seldom leaving his estates, intellectually unsophisticated. Yet the news that he recorded is heavily biased, displaying the Court in a bleak light. His transcripts emphasised Court scandals and corruption – the sex-and-murder melodrama of the fall of Somerset – and on the statements of those who opposed James's pacific foreign policy and, under Charles, the dominance of Buckingham. There was little in his collection that presented the royal policies or entourage favourably, and this imbalance is typical of the bulk of the separate collections and the news diaries of the gentry.[19]

The developing political ideology of the 'country' was symbiotically related to the evolution of two other institutions in which the gentry were vitally involved. The first was Parliament: there were significant shifts in the perception of its role, and the purpose of membership of it. The second involved the changing face of the institutions of local justice and government, particularly the assizes and quarter sessions.

In the Tudor period the gentry 'swarmed' into Parliament. Not only the county seats, but those of the old parliamentary boroughs, and those of towns newly enfranchised by the Crown, were taken by gentlemen. Some 80 per cent of the 372 so-called 'burgesses' in the late Elizabethan House of Commons were country gentlemen. Their reasons for seeking seats were complex: to advance personal or local interests – such as changing the terms of estate settlements, or permitting the draining of land – by passing private bills; to make contact with counsellors or courtiers, and thus to secure a patronage connection with the centre. Some sought an opportunity to sample the pleasures of London and the Court: 'I am one that loves to see fashions and desires to know wonders,' wrote Thomas Bulkeley, announcing his candidacy for Beaumaris. Some saw a seat in Parliament as an essential part of their education; Sir Henry Bagnell begged a kinsman to secure him a seat 'for my learning's sake'. Prestige was also deeply involved, particularly in the elections for the county seats. To be the premier knight of the shire – the man named first on the writ returned by the sheriff – was a high accolade, and competition for the place could be fierce. Those named second on the county return often expressed resentment; those defeated in shire elections were mortified. The gentry allies of Edward Denny of Stortford, beaten in the 1584 Hertfordshire election, writhed as the supporters of the successful candidates celebrated – 'such a ringing of bells as yet sound in my ears'. They consoled themselves by affirming their continued alliance, and contemplating success in 'a new field upon a new occasion'. Finally, we must note that the ideology of the 'commonwealth', or at least its rhetoric, had entered the process of parliamentary selection. Many candidates, seeking the support of their fellow gentry or of the freeholders, announced their desire to serve the public, 'moved in duty,' as a Herefordshire man wrote, 'to her Majesty and the Commonwealth'.[20]

In the early seventeenth century the motives of those who sought a seat in Parliament remained various. Selection was still a litmus of local prestige – a fact nicely caught in Sir Robert Harley's insistence that he should be named premier knight for Herefordshire in 1626; *he* was a knight of the Bath: his competitor, though he had received the accolade before him, a mere knight. Membership was still valued as an educational experience and an opportunity to make or reinforce personal contacts: in 1624 Sir Henry Savile sought a seat out of 'A desire to see my honorable Friends in the South'; two years later Sir George Chudleigh determined to 'give my son a little breeding' in the House of Commons. But the rhetoric of the commonwealth and, beyond it, the polarising language of Court/country, played a greater role. Candidates increasingly emphasised their credentials to represent the country, often in terms of the hostility that the Court had displayed towards them. In the 1620 Yorkshire election, Sir John Savile, alleging that his dismissal from the commission of the peace was a punishment for speaking against Impositions in the 1614 Parliament, presented himself to the voters as 'their Martyr, having suffered for them'. In Cornwall and Essex in 1628 the candidacies of those who had resisted the forced loan was promoted by emphasising that they had 'suffered for their country'. Privy counsellors faced an increasingly uphill struggle to secure election to the shire seats that had been theirs almost for the asking in the Elizabethan period. In the 1620 Yorkshire election it was alleged that Secretary of State Calvert's ties to the Court made him 'not safe to be trusted by the Country'. In 1626 John Winthrop nominated Naunton, his superior in the Court of Wards, as knight for Suffolk, 'I suppose there wilbe no exception against him, except for that he is a privie Counsellor, which may easily be removed by consideration of what he hath formerly suffered for the Commonwealth'. And, he argued further, such a man might be a useful contact for the depressed Suffolk cloth industry. Sir Francis Crane reported a cool response in the county; Naunton's position meant that he would not easily be able 'to speke for the Country', and there was a general reluctance among the gentry to select 'anye cortier'. By 1640 the canard that a man had Court affiliations could be fatal to his candidacy. Sir Edward Dering, reflecting darkly on his defeat in the spring, listed a series of rumours – many contradictory – assiduously disseminated by his opponents: the clincher was 'Is a courtier'.[21]

The changing perspective on the choice of MPs was related to a shift in their self-perception. They were representatives of the country, and their task was to inform the king of the concerns and grievances of the localities that returned them. By 1640 they came bearing petitions from their constituents, often subscribed at the election. Once in the House of Commons they presented these grievances, and they responded to royal requests for subsidies from an ostensibly local perspective, emphasising the poverty of the localities, or assessing the value of the concessions offered by the Crown to their constituencies. In 1614, for example, the King's bills of grace were reckoned inadequate to merit a grant of a subsidy, 'I heard a knight say he would not give 3d for them'. Finally, MPs felt obliged to inform those they represented of the achievements and difficulties of the sessions in which they sat. Sir Thomas Wentworth recognised that the Yorkshire subsidymen would be troubled by the voting of taxes before any legislation had passed, that 'we have given away your money and made noe lawes'. In response, he outlined the proposed statutes, and claimed that the impeachment of the monopolist, Sir Giles Mompesson, was of 'more safety to the Commonwealth' than any six recent statutes.[22]

The term 'country' was an ideal-type. It indicated a concatenation of virtues; it was an evocative symbol, but imprecise and often defined negatively – as anti-Court. It entailed some sense of geographical location beyond innocent rusticity. However, this was, as an analysis of parliamentary rhetoric suggests, of an ambiguous kind. When MPs spoke as representatives of the country, they might mean either the community of the realm, or, more narrowly, their neighbourhoods or localities. Or both conjoined, as in Sir George More's sonorous description of the lower House in 1614 as 'sent hither from all the commons of the kingdom; our principal care to speak from the Commonwealth that continually speaks to us'.[23] A similar ambiguity occurs in relation to the second institutional development, of quarter sessions and assizes, that interacted with the shifting ideology of the country.

The quarter sessions and, more particularly, the biannual assizes, brought large numbers of the gentry together. They were important social occasions. Owen Wynn, writing to his father Sir John from Conway and Caernarfon, described not only the litigation of the Courts of Great Sessions, but the business deals and marriage negotiations that were considered there, and the local scandals that were avidly discussed. William Windham's half-sister, writing about the 1688 Norfolk Assizes, focused entirely on the 'good company' gathered in Norwich, the gossip circulating, the disappointing dearth of 'amours'; she concluded by sneering at the Sheriff's inadequate provision of balls and other appropriate entertainments. Other agendas were less frivolous: the Assizes and Quarter Sessions at Warwick were an opportunity for those with local antiquarian interests to discuss their projects, and to solicit the assistance of their fellow gentry with their research.[24]

Between the provision of royal justice which these meetings were designed to secure, and the socialising and private negotiation that focused upon them as a consequence of the gathering of the local gentry, another class of business developed. Quarter sessions and assizes became forums for the discussion of the public business of the shire, and for the representation of local concerns to the central government. The process is apparent in the reign of Elizabeth. In 1579 the Kentish magistrates, met together at the Assizes, drew up a common response to the Privy Council's demand that money should be raised in the county for the repair of Dover Harbour. From 1589 to 1591 the JPs used quarter sessions and assizes at Norwich and Bury to organise local resistance to Sir Arthur Heveningham's patent empowering him to undertake road repairs in Norfolk and Suffolk, and to rate the counties for this purpose. In 1592 the Cornish fishing industry was subject to the attentions of Captain Henry Warner, whose service to the Queen had been rewarded by a monopoly on the export of salted fish. The fisherman complained to the JPs at the assizes, and the magistrates as a body publicly implored the Privy Council to rescind the patent which was so damaging to local interests. In all these cases the magistrates appropriated the language of the common law and the commonwealth to express their opposition. The Cornish JPs begged the Council to prefer 'the love and weale publicke of us . . . poore subiects' to the enrichment of an individual. The Norfolk and Suffolk magistrates challenged Heveningham to test his patent at law, insisted that the precedent that it created was 'so offensive', and portrayed Sir Arthur as a man from whom 'our commonwelth will still receyve oppression'.[25]

By the 1620s quarter sessions and assizes had developed further as 'focuses for a county's aspirations, as congresses . . . for the formulation of its views, and as institutions through which these views could be communicated to the Council', to quote Professor A.H. Smith. Several counties had begun to employ not just petitions from the magistrates but presentments of the grand jury or the hundred juries to indicate the weight of local sentiment in relation to central policy. In Essex, which had been precocious in this development with the juries being employed to legitimise the county's agreements concerning payments in lieu of purveyance from 1606, the implicit theoretical justification was explicity asserted in 1627. The JPs approached the grand jury, 'being the representative body of this countie and drawne together from all the partes thereof', seeking 'the consent of the countrie' to a royal request for a levy: it was denied. A series of grand jury presentments from a variety of counties critical of royal policy were forwarded to Westminster in the course of the next decade: Hertfordshire and Northamptonshire protested against religious innovations; Somerset, Herefordshire, Staffordshire and Essex against ship-money. The dissolution of the Short Parliament saw more such petitions, yet more daring in their rhetoric. The Berkshire grand jury complained of grievances 'deriving their authoritie from your majestie but beeing directly contrarie to your majesties lawes established in this kingdom'.[26]

Some historians, impressed by the role of quarter sessions and assizes as fora for the discussion and presentation of local grievances, have written of them as county 'parliaments', and seen them as indicative of the intense localism of political culture in an England that can be described as 'a union of partially independent county-states'. Yet while such meetings provided the fullest expression of the corporate identity of the county community they cannot be understood in purely local terms. The prime function of these institutions was the enforcement of a national system of law, and the minutiae and procedures of that system were, as we have seen, increasingly insisted upon by the lawyers who discussed, practised in, or presided over these courts, and followed by the gentry magistrates. The assize judges, chief 'oracles of the law ', were also charged with informing the localities of the law-enforcement, administrative, religious and political priorities of the Crown. So from the mid-1630s Charles used the assizes as an opportunity to promulgate the legal arguments in favour of his right to collect ship-money. Sir Roger Twysden recorded the keen attention paid to Baron Weston's charge on that theme at Maidstone early in 1637, and the 'kind of dejection in their very lookes' with which his fellow magistrates responded to its arguments. The opinions of 'the country' were formally voiced in assizes and sessions through petitions from the bench or grand jury presentments, but these opinions were not those of men blinkered to 'wider political issues', of those 'simply not concerned with affairs of state'. The gentry were well informed, not least by the Crown itself, while responses to unpalatable royal schemes were expressed within the language of common law and the good of the commonwealth.[27]

The degree to which country ideology provided the dominant language of gentry political culture in the first half of the seventeenth century is perhaps indicated by the ways in which it was deployed or cynically manipulated by those intent on the pursuit of personal or sectional interests. In 1624 North Wales was subject to the attentions of a courtier armed with a royal commission to collect fees, long-forgotten and unpaid, ostensibly on the King's behalf. Sir William Thomas and Sir John Wynn discussed their tactics. Should they, as 'good country and commonswealthmen' raise the issue at the highest level and as an issue of principle? Perhaps it would be best to make preliminary moves in this direction, hoping to reach an agreement at a lower rate. 'If I could escape for a small matter,' Thomas wrote, 'I would not stand in opposition.' A similarly keen awareness of the potency of the language emerges in several counties in early Stuart England that were as divided by factional strife as Elizabethan Wiltshire or Lincolnshire. In these later contests both sides sought to appropriate the 'country' accolade, and denounce their opponents as courtiers. Yorkshire was fractured by the feud between Sir Thomas Wentworth and the choleric Sir John Savile, each with his 'bande of reyters' among the gentry. Its spirit is nicely caught in Wentworth's remark during the 1620–1 election campaign: should Savile win 'faith we might be reputed men of small power and esteem in the country'. Both competitors were ambitious of recognition and preferment beyond Yorkshire, and cultivated patronage at the centre. Yet in the county both employed country rhetoric. In 1621 Wentworth ran for election with Calvert, the Secretary of State, and Savile campaigned against the return of a courtier as 'not safe to be trusted by the Country'. After 1625 Savile's careful cultivation of contacts with Buckingham began to pay dividends in the conduct of his feud. Wentworth was appointed Sheriff in 1626 to disable him from seeking election to Parliament, then dismissed from his posts as *custos* and JP. But Court favour had its costs. Savile's active engagement in the King's schemes for raising extra-parliamentary revenue in 1626 and 1627, and Wentworth's resistance to them, enabled Sir Thomas to claim sympathy as a 'Patriot' and 'Martyr', the titles accorded Sir John seven years before.[28]

Somerset politics bore some resemblances to those of Yorkshire, dominated by a feud between Sir Robert Phelips and John Poulett. In origin, the conflict turned on issues of personal prestige. The two men, neighbours and once intimate friends, had fallen out over the 1614 shire election, when Phelips claimed that Poulett's perfidy had occasioned his humiliating defeat. However, the subsequent course of the contest was dictated by Phelips's strong country affiliations. He cultivated the respect of his peers and the countryfolk as a vigorous magistrate, ever prepared to attend to their problems and promote local interests: so in 1635, as 'the countries only friende', Phelips organised the protests concerning the rating of the county for ship-money. In Parliament, and he sat in every session from 1604 to 1629 except that of 1625–6 when the King guaranteed his absence by appointing him sheriff, Phelips was an effective spokesman for country opinion. His 1623 'Discourse . . . betweene a Counsellor of State and a countrey gentleman' was a powerful defence of Parliament, common law and the commonwealth against 'the languadge of the Court'. Phelips's stand obliged Poulett to move ever closer to the Court in the conduct of the feud, and he became a vigorous proponent of Charles's policies in the county. He received some rewards: a peerage in 1628, the effective command of the county's militia – though never the seat on the Privy Council after which he hankered. Yet even in Somerset, where the court–country division was less ambiguous than in Yorkshire, the language could still be used for factious purposes. So in 1628 Poulett disseminated the rumour that his rival had turned courtier, 'upon design,' the exasperated Phelips protested, 'to withdraw the good opinion of the country from me'.[29]

The case of Poulett raises another issue. The polarised language of Court-country might dominate political discussion, even as no more than a smokescreen for private or factional ambitions. But not all the gentry automatically affiliated with the country position. In Parliament in 1628, reflecting on the work of the deputy lieutenants in billeting, raising coat and conduct money, and enforcing the arbitrary loan demanded by the king, Phelips spoke bitterly of a 'decemvirate in every county'. The suggestion that every shire contained a potent clique absolutely committed to the Court's policies is clearly an exaggeration. Yet Phelips's words, not surprisingly, seem apposite to the situation in Somerset, and to some other counties such as Cornwall and Yorkshire. In each case a local boss – Poulett, Savile, and, in Cornwall, Sir James Bagg – who had allied with Buckingham, secured the dismissal of his rivals, and ruled the county in association with a cadre of like-minded gentlemen.

It is tempting to see such men as unprincipled adventurers, ambitious of authority to humiliate local rivals and of access to the pork-barrel of Court patronage. Bagg outdid both Poulett and Savile in this respect, creeping obsequiously to Buckingham, profiting from the abuse of government posts and contracts, purveying venomous gossip to his Court contacts against 'those who love not my Lord Duke'. Some of their close associates were from the same mould. They included men of irascible and violent temper like Sir John Stawell in Somerset and Sir Reginald Mohun in Cornwall, ready to use their power to avenge earlier reverses: and men eager to exploit royal patronage, like Mohun's son, John, whose post in the Stannaries gave him rich opportunities for extortion and who endorsed his official warrants 'to this submit or you will provoke me'. Other counties saw similar figures rise to prominence in the 1620s. Sir Nicholas Sanderson was cordially loathed by his Lincolnshire neighbours for his depredations as a landlord, and for his self-interested abuse of the local offices he held; his behaviour as sheriff, as subsidy commissioner, and as JP had all been the subject of complaints in James's reign. Yet despite his record of partiality and peculation, he became an enthusiastic executor of Charles's policies in Lincolnshire, collecting the forced loan and ship-money in 1627, and the knighthood composition in 1631. Sir Edward Heron of Surfleet, his colleague, if less predatory, was no less self-interested: royal favour was crucial to the various schemes for marsh drainage in the Wash area in which he was involved. Another interest group, those of suspiciously Catholic connection, like Sir Thomas Wiseman in Essex, whose son was a recusant, or Sir William Alford in the East Riding, a gentleman who kept 'company much with Papists', also became active in the execution of Charles's schemes in several counties.[30]

In the 1628 Parliament Sir Richard Grovesnor denounced those gentlemen who had been vigorous agents in the collection of the Forced Loan: 'some papists, some mad men of a more pliable disposition, ready . . . to act whatsoever shall be commanded them'. Papists and mad men is a nice characterisation, apt for men like Alford or Stawell, but it does not incorporate all those who were prepared to administer the policies that followed from the 'new counsels' of the King. Other very industrious administrators in the

1620s, like Sir John Hare in Norfolk, Sir Thomas Jervoise in Hampshire, Sir Ralph Hopton in Somerset, and Sir Thomas Pope in Oxfordshire, seem to have had no obvious personal or sectional axes to grind. Some of these men were intimate with courtiers, like Sir Thomas Denton in Buckinghamshire, the friend of Sir Edmund Verney; others, like Thomas Harington, a diligent justice and the local expert on the financial arrangements within Lincolnshire, were motivated by concepts of duty and service.

A number of those gentlemen who were prepared to serve Charles in the administration of his various fiscal schemes in the 1620s and 30s offered some justification for their actions. They might express their intense devotion to the monarchy, as did Poulett, 'who reverence the Majesty of Kyngs and their government'. They might accede to the constitutional principle, essentially that he was 'enforced by necessity . . . to which noe ordinary rules of law can be prescribed', with which Charles backed his levies. The King's demand for ship-money, Sanderson wrote, was 'unusuall and unexpected', but 'we must obey necessity'. None of this directly threatened, though it might practically subvert, the ideology of the commonwealth and the country to which most gentlemen subscribed. But some went further. Sir Edward Rodney of Rodney Stoke was one of the most vigorous of the Somerset governors in the 1620s. He pressed the 1626 benevolence at a public meeting of the subsidymen in terms of wartime necessity, and he returned to this theme as he sought to justify his actions as a Deputy Lieutenant to the 1628 Parliament, referring to 'the great power of Kings in arms, all which transcends the law'. In 1626 he argued that kings were 'the servants of the commonwealth', and that the good of the commonwealth demanded that the King be supplied. But there was another strand to his thinking, foreshadowed in the 1626 speech. Royal power, he argued, was in its origin patriarchal, and therefore 'the consent of the people was no more necessary than the consent of children to the paternal'. This brought Rodney close to the absolutist theories that had developed in clerical circles, largely in the context of academic dispute with Catholic Resistance theorists, in the early seventeenth century, and which had been deployed by some divines to defend Charles's policies. These views received one of their fullest, most intransigent and influential expositions from the pen of a country gentleman, Sir Robert Filmer. Filmer was not active in local government, but his treatise *Patriarcha*, first drafted in the late 1620s, was circulated among the Kentish coterie of gentlemen scholars of which Sir Robert himself was a member.[31]

Such views found few exponents among gentlemen before 1640, however. Gentry opposition to them emerged in the outright refusal of some to pay such levies as the Forced Loan or, though less frequently, ship-money, and they might rejoice in their subsequent punishment, as did Sir Bevill Greville, in their performance of 'the duty of an honest Englishman'. More might seek to avoid such direct confrontation, making themselves scarce when loans were demanded, or objecting not to the principle of the levy but to the fairness of its execution. Sir Robert Phelips was an adroit practitioner of such tactics, journeying to London as the Forced Loan was put in execution in the county, and complaining incessantly about the sheriffs' rating policies for Somerset's ship-money. Others refused to participate in the practical enforcement of the objectionable expedient. During the Forced Loan many of those nominated as commissioners failed to serve, perhaps after a token show of involvement, once the supervisory role of the Privy Council waned. By July 1628 only two gentlemen were carrying the entire burden of collection in the Holland division of Lincolnshire; their colleagues, they noted with some bitterness, 'perchance have justifiable excuse'. A similar reluctance to act afflicted the Deputy Lieutenants of a number of counties as they were instructed to raise men, money and munitions for the war against the Scots in 1639–40, particularly after the failure of the Short Parliament. In Lincolnshire nine Deputy Lieutenants were initially involved in military affairs in the spring of 1639; the number rapidly fell to three. In June, invited by the Council to investigate the charges of corruption alleged against the professional officers who had taken command of the Lincolnshire militiamen, the Deputies displayed a revived enthusiasm and rapidly constructed a weighty dossier concerning bribery and peculation of Falstaffian proportions. In 1640 only two co-operated in the renewed efforts to raise an army, and their letters indicate their sense of alienation and isolation from their peers. By this time the Merionethshire Deputies had surrendered their commissions and refused to act, while those of many counties claimed that they could make no headway against a tide of popular hostility. In Somerset only three Deputy Lieutenants responded to the frenetic requests from the King: seven of their colleagues, including the 'absolutist' Sir Edward Rodney, refused to involve themselves, relying on a legal technicality, to justify their recalcitrance.[32] Deprived of the support of its 'columnes', the 'noble gentry', Charles's governmental structure collapsed: helpless, he was obliged to call the Long Parliament.

## 6.4 CIVIL WAR

In May 1642 as Thomas Knyvett of Ashwellthorpe was sauntering through Westminster he was greeted by one of the Norfolk MPs and presented with a commission, signed by the Lord Lieutenant of the county appointed by Parliament, instructing him to take command of an infantry trained-band. A few hours later he read the royal Proclamation against the Militia Ordinance, by the authority of which his commission was issued. 'Oh! sweete hart,' he wrote to his wife, 'I am now in a greate strayght what to doe.'[33]

The Long Parliament had met in a spirit of unanimity and optimism in November 1640. Eighteen months later King and Parliament were moving inexorably towards war, against a background of economic dislocation, unprecedented popular awareness of and engagement in the political process, and, in many areas, the breakdown of law and order. The horrors of civil war had been the theme of official propaganda since the sixteenth century, and such dire prophecies were given additional purchase by contemporary events on the continent – the 'German desolation' – and in Ireland. Domestic conflict was, as pamphleteers insisted ceaselessly, 'unnatural war'; it shattered all traditional and organic relationships; it divided families, friends, and neighbours; masters and servants, landlords and tenants. Thomas Knyvett was not alone in his dilemma, 'in a great strayght what to doe'.

Three issues had fractured the unity initially apparent in the Long Parliament. The first was constitutional. The radicals demanded further concessions from Charles, whose alleged involvement in a series of military plots and threatened coups, in 1641 and early 1642, displayed his essential untrustworthiness. In particular, they insisted that high officers of state and privy counsellors should be chosen in Parliament. Moderates believed that this represented too extreme a limitation on royal authority, and that the largely uncontentious legislative restrictions on the King's power – the Triennial Act, the destruction of the King's claim to tax without parliamentary consent, the abolition of the prerogative courts – sufficed. By mid-1642 Charles's advisers sought to portray him as the defender of the traditional balanced constitution, of the 'commonwealth' ideal, now threatened with subversion by radicals who were reducing the King to a cypher by making unprecedented claims for the unilateral authority of the House of Commons. This was the position to which a number of gentry MPs who had vigorously opposed royal fiscal expedients of the 1620s and 30s, men like Sir Francis Seymour and Sir John Strangways, were drawn. It also had some purchase among those gentlemen who were not involved in the debates and manoeuvres at Westminster. In Herefordshire and in Nottinghamshire the gentry informed their MPs – 'men chosen by us and entrusted for us to represent us' – that they could not accept the House's claim to legislate independently of the king, and they required them to vote against any further attempts to 'untwist that triple cord' of the sovereignty of King, Lords and Commons.[34]

The constitutional attitudes of the protagonists concerned the gentry, but their religious positions were of greater importance in the growing disillusionment with Parliament. The majority in the Commons had associated itself not merely with a purge of Laudian innovation but with a wholesale restructuring of the Church, and, in particular, the abandonment of episcopacy. This troubled many gentlemen. Debates in the Long Parliament were heated on this subject, and the defenders of the institution were supported by a series of petitions, often gentry-organised, from more than half the counties. Parliamentary speeches and petitions both stressed the antiquity of episcopacy and sought to difference the order as a whole from the occasional faults of particular men. Further, pro-episcopal opinion insisted, with Sir Henry Slingsby, that 'it were not safe to make alteration'. And here the religious concerns of some of the gentry dovetailed with their fears for the socially subversive consequences of the policies of Pym and his coterie. To assail episcopacy was to challenge an hierarchical institution, defended by tradition and the common law: it was thus an attack on the principle of order. And that principle was already strained. Sectarianism and religious experiment had been encouraged by Parliament's attacks on the Church, and by its countenancing popular involvement in the political process – welcoming petitions, publishing polemical accounts of its dealings with the King to win support. It was in this latter respect that Sir Edward Dering found the vote to publish the Grand Remonstrance so appalling: he 'did not dream that we should remonstrate downward, tell stories to the people'. Sir

Thomas Aston, the organiser of the Cheshire petition favouring episcopacy, best represents the conjunction of fears concerning Parliament's ecclesiastical policies and the challenge to the social order. Aston compared 'the Nobilitie and Gentrie of this Isle' to the drained lands of Holland, 'under the banks and bounds of the Lawes, secured from the inundations of that Ocean, the Vulgar, which by the breach of those bounds would quickly overwhelm us and deface all distinctions of degrees or persons.' For him the attack on the religious hierarchy and establishment was the prelude to a more general assault on privilege that was already beginning; those demanding freedom of conscience 'go higher, even to the denyall of the right of proprietie in our estates. They would pay no fines, do no boons, no duties to their landlords'. Sir John Strangways made the point succinctly: 'If we make a parity in the Church we must come to a parity in the Commonwealth.'[35]

In 1641 and 1642 many gentlemen were becoming disillusioned with the policies pursued by the dominant clique in Westminster. Those who, in Parliament and the localities, accepted the need to uphold Pym's programme even at the cost of civil war, were largely motivated by religious conviction. In counties where Puritanism was entrenched, the established leaders of the godly – Warwick and his long-standing gentry allies, Barrington and Masham, in Essex, that 'place of most life of religion in the land'; Sir Nathaniel Barnardiston in Suffolk – took control and smoothly incorporated the shires into the Parliamentary war-machine. In other areas a zealous minority, led by men like Sir William Brereton in Cheshire, Sir Robert Harley in Herefordshire, John Hutchinson in Nottinghamshire or Cromwell in Cambridgeshire, attempted to seize the machinery of county government in the face of local sentiment that ranged from indifference to outright hostility.[36]

In 1642 a minority of Parliamentarian gentlemen confronted another minority, the Royalists. The motives that led some men to join the King's army or to endeavour to control localities on his behalf in 1642 are more various than those of their opponents. Some had been active proponents of the King's 'new counsels' in the 1630s – Sir John Stawell and Sir Edward Rodney in Somerset; Sir Edward Heron in Lincolnshire. Some were persuaded by the constitutional position argued in Royalist propaganda; Sir Thomas Salusbury, having read Charles's declarations, and consulted both scripture and the chronicles of English history, joined the King. Some were deeply hostile to the religious policies encouraged by Westminster, like Aston, who struggled with Brereton for control of Cheshire. Some believed that personal honour obliged them to maintain the royal cause. Sir Edmund Verney, who carried the royal standard into battle at Edgehill and died there, 'did not like the quarrel', and wished that Charles would accede to Parliament's demands; but 'my conscience is . . . concerned in honour and gratitude to follow my master'. The demands of gentry honour were emphasised more positively by Royalist divines: 'A complete cavalier is a child of honour. He is the only reserve of English gentility and ancient valour, and hath chosen to bury himself in the tomb of honour than to see the nobility of his nation vassalized,' preached Edward Symmonds to the garrison of Oxford. A few acknowledged the ties of deference and clientage to which Newcastle appealed, and followed local magnates into the royal camp; Sir Gervase Scrope, who only narrowly escaped Verney's fate at Edgehill, raised an infantry company in Lincolnshire that he attached to the regiment of the Earl of Lindsey, 'out of devotion and respect to his lordship as well as duty to the King'.[37]

Gentlemen, like Knyvett, who found the choice between the competing sides utterly repugnant were presented with a quandary as the intransigents moved to war. In Staffordshire the majority of the gentry sought to neutralise the county, to prevent its resources being employed by either party; in November 1642 26 JPs agreed to raise a substantial force in the shire to defend it against any incursions. In mid-July a number of the Lincolnshire gentry had subscribed to the raising of 400 cavalry, designed to protect the county from foreign or external invasion, or, significantly, from popular insurrection. This attempt was colonised by a number of committed Royalists as a cover for the raising of troops for the King, but a majority of those who subscribed were not disingenuous in their desire to guarantee 'the peace of the countie'. The latter phrase, or the more telling 'the peace of my country', became the rallying cry of the Norfolk gentry in 1642. Those upon whom the King relied for the execution of the Commission of Array and the MPs charged with the Militia Ordinance agreed to suspend their activities, 'that upon noe . . . directions whatsoever the noyse of a drum might for present bee heard in Norfolk'. While in some areas neutralism took the form of an endeavour to insulate the county from the nascent conflict, even by the threat of force as in Staffordshire, in others, particularly where one or both of the committed minority groups was active, its manifestations were more muted. In several counties petitions to the belligerents were organised, begging them to come to an accommodation. In January 1643 a petition of this kind from Essex was organised by a clique of wealthy gentlemen, many of them leaders of the county's pre-war administration; it was signed by 20 baronets and knights, 63 esquires and 118 gentlemen. Where such collective action was not undertaken, neutralism can be seen in the attempts by individuals either to make themselves scarce, as did Sir Daniel Deligne of Harlaxton, Lincolnshire, who abandoned his house and 'lived privately', or to obey, often casuistically, the direct orders of both sides. In Warwickshire John Fetherstone of Packwood privately expressed his 'distraction . . . being altogether unable to satisfy myself in my judgement and conscience' in the face of the competing demands of King and Parliament for assistance; he resolved his dilemma by attending the muster organised by the Parliamentarian Lord Lieutenant in person, while sending his arms and armour to the Royalists.[38]

Neutralism had little purchase once it became apparent that the war would not be settled rapidly in 1642, either by treaty or victory. The neutrals had to adjust to effective commitment. Hard choices had to be made. In June 1642 a group of 24 JPs in Essex sought to distance themselves from the pro-Parliamentary/Puritan activism of the dominant Warwick–Barrington group. One of them almost immediately attempted to join the King in arms; three subsequently fled the county and lived in territory under Royalist control; 14 remained in Essex, but withdrew from local government – three of these were later accused of Royalist proclivities; six became involved in the Parliamentary war-machine in the county. This latter group, those gentlemen who sought to remain uncommitted in 1642 but who decided to co-operate with the dominant party in their locality and return to their traditional political and administrative roles, were yet more numerous in other counties. In Cornwall the bulk of the gentry 'sat still as neuters assisting neither' while Royalists and Parliamentarians jostled for control; once the former had eradicated their rivals, many of the moderate group abandoned their stance and took up posts in the civil and military administration of the shire. The uncertainties of the bulk of the Kentish gentry were resolved when the shire was invaded by a London-raised force in August; the county's administration was then manned by the tiny group of activists who had declared themselves in the early summer, and by gentlemen whose uncertainties were apparent in their inaction in that period, and occasionally from their correspondence: Henry Oxinden of Deane was 'between Silla and Carybdis' in July as he contemplated the claims of King and Parliament; in the autumn he was an agent of the latter's county committee.[39]

War overtook the gentry, swept them up as military leaders or local administrators. Moderation, the careful avoidance of choice, so apparent in 1642, became ever more difficult, particularly for those gentlemen who had formed the traditional governing élite. In Lancashire 79 per cent of the greater gentry became actively involved in the war effort; only 27 per cent of the lesser, parochial gentry. In consequence losses, particularly in areas over which the war raged, could be heavy: houses burned, estates plundered, men slain. Thirty-four of the Yorkshire baronets or their heirs took up arms; seven were killed in battle or executed, three were seriously wounded. Gentility itself came under attack during the war. Gentry monuments were liable to the assaults of iconoclasts. The memorial at Marholme, Northamptonshire, to 'a curteous soldier', the young Royalist Edward Hunter, concludes with a moving blend of pathos and irony:

> Noe crucifixe you see, noe frightfull brand
> Of superstition's here: pray let me stand.

Radical sectaries, culminating in the Quakers in the mid-1650s, challenged the entire social hierarchy and the relations of deference that were dependent upon it. 'Honours and Titles . . . are but . . . Heathenish distractions not to be retained amongst Christians'; deferential forms of address, such as 'right worshipful', were 'hollow, decitfull, unwarrantable', 'Babylonian', the 'inventions of the beast'. But these assaults were less troubling than a practical consequence of the war and its aftermath – the gradual exclusion of the bulk of the gentry from government.[40]

The advent of war divided the gentry in all areas, but it did not destroy their dominance over the agencies of local government. A substantial group of gentlemen, many from the traditional ruling élite, were, with varying degrees of enthusiasm, prepared to staff the administrative machines established in the localities by Charles and by Pym. By late 1648 that political landscape had almost wholly changed. The shift was most apparent in shires which had been part of the Royalist heartland, and where the defeat of the King had led to the wholesale displacement and sequestration of those who had ruled in his name. But the dominance of local administration by men from beyond the charmed circle of the élite – military adventurers from other areas, representatives of minor gentry families, townsmen and professionals – was also a product of the defection or retirement of those, like the Harley clan in Herefordshire or the Parliamentarian gentry of Wales, who could not identify with the increasingly radical policies demanded by the New Model Army and its allies in Westminster.[41]

This latter process accounts for the social transformation of the administrations of counties that had been controlled by Parliament from the first, the transformation of which Sir John Oglander wrote with such venom:

> We had a thing here called a Committee, which over-ruled Deputy Lieutenants and also Justices of the Peace, and of this we had brave men: Ringwood of Newport, the pedlar: Maynard, the apothecary: Matthews, the baker: Wavell and Legge, farmers, and poor Baxter. . . These ruled the whole Island and did whatsoever they thought good in their own eyes.

While the rhythm of this shift in social profile varied from county to county, we can distinguish some common reasons for it. The members of the élite who initially formed the county committees were increasingly disillusioned by three developments as the war progressed. First, there was the spiralling military burden on their local communities; the seemingly endless demands for supplies, for conscripts and for money. One money-raising scheme was particularly objectionable: the seizure and sale of the goods and the sequestration of the rents of those deemed to be hostile to Parliament. The Norfolk committee were denounced at Westminster as 'remisse and careles' in the work of sequestration; Sir John Holland spoke for his colleagues when, in response, he expressed his abhorrence of being obliged to act against those 'to whome I have the neerest relations of blood and obligations of friendship'. A second reason for gentry disillusionment was Parliament's insistence on the subordination of local interests to the schemes of the centre, to the command of local forces being given to outsiders, to local forces and taxation being employed for purposes other than county defence. Finally, the gentry were troubled during the war by Parliament's refusal to negotiate a treaty with the King, and, after his defeat, with its failure to achieve any religious or political settlement, while the most subversive ideas were being canvassed by the radicals.[42]

In some areas the transformation of local government was accomplished by the direct intervention of Westminster. From mid-1643 the failures of the rulers of Hertfordshire to execute aspects of Parliament's policies – to impose the Covenant; to sequester 'malignants' – had infuriated activist MPs; in December they passed legislation by-passing the old county committee, that had been dominated by 'the principal gentlemen of the county', and empowering a new administrative structure, staffed by 'persons of mean condition'. In others, local coups explain the transfer of power. In Kent Sir Anthony Weldon, an embittered ex-courtier whose 'desire of rule brought him to run with the forwardest', was supported by a narrow clique of extremists in a policy of the most vigorous enforcement of Parliamentary enactments. Those of the committee who did not share Weldon's driving enthusiasm, or who fell foul of his arrogant and vindictive temper, were displaced or retired from the service in disgust. Some of the latter, like Sir Richard Hardres, Sir William Mann and Henry Oxinden of Deane, joined the Kentish revolts in the winter of 1647–8, revolts that were largely directed against 'the tyrannical and embittered spirit' of 'the violent part of the Committee'. In East Anglia the process was more gradual. Here the county committees transferred the more contentious policies for which they were responsible to those who did not share their unease, usually from outside the traditional élite; 'indigent and meane persons' executed the Sequestration Ordinance in Norfolk, 'persons of low and mean condition' in Cambridgeshire; in east Suffolk the work of displacing 'scandalous' clergymen fell to 'meane men', 'men that have neyther good bloud nor breeding in them'. The gentry committeemen originally appointed often found that these deputies, 'Tradesmen committees', then sought to erode their authority, denouncing their 'lukewarmness', their endeavours to shelter men who enjoyed 'relation of kindred and friendship' with them from financial demands or sequestration.[43]

'O the tyrannical misery that the gentlemen of England did endure,' Sir John Oglander wrote during the Civil War, 'They could call nothing their own, and lived in slavery and submission to the unruly, base multitude. *O tempora, O mores*.' By 1648 the majority of the gentry would have agreed with his bleak assessment; from every quarter of England the traditional rulers complained that power had devolved upon upstarts and outsiders: 'men of mean quality' who were 'very hard to the gentry' (Somerset); 'men of so base a condition as renders them unworthy of such trust' (Sussex); men 'of inconsiderable fortunes, others of little or no estate and strangers in our county' (Warwickshire); men who sought to 'subdue the gentry and set beggars on horseback' (Cumberland). The revolutionary events of the winter of 1648–9, and the subsequent experiments that culminated in the collapse into virtual anarchy in 1659, ensured that the situation did not improve dramatically.[44]

A few of the gentry affirmed the radical changes in the fabric of English government after 1648. Many, like Edmund Ludlow and Sir James Harington, were Puritans, zealots who shared a millenarian vision of the immediate working of God in preparation for the last days which were imminent. Forms of government were ephemeral, established and swept away in the tumultuous progress towards the apocalypse – 'but . . . . dross and dung in comparison of Christ', in Cromwell's words. Other Puritans, like Sir Thomas Barnardiston, son of the great Puritan patriarch Sir Nathaniel, who, almost alone among the East Anglian élite, was prepared to co-operate with the rule of the major-generals in 1655–6, were persuaded that radical experiment might advance the cause of 'godly reformation'. A few gentlemen served the various regimes out of a dogged sense that government must be sustained, and that government was still their prime social function. In the decade after the King's execution, Sir Simon Archer was one of the most assiduous of the local governors in Warwickshire, both as a JP and a militia commissioner. It is not easy to see him as a mere timeserver, however. Although Archer tried to avoid commitment in 1642, he was prepared to attack the radical faction that dominated the county committee in 1644, and in the next three years was the most active of the sub-commissioners of accounts who sought to investigate their malfeasance in office; they responded by listing him among 'the Neuter-Malignant party' in the county.[45]

The radical experiments of the Interregnum – the government of the Rump from 1649 to 1653, the rule of the major-generals in 1655–6 – found a few supporters among the gentry. More responded to the conservatism that was always a part of Cromwell's complex character – 'A nobleman, a gentleman, a yeoman. . . That is a good interest of the nation and a great one' – and sought to develop it. In 1654 Cromwell invited those who had been disqualified or who had retired in disgust from public affairs since the regicide to return to their traditional positions in local government: men like Sir John

Palgrave in Norfolk, Sir John Pelham in Sussex or Sir George Booth in Cheshire. After the loathed experiment of the major-generals, this policy was resumed yet more vigorously in 1657; and on this occasion moderate Parliamentarians from the Civil War years were joined in the lists of magistrates and commissioners with the heirs of Cavalier families. While not all those gentlemen invited to serve did so, some were prepared to co-operate, and such men were often behind the scheme to reconstruct kingship, to re-edify the 'ancient constitution' with a new dynasty, the house of Cromwell. While the *Humble Petition and Advice* was largely the work of lawyers and of apparachniks of the Protectorate, some of the gentry, 'a sort of lukewarm, indifferent country knights [and] gentlemen', were also involved in the plan and were rewarded with advancement to the House of Lords, renewed by the *Humble Petition*. In a series of bitterly derisive characterisations, a radical commentator nicely catches the conservative ethos of this group:

> Sir John Hubbard, knight baronet of the old stamp, a gentleman of Norfolk, of a considerable estate . . . Had meddled very little, if at all, in throwing down Kingship, but hath stickled very much in helping to re-establish and build it up again; and a great stickler among the late kinglings, who petitioned the Protector to be King.

The group were an odd and unstable amalgam of supporters of the Rump, those who retired in disgust at the execution of the king, and those, like Hobart, who had played little part in public affairs until the Protectorate. Many undoubtedly shared the views that were attributed to Sir Richard Onslow, who had been purged from the Long Parliament in 1648: 'is fully for Kingship, and was never otherwise. . . And seeing he cannot have young Charles, old Oliver will serve his turn, so he have one'.[46]

A small minority among the gentry co-operated with one or more of the regimes spawned after the regicide. A few gentlemen, more creatively, sought to reflect on the lessons of the war, and to reconstruct both the state and a role for the gentry within it in terms of their reading of history and contemporary events. James Harington and Henry Neville, both the sons of knights from great gentry families with Court connections, the Haringtons of Exton and the Nevilles of Billingbear, were at the centre of this intellectual circle. Harington, in his *Oceana* of 1656, argued that history indicated that the forms of political authority followed the possession of land; the struggle between the Crown and the magnates in the fifteenth century had resulted in a temporary victory for the king, but had exhausted both contestants. The defeat of the king and his nobles in the Civil War indicated that monarchy and aristocracy were no longer options; neither possessed the requisite territorial command or concomitant social power. A republic alone was viable. For Neville, the gentry now held the bulk of landed property, therefore 'the balance is in the gentry'; Harington believed that property was more widely dispersed. Yet he too emphasised the place of the gentry in the new system; their wealth gave them the leisure both for study and reflection, and for a commitment to public service. 'There is something . . . in the making of a commonwealth,' Harington wrote, 'In the governing of her, and . . . in the leading of her armies; which . . . seems to be peculiar unto the genius of a gentleman.' Yet for all Harington's skill in shaping the now traditional ideology of civic humanism to republican institutions, his ideas made few converts. Few of those gentlemen who chose to serve the Interregnum regimes did so on Haringtonian grounds. Most of the gentry remained wedded to the traditional form of government, and to the house of Stuart.[47]

The bulk of the gentry, condemned to political impotence during the Interregnum and either banned from London or no longer finding the attractions that had drawn them there before the war, 'lived most in the country'. Some quite literally cultivated their gardens: Sir Ralph Verney avidly discussed new plants, trees and techniques with a variety of correspondents, on one occasion reporting that 'one villanous Cow in one night spoyled my whole Nursery'. Those with learned interests pursued them. Sir Justinian Isham, though, as he put it, a 'meere rustick', corresponded with Bishop Duppa on topics as various as the conversion of the Jews, the scientific writings of Descartes, the political theory of Hobbes and Harington. For most, particularly those who had experienced sequestration, financial reorganisation and the refurbishment of damaged tenements and dilapidated mansions was the priority. Chesterton House, Warwickshire, had suffered war damage in the 1640s, and Lady Peyto complained of 'mush rumps growing in the topp of the chambers for want of tiling': her son demolished the house and built a Palladian mansion in the mid-1650s.[48]

Banished to their estates, the displaced gentry also threw themselves into the traditional collective rural pleasures: visits and mutual hospitality, parties for hunting and hawking, horse-racing. The agents of the central governments were deeply suspicious of these activities, not without good practical reason. Such occasions could be covers for Royalist plotting. Meetings among the disaffected at the King's Arms in Salisbury, at a series of hunting parties, and at Christmas festivities 'with sets of fidlers', were a prelude to the rising of the Dorset and Wiltshire Royalists in March 1655. But while some of the gentry talked big, few were prepared to challenge the government, with its network of spies and overwhelming military force, outright: the experience of defeat in 1646, in 1648, and, for a few, in 1651, with the inevitable aftermath of sequestration and composition fines, did not encourage activism; and most gentlemen, as Sir Thomas Peyton complained, 'however dissatisfied with the present government, were not willing to incur any danger'. But the regime's antipathy to traditional conviviality was fuelled by more than just pragmatic concerns. The gentry's activities were a statement of their distance from the centre and its agenda of godly reformation. And this was true not just of those Cavaliers whose response to defeat and political impotence was to plunge into a riot of debauchery, violence and excess, as did the Kentish squire, Richard Thornhill of Olantigh – 'the veriest beast that ever was', thought Dorothy Osborne. The point is nicely caught in a speech to the 1656 Parliament by Major-General Lambert: speaking in a thin house on 25 December 1656, he pictured the regime's enemies at their festivities. 'They are, haply, now merry over their Christmas pies, drinking the King of Scots' health, or your confusion'.[49]

Lambert's sense of an antipathy and intransigence to the Interregnum expressed in cultural forms – here, the celebration of Christmas – has a wider significance. The conviviality to which he objected expressed the reconstruction of gentry solidarity after the divisions of the Civil War. Men who had taken opposite paths in 1642 re-affirmed older friendships or ties of family, as did Sir Ralph Verney and his uncle Sir Alexander Denton. Collective activities often followed the seasonal rhythms and the rites of the episcopal Church and its prayer book, obnoxious to and intermittently proscribed by, the regime: Christmas festivities, and the celebration of Easter and Whitsun; baptisms, marriages, funerals. So in December 1652 Anthony Blagrave of Bulmersh, Berkshire, was organising a Christmas dinner for 69 poor folk, and serving as a godfather at the christening of a neighbour's son. Affection for the

Church of England also took other forms: attendance at services conducted according to the prayer book; the building and refurbishment of chapels; the protection and maintenance of those ministers whose loyalty to the established Church had led to their dismissal by the regime. Few gentlemen could match the crusading Anglican enthusiasm of that 'son of the Church', Sir Robert Shirley. His 1653 chapel at Staunton Harold, in the style of a late-medieval parish church, was a powerful statement of his conservative religious affiliations, and he made a substantial financial provision for the displaced clergy from impropriations and Church lands held by his family. But many provided accommodation and small pensions, or chose the tutors of their sons from among that number.[50]

The resigned quietism of the bulk of the gentry posed as significant a problem to the Interregnum regimes as did the plots of the minority. The gentry formed a phalanx, integrated by the reassertion of ties of neighbourhood and commensality and by the development of a common piety, that was coolly distant even to the most conservative of the governmental experiments of the 1650s. The gentry, wealthy, locally respected, politically conscious, held aloof from the central authority. Cromwellian kingship had some appeal, but most of the gentry who favoured the ancient constitution, with Sir Richard Onslow, preferred 'young Charles' to King Oliver.

## 6.5 RESTORATION

The gentry played little direct role in the Restoration. Their feeble attempts to stage an armed rising to take advantage of the feuding among military grandees and civilian republicans that followed the collapse of Richard Cromwell's authority were contemptuously swept aside by the army in August 1659. The return of the King was secured by the intervention of General Monck. The county petitions, for the freedom of Parliament and the peace of the county, as one of the Warwickshire organisers expressed it, with which Monck was inundated in January 1660 and which may have encouraged his decision to re-admit the MPs secluded in 1648, were probably the gentry's major contribution to the return of Charles Stuart.[51]

The gentry may not have played any very active role in the Restoration, but this is not how they subsequently told the story.

19. Staunton Harold Chapel, Leicestershire, built by Sir Robert Shirley, 1653

'The gentlemen were the instrumental cause of the King's Restoration,' insisted Roger Vaughan of Bredwardine in a Commons debate in 1670; 'it was the Cavaleere partie, the loyall gentrie, that brought him home in truth', wrote Sir John Bramston a decade later. Few historians have taken this self-congratulatory and self-serving account seriously. But some have written as though the tale contained an element of truth; arguing that if the gentry were not the engineers of the Restoration, they were certainly its major beneficiaries. Dr Hutton provides a recent, powerful statement of this case: by 1662 the King was 'essentially the president of a federation of communities run by their landowners. . . The 'county' gentry, as a group, gained absolutely from the Restoration'. Professor Fletcher has written of the half-century after 1660 as witnessing 'the triumph of the Stuart gentry.'[52]

This contention would have surprised a major segment of gentry opinion in the immediate aftermath of the Restoration. Those who had suffered during the Civil War, and who sought to rebuild their shattered estates, believed that they had a claim against the beneficiaries of their miseries, and on the monarchy for honours, patronage and perquisites. Charles and his advisers thought otherwise. They insisted on the need to co-operate with the moderate Parliamentarians and Cromwellians, guaranteeing their land purchases; offering them office in the new administration. Attempts in Parliament to recover lands or secure reparations for individual victims were blocked by the government, as were schemes to reduce the rates of interest paid on debts contracted by those who had fought for the king: the government could afford to antagonise neither the land speculators nor the (closely allied) bankers who had fattened on the Royalists during the Interregnum. 'The loyall gentrie' were, with Sir John Bramston, first puzzled, then increasingly embittered, bewailing the insensitivity of the Court and its disregard for their services and their sufferings. Some consoled themselves with embroidered accounts of spotless loyalty and military gallantry. The mythology of the Wyndhams of Kentford, Somerset began with the patriarchal injunction of old Sir Thomas: 'My sons! . . . I command you to honour and obey your sovereign, and in all things to adhere to the Crown; and though the Crown should hang upon a bush, I charge you to forsake it not'. Sir Thomas's five sons heeded this solemn pronouncement: three of them died in the war, and the family, whose material losses were estimated at £73,560, took further risks during Charles's dramatic escape after Worcester. A few minor offices, valued at a mere £1,200 per annum could hardly compensate for such a record of sacrifice: at Edmund Wyndham's funeral the 'hard measure' he received in 1660 was remarked in the sermon, while his son, Sir Hugh's, indignation burns from his tombstone in Watchet Church:

Here lyes beneath this ragged stone
One more his Prince's than his own,
And in his martyr'd father's wars
Lost fortune, blood – gained naught but scars:
And for his suffering as reward
Had neither countenance nor regard.

Such festering resentment was not merely confined to monumental inscriptions. It resulted in much hostility to Clarendon, the progenitor and defender of the policy of Indemnity and Oblivion, and the factionalism and instability of the Commons in the 1660s, that swiftly belied the image of gentry 'union and agreement' emphasised in the April 1661 elections.[53]

Yet despite the indignation of a significant clique among the gentry, discussion of the 'triumph' of the group as a whole carries conviction. Much parliamentary legislation after 1660 can be read as an attempt to defend the values of the gentry as a class, and to guarantee their control of the localities. They were swift to confirm the Long Parliament's abolition of feudal tenures and of the Court of Wards, but did nothing to free their own manorial tenants, particularly copyholders, from similar burdens. They compounded this decision by offering the king, in lieu of his feudal revenues, a sum raised by the most regressive and unpopular of the fiscal experiments of the Civil War years, the excise on liquor: in 1757 Chancellor Hardwicke wrote sardonically of 'the bargain which the nobility and gentry made with the Crown . . . when they purchased out their own burden by . . . wardships, by laying an excise upon beer and ale to be consumed by the common people.' The game laws, that begin their extensive legislative history in 1671, served a similar, narrow interest. The law was a charter for the landed élite: hunting was to be the exclusive privilege of men with freehold estates worth at least £100 per annum and the sons of esquires and those of 'higher rank'. Further, manorial lords, provided they were 'not under the degree of esquire' were permitted to employ gamekeepers and to seize the guns, dogs and snares of those who lacked the statutory qualification. The Game Act of 1671, and a relaxed law of trespass, ensured that the gentry had a monopoly of hunting and could exercise their rights where they pleased; tenants could not protect their crops from the depredations either of the game or of its hunters. But it was not just the rural tenantry that were discriminated against in 1671. The qualification insisted on was not wealth, but the possession of land.[54]

Gentry suspicion of those whose wealth was not based on land, of townsmen, traders and bankers, apparent in the qualifications of the Game Act, emerges in many other contexts after the Restoration. In 1671 the Commons debated an additional revenue to be raised by the Excise. The debates provided much opportunity for the expression of gentry prejudice – fears of the resurrection of the Court of Wards; denunciations of bankers as 'Commonwealth's-men that destroy the nobility and gentry. All tradesmen turn Bankers'. But the discussion of one clause, that would have permitted the excise officers to search private houses, seems particularly significant. The general opinion was that gentry households should, of course, be protected from such intrusion, but not those of townsmen. The 'gentleman must have his liberty', he *deserved* the privilege: he maintained traditional social values, like hospitality; his loyalty was unimpeachable. Not so the towns. 'They keep no hospitality'; at the Restoration 'the Corporations did nothing; infected then, and are since'.[55]

Gentry hostility to the corporations, the spawning ground of that 'company of Tradesmen committees' who had ruled their betters and enriched themselves in the Interregnum had already taken practical form. In April 1662 committees of local gentlemen, whose determining role in the enforcement of the legislation had been insisted upon by the Commons, executed the Corporation Act, purging urban government not only of those who refused to swear loyalty oaths, but of men whose continuance in office was thought, at the discretion of the gentry commissioners, to be contrary to 'public safety'. The *ancien regime* might be thought to have been restored, literally, with a vengeance on this occasion. In 1684 and 1685 the gentry co-operated with the King in another purge of the municipalities, a punishment for their pro-Exclusionist politics during the crisis of 1679–82, and to guarantee the subsequent return of loyalist MPs. On this occasion a number of local squires were added to the governing bodies, even appointed as mayors: Sir Henry Heron, of 'Church of England and the old cavalier principles', became Mayor of schismatic Boston, the town that had insulted and pelted his Royalist father with rubbish in 1642. The Revolution of 1688–9 halted such interventions, but not the hostility and suspicion that underpinned them. This re-emerges clearly in the extended crusade in the Commons to legislate that all MPs, even those for the towns, should be the possessors of substantial landed estates. The Lincolnshire squire, Sir William Massingberd, rejoiced when the Land Qualification Act was finally passed in 1711: 'when landed gentlemen represent us in Parliament and do our business at home in the country we may justly look for better times'.[56]

A sense of the gentry as the major beneficiaries of the Restoration is not a product merely of analysis of their dealings with their inferiors, with farmers and townsmen. Their attitudes towards both Church and King equally suggest that the maintenance of their hegemony was their central priority, despite their ostentatious loyalism and devotion to the Anglican establishment. In 1669, Sir Ralph Stawell, whose father Sir John's zealous Royalism had resulted in his imprisonment throughout the Interregnum and the confiscation and sale of the family estates for £64,000, completed the internal furnishing of the church at Low Ham, Somerset. Upon the ornate chancel-screen, above a frieze of angels, he had carved the biblical verse, 'My sonne serve God and the Kinge and meddle not with them that ar given to change'. This icon catches nicely an aspect of the political culture of the gentry after the Civil War. Kingship and episcopacy, hierarchy and deference, were emphasised as interdependent principles. Yet this idyllic conjunction – 'monarchy, magistracy, ministry' – proved unstable. The tensions between the agendas of the Crown, churchmen and the gentry, and the priority that the last accorded their own interests is apparent in the treatment of religious nonconformity after 1660.

From Breda in April 1660 Charles had promised 'a liberty to tender consciences'. Yet the sectaries immediately found themselves subjected to the hostile attentions of the new JPs and, particularly in the aftermath of the doomed rising by a handful of London Fifth Monarchists in January 1661, of the militia supplemented by gentry vigilantes. Meetings were raided and broken up, individuals mobbed, beaten and imprisoned. 'I would not leave a Quaker alive in England,' an Oxfordshire Deputy Lieutenant snarled on this occasion, 'I would make no more . . . to set my Pistol to their Ears, and shoot them through the Head, than I would to kill a Dog'. In October 1660 Charles had issued a Proclamation designed to accommodate Presbyterian incumbents by not requiring the use of the Book of Common Prayer. Magistrates in many localities would have none of this. In addition to general harassment, a number of Presbyterians were indicted at sessions and assizes for not using the Book. Peniston Whalley, esquire, giving the charge at the

Nottingham sessions, denied the legality of the King's Declaration: the King's excessive concern for 'tender consciences', he noted sardonically, should extend to local JPs and jurors who were morally obliged to enforce the pre-Civil War statutes. In the first sessions of the Cavalier Parliament MPs overrode the King's own views, and neglected his more immediate needs, in their campaign to impose Anglican worship and penalise dissent by legislation. The latter, the so-called 'Clarendon Code', was initially enforced with considerable brutality by the local magistrates. The sectaries again were the favourite targets. A Wiltshire militia officer wrote a jocular letter to his Colonel, the old Cavalier Charles Seymour, MP, describing his troop's 'martial exploits' in smashing up a Quaker cemetery: 'we carried all before us'. On the Isle of Wight, Walter Slingsby sent an English translation of the Koran to the Quaker leaders whom he had imprisoned, hoping that they might convert and thus discredit the whole movement. In Lincolnshire the neglect of due process in proceedings against nonconformists was so flagrant that it earned the JPs a stinging rebuke at the Assizes; the resentful magistrates, headed by Sir Anthony Oldfield, promptly reported the judges to the Council in a missive that emphasised the 'apparant mischeifes' that a policy of legalistic lenience would encourage. Nonconformists might find themselves discriminated against by local magistrates in other matters: when a Dunwich dissenter prosecuted a woman for bewitching him, a Suffolk JP publicly announced that if the witch confined her maleficent attentions to 'such as they are, she should never be hung by him'. Charles's attempt in 1672 to make good his earlier promises with the issue of the Declaration of Indulgence relaxing the penal code against dissent, was indignantly denounced by gentlemen in Parliament, as a betrayal of the Restoration and of 'his father's friends'; 'it did make disturbance in most loyal hearts,' mourned Sir Philip Musgrave. Substantively, objections were not only to the constitutionality of the Declaration, but reiterated the role of the established Church as a bulwark against the poisonous principles of sedition. 'The best foundation of the state is Religion,' said the aged Sir Henry Herbert, 'it makes men more peaceable and better subjects.'[57]

'Church and King' were not always compatible principles, and the gentry apparently preferred the claims of the Church on those occasions when Charles II's policies challenged the intolerant ecclesiastical establishment that they had resurrected and reinforced at the Restoration. Yet the gentry's enthusiasm for the Church was not unqualified, and they had no intention of submitting to the clericist pretensions of another Laud. The restored Church, as its officers complained, had been granted little of its ancient jurisdiction. The Court of Ecclesiastical High Commission was not restored, and the 'creaking machinery' of the toothless diocesan courts could not even enforce their authority over the parochial ministry. The effective prosecution of dissent was deputed to the JPs, and, after their initial vicious pogroms against radical dissenters, their zeal waned. Speaking in the debate on the Declaration of Indulgence, Sir Robert Carr made a telling point in this respect. The penal code, he argued, had been effectively 'dispensed with by justices of the peace' long before the King's intervention. There is much evidence from his native Lincolnshire to support Carr's point. Sir Francis Fane of Fulbeck, Lincolnshire, was 'an old cavalier, and as high for the hierarchy and ceremonies as any man'; yet he became a close friend of a displaced Presbyterian minister, and, in 1678 refused to take any action against a local Quaker, though the man had spurned the parish priest in his own church as 'a false prophet and a hireling'. Two neighbouring JPs, both ex-Royalists were equally complacent in the dealings with the Quaker community: they neglected warrants to arrest suspects and returned distrained goods to their owners. The gentry may have seen persecution as counter-productive, or, more simply, as irrelevant: they no longer felt that their social and political position was at risk from a nonconformity increasingly associated with political quietism. When the Exclusion Crisis and the Rye House Plot resurrected gentry fears of the subversive threat posed by militant dissent, a renewed wave of persecution followed. The Hampshire bench prefaced their 1684 order launching an investigation into church attendance with a denunciation of the 'Daingerous designes' practised by 'Dissenters from the Church of England' against 'the Government both in Church and State'.[58]

Consideration of the creation and execution of religious policies apparently reinforces the argument of the post-Civil War settlement as a triumph for the gentry. Their attitude to dissent was less a product of any affection for the Church of England than of a cool calculation of their class interests. The sedulous loyalty that the gentry expressed to the restored monarchy was also suspect. The abolition of wardship and the restriction of the royal prerogative rights over hunting, the refusal to respect Charles's preferences with respect to religious toleration; all indicated essential gentry priorities. So, too, did the Revolution of 1688–9.

## 6.6 1688: THE TRIUMPH OF THE GENTRY?

The Exclusion Crisis had revitalised the ostentatious loyalism of the bulk of the gentry that had wavered with the revelations of the Popish Plot and in the face of the superior organisation and manipulation of public opinion by Shaftesbury and the Whigs. The county elections to the 1681 Commons were generally contested far more vigorously by those opposed to the policy of Exclusion, who, in many localities, were represented as consisting of virtually the entire gentry community. In Norfolk the 'body of the gentry' opposed Sir John Hobart, who had 'about five gentlemen . . . for him' – though here, as in Yorkshire and in Worcestershire where 'the gentry did their utmost', the unanimity of the local élite was insufficient to carry the election. Upon Charles's abrupt dissolution of that Parliament, the gentry threw themselves behind the monarchy, reviving the persecution dissenters, assisting the King in his policy of purging the municipalities, and organising a series of local petitions in which, typically, they boasted of their sedulous loyalty and accused the Whigs of 'designing . . . to throw us back into the same miseries and confusions we were lately delivered from, by your majestie's happy and miraculous restauration'.[59]

James II's pig-headed determination to force through his pro-Catholic policies at all costs shattered the recently renewed alliance between the Stuart monarchy and the gentry. After the failure of the 1685 Parliament, the King bent all his energies to securing a compliant Commons. Almost all the two hundred or so gentlemen who had been appointed to the corporations were displaced, but this was less troubling than the purge of the county magistracy and the lieutenancy of all who refused to accede to the King's policies. By the summer of 1688 nearly three-quarters of those who had been JPs in 1685 had been outed. What the Bishop of Norwich wrote of Norfolk could stand for all English and Welsh counties: 'indeed, all the most considerable gentry . . . are out of the commission'. The effect on individuals was devastating. Sir John Bramston of Skreens had fought long and hard to advance the royal interest in his county, Essex, with its powerful traditions of Puritanism and Parliamentarianism. His actions made him 'odious to the fanatiques in generall', and they slandered him, accusing him of popery, and backing the accusation with forged documents and perjured witnesses. In 1685 he played leading part at the hustings at Chelmsford, where the Exclusionists, who had carried all before them in the three previous county elections, were badly defeated. Yet in April 1688, Bramston, despite his impeccable Tory credentials, was

> putt out of the commission of the peace, and from beinge a Deputy Lieutenant. With my-selfe were about thirty gentlemen put out . . . few of the old Justices left in Commission . . . In their stead is Colonel Henry Mildmay, Colonell Rich, a leveller, or at least a Commonwealth's man, . . . and many more of the same stamp and principles.

The incongruous appearance on the Essex bench of the old Interregnum Fifth-Monarchist, Nathaniel Rich, was troubling. More galling was the promotion of the 'apocriphal collonell', Henry Mildmay, 'hated by all the gentlemen of the county', 'a rebell as soone as a man almost', Governor of Cambridge in the Civil War, radical knight of the shire for Essex in the three Exclusion Parliaments, and the devious orchestrator of the slander against Bramston's religion. Throughout England men of the proven loyalty of Bramston were displaced by an odd congeries of papists (about a quarter of the new JPs) and dissenters, men 'of no considerable interest' allied only in their mutual 'hatred of the Church of England'. Those few among the gentry who were prepared to support James's policies recognised their suicidal character. Sir John Reresby was appalled when in Yorkshire 'the prime of the gentry', 'the principal gentlemen for estates and interest in their countrys', were replaced by men like John Eyre, who 'can neither read nor write', by worthies who had not 'one foot of freehould land in England'.[60]

James's policies deeply alienated the gentry. A few supported William's invasion. Sir Edward Seymour, that 'man of honour and cordial to the true English interest' joined William at Exeter; Ribston Hall, the house of Sir Henry Goodricke, 'a gentleman of fine parts naturally, and those improved by great reading and travel', was the headquarters of those who plotted to seize York: both men were Tories purged from office in 1687–8. But most gentlemen avoided such active commitment. They simply refused to assist James – and their 'strike' was fatal to his cause. In September 1688, when news of

William's invasion plans reached England, the King reversed his policies, and invited the gentry to take up their positions in local government. The response was half-hearted at best, and, from many, an outright refusal to act. Sir John Bramston typifies the general mood in his reply to the offer of re-instatement to the Essex magistracy and militia. 'I told him he would find gentlemen not forward to take commands; some would thinck one kick of the breech enough for a gentleman.' Bramston confided his doubts about the direction of events to his journal: 'How these risings . . . can be justified, I see not . . . but . . . had not the Prince come . . . our religion had been rooted out.' But, for all his moral qualms, his practical quiescence, and that of the gentry in general, were fatal to James. Even at the height of the euphoria of the Restoration, the ideologue, James Harington, predicted a rapid breakdown in the relations between the gentry and their King. 'Let him come in, and call a Parliament of the greatest Cavaliers in England, so they be men of estates, and lett them sett but 7 yeares, and they will all turn Commonwealthe's men.' Harington's faith in his scientific analysis of political structures resulted in a time-frame that was unduly precipitate, but the overthrow of James II suggests the prescience of his remarks. A King who offended the landed élite, who spurned those 'most eminent for quality and estates', was helpless. It is indeed tempting to think of the 'victory' of a class that relentlessly pursued policies designed to secure its own hegemony at the expense not only of its inferiors, but, in defiance of its stated principles, of the Church and of the King.[61]

Yet, again, such an emphasis sits uneasily with the perceptions of contemporaries. Many country gentlemen in the half-century after the Revolution lamented that the traditional constitutional and social order and, particularly, their role within these was being severely eroded. The 1738 tomb of Percyvall Hart at Lullingstone embodies this embittered nostalgia. The inscription, within a 'Rococo-Gothick' arcade, its tracery bespangled with coats of arms, details his repair and beautification of his parish church, and his care for the Church of England in general as exhibited in his service as knight of the shire for Kent in the last two Parliaments of Queen Anne; it emphasises his practice of traditional gentry virtues – local munificence, hospitality. Hart's 'strong Attachment to the OLD ENGLISH CONSTITUTION . . . abhorring all venality, and scorning to buy the Peoples Voices as to sell his own' disqualified him from parliamentary service after 1715, and he retired to the

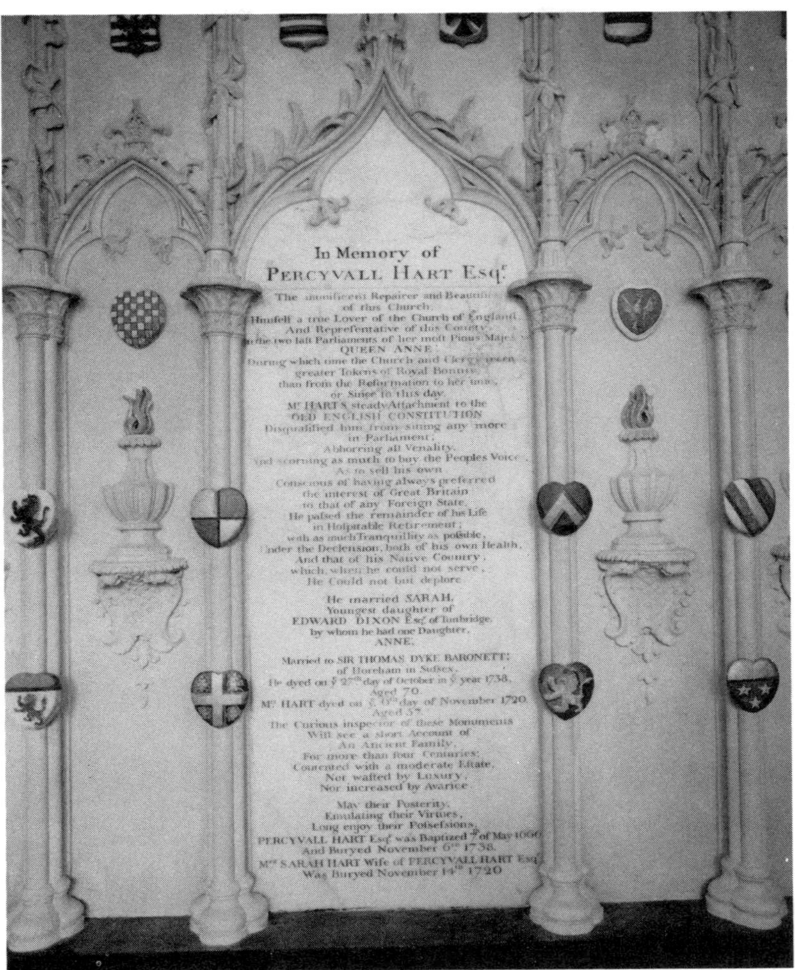


20. Tomb of Percyvall Hart, esquire, d. 1738, Lullingstone Church, Kent

country 'with as much Tranquillity as possible under the Declension both of his own Health and that of his Native Country, which when he could not serve, he Could not but deplore.' We are confronted with a paradox, it seems, of a significant group among the gentry failing to register the 'triumph' for which historians have subsequently congratulated them. Its resolution will depend upon analysis both of the constitutional theory to which the gentry subscribed after 1660 and of the related structure of political authority at the centre.

In 1660 some writers argued a theoretical case for royal absolutism; in 1689 a number played with radical Lockean ideas and the advantages of republicanism. But the dominant strain of respectable political thinking was legitimist and legalistic. At the Restoration and again after the Revolution, the gentry sought to secure 'the ancient fundamental laws', the traditional form of the 'balanced' English constitution. Frequent disagreements concerning the details of constitutional and legal arrangement supposedly enshrined in the historical experience of the English people, apparent in, say, gentry contributions to the debates concerning the repeal of the 1641 Triennial Act in 1664 and its revival in 1692–4, never undermined this mode of analysis. The prescriptive character of the 'ancient constitution' was a commonplace, and most gentlemen would have agreed on its essential characteristics, on what Burke was to call 'the stable, fundamental parts of our constitution'. Legislative sovereignty, the power to alter existing legal rights, particularly those of property, was vested in Parliament; executive power and administration, to be conducted in accordance with legal rules, reposed in the Crown. But this consensus on broad principles did not guarantee a gentry triumph. It left their control of local government insecure, and, more important, the legislative sovereignty of Parliament could be deployed contrary to their interests.[62]

The Crown's right to chose its administrative agents was acknowledged by the gentry, yet it could be deeply subversive of their status and hegemony in the shires. James's wholesale reconstruction of local government, and the consequent antagonism of the gentry united by a common disgrace, had been fatal to his regime. But, as his brother had shown from 1680, the authority to place and displace county magistrates, to reward loyalty and to penalise factious opposition, was a potent political weapon, if employed discriminatingly. The post-Revolution ministers saw the opportunity. In 1696 those thought to be tepid in their support of the Junto regime and its war policies were ousted. This inaugurated a period of government purges and counter-purges, and of wholesale additions to the commissions that gained in intensity in the volatile politics of Anne's reign. In Parliament the country gentry held the traditional view that all members of the local élite, all men of status and property, should be magistrates without respect to factional or party considerations. But their constitutional principles did not permit them to assail the Crown's right of nomination directly. They might petition for the restoration of 'gentlemen of quality and good estates' to the bench; but their only legislative initiative, pursued in the aftermath of both Whig and Tory purges, was the attempt to limit the office to those with a solid landed income; figures of £200–500 per annum were mooted. Local office, it seemed, was the plaything of the turbulent and cynical politics of the centre, and gentlemen 'of quality' might find themselves humiliatingly dismissed or their influence swamped by an influx of 'persons of mean estates'. The sense that magistracy had become tainted and devalued may explain both gentry disillusionment of the kind displayed in Hart's monument, and also the growing reluctance to undertake local office that we have noted before.[63]

The Restoration settlement, reinforced in 1689, guaranteed Parliament's control over the purse-strings. The King had to submit to the Commons' sanction of his administration, and might have to surrender cherished policies to secure financial co-operation. So in January 1667 the Commons delayed both the Poll and the Assessment bills until the government surrendered to their demands for an interdiction of their import of Irish cattle. In the two parliamentary sessions of 1673 speakers explicitly linked financial support for the Dutch war with the redress of grievances; 'begin with grievances and your liberty' insisted the Cavalier hero, 'the loyal colonel', Giles Strangways. 'We have had invasion of Property,' argued Sir John Monson, 'and till Grievances are redressed we cannot proceed any further.'[64] Unless the King was prepared to become a 'Doge of Venice' – an option explicitly rejected by both Charles II and William III – and Parliament the equivalent of the Polish Diet, the institution had to be managed. And its structure, and the resources still available to the Crown, ensured that it was manageable.

The practice of employing the Crown's resources of patronage – honours and, more tangibly, jobs, salaries and pensions – to secure the subservience of individual MPs was begun by the Cabal and raised to a fine art by Danby. The Cavalier Parliament contained a good number of men, often of radically different backgrounds, whose financial necessities left them susceptible to government blandishments. The 'indigent' Sir John Stapley was the son of a regicide and the protector of nonconformists; Sir Robert Holte, whose notorious financial embarrassment was mocked in the Commons and on the stage, was the scion of a distinguished Royalist family and an intolerant Church of England man: both accepted pensions and the Court whip. But if some gentlemen secured financial assistance at the expense of their consciences, most were appalled by the development. In 1675 the 'loyal colonel' Giles Strangways deplored the consequences of venality in the House, of the shifts of those gentlemen 'who speak one way when they have offices, and another when they have none': 20 years later Sir Edward Hussey, a radical supporter of toleration and the Revolution of 1688, made the same point, noting how 'some men by preferment have their mouths gagged up against the interest of the people'.[65]

The growth of a group bound to the government by ties of dependence and patronage revived the potent, divisive language of Jacobean politics: in 1673 Secretary Coventry deplored the attempt 'to make a distinction in the Houses between the country gentlemen and the courtiers'. It also resulted in legislation designed to keep those in receipt of government salaries out of the Commons and to secure the influence of 'the Gentlemen of England'. The first Place bill was introduced, by Giles Strangways, in 1675; a chorus of similar demands exercised Parliament after the Revolution – in 1690, 1692, 1694, 1695 and 1700; all were cut down in the Lords or vetoed. In 1705 Harley undertook a more limited policy that affected only those office-holders whose posts rendered them peculiarly susceptible to government pressure, and obliged them to seek re-election upon their promotion to the office. This proved unsatisfactory to 'country' MPs and in 1711 they reverted to demanding a full-blown proscription; a faint chorus of similar demands echoed into the Hanoverian period.[66]

The 1705 legislation may have been found wanting because the gentry were experiencing an increasingly torrid and expensive time at the hustings. They had effortlessly moved in to the representation of the parliamentary boroughs in the century before the Civil War, but increasingly found that their monopoly was under fire from those prepared to pay heavily for a seat in the Commons as an entry-point to the patronage and favours at the disposal of the government. The aristocratic Bertie family saw a seat in the Commons as the ideal stepping stone to preferment for a younger son; 'courtiers,' Peregrine Bertie wrote, 'must venture their fortunes, and they can have no better lottery than our House to push their fortunes in.' Accordingly the Berties warned off Sir Pury Cust, a local gentleman, with dire threats of the expenses he would face if he challenged their control of the representation of Stamford. Boroughs that had once gratefully accepted the offer of a local gentleman to represent them in Parliament now discovered that they had a vendible commodity. In Anne's reign New Shoreham was described as 'a new whore that is anybody's for their money', while two of the Grimsby freemen hawked the representation of their borough in London, seeking 'such as would give most money': both boroughs had been represented by local gentlemen in the reign of Charles II. Most boroughs were less spectacularly venal, contenting themselves with lavish dinners, doles for the poor, and the provision of public amenities, like Buckingham's Town Hall. Wise or experienced gentlemen warned their heirs of the debilitating financial consequences of electoral contests: in his will in 1733 Sir William Pole solemnly enjoined his family 'never stand as a Candidate . . . for the Borough of Honiton'.[67]

'Between the Army and the City,' an observer commented on the results of the 1715 election, 'there's very little room left for the Country Gentlemen.' Increasingly squeezed out of the Commons, the gentry responded with a chorus of complaint and the abortive Land Qualification Acts designed to halt the influx of carpetbaggers – 'Courtiers, military men, and merchants' – into the constituencies. But their options were limited by their own constitutional premises. In 1690 flagrant corruption in the Stockbridge election led to a suggestion in the Commons that the borough should be disfranchised and an additional two seats given to the county of Hampshire. The proposal was dropped after a debate that emphasised the prescriptive character of the ancient constitution. 'I hope we shall not alter the Constitution of England,' said Sir William Williams; 'the House stands upon ancient Constitutions, and I hope you will not remove old landmarks,' agreed Sir John Trevor.[68]

The gentry had never played a more direct or active role in politics than in the half-century after the Restoration. Their domination of the House of Commons had been secured before the Civil War, but the legislation of 1641, largely ratified in the Restoration Settlement, now gave Parliament an unprecedented role in government. And gentry MPs were responsive to the vociferous and well-informed opinion of their fellows in the localities. Consideration of these circumstances, and of various legislative defences of their class interest, have persuaded some historians of the gentry's political 'triumph' after 1660. Yet in 1716 Addison's squire, the Foxhunter, could argue that, with the exception of some minor refinements of the Game Law, 'there had not been one good law passed since King William's accession'. The gentry's faith in the relationships defined by the 'ancient constitution' did not permit a direct assault on the principle that direction of policy inhered in the Crown, while the structure of the Commons, equally defended by historical prescription, gave the government considerable room for manoeuvre. William III had not invaded England in a spirit of altruistic concern for the local hegemony of the gentry, but to secure English resources in his crusade against Louis XIV. The Revolution ushered in two decades of, in Bolingbroke's phrase, 'the . . . most expensive wars that Europe ever saw'. The gentry found themselves caught in a vicious spiral. War directly benefited military men, munitions contractors and the bankers from whom the government borrowed. War built up the number of jobs and offices with which the government could reward its supporters in the Commons. War encouraged the process whereby its beneficiaries or those would-be courtiers who sought 'to push their fortunes' were prepared to invest heavily to secure a seat in the Commons. And yet war was paid for by a tax of 4 shillings in the pound on landholdings. Their protests in the Commons and at the hustings were loud: 'The country is poor, the nation is racked, the courtiers hug themselves in furs, and the humble country gentleman is half starved'. But they were unavailing. The gentry could not find an adequate answer to the problem, powerfully expressed by Sir John Pakington in 1709, 'how to prevent . . . the moneyed and military men becoming lords of us who have the lands'. Their resentment fuelled the career and the writings of Bolingbroke, the *soi-disant* spokesman for 'the landed interest', in the first decades of the eighteenth century. They became increasingly marginal participants in national politics, the backwoods 'Foxhunters' – praised by one of their clerical allies, counting the stuffed fox-skins at Rydal Hall, as 'an argument of good commonwealth man and a great patriot'; derided for ignorance, xenophobia and dissenter-bashing by Addison. However we read their subsequent contributions, it is clear that any political 'triumph of the gentry' was more limited than some historians have suggested.[69]

# 7

# Education

'Learn', said Christopher Wandesford to his son George, 'to obey when you are young, so that you may be fit to govern when you are old.' He acknowledged that some claimed learning to be fit only for younger sons, and lesser men who had to make their own fortunes, but:

> without learning or manners, you might plow your demesnes and receive your rents; but how to converse with Men of [your] own Quality, how to assist in the Government of your Countrey, and indeed how to behave yourself according to that Degree God Almighty hath placed you in, requires the help of Learning and Prudence, whereby you are made acquainted both with the opinions and examples of elder and wiser times.

The acquisition of such learning and prudence was likely to be a lengthy and painstaking process, beginning in the home with training in temperance, piety and familial loyalty, and continuing through the stages of formal education into a later willingness to study constantly the example of others in the construction of an adult life. Throughout this journey the objects of training concerned Wandesford more intensely than its particular content:

> I would advise you then in general to exercise your self in those studies which tend rather to the Improvement of your Manners, than to the Advancement of your knowledge; I mean, not in Curiosities (which indeed are but the Shells of learning) but rather in such reading as may convey to your Affections rational and fundamental principles, instructing you to know, not only what Virtue is, but how to practise it.[1]

The Wandesfords endeavoured to practise what the head of house preached. In the *Autobiography* of Christopher's daughter, Alice, we have a vivid memorial of this ethic of education in action. All the children were nurtured in a powerful form of Anglican pietism, which remained with most of them throughout life, and in an environment in which the social virtues of the élite were fully articulated. Both parents manifest concern for the public good, generosity to their neighbours and beneficence to the poor. The formal training of the children was much dislocated by the Civil War, but considerable sacrifices were made to ensure that they did not suffer. Alice's two younger brothers, still schoolboys in the early 1640s, were kept at school by her widowed and impoverished mother, and the youngest, Jack, was funded through Cambridge at a time of great family difficulty. The heir to the estate, George, was supported abroad on the Grand Tour until resources ran out. As for Alice herself, she was provided with exactly the education that serious and virtuous parents deemed appropriate for a daughter. She was placed in the company of the Earl of Strafford's daughter Anne, and learned French, singing, dancing, the playing of the lute and theorbo. With her mother she mastered 'working silk, gummework, sweetmeats and other sutable huswifery', but above all from both parents she had full religious instruction, 'tending to the welfaire and eternall happiness and salvation of my poore soule'. She must, coincidentally, have had good basic training in her native tongue, for she writes with fluency, and with a less tortured orthography than many of her female contemporaries. Finally Wandesford must have hoped that when he and his wife could no longer guide the children in their proper duties, his book of advices would befriend them, written as it was in the justifiable fear that he would not live to see his son reach maturity.[2]

The Wandesfords saw their duties to children as ones of training in virtue and understanding suitable to secure them in the station the family already occupied in Yorkshire society. Breeding was to affirm existing hegemony and to lend it civility. The world must have looked rather different to the Welsh squire who wrote an advice for his son at Oxford in the Jacobean period. Cadwalader, his father pointed out, was in 'the fountayne and well head of all learning' as a consequence of much sacrifice, the only one of a large family who could so benefit. It therefore behoved him to address himself to his books and keep away from the evil company of those students who drank and took tobacco 'to their own losse and discredit of their friends and parents whoe sent them to the University for better purposes'. No extra costs were to be incurred – no servitor, no elaborate clothes – by the way, he adds, what has become of Cadwalader's russet coat? Above all, his son should associate with English, not Welsh, companions: 'thereby you may attaine and freely speak Englishe tongue perfectly. I hadd rather that you should keepe company with studious honest Englishmen, than with many of your own countrymen, who are more prone to be idle and riotous than the English'.[3]

There is plenty of brusque affection in Cadwalader's father's letter, and a serious conviction that the accumulation of knowledge led to moral and spiritual virtue. He advises on proper note-taking technique at sermons and disputations, since any scholar of quick understanding can profit from assimilating and digesting the words of preachers and teachers. However, his philosophy of education is a good deal more materialist and mechanistic than that of Christopher Wandesford. Behind the words of his advice is a barely concealed assumption that education is an investment, a means of upward, and geographic, mobility, worth purchasing at considerable cost to the rest of the family. Cadwalader has been thrust from the fastnesses of rural Wales, and it would seem that his father has no intention of letting him lapse once again into the Welsh squirearchy. Here education provides access to the metropolitan culture, to a new social environment, perhaps to wider political influence.

It should by now be no surprise to find gentry attitudes to issues of culture both inherently conservative and sufficiently plastic to accommodate the facts of social mobility and rapid economic transition. The élite shared with other groups in Tudor and Stuart society a logical desire to acculture their young to the roles they would perform in adulthood, roles which contemporary theory described as relatively invariant and determined. The gentry, to quote Wilson, 'be fit to be called to office and authority in their country where they live'. But rulership was inherently complex, and in the literate and enlarged society of the sixteenth century came to demand extended skills that were taught in a more elaborated educational system. The construction and extension of such a system in its turn obliged the élite to hone their cultural skills in order to maintain their social and political hegemony. Wandesford's notion that his sons must be able to 'converse with men of their own quality' in learned discourse is the logical outcome of this process. At the same time education was an acknowledged route to mobility and many of the established families of the period had fairly recent memories of backgrounds like the Ishams, where the yeoman Euseby and his wife 'did so cut his cloth' that all five sons were schooled and became lawyers, clerics or prosperous merchants, three later gaining access to land and the ranks of gentility. The social theorists of Elizabeth's reign were also aware that transformations of this kind existed: men whose fathers were content 'to be counted yeomen and called John or Robert (such an one)' acquired good clothing, admission to an Inn of Court and 'must ever after think scorn to be called other than gentleman'. Established families might not approve, but they could scarcely deny the relationship between education and mobility, since their own younger sons were often dependent on good training to, as Sir John Oglander put it, 'do themselves good'.[4]

Training for a life of power and social authority; training to acquire these advantages for those who by position or family background had no automatic access to them: these are the recurrent themes in any discussion of education and the élite. The emphasis, moreover, was on life: although much of the following discussion inevitably focuses on the formal institutions of training – school, university, the Inns of Court – these were in practise integrated with the broader concept of breeding a gentleman and internalising the values and behaviours proper to rank. A familiar form of will request was that children be educated 'according to their degree and quality'. This had its dangers, as Thomas Fuller observed, for foreigners often commented that 'Englishmen by making their Children Gentlemen before they are Men, cause they are so seldome Wise-men'. Younger sons, of course, needed serious instruction in career skills, but even here the inculcation of piety, of obedience to others, of good manners and of appropriate familial pride were accounted of great importance. Another common form of will request was that children be reared up 'virtuously, in good learning and conversation'. Dame Anne Newdigate requested in her testament that all her children be 'bred up in vertuous and godly life', though for the boys she also added 'good learneing'. Education, in this very broad sense of breeding, should be regarded by the gentleman as second nature, says Brathwait, 'which (such innate seeds of goodnesse are sowne in him) ever improves him, seldome or never depraves him'.[5]

In the radical 1960s it was fashionable to talk of the early modern period as one of revolutionary change in education, when the access of large sections of the populace to literacy and learning was greatly increased, and when the lay élite suddenly acquired a humanistic concern for classical education in the universities. The historiographic pendulum has now swung away from the notion of seismic change: medievalists stressing the continuities of educational provision, early modernists doubting the substance of intellectual advance for the majority of the landed classes. Notions of continuity have much to commend them, especially in the analysis of gentle assumptions about training. Breeding of children in virtue and godliness, providing them with fit opportunities to display leadership in later life, inculcating good manners – these remained rather obvious constants in parental concern between the fifteenth and seventeenth centuries. Peter Idley's rambling advice to his son, translated from earlier sources in the 1450s, urges love of God and devotion to his service, prudence in speech and action, the avoidance of such dangers to youth as women, taverns and good fellowship and gives guidance on how later to manage a wife and household. There is little emphasis on formal education, but the young Idley is expected to learn wisdom from the ancients, and to have all the practical knowledge that ensures self-control. This advice differs little in fundamentals from the type current in the later seventeenth century. In the anonymous *The Advice of a Father, or Counsel to a Child* (1688), for example, piety, good living, beneficence, self-government and good estate management are the key themes: only a greater respect for book learning really differentiates the text from its medieval predecessor.[6]

## 7.1 EARLY AND HOUSEHOLD TRAINING

Many of these basic assumptions about manners, morals and proper behaviour were obviously to be taught by parental example and precept – hence their prominence in the literature of advice. Lawrence Humphrey argues that it was essential that the young noble or gentleman learned his social skills:

> . . . at his owne home, as in a free schoole, shape and forme himselfe; before thence he be thruste abroade as into an open stage before he determine with others in the churche divine ordinances religiously, and civile duties towards all and every man.

The first and best teachers in the household were parents. 'Beware', said Walter Mildmay to his son in 1570, 'what thou sayest and doest in thine own house, for thine example is a guide to thy wife, children and family'. Simonds D'Ewes, whose own parents had been somewhat negligent, believed that 'parents are . . . especiallie bound to instruct . . . children, pray for them and traine them upp in the feare of God because they drew originall corruption from ther loines'. This implied intimacy and proximity. Ideally, observed the *Glasse for Householders* (1542), children should be kept close to parents, sleeping in their bedchamber and eating with them at table, for only so could they fully absorb the moral example of their elders. John Kaye described for his descendants how children should be educated 'at playe and meale' by their parents to distinguish good from bad. In the consciously godly household such close supervision of a child's early moral development was a religious duty. Gervase Disney and his siblings were reared by devout parents, who watched them closely and 'moderated betwixt the Extreams of unwarrantable Indulgence and cruel rigor.'[7]

Such intimacies were by no means guaranteed among the gentry, even in the seventeenth century when methods of childrearing had been softened by humanist and Protestant advice. Large households and frequent parental absence inevitably contributed to social distance, and the practise of wet-nursing no doubt raised barriers to early bonding. In practise the young were frequently left to the not-so-tender mercies of servants like those who allowed Simonds D'Ewes the run of his grandfather's cellar, thereby 'enflaming his blood'. Grace Sharington's governness had to warn her charges to avoid the serving men, who were both bold and ribald. John Aubrey was passionately opposed to education in the home for boys, partly because they would be 'flattered by the servants and dependents of the family' and distracted by domestic contretemps. In 1671 Lady Harley urged her husband to send her young sons away to school, since at home they could not be prevented from mixing with the servants and acquiring strange clownish speech and behaviour.[8]

Proper governance and discipline was in the hands of the head of household and much of the literary discussion about early rearing revolved around the degree of sternness he should display to the young. The most widely shared position throughout the early modern period was that to spare the rod was to spoil the child. If evil habits were allowed to flourish in infancy, said John Kaye, they would never be eradicated, and the usually mild John Oglander spoke with passion when he insisted that 'nothing undoeth children more than the fondness of parents when they are young, breeding them so tenderly and keeping them from hardness and labour that they seldom prove good for anything afterwards'.

Children, said Grace Mildmay, are governed by 'the terror of punishments'. The theorists generally concurred, although the unanimity of the disciplinary view inherited from the Middle Ages was gradually shaken by post-Erasmian writers. *The Glasse for Householders* was already advocating the stick and carrot approach to learning, and by the early seventeenth century Dorothy Leigh could argue as a commonplace that gentleness was the best persuasion to good behaviour. However, most writers remained deeply suspicious of the old Adam in children, and of the weakness of parents, especially mothers, who would 'cocker' their young. Some fathers reacted against any notion of such tenderness with vigour, like Sir William Carew, who hauled home his truant schoolboy son from Exeter in 1526 'like a dog' and tied him to one of the family hounds to teach him penitence. This would probably have been deemed inappropriate a century later, but severe discipline in the home was still so normal as to occasion little comment from those, like Christopher Guise, who experienced its daily effects. Sir John Holland's daughter recalled that when she failed to learn her catechism her father 'debarred me from my meat' and the usually indulgent Harbottle Grimston argued that both servants and children must be chastised severely if they 'offend grievously'.[9]

Household discipline was intended to combine crucial training in piety, manners and early civility with some introduction to formal learning. The father might take some role in the latter, as did Judge Whitelocke, who not only talked seriously to his son from the age of three onwards, but began to offer him 'solid instruction' from the age of eight. Sir Henry Slingsby experimented with teaching his four-year-old son Henry Latin by speaking the language, though he had a tutor and chaplain to assist him. Puritan fathers took predictable interest in religious training: Sir Nathaniel Barnardiston cared for his children 'by a constant and serious study for their Education in the most exact and strict way of pure and paternal Religion'. Learned fathers often reserved their serious efforts for later instruction when, like Sir John Holles or Sir Edward Dering, they would write to their sons in several ancient and modern languages and expect responses in kind.[10]

But many of the tasks of household teaching, at least before the age when children emerged from the nursery, devolved upon the mother. In the early years of training there seems to have been little that was overtly gendered about education, except in those establishments where parental ambition pushed sons into precociously early work in the classics, like the unfortunate Richard Evelyn, who could read English, French and Latin before his death at the age of five. Reading, early religious study, and perhaps some access to language were in the hands of those women who had sufficient skills themselves. Gervase Holles lost his mother when an infant, but was given a good training in the reading of English by his grandmother before going to grammar school at six. Bulstrode Whitelocke's mother, a lady of considerable learning, taught her son the rudiments of 'his book' and it would seem some of the French in which she was expert. Sir Henry Slingsby's wife instructed her daughter Barbara in her catechism, and reading and writing. The number of 'advices' from mothers to their children (usually male) after the turn of the sixteenth century suggests the seriousness with which they regarded these duties. Although levels of female illiteracy may have made formal teaching more difficult a century earlier, there was some continuity of expectation that mothers should educate their young: St Anne teaching the Virgin to read was a favoured theme in late medieval art.[11]

It was within the household that these early directions were gradually superseded by a more obviously gendered approach to training. Both sexes had to learn obedience – standing before parents, kneeling for daily blessing, offering deference to those of high rank and greater age. The formality of such gestures diminished during the seventeenth century, so that Aubrey could regard as old-fashioned the habit by which married women still stood in their mothers' presence, but the basic principle of obedience was upheld. However, the control of the will led in very different directions for boys and for girls of the élite: boys had to make the transition from habits of obedience and internalised self-discipline to those of authority and command. A delicate balance had to be achieved between the former and the latter, one that necessitated a fairly early addition of formal, external instruction to direct parental guidance. In the case of girls an even more difficult feat had to be attempted, since the breeding process had to inculcate modesty, chastity and submissiveness, qualities which, as Linda Pollock observes 'were not innate, but had to be taught'. Lady Grace Mildmay vividly described how her mother had taught her 'not to subject my self unto mine own will, and frame me to bear patiently whatsoever adversity should assault me in this world'. Moreover, it was not in the case of women simply a question of breaking the will and achieving these goals; rather the gentlewoman had to combine a life of dutiful conformity with the ability to manage a household, discipline servants and act as the alter ego to her husband in any necessary circumstances. She had to learn the tripartite skills of submissiveness to authority, internal self-discipline and an ability to command. Most parents continued throughout our period to believe that these were best taught within a household context, as the 'natural' environment of the female.[12]

In practise these aspirations meant that the training of women changed less markedly than that of men during the early modern period. The constant goal was good breeding: Sir Edward Molineux's daughters, for example, were sent to a cousin to be reared in 'virtue, good manners and learning to play the gentle-woman and good housewives, to dress meat and oversee their households'. Such breeding up might be achieved within the parental home, with the importation of private tutors when necessary. Humphrey Jones advised Sir John Wynn in 1621 that he had an excellent music teacher, who had already trained several young Welsh ladies not only in singing and instrumentation, but in writing a 'faere Romane' hand and reading English. He suggested that he be retained for Sir John's grand-daughters. In household with a learned father or mother this was probably a satisfactory arrangement: William Blundell kept his daughters at home and gave serious attention to their training, assisted by his unmarried sister Frances. Home training should also have had the advantage of preserving the prized virtue of daughters, though even then there was the danger of an unsound teacher, like the music tutor with whom Katherine Cholmley fell in love. The day she was to marry Lord Lumley she begged her father not to force her to the match and, remarkably for an Elizabethan parent, Sir Richard 'in some sort connived at' marriage to the tutor, when it seemed too late to prevent it. The amorous potential of music teaching is well evoked in the autobiography of the madrigalist Thomas Whytehorne, though he constantly presents himself as innocent victim of the seductive wiles of his female employers.[13]

Even in the parental home it should not be assumed that female education was a simple process. The acquisition of the list of skills required by Molineux was no doubt as time-consuming as those required of boys. The avoidance of idleness was required of both genders, and moralists were much afflicted by the fear that women in particular would be reared with too much indulgence. Ralph Verney, in a famous comment on his daughter Peg complained that 'she grows a great girl and will be spoiled for want of breeding . . . being a girl she shall not learn Latin, so she will have the more time to learn breeding hereafter; and [needle]work too'. It was also Ralph Verney who was keen to restrict his intellectual god-daughter Nancy Denton to the Bible and the Book of Common Prayer as her principal reading matter, though here he seems rather traditionalist by the standards of seventeenth-century gentlemen, since pride in the intellectual achievements of daughters was also common. Sir Thomas Meautys expressed pleasure that his eldest girl was 'of a good memory and learnes more than I can find meanes to have tought hir'.[14]

Education, especially if parents were conscientious about the acquisition of a range of practical, social and intellectual skills, was inevitably burdensome, and at least its later stages were often acquired elsewhere. Here the pattern of opportunity for girls did change somewhat over time. Before the Dissolution of the Monasteries parents had the choice of other households or a nunnery; in the seventeenth century boarding schools began to play a role not dissimilar to the latter. Between those dates the only serious choice available to Protestant parents was another élite household. It might, indeed, be assumed that private establishments had some advantages for girls, since they provided visible role models of adult female behaviour, alternately exercising authority and living under subjection. But it was not always possible or convenient to turn to other individuals, and many gentry parents seem to have looked to formal structures when they had the opportunity. Sometimes one system followed the other: in the late medieval period a familiar pattern seems to have been a nunnery until a daughter was about fourteen, and then a household for finishing and service of the lady. The popularity of the nunnery is suggested by the report of the Dissolution commissioners that at Polesworth Abbey between 30 and 40 gentlemen's children were being reared and that St Mary's, Winchester, housed 26 girls from local families. By the end of the seventeenth century there were boarding establishments in London, but also in most provincial centres of any size, and they had become a standard resort for the daughters of the gentry.[15]

Some gentlewomen experienced training in households that were likely to be better equipped for the serious development of the young than any nunnery or girls' boarding school. Lady Margaret

Hoby was reared with the Countess of Huntingdon in an atmosphere of Protestant learning and godliness, though the practical abilities revealed in her diary show that housewifery was not neglected. The Countess prided herself on her training of the young: in 1618 she observed 'I think ther will none meke questen, but i knoe how to breed and govern yong gentlewomen'. Margaret in her turn took in daughters of local families for service and education. Sir Hugh Cholmley's wife was 'desired' by various local men 'to have their daughters in service with her; so as being dismissed with many good qualities, they did communicate them to others'. On the Isle of Wight Mistress Milles, the widow of Mr George Milles of Heasley, 'brought up most of the young gentlewomen in the Island and had the sway of the Island for many years'. Alice Thornton, as we have seen, learned her formal skills in the household of the Earl of Strafford.[16]

The content of the education offered to girls in these various establishments is not easy to categorise in detail. Since there was a persistent emphasis on life skills and manners it would be dangerous to assume that training automatically became more formal or intellectual during the course of the sixteenth and seventeenth centuries. Indeed it has been suggested that the boarding establishments in particular were retrograde in placing increased emphasis on social graces and denigrating even those subjects such as modern languages that had been thought appropriate to women. The Latinity of a small minority of noblewomen does not offer effective insights into the training of the rest, since they were being specifically trained to transcend their gender, possibly to rule. The most obvious shift in general instruction for the gentry was that basic literacy, already an expectation for many in the late Middle Ages, was gradually supplemented by training in writing and general clarity of expression that had previously been less widespread. At the end of the sixteenth century women often show more elegant command of an italic hand than do men, but their spelling and general control of language still betrays a lack of access to high culture. Yet it would, by the mid-seventeenth century, be uncommon to find a woman of the élite who could not handle her own correspondence or use formal accounting methods in the organisation of her household.[17]

The type of parents who have left literary records about childrearing are also likely to have been those who cared most about their daughters' education. They bred up girls who often had a wide range of knowledge and skill, even if only a small minority had access to full Latinity. Elizabeth Cholmley, born a Twysden, had as her chief pleasure 'her book' and the reading of histories; Hannibal Baskerville's grandmother, a Throckmorton, was learned in several tongues, and many godly ladies were passionate note-takers at sermons (another skill, incidentally, which Sir Ralph Verney believed should be beyond women). Even in the early sixteenth century a number of gentry wills ask for girls as well as boys to be 'put to school' or 'brought up in erudition'. Fragmentary evidence from household accounts suggests that there was a willingness to invest heavily in the training of daughters. Some girls, like the two grand-daughters of Sir Ralph Worsley, cost more to put through school than their brothers. Even a minor gentleman such as Thomas Congreve of Staffordshire was prepared to face the cost of boarding school in the Cotswolds for at least one daughter. Gentlemen of Congreve's kind often seem to have compromised giving younger girls in the family a more formal education, perhaps because the loss of a mother made alternative arrangements desirable, while keeping the oldest girl at home in anticipation of early marriage. We know, for example, nothing of the education of the two daughters of Sir John Wynn, both early arrivals in the family, who seem to have been regarded as fodder for suitable marriage alliances, though Mary at least acquired some intellectual skills before she became a Mostyn. The Kaye girls also came early in their family, and John is alarmingly silent about their training in his proud writings on financing the education of his sons. And no doubt there were many parents who simply did not see the point of excessive instruction for girls. Dorothy Kaye's mother can scarcely have valued academic skills, if we are to believe the verse accompanying her daughter's portrait:

> To lyve at home in howsyverye
> To order well my famylye
> To see they lyve not Idillye
> To bryng upe children vertuslye.[18]

## 7.2 VOCATION AND SCHOOLING

The essence of female education was that it should fit daughters for the complex vocation of wife and mother. With boys there were problems of other kinds, the most obvious of which was the issue of how narrowly vocational training should be. Many assumed, as Wandesford reminds us, that education towards a calling was a necessary gift to younger sons, while the eldest, heir to a secure estate, might be permitted less concentration on study. But life in early modern England was full of vicissitudes, and gentry fathers spoke from experience and observation when they argued that all sons needed to acquire skills, not only to maintain their social state, but to secure their future. 'For good husbandry in thy children', said Oglander, 'be sure to bring them all up in a vocation. . . Make them but scholars and they are fitted for any employment'. 'Fine feathers make fine birds' was Theophilus Leigh's view of his son, 'Riding the great Horse and Dancing may make him a beau but I doubt will conduce little to making his fortune in the world'. When these practical anxieties intersected with humanist insistence that education was necessary for the life of virtue, the influx of gentlemen into schools, universities and Inns of Court becomes comprehensible.[19]

Concerns about career structure, particular pressing for younger sons and for those on the margins of gentility, are one of the most visible forms of parental involvement in education. It would seem that for the former group familial interest was often expected to transcend personal preference or even ability. The image of the sons of the Knightley family arrayed on their father's tomb in the vestments of their calling is a striking evocation of this perception. There is, even in the seventeenth century, a recurrent tendency to destine the second or third son for the law, the next for the Church and the youngest for trade, a patterning that must transcend any understanding of the needs of the individuals concerned. Sir John Wynn, in his characteristically patriarchal way, seems to have had an arrangement of this general type in his mind, and much of the Wynn correspondence is concerned with the attempts of his sons, often supported by their Uncle Ellis, to persuade him to be more flexible. Sir Patience Ward, Lord Mayor of London during the Exclusion Crisis, described how his pious mother had destined him for the ministry, and trained him, even in his infancy, to participate in her private prayers.[20]

Educational theorists from Erasmus onwards spoke against these parental reflexes: William Perkins argued that two things must be considered before choices were made for children 'first, their inclination, secondly, their natural gifts'. John Kaye was a

21. The sons of Sir Richard Knightly, d. 1534: panel from monument, Fawsley Church, Northamptonshire

gentleman who understood this message, for he urged parents to 'ponder . . . indifferentlye, to what thy childe ys bente'. A wise parent or grandparent allowed the natural inclinations of children to emerge in the early years of schooling, and listened to any advice his teachers could give. Thus Jonathan Rashleigh's grandsons were ordered according to the suggestions of their schoolmaster: John, though no natural intellectual, would benefit from time at the university, Philip was a scholar by disposition, while Charles 'is cut out for a Merchant which his genius carries him too'. An extreme example of a willingness to suit boys to careers comes from the Gawdy family where Sir William allowed his second and fourth sons, who were both deaf-mutes, to be apprenticed to the artist Peter Lely. It is predictable that parents usually found it easier to accommodate themselves to sons who sought careers in the law than in the Church or trade. It would be difficult to demonstrate any *general* hostility to either of the latter, but anxiety about future prospects sometimes afflicted families. Much thought was given to the suitability of masters, and there are examples of parental resistance to sons' requests for a practical training, like that of Sir Ralph Verney, who took three years to yield to his second son Jack's desire to be an apprentice. 'I doe know,' the latter pleaded, 'Lords sones which must be apprintices, and theire elder brother is worth 5 thousand pounds a yeare'. Not many aristocrats were bound apprentice, but Jack was correct to argue for the growing respectability of trade: by the mid-seventeenth century over a third of the apprentices to the London Grocers' Company claimed gentle status, as did nearly 50 per cent of the Drapers of Shrewsbury.[21]

Whether restrictive or permissive about future life choices, most serious gentlemen would have endorsed Perkins's view that it was their duty to guide children into a proper calling, for their own advancement and the avoidance of the sin of idleness. One fear was of the wastrel younger son, like Francis Wilson of Sussex, who moaned that he 'must study to get money to buy bread', but always returned to batten on his father until he finally found an outlet in the Dutch and Swedish armies of the Thirty Year's War. Or there was the anonymous, flippant, young man, who besieged his mother with vaporisings on his career choice having 'turned-over twenty eight gret leaves of the littell volume of my life'. Sir Nathaniel Bacon apparently threatened on one occasion to lock his grandson in an unheated chamber 'to make him leve his house and betake him to some calling'. Another fear was of the indolent heir, bent on hunting and drinking rather than on the protection of the family estates and the securing of the family's name in the commonwealth. The impulse to provide an increasingly formal, academic education for all sons probably owed as much to the desire to 'keepe them from idleness which is the route of all evil' as it did to the explicit preaching of humanist educationalists. 'I myself', said Sir John Wynn in 1603 'have had the breeding of a gentleman, and I am fre thank God from drunkeness and frenzy'.[22]

The old style of household training, which was by no means dead in the sixteenth century, was not wholly deficient in formal teaching, but, with its emphasis on physical pursuits and shared conviviality, perhaps reinforced too strongly the existing habits of the gentry. Yorkshire gentlemen, complained James Ryther to Cecil, 'generally have actyve bodies . . . but by the remysse educacion of indiscreet parents they fall to rude pastymes befor they learne cyvill behavior'. Sir John Perrott, reared in the old traditions of 'gentleman-lyke exercises' under Henry VIII showed, according to his descendant, the virtues of magnanimity and 'greetness of body', and added a good natural wit in languages, yet in matters of state could only behave as 'a Man not professing Learning'. As Stone points out, the shortage of surviving gentry correspondence for the first three-quarters of the sixteenth century suggests that traditional education did not in general foster learned habits. It even confined some of the lesser gentry to illiteracy: in the 1560s 92 out of 146 gentlemen of Northumberland failed to sign their names on the Supremacy Oath. When times had changed, Sir John Reresby could speak with disapproval of his great-grandfather for giving his grandfather 'private education and not much learning'. A certain defensiveness also pervades the account that Gervase Holles gives of ancestors not subjected to the full rigours of a classical education. Gervase's maternal grandfather 'had great disadvantages of education, which comonly young wardes have . . . I have heard him say yt he had proceeded at the schoole no further than Ovid's Metamorphoses before he threw away his books and got him a kennell of houndes'.[23]

By the mid-sixteenth century the best secondary education for boys, whether conducted in household or school, was determinedly classical and a deliberate preparation for higher education. The choice of environment was dependent on wealth, religious preference, availibility of schools and, in some measure, fashion. The sons of nobles, on the first and last grounds, tended to be trained by private tutors, or at one of the great schools such as Eton. Catholics, especially from the later Elizabethan years, opted for private tutors when they did not choose to send sons and daughters abroad. The children of conformist gentlemen were most likely to attend grammar or private schools. A breakdown of the schooling of 310 Yorkshire gentlemen between 1558 and 1642 shows that over a third were trained in local grammar schools and another 37 in local private schools. As many as 85 were given private tuition, but of these no less than 70 were from Catholic families. A similar impression, not so clearly expressed statistically, can be gained from work on Durham, Gloucestershire and Wales, where local or regional schools like Shrewsbury, predominated. From a different perspective, the matriculation registers of Caius College, Cambridge, show that an overwhelming proportion of the gentry entering the college had formal schooling behind them: a sample of 153 cases for the late sixteenth century provides only 14 examples of full education at home and a strong preponderance of local and regional schools among the matriculants. Grammar schools often had a large percentage of gentry students: at Bury St Edmunds in 1656, for example, 52 per cent of those on the roll were from gentry backgrounds, and even at less fashionable Colchester the admission registers from 1637 to 1645 show 31 per cent gentlemen.[24]

The story is slightly different if the period is extended to include the early sixteenth and late seventeenth centuries. In the earlier years household education was still a vital force: a number of Gloucester gentry of the Henrician years gained their education through the royal Court, for example. These were the years when interesting experiments like Sir Humphrey Wingfield's private household school in Ipswich sought to integrate humanist ideas into the training of the élite. Men as distinguished as Roger Ascham, Queen Elizabeth's tutor, and John Christopherson, one of Mary's bishops, passed through Wingfield's hands before going to university. Households and formal educational establishments were still not fully distinct entities in some parental minds at this date. John Basford, stepson to Sir Thomas Pope, founder of Trinity College, Oxford, was a reluctant attender at university 'to have the Latin tongue'. His mother, who was determined to educate him for some employment, offered the alternative of Sir Richard Southwell's household 'to learn there among his children'. A minority of gentlemen continued to pursue private humanist education for their children in the next hundred years, despite the general dominance of the grammar schools. The sons of Sir John Newdigate, for example, were bred at home in the latest learning by Henry Simpson, whom Dame Anne described as 'a most honest, civil, fair-conditioned man . . . a greater scholar . . . and a good divine'.[25]

In the later seventeenth century the grammar schools lost some of their popularity, both because they were seen as subversive of orthodoxy, and because they were not always deferential to status. Christopher Guise found it instructive that at Wootton school he was 'on the playne ground without any advantageouse rise of aliance or preheminence of extraction', but many gentlemen sought exactly these latter benefits for their offspring. By the Restoration the private tutor with an ability to teach the classics was a common feature in the gentry household. On the other hand, such enclosed education might retard the socialising process: Aubrey spoke bitterly of the 'kind of park' in which his father reared him, far from children of his own age, and of the need for 'affronts' and 'some beatings' to civilise children. Some sensitive elders began to doubt whether the beatings liberally administered by the great schools were desirable: Mrs Sacheverall advised her brother not to send her mild-tempered nephew to a public school, but to choose a private master 'who usually considers a childs disposition more'. But such 'advanced' educational theory was not widely accepted. Many of the greater gentry continued to see sociability as desirable, and sent their sons to public school: Dr Busby's regime at Westminster during the Civil War, for example, confirmed the pre-eminence of that school in the capital and encouraged a number of nobles, as well as gentlemen, to send their sons there.[26]

Information from the gentry themselves about their schooling tends either to reminiscences, often negative, about grammar school existence, or endless parental correspondence about fees, damp air and clothing. It is, however, possible on occasions to reconstruct some of the attitudes that encouraged parents to despatch their sons to school. The correspondence of Sir John Wynn is replete with material on the education of his sons, all of whom left Wales relatively early to attend big schools in south-east England. His heir John was at Bedford in 1604, where he was able to pursue not only Latin grammar, but Greek and Hebrew, instrumental and vocal music, French and Italian. It may be assumed that John gained some competence in the last two, since on his Grand Tour in 1615 he shows linguistic skill. Wynn's objective for his son was not university, but the Inns of Court, but his own wide culture would have predisposed him to a good foundation in the humanities for John. The high value that he placed on education is suggested by the existence of an informal school in his home at Gwydir. John was followed by Richard, who may also have been to Bedford, and then by Owen and Robin who, after dithering by their father that lasted over two years, were sent to Westminster. It was during this period of uncertainty in 1605 that Sir John wrote to his London agent asking for assistance in finding rooms for the winter, saying that he intended to bring up Owen and Robin 'for Eaton, and so the rest of my children I mean to place thereabouts for Educatyon and course of lyf'. He was, with much complaint about cost, investing in a future for his younger children around the capital, since Wales yielded little to their advantage. Westminster was selected in the end because Wynn's brother Ellis went there 'which was the cause of his good fortune'. However, a few months later Sir John moved the boys to Eton, on the grounds that the air of London was damaging to their health. Robin was the only child who was seriously intended for university, perhaps in this case because Wynn had recognised his genuine academic bent. The younger sons were educated partly in Wales, but then Ellis and Henry were sent to the Free School at St Alban's. This, their older brother Maurice reported, was a good school for learning and manners, but the boys were corrupt, and likely to spoil others. For these younger boys Wynn seems to have regarded schooling primarily as a feeder for a career in law, his own advancing years making it necessary that they should be 'placed' as soon as possible.[27]

## 7.3 UNIVERSITY AND BEYOND

Sir John Wynn's practical spirit, combined with the constant impecuniousness of his purse and the need to provide for a large family, led him to favour training that would secure a return, largely that provided by the Inns of Court. We have no evidence of his views on the universities, but it might be reasonable to infer that, despite his own wide culture, he regarded them as appropriate primarily to scholars and future clerics. Parents who chose one of the ancient universities as training ground for their young after school days presumably saw additional qualities in the institutions, but even they were subject to anxieties and doubts about Oxford and Cambridge. In the first place there was the moral danger to children presented by those 'tobacco-takers, drinkers and swearers' against whom Cadwalader's father had been so careful to warn. The sort of youth who participated in throwing a brick-bat in at the college window where a group of Sir Roger Townshend's godly friends were assembled at prayer, were an ever-present threat to good order. 'If you fall into lewed companie and delight in them,' said Jonathan Rashleigh to his son, 'I shall account you as a lost child.' Not only were there the predictable moral dangers of dissipation, but the deliberate exploitation of the innocent and prosperous by those whom Christopher Wandesford claimed waited to lead eldest sons into riot and expense. Some parents who risked these moral perils found their fears had been amply justified: 'you have goseled and goodfelloed it more then yow have studied' complained Sir John Holles to his son Denzil. Even sober students acknowledged that these parental anxieties were often justified: Sir Simonds D'Ewes, for example, described Cambridge in the Jacobean period as swarming with the 'debauched and atheisticall'. Christopher Guise knew well that 'the vice of Oxford scollars is theyr frequenting tipling houses', since he had himself been one of the merry rout. Patience Ward claimed that he had been so horrified by old school-friends who had 'told him the methods and course' of Civil War Cambridge that he immediately departed for London to seek an apprenticeship.[28]

The other major disadvantage of the university was that it was costly, more costly than many parents seem to have anticipated when they first despatched their boys. An archive could be constructed out of the anxious correspondence between parents, boys and tutors on the financing of the young. Justice Silence spoke for many when, in response to Shallow's questions – 'I dare say my cousin William is become a good scholar? He is at Oxford still is he not?' – he replied with feeling 'Indeed sir, to my cost'. Lady Meriel Littelton was particularly burdened by the need to redeem her Worcestershire estates after the condemnation of her husband for his part in the Essex Revolt, keep a son at Oxford and two at school, and moaned to her aunt 'more charge I have found yt then happily others will beleeve or truly I did myself expeckt. Yt is a deare time . . . to trayne uppe youth in'. Average costs for an undergraduate at the turn of the sixteenth century have been reckoned at between £30 and £50 a year, a figure that would strain the resources of an ordinary squire, or anyone with several sons to promote. Those squires who did succeed in funding children through university clearly prided themselves on their managerial skills: John Kaye recorded that he had spent £120, £53 and £130 on his three university-trained sons. Richard Wilton of Topcroft Hall, Norfolk, sent his son Robert to Cambridge in 1615 with an allowance of only £30, and spoke in his commonplace book of that which Providence had provided which 'I besich maybe effectually expended to Gods glory'.[29]

Given the costs of provision, parents were understandably suspicious of the ability of the young to manage their resources. 'As I am wilinge to paie my monie for your learninge', said Sir Henry Slingsby to his son in 1619, 'soe you ought to be carefull my monie be not loste by your childish negligence'. Thomas Isham thought that while necessary items should be purchased 'unneedfull things I would have spared' since he was about to conclude a marriage treaty at home for one of his daughters. Boys, in their turn, thought as ever that parents had a wholly unrealistic understanding of the charges of a university. Simonds D'Ewes was typical in constantly complaining about his small allowance, as was Harvey Bagot in plaguing his father with requests for extra subvention. It was predictable that Sir John Wynn should fail to give Robin a 'competence of living' while he was at St John's, Cambridge. Tutors sometimes took the side of the young in these disputes: Elias Travers, tutor to young Thomas Knyvett, told his grandmother on several occasions that she did not allow him monies 'sutable to his place and ranck' and that he had endeavoured to live as frugally as was compatible with that state. James Oxinden's tutor remarked to his brother Henry with some asperity that the former 'is well enoughed cloathed for a poore scholler in St. John's College: but short of a Kentish gentleman'.[30]

These arguments between parents and children have for us a universal air. But they can only have developed when the practise of educating in households gave way to formal training in professional institutions. Although in the case of the gentry the habit of attendance at university stretched well back into the Middle Ages, more sons were being given this education in the later sixteenth century than previously. Some of the perceived increase in gentlemen attending the universities from the mid-Elizabethan years onwards is undoubtedly an illusion created by the keeping of matriculation registers, but the real influx of prosperous commoners seems well attested. One of the latest contributions to a flourishing historiographical debate on this problem – McConica's study of

Corpus Christi, Oxford admissions – shows that there was steady recruiting to the foundation from gentry families throughout the sixteenth century, but that the few commoners admitted under Bishop Fox's original statutes were strongly afforced in the last two decades. Stone's figures, based on the matriculation registers of Oxford, show the average annual admissions of sons of peers, baronets and knights rising from 7 in the 1570s to a peak of 45 in the 1630s: the size of this group increased approximately three-fold between 1603 and 1640, the number of those they sent to Oxford four-fold.[31]

The story is unlikely to have been very different in the broader ranks of the richer gentry: if we examine this from the perspective of the counties we find that in Gloucestershire, for example, almost all MPs and JPs from the early decades of the seventeenth century had been trained at Oxford. As early as the 1570s between 17 per cent and 26 per cent of a sample of 470 Norfolk gentlemen had attended university. In the case of Yorkshire gentlemen it is possible to discern a rough correlation between size of estate and commitment to higher education: only 172 of the 679 heads of house alive in 1642 had attended a university, but if only Protestant squires worth more than £500 per annum are isolated it transpires that a majority, often plus their younger brothers, had been to Oxford or Cambridge. In Havering in Essex the greater gentry were already sending some of their sons to university under Elizabeth, but it only became common for those of less wealth to do so in the Jacobean age. By the later seventeenth century when Stone's so-called great depression in university education had begun, the Glamorgan gentry continued to send about 25 sons a year to matriculate at Oxford from a county which had only 60 to 70 families with incomes over £150 per annum.[32]

So what induced so many careful parents to send sons into an expensive and morally threatening environment that offered few immediate rewards or career prospects? It may run counter to the spirit of our initial argument, as well as much secondary literature on the subject, to suggest that parents first sought learning, or rather the wisdom that comes from knowledge, as a serious goal. All the sententious advice descending on the heads of the young urged serious application to study, and to the godly instruction so readily available at Oxford and Cambridge. We have encountered the Welsh squire on the subject of sermon notes, and Rashleigh's anxiety lest his son be distracted from study by idle company. Dame

Katherine Paston wanted her son kept at university 'until thy mind be furnished with . . . liberal sciences'. Concerned parents often sought a combination of subjects that were part of the university syllabus and humane disciplines. Sir William Wentworth suggested that his son take the advice of some learned 'judicial man of the university' and study logic, philosophy, cosmography and especially histories; Christopher Wandesford that his son follow university learning, but that histories should be his prime concern. Thomas Isham observed to his son John in 1600 that he would be wise to continue with the study of poetry since he did not think 'hym to be a sufficient scholler that is not somewhat practised therein'. Sir Roger Twysden told his rather older son Charles in 1665 that he must buckle to the study of Greek so that 'you may make yourself fit for any employment at home or abroad.' Ellis Wynn, when advising his brother on a suitable university for Robin, thought that the crucial issue was finding a good tutor in logic and philosophy – a much easier task, he claimed, at Oxford than at Cambridge. It may be that the surviving set of correspondence is unrepresentative, but there is scarcely a parent or guardian who does *not* seek to persuade their charges of the need for serious application to intellectual duty.[33]

This language of academic concern from parents fits with arguments recently advanced that the distinction between types of early modern undergraduate has been overdrawn by historians. Older and younger sons, those with scholarships on college foundations and those who were prosperous fellow commoners, may have had more in common than has been supposed. Before the Elizabethan era many of the gentry who studied at university were scholars, and they included their share of heirs as well as younger sons. Among 51 gentlemen who passed through Corpus in the sixteenth century, and were landowners in later life, almost half entered the college as scholars. In all there were 42 gentry on the foundation, and 11 of them were eldest sons. The evidence of book purchasing by Joseph Mead's pupils at Christ's College, in the early seventeenth century, shows the prosperous fellow commoners, few of whom were destined for an academic career, buying more per quarter than the pensioners, the group including many future clerics.[34]

If any description of studies can be woven from recent research on undergraduate education it is that initially many students of all categories followed fairly closely upon university requirements in logic and philosophy. This is suggested by the pattern of book-buying at Christ's, by sources such as the undergraduate account books of the Carnsew brothers in Elizabeth's reign and the Newdigates in the next century, and by individual reminiscences like that of Bulstrode Whitelocke. Whitelocke, at St John's, Oxford, under Laud 'closely followed his study of Logick and Philosophy' and conversed on these with his tutor Dr Parsons. Sir George Courthop, recalling his years as an upper commoner at University College, Oxford, noted that the Master 'kept us to do as much exercise in the house, as any poor scholar or Servitor' and had such an influence on this oldest son that he stayed three years to complete his BA and almost fulfilled MA requirements. After the first year of study it may well be that for most there was a greater polarisation between the 'professional' student, constrained to spend much time on the university syllabus, and those who were intended to spend only two years or so in the system. Mead's students in this latter position seem to have bought fewer books in physics, Hebrew, theology and geometry, more in Latin and arithmetic. Even a student like Whitelocke, who had some aspirations to proceed to BA, spent much time reading history as well as pursuing the required syllabus. The Newdigates bought key historians such as Tacitus and Livy, as well as a number of texts necessary for the early stages of the formal syllabus. Some gentlemen, like Randolph Cholmondeley, son of a Cheshire knight, seem to have managed to concentrate almost entirely on classical rhetoric.[35]

The consequence of such training, if parents were fortunate and the young disciplined, was the construction of men of serious academic ability, the sort of men to whom Reginald Scot could appeal when he addressed his *Discoverie of Witchcraft* to gentlemen who would be 'very sufficiently informed' about the great range of sources in 'divinitie and philosophie' which he invoked. The circles of learned and godly gentlemen, such as the Elizabethan Society of Antiquaries, the Puritan gentry of Northamptonshire, or the scholarly men of early seventeenth-century Norfolk and Kent, did not garner all their knowledge at the universities, but a majority had attended Oxford or Cambridge and must have had their formal training enhanced there. A character in Henry Glapthorne's play *Wit in a Constable* (1639) shows the gentleman turned scholar: 'I have been idle' laments Jeremy Holdfast, 'Since I cam up from Cambridge, goe to my stationer And bid him send me Swarez Metaphysickes'. Even D'Ewes, who despised many of his fellow-

22. Sir Thomas Lucy III, d. 1640, with his books: detail from monument, Charlecote Church, Warwickshire

students, was deeply attached to his tutor Richard Holdsworth, and gained both increased knowledge of the classics and a firmer theological foundation during his years at Cambridge. The construction of the learned country gentleman, so beautifully exemplified by the Sir Thomas Lucy III, who had his classical texts carved behind him on his tomb, and whose epitaph spoke of the welcome he always gave to those who could talk of theology and literature, was at least in part the achievement of the ancient universities in the century after the Reformation.[36]

But it would be unwise to react too vigorously against the familiar argument that the universities were seen as finishing schools and places of social advantage by both parents and children. For every earnest parent who sought pure godliness or scholarship from their investment – 'my greatest care . . . hath been, and still is, to breed my son a scholar', said Sir Thomas Fairfax in 1614 – there must have been many who saw the life of the mind as only one of the offerings available. Tutors were sensitive to such concerns: Thomas Atkinson, for example, wrote in 1624 of his charge Thomas Smyth to his father 'when you left him here I took upon mee the Charge of a Gentleman, I shall blush to returne him you again a meere Scholler'. The extra-curricular activities of dancing, music, fencing and hunting were all accepted as appropriate additions to formal study. These might easily become a distraction, as they did for the unfortunate Simon Forman, who had to accompany his upper-class patrons on endless excursions into the Oxfordshire countryside. But the construction of the gentleman demanded such training, so that, in Clarendon's words, the universities should combine 'the lighter with the serious breeding'. 'I would have you learne to dance', said Rashleigh to his son, having given him fierce instructions on not wasting study time. Even scholars might need to reveal some of these attributes of gentility. Thomas Cranmer's father, who intended his son to be bred a scholar, nevertheless also ensured that he had skills in riding and hunting, which he continued to exercise at university. When Bulstrode Whitelocke was at St John's he frequently hunted in company with Dr Juxon, then a commoner of the college.[37]

It was unlikely, however, to be extra-curricular training tacked to the edges of the collegiate system that most attracted parents. Rather it was the chance to mix and mingle with 'all sorts and conditions of men', to make the social contacts and to gain the experience that were to be important in adult gentry existence. Sir Nicholas Le Strange made this very explicit in his advices to his son Hamon at the turn of the seventeenth century:

> I carryed you to Oxford upon the same wise Reasons as Sr Christopher Calthorp plac'd me there, where you might have a new acquaintance wholly to choos, and I hope you have

contracted it with such sober and discreet young persons, with whom you may spend some houres of buisiness with advantage, and your Times of Leisure with Innocence.

'You shall meet', said Wandesford, 'a Multitude of new Faces collected together from all Quarters of the Kingdom', and must be correspondingly prudent in the choice of friends. Such contacts may have been made first within a student's own college or hall, and sometimes have depended upon those regional networks which a proportion of colleges came to represent. It was natural that Bulstrode Whitelocke should make his friends through the music society and the hunting fraternities of St John's, as it was for the 'tall raw-boned Cornish and Devonshire gentlemen' who came up to Exeter College, to cling together in comforting groups. Yet there is ample evidence that shared interests led youths to transcend their regional backgrounds and even collegiate affiliations. The Trinity friendships developed in the circle of the Newdigates and Gilbert Sheldon, the future archbishop, seem to have owed very little to localist connection. Groups of the godly had assembled from the time of the White Horse Tavern onwards: Thomas Wadsworth, for example, belonged to 'an honest club of scholars of his own and other colleges'. Sir Roger Townshend and D'Ewes both associated with a wider circle of like-minded friends than those merely from their own colleges. It is impossible to establish how the future Lord Herbert of Cherbury and Sir Thomas Lucy III became friendly at Oxford, but probably through shared intellectual and cultural concerns.[38]

Either within or between colleges status might be a more relevant issue than geographical background or intellectual taste. Sir Henry Slingsby was most concerned about the standing of those with whom his son would associate at Queen's. He was delighted when he heard that the Earl of Lincoln's son was to be tutored by John Preston, and his son must have known he was playing to parental sensibilities when he talked of the fellow commoners acquired by Preston since his arrival – two sons of Sir Henry Yelverton, and two sons of Sir Henry Capel. The tutor deliberately cultivated this snobbery in the interest of promoting his vision of godliness: two years later Slingsby was writing to his father that he would only take those who were of 'a stayd sober carrage' and 'an elder brother'. Sir Simonds D'Ewes advised his brother Richard, who was at St Catherine's: 'You are maintained with the best of your ranke;

dehonorate not yourselfe by your unseemlie associating with pensioners and subsizers though of other colleges.' Lesser men experienced the same pressures: Elizabeth Smyth, for example, expressed her delight that her son Thomas had been a social success on a recent visit to London from Oxford, and stressed that he should continue in the best company since 'it will prove most advantageous to you'. Even so, the universities did not meet the most snobbish standards of gentry elitism: Aubrey believed that new academies were necessary partly because 'gentlemen are the fittest persons to breed gentlemen'.[39]

We are accustomed to think that the gentry followed university by the Inns of Court in a routine that was almost predestined in the century after 1550. But such head-counting as has been done suggests caution is necessary: the figures for Yorkshire heads of house in 1642 show that only 70 attended an Inn of Court, as against 79 who went only to university and 92 who had time at both. In Somerset the comparable figures for Elizabeth's reign are 18, 26 and 36. Later calculations for Glamorgan, which include all gentry entrants, shows consistently higher numbers only attending university: in the decade 1631–40, which seems fairly typical, 23 matriculated at Oxford, 9 entered the Inns of Court and only 6 attended both. In so far as a trend can be claimed for this and other data, it indicates that the universities tended to be the favoured resort for parents, although the literary evidence often suggests the opposite. The contrast may be explained partly by patterns of age at admission: although there was no consistency at either set of institutions there was a tendency for gentle youths to be entered at university at about 15, while the standard age of admission to the Inns seems to be between 16 and 20. It may have been more difficult, simply on grounds of cost, to sustain both forms of tertiary education, or to hold a son in schooling until such time as he was sufficiently mature to move directly to an Inn. Some parents, even in the early seventeenth century, saw the Inns as only a second-best choice: Sir Henry Slingsby planned that his sons should go to France after university 'except yt shalbe thought fitter that they . . . applie themslves to the studie of the common law'. The death of a father, or simply a change of plan, like that experienced by Sir George Courthop when he was sent off precipitately on the Grand Tour, might also preclude an interlude at the Inns.[40]

Nevertheless, many gentleman's sons did undertake some legal training after university, and others, like the sons of Sir John Wynn or some of the Oglanders, went there directly from school. From at least the mid-fifteenth century the Inns had, according to Sir John Fortescue, provided training not only for professional lawyers, but also for sons of the aristocracy 'although they do not desire them to be trained in the science of the laws'. Since Fortescue was writing for the eye of the prince, he may have exaggerated the noble quality of the Inns, but sons of knights and gentlemen were certainly to be found in the admissions registers of Lincoln's Inn. By the later sixteenth century, when full admissions calculations become possible, 40.6 per cent are of those from backgrounds from peer down to esquire, a further 47.8 per cent are sons of gentlemen. It is not easy to divide these figures between those who were destined to practise law, and those who used the Inns as a general form of higher education, but some help may come from the statements of position in the family at admission: 64.4 per cent were described as elder or only sons, 33.2 per cent as younger sons. The latter group were clearly more likely to have to regard the law as a career than were heirs.[41]

Many of the observations already made of the universities are equally applicable to the Inns of Court. The latter were costly for parents – an accepted minimum at the end of the sixteenth century was £40 – and the moral and social dangers of youth en masse were enhanced by the seductive presence of London and the absence of a tutorial system. Sir John Holles observed sarcastically to his brother Thomas that he could understand that £30 seemed too modest an allowance 'for a mongrel course betwixt a student and a reveller'. Sir Hugh Cholmley admitted, with some show of regret, that, after wasting three years at Oxford, he consumed another three in partial idleness at Gray's Inn. George Oglander, his father's darling, frittered away his London time, despite Sir John's immense pride in his one law moot. Sir John Reresby, though he claimed that at times he followed the exercises closely, acknowledged, with some understatement, that he was not 'at that age the most stanche man in the world' – alcohol and quarrelling seem to have been major occupations. Regular injunctions from Sir John Wynn to his sons to keep to their book suggests that he knew the temptations from his own experience. What memorialists and letter writers could not confess was that dissipation had its charms: William Welby of Gedney, for example, found himself in Star Chamber, when he and his drinking companions from various Inns resolved 'to do something that they may be spoken of when they are dead'. This bold deed was an attack on the Swan at Lambeth Marsh, a house of ill-fame, where they ended by breaking the windows. 'Jesu, Jesu, the mad days I have spent!', says Shallow.[42]

The motives for sending youth to the Inns instead of, or as well as university, again revolved around a combination of intellectual training and social advantage. Younger sons, and the few elder who showed real disposition for the law were believed, often correctly, to be launched on the most profitable of early modern careers. John Savile, though heir to a modest estate, was so eager to embark on the enhancement of his fortunes that, detained at home in Yorkshire by the great plague of 1563, he read Littleton, the Statutes, Rastall's *Abbreviamenta* and some of the Year Books 'once and again'. His instincts were correct: he died Sir John Savile of Methley and a Baron of the Exchequer. For most heirs, however, there was less emphasis on intellectual discipline than at Oxford or Cambridge. The boys were generally older, they had access to a far wider range of interests in London, and there was some mismatch between the species of law offered for professional training and that valued by the country gentleman. The sheer difficulty and obscurity of the subject could, moreover, daunt even the most able student. Stephen Powle, later a highly effective clerk in Chancery, complained to his old schoolmaster in 1578 that he had 'small liking for this study, which I account for the knowledge rude, for the order confused, and for the language barbarous'.[43]

Yet the conviction that a man should show some learning in the law if he was to govern his own society seems to have moved many parents to hold their children in London. Sir John Oglander derived his faith in this system from his grandfather who 'affectinge the studie of the lawe was called to the barr', though he never practised. Instead he 'did mutch good amonge his neyghbours' and clearly gained social standing through legal knowledge. Thomas Isham, as we have seen, was convinced that his son's legal studies would benefit the family, though he also argued for profit to 'the cuntry' from John's learning. 'Have some insight in the laws' advised Sir William Wentworth, 'for it will be a great contentment, comfort and credit and quiet for you'. 'Labour cheefly' said Sir John Strode, 'to understand, in sum good measure . . . the lawes by which thou art governed'.As the reverence for legal culture gained a grip upon the English gentry these views acquired almost mystical overtones. It was the view of Sir William Twysden that there were only two worthy subjects of study, 'the law of God, to teach [a man] the way to heaven; [and] . . . the law of the nation, to direct him how to deport himself in this life, and to manage his civil affairs'.[44]

Whatever the reality behind these optimistic parental statements, there were material benefits to all concerned from residence in London. The young acquired cultural and social skills, and extended and enhanced those networks of friendship begun at university. The environment was even more conducive to the formation of proper connections because of the social exclusiveness of the Inns. Here the barriers imposed by membership of a particular Inn meant little, despite certain regional biases in the recruitment of members. Bulstrode Whitelocke, deep in the serious study of law, made his intellectual contacts among his immediate fellows, but also in other Inns and through his general activities of music and classical learning. Another serious lawyer, Thomas Egerton, held William Lambarde, Francis Thynne and others in 'one chain of amity' despite their diverse backgrounds. The Newdigate account book indicates that John, the elder brother, gave no attention to the law, but assiduously cultivated 'connection', with extended kin, with local families, with new gentry acquaintances, with professional lawyers. The account book also suggests that residence at the Inns was of advantage to the family back home, since sons could monitor the progress of legal disputes and evaluate those who might provide professional services. They often found themselves pressed by fathers to perform these types offices for the collective good, to their own detriment. Sir John Wynn, in particular, constantly harried his sons: Ellis begged in 1618 that he should be troubled with no further business 'that may not be effect in once going abroad at som idle time'.[45]

Edward Waterhouse saw the Inns as 'schools of civility and chivalry, as well as law'. But the problem, as his contemporary William Higford pointed out, was that the élite were by the period of the Restoration beginning to think of other ways of acquiring cultural polish so that 'when their sons leave the universities, [they] omit the innes of court, and send them across the seas'. Only younger sons, and men of small fortune who intended to become rich by the law, it was said, still resided at the Inns. The complaints, especially this early, were exaggerated, but at the end of the seventeenth century the patterns established under Elizabeth, James and Charles were breaking down. The Civil War, which forced many Royalists upon their travels, and made London of less attraction to the rest, was an obvious solvent of change. Beyond this it is usual to follow the moralists and argue that the development of the Grand Tour for heirs to large estates was the key explanation for change. Yet it might be more appropriate to suggest that the European visit was only the most obvious manifestation of a much more complex move away from academic institutions and towards environments in which social and cultural graces could best be cultivated. The 'finishing' of a gentleman now entailed less mastery of Tacitus, Cicero and Littleton, more subtle understanding of mores and aesthetics.[46]

These were precisely the qualities that extended European travel was thought to inculcate into the fortunate few; though they could also be mastered at home in the cosmopolitan environment of London. Englishmen had long been habituated to thinking that all developments, good and ill, in manners derived from Italy or France. Under Elizabeth and the early Stuarts many English squires regarded these either as wholly pernicious – 'rarely is a man bettered by his gadding abrode' said Strode – or at best irrelevant to the career an eldest son should pursue. Sir Arthur Capel refused to send his grandson overseas because 'his callinge is to be a countrey gentillman, wherin ther is lytell or no use of forrane experience'. Sons who did manage to undertake the Grand Tour at this period were expected to follow the advice of Lord Burghley and Sir Philip Sidney and gain linguistic skills and 'civic' knowledge. George Stradling, who travelled abroad in the 1630s, insisted at the end of his life that he had done so in order to study history and politics, not 'old walls, ruined amphitheatres and antiquated coins'.[47]

Some of the later advice given by fathers to sons departing for a European journey shows an interesting conjunction between these 'civic' values and the 'civil' concerns that were beginning to succeed them. Sir John Holles, writing to his son who was leaving for France in 1614, began sternly: 'yow are to call to mind the end of your travell, which is to enable your self to your cuntries service', but then he turned to more personal skills, such as the need to learn from the French 'assured, free and civill conversation'. Sir Henry Savile aimed to make his kinsman John 'an acomplisht traveller', though he wrote gloomily to Sir Dudley Carleton that he feared 'nature did more enclyne [him] to make a plodding common lawyer'. When Sir John Reresby went on his extended travels he learned music, mathematics and fencing from the Italians, dancing, guitar and lute from the French. Architecture, that late seventeenth-century passion of the gentry, was best learned from the Italians, and other elements of virtuosi behaviour like art collection were largely a consequence of continental contact. Aubrey, as usual, finds the correct language in which to sum up the beliefs of his contemporaries: 'travel does much to open the understanding, and besides gives a good address'.[48]

Not everyone was happy with the gradual movement of the élite away from those concerns with the intellect and with the construction of the 'civic' man that had been important before the mid-seventeenth century crisis. Proposals for the reform of the education of gentlemen flowed in abundance and often concentrated upon the introduction of the élite to the 'modern' disciplines of mathematics and natural science. Erudition of a high order was still valued among the cultivated gentlemen of the last decades of the century, a world wonderfully evoked in Evelyn's *Diary* or in the early proceedings of the Royal Society. Yet something had been lost: the integrated vision of a training in manners, morals, piety and learning, a synthesis of medieval chivalry and humanist and Protestant scholarship that had infiltrated the imagination of an élite bent on sustaining its control over English society. Perhaps the very completeness of the gentry's political success after 1660 made it less necessary to invoke learning as a route to power. Now civility, always a part of the training of a gentleman, became an essential means of differentiation from the ruder sort who had so disturbed the years without a king. The forms in which this civility was expressed will be a major theme of the following chapter.[49]

# 8

# Civility, Sociability and the Maintenance of Hegemony

John Aubrey believed that the education of a young gentleman must be completed by the age of 25 at the latest. Thereafter 'the management of his estates will take up most of his time, besides visits and returns of visits'. The construction of the gentleman might have been an arduous and costly process, but the result at best was an individual who could combine political leadership and intelligent financial management with courtesy, magnanimity and cultural sophistication in daily living. The ideal varied with time, place and circumstance: in the hands of John Kaye in Elizabethan Yorkshire, for example, it was a very externalised image of the prosperous householder, providing for his 'friend, He hath his desyer', serving the king with ready armour and the Deity with daily prayer. He then conceded a little to civility by adding to his portrait 'wisdom, aptnes and curtesey, are the nursses of all gentry'. William Vaughan agreed that the gentleman must be affable, courteous and liberal, but added courage and willingness to forgive injury to his list of necessary qualities. At the other extreme Richard Brathwait's gentleman is constructed from inner qualities of mind, afforced by good training, so that 'he admires nothing more than a constant spirit' and 'amongst men he hates no less to be uncivill, than in his feare to God-ward to be servile'. The moral, civil and social qualities of the gentleman had constantly to be displayed in his adult being. They were revealed in the transactions of life in the country estate or in city and Court, transactions in which his peers and inferiors provided the social opportunity for exchanges of honour. The complex layers of these social worlds were as significant to the gentleman as his political hegemony or economic power.[1]

## 8.1 THE GENTLEMAN ALONE

Lineage, family and household were the abiding constants of the life of the country gentleman. But gentility, as has constantly been stressed in earlier chapters, came to depend upon the moral qualities of the individual, as well as his house and descent. From the Elizabethan period onwards Stoic influences on contemporary thought extended this humanistic argument into the perception that a true gentleman was independent of his social environment. 'For though a vertuous man doth walke alone . . . hee shalbe honored . . . because it is the vertue of minds, and not the guifts of fortune, that honor is due unto.' This idea afforced an older concern for the contemplative life as the most inherently virtuous that the élite could pursue. Contemplation in the countryside was readily contrasted with the babbling intercourse of the Court. When the poet Wyatt was banished from the Henrician Court he decided in his 'First Satire' to render the tedious tolerable by praise of retiredness in Kent and Christendom, 'among the muses where I read and rhyme'. Sir John Harington engaged in a typical exercise when he wrote *The Prayse of Private Life,* advocating retirement from the city and separation from the daily business of men. In these circumstances the cardinal virtues of temperance and prudence could be nurtured in a reflective environment, in which man 'doth all thinges with deliberacion, never forgettinge such circumstances as appertaine to everie accion, and chiefly . . . prepared for Death'. Or, as William Cornwallis noted more practically, solitariness and contemplation 'keepe your house sweet'.[2]

The actual lives of Wyatt and Harington, catapulting between success at Court and banishment and disgrace in the country, should serve as a warning against taking this literary posturing too seriously. There were, however, ways in which ordinary gentlemen might have come to place positive value on solitude in these years. No doubt many followed the suggestion of Lady Fanshawe that a man should reserve time 'to examine [himself] and his fortune . . . or [he] will certainly shipwreck [his] mind'. An academic training, allied to a growing range of intellectual interests, encouraged many to an abiding study of their books. 'The learned Man, at all tymes, and in all places, can intertayne himselfe with readinge, or rumynatinge upon somewhat he had formerly founde in bookes', says Harington. Scholarly interests might be shared and convivial, but their pursuit also necessitated some hours of isolation. The extensive memoirs, diaries and geneaological notes on which the present study draws so extensively betoken a body of men who were self-sufficient in the pursuit of knowledge.[3]

The separation of the learned and serious gentleman from his household has its physical expression in the construction of rooms specifically designed for intellectual activity: at first closets and studies and then later libraries. Vincent Mundy, listing his rooms at Markeaton, Derbyshire, in 1545 included a study in which he kept his books, coffers of evidence and weights and measures. Sir William More had a closet beside his bedchamber at Loseley, Surrey, in which he kept his book collection in the 1550s. In 1597 John Wynn, engaged in a variety of building projects, noted that he must finish the dining chamber and his own study at Caernarfon: a few years later Sir Arthur Ingram was building separate studies for himself and his wife in his York establishment. Neither these, nor any contemporary examples, survived unchanged, but we may imagine that the best of them had some resemblance to the unique Kederminster Library in Langley Marish Church, Buckinghamshire. Henry Peacham also evokes the physical appearance of such a room when, in the *Compleat Gentleman*, he advised that a study should face east in order to avoid mould and damage to books and pictures. By the 1630s many large gentry households listed separate rooms for books and papers in inventories, though it is probable that it was later in the century before the 'trickle-down effect' led to their construction in more average homes. For example, Edward Sheppherd was the first middling gentlemen of North Norfolk whose inventory, dated 1676, includes a room with a desk and 'all the books'.[4]

Closets and libraries imply large numbers of books. Gentry libraries have been researched only patchily for our period: the basic listing of English Renaissance libraries records 17 gentry collections for the period up to 1600 and a further 36 before 1640. A number of other examples have been revealed by more recent specialist studies, but gaps still remain. Many of the listings that do survive are equally clearly incomplete – for example, music volumes are recorded for Sir Thomas Kitson of Hengrave, Suffolk, but nothing else. We cannot begin to reconstruct the reading matter that most country gentlemen had on their shelves. However, we can point to some early libraries suggestive of very scholarly habits of mind among their owners. Sir William More left over 400 volumes in the mid-1550s, and at about the same date the sophisticated collection of

23. The Kederminster Library, 1631, Langley Marish Church, Buckinghamshire

Sir John Prise contained at least 100 manuscripts and a substantial number of printed books. One of the largest sixteenth-century gentry lists is the 413 volumes left by Richard Stonley, that minor Exchequer official and landowner whose goods were seized by the Crown in the 1590s. All of this, however, pales into insignificance beside the library left by Sir Thomas Knyvett of Ashwellthorpe, Norfolk, in 1618: 1,400 volumes covering the full map of contemporary knowledge, written in five languages. This seems to the most important gentry collection built up mainly before the Jacobean era. From the 1620s such great accumulations began to become common among the learned and wealthy.[5]

Libraries do not automatically imply scholarly habits or deep reading; they may say more about social convention. Aubrey's description of Sir Henry Blount juxtaposed his great book collection and his 'not . . . very much reading'. Some of the large accumulations of the late seventeenth century no doubt owe much to the notion that great houses should now possess book-lined walls. Yet love of books is constantly attested amongst seventeenth-century gentlemen: Sir Thomas Lucy III, as we have seen, chose to have himself portrayed on his tomb with his volumes behind him: Sir Peter Leicester, having itemised his library in affectionate detail, laid upon his descendants the charge that they alienate none of the books, but treat them as an heirloom not to be sold away or even loaned to others. Sir Thomas Knyvett harried his unfortunate brother Henry, who acted as his London agent, about the acquisition of choice texts, and was irritated by his failures. A Welsh squire, Humphrey Matthews of Castell-y-Mynach, was prepared to pay £500 to the London dealer Thomason for a manuscript collection. Book fanatics were willing to fight for particularly desirable collections: Thomas Mostyn insisted that none of the books of his neighbour Robert Vaughan, should be 'disposed of without my knowledge'. Even women can on very rare occasions be glimpsed as serious collectors: Frances Wolfreston of Statfold, Staffordshire, wife of a middling gentleman, owned at least 100 volumes of contemporary literature, theology and history in the mid-seventeenth century.[6]

Scholarship could be a gregarious business in Tudor and Stuart England, a matter of attending meetings of the Society of Antiquaries, exchanging notes on heraldic matters, or discussing theology and law at the dinner table. Nevertheless, the gentleman scholar also worked alone, constructing a private role within his household of a kind previously associated mainly with learned clerics. 'In you', said William Higford to his grandson, 'it were noble to vindicate from sleep and sports some hours every day, and to dispose them in the exercise of learning.' Glimpses of this role emerge from the notes of Sir John Oglander. Oglander uses his

24. Sir Nathaniel Bacon, 'Self-portrait', *c.* 1625

study in part to preserve his evidences methodically: he records in 1626 that he had hidden the large sum of £2,250 needed for various transactions behind the books and in 'the Parliament boxe'. On another occasion he asks that a search be made for some missing evidences he needs. But the study was also the retreat in which he scribbled at his various advice books, and accumulated copies of the evidences of island families towards a 'tract of the Antiquities of the Island'. Another glimpse of the gentleman-scholar at work comes from Alice Thornton's description of her father at work on his *Instructions*. A household servant watched each night as he wrote in his closet in Ireland after transacting his business as Strafford's deputy, and was so intrigued by the labour that he copied the text, thereby saving it, since the original was lost in the Civil War. Books and writings were, as Henry Peacham said, 'companions' in themselves, and the best means of avoiding idleness.[7]

Other solitary and contemplative activities, such as gardening, painting and fishing, also protected gentlemen from the constant press of business and sociability which was their normal lot. Collectively they established the image of virtuosi, cultivating civility, each within his own private world: an image beautifully exemplified by Sir Nathaniel Bacon's self-portrait in his study. But the demands of honour and reputation, as well as the practical exigiencies of estate management and life in a large household, meant that they were usually defined as the luxuries of leisure. Dearth and tenurial problems on his Lincolnshire estate, complained Sir William Pelham in 1623, 'draweth me wholly from a contemplative life, which I most affected'.[8]

## 8.2 THE GENTLEMAN IN HIS HOUSEHOLD

### Hospitality

While poets and moralists might praise solitude and contemplation it was *negotium* that regularly triumphed over *otium* in Renaissance discourse. Gentlemen were not born and bred for a private and retired life, but for society and action in the commonwealth. This prescriptive view matched social practice. While the continued pursuit of scholarly interests and individual concerns into adulthood achieved growing legitimation in Stuart culture, they were not considered as an alternative to the cultivation of society. Both obsession with learning and withdrawal from public duty were sternly reproved: 'Be not so Bookish, as to neglect thy Estate', says one advice author. Francis Willoughby, a distinguished student of natural history, and collaborator with the biologist John Ray and 'from his childhood adicted to study', had to be reminded forcefully by his relative Sir Thomas Wendy that when he inherited Wollaton he must 'settle himself and bear a share in publick imployment'. A major objection to the flight to London after the 1590s was paradoxically that it was motivated by a desire to live a solitary, and hence selfish, existence. 'They [the gentry] get themselves into remote places, where they may live to themselves alone and their pleasures.'[9]

Instead it was the duty of the gentleman to live upon his estates, and to conduct his life in and through his family and household. The cardinal virtues of prudence and temperance, much lauded by the humanists, could be manifest in solitude, but their ideal context was the household, while their companion qualities of justice and fortitude or magnanimity positively demanded a social environment. Honour and reputation were best displayed in the theatre of the household. This metaphor is used with some frequency to express this vision of gentility in action, most famously in Sir Henry Wotton's description of the household as 'the theatre of our hospitality'. The construction of a gentleman had become a matter of art and artifice, of self-fashioning some commentators would say, and he required a stage on which to act the role he had learned.[10]

All this may suggest a self-awareness that was hardly likely to inform the routine behaviour of the gentleman on his estate. But most members of the landed élite no doubt conducted their daily affairs with some reference to their standing among their neighbours. Throughout the sixteenth and seventeenth centuries this was most readily done by generous housekeeping, the most visible element in that 'port' required of the gentleman. This long period saw some shifts in domestic organisation and values, but the image of generosity and openness was sustained wherever the family concerned was in quest of social influence. Through what writers often called 'the good old hospitality' reciprocal exchanges of honour could occur and loyalties be affirmed. Few would have dissented from the prescription of the anonymous *Institucion of a Gentleman* (1555) that 'good housekeping is a thinge in all Gentlemen required'. Gentry households tended to be structured around these assumptions about public display and openness. Until at least the turn of the sixteenth century servants included a number of 'tall fellows', servicing their master primarily as images of his power in hall, chamber and when out riding, rather than as specialist domestics. Liveries were dispensed liberally in order to enhance this vision of largesse: Sir William Holles, the younger, was said to have appeared at Edward VI's coronation with 50 servants in blue coats and badges; Sir Edward Rodney's mid-Tudor ancestor Maurice was the 'first in his county that gave livery Cloakes to his men'. The slowness of the process by which servants were banished 'below stairs' is also revealing. Although the hall had ceased to be used for family dining in most large households by the beginning of the sixteenth century, it was not until the period before the Civil War that the servants were expelled. Until then they ate in public, and occupied the hall space between meals in anticipation of the need to receive guests. A few antediluvian gentry even perpetuated the habit until the late seventeenth century in the belief that it showed their adherence to good old customs: Sir John Norton who died in 1687 was praised by the preacher of his funeral sermon for ensuring that the substantial provisions served in his parlour 'afterwards feasted the Hall, and plentifully reliev'd the Poor at his Gates'.[11]

The configuration of domestic architecture provides physical evidence of this concern for open service and entertainment. The arrangement of a hall range with the family rooms at the dais end of the hall, entrance screens at its lower end and services beyond, seems firmly locked into the consciousness of the gentry and their masons for most of the sixteenth century. It possessed practical convenience, especially in proximity of hall and kitchens, but this diminished as prestige food was required at the further end of the establishment. The perpetuation of this plan seems to depend above all on the need to use the hall as ceremonial space and formal access to the inner household. The courtyard arrangement commonplace in the early Tudor house, while conceived partly for defensive reasons, also afforced the image of generosity intended by the master. Access through a gateway, often decorated with heraldic devices, could be made more or less ceremonious, more or less easy, according to the status of the guest. The poor, especially the alien poor, could be 'relieved constantly at the gates', while others moved inwards, to be received in buttery, hall or chamber as was most appropriate. Within the household proper the awkward problem of moving food over some distance could also provide the opportunity for display, though perhaps only the greatest gentlemen would have gone as far as Sir Francis Willoughby, who ordered that the hall usher was to proceed the food service saying in a loud voice '"Give place, my masters", albeit no man be in the way'.[12]

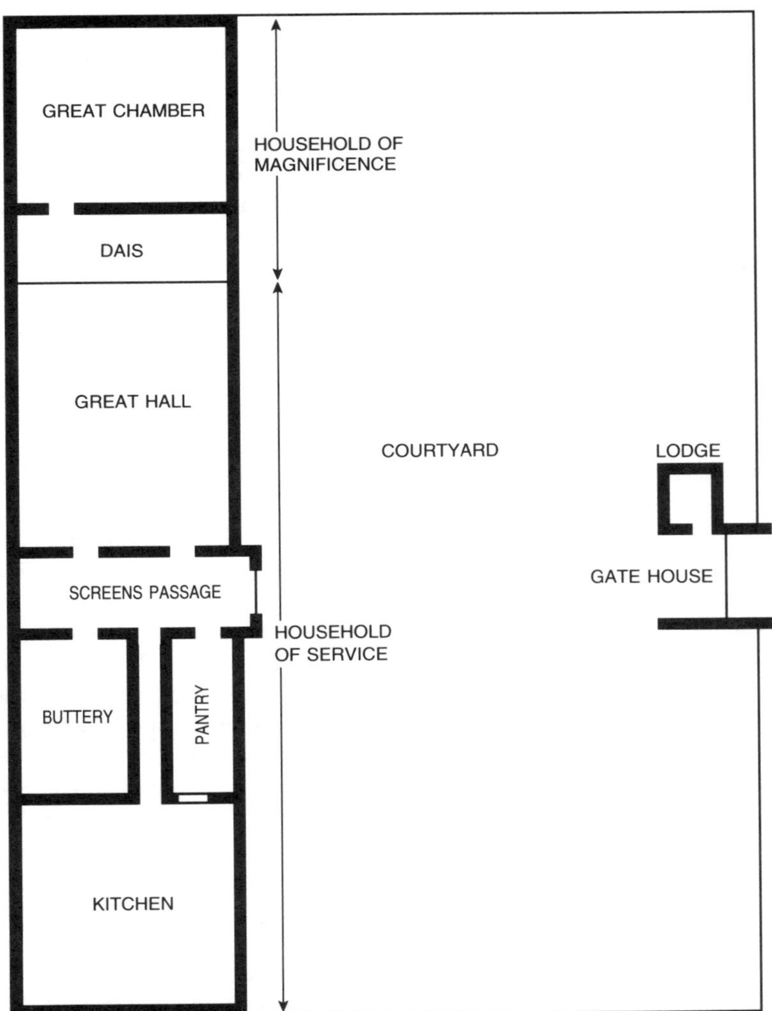


25. Plan of a typical sixteenth-century gentry house

Even when new architectural influences began to permeate English domestic building in the later sixteenth century there was a great reluctance to abandon the basic internal designs shown in Illustration 25. Halls were gradually truncated, or turned through 90 degrees to aid symmetrical design, specialist chambers were increased in number, and dining and socialising were separated for the gentry family. Courtyards, and eventually gatehouses, were slowly abandoned. Visual display, once largely confined to gatehouses and specific features such as windows, engulfed those houses that followed Elizabethan prodigy architectural style. But most gentry builders were reluctant to rethink their designs and consign the services to a basement, or the hall to a mere vestibule. It is reasonable to infer that many of them felt, with Sir Henry Wotton, that 'by the natural hospitality of England, the Buttery must be . . . visible; and we need perchance for our ranges, a . . . spacious and luminous kitchen'.[13]

Entertainment offered by the gentry household served contrasting objectives for different social groups. For the poor it provided Christian beneficence and was one of the many means by which the élite could discharge their social obligations to the community. Here a marked shift occurred during the early modern period. Much of the charitable giving of the early Tudor gentry was focused upon the food, clothing and money doles handed out at the gate. Their importance is suggested by the insertion into the 1536 Poor Law of a clause permitting the alms of noblemen to be given 'to poor and indigent people of other parishes as of the same parish', when the Act itself endeavoured to circumscribe indiscriminate doles. Shifting economic circumstance and changing ideological approaches to charity gradually displaced the household as the prime focus of giving. By the early seventeenth century a gentleman like Sir Edward Lewkenor, who deliberately nurtured the poor by providing a dining room at his gates, must have been considered something of an oddity. Most conscientious donors channelled giving through local institutions, and placed almost exclusive emphasis on the needs of the poor in the community. However, charity as hospitality could never wholly be abandoned, since the honour of the gentleman demanded that he showed beneficence to those in need, and even post-Restoration households still offered their scraps at the kitchen door.[14]

Tenants and other contacts of inferior social status presented fewer problems than the poor. By long-established medieval precedent gentlemen believed themselves obliged to provide a tenant feast at Christmas, spreading the burden over several days if they were owners of broad acres. In 1551 it took Sir William Petre at least five days out of the twelve of the feast cycle to receive all his tenants; in 1570 Sir Marmaduke Constable crammed his into three days, but only by inviting four townships on 26 December and five on 28 December. The tenant feast was in origin a reciprocal *gestum*, or reward for services rendered, and in the sixteenth and seventeenth centuries was still provisioned partly by the tenants' own gifts. Even a mourning household found it difficult to ignore this reciprocal occasion; when Lady Sarah Wynn lost her father in December 1666 all celebration of the festival was deferred except that 'the poore tenants we must byd ells we shall not know what to doe with the provistion they bring in'. By the seventeenth century gentry voices are sometimes raised in distaste at these rituals: Lady Pelham mocked the local rustics who 'dance galliards of there owne invencions which agrede best with there clowted shoes and bootes'. But concern for civility had to yield to the imperatives of generosity: no landowner was wise to ignore the expectations of his dependents and lesser neighbours, and even outside the Christmas season the conscientious had an open buttery door and were likely to permit entertainment in the hall on regular occasions. The hall, indeed, could provide the ideal environment in which to impress a gentleman's worth upon his inferiors: in James Shirley's play *The Witty Fair One* the pretentious knight Sir Nicholas Treedle proposes that a newly purchased globe shall 'stand in my hall to make my tenants wonder instead of the Book of Martyrs'.[15]

Set-piece entertainment in 'the theatre of our hospitality' extended much further up the social scale to embrace grand rites of passage and other feasting. When Elizabeth, daughter of Sir John Neville, was married to Roger Rockley in 1536 the celebrations lasted a week, the main banquet consisted of 110 dishes and the entertainment consisted of masques and plays. This was probably hospitality of a kind unusual among the gentry, but there was a general sense that the entertainment on these occasions had to exceed the normal liberality and display a measure of magnificence. Visiting nobles and figures of political influence had to be received with multiplied gestures of deference and correspondingly large expenditure, which is presumably one reason for the continual advice given to sons not to associate too freely with superiors. 'Occasionall entertainment of men greater then thy self,' says Thomas Fuller, 'is better then solemn inviting them'. Most punishing of all was a royal visitation, when a mere knight might have the pleasure of the full company of the Court for several days. Few of the nobles or the senior gentry of the southern counties escaped the obligation to provide this service at some time during Elizabeth's reign.[16]

But in the general pattern of gentry living hospitality probably meant above all the relatively routine entertainment of one's peer group and extended kin. Wherever account books and correspondence offer quantifiable information it is these groups that predominate. An early sixteenth-century kitchen book for the Le Stranges of Hunstanton in Norfolk shows endless exchanges with men from within the county, with a preponderance of relatives involved. A century later the accounts of Sir Nathaniel Bacon and his Townshend heirs show a very similar pattern from the same corner of Norfolk, though with an even stronger emphasis on the kin group. Gregariousness of this kind was expected: even a stern advice writer like Sir John Strode urged 'let thy doores be (at all seasonable tymes) opon to thy kinred and friends'. A paradigmatic portrait of gentry hospitality is provided by Thomas Delaval, who says of his father Sir Ralph 'he delighted much in the company of his kinsmen and friends and entertaining strangers in his house'. Richard Carew offers a wonderful image of Cornish gentlemen, all apparently interrelated, who moved from household to household gathering numbers as they went 'in which progresse they encrease like snowballs, till through their burdensome waight they breake againe'.[17]

Such conviviality seems natural enough, but the scale of exchanges between households is something with which we are culturally unfamiliar. A system of entertainment in which the host rarely sat at a meal without guests, in which relatives often stayed for weeks on end, and in which both friends and casual contacts could appear uninvited, is distinct from most modern Western categories of sociability. Sir William Holles was said never to have sat down to dine until the late hour of one o'clock since 'for ought he knew there might be a friend come twenty miles to dine with him and he would be loth to lose his labour'. William Carnsew, conforming to the image of Cornishmen, often turned up on neighbours and friends wholly unannounced, and was mildly surprised if they were not at home. The practical implications must often have been as described by one author in the 1580s '[guests] for the moste parte bee so careles, or slovenly, as they will make quicke speede to weare out not only our linnen, but also our hanginges, Curtains and Canopies of silke'. Even if material damage was minimised, the financial implications of such openness could be dire, hence the constant reminders to heirs to balance liberality with prudence and not to spend more than a third of their income on housekeeping. And it was bad for the liver and patterns of sleep as well: in the late seventeenth century Sir Nicholas Le Strange worked hard to impose social order on his Norfolk neighbours, whose habits of carousing to the early hours were 'attended . . with so great irregularity'.[18]

**Recreations**

'Visits and visiting' might thus have many disadvantages, but gentlemen, and gentlewomen, often convey the impression that they were the only way of surviving the ennui of rural existence. John Bourne, having laid his books aside for rural labour, begged his friend Francis Yaxley to come and visit him 'for goddes saak . . . and if mo good frendes and old felowes come with you, I woll mak good chere the better'. Such boredom must be held at bay not only with eating, drinking and conversation, but with plays, cards and gaming in the evening and the endless pleasures of the hunt in daytime. A major reason for summoning your neighbours and kin was to provide a quorum for these activities. In particular the hunting party, not so very dissimilar one suspects from its nineteenth-century successor, was a strongly established feature of élite sociability: a mid-seventeenth-century painting of the Carlile family at the hunt conveys something of its atmosphere

Sir William Cordell also wrote to Yaxley in 1560 describing a three-day visit by Sir Thomas Cornwallis, Lord Windsor and many others 'hunting and making mery with me'. In 1571 Sir Marmaduke Constable's kitchen accounts show that in mid-July there was a large assembly of local gentlemen and their wives, headed by Sir John and Sir Richard Constable, who must have occupied their time in hunting within the Everingham park. On 10 July they had killed one sorrel deer and one 'prycke': the latter was divided by the kitchens, half being made into pasties and half roasted 'in the hall', suggesting rather primitive cooking arrangements. A week later another buck was killed, and divided between the visitors who had taken it and the household. Most detailed household accounts for the sixteenth and early seventeenth centuries record occasions of this kind, often the moments of greatest conviviality outside the Christmas season.[19]

Hunting and hawking, the most routine of diversions for the gentry, attracted conflicting value-judgements from moralists and

26. J. Carlile, 'Sir Justinian Isham and the Carlile family hunting the stag', mid-seventeenth century

commentators. Of themselves they were widely accepted as proper marks of gentility, and suitable recreations, but the passion with which the English gentleman massacred his fellow creatures was often condemned because it excluded other, more serious, preoccupations. Attacks on the 'huntin' and shootin' ' squire became one of the stock-in-trades of humanist rhetoric, later appropriated by satirists like Jonson and the 'character' writers. 'What need we to know', asks the gentleman in Jonson's *Speech According to Horace*, 'More than to praise a dog or horse? Or speak the hawking language?'. All too often, according to Robert Burton, the wealth of country gentleman ran away with their hounds, and their fortunes flew with their hawks. The image, while obviously exaggerated for the moralists' purposes, has a substratum of truth. The most famous of early hunting diaries, that of Nicholas Assheton from the Jacobean period, shows the Lancashire squire oscillating between chasing otters, foxes, rabbits, ducks and hares, fishing for salmon and tippling with his companions. Sir William Kingsmill's passion for the chase extended to verse: in a lengthy 'Georgic' on ten hunts in the Hampshire countryside he included such immortal lines as 'Full fifty Bucks I kill'd with hounds in last two seasons space'. Several of the memorialists, warning their descendants about profligacy, produced family examples of men obsessed by hunting. Gervase Holles, as we have seen, criticised his maternal grandfather who threw away his books at an early age and 'got him a kennell of hounds'. He became gentleman of horse to the Earl of Rutland, and lived lavishly, entertaining his master and hunting. General profligacy, as much as hunting, seems to have ruined Kingston, but his preoccupation with the chase was obviously a contributory cause. He sold much of his land before he abandoned hunting, indeed only a major riding accident in old age finally deterred him. Three generations of Cholmleys spent, in Sir Hugh's opinion, too much on 'fleet hounds and horses'.[20]

Zeal for the chase could also lead to social folly: Sir Thomas Shirley was in trouble with the Privy Council in the 1620s because he pursued his hawk onto the Earl of Huntingdon's land, and when challenged retorted 'he cared for never a lord in England except the Lord of Hosts . . . if my hawk had flown into any lord's parlour, I would have followed my hawk'. Similar enthusiasm routinely carried away gentlemen whose dogs pursued deer wandering out of parks and forests: Sir John Carew, for example, complained that his tenants on the edge of Exmoor constantly suffered damage from those chasing the forest deer. One of the accused piously observed that he acted only under the guidance of Sir Hugh Pollard, the chief forester. Beyond these cavalier gestures lay the murky world of poaching which regularly led both to bitter aristocratic feuding and to organised incursions into the royal forest and noble parks by lesser gentleman who believed passionately that there should be 'a little Nimrod in every manor'.[21]

An engagement with such rural pastimes was often seen as a test of gentility: 'if a young childe loveth not an Hawke and a Dogge . . . it is a token, saie they, he degenerates'. The multiplication of printed texts on hunting, and the great popularity of an early work like the *Booke of St Alban's*, which ran through 22 editions between 1486 and 1616, is indication of the concern for sophistication in this field. The language of the chase, it has been suggested, was a necessary 'grammar' for upward mobility and indeed the concept of gentility itself was often more closely linked to these arts than to the ethics of the humanists. Sir Thomas Lucy III, who we have encountered as a model of learned gentility, was also a passionate rider and huntsman: his death resulted from a fall from his beloved 'great horse'. A good stable and kennel could be as significant a status symbol as proper servants: a character in one of Sir William Davenant's dramas claims to be 'an arrant gentleman, in's scutcheon, gives horns, hounds, and hawks, hunting nags, with tall eaters in blue coats, sans number'. All of this, with the obligations of status, sociability and reciprocity that it entailed, made it exceedingly difficult for a rural gentleman to eschew hunting. Even Sir Edward Lewkenor, that model of godly Puritanism, was thought justified in retaining his hawks and hounds 'not onely in regard of the abilitie of his estate, but ablenesse of his minde, who knew right well to put a difference between the use and the abuse'. The Jesuit John Gerard derived great advantage from his youthful training in the hunting arts when he moved disguised through Norfolk society. His expert talk of hunting and falconry allayed the suspicions of one Protestant gentleman, and he later endeavoured to teach his colleague Southwell, so that he could communicate with gentlemen 'who had practically no other conversation'.[22]

While the hunting zeal of the rural élite remained undimmed throughout these centuries, there were signs of change in the structure of their sports. The most significant was the gradual shift from deer to fox hunting, only completed in the early years of the eighteenth century and attributable both to the positive costs of maintaining deer and the accessibility of more open pasture across which the fox could be chased. Disparking had become attractive in some areas by the end of the sixteenth century when, in Carew's vivid phrase, Cornish landlords made 'there Deere leape over the pale, to give the bullockes place'. The strengthening of the game laws in 1671 protected, and thereby made more exclusive, hare coursing and pheasant and partridge shooting, which were now forbidden to those with less than £100 freehold per annum. Fashion also played a part in change: hawking diminished in popularity, while other forms of trapping gained. Hentzner observed in 1598 that 'hawking is the common sport with the gentry', but a century later this remark would more likely have been made of hunting or shooting. Individuals were often fickle in their loves: Thomas Oxinden sold his hawks in 1635 and chose spaniels for water-

27. Sir Thomas Lucy III, d. 1640, on his great horse: detail from monument in Charlecote Church, Warwickshire

fowling instead, but then changed his mind and returned to hawking. Impressing his neighbours with the quality of his animals was not the least of his objectives.[23]

Among other outside activities associated with the household, bowling is the only one that need detain us. George Owen wrote that it 'yelds more exercise to mans bodie then anye other' except perhaps tennis, and a belief that it was a sport with Roman roots helped to make it fashionable among the Tudor and Stuart gentry. The provision of a bowling alley became one of the marks of a generous host; an especially domestic gesture since in theory public alleys were outlawed by 1541 legislation compelling the populace to practise archery instead. Chauncy describes the green at Pishiobury, Hertfordshire, laid out by Sir Walter Mildmay in the 1580s as 'enclosed with a brick wall topped with stone, and balls upon it'. Sir Arthur Ingram was anxious to have his alley completed in 1628, so that he could entertain adequately at Temple Newsam. Many of the commissioned portraits of houses and their gardens dating from the later seventeenth century show these alleys as an integral part of the grounds. Sir Roger Townshend's innovative garden at Raynham had a bowling green alley as one of its essential features, and Sir John Oglander took it for granted that his beloved Nunwell had to have an alley. Bowling, together with fishing, was one of the few relaxations that the rigorous Lady Margaret Hoby permitted herself. Tennis, the other favoured sport of the élite, was less likely to be played in the homes of even the greater gentry, since it demanded the lavish resources of an indoor Court.[24]

Within doors social diversion was provided by music and drama, which met with general moral approbation, and gaming, which did not. It would be unwise to succumb too readily to the renaissance image that all gentlemen were well versed in music, but a measure of skill was certainly expected of women as part of their training, and part singing was normal entertainment in the greater households. Inventories and household accounts routinely contain references to instruments and written music especially from the Elizabethan period onwards. Although the sources are biased towards the greater households, it is not uncommon to find that a mere gentleman, like Christopher Cooke of Keverstone, Durham, owned a 'great pair of virginals'. Philomathes, a character in Thomas Morley's dialogue *A Plaine and Easie Introduction to Practicall Musicke,* finds himself acutely embarrassed when he cannot take a part in singing after supper at a friend's house. Cultured persons exchanged music, as they exchanged the other products of Renaissance learning: in 1602, for example, Philip Gawdy sent his sister-in-law 'two songs for the viol, that were given me from a very worthy musician at Court'. Richard Brathwait's figure for Recreation on the title page of *The English Gentleman* is 'expressed playing upon a Violl, with a Song-booke before him'.[25]

And in addition to the general expectation that music was a part of the civilised household, there were some in which it was a consuming passion. A few great gentry families kept chapel choirs in the early sixteenth century: the Willoughbys and the Devonshire Champernownes among them, and the last at least preserved some religious music throughout the Reformation. After the mid-century household accounts begin to document the serious musicality of families like the Kitsons of Hengrave, the Petres, the Pastons and the Cornwallises. Most kept one or more resident, professional musicians, and some supported the type of consort of strings illustrated on the frieze at Gilling Castle, Yorkshire. This sort of patronage was costly, and probably within the range and interest of rather a small minority. It is tempting to think of the major patronage as emanating from Catholic families, unimpeded by anxieties about the propriety of religious music, but there are enough examples of Protestant patronage to question any narrow causal association of this kind. The Willoughbys remained great patrons throughout the sixteenth century, and Sir Henry Fanshawe kept 'many gentlemen well qualified' in music. James Whitelocke's enthusiasm led him to keep a full-time organist and seek out servants who were good musicians. His son Bulstrode describes how, when he was visited by any of his father's old servants 'who were musitians, they had good musicke in memory of the Judge'.[26]

The only criticism of music as pastime came from Sir Thomas Elyot who, still instinctively identifying musicians as servants and wanderers, warned that performance before a 'commune audience' impaired a gentleman's reputation, since 'the people forgett . . . reverence'. Drama as domestic entertainment rarely risked this ambiguity, since it usually remained the prerogative of travelling professionals: though in specific circumstances, like those of Milton's masque *Comus*, members of the élite themselves might be participants. From the mid-seventeenth century onwards references to gentry involvement multiply: Dorothy Osborne was called upon to play a part in 'The Lost Lady' on her brother's Kentish manor; a little later Lady Elizabeth Kingston was organising her aunt's servants to perform with her in Guarini's *Il Pastor Fido*. It is, however, more characteristic to find that the houses of the greater gentry, like those of the peers, were visited by players during the Christmas season, and on several other occasions during the year. Much of the interest of drama in the household lies in the ability of a host, like Hamlet, to command a particular performance. In an extreme case Sir Edward Dymock employed an actor to impersonate his great rival Henry, Earl of Lincoln: like Don Giovanni the latter was carried off to hell, with the additional amusement of a dirge by a chorus of whores. This was too much, and landed its promoter in gaol. More insidious were the activities of various theatrical groups in Jacobean Yorkshire, who played in the houses of local gentlemen and, when asked, could present good anti-Protestant propaganda. Sir John Yorke of Nidderdale was in particular trouble for encouraging the Egton players to perform an interlude of a disputation between a Protestant minister and Catholic priest. At the end there were flashes of fire as the devil carried the minister away 'whereat all the people greatlie laughed'.[27]

The other habitual domestic entertainments of dicing, cards and other forms of gaming were quite another matter. Moral opinion varied from outright condemnation, by no means a monopoly of the Puritans, to cautious acknowledgement of gaming as a social necessity that must be kept within well-controlled bounds. The latter position is articulated by Anthony Fitzherbert who acknowledged 'it is conveniente for everye man, of what degree that he be of to have playe and game accordynge to his degree', but not to play for the stakes that enabled a man to 'lose a month's food' in one night. This is echoed by many of the advice texts: 'know play to make thee sociable but sett not thy heart upon it' says Mary le Despenser, 'spend not too much time, nor venture too much Money at Gaming' Thomas Wentworth advised Sir William Savile. Even the earnest Sir John Strode admitted the possibility of card play, 'so allways the game be smale, the tyme litle, and the mony less'. The godly predictably could not tolerate such moral relativism: Sir Thomas Hoby would not accept cards in his house, and John Bruen was so incensed at the cards found on his lodger Sir John Done that he removed the four knaves and burned them. Thomas Shepard, a Puritan preacher from Essex, was horrified at his first entry into the supposedly godly household of the Darleys in Yorkshire, to find members of the family at cards and dice. Some of the advice writers approved this type of behaviour because of the weakness of gamblers: Sir William Wentworth advocated total avoidance of play and game, and Sir Peter Leicester observed bluntly that drink ruined an individual, gaming his family.[28]

In practice the rigidity of a Bruen or Hoby clearly set them apart from the ordinary sociability of their neighbours. Most prudent gentlemen are more likely to have endeavoured to follow the views of Strode: Christopher Wandesford, for example, prided himself on playing rarely, for low stakes, and on having lost less than £200 in his adult years before he left for Ireland. John Gerard, forced, he claimed, to play cards as part of his disguise, was on one occasion thought by his hostess to have been 'at the game for a long time' like a courtier. He felt ill at ease with the gambling element involved, for when he played with Catholics every player got his or her money back at the end, and the loser had to say an *Ave Maria* for every counter returned. The problem with such prudential attitudes was that they ran counter to the inherent competitiveness and concern for honour that were integral features of gentry life. The rapid growth in spectacular gambling that was a feature of the Jacobean Court, or the elaboration of wagers within provincial society in the early seventeenth century, were means by which the élite expressed this competition. But the context was perhaps more often 'public' than 'private': in his own home it often seems that the gentleman's gravest problem was not with his guests, but his retainers. Idleness and gaming were constantly associated in the sixteenth century, and the 'tall' fellows who decorated a gentleman's hall frequently wasted their time in dice-play and the like. Judge David Lewis complained to Walsingham in 1576 that the Glamorgan gentry all too often nurtured idle supporters who passed their days in 'play at cards', waiting to further their masters' quarrels.[29]

**Building and gardens**

The character of a gentleman could be displayed by the company he kept and the forms of leisure he pursued. But these were ephemeral. When he reflected on how he and his lineage might more permanently manifest their influence on their environment it was likely that he would turn to new building: 'a sober entertainment and doth not impeach the health' claimed Roger North. Sir Thomas Cockayne's mid-sixteenth-century tomb at Ashbourne in Derbyshire noted

> Three goodly Houses he did build to his great praise and fame . . .
> He did his House and name renew and eke restore
> Which others had with negligence in time decayed before.

The 'great rebuilding' of the later sixteenth century was of particular importance among the gentry – a survey of Derbyshire, Essex,

Shropshire and Somerset suggesting that more country houses were built between 1570 and 1620 than in any subsequent 50 years. Stone's figures also show sharp increases of country-house stock in Hertfordshire and Northamptonshire in the same decades. Building continued into the 1630s, though not at the same pace, and after the 1660s the building of small country mansions was particularly popular. All new gentlemen needed new homes and no old gentleman of any worth could content himself with the home that his ancestors had tolerated.[30]

New building provided a wide range of opportunity to display gentility. In the sixteenth century this often took the most literal and narrow form of gatehouses adorned with heraldic devices, halls lit by stained glass armorial windows, and such ornaments of status as crenelation and porticoed entries. But as social and aesthetic pressures combined by the Elizabethan age to make many gentlemen 'continual builders', there was a growing awareness of building and grounds as evoking the character of their owner. Sir Thomas Tresham's 'device' of the Triangular Lodge at Rushton, Northamptonshire, is the extreme example of personality and ideology displayed in stone, a total expression of his devotion to his faith in its Trinitarian aspects. John Talbot, the owner of Grafton Manor, Worcester, was even more explicit: he used a window refurbished in 1567 to display his view of social hierarchy: 'Plenti and grase bi in this plase whyle everi man is plesed in his degre there is both pease and uniti. Salaman saith there is none acorde when everi man would be a lorde'. By the end of the next century, however, Roger North claimed to be able to read a man's worth through his building without such obvious verbal clues:

> If he hath bin given to parsimony or profusion, to judge rightly or superficially, to deal in great matters or small, high or low; his edifices shall be tincted accordingly, and the justness or imperfection of his mind will appear in them.[31]

Such an identity was possible partly because of the expectation that the gentleman could still be 'his owne surveyor', or at the very least that his close personal attention was an essential part of any major building project. While the greatest courtiers and nobles might turn to the new 'profession' of architect, gentlemen's houses, to quote Summerson, 'grew out of irregular discussions between owners and artificers, and possibly a surveyor or two thrown in'.

Written advice on the theory and practice of architecture became readily available by the seventeenth century to assist those gentlemen who could not travel to view new developments for themselves. The advice often embodied the contradictory pressures under which élite builders worked. Men like Bacon and Sir Henry Wotton emphasised the importance of use over aesthetics: 'houses are built to live in, and not to look on', and there was much nostalgia for 'the good old days' when all that mattered was a full hall and smoking chimneys. On the other hand even cautious authors acknowledged that a gentleman could now make effective statements about power and honour through his aesthetic choices. The mansion house, says Wotton, is 'a kind of private princedom . . . [and] may well deserve . . . according to the degree of the master, to be decently and delightfully adorned'. Slowly gentlemen began to realise that in these matters they must follow the lead of the Court and engage in visual competition. 'We see', said Slingsby of his native Yorkshire, 'an emulation in the structure of our houses'. By the late seventeenth century, when a gentleman was not prepared to compete he risked a serious loss of reputation. North complained that after the Civil War many gentlemen relied on models 'by profest builders', especially from London, to save money, so that they 'creep after the meanness of these town builders'. But even such cheapjack methods were preferable to an ignorance of architectural fashion, of the kind still displayed in some northern and western backwoods.[32]

The particular aesthetics of country houses were obviously influenced by Court style, international contacts and neighbouring example, but often displayed a distinctive individualism stamping them as the product of a specific gentry mind. Sir Roger Townshend's rebuilding of Raynham in Norfolk is an obvious example. Townshend took a serious interest in design, perhaps initially encouraged by the involvement of his father-in-law Sir Nathaniel Bacon. He is known to have travelled to look at examples of other houses of innovative design – Wimbledon, Somerset House and Hatfield, as well as gaining information on buildings by Inigo Jones. He was not his own surveyor – that task was performed by a specialist, William Edge, but the conception was essentially his, and he was deeply involved in the process of construction. The result has been claimed as one of the most imaginative country houses of the early seventeenth century. Roger North's description of his own rebuilding of Rougham Hall, Norfolk, in the 1690s reveals similar

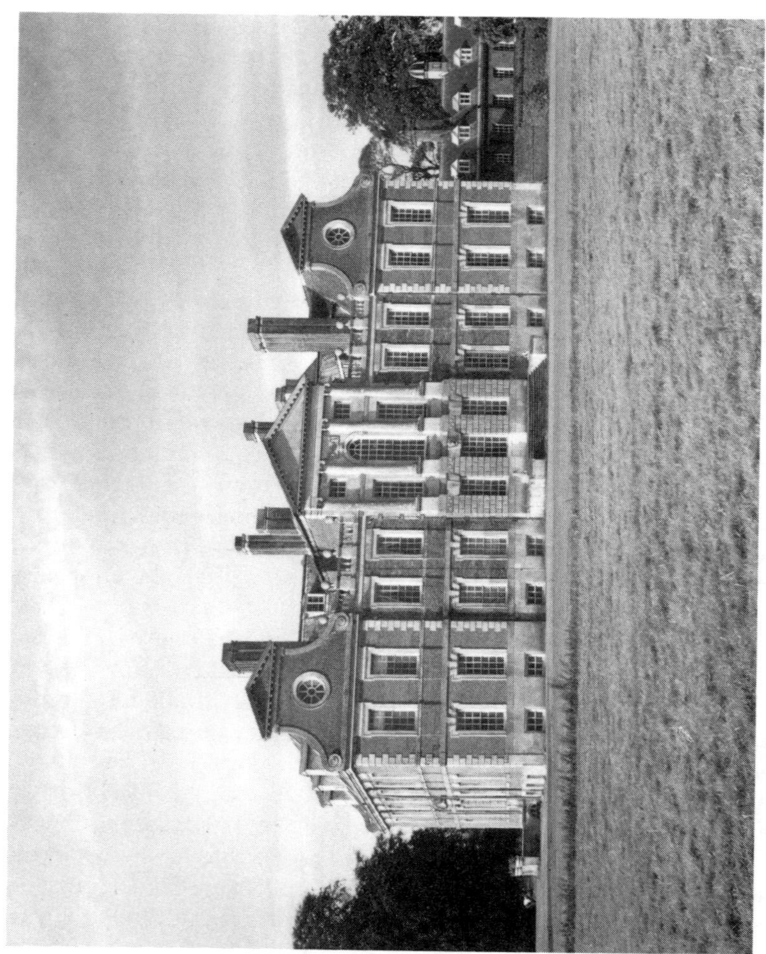

28. Raynham Hall, Norfolk, begun by Sir Roger Townshend, 1622

determination: he stretched a skin of external symmetry over an 'ancient manor-house', achieving elegance within and imposing style without at a relatively modest cost. Such total engagement was unusual: not all country gentlemen had the time, money, capacity or interest to build so adventurously. Among the middling and lesser sort of gentleman there might be little to distinguish dwellings from those of prosperous yeomen except for the detailing on, for example, gables or doorways, that spoke of status. But pride in aesthetic achievement was widespread, as was anxiety not to be excluded from new developments: David Papillon, advising Sir Justinian Isham on a new house in 1652, must have touched a sensitive nerve when he described the existing Lamport structure as 'repugnante aux reigles de cet Art . . . [sans] profit, honneur, ou contentement'.[33]

Greater architectural formality was matched by the emergence of the centrally planned house, focused around the entrance hall, and fully divided between 'upstairs and downstairs' in the manner advocated by Sir Roger Pratt. Pratt's ideals – the separation of family, guests and servants; the construction of symmetry in internal as well as external design; a compact basic structure; and rooms arranged in an enfilade for the proper ceremonious circulation of guests – all appealed strongly to the post-Restoration gentry. From the time of Charles II, says North, the old ways of organising social space, with servants mingled promiscuously in the upper household, has become moribund and 'scarce any [house] of that intention hath bin built'. Belton House, built for Sir John Brownlow in 1685, is the perfect embodiment of the new principles: its external regularity, as shown in the painting attributed to the steward Henry Bugg, mirrored its internal order, which was probably copied from Pratt's 'double pile' houses such as Horseheath in Cambridgeshire.[34]

As aesthetic preoccupations with building form intensified, so did concern for the total environment provided by mansion, park and garden. The early Tudor propensity to site farm and outbuildings close to the house yielded to a concern for formal space, vista and railed enclosure. These transformations wrought in the immediate environment of houses were in many ways as significant as changes in the buildings themselves. Aubrey's 'before and after' sketches of his family home show the crucial visual importance of terracing and formal gardening in displaying the house and enhancing its owner's status.

29. Henry Bugg, attrib., 'Belton House, Lincolnshire', *c.*1690

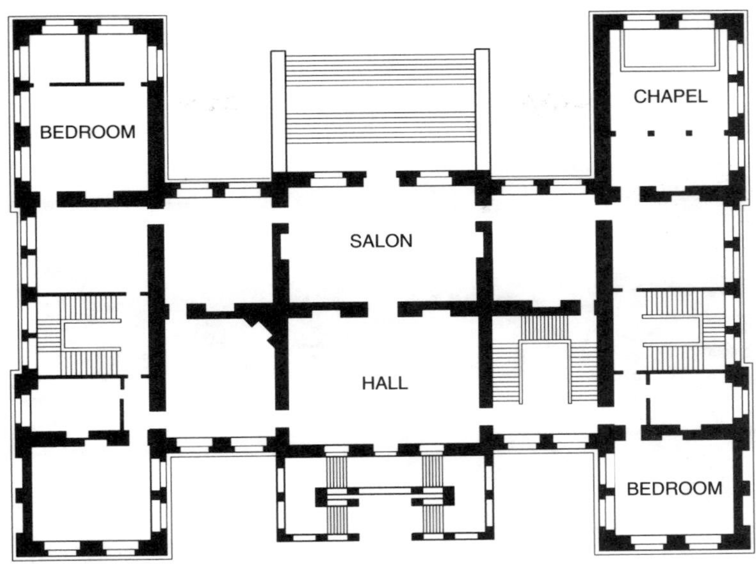


30. Ground-floor plan of Belton House, Lincolnshire, 1680s

Other late seventeenth-century illustrations, especially the elegant series of engravings included in Sir Henry Chauncy's study of Hertfordshire, demonstrate the same integrity of house and garden, the perspectives stretching away into parkland to convey the image of eminent domain. The wonderful naive painting of the squire's house and garden at Llannerch, Denbighshire, dating from about 1662, suggests that the garden, here designed in the new Italian style, could take priority over the house as a source of pride.[35]

Sir Thomas Hanmer, writing in the 1650s, argued that 'the rich among us are not satisfied with good houses and parks . . . their ambition and curiosity extends also to very costly embellishments of their gardens'. The last is often overlooked because changing fashion has swept away all original garden arrangements from the period and reconstructions are dependent on illustrations and literary descriptions. The Grand Tour, and access to France and Holland for many gentlemen during the difficult years of the Interregnum, provided the ideas upon which the ambitious could

31. John Aubrey's sketch of the family home, Easton Percy, Wiltshire, before reconstruction

32. John Aubrey's sketch of the family home and gardens, Easton Percy, Wiltshire, after reconstruction

33. Llannerch, Denbighshire: house and gardens, *c.*1662

build their vegetable creations. New garden theory, and the growing prestige attached to good landscaping, encouraged substantial investment. Already in the mid-sixteenth century continental contacts stimulated gardening ambitions: the Carews, for example, imported a large number of orange trees to Beddington in Surrey and built special shelters for their winter protection. The multiplication of books on horticulture – only about 19 new titles in the sixteenth century, but 100 in the next – is one sign of the growth of gardening enthusiasm. William Harrison believed that even under Elizabeth the beauty of gardens had greatly increased 'so that in comparison of this present the ancient gardens were but dunghills'. By the Jacobean period Court involvement in land-scaping and new species stimulated a response from the landed classes. Sir Roger Townshend seems to have laid out no less than eleven acres of park to formal garden at Raynham, the scale of his endeavours being suggested by the planting of 1,400 elms and 4,000 lime trees in 1620–1. Further down the social scale Sir John Oglander planted over 100 elms and ashes, plus 100 quinces and many apples, cherries and plums on his Nunwell estate. Social emulation encouraged these extravagances but gardens cannot be read solely as a source of display: then as now many individuals were consumed by a passion for their environment. Oglander confessed to spending 'more money than a wise man would have done in flowers for the garden', because for him the garden was his individual solace from study and labour. He was aware its contribution to his standing – he had made Nunwell from a 'rude chase' into a 'fit place for any gentleman' – but his garden was clearly a work of love. At the very margins of gentility, the Shann family of Methley, Yorkshire, showed a passion for trees, beautifully exemplified at a moment when a mulberry is planted by three generations, the grandson still a babe in arms assisted by his mother. John Evelyn revealed his obsession with gardens long before he wrote on them, when he redesigned part of his brother's gardens at Wotton, Surrey. Sir Thomas Hanmer, himself a great collector, told Evelyn in 1668: 'we have within these few years in Flintshire . . . many gentlemen that have upon my instigation and persuasion fallen to plant both flowers and trees'. For such men the garden was no doubt both a source of fascinating experimentation and of spiritual solace, that 'purest of human pleasures' of which Bacon had written so eloquently.[36]

## 8.3 THE GENTLEMAN IN COMPANY

Rural sociability focused largely upon the great house, but was not confined to its bounds. Just as much of a gentleman's political obligation was discharged in the public fora of town and city, so a part of his social intercourse was conducted in these collective contexts. Politics and sociability were directly linked through the entertainments associated with assize and quarter sessions, and lesser judicial occasions. As the frequency and complexity of such meetings increased during the course of the sixteenth century, so did the enhanced opportunities for sections of the 'county community' to find entertainment together. The larger towns in their turn often cultivated the rural élite for profit and social cachet: already in the early sixteenth-century York and Chester saw their pageant cycles and processions as important moments for the entertainment of the gentry, offering wine and 'treats' as an accompaniment to the day. When this source of contact was lost after the Reformation, there were conscious efforts to find substitutes. Norwich had considerable success in transmuting its St George's Day celebrations and also promoted its Florists' Feast. The latter was described in the 1630s as celebrated 'by such a conflux of Gentlemen of birth and quality, in whose presence and commerce . . . your cities welfare partly consists'. Chester had some success in the development of horse-racing, to which we shall return, and York oscillated between racing and a midsummer show, though the latter was never wholly successful. Such constructed moments of sociability were no substitute, however, for a regular focus of entertainment in the towns, which really waited upon the changes of the later seventeenth century.[37]

Meanwhile, many of the opportunities of the town must have been of the more mundane variety summarised in Heywood's *The English Traveller* (1633) when Delavill thus describes the excitements of Barnet market:

> This Barnet is a place of great resort;
> And commonly upon the market dayes
> Heere all the Countrey Gentlemen Appoint
> A friendly meeting: some about affaires
> Of consequence and Profit; Bargaine, Sale,
> And to conferre with Chap-men, some for pleasure,

> To match their Horses; Wager in their Dogs,
> Or trie their Hawkes; Som to no other end
> But onely meet good Company, discourse,
> Dine, drinke and spend their Money.

The inn provided the focus for such miscellaneous activities, and the gentry were liable to end the day the worse for drink and ill-tempered, like the two groups of young Norfolk gentlemen who ended a day's drinking at the King's Head, Norwich, in 1615 with a series of challenges to duels that put them into Star Chamber, prosecuted by the Attorney-General. Oglander remembered with some affection the merry gang of Isle of Wight 'good fellowes' who, like Falstaff, 'loved a coupp of sacke and a wenche' and were prone to reel down Newport High Street proving it.[38]

Sociability was more explicitly fostered at encounters of a sporting kind, such as bowling, cock-fighting and horse-racing. William Carnsew, in his Cornwall diary of the 1570s, describes bowling in public places as well as with gentlemen friends. Under James bowling was *de facto* if not *de jure* liberated from the constraints of the 1541 statute when the King granted the right to license alleys to one of his household, and public alleys became popular with the gentry. Anthony Ashley Cooper identified Hanley bowling green as a major meeting place for the gentry of east Dorset before the Civil War: 'though neither the green nor accommodation was inviting yet it was well placed for to contrive the correspondence of the gentry in those parts'. Oglander said much the same about the twice-weekly bowling meetings on the Isle of Wight downs, where 30 or 40 knights and gentlemen met, and there was an inn for their entertainment. Sir John speaks nostalgically of amity on these occasions, though Richard Brathwait noted that even 'bowlings' provided occasion for the quarrelsome 'to make differences amongst men of qualitie'.[39]

If the bowling green was thought often to foster a measure of co-operation and shared identity, the cockpit and the racecourse were generally believed to nurture competition, conflict and heavy betting. Cockfighting is of interest as a sport which still integrated gentlemen and their inferiors, cutting across social boundaries already well established in areas like hunting. Oliver Heywood has a vivid description of cocking in Halifax in the 1680s, in which the men of Halifax matched their birds against the local gentry and 'generally beat the gentlemens', though only after some participants had come to blows about the social propriety of the occasion. Some matches were on the grand scale, like the fight between the cocks of Lancashire and Cheshire on the one hand, and those of Shropshire and Wales on the other, held at Shrewsbury in 1598 and attended by 'lords, knights and gentlemen' as well as some Londoners. Much money was won and lost on this occasion, as no doubt it was at the Chester cockpit built by the fifteenth Earl of Derby, 'to which resorted gentlemen from all parts and great cocking was used there'. Regional rivalries were expressed in these conflicts, but fights and betting were also reflections of the individualism of gentry culture. One of Nicholas Le Strange's jests has Sir Thomas Jermyn gulling the London punters with a dunghill cockerel proudly trimmed. Men bet on Jermyn's cock, he says, simply because of the reputation of the gentleman. The status and courage of a gallant was supposed to be mirrored in his bird. Sir William Kingsmill, who failed to produce his cock for an arranged fight in 1688, was perceived as behaving almost as dishonourably as though he had refused to duel.[40]

Horse-racing, which began as little more than an occasional alternative to the leisure activities already discussed, came to outstrip most of them in popularity during the seventeenth century. It combined the gentry's love of vigorous riding with enthusiasm for horse-breeding and ideal opportunities for competition and wagers. The modest beginnings of organised meetings, as against simple competitive riding, seems attributable to some of the northern towns, especially Chester, which saw racing as a means of restoring part of its economic fortunes after the Reformation. At Chester the Easter Monday shooting match was gradually replaced by the Easter Tuesday race under Elizabeth, the town providing one of the earliest recorded prizes. The other key influence was the Court, where the royal interest in bloodstock in Henry VIII's reign stimulated competitive riding. By Elizabeth's reign there are scattered references to meetings sponsored either by towns or nobles and gentlemen from various parts of the country, though already with a preponderance of northern examples. By 1600 Doncaster had a full racecourse and structure of meetings, and other places rapidly followed under the influence of James's royal enthusiasm for the sport.[41]

Racing was inevitably a sport of the élite, one in which the younger members of many great households were eager participants and their elders provided prize money. A well-documented encounter at Gatherley Moor, near Richmond, Yorkshire, in 1622, involved six horses, ridden by members of the Bowes, Wandesford, Wharton, Brough and Loftus families, seconded by other North Riding gentlemen. A thorough listing of those contributing to prize money at Etton races in about 1617 is a roll-call of the leading gentlemen of the East Riding, under the patronage of a few of the great such as the Earl of Cumberland and Viscount Dunbar. The growing elaboration of racing provided a relative novel context for gentry encounters, one that presaged the far more general 'public and civil' culture of the eighteenth century. This novelty also invested the races with a powerful function as a 'theatre of honour', as more attractive occasions for wagers and competition than other forms of sociability. Only gaming and card play had similar appeal as ways of losing money, for as Burton sourly observed 'many gentlemen by such means gallop quite out of their fortunes'. Levels of wager are not easy to determine from surviving sources, though the second Earl of Salisbury sometimes staked several hundred pounds on a horse. Gervase Markham included in his text on horsemanship a section on the making of wagers, both for hunting contests and races, since many gentlemen 'will make matches'. At least the gradual regulation of races eliminated some of the worst effects of this private gambling: like the famous disaster of the race around Faringdon, Berkshire, between two Fettiplace cousins, which ended in one murdering the other. There are examples of assaults committed at race meetings: Gervase Holles's father engaged in a quarrel on a kinsman's behalf at Grimsby races, and his opponents planned revenge at the next meeting, only to be thwarted by a strong display of gentry solidarity. More often, however, competitiveness seems to have been contained within the structure of wagers on the event itself.[42]

These forms of provincial sociability affirmed a sense of élite masculine identity by providing meetings of approximate equals not constrained and defined by the roles of host and guest. In the grand encounters of assizes and quarter sessions, or great cocking matches or race meetings, this identity may have been as broad as the county or even the region. On a more routine basis it probably followed 'the Barnet model' and secured contacts within a sub-region defined by the nearest market town or a manageable day's ride. Gilbert Littelton, as we have seen, was proud that he had made Stourbridge, Worcestershire, such a centre for 'cocke fights and other pastimes' under Elizabeth. Elite identity (or competition) of this kind could have its dangers for those in authority. The

Gunpowder Plotters used the occasion of a general hunt at Dunchurch in Warwickshire to pull together disaffected gentlemen. As we have seen, the Interregnum regimes were particularly sensitive to the dangers of these public meetings, which could provide the opportunity to orchestrate opposition.[43]

Provincial sociability of this kind also performed a useful function since it could transcend social boundaries and offer opportunities for an integration of popular and élite culture. This could be merely a matter of traditional habit, but in the divided England of the seventeenth century it might also be a deliberate statement about the values of the political culture. The famous Cotswold Games of the pre-Civil War period were orchestrated and supported by the élite and were also a deliberate affirmation of popular culture in the face of Puritan hostility. After the Restoration, support for cock-fighting, bowling and other popular pastimes became identified with both an 'Anglican' and a 'country' resistance to the twin pressures of the godly and the metropolis. Recreations and entertainments were not automatically charged with such meanings, but the public standing of the gentry meant that they could not escape forms of political identity even at the inn or on the bowling green.[44]

## 8.4 THE GENTLEMAN 'ABROAD'

The country/county was perceived by the moralists of Tudor and Stuart England as the natural sphere of gentry activity. Beyond their own localities gentlemen might have legitimate duties: education, litigation, military responsibility and political representation being the most obvious. But these were the particular branches and fruits of a tree firmly rooted in a rural estate and local government. James I is supposed to have compared a gentleman to a sailing vessel, which looks formidable when seen on a river, while it may be lost in the vastness of the ocean. Of course the monarch and his fellow commentators did not have in mind any old ocean in this simile. Gentlemen did wander far beyond England, and widely within their own realm, but the social phenomenon that most concerned Englishmen was a particular migration, the movement to London. London, in the jaundiced view of James, would soon devour all England, since the gentry were no longer willing to live 'as every fish lives in his own place, some in the fresh, some in the salt, some in the mud' but all would seek to crowd into the city and to the Court.[45]

It is relatively easy to generalise about the broad influence of the metropolis on gentry culture and behaviour, though more tricky to flesh out the detail. The growth of London as a centre of conspicuous consumption and of political and social activity for the élite has a starting point long before our period, and a certain linearity through these two centuries. In the first half of the sixteenth century the major stimulus was political and administrative centralisation – the growth of the Court as a focus of competition, the extended role of Parliament and above all the enhanced activity of the law courts. The political difficulties of the mid-century may have curtailed some gentry enthusiasm for the 'great wen', but from the Elizabethan period the political and legal trajectory of growth was resumed. At some time in the Queen's late years the social pull of the capital became more intense, and something like a 'season' was initiated. Despite the hostility of the early Stuart regimes, and the series of proclamations that attempted to confine London residence by the gentry to the law terms, the magnet-force of the capital intensified before the Civil War, assisted by the programme of building that created Covent Garden and parts of the West End. Civil war obviously inhibited expansion, but even before the Restoration the scale of engagement was once more increased, and in the last years of the century the London season became a critical part of the experience of the élite.[46]

All of this may appear as natural to the historian as it appeared reprehensible to many contemporaries. When the political and legal institutions and specialist services of the realm were so intensely concentrated on the capital, it seems logical that those with the appropriate wealth and leisure would be found there. Indeed what might need explanation is why the élite continued to be partially resident in the country, why they did not surrender to the charms of urbanity as did, for example, so many of the French nobility. However, even the apparently inexorable drift of the gentry to London is not without its explanatory problems. For example, the growth of many of the specialised functions mentioned above long preceded routine residence in the capital, and well into the Stuart period there seems a reluctance by many gentlemen to make any long-term investment in the city.

The prevailing impression from the limited sources available before the 1580s is that the gentry did not reflect very closely on the problem of the metropolis. An occasional voice is raised in warning about the corrosive effects of London living: for example in the advice given to John Gostwick in the 1540s not to take his wife to the capital because of her fondness for gambling. The discourse of city versus country was already part of the vocabulary of Henrician courtiers and poets, but in practice it was the contrast between Court and locality that engaged men like the elder Wyatt, and this was a dilemma that impinged on a rather small and rarefied section of the gentry. Otherwise the city was mainly a fertile source of complaint about cost and poor lodging from gentlemen conducting legal or political business. Late in Henry's reign, William Paston, for example, complained to his grandfather that he could not stay in the city because of the high cost of living and 'the diabolicall covetousnes . . . among allmen'. Yet despite the grumbles many were drawn to the capital: some crude sense of this may be drawn from an extended will sample from 1500 to 1540 in which at least 37 among 200 gentry wills show testators either making their wills in London or anticipating that they might die there. Among the groups most prominent in this sample are lawyers and royal officials, but there is also an interesting clutch of widows, perhaps the prototypes of those later single women who found the resources of the town peculiarly congenial.[47]

It is only in the later half of Elizabeth's reign that literary sources begin to develop the trope of London as the seductress of the landed élite. A city which had been perceived largely as a necessary resort of those pursuing honest business now acquired the reputation for giddy entertainment, cozening, 'pomp, pride and luxury'. A priggish young Puritan like James Harington of Ridlington found himself 'almost suffocated with ill scent of pride and vanity'. Writers for the public stage constantly portrayed the foolish country gentleman bent on cutting a figure in the city. And life could imitate art: as with the poor Welsh knight who in 1620 was robbed of his wealth by his servant, and on his attempt to pursue it 'all the women in the street hard by Holborn Conduit did beat him very sore and abuse[d] him vilely: they called him "the foolish Welsh justice"'. Such dramas reflect not only the age-old polarity between town and countryside, but also an awareness that a substantial change in élite behaviour was occurring. By the 1590s there were the beginnings of a term-time season, focused in the autumn or early spring, when gentlemen were in town in large numbers. James I was later to associate the change with the presence of wives, and to blame their passion for entertainment:

You dreame on nought but vizitts maskes and toyes
And thinke the cuntrey contributes noe ioyes

No doubt he was in some measure correct. We can observe just such a feminine passion at work when, in about 1590, Sir Edward Aston complained bitterly that his wife had twice compelled him to town at the cost of £200 on each occasion. 'Ther is no talk but I must goe ly at London and brave it owte: it is base lyinge in the countrey.' Of course men also sought to escape the countryside: William Johnson told Sir Edward Dering that, having 'worne out a melancholie winter' in the country, he longed to go to London 'as those poore men who were left in Greenland a whole winter, did long for a summer fleet to carrie them home'. However, this possibility had always been available to the more prosperous among them: its extension to their wives was a far greater novelty.[48]

Though the female desire for company drew them to London, it was husbands who held ultimate control over their mobility, and most would not have acceded to these pressures without some inducement beyond the merely social. The most likely catalyst was the law: the season grew up around the law terms and derived much of its vitality from the litigiousness of the landed gentry. For much of the seventeenth century the gentry moved in flocks: out of term they migrated back to the countryside and, as one contemporary observed: 'methinks this towne is becum a wildernes, none therin lefte but lawiers and prentises, from whom good Lord deliver me, and every honest cuntry gentleman'. A wife might be of direct utility in the prosecution of suits, as it seems Lady Margaret Hoby was when she came south from Hackness in 1600 to support her husband's vendetta against the Eures. Or, if her specific support was not required, she might provide valuable companionship during the long delays to which the courts were subject. We may infer from Sir Hugh Cholmley that his father's residence in London owed much initially to his endless litigation with Hoby which 'occasioned many expences and increase of debts'. Much of our knowledge of affectionate marriages in early Stuart England derives from the correspondence of husbands and wives separated by the demands of the law on the former. Neither party usually found this attractive, and the logic of the situation must have suggested that if a wife could be spared from the country she should accompany her spouse. 'There is no reason,' wrote Sir Robert Sidney to his wife in 1594, 'to leave you where you are at Penshurst without company in the winter'.[49]

If the demands of law were a major catalyst for change they were strongly afforced by a series of other incentives that ensured the permanence of the social shift. The development of the private coach was the instrument for mobility that secured wives a more comfortable access to the capital, and in the early seventeenth century its ownership was rapidly diffused, until in 1623 it was solemnly reported to Joseph Mead that 1,400 coaches had left the city at the Christmas season. They were certainly felt to clog the city by the same period, for John Taylor expressed relief that the streets were suddenly cleared of vehicles. Once these major inducements to change were in place, others followed pell-mell. London gave access to specialist services, of which medicine and education were probably the most important, and it became routine to employ these rather than depend on the provinces. In medicine the remarkable clientele acquired by Sir Theodore Mayerne under James I and Charles I is indicative of provincial as well as urban demands. Women, in particular, flocked to London physicians, and many of the licences that the Crown issued to permit residence in the capital were for medical treatment. Education not only brought youth to the city, but might persuade parents to follow them, as when in 1605 Sir John Wynn resolved on winter residence in London, since 'I mean to place [my children] thearabouts for Educatyon and course of lyf'. Beyond these serious needs London offered all the luxury services of fashion and culture and was, in the vivid phrase of Sir Anthony Denton 'the garden of England, whear wee may all live together'.[50]

The scale and consequences of this growing metropolitan access are not easy to estimate. No effective count of ordinary gentlemen visiting, or resident in, the city can be made for the seventeenth century, and even Stone's calculations that approximately a hundred peers had London accommodation in the 1630s are probably not exhaustive. As many as two dozen Kentish justice families may have had regular London residences by the eve of the Civil War: 13 of the 38 magisterial families of Berkshire were also property owners in the metropolis. The most promising sources for mere gentlemen are the lists of residents drawn up at the Crown's behest in 1622 and 1633 with the object of expelling those with no legitimate claim to be in the city. In the major sweep of 1632–3 nearly 250 gentlemen and women were found to be in violation of the royal Proclamations, which provides us at least with a core of determined Londoners. A common feature of surveys and prosecution lists is a weighting towards the upper end of the élite: 93 of those listed were knights, plus 21 women of the same status, and approximately half the rest were listed as esquires. This is no doubt in part because the Crown wished to make an example of those senior gentry who were office-holders in their own shires, but it also indicates a predictable division between the 'county' gentry, who had the resources to live in London, and the majority of mere gentlemen. The point can be reinforced by looking at London residence from the county perspective. When estreats were taken in Warwickshire for the fine for the knighting of Prince Henry in 1609 a list of five of the senior gentry were either absent in London or about to depart. The Pelhams stand out from their contemporaries in mid-century Sussex as a family that chose to be seduced so completely by London pleasures. Sir Humphrey Mildmay's recorded London associates were largely Essex men of high standing. Later in the century, when the season had become routinised, it was still the greater gentry who were able to afford its pleasures. Glamorgan men, ever slow to follow general fashion, were gradually following the season by 1700, but there was approximately a half century gap before middling gentlemen began to follow their richer colleagues.[51]

The London market and London culture created a national response to fashion and consumption among the élite, generating a response even among those who chose not to spend time in the capital. Gentry memoirs may be replete with nostalgia for the simple ways of their ancestors, but few failed to enquire after the latest fashion, or to take advantage of current developments in taste. Most of the families with surviving correspondence had London agents who sought out luxury goods and ordered clothes for them, though a few like the Wynns depended heavily on members of the family living in town. Sometimes country gentlemen still needed persuasion before yielding to the tyrannies of taste, but their London contacts were adamant: 'I have sent you', says Stephen Smith to Sir Hugh Smyth 'a paire of hangers of the newest fashion, and such as are now in use by men of the best fashion'. But following style at a distance was no substitute for London living since, as Edward Waterhouse admitted, only in the city could you find 'pleasant houses, good diet, fashionable furniture, pleasures and profits the best of all sorts'.[52]

Behind this construction of material conformity lies the more interesting development of a civil culture, one in which values originated in urban society become defining for the whole of the social élite. This is a complex process, born of the intersection of Court, city and gentry in the half-century before the Civil War, but not fully visible until after the Restoration. Individual voices defending the life of the city as superior to that of the country had been heard from the earliest reception of Renaissance texts. By the early seventeenth century it was no longer thought curious to defend the proposition that cities are 'fullest of knowledge and good manners', though the defenders of the rural idyll still spoke more vociferously. The greater gentry acted rather than theorised, and modelled themselves on the cultural behaviour they observed on their peregrinations, accepting complex rules for polite society and transmitting them to their localities on their return. What the very rich learned in one generation was by the next transmitted to lesser men, and not only to lesser gentlemen, but to the burgeoning middling and professional sorts, who often had easier access to urban values than rural squires. The society of manners was afforced by that of virtuosity: although the latter owed most to the Grand Tour it was in London that the intellectual contacts that sustained collecting and connoisseurship were to be found. John Evelyn's diaries are powerful testimony to the growth of this culture after the Restoration. In a typical week in February 1665 he saw a masque at Court, heard two sermons from a Scottish preacher and his own curate, dined with the Earl of Southampton in Bloomsbury where he evaluated the new architecture, and engaged in a scientific study of the wildfowl in St James's Park. It would be foolish to suggest that Evelyn was a typical gentleman, but the diverse worlds to which he had access in the city are exemplary of the enlarged opportunities of the post-Restoration world.[53]

Spas, provincial capitals and the European Grand Tour all contributed to the construction of civility in the post-Restoration world. They also reinforced that sense among the gentry that, if they remained in their rural estates, they would 'be taken for Justice Silence or Justice Shallow'. By the end of the seventeenth century there was perhaps more risk that the English élite would follow the French pattern and flee the countryside almost completely than some commentators allow. In the next century Dr Johnson, that ultimate Londoner, could claim 'there was not now the same temptation to live in the country as formerly. The pleasures of social life were much better enjoyed in the town, and there was not now in the country that power and influence in proprietors of land which they had in olden times'. It was in the last comment that Johnson was most astray: much power, as well as wealth, still rested in tenurial relationships in the countryside, and it was there that social hegemony most needed to be displayed. While this could be combined with the merry massacre of the unfortunate fox, the masculine half of English élite were unlikely to abandon their rural estates completely for the pleasures of civil society abroad.[54]

# 9

# The Gentry and the Church

Sir Henry Spelman, the great legal historian, was in some ways a characteristic learned gentleman of the early seventeenth century. He exchanged notes and writings on heraldry with his fellow antiquaries, participated efficiently, if not vigorously, in the political affairs of his county of Norfolk, and sat as an MP in the Parliaments of 1597 and 1625. Like many of his contemporaries, Spelman was also involved in much litigation for the preservation of his estate, including long and bitter conflicts about his claim to property formerly held by the abbeys of Blackborough and Wormegay. The dispute ground through Chancery for two decades until it was finally compromised by Lord Keeper Coventry. And there the matter would probably have ended had the antiquary not been in other ways a very untypical gentleman. Instead he expressed relief to be 'out of the briars', but drew from his experiences the unusual conclusion that he had been taught 'the Infelicity of meddling with consecrated places'. From this beginning Spelman began to accumulate evidence of the disastrous effect that possession of former Church property had had on the families of his native county, evidence that was published long after his death in *The History and Fate of Sacrilege*. An interim statement of his views on sacrilege did, however, appear in 1613 in *De non temerandis Ecclesiae*.[1]

Spelman analysed the families who lived in close proximity to his Norfolk home, including in his survey 24 mansion houses where, before the Reformation, approximately the same number of monastic establishments had existed. Systematically he revealed that none of those who had taken ecclesiastical lands had prospered: families had not reproduced themselves, heirs had run mad or been killed in accidents, heads of houses had been imprisoned for debt. Even relatively virtuous families like his friends and kinsmen the Townshends had been blighted by their possession of monastic lands, in this case those of Coxford Abbey. Sir John had been killed in a duel just after the turn of the century, and his heir, Sir Roger, had been cursed by two accidents, for a workman was killed as he was demolishing the steeple of the abbey and the foundations of his new house cracked. The rapid turnover of families, which historians would see as a part of the contemporary demographic regime, was to Spelman clear evidence of Divine judgement upon those who had turned sacred property and goods to secular uses, making, as he says in one extreme case, an 'appropriate Parish-Church a Hay-house, or a dog-kennel'.[2]

Since the sins of the fathers would be visited on the children Spelman did not believe that the damage of the Reformation period could be fully atoned for, nor did he advocate the impossible for a Protestant, the restitution of monastic lands. But something could be done, and from the time of the publication of *De non temerandis* he campaigned to persuade his fellow gentry to return impropriations – those lay rectories transmitted to them by the Crown as part of the distribution of monastic goods – to the Church. Sir Roger Townshend was one of those who responded: 'he hath', Spelman recorded, 'very nobly and piously endeavoured to expiate [his guilt]; for he hath given back to the Church three or four Appropriations'.[3] Only when such gestures were made by the majority would God's judgement be turned from the leaders of Stuart society. The antiquary did not live to see the outbreak of the Civil War, but it is obvious that he would have seen the collapse of the traditional order as confirmation of his most dire warnings.

It must be said that Sir Henry Spelman's was a distinctive, if not quite unique, lay voice in pronouncing jeremiads upon the gentry for their appropriation of Church wealth. Clerics of all persuasions might thunder against greed and sacrilege, but most gentlemen preferred to believe that what had been done with Crown sanction should never again be undone. If they did contemplate restitution it was within the very different context of godly Puritanism: to fund a preaching ministry which would probably organise itself by a presbyterian discipline. This was the vision of Sir Anthony Cope, one of the promoters of the famous Bill and Book introduced into the Parliament of 1586–7, which would have swept away the entire existing structure of the Church of England, and replaced it with a Genevan constitution. Such a complete *tabula rasa* of a Bill, as Neale calls it, was doomed to immediate extinction. However, in one of the speeches that buried it for the benefit of MPs, Sir Christopher Hatton vividly evoked the perennial anxieties of the gentry about their power over the Church. Patronage of Church livings would be transferred to presbyteries; each parish would have to increase its paid personnel with pastors, doctors and deacons, and payment could only come from the impropriated tithes; finally, former abbey lands would be needed to fund the edifice proposed in the Bill. 'They call us', said the Chancellor, identifying himself with gentry interests, 'Church robbers, devourers of holy things, cormorants etc.' while aiming at patronage, impropriations and land, so that the Bill 'toucheth us all in our inheritances'. The appeal to self-interest was unsubtle, but presumably compelling, especially when linked to the obvious charge that Cope and his fellows sought to create 'a barbarous equality' in the Church, and therefore why not in the State? Few gentlemen were immune to fears of levelling and/or financial expropriation. Hatton could safely affect amazement that the ideologue Cope could be so obtuse about the interests of his class: 'the honest, zealous gentleman of this House [who]. . .hath been slily led into this action'.[4]

Spelman and Hatton do more than simply remind their audience of the economic advantages they had derived, legitimately or not, from the Church. They indicate that power, in its political and social forms, was indissolubly linked to the acquisition of these material benefits. The 'inheritances' of Hatton's speech include patronage, and hence command over men: the 'sacrilege' discussed by Spelman includes the abuse of responsibilities that had been inherited with the monastic estates, such as the duty to appoint good ministers and to give hospitality. The story of the relationship between the gentry and the Established Church in England requires that primary attention be given to these issues of power and wealth, since they provided the framework within which religious beliefs normally operated. The gentry were public figures with a visible position to maintain within the commonwealth, and this immediately involved them in a network of obligations and interests that were not necessarily godly.

## 9.1 BEFORE THE REFORMATION

It is tempting at first sight to argue that the power relationships between gentry and Church shifted fundamentally at the Reformation. The lands with which to become sacriligeous only became available at the Dissolution of the Monasteries; impropriations were similarly released by that movement and patronage, though not new, was massively increased. Discipline exercised over the Church by laymen would have been unthinkable among the orthodox before the break with Rome. But to understand what happened in the 1530s we need to consider the continuities from the past, rather than the sharp contrasts. It seems particularly important to consider these links as a way of understanding why almost everyone of sufficient standing and wealth was prepared to participate in the dismemberment of the old structures, regardless of their ideological views. It has frequently been remarked that families who later became impeccably Catholic were amongst the most zealous in the scramble for monastic lands and parish patronage. Sir John Tregonwell, Sir John Arundell and Sir Anthony Browne were all among the leading expropriators: not much evidence of fear of sacrilege was evident among them.[5]

The typical landed gentleman of the early years of Henry VIII's reign already had associations with the Church far beyond the narrowly spiritual. At the most personal level he was likely to be an employer of clerical labour, via household chaplaincies and chantry foundations. While the bishop maintained powers as ordinary over such clergy, in practice a gentleman could hire and fire almost at will. More, in his *Dialogue Concerning Heresies* complained that 'every meane man must have a preste in his house to wayte uppon his wyffe' and Christopher St German pointed out that irresponsible employers could command chaplains 'to go huntyng, hawkynge, and suche other vayne disportes. And some wold lett them lye amonge other laye servauntes where they could neyther use prayer nor contemplation'. No doubt most masters did not behave in such an extreme manner, and it would be foolish to regard as typical the few cases in Chancery and Star Chamber in which priests aided and abetted their masters in their supposed misdeeds. But the power relationships between priests and masters were obvious, and could not easily be modulated by the intervention of clerical superiors. The 'tone' of a conscientious, but authoritarian, master is heard in Sir Thomas Lucy's arrangement that Richard Ilshawe should have money to train as a priest, provided that he then 'doo service . . . to my said wife'.[6]

Command over parish priests was less likely, yet lay patronage already represented a significant element in the English Church. In the decades immediately before the break with Rome nearly 36 per cent of the presentations in the huge diocese of Lincoln were made by laymen, the gentry doubtless prominent among them. A similar calculation for Canterbury estimates only 16 per cent of livings to be in lay hands, but this does not take into account the tendency of monasteries and bishops to grant the right of presentation for one turn to a suitable purchaser. Little evidence about gentry attitudes to their livings survives for this period, though there is the earlier Paston letter which 'advertises' the virtues of the family living of Oxnead: 'the cyte off Norwych is with-in vi myle'. . . 'it is butt an esy cure to kepe, for ther ar nott past xx persons to be yerly howselyd'. Whether a patron or not, a gentleman already had views upon the interior of his local church and its arrangement for his benefit: pewing, which became such a major issue in the later sixteenth century, was well established in many areas before the Reformation, and the gentry could already expect to sit either in their own chapel or in the chancel itself. In the embellishment of their parish churches we should no doubt credit members of the élite with a positive commitment to the corporate aspects of their faith, but some of the most impressive remains for this period are the distinctive burial chapels which label a section of the fabric with a familial identity. As Sir John Oglander was later to put it:

> The South Chawncell of Brading was fownded by my Awncestors, only for a place of Buriall, where they lie all interred. I have mayntayned itt at my owne chardges and in that respect I am freed from payinge of mortuaries . . . I am also freed from payinge any thinge for breakinge of grownd to the parish, which of others they have

This sense of a right to instruct cleric and wardens on the proper deference due to a gentleman is nothing new: already in the fifteenth century honour and precedence in church was a sensitive issue for the élite.[7]

The tradition of *eigenkirche* and of the influence of founders was even more explicitly manifest in the monasteries than in the secular Church. It was in the monasteries that founders' and benefactors' rights were at their most intrusive: the ability to appoint corrodians, to secure obits and to elicit hospitality may not have been so disruptive as some of the older commentators suggest, but they reinforced a proprietorial sense that was to have major consequences at the Dissolution. They certainly encouraged laymen to act in the broadest sense as patrons, defending houses when they needed political support, involving themselves in internal disputes if there was sufficient excuse. Thus Sir William Courtenay became heavily engaged in faction fighting at Launceston Priory, and was apparently guilty of a simonaical transaction with John Shere for the latter's election to the Prior's seat. Courtenay denied the charge, but admitted to Cromwell that since Shere's promotion 'I have had 200 marks of him, and as God shall help me without any promise of him or any man for him'. Since Courtenay became engaged in a similar contretemps at Hartland Priory, this time with Sir Thomas Arundell against him, his pleas of innocence sound dubious. There was more legitimacy in the actions of John Scudamore in relation to Monmouth Abbey, since he was appointed receiver in 1534 when the house was at the point of collapse through mismanagement and internal dissension. Scudamore organised the lease of the abbey buildings in order to meet the commitments of annuities and other payments that had been incurred, thereby effectively secularising the institution. However, it is the style, rather than the content of his actions that is of interest to us, since he had no hesitation in conceiving the the monastery as a financial institution with obligations that had to be met.[8]

The roles of the gentry as stewards to monasteries, and as lessees of their property, brought them into ever more intimate contact with the wealth they were so readily to appropriate. The management of many monastic estates was, by the eve of the Dissolution, almost entirely in the hands of laymen, either as lessees or administrators. In Leicestershire the local élites were so entwined with the monastic houses that there is logic in Thomas Billesden's complaint about Launde: no justice could be had of the Prior at the Assizes because all the great men of the county were in his employment. In many cases there was a direct correlation between these pre-Reformation roles and land purchase after the Dissolution. In Lincolnshire, for example, Sir John Heneage bought estates that had previously belonged to Bardney, of which he was steward, and George St Paul and Edward Skipwith did the same at Thornton. Elsewhere the connection is less precise, as in south-east Wales, where slightly different social groups appear to have been administrators and purchasers. The crucial point, however, is that taboos against the exploitation of church property had already been weakened by the economic and political circumstances of the first years of the sixteenth century. Even the first essay in dissolution, that of Wolsey's 1525 closures, already attracted ambitious gentry like the Kentish Guldefordes who sought land from the houses of Bayham and Bilsington.[9]

Traditional Protestant views of the Reformation would have associated these incursions into the power and property of the Church with a contempt for, or at least mistrust of, the clergy themselves. It is no longer so convincing to talk of anti-clericalism as a blanket concept, capable of explaining all the problems of the Reformation years. The emphasis in recent work has been on the general acceptance of the clergy as performing adequately within their defined roles, with rather limited criticism of their education, morality or assiduity. The gentry still believed that they could recruit worthy chantry priests, and often went to some lengths in their wills to specify that they should be 'sober' or 'of good conversation'. Many gentlemen left bequests to their local cleric, and a substantial minority of these were more than mere tokenism, but gave significant sums, or referred with apparent affection to 'my ghostly father'. Household accounts for the period, such as those of the Le Strange family of Hunstanton in Norfolk show the clergy as routine and apparently popular guests at their tables. The Prior of Coxford seems to have been particularly popular because of the generosity of his food gifts to the Le Stranges. A reflex anti-clericalism is sometimes encountered in the lay élite, as in the crisis over the Hunne Case, but this is more than matched by the evidence of collaboration. Bishops and leading gentlemen co-operated in the governance of the localities with no more strain than might reasonably be expected between two rival jurisdictional groups.[10]

Yet the absence of constant conflict, and the rather limited role that appears to be played by anti-clerical sentiment may be of little utility in explaining the circumstances of the Church on the eve of the Reformation. It seems likely that leading laymen were already adept at separating their political and economic interests from their devotional lives, and that the generally subservient status of the clergy did nothing to challenge this process. It was often the clergy themselves who invoked lay assistance, because they lacked the resources or power to resolve issues themselves: this was particularly true of the monasteries which, in the last ten years of their existence, increasingly depended on lay interventions in elections and the like when conflict arose. A powerful bench of Henrician bishops made some headway in resisting lay incursions, but also alerted the King and his leading subjects to the threat of ecclesiastical power. Essentially the lay élite had been accorded considerable *de facto* power within the framework of the Church, and intended to seize the opportunities of profit and power offered without any very visible signs of guilt.[11]

## 9.2 DISSOLUTION, ACQUISITION AND IMPROPRIATION

Although continuity both of power relationship and attitudes do much to explain the response of the gentry to the Dissolutions, a very real shift in influence did occur at the Reformation. Ex-monastic land, the most tangible manifestation of that power, did not pass in any neat or ordered fashion into the hands of one section of the élite, but few of those historians who have followed the convoluted evidence for its dispersal would contest that much of it went to afforce the landed wealth of the ranks below the peerage. In most of England and Wales the greater part of the monastic lands had left royal hands by 1547, and much of the rest had been dispersed by 1558. The effects on the pattern of landownership varied in different areas: in counties close to London, such as Essex, an already mobile élite was afforced by grants to courtiers and royal officials. A few very determined and successful families used political influence to carve great territories out of the monastic estates, the most notable examples being the Russells in the south-west and the Wriothesleys in Hampshire. Mercantile wealth moving into land influenced the pattern of sales in south-west Wales and elsewhere, while lawyers were active purchasers in many parts of the realm.[12]

It is very difficult in these circumstances to identify the typical outcome of monastic sales. However, two local studies of counties may give some sense of the pattern of change. In Norfolk just under 270 monasteries and other ecclesiastical estates were sold by the Crown between 1536 and 1566. Over 200 of these grants had gone to gentlemen, only fifteen to peers, and most of the grants to peers were made before 1545. It is easy to see why Spelman could use Norfolk as his example for sacrilege. In Devon by 1558 over half the monastic lands dispersed by the Crown were in the hands of local gentlemen, with incoming gentry accounting for less than a further 10 per cent. In Devon, and it would seem elsewhere, two types of gentleman were particularly likely to take advantage of the ex-monastic lands and of the general stimulus that their sales gave to the land market. First there were the established families whose lands were inconveniently located, and who were given the opportunity to consolidate property nearer home. Secondly there were the cadet branches of existing gentry families who seized the chances offered to establish themselves independently. Few, whatever their initial position, could afford to be left behind in the quest for property for, as Sir Richard Grenville put it in a famous letter to Cromwell, 'I do this for no covetousness, but to stand in the case of others. And the lands stand not far from my lands'.[13]

For contemporaries one of the most dramatic manifestations of lay ascendancy must have been the reconstruction of domestic dwellings out of the monastic remains. Presumably changes that were made with great rapidity, or that involved a very explicit re-exploitation of the old buildings must have made greatest impact. The most famous example both of speed and adaptation is Titchfield Abbey in Hampshire, reconstructed from its abbatial style by the brutal device of driving a gatehouse entrance through the nave of the great church. This is also a rare case in which we know the issue of sacrilege was raised, since John Crayford's correspondence with Thomas Wriothesley survives. Crayford made it clear that by adaptation Wriothesley could have a house in which to entertain the King 'within reasonable charges'. He then continues:

> Mistress Wriothesley, nor you neither, be not meticulous to make sale of such holy things [the remains of altars etc.], having example of a good, devout bishop of Rome called Alexander [VI] . . . As for plucking down of the church [it] is but a small matter, minding (as we doubt not but you will) to build a chapel.[14]

Few grantees were as bold and swift as Wriothesley (a good conservative in matters of religion) in the adaptation of churches, but there are some other startling examples of conversions such as Buckland Abbey in Devon where the body of the old church became part of a house constructed by the son of that Sir Richard Grenville who thought himself entitled to his share of monastic loot. Most of the major alterations were undertaken by courtiers or office-holders best equipped to profit from the monastic scramble, like Sir William Sharington, who was a groom of the Privy Chamber at Lacock Abbey. But some lesser figures managed to rebuild within the cloisters – Robert Gostwick at Warden Abbey, Bedfordshire, and Sir John Byron at Newstead Abbey, Nottinghamshire. Employment of the monastic churches was officially forbidden, since the Royal Commissioners were ordered to see them pulled 'all down to the ground', but occasionally the gentry seem to have made very deliberate gestures in using sacred precincts as chapels: Tregonwell did this at Milton Abbas, Dorset, and Gregory Cromwell at Launde, Leicestershire, with, one would assume, very different religious motives.[15]

The issue of the monastic lands forms the continuo in relations between the lay élite and the Church. Loss of possession was a recurring anxiety, a nightmare to be invoked when the Crown needed allies, as Hatton's speech shows. But the lands were decisively alienated from the Church after 1539 and it was the secular clergy who were now of daily relevance to the gentry. Here the major transition, though one whose significance was only slowly recognised, was the transference of appropriated benefices, usually with their accompanying advowson or right of presentation, to the laity. Even though many of the tithes were already in lay hands by lease this change of ownership was, in Hill's words 'a slight social rearrangement . . . pregnant with vast consequences'. The number of impropriated livings in the early seventeenth century was variously estimated by the bishops and by Henry Spelman at 3,849 and 3,845 out of a total number of English and Welsh livings of 9,284. Since the market in ex-monastic property was volatile, and impropriations less immediately attractive than the prime lands of the orders, it was not until the Elizabethan period that a more settled pattern of holdings among these impropriations began to emerge. No specific analysis has been made of the proportion controlled by the gentry: though it has been estimated that over 800 were in the hands of ecclesiastics and the Crown held a fluctuating number of around 1,000. A crude guess might put gentry impropriations at at least 1,500 by the late sixteenth century. Patronage rights extended far beyond this: in Worcester by the end of the sixteenth century 102 out of 176 benefices were owned by laymen; in Lincoln diocese 788 livings out of 1,271 were held by the laity. Only in Welsh sees like St David's did the laity play a comparatively small part: there George Owen calculated that there were only 11 lay impropriations and about 30 livings in patronage. When the increased propensity of rectors to lease their tithes and/or glebe to substantial laymen is included it becomes obvious that the lay élite had a massive investment in the economic and social structure of the Church. The consequences could be dire. Robert Claphamson, a proctor in the East Riding, told the Archdeacon John Cosin in 1626 that impropriations were the ruin of the jurisdiction: owners were often absentee southerners, several might have rights in one rectory, and curates were abominably paid and supplemented their income by performing clandestine marriages. Meanwhile the good Catholic and antiquary, Thomas Habington, spoke with predictable horror of impropriations 'wasted in supportinge greatenes or ryott of lyfe'.[16]

Such an enhancement both of the quantity and nature of secular power must have had an influence upon attitudes to the Church. Boundaries between the sacred and the secular were redefined as influential laymen and uncertain clerics sought to establish themselves within the new environment of Protestantism. The most likely local consequence was that religious change intensified that proprietorial approach to parish life which we have already observed in the earlier period. To the lay possession of some patronage and some control over chapels, pews and the like, was added the ability to manage tithe, either through impropriation or leasing, greatly enhanced patronage and perhaps the holding of local monastic or chantry lands. The use to which these powers were put were as diverse as the gentry themselves: it is possible to find ample evidence of the careful use of patronage to further an ideological position, of practical assistance from impropriated tithes for vicars on lowly stipends, of ruthless exploitation of property and of complete indifference to patronage rights. Sir Richard Knightly is often cited as an example of a godly Puritan who used his patronage rights to change the religious complexion of western Northamptonshire. John Bruen, an equally godly gentleman, believed that his patronage of his local church gave him the right to strip the buildings of the relics of popery as well as providing godly clerics and preachers. There were those who saw their power as an ideal opportunity to secure family interest, like John Harington of Stepney who in 1565 promoted his nephew to the living of Kelston when he was only eighteen, several years below the canonical age for the ministry. Catholic patrons were peculiarly prone to cynicism after 1559 because of their inability to use their power for their own religious objectives. At its most extreme the system spawned patrons who were involved in simonaiacal transactions, like Mr James Calthorpe, who persuaded an ex-chantry priest to take a living to supplement his pension, provided that he leased the tithe and glebe to the impropriator. Such abuses were an almost inescapable consequence of the reciprocal relationships between cleric and patron: as that good business man Sir John Lowther wrote, when a fit younger son was offered promotion in the Church 'he is bound to a thankfullnes to the patron and may contract for it'. In the next century Sir Thomas Freke was thought so charitable a patron that his memorial inscription recorded 'Hee alwayes presented orthodox men to his tenn churches FREELY'.[17]

If one generalisation can be made about these widely divergent attitudes it is that the gentry were determined to regard their rights within the Church as property, covered by all the protections of the common law, and in most cases in their absolute disposal. This was most obviously true of impropriations, over which the Church had lost all legal control. The gentry litigated about impropriations in the common law courts, Exchequer and Chancery: only when repairs to the church fabric were at issue were the Church courts normally involved. As Claphamson's comment indicates, impropriations were a fertile source of litigation because of the complex manner in which they had been transmitted from monastery, to Crown, to laymen. There was sometimes uncertainty about whether the advowson and impropriation were indissolubly bound together, and ownership of different aspects of the rectory could indeed be fractionalised between several individuals. Rectorial leases, and leases of partial rights to tithe collection, although ostensibly under greater ecclesiastical control, were equally productive of lay aggression and potential litigation.[18]

Some sense of both the legal complexities and the tenacity of the gentry can be gained from the case of the Monins family and Waldershare Rectory in Kent. Waldershare was an impropriated benefice, which had originally been part of the possessions of the Abbey of West Langdon. Along with many of the other benefices of that house it passed to the archbishops of Canterbury in exchange for several manors at the Dissolution. But the Monins family, who resided in Waldershare, already had interests in the living via a lease of the rectory given them by the abbot, and the patronage of the church, which they claimed to have been awarded in perpetuity in 1532. The lease of the rectory clearly lapsed, though the family continued to lease part of the tithes, and to be involved in minor disputes on their collection for much of the subsequent century. The key issue, however, was patronage: whether the Monins's rights of presentation could be upheld. The legal disputes that this generated must have much enriched Chancery and other lawyers under Elizabeth, James and Charles: the family pressing for disappropriation – a separation of advowson and patronage – the archbishops and their lessees opposing them. A further complication was introduced when, in 1591, one Richard Thornhill, esquire, purchased the manor of Langdon from the Crown, and claimed rights of his own in part of the benefice. In the 1630s the complex litigation took a new turn when Archbishop Laud showed a predictable determination to reassert the patronage rights of the see and settle the issue once and for all. He brought a case against Sir Edward Monins in Common Pleas, which was still pending when he was executed, and the whole problem was shelved until after the Restoration. Meanwhile, Monins resurrected a compromise by which he claimed an entitlement to present by turns with the archbishop. In 1662 there was a decision against the family, but it seems that litigation continued in a desultory way until Sir Edward's death the next year divided the estate among female co-heirs.[19]

The anxiety of the archbishops to protect their claims is understandable, part of that defensiveness of ecclesiastical rights that is so important a theme of early seventeenth-century history. It is, however, the motives of the Monins that are of more interest here. Under Elizabeth at least one branch of the family had Catholic sympathies: a cousin, Edward, was one of the few Kentish gentlemen to appear on the recusancy rolls of the Exchequer. By the Civil War they were firm Protestants, and espoused a moderate Parliamentarian position. It is possibly indicative of changing sympathies that after raising few challenges to the archbishops (on one occasion Parker presented to the living by lapse), they became active defenders of their rights at the end of the century. The head of the family at the Restoration offered the following revealing defence of his actions: '[My] cheefe seate is in the parish of Waldershare, and . . . [I] desire only to have the cure well served by an able minister'. He might have added that the proprietorial rights of the family were so long established that he regarded the intrusion of the archbishops as a costly irrelevance: one of the disputes with Thornhill reveals that as early as Richard III's reign the Monins were exchanging and leasing lands with the monastery of Langdon. At least three generations of the family showed absolute determination to defend their interest in Waldershare and its connected lands with an intense territoriality. But this did not necessarily preclude a serious interest in the patronage of the living. In 1638 Jane Thornhill, a Monins married into the rival family of landowners, urged her father to promote the interest of Mr Walton, her domestic chaplain. Sir William Monins endorsed her request, urging his son that 'we cannot have a better' and suggesting that family pride be swallowed and the chaplain presented to the Archbishop because he was determined to assert his rights.[20]

Impropriated tithes, rectorial leases and parish patronage might be important to the local sense of honour and power of a gentry family, but they were essentially pieces of property and could be perceived in narrowly economic terms. In 1598 Sir John Holles was unwilling to pay 20 years' purchase for a neighbouring rectory, but suggested instead 15 years as a bargaining position to the impropriator, Mr Poplewell. They could also in some circumstances form a significant part of the landed inheritance of a family, especially in Wales, where a number of benefices were impropriated and gentlemen impecunious. William Maurice of Clenennau received £75 per annum from two Anglesey rectories, to which he later added more than £100 from Holyhead and an annuity of £320 mainly from two south Welsh parishes. He could scarcely afford to do other than defend his acquisitions. Gentlemen were quick to see the commercial advantages of rectories, as when Sir John Oglander noted that he would like to buy the parsonage of Brading in order to increase his control over fertile land north of the downs. On the other hand, the ferocious conflicts between Sir John Wynn and the bishops of St Asaph and Bangor about the leases of the rectories of Llanrywst and Llanfair were probably typical in combining direct financial ambition with an assertion of power. The testy gentleman was prepared to show himself as a friend of the Church in north Wales *provided* that proper dependence and deference was shown to him within what he regarded as his property.[21]

It was this sense of propriety which posed so many difficulties for ordinary incumbents, who lacked the distance and financial resources to oppose the local élite. The parson's freehold offered a measure of security, but even that was capable of manipulation by a determined patron. John Oswald, Vicar of Much Waltham in Essex, complained that Sir Hugh Everard and his adherents had forced him from the parish, putting a curate in his place; tactics which 'will . . . make the livings of all clergymen precarious and dependent upon the uncertain Tenure of any angry Gentleman's Arbitrary Will and Pleasure'. When patron and incumbent were at odds, the latter had little chance of securing his rights: Thomas Hassall, Vicar of Amwell in Hertfordshire, had the misfortune to be appointed by a patron who then sold the benefice without revealing to the purchaser that a new nomination had been made. When Hassall asked for a pension customarily paid to the vicars, he was told by the new patron that 'it was the love and charity of the patrons to theyr chaplaynes . . . but yow are no chaplayn of myne . . . therefore I find no reason to extend any such kindnes towards yow'. A curate, without even such security, was even more vulnerable to harassment: Sir Benjamin Pellatt, for example, conducted a campaign against the Curate of Bolney, Sussex, which included bribery, intimidation and setting him in the stocks, as well as binding him to appear at the assizes.[22]

Extreme behaviour of this kind was no doubt less significant than the more routine manifestations of social power that mark exchanges between patrons and clerics. Letters from candidates for promotion are rarely free of elements of servile deference: a characteristic effusion is that of John Ridley to Edward Monins praising his 'great Civility' and his 'greater Pyety' which had 'affected his heart' to bless the Lord. In this case it did not work; Ridley was politely rejected. Patrons in quest of clerics often took their ideological position and professional qualifications seriously, but also sought civility, humility and peace. Lady Bridget Kingsmill indignantly denied her son's charge that she was thinking of taking money for the parsonage of Titchfield [though it would have been characteristic of the lady], claiming that she merely sought an honest man 'that will not be like to give me trouble at present, nor you hereafter'. A much more conscientious lady, Meriel Knyvett, could still, in seeking a new incumbent, ask for a man 'as is of good fellowship, neither over precise nor yet dissolute'. Francis Cheynell reckoned that he lost a golden opportunity for promotion in Northamptonshire in 1636 because the patrons disapproved of his preaching that it was good for a man 'to bee constantly orthodox and not basely popular'.[23]

When a cleric was safely in post, he still depended on the support of patron and squire, and its loss could fatally weaken his local position. Men of the cloth, observed one of Sir John Isham's correspondents in 1608, 'need of the favor and countenance of the greatest and best; els shall they be overcrowed by every Coridionicall hoiden'. The same Lady Bridget Kingsmill fell out with William Frenche on some unspecified issue, and provoked a pathetic letter begging for renewed favour for 'I ame verily persuaded, that yor Ladyshippe never meant, by the disgracinge of me, to incourage those, that alwaies hate our callinges'. Sir Simonds D'Ewes conducted a long and bitter feud with the incumbent of his Stow living, Mr Danford, in which both parties seem to have displayed an excess of obstinacy in defence of their rights. D'Ewes sententiously recorded Danford's 'malicious practices' against him in his *Autobiography*, but the minister had ample grounds for grievance against one who believed in reorganising the spiritual life of the community to suit his doctrinal tastes. Catholic patrons, especially in areas of weak political control like the North Riding, were often accused not only of absenting themselves, but of encouraging lewd behaviour by others and thereby subverting the authority of the established Church. Sir John Yorke's tenants and servants were said by his enemies to have a piper with them on a Sunday in the churchyard and to make such a noise that the minister could not be heard. Richard Cholmley was accused by the minister of Whitby of allowing some of his servants to enter the church with a lord of misrule, and also to organise horse-races in time of divine service.[24]

Another major source of disharmony between resident gentlemen and the clergy was tithe. It is now a commonplace of Reformation scholarship that tithe conflicts increased sharply after the 1530s, partly because of the general decline in ecclesiastical power, partly because economic dislocation made such conflicts inherently more probable. In the case of the gentry, the active land market, and their constant purchases, leases and other transactions created genuine doubts about obligations which were then underpinned by their inherent determination to protect their possessions through litigation. Sometimes the gentry found themselves in conflict with others, impropriators or farmers of tithe: at the turn of the sixteenth century Sir Robert Delaval was in the interesting position of driving a hard bargain with Mr Wycliffe, a lay farmer, for tithes owed on Hartley, Northumberland, while himself seeking to lease Elwick tithe to Arthur Gray for seven years. But the more damaging disputes for the Church directly involved the clergy: for example, Thomas Benson, Vicar of Wath, was rash enough to take on Sir Thomas Wentworth, who promptly refused all tithe payment and wrote to the Archbishop of York denouncing Benson as a usurer. When a tithe commutation, or *modus decimandi*, was involved, conflict might be even more complex: it was sometimes possible for an incumbent to overturn a prescriptive *modus*, but only at great cost and effort. Thus the Rector of Boothby Pagnell, Lincolnshire, recovered tithe in kind on the demesnes from the patron but only with 'his extreame chardges, and to the empoverishinge of his state, not longe before his death'.[25]

The corrosive effects on parish life of tithe disputes are well shown by the conflicts between Sir Edward Dering and John Copley, Vicar of Pluckley Church in Kent. Dering's father Sir Anthony had already been at odds with Copley about tithe commutation, a ruling of 1618 allowing him a year of tithe in kind, so that the proper cost of a *modus* could be ascertained. This agreement did not hold, and in the 1630s Copley was appealing to Laud for assistance. Meanwhile, the breakdown between vicar and squire ensured that they would take opposing sides on the other issue that had been dividing the parish since the previous century, the struggle for local supremacy between the Derings and the Bettenham family. Much of the feud had no bearing on the church, but so bitter a tension was bound to express itself in the most public of local fora, and on the most obvious hierarchical issue, the possession of pews and burial places. The Derings, no longer content to share the head of the church with the Bettenhams, had endeavoured to oust them by force, and initiated a series of suits not fully resolved before the Civil War. Then Edward Dering's construction of a new burial aisle and defacing of Bettenham arms on the font fuelled further tension, and Copley identified with Bettenham's cause. He allegedly told Dering that he was 'voyde of the grace of God . . . the proudest man in the world . . . [and] . . . ill bred', grave charges indeed against a gentleman. Dering returned the compliments in kind, calling Copley 'unpeaceable and malignant' and demanding that Laud place him in some other parish because 'he cannot be at peace with our ashes'. Copley was not removed, although Dering persisted in his attempts to the end of the decade: the effect on the spiritual life of Pluckley can only be imagined.[26]

## 9.3 THE GENTRY AND THE PARISH CHURCH

The Dering example may also serve to remind us how often the relationship between the gentry and the Church was articulated physically: expressed through the fabric of the parish building where a series of lessons in authority (and its abuse) were presented to ordinary parishioners. First there was the formal duty of gentleman impropriators or their farmers to maintain their share of the structure itself – the chancel. The later sixteenth century was not a happy period for the fabric of the English Church, and gentry impropriators bore a heavy responsibility for the neglect. Wardens constantly reported deficiencies in church repairs, especially from absentee lay rectors. At Astley in Warwickshire the rather humble gentleman who married Lady Frances Grey, the widowed Duchess of Suffolk, proceeded to remove much of the lead from the roof not only of the chancel, but the spire and aisles, with the consequence that much was left exposed to the elements and that in about 1600 the tower fell down, demolishing part of the church en route. This was so dire a situation that the impropriator, Richard Chamberlain, did undertake some reconstruction with the help of a collection from the county, but he drastically foreshortened the church, made the choir into the nave and a small chapel the chancel, destroying much of the rest. Such cavalier treatment of structure can be found elsewhere: Sir Francis Walsingham demolished the chancel of Carisbrooke Church, telling the townsmen that they had ample chancel already. Sir Nicholas Bacon is said to have turned the chancel of Egmere, Norfolk, into a stable. Most examples were less spectacular: leaking roofs, unglazed windows and the like recur endlessly in churchwardens' complaints, especially in the years before the 1590s.[27]

Resident squires sometimes did better: John Kaye, for example, listed with pride his family's contributions to local churches. They had renovated the chapels at Slaithwaite and Honley 'that the people may have the more rowme to pray', had bullied Archbishop Sandys into making the patron of Almondbury repair the chancel and had presided over the re-pewing of no less than four local churches and chapelries. Francis Winchcom, esquire, rebuilt the chancel of Bucklebury, Berkshire, in the 1590s and Shipton in Shropshire was re-edified by John Lutwich in the previous decade. A handful of other surviving or documented examples of substantial sixteenth-century reconstructions can be attributed to the gentry. In the first half of the next century there was further improvement, with fine examples of reconstruction emanating from strong individual beliefs: Low Ham in Somerset, built by the well-known justice Edward Hext, is an early instance, that of Iwerne Courtney in Dorset a slightly later one. At Iwerne Courtney Sir Thomas Freke married devotion to 'orthodoxy' to family piety, by building the church as 'the MONUMENT set upon his FATHERS SEPULCHRE'. Elsewhere evidence suggests that the worst of neglect may have been over by the end of the sixteenth century: for example, wardens in the large archdeaconries of Lincoln and

Stow could report four-fifths of the churches in good repair by the late 1590s. The gentry, however, remained less than generous in their building programmes and their model cannot always have inspired ordinary parishioners to proper investment in the rest of the fabric.[28]

The second material manifestation of the gentleman in church was that presented by his pew. The passion of the Dering conflict with Bettenham, in which armed men hauled one another from church pews Sunday after Sunday, led an ecclesiastical official to remark with a fine sense of understatement that 'theyre poore neighbors may indure some brunt or incunveniences'. The squire's pew, properly placed at the head of the nave, in a personal side chapel, or sometimes (to Laud's disgust) still in the chancel, solid with height, status and the manifestations of armigerousness, was the very embodiment of local hierarchy. Sir Thomas Gawdy's pew at Redenhall in Norfolk was described by a hostile ecclesiastic as 'of a monstrous hight, curtayned like a bedstead, and encroach[ing] upon the Ally'. Lesser gentlemen might not manage anything so garish, but they could at the least expect to sit prominently in aisle and transept ahead of their neighbours. The Church gave to the

34. Early seventeenth-century box pews for the James family, Ightham Church, Kent

wardens the normal duty of ordering and allocating seating, unless a prescriptive right could be claimed through the obligation to repair the structure. It need hardly be said that the gentry normally exercised such prescriptive rights. In some contexts they regarded these claims as so ample that they even permitted the buying and selling of seatings: the Welsh had a particular conviction of their absolute possession. In 1612 Sara Snead of Hope, co. Flint, conveyed to Robert Davies, esquire, all her rights to 'seates, roomes, benches, kneelinge places, burialls and burying places in the south Ile of the parishe church of Mould'. This was unusual, but the proprietorial attitude it embodies was common enough: Welsh feuds often took pews as their symbolic focus, as when the Nanneys and Owens engaged in an orgy of destruction in Dolgellau Church as part of their long-running conflict. Encounters were usually less violent in England, but a sensitivity to status was always present and led to some incredibly vulgar displays, like the Cholmley pew at Whitby, which completely straddles the chancel arch, or the Shirley pew at Breedon, Leicestershire, described in 1632 as 'like the skreen of a great man's . . . [hall]'. Archbishop Laud's determination that pews should be uniform, while only partially enforced, was guaranteed to offend against the cherished sense of local propriety which these constructions expressed. For most of our period the Church authorities saw no virtue in antagonising gentlemen about seating and often proved remarkably accommodating when they wished to rebuild part of the structure for their own benefit.[29]

The third form of material display was that which most routinely survives for us, the tombs of the gentry. The continuities from the past are self-evident: although monuments themselves reached an apogee of lavishness under James I, it is probable that more separate burial chapels and aisles were erected in the century before the Reformation than at any point thereafter. New aesthetic fashions, increasingly dictated by the influence of the national sculptors' workshops in Derbyshire and at Southwark, led to the elaborated representation of figures on tomb chests and kneeling before prayer desks. The crucial concern to express lineage identity through the memorial has already been discussed in an earlier chapter: here we should stress instead the desire to preserve the social body of those represented, and to make them constantly a part of the parochial environment. Much of the greatest ostentation might be 'privatised' within family chapels, but in many churches the vital effigies of the dead join the living in worship in chancel and aisle. As

35. Shirley family pew (1627), Breedon-on-the-Hill Church, Leicestershire

representation became more plastic in the early seventeenth century this sense of interconnection was afforced by figures sculpted in reclining postures looking, and even gesturing, outwards to the church. As Bosola observed in the *Duchess of Malfi*, princes' images now lie with hands under cheeks, 'as if they died of the toothache: they are not carved with their eyes fixed upon the stars; but as their minds were wholly bent upon the world, the selfsame way they seem to turn their faces'. This expression of the shared identity of living and dead was obviously intended when, as often, family chapels were used for burial and pews. An elaborate will request of Henry Brook, esquire, in 1558, asks for a tomb of alabaster to be erected in his chapel, displaying him in full armorials, with a dearly beloved daughter carved at his feet on the same slab. In the chapel two new pews were also to be built, one where his wife had her 'kneeling'.[30]

There were, it would seem, those who had reservations about this intense physicality and ostentation. Weever, writing in the 1630s, criticised tombs that were so vast that 'they take up the church, and hinder the people from divine service'. From the late fifteenth century onwards a small minority of gentlemen and women requested burial without elaboration, and presumably thought the same about their monuments. Aesthetic, and/or religious sensibilities, led other minorities to confine themselves to wall tablets, and a lack of figural representation: some, but by no means all, Puritan families seem to have adopted this position. The Rector of Kedington, Suffolk, pleaded with Lady Barnardiston in 1653 that she add to her husband's memory:

> no pictur'd stone
> Lest whilst within the Church my vows I pay
> I to the Image of this Saint should pray.

By the late seventeenth century a few voices spoke against burial in church, even for the élite. Sir Richard Browne, John Evelyn's father-in-law, ordered that his body be buried in the churchyard adjoining the family chapel 'he being much offended at the novel costome of burying everyone within the body of the Church and Chancel, that being a favour heretofore granted only to martyrs and greate persons'. Browne, dying in the 1680s, here stands perhaps at the beginning of a new period, when reservations about monuments of power increased and the practicality of churchyard burial became more obvious. Before that date the desire to represent the individual and his or her lineage in the most tangible way in the most sacred ground available usually moved the gentry. Even Catholic families were committed to church memorialisation, though occasionally they engaged in curious compromises such as the closed aisle in Mapledurham, Oxfordshire, which sealed the family tombs away from the contagion of the Anglican service.[31]

The visual representation of élite power extended even to the smaller items of church furnishing, such as plate and bells. Here the original contribution made before the Reformation has been lost to us, though it can in some measure be reconstructed from wills. In the gentry will sample for the first half of the sixteenth century there were some lavish donations of plate, often associated with chantry chapels. For example, John Browne of Eltham left plate and other equipment to the lady chapel of his parish church, but only on condition that his executors supervised its proper use. Sir John Gostwick loaned his private chapel vessels to Willington Church,

Bedfordshire, at the great festivals. Other bequests seem to be more generally directed at the parish and to be used to sustain the physical link between family and community. George Barrett, esquire, left Aveley, Essex, his home parish, two candlesticks, inscribed with his arms and those of his wife. He also left clothes to be made into vestments for a Hertfordshire chapel of which he was patron, and for Strethall Church, where his father was lord and patron. It was, in fact, clothing to be made into vestments that predominated in physical bequests to churches – velvet gowns from gentry wardrobes were constantly being reworked for the benefit of local priests. A cynical interpretation might be that it was less costly to employ second-hand clothing as gifts than to surrender plate, but it may be that we should also associate the personal intimacy of the gift with the transmission of very specific devotion from the donor to the church.[32]

If this is so, yet one more physical expression of commitment was foreclosed by the Reformation: thereafter plate was one of the few meaningful donations from the gentry to the church fabric. The history of such gifts belongs exclusively to the second half of our period: under Elizabeth the great refashioning of the parish plate for the new communion seems to have taken place without any explicitly identified donations from the gentry. Thereafter gifts began slowly to increase, with the 1630s and 1670s onwards yielding significant quantities of inscribed and dated plate. The gentry commemorated their donations with arms as well as inscriptions, showing little reticence about 'badging' even the communion cup as evidence of their role in the community.[33]

## 9.4 GENTRY–CLERICAL RELATIONSHIPS

It would be easy to conclude that relationships between the gentry and the Church were based on material considerations, and were essentially hostile in the long century after the Reformation. The painful 'birthpangs of Protestantism' and the profound dislocation introduced by resurgent clericalism in the 1630s fostered in the gentry that anti-clericalism that had been dormant in the late middle ages. A significant minority was wholly alienated from the establishment by Catholic belief: radical Protestants offered only conditional support. Even so serious a son of the established Church as Sir Henry Slingsby could mutter darkly in his diary against the clergy as covetous, contentious and ambitious. When devout men urged their children to be obedient to God's ministers, they showed awareness of how unusual they believed their sympathies to be. 'Although', said Sir John Strode, 'sum of them be heddy, high mynded, covetous, unpacient, vicious and the like, yet so long as they ar the messengers of God let them not be despised or dishonored by thee.' Since the Church must be defended, wrote Sir Justinian Isham in 1642, his daughters should garner what good they could from the clerics, and if they were so fortunate as to find a wise and learned one among them 'to account him a treasure'. George Herbert's admirable *The Priest to the Temple* actually has a chapter devoted to 'The Parson in Contempt' in recognition that anti-clericalism was a routine problem that would be faced by any parish cleric. If the cleric was not seen as ambitious and proud, he would all too often be regarded as a menial. Sir John Wynn's chaplain was instructed to take household prayers, catechise and preach, but also to amuse his master socially when no better company was at hand. 'If I go to bowles, or shuffel board, I shall lyke of your company, if the place be not made up with strangers.'[34]

We must, however, be careful not to overdraw the image of the gentry's rooted contempt for, or exploitation of, established religion. Political circumstance demanded that lay élite and clergy had to work together for the maintenance of conformity and order. Moreover, at a personal level, contempt and superiority were not the only, or probably the dominant, traits that marked gentry attitudes to ministers. The slow emergence of a learned profession, which put university men into most parishes by the Civil War, served to foster identity and sympathy. Sir Henry Slingsby might speak slightlingly of the priesthood, but he had close friendships of intellectual equality with particular ministers: Sir Edward Dering had no love for John Copley, but a warm attachment to John Reading, Vicar of St Mary's, Dover. The intimacies developed at university often persisted for a lifetime, as witness the friendship of the Newdigate boys and Gilbert Sheldon. Serious Puritan parents and grandparents like Brilliana Harley and Meriel Knyvett urged their young to associate with godly and sober youths at college – future clerics no doubt among them. Ministers seeking promotion had to play roles of suitable deference but, at least in the later seventeenth century, they must have been aware that they offered rare intellectual companionship to the parish gentry. Sir Geoffrey Copley was seeking in 1678 for such an incumbent when he asked for a man of exemplary life and learning, who would also be an agreeable neighbour. Paul Foley, seeking the advice of Sir Edward Harley in 1684, hoped to find a Calvinist divine for the rectory of Stoke Edith, Herefordshire, with whom he could 'heartily converse'.[35]

Nor is it really necessary to argue that this companionate connection between gentry and clerics is automatically a product of the growth of the learned profession. At least at the level of the parish it often appears as general sociability logical between those who were distinct from the ordinary yeomanry. The diaries of Richard Stonley and William Carnsew, both mid-Elizabethan records of the very different counties of Essex and Cornwall, note constant interchange with local clerics and interest in their well-being. Carnsew shows a lively engagement with men of his own kind as he records the personal crises that befell the father and son who held his local benefice in succession.[36]

It is perhaps easiest to 'read' relations between clergy and gentry at the superior level of the episcopate, where the petty animosities and friendships of the parochial scene were of less relevance than broader questions of politics and ideology. Here there is no consistent image of co-operation or conflict. The mid-Tudor years, part of the early Elizabethan period, and of course the 1630s, produced widespread tensions consequential on the need of the episcopate to enforce unpopular governmental policies, or on the assertiveness of the order itself. Even in such periods, however, there was a marked difference between individuals: under Elizabeth, for example, Jewel and Grindal handled their leading laymen with exemplary tact and skill, while Bishop Curteys of Chichester brought the whole county of Sussex about his neck with ill-judged attempts to enforce high Protestant standards. The same contrast can be seen in the 1630s between the elaborate caution and courtesy of Bishop Williams of Lincoln on the one hand, and the highhandedness of Wren of Norwich on the other. The latter was claimed by an offended gentleman to have said 'he hoped to live to see the day, when a minister should be as good a man, as any upstart Jack gentleman in England', which, if not accurate reportage, seems a true enough summary of the prelate's feelings.[37]

Between these difficult periods of ideological conflict prelates and gentry were more likely to establish adequate *modi vivendi*, provided that the former accepted the reality of the latter's power in the localities. The gentry had to be humoured, consulted and entertained: tasks at which successive archbishops of Canterbury showed themselves adept until the coming of Laud. Particularly warm relationships seem to have marked a number of incumbents of the northern sees of Chester, York and Durham in the early seventeenth century: Morton and Mathew, for example, had high reputations for their generosity. In return, prelates could exercise influence both ideological and personal over individual gentlemen still conscious of their standing in Church and state. George Lloyd, the Jacobean bishop of Chester, took upon himself the task of counselling Sir Richard Brereton about his notorious 'familiarity' with Lady Townsend, walking with him in his bowling alley, and reducing him to a tearful agreement to abandon her, since she had 'bewitched him'.[38]

Intense lay/clerical bonds, however, were most often associated with shared ideologies. Puritans who grudged any supplement to a 'dumb dog' of a cleric would protect their own kind through chaplaincies and lecturerships at considerable personal and economic cost. A famous case is that of John Dod, who was protected by the Northamptonshire families of Dryden and Knightley first in the exempt peculiar of Canons Ashby and then in the household at Fawsley. A high Calvinist doctrine of the ministry might well bond cleric and patron together in mutual support against an indifferent or hostile community. Lady Joan Herrick gave vigorous evidence of her support for her Puritan minister John Bryan at her living of Woodhouse, Leicester: she was reputed personally to have broken an idolatrous window for him. Some of the godly also understood the need for financial sacrifice: the actions of the Feoffees for Impropriations showed this collectively in the 1630s, and there were also grand individual gestures, like Sir William Doddington's restoration of six impropriations from his own estate, with a yearly value of £600. Even humble ministers, like John Spofforth, a Yorkshire curate, who could be relied on as 'preacher[s] of the Word of God' might find impropriated tithes returned to them by committed patrons.[39]

Conformists were more likely to be moved by arguments that the Church was being brought into social contempt. Spelman's calls for augmentation began to stir devout men in the early seventeenth century: Sir Ralph Hare, his Norfolk neighbour, restored the impropriatium of Stow Bardolph and gave the perpetual advowson to St John's College, Cambridge, to prevent his heirs from changing his dispositions. Viscount Scudamore restored impropriations taken by his great-grandfather and reconstructed the church at Abbey

Dore – a monument to lay Laudianism. Sir John Osborne conveyed the impropriation of Haynes, Bedfordshire, to trustees to increase the maintenance of the vicarage, and a variety of informal gestures of supplementation were made by men like Sir Edmond Allen, who had made considerable profit from Church livings. But it required the threat to the Church to become visible before a much clearer identity of interests began to bind gentry and clergy. Devout Anglicans learned to respect and support those who suffered under the Commonwealth, relearning the lessons of the Catholics and Puritans. Sir Robert Shirley gave the revenues he had derived from impropriations for 'orthodoxall and distressed clergie men', actually employing Dugdale to hunt out evidences for any of his land once owned by the Church. The houses of the Royalist gentry were a haven for those excluded from their livings. By the 1650s, as we have argued above, a much larger group of the ruling élite came to see the clergy as a principal bulwark against further revolution, and to accept the structural alliance that this implied.[40]

Few of the problems we have considered in this chapter were fully resolved by the Restoration: even in the 1690s a jaundiced young curate could write bitterly that the House of Commons was made up of those who 'vallues the weal politic above the ecclesiastic, and their own wordly ends above their own salvation'. 'Sacred things,' he said, were not safe in the hands of such 'a company of irreligious wretches who cares not . . . what becomes of the Church . . . if they can but get their hawkes, houndes and whores, and the sacred possessions of the Church.' The gentry were not necessarily intellectually reconciled to the old ways: many of them, complained a Restoration author, 'are grown more inquisitive in religious things' and were unwilling to be guided by the clergy. Mockery and scepticism were forms of discourse that were widely accepted after 1660. But there was also a recognition that a bound had to be set to the articulation of such sentiments if the Church was to be a defence against disorder. These more positive sentiments were aided by the development of a distinctively Anglican piety, one of several manifestations of lay belief to which we must turn in the final chapter.[41]

# 10

# Piety and Belief

> What is a Gentleman without the true Faith of Christ in his heart, and the holy fruits thereof in his life, but a meere Gentilman without Christ, an alien from the common-wealth of Israel, and a stranger from the Covenant of promise, without hope and without God.
>
> William Hinde, *A Faithfull Remonstrance of the Holy Life and Happy Death of John Bruen* (1641) pp. 4–5

Sir Henry Slingsby, the first baronet and Royalist martyr, modelled his *Diary* on 'the advise of Michael de Montaigne', setting down such 'accidents as befall me' without method or order. Like Montaigne, however, Slingsby in practice gave considerable thought to his scribbling; weaving a philosophy of living out of the apparently insignificant doings of a gentry household in Yorkshire in the 1630s. On matters of religion Sir Henry divided his attention between the practical and the theological, and built into his observations a clear vision of the pious life of the Christian gentleman. An encounter with Timothy Thurscross, a prebendary of York, caused him to reflect on the dangers of simony in the contemporary Church, for Thurscross had resigned a benefice which he had gained by simonaical means. Since the cleric was now a man of reformed and exemplary behaviour, Slingsby was puzzled by his commitment to Laudian ceremonial which 'I thought came too near idolatory to adore a place with rich cloaths and other furniture and to command to use towards it bodily worship'. But, like the moderate man he was, Slingsby refused to condemn the prebendary: instead the qualities of his Christian witness prompted his admiration, as well as the observation that it was 'a hard thing to be a good christian'.[1]

The hardness of the daily Christian life much preoccupied Slingsby, who was deeply concerned to reconcile high religious standards with his 'honour and credit' as a gentleman. This was no passing anxiety: he had from his youth been reared by a pious father to examine his conscience, and to endeavour to live in conformity with Christ's example. In his letters to his son at Cambridge the older Sir Henry was always eager to ensure that he behaved with due sobriety and morality, but to this he added specific advice on the hearing of sermons and on proper preparation for communion 'the great misterie of your salvacon'. At home the family was regular in its devotions, and Sir Henry senior proved that his piety was not merely verbal by building an elaborate domestic chapel attached to the Red House, Moor Monkton. Although the chapel was never consecrated (for fear of conventicles says his son) it became the centre of family worship, and the younger Sir Henry ventured to hear sermons there 'altho' contrary to ye orders of ye Church'.

This combination of serious interest in ideas, and attachment to the basic rhythms of family worship remained with Slingsby throughout his life. On the eve of his execution he passed a volume of meditations to his daughter Barbara, who subsequently transcribed them as a memorial. Prayers and hymns are interspersed with catechitical examinations of contrition and absolution and discussions of meditative techniques. The examination of conscience three times a day was advocated, as well as more systematic reflection each Saturday and on one day of the month. Slingsby's attachment to moderate Anglicanism did much, no doubt, to determine his Royalist sympathies during the Civil War, even though he remained critical of Laudianism. The clergy, as we have seen, he mistrusted, unless they were personally known and respected: 'for the most part,' he wrote, 'we shall receive no benefit, but rather harm' from the company of clerics, 'being covetous, contentious, proud, boasters, ambitious'. But the relationship between the individual and God, aided by the wise guidance of a few chosen authors and personal mentors, was for him at the heart of the proper life of the gentleman.[2]

Sir Henry Slingsby's practical Christianity, to which he added an intelligent interest in theology born of formal academic training, is an appropriate exemplar of gentry piety in our period. It is not easy to label the baronet: indeed there is an eclecticism in his approach to faith which is reminiscent of the methods, if not the ideology, of Montaigne. His mind seems to combine the intensely serious with the rather detached, thus avoiding the fervent religiosity often

36. The Red House Chapel, Moor Monkton, Yorkshire, built by Sir Henry Slingsby, 1618

found in the most Catholic or Puritan meditations on the Divine. Sir Henry clearly spent proper time in worship and reflection, but his days were not one long round of prayer and reading as were those of some of the most devout of gentry wives. His life moreover is a salutary reminder that godliness and personal piety were not the prerogative of those who opposed the established Church.

Slingsby's *Diary* also provides some insight into the cultural parameters of élite religious behaviour in early modern England. Formal instruction in youth, and particularly the influence of the universities, were of great importance in securing more than a conventional adherence to the faith. Sir Henry was at Jacobean Cambridge, and so exposed to the presentation of that moderate confessional Puritanism which we associate with Perkins and his followers. He was under the direct tutelage of John Preston at Queen's. This background must have served to modify the anti-clericalism revealed in his writings by positive contacts with particular clerics who helped to develop a model of godly behaviour for the laity. Slingsby's observations also suggest that a gentleman's awareness of his social and political duties, that public life to which God and his country committed him, could afforce a sense of religious calling and provide a further stimulus to inner devotion and reflection. He was not so aggressively godly a magistrate as some of his contemporaries, but he was deeply aware of the interdependence of the private and public duties he had been called upon to assume. Finally, there is a clear linkage in his thought between piety and true belief on the one hand and correct social behaviour on the other: proper prayer would issue in right doing. Thus he continued to adhere to that blend of humanist, neo-Stoic and Protestant thought that informed so much élite behaviour in our period.[3]

## 10.1 BEFORE THE REFORMATION

Sir Henry Slingsby was the very model of a Protestant gentleman. Yet there is much in his behaviour and experience that can be applied more generally to individuals who were serious about their faith both before and after the Reformation. Although there is little evidence on the *intensity* of spiritual commitment in the late medieval period to compare with the personal sources such as diaries and letters later available, we can infer from what does survive that informed lay piety was an anticipated pattern of behaviour. A rare vignette suggests that serious devotion was accepted as unremarkable: the description in the Paston letters of the death of Sir John Heveningham, who heard three masses in the morning and then walked in his garden in private meditation before illness suddenly overcame him. The equally chance survival of a series of fifteenth-century instructions by a confessor to his gentleman patron urges constant meditation in a private closet, daily attendance at mass, and a day dominated by self-denial, reflection on unworthiness and the saying of 'Hail Marys'. Robert Constable, a fifteenth-century Yorkshire gentleman, bequeathed his son 'my Portative which I say upon my self' and his friend Thomas Witham the diurnal which 'I bear in my sleeve'. By the early Tudor period this concern for personal piety was fed by the growth of published texts suitable for lay devotion: the translation of the *Imitatio Christi*, advice on the art of dying well, and finally Richard Whitford's *A Werke for Housholders*. Above all, the primers offered access to a vast extension in the pattern of prayer and meditation for the laity. Although some of these writings seem directed first and foremost to an urban audience, they were intended to appeal to the articulate and committed laity wherever they were to be found.[4]

Gentry wills can be employed with due caution to reveal associated evidence of learned piety and an individual view of faith. Preambles, those formulae dedicating the soul to God, have had a very bad press from historians of late. They have been solemnly exposed as formulaic and more dependent on the choices made by cleric or scribe drafting a deathbed document than on the personal views of the testator. Nevertheless, literate gentlemen were more likely than their inferiors to draft their own wills, and their scribes were often household chaplains, those who shared and inspired their devotional life. When a minority therefore deviate from the common dedication of the soul to God, the Virgin and the company of heaven we may infer that this was intentional. Evidence can be found of firm Christocentric devotion clearly associated with contemporary literary pietism. For example, that of Sir William Boleyn, who died in 1505, begins:

> First gracious Jhesu I as a synfull creatur knowyng verely my synfull soule by reason of my merites not worthy to be accepted to the holy company of heven to contenew in that blessed place lord withoute thy grete and large mercy and grace.

and continues in the same vein for a further three sentences.[5]

Such precision and depth is a rarity in will preambles, but many invoke particular saints – St George, St Katherine and St Dorothy being the favoured cases – and God was often changed to the Trinity or to Christ. Another distinctive form of dedication and benefaction that appears to be gaining ground during the Henrician years is an insistence on the corruption and irrelevance of the flesh, and a consequent request for modest funerals. John Broughton, esquire, asked in 1517 that there should be little charge 'about my corruptible body for any worldlye pompe', and Dame Katherine Bray, the widow of Sir Reginald, insisted that 'all worldlie pompe and superfluous vanitie [be] clene sett aside'. These examples seem to reflect a sober strain in gentry piety that has been identified as early as the fifteenth century, though such requests for restraint only become commonplace in the mid-sixteenth century.[6]

Will benefactions, and those made *in vivos* should in theory offer afforcement of gentry concerns for piety. Some gifts do indeed seem to speak volumes about the priorities of their donors. Sir Robert Throckmorton of Coughton, Warwickshire, was a lavish supporter of his local church both in life and in his will. Leland later described Coughton as 'very faire, excedyngly well glassyd and adornyd', largely through the efforts of Sir Robert, and his will shows his own devotion to a specific band of saints. But our confidence in Throckmorton's piety derives mainly from his departure in 1518 on pilgrimage to the Holy Land: he died in Rome before reaching his destination. Few members of the Tudor élite died on pilgrimage, but others shared much of Throckmorton's material generosity: the Tame family gave Fairford Church in Gloucestershire much of its jewel-like glass in the first decades of the sixteenth century, and St Mary's at Launceston in Cornwall was completely reconstructed in consequence of a vow by Sir Henry Trecarrel.[7]

There is an abundance of further evidence that the gentry were prepared to invest heavily in their faith. All the traditional forms of benefaction continued to flourish on the eve of the Reformation. Funding for prayers for the dead, one of the more weighty indicators of individual religious attitudes, remained well-nigh universal among the prosperous. Among 252 wills in a sample from 1500 to 1547, 111 tried to leave an adequate endowment for a singing priest, and many of the rest asked for observance of dirges, trentalls and obits. Apart from nuncupative wills, and those obviously conceived and signed in haste before an unexpected death, only a handful omit some gesture for the soul. A significant minority invested heavily in such prayers. John Thaccher, gentleman, of Ringmer in Sussex, tried to establish a chantry in perpetuity, avoiding the difficulty of gaining a licence to alienate land in mortmain by giving the Prior of Lewes a lump sum to invest. Fourteen other testators tried for such perpetuities, some, like Edmund Tame of Fairford and William Teye of Colchester employing all the ingenuity of their lawyers to protect their investment. A recent study of the Warwickshire gentry found that 5 out of a sample of 42 sought to establish a perpetual chantry. Another form of ostentatious pietism comes from those testators who wished to number their prayers and good works like the grains of sand. Widows excelled here. Dame Elizabeth Biconyll, who died in 1504, offered precise directions for every dirge, beginning at daybreak on the morning after her death and continuing remorselessly until her anniversary was past. She left money to a variety of friaries for prayers, to local churches, to poor householders, to the upkeep of highways and to scholars at Oxford, all intermingled with small gifts to her extended kin and friends. She also left detailed guidance for the prayers to be said by her chantry priest, who was constantly to remember her family, her charity extending as far as her husband's first wife. Dame Agnes Burton of Taunton went even further in her concern for particular masses for herself and her kin: the priest was, for example, to say the mass of the five wounds every midsummer, and once a month to rehearse the psalms of the passion.[8]

Wills inevitably reflect the most pious of sentiments their makers can muster in the face of death. Their relationship to the life as lived is at best ambiguous: it may well be that ostentatious piety on the deathbed reveals as much about guilt for a misspent life as about spiritual intensity. The most that can be said is that the English gentry regarded some sacrifice of familial interests as necessary at this stage of their careers, in genuine concern about the world to come. But even religious benefactions, provided that they were appropriately directed, could enhance family standing as well as offering evidence of individual piety. The chantry or the tomb had some advantages over the house which, in Christine Carpenter's vivid phrase, 'impressed only the neighbours' while the tomb 'could impress the numberless hosts of heaven as well'.[9]

Another route through which to approach the nature of gentry devotion before the Reformation is that of the household. It was the household and the domestic chapel that formed a major focus for the worship of the élite, sometimes providing a liturgical life that was virtually self-sufficient. This is the image offered by the surviving ordinances of the greatest households, such as those of the Earls of Northumberland. These suggest a pattern of worship more elaborate than that of most parish churches, with the household functioning as a spiritual unit under its lay head. Accounts and ordinances show at least that the cycle of fast and feast ordained for the week and the sacred year were observed, and that devotion to particular saints or festivals can be identified in particular families. The physical expansion of many household chapels in the fifteenth century may indicate the need to accommodate a larger household, but it is surely also an ostentatious reminder of the piety of the lord. We should not necessarily associate the private chapel with a retreat from the parish church; the gentry remained concerned with public worship, in both senses of that latter phrase. It does appear, however, that during the fifteenth century the licensed oratory became an essential feature of the élite household. Carpenter can cite 17 examples from fifteenth-century Warwickshire, and this seems in no way untypical. The seriousness with which the chapel was taken in building of the early Tudor period is indicated by the elegance of surviving examples such as Cotehele in Cornwall or The Vyne in Hampshire., Wills routinely mention chaplains, and it seems unlikely that many gentle households were without the services of at least one cleric.[10]

Since personal closets for the saying of private prayers seem also to have become commonplace, the élite apparently possessed the ideal environment for the cultivation of that domesticated religion that is seen as precursor to Reformation devotion. But neither the circumstances of the open household, nor the attitudes of a majority of the ruling classes, necessarily conduced to this intensity. Cavendish's image of Thomas Cromwell having to snatch a moment in a window to say 'Our Lady's Hours' while he was part of Wolsey's household, is evocative of the difficulties in seeking isolation. Most gentry acts were still a matter of public performance, and a confessor who valued privacy in devotion had to urge this very strongly, as did the writer of the advice to a literate layman. There such expressive gestures as arranging breadcrumbs to exemplify the Five Wounds of Christ at the dinner table are read as needing secrecy for their performance. This constant interrogation of conscience can scarcely have been the characteristic mode

37. The chapel, Cotehele House, Cornwall, built by Sir Richard Edgcumbe, *c.* 1488

even of the devout gentleman. The latter was more likely to combine some meditation, aided by breviaries and books of hours, with a serious cycle of worship both at home and in the parish church.

Some reconciliation of the private, the familial and the public was an essential feature of élite behaviour.[11]

## 10.2 THE COMING OF REFORM

Little in this expressive and rather solemn world of Catholic piety can have done much to prepare the gentry for the traumatic consequences of the Break with Rome. While an aversion to pomp or a passion for the study of religious texts might predispose an individual to question established orthodoxy, they might equally reinforce an informed belief in traditional ideas. The choice of religious allegiance must often have been made according to family affinity, factional alignment or educational accident. Parents who chose to send their sons to Court in the 1530s, or to Cambridge in that or the next decade, probably thought little, if at all, of the religious consequences. However, these environments proved fertile ground for the inculcation of serious ideas of reform, while access to some Oxford colleges, or to parts of the Inns of Court might have the opposite effect. The influence of Cambridge can be traced through the biographies of the Marian exiles and the alliances that came to power under Elizabeth. The Court's fundamental contribution was no doubt the construction of élite groupings dedicated to self-advancement through the new gospel. However, it also offered an environment, especially in the circle of Catherine Parr, in which Erasmian piety could be integrated with an evangelical commitment to the Scriptures to create a devotional pattern appropriate for the ruling classes.[12]

It seems that these novelties, especially in their more radical forms, appealed particularly to the young, who had greater exposure to formal training than their elders, and who also presumably possessed the general adventurousness of youth. The example of William Roper's heretical leanings, and the subsequent struggle by Sir Thomas More to recapture him for Catholicism, is well known. Robert Plumpton, resident in the Inner Temple in the 1530s, was converted to the new beliefs and sought to change his Yorkshire family as well. He urged his mother to read the New Testament, 'that ye will take heede to the teaching of the Gospell, for it is the thinge that all wee must live by'. 'You have,' he continued, 'muche to thanke God that it woulde please him to geve you licence to live untill this time, for the gospell of Christe was never so trewly preached as it is nowe'. It is unlikely that his mother agreed: the family remained identified with the old faith and Robert himself eventually married into the conservative Norton family. Other gentry rebels included Robert Jermyn, who reacted against his father's conservatism at Matthew Parker's Corpus, and Sir Clement Higham's son who did the same at Trinity Hall. A moving testimony of an unknown gentleman to his abiding Catholicism, probably written in the early years of Elizabeth's reign, acknowledges that his Protestant children have chosen the path of youth.[13]

Intense experiences of conversion bred predictable division within élite families. A spectacular case is that of Mrs Elizabeth Bowes who, in Collinson's words 'stand[s] out as the first Protestant of her sex and class in the whole north-east of England', who deserted her husband and followed her son-in-law John Knox to the purer environment of Geneva. Few went this far, either ideologically or geographically, but disputes about belief were common. The Stonors were alienated father from daughter after the latter's marriage to Sir Philip Hoby in the early 1540s. Stonor found her an irritating evangelist 'much geaven to the Scryptures and . . . alwayes . . . arguyng and contendyng with hym yn the same, the which thyng he cold in no wyse bere and specyallye at hur handes'. Other members of the Hoby circle may have had similar problems: Richard Scudamore, for example, was not mentioned in his conservative father's will when it was made in the 1570s. At other times we may legitimately infer conflict from what is known of allegiances. The Brudenells of Deene were divided in the mid-century, between a husband who supported the Edwardian regime with enthusiasm and a wife who apparently maintained Catholic ritual and educated her children in the old faith. And this was no mere nominal adherence on either side: the will of Sir Thomas, who died in 1549, is full of testimony to his new faith, including an insistence on sermons based on collects from the new Book of Common Prayer.[14]

Despite these compelling examples of division and tension it is likely that the strength of lineage identity and family loyalties often constrained cadets and descendants to identify with the position adopted by a determined ideologue in these early years of religious change. Thus the Throckmortons of Coughton, with their particularly intense devotional life pre-dating the break with Rome, appear destined for their later recusancy. Conversely, the descendants of William Tracy, a Gloucestershire gentleman, were identified with the early and trenchant Protestantism which he had displayed in his 1530 will. Archbishop Warham had his remains exhumed and the Worcester diocesan authorities burned them for heresy. His younger son Richard showed a proper sense of kin loyalty when he persuaded Cromwell to investigate the case, which had brought shame on the family, but his sympathies also extended to writing on those religious causes to which his father had been committed. A century later the Tracys were still immeasurably proud of their early Protestantism. Once a decision about religious identity had been made, for whatever motive, family interests, and the further influence of tutors and spiritual counsellors, could reinforce the choice. In the Lucy family of Warwickshire a continuous history of support for the reformed faith seems to emerge from William Lucy's friendship with Latimer and acceptance of his advice that his son should be tutored by John Foxe.[15]

When powerful clerical guidance was available to the laity they often responded: Latimer had a particular reputation as a spiritual counsellor, and men like Saunders and Bradford attracted coteries of the devout. A small section of the gentry clearly reacted to the traumas of the mid-Tudor decades with religious engagement far beyond any immediate economic or political self-interest. Thus Christine Garrett calculated that 166 gentlemen went into exile under Mary 'for their faith', and even if we eliminate those difficult to identify and those whose main motive seems escape from failed rebellions, we still have a figure of approximately 90. But zealous Protestant preachers could provoke negative responses as well, both because of their challenge to old values and because they often failed to make concessions to the social susceptibilities of the gentry. Latimer was as unlikely as John the Baptist to respect hierarchy. In the 1530s he wrote to a Warwickshire JP: 'O Lord God, who would have thought that Master N. had been so impotent that he would not hear a godly monition for the wealth of his soul? I have in use to commit such trespass many times a year with your betters by two or three degrees'.[16]

For these reasons deep ideological engagement with the new order must have been the prerogative of a small minority in the Reformation years. Instead the gentry and their spiritual advisers were beseiged by confusing religious signals, and complex threats to traditional order and responded with predictable evidence of uncertainty. In the 1540s and 1550s the will preambles of our sample show a rapid fall in the percentage of traditional Catholic formulae, a rather slow increase in full Protestant forms and much use of the 'neutral' dedication of the soul to God only. More interesting is the increase in variant forms of dedication, not easily classifiable as the above: in the 1540s 22 per cent of the 102 wills could be said to deviate from the recognised norms. Variant forms are by definition difficult to categorise but it is striking how often these wills seem to be endeavouring to assimilate the old and the new. In 1541 Thomas Braybrooke, gentleman, of Abingdon, Berkshire, avoided any request for the intercession of the Virgin, but desired that he might be 'in company with the virgin Mary and all the elect people of God'. George Thomson, gentleman, of Bishop's Stortford, making his will in the first year of Mary's reign, dedicated his soul to God and Christ 'through him trusting to be associated withe the holie saintes in heaven, whome I beseche to pray with me and for me'. Most apparently confusing was Sir Christopher Barker, Garter King of Arms, who made a will at the end of 1549 that spoke in the same words as Sir William Boleyn of Christ's passion, sought the intercession of the Virgin and saints, expressed the hope that he would be received into the bosom of Abraham and then concluded 'whereunto I truste by thinfynyte mercye of thew mercyfull god to be prepared elected and predestynated amonge thellecte Chrystyans'. This could all be assimilated to ideas legitimated in late medieval Catholic devotion, but it seems more likely that Barker was indeed seeking to integrate the old and the new theology. In other cases there may be a desire to express distinctive commitments while remaining on the correct side of the ecclesiastical authorities or a simple confusion about what to think and say, but a reluctance to be merely formulaic.[17]

Among the varied responses that the serious and devout might offer to the vicissitudes of Tudor religious policy we may distinguish three which were to have currency among the gentry until at least the Restoration period. The first emphasised personal pietism, and the living of the virtuous Christian life, regardless of doctrinal niceties which were better left to trained theologians. This quietist, Erasmian strain of devotion, is mediated through such humanist sources as Ascham and Cheke, though voices raised in its favour among the gentry themselves are usually of a later date and often connected with emergent Anglicanism. A second approach did not necessarily seek to minimise ideological division, but endeavoured to separate this from other relationships and obligations. This is well exemplified in a story told by Sir John Harington from his Stepney childhood in the 1560s. His parents, members of the Edwardian and Elizabethan Court Protestant élite, were committed and devout, especially his mother who was 'ever zealous in her faith'. Her brother, a far more conservative figure, brought Lord Hastings of Loughborough to dine, and while prayers were being said he removed himself to the garden. This provoked Mrs Harington to say that guests 'that scorned to pray with her, she should scorne they should eate with her'. Despite this brief outburst, the Haringtons continued to adhere to the basic principle that 'Religion brake not freindshipp, brake no Allegance, bard no good opinion'. The third position was that of the truly zealous: those for whom the Lord and/or the Church became parent, kin and ruler. It was in this spirit that Sir Francis Hastings counselled a female friend to act when she faced the overwhelming displeasure of her Catholic parents on her conversion. Quoting Matthew 10:37, 'He that loveth father or mother more than me is not worthy of me', he urged, 'let neyther losse of frendes, losse of living, no nor losse of life draw you to deny the truth, for what can all the frendes in the worlde doe for you, if the Lord Jesus forsake you?'[18]

## 10.3 POST-REFORMATION PIETY

The decade of the 1570s represents a more convincing turning-point in the story of the gentry and faith than does the beginning of Elizabeth's reign. Only when the major elements of the Elizabethan Settlement had been in place for some time, and the mechanisms of enforcement were invoked in earnest, do divergent opinions among the laity begin to be crystallised. For the Catholic community this was the first of the testing decades: the beginning both of serious persecution and of the missionary effort. For conformist and godly gentlemen this was the decade in which the effects of Protestant education first began to percolate fully into the adult community. What was begun here affected critical sections of the élite to the Civil War, and beyond it as far as the Restoration.

In this near-century political and cultural circumstance conspired to persuade those gentlemen and women who had any impulse to spiritual seriousness to a strong commitment to their faith. The English Crown's drives for conformity, and the crises of national and international politics provided one obvious context. Sustained religious education of the lay élite, afforced by the insistence of both Protestant divines and counter-Reformation missionaries on the spiritual duties of the individual, provided the other. These demands placed great burdens upon the conscientious gentleman or woman, but also flattered him or her by offering involvement in the great tasks of promoting religious unity or protecting the Church Catholic. One recent commentator on the continental Reformation has suggested that the success of the Protestants lay in precisely this willingness, often more apparent than real, to take the laity into spiritual partnership. Following this reading we might suggest that the English gentry found themselves doubly flattered, for they were offered a measure of leadership in matters of religion both by a Crown in need of instruments to enforce conformity and by clerics anxious for patronage and protection.[19]

A major consequence of these new circumstances was the construction of a more elaborate notion of godly living than that which had conventionally obtained in the first half of the Tudor period. The basic tools were, of course, the imported theologies and devotional writings of continental divines. Calvinist theology, with its concern for election and sanctification, and its insistence on the examination of the conscience, was of overwhelming importance. Among Catholics, the *Spiritual Exercises* of Loyola and the devotional writings of the Counter-Reformation played a less dramatic role, but nevertheless offered similar support to those who struggled to internalise their faith. By the early seventeenth century these prime influences from abroad were afforced by the flowering of English devotional literature of all confessional varieties, with William Perkins as the unquestioned doyen of Puritan spirituality, Lancelot Andrewes as key expositor of Anglican pietism and men such as Robert Southwell offering Catholics a more local access to the new routines of the Counter-Reformation.[20]

The choice of literary mentor made by the gentry was contingent first upon religious identity, and then no doubt on personal preferences about style and intellectual complexity. No one text can stand as model for the group as a whole. However, there are a few writings that had a sufficiently wide appeal to offer some broad insight into expectations, at least among Protestants. Perhaps the best example is Bishop Lewis Bayly's *The Practice of Piety*, a devotional work by a moderate Puritan prelate which first appeared in 1612. Before 1640 there had been at least 38 editions of the book and translations into various languages including

Polish, and in the 1660s even the Pequot Indians were given the benefit of Bayly in their own tongue. It seems to have particularly attracted a gentry readership: Sir John Wynn recommended it to his son Maurice as something on which he should meditate, it appears regularly on book lists such as that of Judith Isham, and Ann Rashleigh's husband read to her from the text in her dying moments. On one occasion it even became a weapon in a domestic battle: Sir Edmund Skory bequeathed his wife Dame Silvestra his Christian forgiveness for her wickedness and 'a praier Booke called 'The practice of piety' desiring that she better love and affect the same then hitherto she hath done it'.[21]

The structure of Bayly's popular text offers insight into the expectations that the clergy entertained about the pious life of the virtuous householder. Bayly leaned upon the example of his sixteenth-century predecessors in offering a work programmed to the active life of the busy layman. He also included gestures more obviously directed to a social élite. The frontispiece shows a gentleman at prayer, behind him the Bible open upon a table, before him his words ascending to the heavens. Such a man must begin with an understanding of the faith and its basis in revelation: so the first part of the text is dedicated to an exposition of the theology of the Trinity, of the attributes of the Deity and of election. This last is pursued at length through sections on the strivings of the saints, the miseries of hell and the joys of the elect. From knowledge must come action: a willingness to search the conscience daily, to read the scriptures, to show the fruits of faith. Such action commences in the private devotions of the closet and bedchamber, and in the inner meditations the individual conducts with his soul during the working day. Bayly offers his readers a detailed structure of private prayer and reading which could have consumed many waking hours, though the good Bishop had the wisdom to vary the length of his prayers for the circumstances of different individuals (hence perhaps his appeal). Private prayer leads on to household devotion, with godliness in the household as a chief means to the preservation of families and commonwealths. In a moment of particular address to the gentry he describes religion as 'the best building and surest entailing of House and Land to a man and his posterity'. Public worship, and a full form of sabbatarianism, were also essential features of the devout life, as were the Second Table duties of charity and beneficence. Finally, Bayly offered one of the most extended late contributions to the *ars moriendi*, counselling the

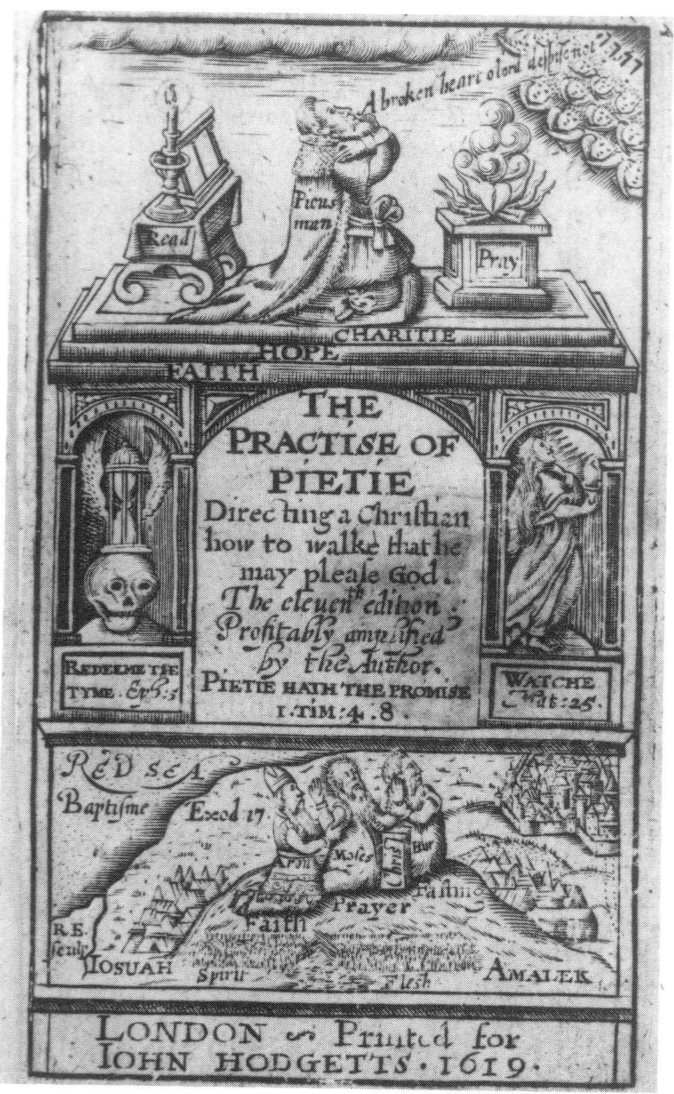


38. Lewis Bayly, *The Practise of Pietie* (1619): frontispiece

departing against despair and advocating communion on the deathbed.[22]

Most of the elements of the Bishop's advice can be found in the routines of godly individuals and households under Elizabeth, James and Charles. The regular examination of conscience through prayer and meditation is its most intimate feature. This was a constant expectation in the advice literature, whatever the religious persuasion of the author. Oglander veered to the perfunctory when he told his son George merely to pray 'every morning and evening privately in thy study'. Wandesford more explicitly defined circumstance and motive for his children:

> Let his [God's] service be the first Work you begin withall in the Morning, and the last you conclude the Day withall, when you goe to your Rest. Neither doe it for Fashion's sake . . . but with hearty Affection and Humility . . . I say with Humility; for all outward Reverence must be used in these Exercises both in public and private.

The highly pre-selected evidence of diaries and memorandum books suggests that these advices were often followed, at least in externals. Richard Stonley always concludes his day's entry with a note on prayers and then bed: Henry Ferrers, from the Catholic end of the religious spectrum, observed the habit of private prayers in his bed before the curtains were drawn aside in the morning. Sir John Newdigate devised for himself prayers that should be said on waking and sleeping. On the other hand it is difficult to believe that scapegrace squires like Nicholas Assheton or Humphrey Mildmay were regularly to be found on their knees before they tumbled drunk to bed. Dorothy Osborne was rather shocked to find that her sister-in-law ran her household in the 1650s in such a way that 'we go abroad all day and play all night, and say our prayers when we have time'. Habituation from childhood to routines of devotion was an obvious protection against such dissipation and neglect. It was therefore one of the prime duties of the mother to inculcate good practices into her children, and in the rare cases in which female advice survives it often revolves around the routines of private prayer. At a rather later stage of their careers young men were subject to constant reminders of the need to pray effectively; advice such as that offered by Sir Henry Slingsby to his son at Cambridge being available in abundance.[23]

But habituation to these basic routines can scarcely be equated with deep pietism. Both the extent and the nature of private devotions have to be examined as indices of a fuller involvement in the godly life. Bishop Bayly remarked with some scorn that the Protestant did not need the multiplied and obsessive devotions of the papists, yet many seem to have sought exactly this. It is inevitable that this form of religiosity is particularly associated with women, those wives and widows whose circumstances permitted a daily round of worship, reading and meditation rarely achieved by the most conscientious man. Lady Margaret Hoby must have consumed two-thirds of her waking hours in religious acts, and Ann Montagu's guidance to her children suggests similar preoccupation. Ann Wen Brynkir, of the North Welsh Maurice family, was described by a friend as 'altogether given to godly prayers and religious exercises'. Puritan gentlewomen such as Mary Strode, Margaret Wroth and Mary Armyne were credited with spending several hours a day in their closets at private devotions and meditations. Catholic ladies were equally given to these routines: John Gerard described one of his Catholic hostesses, Jane Wiseman, as devoted to all kinds of good works and worship; Mary Gifford, a Staffordshire gentlewoman, was said to have worn holes in her dresses from her constant kneeling at prayers. Clerics preaching funeral sermons were obviously prone to stereotype their female subjects: their comments are replete with descriptions of lives given wholly to faith and good works. But members of the women's own families also frequently emphasised female holiness: Alice Thornton described her mother as laying out all her goods 'for God's service and glory', and Sir Roger Twysden believed that his mother Lady Anne had such a delight in Christ that she 'contemne[d] the world'. The immediate reality behind these images no doubt varied, but their sheer consistency made them a powerful social construct, with much ability to influence actual behaviour.[24]

The content of such female piety varied from the development of personal patterns of prayer, based, especially in the case of serious Calvinists, on close examination of conscience, to the rehearsal of ideas drawn from sermons, either privately or in the company of maidservants. Lady Strode, according to the preacher of her funeral sermon, repeated 'in her Chamber . . . to her Maidservants, the sermons shee had heard and penned'. Bible reading was clearly an essential, and was often undertaken to a systematic yearly plan, and other books were at least recommended to women. Sir Justinian

Isham, who took a higher view of female learning than many of his contemporaries, urged his daughters to prayer and meditation and to the reading of St Augustine's *Meditations*, Thomas à Kempis and Daniel Featley's *Handmaid to Devotion*. Elizabeth Isham recorded in her diary that she began to read the Bible at the age of 10, to study it systematically in a daily routine of meditation at 16 and added the Augustinian texts when she was in her early twenties. Lady Mildmay's mother had been more restrictive, commending only the Bible, à Kempis, Foxe and Musculus's *Commonplaces* to her daughter, but these had been sufficient to construct a pattern of life-long devoutness. When John Evelyn had the melancholy task of sorting the papers of his close friend Mrs Godolphin, who died in her mid-twenties in 1678, he provided the following summary:

> [they] consisted of Prayers, Meditations, Sermon-notes, Discourses and Collections on severall religious subjects, and many of her owne composing, and so pertinently digested, as if she had ben all her life a student in divinity.

Meanwhile Catholic ladies were perhaps less likely to take the Bible to their closets, but were embarked by their confessors into a cycle of prayer centred upon the physical presence of Christ in the Sacrament. John Gerard also talks of giving 'ascetical works' and Loyola's *Exercises* to devout female converts.[25]

The expectations of private male piety were not significantly different: patterns were gendered by outcome more than by initial intent. Bible study, extempore prayer and serious reading were expected of both sexes, as the advice of Brathwait's *English Gentleman* and *English Gentlewoman* indicates. Sir George St Paul was one of many who endeavoured to sustain a thorough programme of devotion, reading the Bible each day and using Monday to rehearse all he had learned on the Sabbath. But men had the opportunities and responsibilities of their public life, and, for most, private hours for meditation must have been uncommon. The diversity of their religious duties also perhaps reduced the incentive to exercise spiritual discipline and control from the sanctity of the closet. Only in prison, or in other confining circumstances, could they aspire to the devotional rounds of a Lady Margaret Hoby. Sir Thomas Tresham maintained his sanity in gaol by hearing readings each night from such sources as *The Christian Resolution* and other treatises on the existence of God, and by planning that distinctive offering to the Trinity, his triangular lodge at Rushton (see illus. 16, p. 138). Incarcerated in the discomfort of a Tudor prison even men less visibly devout than Tresham were likely to turn to meditation and prayer: Sir John Conway published his *Poesie of Floured Prayers* after a spell in the Tower, and managed to combine serious reflection on the Lord's Prayer and other key texts, with pleas to Elizabeth to forgive him his offences.[26]

Otherwise the godly endeavoured to maintain routines of meditation which, as Sir Thomas Wodehouse wrote, 'is an intention and application of spirit to devine things' but often found the strain of conflict with other activities. Sir Simonds D'Ewes found himself compelled to reduce his humiliations and fasts to one session a quarter and Sir John Newdigate often reproved himself for inadequate time given to private study and meditation. Men with a less stern and disciplined view of life were even more prone to distraction: William Carnsew read good Protestant authors and meditated, especially on a Sunday, but secular thoughts crept in. In August 1576 he gave over one Sunday to reading, but was disturbed by '2 grett swyne [who] dyed in the lust of eatting poysonyd rats, I thynke'. On another occasion his sober reading of Foxe only resulted in nightmares about Bishop Gardiner.[27]

Diaries, used with proper caution, allow us to test the intrusion of spiritual reflections into everyday experience. Here the godly Protestant, though not necessarily only the nonconformist, is usually set apart from his or her contemporaries by the belief in special providences and by a daily concern for evidence of sanctification. Diarists record, often as selfconscious reminders to themselves and their readers, the ever-present hand of the Deity. A diary like that of John Harington, the Puritan MP and son of the witty Sir John, is so steeped in these preoccupations that, as his editor remarks, even his dreams appear to have been religious. In 1650, for example, he dreamt of being 'shy of full holiness'. The well-known Puritan families of the pre-Civil War period, the Harleys, Veres, Barnardistons and Barringtons all exhibit in their correspondence this questing after the affirmation of faith as daily experience. Such anxieties readily transmuted into a superstitious quest for evidence of Divine providence, and cuts across ideological and political divisions. For example, Alice Thornton, who during the Civil War and beyond was a passionate adherent of the Anglican cause, spilled much ink on the special providences that had secured herself and her family from a variety of disasters. After a vivid description (recalled of course in tranquillity many years later) of her escape from a fall in Ireland, she ejaculated 'But oh! what great cause have I to cast my selfe downe att the feete of the great and dreadful Lord God, who am but dust and ashes, made by his power and preserved by His Providence ever since I was borne'.[28]

Private meditation was the prelude to public worship within the household: and this was essential 'if thou desirest to have the blessing of God upon thy selfe and upon thy family', says Bayly. We have already seen two important examples of the family at prayer: that of the Hoby establishment and that of the Haringtons. Evidence for religious observance is of course unquantifiable, but seems to point consistently towards some form of public household devotion. Incidental comments on domestic worship are perhaps more revealing than the set-piece descriptions of the godly. One of Sir Nicholas Le Strange's jests involves a gentleman's younger son, called upon to read a lesson at household prayers, who inverts bread and beard and reads 'how many hired servants in my Father's house have beard, and I have none'. A major contretemps between husband and wife in the household of Sir John Norris revolved around collective prayers. Here there was no domestic chaplain and, depending on whose story in the subsequent litigation is to be believed, either a senior servant read prayers 'accordinge to the ordinary custome used in the house' or else a local cleric was imported. On one occasion husband and wife were undoubtedly present with the sermons when Sir John, peeved by his wife's behaviour, arranged that a chapter of Ecclesiastes on the obedience of women should be read. Lady Norris, on her own admission was so incensed that she sent for the Bible and tore a page from it (trampling it underfoot says her opponent for good measure). It was the quasi-public nature of household prayers that rendered them so important as a demonstration of gentry devotion. When that piety was challenged, the honour of the head of house was affronted; as Sir William Springett affronted his uncle Sir Edward Partridge, with whom he resided, by insisting on conducting his own form of godly worship in his chambers 'which wrought great discontent in the family'.[29]

If the routine of daily prayer for the whole household was a norm for the gentry, it cannot be assumed to have covered the variety of religious and personal experience of the whole social group. There were, as usual, the extremes of enthusiasm. Richard Sedgwick's praise of Sir Edward Onslow, who prayed with his husbandmen at six in the morning and catechised the family after prayers at night 'wherein he used no respect of persons', implies that such dedication was unusual. Bruen organised his household around religious devotions, expounding a chapter of the Scripture every night for the benefit of his servants and having a godly preacher every Sunday in his chapel. Sir Anthony Cope was said to have 'shamed himselfe' in his prayers with his household by 'confession of his owne most speciall sinnes'. Recusant households could not proceed so publicly, but the accounts of the missioner priests testify to a passionate enthusiasm for household mass when it was available. A key feature of the ideologically committed is that they tended to assume active responsibility for the spiritual welfare of their households alongside, or instead of, a professional minister or priest. They catechised, rehearsed sermons, organised the cycle of feast and fast, even preached or expounded if, like John Bruen, they felt that no godly minister was available. It is interesting that Bishop Bayly was willing cautiously to legitimate this last practice: he suggests that heads of household, having called their families together and read a chapter of Scripture may 'if leisure serve, . . . admonish them of some remarkable good notes'.[30]

Household holiness, while ostensibly the preserve of the individual gentleman, became a matter of public debate and concern in the century after the Reformation. The Puritan divines saw it as a prime witness to élite belief, and were constantly warning of the need for activism. Catholic households faced a major dilemma since, from time to time, the government chose to insist on Prayer Book devotions as a test of domestic loyalties: so some heads of house used the Prayer Book in the morning in order to secure quiet for Catholic devotion thereafter. Some Catholic households resolved the problem by avoiding any collective worship: Henry Ferrers pursued his private prayers, but does not seem to have insisted on any for the servants.

Private chapels continued to be consecrated in the first decades of the seventeenth century, most bishops apparently depending on the safeguards for parochial worship built into the legal registration of such buildings. The detailed descriptions of the ceremony provided when Edmund Style's chapel was consecrated at Langley, Kent, and that of John Strode at Chantmarle, Dorset, seek to protect parochial worship and orthodoxy. The family, women as well as men, had to sign an engagement to attend the parish church from time to time, communicate twice yearly, and pay all tithes. After the Royal

Instructions of 1629, which required strict enforcement of the Henrician statute on chaplains, Neile, Laud and others seem to have pursued a systematic policy of refusing chapel consecration, except to the favoured few in the élite. Hence Sir Henry Slingsby's grievances about the Red House chapel, which he was particularly eager to consecrate since his house was so far from the parish church. It was characteristic of Bishop Williams that he chose to ignore this aspect of Laudian policy and consecrate Judge Whitelocke's chapel at Fawley Court, Buckinghamshire, with maximum ostentation and minimum attention to altars and rails. The main object of the prelates was to assail nonconformity, but Laud and Wren also seem to have seen this pressure on the gentry as an inducement to fully public worship in the parish church. Private chapels were out of ecclesiastical fashion, and could be employed, as Henry Hastings did, for storing hams for hospitality.[31]

While household worship was universally recognised as a prime responsibility of the man of substance, public attendance at church became the test par excellence of religious affinity. Bishop Bayly offered the ideological justification: 'Almighty God will have himselfe worshipped . . . in a . . . publique sort, of all the godly ioyned together in a visible Church', but the state was also acutely aware of the desirability of afforcing divine wishes. Conformity could scarcely be expected of the lower orders if the squirearchy held themselves aloof. The gentry at prayer, dutifully listening to their ministers, properly attendant to the wishes of the government, were the true supports of the hierarchical commonwealth. It is precisely because the need for this external conformity was so great that it is extraordinarily difficult to describe the public religious behaviour of the élite in terms of devotion or ideological commitment. Gentlemen themselves, unless they had taken the route of overt resistance, also had powerful reasons to appear conformist and devout. Long before the Reformation they had employed the parish church as the environment in which to display their manorial and familial authority. The church provided the most visible local articulation of the social order and multiplied the opportunities for deference. In the overturning times of the sixteenth and seventeenth centuries such articulation became ever more important. Nicholas Le Strange has a nice story of the minister who inveighed against the commonalty for rising when great persons came into church, 'even in the midst of their devotions'. 'Sayes he, [the minister] I like an Holy-Rowly-Powliness; for there sure if anywhere, we ought to be Haile Fellows well mett'. Such egalitarian sentiments were hardly likely to appeal to the majority of the gentry: even those godly families who rejoiced in the community of the saints were rarely immune to public gestures of deference.[32]

Some indicators of gentry commitment can, however, be sought in enthusiasm for preaching and in the seriousness with which preparation for the sacrament of the Eucharist was viewed. The evidence on preaching is well known: the godly were eager to fund a preaching ministry, and gentlemen offered powerful support of suitable clerics, either through direct parish patronage or via lectureships. The zealous and potentially nonconformist were obviously the leaders in this direction, but the thirst for sermons extended well beyond their ranks, and in the patronage negotiations discussed in the last chapter the most serious 'religious' questions almost always concerned ability in the pulpit. When Edward Waller was recommending a Mr Powell for the living of Wrestlingworth, Bedfordshire, in 1625 he assured the patron, William Hale, that Powell was a 'very good preacher' and was willing to display his skills on the following Sunday. Sir John Strode not only heard his candidates, but sometimes chose the text on which they should expound. Lay sympathisers with Laudian innovation might occasionally dethrone sermons in favour of liturgy, but the demand for preaching continued unabated throughout the period of religious crisis and beyond. Even the derelict Nicholas Assheton often noted that he had attended sermons, though with what profit is unclear. John Kaye exemplified the attitude of the age when he described his new pew in Almondbury Church as having been constructed 'to heare sermons'.[33]

Evidence for eucharistic enthusiasm is less consistent. Here the 'Anglican' wing of the seventeenth-century Church is of most relevance, though it would be a mistake to see this of a concern only of the ceremonialists. Sir Henry Slingsby the elder was, as we have seen, particularly insistent that his son prepared himself adequately for this 'great misterie of your salvacon', and Ann Montagu devoted much of her religious advice to the Eucharist:

> With reverance the sacrament
> receive as oft as may
> it will your faith increase and strength
> bee to your soule a staye.

Sir Simonds D'Ewes's fury with Mr Danford of Stow focused at one point on his denial of communion to the congregation, and the godly Bruen made a particular point of commending his kinsman Thomas Wilbraham's regular attendance at communion. Lady Mildmay, whose extensive meditations allow an unusual access to her ideas, was deeply influenced by aspects of Calvinist doctrine, yet showed no interest in sermons, while describing the sacraments as 'the heavenly food and sustenance of our souls'. The growth of a distinctively Anglican piety amongst leading laymen by the 1630s afforced this preoccupation with eucharistic reception, while complicating it by identification with Laudian ceremonialism. Alice Thornton's mother constructed several prayers 'proper for the time of the Holy Sacrament', which she must have employed as one of her forms of religious comfort during the dark days of Civil War. The need for access to the Eucharist during the Interregnum led devout Anglicans like John Evelyn to take risks more normally associated with Catholics. On Christmas Day 1657 Evelyn was one of those arrested while Gunning was administering the sacrament in Exeter Chapel, London, by army officers bent on the suppression of Christmas celebrations.[34]

The moments of devotion, in closet, hall or chapel and parish church were seen as the expression of the godly life, providing, when properly undertaken by the gentry, a model for the rest of the commonwealth. But practical manifestations of faith were of more immediate efficacy for the community. 'As therefore,' says Bayly, 'Christ ioyned Fasting, Prayer and Almes together in Precept, so must thou ioyne them together . . . in practice.' The fruits of faith must be a lively doing of good works. The consequences for the pious gentleman or woman would be the generous performance of Second Table duties especially towards the neighbourhood. The sick must be visited, the poor fed, almshouses constructed. John Kaye, a decent enough Calvinist in his views on election and salvation, rhymed these social duties in a way that suggests a firm belief in his reciprocal duties to the deity:

> Fyrste serve thy God early, kepe holie his day,
> Vysytt his temple, learn others to pray,
> Among thyne howshold banysh all stryfe,
> As lying and swering and vile trails of lyfe,
> To servants and Hierlings pay dew their Hier,

Provyde well in somer, for wynter and fyer,
The poore and the naykd, yll Hungrid and Cledd
Willingly Releve, with cloth and with Bread,
Then shall the Lord blesse both the and thy store,
As he hath thyne Elders that dwelt here before.[35]

Such charitable duties were still performed with much seriousness by many of the Stuart gentry. While casual almsgiving and hospitality suffered from contemporary suspicions of the wandering and indolent poor, generosity to the community remained a major manifestation of gentility. By the early seventeenth century a typology had emerged on funeral monuments, in sermons and memorials, which identified piety, honesty in social dealing, liberality and charity as the construct of the virtuous gentleman. Much the same was true for the gentlewoman, though as usual with less emphasis upon public qualities. These models speak of a concern for beneficence in the community which was one of the hallmarks of the landed gentleman in Tudor and Stuart England. We do not need to accept W. K. Jordan's precise monetary calculations to acknowledge his general argument that structured provision for the poor and for education by the gentry among others increased greatly from the reign of Elizabeth to the Civil War. In Buckinghamshire, for example, 22 almshouses were established during this period, approximately half of them by the gentry. Jordan's figures for the three counties of Buckinghamshire, Norfolk and Yorkshire show the gentry as consistently the greatest benefactors: no great surprise, given their numbers and wealth in this period, but some confirmation of the preoccupation with beneficence. Sir John Wynn, so tightfisted in his estate management and the control of his family, was nevertheless an almshouse founder. Of his establishment at Llanrywst he said to his son: 'I ment hit to a good end, god grant hit so be, and that posterity do not for covetousenes sake . . . abuse hit'.[36]

Some of this behaviour emerges as concern for public virtue, afforced by the conviction that once such duties had been performed 'God will . . . prosper thee and thine in this world'. In a social group so profoundly committed to family continuity as the gentry this notion of intergenerational reciprocity must have been a powerful inducement to piety. Practical piety also focused upon the preservation of order in the commonwealth where, as Arthur Gregory remarked, 'the feare of god . . . only preserves the society of men'. But even 'Anglican' gentlemen frequently transcended these conventional and communitarian perceptions of the faith. Christopher Wandesford, with his deep concern for religious duties combined with neighbourhood identity, or Sir Henry Slingsby, typify this reflective approach to belief in action. Wandesford specifically advised against engagement in religious controversy and 'scholastic distinctions [wherein] much of perplexity and Danger may come by it, little of satisfaction to your Mind, nothing at all to the amendment of your life'. Instead he urged the performance of those duties that emanated from love of God and neighbour, mediated through constant reference to the Scriptures. Slingsby, despite his academic interest in theology, saw the routines of daily life as providing his prime witness as a Christian. The more Puritan Sir Edward Montagu advised his son 'for your religious and Civill carriage study well Salomans workes', and, 'lett Equity, the Rule of our Saviour Jehsus Christe be your rule'. Sir John Newdigate, reminded himself in his notebook 'do that thou are fittest for with constancy and perseverance. That is, serve and govern my household and labour, to be fit to serve my country and . . . my neighbour'. No one ideological position bound these men, especially in ecclesiology, but they seem to have characterised a mainstream position among the élite which could be identified as moderate, often Calvinist, and possessing a moral earnestness that may have owed something to Stoicism as well as Protestant teaching.[37]

For a minority, or rather several minorities, this earnest performance of Second Table duties could never be sufficient. As Sir John Strode expressed it to his son 'as thou hast all from God, so be thou all his'. For the zealous godly, and indeed the powerfully committed Catholic, a man's life should be lived wholly in the knowledge and fear of the Lord, and hence in pursuit of his purposes. A gentleman's commitment would also stand as an exemplar to many. Barnaby Potter, preaching the funeral sermon of Sir Edward Seymour in 1613, reminded his children that:

> the goodness of a private man is his owne, and his sinnes seldome hurt any but himselfe, but the goodnesse of a principall man is the whole countries, and his sinnes infectious unto many.

In the century between the Reformation and the Civil War such zeal and concern for good example had ample outlets. No longer were the clergy alone left to determine doctrine, religious loyalties or the spiritualisation of the society. Gentlemen like Sir Edward Dering wrote learned theological polemics; ladies like Magdalen, Lady Montagu, or Elizabeth Vaux provided the new paradigms of Catholic sanctity; MPs like Sir Anthony Cope or John Harington fought for spiritual regeneration through legislation. Occasionally these commitments were expressed visually, as in the fine portrait of William Style of Langley, Kent, apparently the perfect virtuosi, until the emblems are read as a rejection of worldly possessions and a turning to inward devotion, much of it inspired by Counter Reformation models. The behaviour of these men and women, although the subject of some contempt and derision among the unregenerate – the world, as Bruen's biographer remarked was full of 'mockers, contemners of God, and despisers of good things' – nevertheless provided a standard of lay devotion against which all their peers were constrained to judge themselves. No doubt most neither aspired to nor desired such rigorism and self-sacrifice, but a cultural standard was established in this period that challenged the rest of the gentry to explicit response. The paradigm of intense godliness was only subverted when its full destructive potential had been tested in Civil War.[38]

## 10.4 RESTORATION

The years after the Restoration are something of a postlude in the story of gentry devotion and belief. Circumstances inevitably subverted some of that zeal to actualise godliness in daily assaults on the unregenerate that had marked the period of the Civil War. Godly magistracy became unfashionable because of its identity with religious extremism and political instability. The dual pressures upon the gentry, from the Crown to conform to a particular form of settlement, and from the zealous clergy to initiate godly rule, were rapidly dissipated. The drive for external conformity was now of a different order; largely a construct of the gentry themselves as an opportunity to secure the success of the Established Church.

It would be unwise to suggest that the commitment of the gentry as a class to religious exercises therefore also diminished. The literature of spiritual advice continues to advocate prayer, meditation and bible reading as necessary foundations of the life of a gentleman, and family prayers remained a recognisable part of the daily domestic routine. Determined godliness of the kind

39. Portrait of William Style, esquire, of Langley, Kent, 1636

common under James I and Charles I is still revealed in some of the correspondence, memoirs and advices of these years. A notable example is that of Matthew Hale, the judge, who still sternly enjoined sabbatarianism and spiritual discipline. Funeral sermons continue to describe lives of godly virtue: Lady Anne Burgoyne, widow of the Presbyterian Sir Roger, not only overcame her early aversion to Anglicanism, but acquired an especial devotion to the Lord's Supper and never allowed 'Publick Prayers . . . [to be] delay's one quarter of an Hour upon her account'. John Evelyn's diary is a powerful testament to devout Anglicanism experienced amid rich worldly distractions. These beliefs were supported by a rich crop of devotional writing, especially on the central rite of the Lord's Supper, that found a ready market.[39]

The godly household, of whatever particular doctrinal persuasion, continued to support a life of domestic prayer identical to that of the pre-Civil War Years. Gentlemen still employed private chaplains, and in the calmer atmosphere prevailing between bishops and leading laymen, it was easier to patronise them without conflict. Domestic chaplains, providing services unmonitored by the ecclesiastical hierarchy, offered a spiritual outlet for gentlemen who now conformed to the Church of England, but whose instincts were still Presbyterian. Sir Richard Hoghton of Hoghton Tower, Lancashire, was claimed as orthodox at his burial in 1678, but maintained a steady preaching ministry in his household, serviced by men ejected from their livings. It also became more acceptable to construct private chapels and have them consecrated. Such buildings could be powerful statements of loyalty to revived Anglicanism, that built by Sir Peter Leicester at Nether Tabley, Cheshire, at a total cost of almost £800; or the chapel at Gwydir constructed by Sir Richard Wynn the younger.[40]

There were, moreover, residual manifestations of zeal: the Popish Plot and its aftermath generated acute anxiety, as in the case of Thomas Mostyn of Mostyn, North Wales, who drafted a will attempting to keep his children away from the evil influence of their Catholic relatives or 'such others as may seduce them to popery'. An education under the famous Dr Fell at Oxford may help to explain Mostyn's intensity, though it should be noted that it had not prevented him from marrying a Catholic wife. The influence of churchmen such as Fell was no accident: ecclesiastical dignitaries deliberately cultivated the young members of the élite, hoping thereby to steer them away from the corrosive vices of the age.[41]

40. Chapel at Nether Tabley House, Cheshire, built by Sir Peter Leicester, 1675–8

Despite these continuities a cultural sea-change seems to have overtaken late seventeenth-century devotion, as it did other intellectual forms. That concern for the reasonable life lived according to sound principles of belief, which we have already identified in men such as Wandesford and Slingsby, now became the dominant mode of description in advices and sermons. A 'sober morality', offering a calm and reflective vision of faith was that which attracted many of the more serious members of the élite. Loyalty to the Established Church was to be integrated with civility in religion as well as secular society. The tone is exemplified by Sir John Reresby's prayer to be preserved from 'the two Rocks of

Popery and Pelagianisme, and . . . that in the Orthodox profession of Protestancy I may live soberly, righteously and godly in this present world'. The cynicism induced by years of religious conflict also took its toll. Francis Osborne's advice to his son is redolent of the disillusion of these years:

> Oppose no Religion you find established, how ridiculous soever you apprehend it: For though like David, you may bring unavoidable Arguments, to stagger a popular error, None but the Monsters owne sword can cut off the head of one universally received.[42]

# Conclusion

In the second half of our period the gentry were able to enjoy continental travel to an extent not customary in earlier centuries. What they saw and did was solemnly recorded in journals which rarely reflected explicitly on society at home, but which are intermittently revealing of the way they saw their own situation. France provided the greatest food for thought: culturally accessible for the well-trained gentleman, yet noticeably different to the English polity. Robert Dallington, writing his *View of France* at the turn of the sixteenth century, admired the valour of the French nobility. However, he suggested that it could be said of most of them, adapting Plato's words, 'Hee was a very tall man at armes, but he had no good quality besides'. Those good qualities, by implication the possession of the English élite, included the ability of an individual to 'serve his Countrey both in peace and warre' and to match valour to wisdom 'for if he have not valour to dare and wisdome to knowe how and when, he wanteth one of the principall supporters of his honour'. Others were firmly of the opinion that the French *noblesse d'epée* lacked learning: Sir John Reresby noted that they were taken from school by the age of 14 and bred up in cultural pursuits and military service which 'trains them up to a great confidence, which often puts an handsome gloss upon mean parts'. Fynes Moryson argued that contempt for the formal learning of the universities was common among the continental nobility: a German gentleman 'perceiving I spake Latin better than he thought a gentleman [should] . . . did after esteem me as a Pedant'.[1]

English gentlemen therefore seem to have discovered rather to their surprise that they had absorbed humanist arguments for learning more fully than their neighbours. The reverse was true of social polish. John Evelyn agreed that the French lacked academic training and hence proved less intellectually curious than the English or Dutch, but contrasted this with the civility they acquired from urban living. They did not 'suffer themselves to be eaten up at home, in the country, in the likenesse of beef and mustard, among their unthankful neighbours'. They used style as a route to power as well as social standing: Reresby believed that lesser title of nobility could be gained without land: 'good clothes and a splendid equipage creates them daily'. The rusticity, and lack of cultural polish were equally often the burden of foreign travellers' comments on the English. Beat Muralt, a Bernese who observed English society rather closely in the 1690s, tactfully described the gentry as men 'whose Birth no way subjects them to any Nicety, or troublesome Punctilio, so that they may follow any kind of Business in case of Need', then destroyed the effect of his statement by noting that 'Debauchery and Hunting are their usual Employments'. Genteel behaviour, which in other countries would serve to separate the nobility from the rest were, in Muralt's opinion, quite neglected by the ordinary English gentry. National stereotypes of course play a part in these observations, but they were offered by men who had experience of diverse cultures and cannot wholly be dismissed.[2]

Contrasting political cultures was a more sensitive business. It was not difficult for an English gentleman to envy the privileged status of his continental counterparts. Evelyn remarked the advantage of the *petit noblesse*, not only in France, but elsewhere on the continent: 'nor indeed is there in any kingdome (save ours onely) that severe distinction of *minores* and *majores* amongst the Nobility, a difference which some think neither suits with true policy or justice'. Although informed observers recognised that French society was mobile, and that, as Northleigh suggested, 'they have a Vanity among them of passing themselves for Counts or Marquesses, when indeed they are none; and so Monsieur *le Count* carries it many times by Courtesie, like an English Esquire', there was an undoubted attraction in title. The French in their turn thought that the English compensated for their lack of legal privilege by a greater concern for deference and ceremoniousness. They despised, says Moryson, the English for wearing great lords' liveries and for showing undue reverence for superiors. But there was consolation for the English gentleman when he saw the alarming gulf that lay between the nobles and the rest in France. 'We are', says Evelyn, '. . . in this Dominion to take the *Noblesse* (that is the Gentry) for the sole visible body, and consequently the Plebeians of a far more vile and naturally slavish genius, then they really are in any part of Christendome besides'. And, as Northleigh added, 'The Body of this vast people is not compos'd of the Gentry and Yeomanry, that with us, like Ziba and Mephibosheth, are to divide the Land'. Thus observation of their neighbours had already launched the English élite into that self-congratulatory mode which rationalised their lack of privilege by a praise of openness. France and Italy, said Thomas Fuller, are 'like a die which hath no points between cinque and ace, – nobility and peasantry'. While 'In England, the temple of honour is bolted against none who have passed through the temple of virtue'.[3]

Thus looking at their neighbours gave gentlemen travellers some reasons to be complacent about their own class and its place in society. They claimed a superiority in learning, a stronger sense of service to the state and a less exploitative role in society. They *may* have had to pay the price of weak formal privilege by courting nobles assiduously in pursuit of office and influence, but, as Muralt remarked, they could also live 'as little kings in their Country Houses' and eschew place-seeking. Perhaps continental journeys left the sophisticated member of the élite less certain than his ordinary countrymen that 'the English were the best people in the world'. They do not seem to have dented the belief that travel was for the acquisition of cultural polish, not to change mens' minds about their own social environment.[4]

The English gentry may have possessed a basic confidence in their situation, but complacency had to be tempered by an ability to respond to circumstance. The remarkable feature of the social group in the *longue durée* was its adaptivity. In our two centuries adaptivity was tested by Tudor state building, religious conflict, price inflation, civil war, and declining rent-rolls. Each of these tests found individuals and families that were wanting; each served to confirm that the majority of the landed had a remarkable capacity to weather the storm. When the language of 'the rising gentry' or 'the crisis of the aristocracy' has been employed to explain the social changes of the century between 1540 and 1640 it has been at the expense of this powerful evidence of continuity. Durability does not, of course, exclude major elements of change: the number of gentry increased sharply in this century, their political role was greatly enhanced, their behaviour was in many ways dramatically modified. But they remained in fundamentals at the end of the period what they had been at the beginning: a landowning élite without significant legal privileges, able to adjust to prevailing circumstance. Natural losses and failures were recruited through the permeable membrane that distinguished the gentry from other status groups. At the lower end of the social hierarchy, relatively easy access to land, and the importance of genteel behaviour as a test of status, secured the appropriate flexibility for group survival.

We should not presume, however, to apply this image of adaptivity too closely to individual familial experience. While the numerous strategies for family survival have been considered in our text we have also shown how often they failed, either as a consequence of one of the crises listed above, or of the cruelties of biology. If we return finally to the magnificent gentry tombs that have been a significant part of our story, we might consider them as a metaphor for the experience of the English gentry. All too often their pomposity and pretension, their pride in lineage and their display of proper virtue is mocked by the rapid failure of their descent, the decay of all their hopes. Like Shelley's Ozymandias, their demand to the traveller to 'Look on my works' echoes hollowly in an empty church. Yet the collective impact of the great tomb-building tradition of these centuries is to fix in the mind of the observer an image of confidence and power, of gentility triumphant not only over individual adversity, but over the local society to which they are displayed.

This has been a study both of a social group and of the attitudes of the individuals who composed it. It is therefore fitting to end with the observations of two of those articulate individuals; men who had to wrestle with the paradoxes of fragility and endurance in their own families. Sir Edward Rodney, writing of his lineage in the 1650s, was addressing the daughters who were his only surviving heirs. Not only were his five sons dead, but the estate was burdened with old debt, and with the costs of sequestration and composition. It was little wonder that Sir Edward quoted Job 'many things have made mee weary of the world'. Yet he acknowledged the need for thanksgiving and hope. A 500-year inheritance was given to his daughters with 'thanksgiving to God that it hath lasted so long, and that through so long a tract of time it hath not contracted any blemishes or spots of infamy'. That spotless descent would benefit his daughters and their lineage, since 'they are as likely to derive good qualities with their blood as all other irrationall and inanimate creatures'. And maybe, he concluded, God would judge his house kindly so that 'some of my Brothers Sonnes may continue his true worship in our name to another period'.[5]

Eighty years later the good old Tory, Percyvall Hart, esquire, also faced descent to an heiress and the loss of his name and worship. But he spoke with some confidence from his tomb into a church filled with the monuments of his ancestors of the values that he, his lineage and his social class had at its best embodied, and of the power they therefore had a natural right to retain:

The curious inspector of these Monuments
Will see a short account of
An Ancient Family
For more than four centuries
Contented with a moderate Estate
Not wasted by luxury
Nor increased by Avarice.
May their Posterity
Emulating their Virtues
Long enjoy their Possessions.[6]

# Notes

**Abbreviations used in Notes**

*AgHR* *Agricultural History Review.*
*AHEW* *The Agrarian History of England and Wales*, ed. J. Thirsk, vol. 4 (Cambridge, 1967); vol. 5, 2 parts (Cambridge, 1984–5).
*AHR* *American Historical Review.*
*Barrington Letters* A. Searle (ed.) *The Barrington Letters*, Camden Soc., 4th ser., 28 (1983).
*BIHR* *Bulletin of the Institute of Historical Research*, since vol. 60 (1987) published as *Historical Research.*
BL British Library.
Blackwood, *Lancashire* B. G. Blackwood, *The Lancashire Gentry and the Great Rebellion, 1640–1660*, Chetham Soc., 3rd. ser., 25 (1978).
Bod. L Bodleian Library, Oxford.
Cholmley Sir Hugh Cholmley, *Memoirs* (1787).
*Clenennau Letters* T. Pierce (ed.) *The Clenennau Letters in the Brogyntyn Collection, National Library of Wales Journal*, ser. iv, pt i (1947).
Cliffe, *Puritan Gentry* J. T. Cliffe, *The Puritan Gentry: The Great Puritan Families of Early Stuart England* (1984).
Cliffe, *Yorkshire* J. T. Cliffe, *The Yorkshire Gentry from the Reformation to the Civil War* (1969).
CRO Cornwall Record Office.
*CSPD* *Calendar of State Papers Domestic.*
CUL Cambridge University Library.
*D'Ewes* J. O. Halliwell (ed.) *The Autobiography of Sir Simonds D'Ewes*, 2 vols (1845).
*DNB* *Dictionary of National Biography.*
DRO Dorset Record Office.
*EcHR* *Economic History Review.*
*EHR* *English Historical Review.*
Fletcher, *Sussex* A. Fletcher, *A County Community in Peace and War. Sussex, 1600–1660* (1975).
FSL Folger Shakespeare Library, Washington DC.
*Guise Memoirs* G. Davies (ed.) *The Autobiography of Thomas Raymond and the Memoirs of the Family of Guise of Elmore, Gloucestershire*, Camden Soc., 3rd ser., 28 (1917).
*Harley Letters* T. T. Lewis (ed.) *Letters of the Lady Brilliana Harley, wife of Sir Robert Harley*, Camden Soc., old ser., 58, (1854).
HHL Henry Huntingdon Library, San Marino, California.
Higford William Higford, *Institutions, or Advices to his Grandson* (1660) in T. Park (ed.) *The Harleian Miscellany*, 10 vols (1806–15) ix, pp. 580–99.
*HJ* *Historical Journal.*
HLMP House of Lords, Main Paper Series.
*HLQ* *Huntingdon Library Quarterly.*
*HMC* *Historical Manuscripts Commission.*

Holles Gervase Holles, *Memorials of the Holles Family*, ed. A. C. Wood, Camden Soc., 3rd ser., 55 (1937).
Holmes, *Lincolnshire* C. A. Holmes, *Seventeenth-Century Lincolnshire* (Lincoln, 1980).
Hughes, *Warwickshire* A. Hughes, *Politics, Society and Civil War in Warwickshire, 1620–60* (Cambridge, 1987).
IOW RO Isle of Wight Record Office.
*JBS* *Journal of British Studies.*
*JEH* *Journal of Ecclesiastical History.*
Jenkins, *Glamorgan* P. Jenkins, *The Making of a Ruling Class: the Glamorgan Gentry 1640–1790* (Cambridge, 1983).
KAO Kent Archive Office.
LAO Lincolnshire Archive Office.
*Letters of John Holles* P. R. Seddan (ed.) *The Letters of John Holles, 1587–1637*, 3 vols, Thornton Soc. Record Ser. 31, 35, 36 (1975–86).
*Lowther Family* C. B. Phillips (ed.) *The Lowther Family Estate Books*, Surtees Soc., 191 (1979).
*LP* *Letters and Papers Foreign and Domestic of the Reign of Henry VIII, 1509–1547*, ed. J. S. Brewer *et al.*, 21 vols (1862–1932).
MacCulloch, *Suffolk* D. MacCulloch, *Suffolk and the Tudors: Politics and Religion in an English County, 1500–1600* (Oxford, 1986).
m.i. memorial inscription.
*NA* *Norfolk Archaeology.*
NLW National Library of Wales.
NorfRO Norfolk Record Office.
NRA National Register of Archives.
NRO Northamptonshire Record Office.
NUL Nottingham University Library.
*Oxinden Letters* D. Gardiner (ed.) *The Oxinden Letters*, 2 vols (1933–7).
*PP* *Past and Present.*
PRO Public Record Office.
PROB Public Record Office, Probate Records.
*PSIA* *Proceedings of the Suffolk Institute of Archaeology.*
*RCHM* *Royal Commission on Historical Monuments.*
Reresby A. Browning (ed.) *The Memoirs of Sir John Reresby*, 2nd edn with additional material by M. K. Geiter and W. A. Speck (1991).
RO Record Office.
*Royalist's Notebook* A. Bamford (ed.) *A Royalist's Notebook: the Commonplace Book of Sir John Oglander* (1936).
*SAC* *Sussex Archaeological Collections.*
SBT Shakespeare Birthplace Trust, Stratford on Avon.
Slingsby Sir Henry Slingsby, *The Diary and Correspondence*, ed. D. Parsons (1836).
SomsRO Somerset Record Office.
SRO Staffordshire Record Office.
*STC* *A Short-Title Catalogue of Books printed in England, Scotland, and Ireland, and of English Books printed abroad, 1475–1640*, ed. A. W. Pollard *et al.*, 2nd edn. (1976–1990).

Stone, *Crisis* L. Stone, *The Crisis of the Aristocracy, 1558–1641* (Oxford, 1965).

Stone, *Family* L. Stone, *The Family, Sex and Marriage in England, 1500–1800* (Oxford, 1977).

*Thornton* C. Jackson (ed.) *The Autobiography of Mrs Alice Thornton*, Surtees Soc., 62 (1873).

*TRHS* *Transactions of the Royal Historical Society.*

UCW University College of Wales.

*VCH* *Victoria County History.*

*Verney Memoirs* F. P. Verney and M. M. Verney (eds) *Memoirs of the Verney Family during the Seventeenth Century*, 2 vols (1925).

*Wandesford* T. Comber (ed.) *A Book of Instructions by Lord Deputy Wandesford* (Cambridge, 1977).

*Wentworth* J. P. Cooper (ed.) *The Wentworth Papers, 1597–1628*, Camden Soc., 4th ser., 12 (1973).

*Whitelocke* R. Spalding (ed.) *The Diary of Bulstrode Whitelocke, 1605–75*, British Academy Records of Social and Economic History, 13 (Oxford, 1990).

WRO Warwickshire Record Office.

WYRO West Yorkshire Record Office.

*YAJ* *Yorkshire Archaeological Journal.*

YAS Yorkshire Archaeological Society, Leeds.

Place of publication is London unless otherwise stated.

**Introduction**

1. Hoby has attracted the attention of a number of historians. The best introduction to his life is to be found in the preface to the edition of his wife's diary, D.M. Meads (ed.) *The Diary of Lady Hoby* (1930); some detail in the following account is from this work.
2. G.C.F. Forster, 'North Riding Justices and their Sessions, 1603–1625', *Northern History*, 10 (1975) pp. 102–25; *CSPD Eliz. 1599*, 270, p. 99.
3. PRO, STAC 5/H16/2, H22/21, H50/4.
4. *HMC Salisbury*, x, pp. 302–3; xi, pp. 456, 546; PRO, STAC 5/H22/21.
5. H. Aveling, *Northern Catholics: the Catholic Recusants in the North Riding of Yorkshire, 1585–1790* (1966) pp. 120–2; PRO, STAC 5/H22/21; G. C. F. Forster, 'Faction and County Government in Early Stuart Yorkshire', *Northern History*, 11 (1976) pp. 74–6.
6. PRO, STAC 8/12/11, 104/15, 175/4; T.H. Brooke, 'The Memoirs of Sir Hugh Cholmley', Univ. of Oxford, B.Litt. thesis, 1937, pp. 43–6, 193; BL, Add. 4275, fos 99, 236; Cliffe, *Yorkshire*, p. 276; WYRO, TN/C/1/321.
7. R.H. Tawney, 'The Rise of the Gentry', 1558–1640', *EcHR*, old ser., 11 (1941) pp. 1–38; H.R. Trevor-Roper, 'The Gentry, 1540–1640', *EcHR*, supplement 1 (1953). For other contributions to the now-defunct debate on the gentry see J.H. Hexter, 'The Storm Over the Gentry' in his *Reappraisals in History* (1961); D.C. Coleman, 'The "Gentry" Controversy and the Aristocracy in Crisis', *History*, 51 (1966); G.E. Mingay, *The Gentry: the Rise and Fall of a Ruling Class* (1976).
8. Sir F. Pollock (ed.) *Table Talk of John Selden* (1927) pp. 50–1; F.J. Furnivall (ed.) *Harrison's Description of England in Shakespeare's Youth*, 4 pts, New Shakespere Soc. (1877–1908) i, p. 128; Tawney, 'The Rise of the Gentry', p. 37; the most important recent analysis of the evolving connection between gentle status and authority over land is in C. Carpenter, *Locality and Polity: a Study of Warwickshire Landed Society, 1401–99* (Cambridge, 1992) pp. 35–95; see also S. Payling, *Political Society in Lancastrian England* (Oxford, 1991) pp. 20ff; for the heralds' difficulties in establishing gentility at the margins of the group see G.D. Squibb, *The High Court of Chivalry* (1959) pp. 171–5.
9. But note that Wilson, writing in 1600, endeavoured to assimilate his professionals into the appropriate rank of gentility: J. Thirsk and J.P. Cooper (eds) *Seventeenth Century Economic Documents* (Oxford, 1972) pp. 755, 766–8.
10. A. Everitt, *Landscape and Community in England* (1985) pp. 27–8, 254–6; DRO, D53/1; for Bond's career see D. Underdown, *Fire from Heaven: Life in an English Town in the Seventeenth Century* (1992) pp. 42–54; J.G.A. Pocock (ed.) *The Political Works of James Harrington* (Cambridge, 1977) p. 405; for other good examples of contemporary movements in and out of mercantile wealth see the cases from Hooker's 'Description of Exeter' in D. Palliser, *The Age of Elizabeth: England under the Later*

*Tudors 1547–1603* (1983) pp. 91–2; J.S. Morrill, 'The Northern Gentry and the Great Rebellion', *Northern History*, 15 (1979) pp. 73–4; Celia Fiennes *The Illustrated Journeys, 1685–1712*, ed. C. Morris (1982) p. 186; Daniel Defoe, *A Tour Through the Whole Island of Great Britain*, ed. P.N. Furbank, W.R. Owens and A.J. Coulson (New Haven, 1991) p. 91.

11. Thomas Adams, *Works*, 3 vols (1861) i, p. 153; Sir Thomas Smith, *De Republica Anglorum*, ed. M. Dewar (Cambridge, 1982) p. 73; Morrill, 'The Northern Gentry', pp. 71–2; on the close association between land and authority in seventeenth-century Cheshire and Shropshire see M.G.D. Wanklyn, 'Landed Society and Allegiance in Cheshire and Shropshire in the First Civil War', Univ. of Manchester, PhD thesis, 1976, pp. 392ff.
12. One of the best discussions of changing perceptions of gentility is to be found in J.P. Cooper, *Land, Men and Beliefs*, ed. G.E. Aylmer and J.S. Morrill (1983) pp. 43–77; John Ferne, *The Blazon of Gentrie, Comprehending Discourses of Armes and of Gentry* (1586) pp. 12–13, 100; Edmund Chamberlayne, *Angliae Notitia* (1669) pp. 479–80; A.R. Wagner, *English Genealogy* (Oxford, 1960) p. 105; Matthew Carter, *Honor Redivivus* (1659); Richard Gough, *The History of Myddle*, ed. D. Hey (1981) pp. 116, 144.
13. J.E. Hollinshead, 'The Gentry of South-West Lancashire in the Later Sixteenth Century', *Northern History*, 26 (1990), pp. 82–3; N. Wright, 'The Gentry and their Houses in Norfolk and Suffolk from ca.1550–1850', Univ. of East Anglia, PhD thesis, 1990, pp. 13–15, 506–8; *CSPD 1641–43*, p. 66; H. Horwitz (ed.) *The Parliamentary Diary of Narcissus Luttrell, 1691–1693* (Oxford, 1972) p. 353.
14. Cliffe, *Yorkshire*, pp. 5ff; Carpenter, *Locality and Polity*, p. 90; Hughes, *Warwickshire*, p. 27; C.G.A. Clay, *Economic Expansion and Social Change: England 1500–1700*, 2 vols (Cambridge, 1984) i, p. 158, citing research undertaken by M.A. Havinden; Blackwood, *Lancashire*, pp. 4–10; J. Bedells, 'The Gentry of Huntingdonshire', *Local Population Studies*, 44 (1990), pp. 35–6; in the short term the crisis of the Civil War certainly influenced numbers: for example, the gentry of Cumberland and Westmorland declined from 180 to 169 between 1642 and 1665: C.B. Phillips, 'The Gentry of Cumberland and Westmorland, 1600–1665', Univ. of Lancaster, PhD thesis, 1973, p. 10.
15. Thirsk and Cooper, *Economic Documents*, pp. 755, 766–8; Cooper, *Land, Men and Beliefs*, pp. 20–42.
16. Cooper, *Land, Men and Beliefs*, pp. 18–19; Mingay, *The Gentry*, pp. 14–15; Clay, *Economic Expansion and Social Change*, i, p. 143; A. Everitt, *Change in the Provinces: the Seventeenth Century* (Leicester, 1969) pp. 18–19.
17. L. Stone and J. Stone, *An Open Elite? England 1540–1840* (Oxford, 1984) p. 462; Jenkins, *Glamorgan*, pp. 21–2; MacCulloch, *Suffolk*, pp. 25–6; Hoskins estimated that in the 1520s only one in every six or seven Leicestershire villages had a resident squire: W.G. Hoskins, *Essays in Leicestershire History* (Liverpool, 1950) p. 127; Palliser, *Age of Elizabeth*, p. 72; for explorations of the consequences for popular politics see MacCulloch, *Suffolk*, pp. 295–7; D. Underdown, *Revel, Riot and Rebellion* (Oxford, 1985).

18. J. Cornwall, *Wealth and Society in Early Sixteenth Century England* (1988) pp. 21, 145–6; Cooper, *Land, Men and Beliefs*, p. 20; Cliffe, *Yorkshire*, pp. 27–9; Everitt, *Change in the Provinces*, p. 55; Stone, *Crisis*, p. 762.
19. G. Jones, *The Gentry and the Elizabethan State* (Llandybie, Dyfed, 1984) p. 32; T. Birch (ed.) *A Collection of the State Papers of John Thurloe*, 7 vols (1742) iv, p. 316; Fiennes, *The Illustrated Journeys*, p. 128; Wanklyn, 'Landed Society and Allegiance', pp. 132–3; Clay, *Economic Expansion and Social Change*, i, pp. 157–8.
20. Phillips, 'The Gentry of Cumberland and Westmorland', p. 24; Jenkins, *Glamorgan*, pp. 32–5; Wanklyn, 'Landed Society and Allegiance', pp. 72ff.
21. See for example M. L. Bush, *The English Aristocracy: a Comparative Synthesis* (Manchester, 1984) pp. 2–4; Smith, *De Republica Anglorum*, p. 66; Holles, p. 41; F. Heal, *Hospitality in Early Modern England* (Oxford, 1990) pp. 61, 92.
22. Smith, *De Republica Anglorum*, p. 73; Morrill, 'The Northern Gentry', p. 72.
23. William Shakespeare, *The Winter's Tale*, Act 5, sc.2; Richard Brathwait, *The English Gentleman* (1630) and *The English Gentlewoman* (1631).

## Chapter 1 Lineage

1. The quotations from Oglander are from *Royalist's Notebook*, pp. 3, 106, 109, 110, 163, 212, 250–1, and IOW RO, OG\AA\16 – no pagination, *sub* Boorman; Higford, pp. 584–5, 595.
2. We owe the general figures on inheritance, based on analysis of the Inquisitions Post Mortem, to a seminar paper by Dr Simon Payling; the baronetcy calculations are our own. The Nottinghamshire information is from S. Payling, *Political Society in Lancastrian England* (Oxford, 1991) pp. 66–7; for Yorkshire, see Cliffe, *Yorkshire*, p. 16: for Glamorgan, see Jenkins, *Glamorgan*, pp. 38–41.
3. *VCH Berks.*, IV, pp. 457, 458; *RCHM Essex*, IV, p. 100; Holmes, *Lincolnshire*, pp. 66–7.
4. Holles, pp. 30, 34, 35; *Guise Memoirs*, pp. 108–9, 132–3.
5. Cliffe, *Yorkshire*, pp. 145, 156–7.
6. An analysis of most of the figures available in 1978 is provided by Blackwood, *Lancashire*, pp. 21–3; for Dorset, see J. P. Ferris, 'The Gentry of Dorset on the Eve of the Civil War', *Genealogists' Magazine*, 15 (1965–8) p. 104; for Leicestershire: D. Fleming, 'Faction in Civil War Leicestershire', *Leics. Arch. & Hist. Soc.: Trans*, 57 (1981–2) p. 31; for Warwickshire: Hughes, *Warwickshire*, pp. 28–9. The Lincolnshire figures are our own calculations.
7. General discussion relies on Stone, *Crisis*, pp. 65–71; P. J. Styles, 'The Heralds' Visitation of Warwickshire 1682–3' in his *Studies in Seventeenth Century West Midlands History* (Kineton, 1978) pp. 108–49; additional material from G. D. Squibb, *The High Court of Chivalry* (1959) pp. 80–3; A. R. Wagner, *Heralds and Heraldry in the Middle Ages* (Oxford,

1939) pp. 9, 79. For Harris, see G.W. Fisher, 'Sir Thomas Harris of Boreaton', *Trans. Shrops. Arch. & Nat. Hist. Soc.*, 2nd ser., 10 (1898) pp. 77–92; G.D. Squibb (ed.) *Reports of Heraldic Cases in the High Court of Chivalry 1623–1732* Harleian Soc., 107 (1956) pp. 1–5.

8. Thomas Smith, *De Republica Anglorum* ed. M. Dewar (Cambridge, 1982) pp. 70–3; and see the discussion of Smith in J.P. Cooper, 'Ideas of Gentility in Early-Modern England' in the volume of his essays, *Land, Men and Beliefs: Studies in Early-Modern History*, ed. G.E. Aylmer and J.S. Morrill (1983) pp. 62–70.
9. Erdeswick's comments are printed in William Dugdale, *The Antient Use of Bearing such ensign of Honour . . . call'd Arms* (Oxford, 1682) p. 32; John Ferne, *The Blazon of Gentrie, Comprehending Discourses of Armes and of Gentry* (1586) pp. 3, 10–11, 13–15, 47–9, 97, 99.
10. This discussion is very much influenced by Cooper, 'Ideas of Gentility', pp. 43–77.
11. Ferne, *Blazon*, pp. 12, 15, 19–20, 32–58; Francis Markham, *The Booke of Honour* (1625) pp. 11, 44, 47–49: for Shallow, see below, p. 169.
12. FSL, Z. e. 27, fo.1v; *Proc. of the Somers. Arch. & Nat. Hist. Soc.*, 38, part 2 (1892) pp. 59–71.
13. For the divines see: John Wilford, *Memorials . . . of Divers Eminent and Worthy Persons* (1741) pp. 520–1; Cliffe, *Puritan Gentry*, pp. 64–5, 128, 130; Thomas Froysell, *The Beloved Disciple* (1658) pp. 2–3; William Hinde, *A Faithfull Remonstrance of the Holy Life and Happy Death of John Bruen* (1641) pp. 2–3; M.C. Cross (ed.) *The Letters of Sir Francis Hastings, 1574–1609*, Somers. Rec. Soc., 69 (1969) p. xix; A.J. Jewers, 'Heraldry in the Manor House of North Cadbury', *Proc. of the Somers. Arch. & Nat. Hist. Soc.*, 36, part 2 (1890) pp. 136–67; H. Aveling (ed.) 'The Recusancy Papers of the Meynell Family of North Kilvington . . . 1596–1676', *Miscellanea*, Catholic Record Soc., 56 (1964) pp. 4, 9–13.
14. *D'Ewes*, i, p. 6; J.H. Round, *Family Origins* (1930) pp. 62–72; Sir John Wynn, *History of the Gwydir Family and Memoirs* ed. J.G. Jones (Llandysul, 1990) p. 35.
15. E.J. Payne, 'The Montforts, the Wellesbournes and the Hughenden Effigies', *Records of Buckinghamshire*, 7 (1896) pp. 362–402; *The Ancestor*, 3 (1902) pp. 14–35 [Lambert]; J.H. Round, *Peerage and Pedigree* 2 vols (1901) ii, pp. 134–213 [Smith/Carrington]; ibid., p. 91 [Staunton]; *The Genealogist*, 3 (1879) pp. 129–32 [Wodehouse]; Round, *Family Origins*, pp. 35–42 [Churchill]; Bod. L., Ashmole 850, p. 56; *The Genealogist*, 4 (1880) pp. 99–102.
16. In general, see Stone, *Crisis*, pp. 23–5. Details from D. MacCulloch (ed.) 'Henry Chitting's Suffolk Collections', *PSIA*, 34 (1977–80) pp. 105–6, 109–10, 117, 119; Bod. L., Ashmole 850, pp. 20–1, 63, 120–2, 137, 226; H. Norris, *Tamworth Castle* (1899) pp. 15–19, 26–7; A.R. Wagner, *The Records and Collections of the College of Arms* (1952) pp. 15–16; F. Jones, 'An Approach to Welsh Genealogy', *Trans. of the Honourable Soc. of Cymmrodorion* (1948) p. 312.
17. M. Maclagan, 'Genealogy and Heraldry in the Sixteenth and Seventeenth Centuries' in L. Fox (ed.) *English Historical Scholarship in the Sixteenth and Seventeenth Centuries* (1956) pp. 31–48: CUL, Hengrave

76/1: for Digby, see Round, *Peerage and Pedigree*, ii, pp. 39–42; for Temple, *Herald and Genealogist*, 3 (1866) p. 385. Round noted some of the Dering story in *Peerage and Pedigree*, ii, p. 112. For more on Dering's claim to Saxon ancestry see FSL, Z. e. 27; KAO, U350 F15: for his creative alterations in Pluckley Church, KAO, U 350 Q1/2, 4–6. For Phillpot, see *Sussex Arch. Coll.*, 69 (1928) pp. 53–70; 70 (1929) pp. 19–31.

18. *Guise Memoirs*, p. 107; Holles, pp. 11–12.
19. Styles, 'Heralds' Visitation of Warwickshire', *passim*: quotation from pp. 110, 138, 145.
20. 'The Family of the First Countess of Coventry' in *Herald and Genealogist*, 7 (1873) pp. 97–115: E. Mercer, *English Art, 1553–1625* (Oxford, 1962) pp. 217–52; K. A. Esdaile, *English Church Monuments, 1510–1840* (1946), particularly pp. 55–56, 75–76; S. A. Jeavons, 'The Church Monuments of Derbyshire: the Sixteenth and the Seventeenth Centuries', *Derbys. Arch.* J., 84 (1964) pp. 52–80, esp. p. 58.
21. Sylvanus Morgan, *The Sphaere of Gentry* (1661) p. 101; Edward Waterhouse, *The Gentleman's Monitor* (1665) pp. 28–31, 70–2, 115, 118–25, 170, 175, 452; and see A. Sharp, 'Edward Waterhouse's View of Social Change in Seventeenth-Century England', *PP*, 62 (1974) pp. 27–46.
22. Holles, p. 12; Squibb (ed.) *Reports of Heraldic Cases*, p. 103; Styles, 'Heralds' Visitation', p. 146; C. E. Welch, 'The Turnour Chapel at Little Wratting', *PSIA*, 27 (1958) pp. 37–40; *Canons Ashby*, National Trust guide (1986) p. 45.
23. William Lambarde, *A Perambulation of Kent* (1596) pp. 12–14; Thomas Habington, *A Survey of Worcestershire* ed. J. Amphlett, 2 vols (Oxford, 1895) i, pp. 34, 305, 395; ii, p. 188; Robert Atkins, *The Ancient and Present State of Gloucestershire* (1712) p. 21; Sampson Erdeswick, *A Survey of Staffordshire* (1717) appendix, p. 1; *Harleian Society*, 19 (1884) pp. 206–08.
24. Waterhouse, *Gentleman's Monitor*, p. 452; Sharp, 'Waterhouse's View of Social Change' *passim*: Dr Sharp sees the theme of mutability as a commonplace which is merely 'revivified' by the Civil War (p. 38); we would argue that the Civil War had a transforming effect, obliging the gentry to incorporate a recognition that, while troubling, had not previously been permitted to disturb the symmetry of their conceptual framework.
25. The literature on estate settlement, both in its legal and its social aspects, in the early modern period is voluminous. An excellent introduction is provided by Stone, *Family*, pp. 156–7, 242–4; see also the very suggestive discussions by L. Bonfield, 'Marriage, Property and the "Affective Family"', *Law & History Review* 1 (1983) pp. 297–312, and by J. P. Cooper, 'Patterns of Inheritance and Settlement by Great Landowners from the Fifteenth to the Eighteenth Century' in J. Goody, J. Thirsk and E. P. Thompson (eds) *Family and Inheritance* (Cambridge, 1976) pp. 192–327.
26. LAO, Monson 7/14/157, 159, 160; Altham MS 1 fos. 70–9; PROB, 93 Huddleston.
27. NLW, MS 9080E, fo. 51.

28. *Guise Memoirs*, pp. 108–109; John Smyth, *The Berkeley Manuscripts* ed. Sir J. Maclean 3 vols (Gloucester, 1885) iii, p. 166; HLMP Box 179/17.
29. This incident is discussed in the family history written by Sir Edward Rodney in 1655, and published in *The Genealogist*, 16 (1899–1900) pp. 207–14; 17 (1900–1) pp. 6–12, 100–106.
30. IOW RO, OG/SS/1, fos 30–3.
31. L. Bonfield, *Marriage Settlements, 1601–1740* (Cambridge, 1983) p. 122; SBT, DR 37/87 unfol., John Ferrers to Thomas Archer, 14 Feb. 1679–80.

**Chapter 2 The Family**

1. Bod. L., Eng. Hist c.287, fos 129–34v; *HMC Portland*, ix, pp. 124–6: this latter conflict is principally about jointure and access to lands which Lady Stanhope claimed had been secured to her by her husband; Sir Clement Markham, *Markham Memorials*, 2 vols (1913) i, p. 131.
2. Cholmley, pp. 3, 82–92; m. i. to Sir Hugh, East Peckham Church, Kent.
3. BL, Add. 37719, fo.167; B.G. Charles, *George Owen of Henllys* (Aberystwyth, 1973) pp.28–9, 45; in the Rodney family the crisis was that of a failure of surviving male heirs out of 13 children, though 6 daughters lived: Sir Edward Rodney, 'The Genealogy of the Family of Rodney of Rodney Stoke', *The Genealogist*, 17 (1900–1) p. 104. Training within the family is considered below in Ch. 7.
4. H.E. Lippincott (ed.) *Merry Passages and Jeasts: a MS. Jestbook of Sir Nicholas Le Strange (1603–55)* (Salzburg, 1974) p. 21.
5. *Lowther Family*, p. 200; A.T. Friedman, *House and Household in Elizabethan England: Wollaton Hall and the Willoughby Family* (Chicago, 1989); NLW, MS. 9080E; Sir John Strode to his son, IOW RO, OG/SS/1, fo. 86; Stone, *Crisis*, pp. 661–2, estimates that about 10% of all peerage marriages between 1570 and 1659 ended in estrangement or full separation.
6. *Oxinden Letters*, i, p. 219; *Royalist's Notebook*, p. 5. There is a vast literature on the structure and ideology of the English family. The opposing positions on ideology and 'affect' are most clearly expressed in Stone, *Family*; R.A. Houlbrooke, *The English Family, 1450–1700* (1984); A. MacFarlane, *Marriage and Love in England, 1300–1840* (Oxford, 1986); for a persuasive argument in favour of continuity in the advice literature see K.M. Davies, 'Continuity and Change in Literary Advice on Marriage' in R. Outhwaite (ed.) *Marriage and Society: Studies in the Social History of Marriage* (London, 1981) pp. 58–80.
7. On funeral memorials in general see K.A. Esdaile, *English Church Monuments, 1510 to 1840* (1946); N. Llewelyn, *The Art of Death* (1991) pp. 101–27. Stone suggests that the careful recording of children is a feature of the early seventeenth century: it was certainly most common then, but examples are available in some quantity from the early sixteenth century onwards; Stone, *Crisis*, p. 593. For an interesting discussion of the role of children on tombs see E. Mercer, *English Art, 1553–1625* (Oxford, 1962) pp. 226–39; their relatively early appearance on brasses is discussed in J. Page-Phillips, *Children on Brasses* (1970)

pp. 15–17; T. Fuller, *The History of the Worthies of England*, 2 vols (1811) i, p. 282.

8. On the importance of familial identity expressed on tombs see J. Wilson, 'Icons of Unity', *History Today*, June 1993, pp. 14–20; Stone, *Family*, pp. 411–12; Page-Phillips, *Children on Brasses*, figs. 53–5 illustrates brasses with family scenes in a very similar *memento mori* convention.
9. L. Pollock (ed.) *With Faith and Physic: The Life of a Tudor Gentlewoman* (1993) p. 47; NRO, IC 353; *Lowther Family*, p. 41; *Wandesford*, p. 51.
10. M. Slater, 'The Weightiest Business: Marriage in an Upper-Gentry Family in Seventeenth-Century England', *PP*, 72 (1976) pp. 25–54. There are good general accounts of the formation of marriages, though with very different interpretive biases, in Stone, *Family*, and Houlbrooke, *English Family*; on maternal roles and on kin networks see R. Priestley, 'Marriage and Family Life in the Seventeenth Century', Univ. of Sydney, PhD thesis, 1988, pp. 48–51, 64–71; on ideology and marriage see Cliffe, *Puritan Gentry*, pp. 63–7.
11. MacCulloch, *Suffolk*, pp. 420–1.
12. NRO, IC 1391; IOW RO, OG/CC/22; F. Peck, *Desiderata Curiosa*, 2 vols (1732) i, p. 65; C. Aspinall-Oglander, *A Nunwell Symphony* (1945) p. 48; see also John Strode's advice, IOW RO, OG/SS/1; Bod. L., Rawl. D 859, fo. 1.
13. KAO, U275/A3; U350, C2/43; *Royalist's Notebook*, p. 87; NRA, Firle Place MSS, Box 21; DRO, D124/Box 233.
14. BL, Add. 70,001, fos 57, 59, 62, 66, 69; J. Eales, *Puritans and Roundheads: The Harleys of Brampton Bryan and the Outbreak of the English Civil War* (Cambridge, 1990) pp. 20–2.
15. CRO, DD CY/7042–3; FSL, L. a. 68; *Lowther Family*, pp. 40, 122–3; Bod. L., Rawl. C 929, unfol; PROB, 11/26 Porch; L. Campbell, 'Sir Roger Townshend and His Family: a Study in Gentry Life in Early Seventeenth Century Norfolk', Univ. of East Anglia, PhD thesis, 1990, pp. 134–45; Holles, p. 194; E. A. Parry (ed.) *The Letters from Dorothy Osborne to Sir William Temple* (1914) p. 35.
16. NLW, Wynn, nos. 68, 72–3, 90, 152.
17. NLW, Wynn, nos. 685, 702; Lord Mostyn and T. A. Glenn, *History of the Family of Mostyn of Mostyn* (1925) pp. 103–4.
18. NLW, Wynn, nos. 187, 266–7, 284, 288, 290, 312, 317–18, 326, 332–5, 361, 429.
19. NLW, Wynn, nos. 686, 694, 699, 701, 765–70, 776, 786, 792, 841.
20. NLW, Wynn, nos. 830, 834, 1072, 1377–9, 1532.
21. NLW, Wynn, nos. 2718, 2748, 2752–4, 2779, 2763, 2766, 2771, 2773–4, 2780, 2782.
22. Friedman, *House and Household*, pp. 54–9; J. Wake, *The Brudenells of Deene* (1954) pp. 68–71.
23. NRA, Gage MSS, Box 21; *Lowther Family*, p. 155; KAO, U1713, A/1; H. H. E. Craster (ed.) *A History of Northumberland*, 10 vols (1909) ix, p. 158; SRO, D1057/O/1, fo. 57; M. F. Bond (ed.) *The Diaries and Papers of Sir Edward Dering, 2nd Bt., 1644–84*, House of Lords Record Office occ. pub., 1 (1976) p. 110: this shows Dering living with his mother-in-law

for four years; NLW, Wynn, nos. 415, 419, 429, 1188; A. H. Smith, G. M. Baker and R. W. Kenny (eds) *The Papers of Nathaniel Bacon of Stiffkey: vol 1, 1556–1577*, Norfolk Rec. Soc., 46 (1978–9) pp. 8–10; Friedman, *House and Household*, p. 56; *Thornton*, pp. 75ff; V. Larminie, *Wealth, Kinship and Culture: the Newdigates of Arbury, c.1585–c.1685*, (forthcoming) Ch. 1.

24. Cholmley, pp. 39, 93; KAO, U275A3, pp. 12–14; Campbell, 'Sir Roger Townshend', pp. 141–3; FSL, L. a. 21; A. Fairfax-Lucy, *Charlecote and the Lucys* (1958) pp. 87–9; SRO, D1057/O/1, fos 69ff.
25. Houlbrooke, *English Family*, p. 104; *Clenennau Letters*, p. 64; KAO, U350, C2/26; CRO, R(S), 1/40; NLW, Wynn, no.864.
26. Holles, pp. 230, 233–4; A. Clifford (ed.) *The Tixall Letters*, 2 vols (1815) i, pp. 190, 196.
27. On the use of gender roles in successful marriages see A. Wall, 'Elizabethan Precept and Feminine Practice', *History*, 75 (1990) pp. 23–38, where the ability of women to adapt their roles to suit their own purposes is stressed; M. Slater, *Family Life in the Seventeenth Century* (1984) pp. 64–72, which emphasises, but also exaggerates, the gender inequalities in the Verney relationship; see also *Verney Memoirs*, i, pp. 346–69.
28. PRO, STAC 8/297/12; NLW, MS 9080E; NLW, Wynn, no. 45A; L. Stone, *Road to Divorce: England 1530–1987* (Oxford, 1990) pp. 183ff; B. Hale Wortham 'An Ancestral Scandal', *The Ancestor*, 5 (1903) pp. 73–80; V. Salmon, 'The Other Elizabeth Drury: a Tragic Marriage in the Family of John Donne's Patron', *PSIA*, 29 (1962–4) p. 204; R. Gough, *The History of Myddle* ed. D. Hey (1981) p. 159; on the other hand much comment on wifely adultery appears to pander to age-old male sexual anxieties: see for example the apparent determination of all Thomas Whythorne's gentlewomen employers to seduce him, while he merely wished to make music, J. A. Osborn (ed.) *The Autobiography of Thomas Whythorne* (1962).
29. Cholmley, p. 10; J. M. J. Tonks, 'The Lyttletons of Frankley and their Estates, 1540–1640' Univ. of Oxford, B. Litt. thesis, 1978, pp. 47ff; BL, Add. 23,212, fos 3ff; Bod. L., Rawl. D 859, fos 3–4; NLW, MS 9080E, fo. 51.
30. See above pp. 48–9; FSL, L. a. 21; PRO, STAC 8/138/18; BL, Eg. 2715, fo. 55; Friedman, *House and Household*, p. 61.
31. Mostyn, *History of the Mostyn Family*, p. 107; *HMC Salisbury*, v, p. 480; Campbell, 'Sir Roger Townshend' p. 128.
32. J. Harvey Bloom, *The Griffins of Dingley* (1921) p. 22; BL, Add. 23,212; CRO, R(S) 1/62; on the finance of marriage see below pp. 141–3.
33. YAS, MS 178, p. 5; *Wandesford*, p. 91; *Royalist Notebook*, p. 241.
34. On wet-nursing see Houlbrooke, *English Family*, pp. 132–4; Stone, *Family*, p. 428; D. McLaren 'Marital Fertility and Lactation, 1570–1720' in M. Prior (ed.) *Women in English Society 1500–1800* (Oxford, 1984) pp. 22–53; Larminie, *The Newdigates*, Ch. 6; L. Hutchinson, *Memoirs of the Life of Colonel Hutchinson*, ed. J. Sutherland (Oxford, 1973) pp. 287, 289; *Thornton*, pp. 142, 186; Campbell, 'Sir Roger Townshend', p. 171; *CSPD Eliz. 1601–3*, p. 283; B. Anderton (ed.) 'Selections from the

Delaval Papers', *Public. of the Newcastle upon Tyne Rec. Comm.*, Misc. 9 (1929) pp. 161–2.

35. Larminie, *The Newdigates*, Ch. 6; Stone, *Family*, pp. 105–9; *Thornton*, pp. 124–7, 150–1; funeral sermons were preached for two of the Thornton children who died in infancy; Altham MS. 1, fo. 11; E. K. Bennet, 'Notes from a Norfolk Squire's Note-Book', *Camb. Antiq. Soc.* 43 (1883) p. 207; E. Cust, *Records of the Cust Family . . . the Brownlows of Belton* (1909) pp. 120–3; see for example Holles's lament for his two-year-old heir: Holles, p. 235; Slater, *Family Life*, p. 121.
36. Stone, *Family*, pp. 105–16; *D'Ewes*, i, pp. 27ff; Sir John Bramston's grandmother, Mary Hill, was one of those who acquired charges in this way: P. Braybrooke (ed.) *The Autobiography of Sir John Bramston*, Camden Soc., old ser., 32 (1845) pp. 13–14; C. E. Whiting, 'Sir Patience Ward of Tanshelf', *YAJ*, 34 (1939) p. 245; M. Blundell (ed.) *Cavalier: Letters of William Blundell to his Friends* (1933) p. 44; NUL, Clifton c.48; Slater, *Family Life*, p. 121; Llewelyn, *The Art of Death*, pp. 28–30; Page-Phillips, *Children on Brasses*, p. 17.
37. See below, Ch. 7, for the figures on education.
38. *Verney Memoirs*, i, p. 78; NRO, IC 3951; IOW RO, OG/AA/27, fo. 78v; *Royalist's Notebook*, pp. 82–3.
39. YAS, DD56 M2 bundle 1589–1634, unfol.; SomsRO, DD/PH/224/1, 3–6, 228/13–14, 18, 229/1; BL, Add. 29,599, fos 38–39v; YAS, DD56 M1/6; BL, Add. 11,044, fo. 237.
40. FSL, L. a. 240, 1006; *Lowther Family*, pp. 181–2; NLW, Wynn, nos. 820–2.
41. *The Genealogist*, 11 (1894–5) pp. 65–7; SomsRO, DD/PH/224/45; HLMP, Parchment Box, 12 May 1641; PRO, STAC 8/228/12; HLMP Box 179/17.
42. H. A. Wyndham, *A Family History, 1410–1688* (Oxford, 1939) pp. 278–9; Hutchinson, *Life of Colonel Hutchinson*, pp. 24–5; KAO, U1107 C21, U133 C1/2, U350 C2/103; Edward Dering, *Autobiography*, p. 10 in Bond, *Diaries*, p. 108; Priestley, 'Marriage and Family Life', pp. 358–65.
43. NRO, Montagu 3, fos 153–5; LAO, Monson 7/13, no.31; T. T. Lewis (ed.) *The Letters of the Lady Brilliana Harley*, Camden Soc., old ser., 58 (1854) pp. 16–17, 22–3, 27; J. Bettey (ed.) *Calendar of the Correspondence of the Smyth Family of Ashton Court*, Bristol Rec. Soc., 35 (1982), pp. 67–79; Campbell, 'Sir Roger Townshend', pp. 148, 187.
44. NLW, Wynn, no.1188; WRO, CR 1998, Strongroom Box 60, folder 1, no.6; SBT, DR37/Box 88, unfol.; SomsRO, DD/PH/229/16A; Campbell, 'Sir Roger Townshend', p. 227.
45. Tonks, 'The Lyttletons of Frankley', p. 119; NRA, Kingsmill MSS nos.1371, 1376, 1379; SomsRO, DD/PH/224/97, 229/11, 229/13; NLW, Wynn, nos. 1550, 1554, 1573–4: at one point in the dispute Ann Bulkeley likened her son to Nero; N. Johnson, 'History of the Family of Foljambe' (1701) in *Collectanea Topographica and Genealogica*, 2 (1835) pp. 79–80; Cassandra, Duchess of Chandos, *The Continuation of the History of the Willoughby Family*, ed. A. C. Wood (Eton, 1958) pp. 112–3, 120–4; T. H. Hollingsworth, 'The Demography of the British Peerage', *Population Studies*, supplement 18 (1964) p. 22; *Reresby*, p. 2.

46. For the traditional view that younger sons were 'angry young men' see J. Thirsk, 'Younger Sons in the Seventeenth Century', *History*, 54 (1969) pp. 358–77; this is questioned by L. Pollock, 'Younger Sons in Tudor and Stuart England', *History Today* (June, 1989) pp. 23–9; F. J. Fisher (ed.) *The State of England anno dom. 1600, by Thomas Wilson*, Camden Soc., 3rd ser., 52 (1936), p. 24; NLW, Wynn, no. 1188; PROB 11/1 Welles; SRO, D1057/0/1, A & B; BL, Add. 33,572, fos 22ff.
47. D. R. Hainsworth, 'The Lowther Younger Sons, a Seventeenth Century Case Study', *Trans. of the Cumb. and Westmor. Arch. Soc.* (1988) pp. 149–60; Pollock, 'Younger Sons', pp. 25–9; I. H. Jeayes (ed.) *The Letters of Philip Gawdy* (Roxburghe Club, 1906) pp. 78, 82, 104–5, 131, 156; Larminie, *The Newdigates*, Ch. 4.
48. SomsRO, DD/PH/224/37; NLW, Wynn, nos. 865, 878, 923, 997, 1132, 1419; Cassandra, Duchess of Chandos, *History of the Willoughby Family*, pp. 36–52.
49. NLW, Wynn, no.963; Altham MS., 2, fos. 122, 128; YAS, MD 237/6; CRO, R(S) 1/24; E. Cope, *The Life of a Public Man*, Proc. of the American Phil. Soc., 142 (1981) p. 70.
50. Houlbrooke, *English Family*, pp. 186–8; Bod. L., Rawl. D. 859, fo. 12; NLW, Wynn, no. 497; Friedman, *House and Household*, pp. 67, 136–7; Campbell, 'Sir Roger Townshend', p. 132; SRO, D1057/O/1 A, fos 73, 78, 84.
51. UCW Bangor, Mostyn, 9068, no. 29, also nos. 45, 48–50; YAS, DD56 M2, unfol.; *Oxinden Letters*, ii, p. 113; Holles, p. 118; NRO, IC 184, 186–8, 199–200; M. E. Finch, *Five Northamptonshire Families, 1540–1640*, Northants. Rec. Soc., 19 (1956) p. 34; Priestley, 'Marriage and Family Life', pp. 51–5.
52. J. Nicholas (ed.) *The Memoirs of Lady Fanshawe* (1829), p. 35; *Thornton*, pp. 103–4; IOW RO, OG/CC/63, 66; PROB, 38 Noodes; m.i. in Stoke Mandeville Church, Buckinghamshire.
53. Bod. L., Rawl. D 859, fo. 72; cf. Carew's famous remark on all Cornish gentlemen as cousins: R. Carew, *Survey of Cornwall* (1602) fo. 64v. Houlbrooke points out that in areas of partible inheritance, like the Celtic fringe and Kent, cousinage networks arose from the ability to construct an unusually large number of cadet branches of gentry houses: Houlbrooke, *English Family*, p. 51.
54. Holles, pp. 34–5; BL, Add. 29,599, fos 45, 47; for examples of tabling see the early sixteenth-century Le Strange accounts, *Archaeologia*, 25 (1834) pp. 481ff; SRO, D1057/0/1, fo. 50; *Wentworth*, p. 13; Bod. L., Rawl. C. 929, unfol; *The Memorandum Book of Richard Cholmeley of Brandsby, 1602–23*, North Yorks. County Record Office Public., no. 44 (1988) pp. 41, 45, 47; for a valuable discussion of the uses of kinship see Houlbrooke, *English Family*, pp. 45–50.
55. Larminie, *The Newdigates*, Ch. 9; BL, Eg. 2715, fos 96, 101, 114; BL, Add. 34,169; *Lowther Family*, p. 62; Campbell, 'Sir Roger Townshend', p. 153; on children listed with godparents see DRO, MW/M4, fo. 1 [Sir John Strode], Bennet 'Notes from a Norfolk Squire's Notebook', pp. 206–7; BL, Add. 34,169, fo. 32; *Verney Memoirs*, i, p. 355; on the issue of

godparents during the Commonwealth see C. Durston, *The Family in the English Revolution* (Oxford, 1989) pp. 116–20.

56. Durston, *The Family in the English Revolution*, is an example of an approach deeply opposed to the *longue durée*. He argues that the family can be studied effectively during a brief period of upheaval, in this case the Civil War and Interregnum, but the argument is not wholly convincing.
57. M. MacDonald, *Mystical Bedlam: Madness, Anxiety and Healing in Seventeenth Century England* (Cambridge, 1981) pp. 88–9; for an interesting discussion of the family and performance see B. Gottlieb, *The Family in the Western World from the Black Death to the Industrial Age* (New York, 1993) pp. 259–67.

**Chapter 3 Wealth: Income**

1. *Barrington Letters*, pp. 20, 42, 56, 84, 90, 98, 113, 114, 120, 144, 206, 256; HLMP, 1640, 30 Nov., petition of Eusebius Andrewes; G. D. Squibb, *The High Court of Chivalry* (1959) p. 59.
2. F. W. Steer (ed.) *A Catalogue of the Earl Marshal's Papers at Arundel Castle*, Harleian Soc., 115, 116 (1964) p. 13; Higford, p. 585; Holmes, *Lincolnshire*, p. 68.
3. *Guise Memoirs*, pp. 108–9; Cliffe, *Yorkshire*, p. 119; *Collectanea Topographica & Genealogica*, 2 (1835) pp. 80–1 [Foljambe]; Holmes, *Lincolnshire*, p. 71 [Ayscough]; R. Meredith, 'The Eyres of Hassop, 1470–1640', *Derbys. Arch. J.*, 85 (1965) pp. 69–78: E. P. Shirley, *Stemmata Shirleiana* (Westminster, 1873) pp. 63–4; Thomas Habington, *A Survey of Worcestershire* ed. J. Amphlett 2 vols (Oxford, 1895) i, p. 49; ii, pp. 28–9.
4. The statistical information on prices is from *AHEW*, 4, pp. 862, 865; 5 sect. 2, pp. 856, 879.
5. Cliffe, *Yorkshire*, pp. 33, 125; BL, Eg. 2713, fos 40, 45; W. Knowler (ed.) *The Earl of Strafforde's Letters and Speeches* 2 vols (1739) i, p. 169; A. Simpson, *The Wealth of the Gentry* (Cambridge, 1961) pp. 12–14, 59, 73.
6. Higford, pp. 585–6, 587, 589–90; *Lowther Family*, p. 27.
7. Holles, pp. 214–24.
8. Samuel Hartlib, *The Compleat Husbandman* (1659) p. 2. Prices are from *AHEW*, 4, pp. 862, 865; 5 sect.2, pp. 856, 879; population figures are from E. A. Wrigley and R. S. Schofield, *The Population History of England* (1981) pp. 208–209.
9. *Glamorgan County History*, IV, p. 104; *Wentworth*, pp. 18–19.
10. FSL, V. a. 180 [Mildmay]; Bod. L., Rawl. C 929, fo. 30v [Cornwallis]; IOW RO, OG/SS/1 fo. 88v; *Wandesford*, p. 91.
11. L. Stone (ed.) 'Sir Edward Montagu's Directions to his Son', *Northamptonshire Past and Present* (1958) pp. 221–3; Cliffe, *Yorkshire*, p. 46 [Tempest]; Higford, pp. 589, 590. For Sanderson, see *DNB* and Holmes, *Lincolnshire*, pp. 23–7, 52, 61–3, 72–3. The quotations are from W. Jacobson (ed.) *The Works of Robert Sanderson D.D.*, 6 vols (Oxford, 1854) ii, pp. 204, 314, 344; iii, p. 84.

12. PRO, STAC 8/10/4.
13. Simpson, *Wealth of the Gentry*, Ch. 2, especially pp. 78–9; J. M. J. Tonks,'The Lyttletons of Frankley and their Estates, 1540–1640', Univ. of Oxford, B. Litt. thesis, 1978, pp. 14–37.
14. M. E. Finch, *Five Northamptonshire Families, 1540–1640,* Northants. Rec. Soc., 19 (1956) pp. 67–72.
15. P. Rutledge, 'Sir Thomas Knyvett and his Norfolk Manors, 1577–1591', *Norfolk Archaeology* 32 (1961) pp. 343–52; Tonks, 'Lyttletons of Frankley', pp. 14–37.
16. Finch, *Northamptonshire Families,* pp. 67–76.
17. For a general introduction to the problems associated with copyhold tenure, see E. Kerridge, *Agrarian Problems in the Sixteenth Century and After* (1969) chaps 1–3; R. W. Hoyle, 'Tenure and the Land Market in Early Modern England', *EcHR,* 2nd ser., 43 (1990) pp. 1–20. For Cotton, R. B. Manning, 'Antiquarianism and the Seigneurial Reaction: Sir Robert and Sir Thomas Cotton and their Tenants', *BIHR* 63 (1990) pp. 277–88.
18. R. B. Manning, *Village Revolts: Social Protest and Popular Disturbances in England, 1509–1640* (Oxford, 1988) p. 265 [Condover]; H. A. Lloyd, *The Gentry of South-West Wales* (Cardiff, 1968) p. 67 [Walwyn's Castle]; W. G. Hoskins, *The Midland Peasant* (1957) pp. 104–9 [Wigston]; P. Large, 'Rural Society and Agricultural Change: Ombersley 1580–1700', p. 114, in J. Chartres and D. Hey (eds) *English Rural Society, 1500–1800: Essays in Honour of Joan Thirsk* (Cambridge, 1990); A. B. Appleby, 'Agrarian Capitalism or Seigneurial Reaction? the North-West of England, 1500–1700', *AHR,* 80 (1975) p. 584 [Loweswater].
19. Hoyle, 'Tenure and the Land Market', pp. 12–17: examples are from Hoyle, except those of Wigston Magna: Hoskins, *Midland Peasant* p. 104; Chippenham: M. Spufford, *Contrasting Communities: English Villagers in the Sixteenth and Seventeenth Centuries* (Cambridge, 1974) pp. 75–8; Claydon: J. Broad, 'The Verneys as Enclosing Landlords', pp. 30–31, in Chartres and Hey, *English Rural Society*; and Aynho: N. Cooper, *Aynho: a Northamptonshire Village,* Banbury Hist. Soc., 20 (1984) pp. 41–2, 61; for the northern Royalists, see C. B. Phillips, 'Landlord–Tenant Relationships, 1642–1660', in R. C. Richardson (ed.) *Town and Countryside in the English Revolution* (Manchester, 1992) pp. 242–5.
20. Finch, *Northamptonshire Families,* pp. 6–20, 39–48.
21. For Weston, see *DNB*; *AHEW,* 5 sect. 2, pp. 541, 545–6; A. R. Michell, 'Sir Richard Weston and the Spread of Clover Cultivation', *AgHR,* 22 (1974) pp. 160–1. For Lawrence, J. H. Bettey, 'The Development of Water Meadows in Dorset during the seventeenth century', ibid., 25 (1977) pp. 37–43; for Vaughan, M. Delorme, 'A Watery Paradise: Rowland Vaughan and Hereford's Golden Vale', *History Today,* July 1989, pp. 38–43; for cider, M. Stubbs, 'John Beale, Philosophical Gardener of Herefordshire', *Annals of Science* 39 (1982) pp. 466–7, 475, 479; J. Thirsk, 'The Fashioning of the Tudor–Stuart Gentry', *Bulletin of the John Rylands Lib.,* 72 (1990) p. 82; for Dymoke, *AHEW,* 5 sect. 2, pp. 547–8, 552–3; J. Thirsk, 'Plough and Pen: Agricultural Writers in the Seventeenth Century', in T. H. Aston *et al.* (eds) *Social*

*Relations and Ideas* (Cambridge, 1983) pp. 301–5: V. Larminie, *Wealth, Kinship and Culture: the Newdigates of Arbury, c.1585–c.1685*, (forthcoming), Ch. 1; B. A. Holderness, 'The Agricultural Activities of the Massingberds of South Ormsby . . . 1638-*c*.1750', *Midland History*, 1 (1971–2) no. 3 pp. 15–22.

22. Thirsk, 'Fashioning of the Tudor–Stuart Gentry', pp. 79–80; Kerridge, *Agrarian Problems*, pp. 103–8; Hoyle, 'Tenure and the Land Market', p. 13 [Gretton]; D. R. Mills, 'Enclosure in Kesteven', *AgHR*, 7 (1959) p. 86 [Swinderby]; J. Thirsk and J. P. Cooper (eds) *Seventeenth Century Economic Documents* (Oxford, 1972) p. 149 [Ashby Magna]; A. Gooder, *Plague and Enclosure: a Warwickshire Village in the Seventeenth Century* (Coventry, 1965) p. 18 [Clifton].
23. Manning, *Village Revolts*, Ch. 5 and pp. 237–4; Kerridge, *Agrarian Problems*, p. 100; Lloyd, *Gentry of South-West Wales*, p. 70 n.1; LAO, Cragg 2/8 fo. 69; 5/1 nos. 196, 197; LAO, Court Papers 62/2/19; PRO, STAC 8/217/4; 279/8.
24. PRO, STAC 8/10/12: for a similar pattern at Cotesbach see L. A. Parker, 'The Agrarian Revolution at Cotesbach 1501–1612', *Trans. Leics. Arch. Assoc.*, 24 (1948) pp. 41–76.
25. Simpson, *Wealth of the Gentry*, pp. 179–216; W. H. Hosford, 'An Eye-Witness Account of a Seventeenth-Century Enclosure', *EcHR*, 2nd ser., 4 (1951–2) pp. 215–20; IOW RO, OG/TT/31 sub Nov. 1635.
26. J. W. F. Hill (ed.) 'Sir George Heneage's Estate Book, 1625', *Lincs. Architectural and Arch. Soc.: Reports and Papers*, 1 (1938–9) pp. 41, 57–9, 73–4, 202, 215–16; NLW, Wynn, nos. 597, 713–18, 823; LAO, Cragg 2/8; PRO, STAC 8/279/8.
27. Finch, *Northamptonshire Families*, pp. 14–17; Manning, *Village Revolts*, p. 265: see also the activities of the London financier, John Quarles, at Cotesbach – Parker, 'Agrarian Revolution', pp. 60–76.
28. Large, 'Rural Society and Agricultural Change', pp. 114–20; for Samuel Sandys: Spufford, *Contrasting Communities*, pp. 121–7; C. Holmes, 'Drainers and Fenmen' in A. Fletcher and J. Stevenson (eds) *Order and Disorder in Early Modern England* (Cambridge, 1985), pp. 182, 193, for Sir Miles.
29. W. A. Leighton (ed.) 'Early Chronicles of Shrewsbury', *Trans. Shropshire Arch. Soc.*, 1st ser., 3 (1880) p. 259; Habington, *Worcestershire*, i, pp. 378–88; ii, p. 256; MacCulloch, *Suffolk*, pp. 311–12.
30. M. Burrows, *The Family of Brocas of Beaurepaire* (1886) pp. 208–23; PRO, STAC 8/8/11, 10/20, 82/3 [Brocas]: PRO, STAC 8/181/17; LAO, Monson 10/1/10, 22, 28 [Dallison]; Holles, p 162; *The Memorandum Book of Richard Cholmeley of Brandsby*, North Yorks. County RO Publication, no. 44 (1988) pp. ix, 46.
31. SBT, DR 37/87 unfol., letters from William Fetherton to Andrew Archer; Thirsk and Cooper (eds) *Economic Documents*, p. 24. In general, see P. J. Bowden, 'Fluctuations and Trends in the Agrarian Economy', *AHEW*, 4, pp. 617–49.
32. C. Clay, 'Landlords and Estate Management', pp. 119–35; and P. J. Bowden, 'Agricultural Prices, Wages, Farm Profits, and Rents', pp. 75–81, both in *AHEW*, 5 sect. 2; M. G. Davies, 'Country Gentry and Falling

Rents in the 1660s and 1670s', *Midland History*, 4 (1977–8) pp. 86–96; P. Roebuck, *Yorkshire Baronets, 1640–1760: Families, Estates, and Fortunes* (Hull, 1980) pp. 7, 32, 115–16, 163–4, 169; J. V. Beckett, *Coal and Tobacco: the Lowthers and the Economic Development of West Cumberland, 1660–1760* (Cambridge, 1981) p. 31; Holmes, *Lincolnshire*, p. 25; LAO, Monson 7/12/46; Clay, 'Landlords and Estate Management,' pp. 211–12, 214, 222, 232–5.

33. J. Thirsk, 'Agricultural Policy: Public Debate and Legislation', *AHEW*, 5 sect. 2; pp. 328–32, 346–56; P. Seaward, *The Cavalier Parliament and the Reconstruction of the Old Regime* (Cambridge, 1988) pp. 243, 249–54, 296–7; Holmes, 'Drainers and Fenmen,' p. 175.
34. *Royalist's Notebook*, p. 75: this comment has been much discussed since its employment by Professor Trevor-Roper as a central pillar of his pessimistic argument about the difficulties of the 'mere gentry' in the early-modern period. See his *The Gentry 1540–1640*, *EcHR*, supplement 1 (1953) p. 26.
35. NLW, Wynn, nos. 455, 456, 460, 462, 466, 467, 470, 471.
36. John Smyth, *The Berkeley Manuscripts*, ed. Sir J. Maclean, 3 vols (Gloucester, 1883) iii, p. 42; J. U. Nef, *The Rise of the British Coal Industry*, 2 vols (1932) i, pp. 33, 324; ii, pp. 8, 65–78; Hughes, *Warwickshire*, pp. 10–12; Cliffe, *Yorkshire*, pp. 57–62; Roebuck, *Yorkshire Baronets*, pp. 39, 116, 208, 216, 324–5; Stone, *Crisis*, pp. 340–2, 390; R. S. Smith 'Huntingdon Beaumont: Adventurer in Coalmines', *Renaissance and Modern Studies*, 1 (1957) pp. 115–53.
37. Nef, *Coal Industry*, i, p. 59, 110, 219; Cliffe, *Yorkshire*, pp. 58, 60, 62, 150, 208; A. J. Hawkes, 'Sir Roger Bradshaigh', *Chetham Miscellany VIII*, Chetham Soc., new ser., 109 (1941) pp. 14–19.
38. Beckett, *Coal and Tobacco*, pp. 14–46, 158–9; Jenkins, *Glamorgan*, p. 59.
39. Roebuck, *Yorkshire Baronets*, pp. 22, 265; NLW, Wynn, nos. 905, 922, 933, 973, 990, 993, 1017, 1031, 1060, 1078; T. Coker, *A Survey of Dorsetshire* (1732) pp. 46–7.
40. Roebuck, *Yorkshire Baronets*, pp. 204, 208–9; Meredith, 'Eyres of Hassop', pp. 26, 29–39, 43; Fletcher, *Sussex*, pp. 17–20; A. L. Rowse, *Tudor Cornwall* (1941) pp. 54–5.
41. Nef, *Coal Industry*, i, p. 219; ii, pp. 17, 31; Hawkes, 'Sir Roger Bradshaigh' pp. 19, 20; Cliffe, *Yorkshire*, pp. 52–3; Roebuck, *Yorkshire Baronets*, p. 37; E. A.B. Barnard, *The Sheldons* (Cambridge, 1936) pp. 13–14, 26; A. M. Mimardiere, 'The Finances of a Warwickshire Gentry Family, 1693–1726', *Univ. of Birmingham Hist.* J., 9 (1963–4) p. 133.
42. Holmes, *Lincolnshire*, pp. 31–2; Perry Gauci, 'The Corporation and the Country: Great Yarmouth 1660–1722', Univ. of Oxford, DPhil thesis, 1991, pp. 146–68.
43. Cliffe, *Yorkshire*, pp. 53; Tonks, 'Lyttletons of Frankley', pp. 67–8; Beckett, *Coal and Tobacco*, pp. 181–90.
44. Finch, *Northamptonshire Families*, pp. 11–14, 32–4; Cliffe, *Puritan Gentry*, pp. 114–17; *D'Ewes*, i, p. 354; ii, pp. 96, 153; Holles, pp. 121–2; N. Jones, *God and the Moneylenders* (Oxford, 1989) pp. 158–9; Robert Filmer, *A Discourse Whether it May Be Lawful to Take Use for Money* (1678) sig. B4v.

45. Lincolnshire Archives Committee, *Archivists' Report, 1954–55*, pp. 33–4; Cliffe, *Yorkshire*, pp. 150, 373; A.R. Maddison, 'The Making and Unmaking of a Lincolnshire Estate', *Associated Architectural and Arch. Socs. Report*, 27 (1903–4) pp. 337–73; PRO, STAC 8/83/13.
46. Roebuck, *Yorkshire Baronets*, pp. 116, 121, 123, 182–3, 212–16, 230–1; Mimardiere, 'Finances of a Warwickshire Gentry Family', pp. 134–5.
47. HHL, HM 30665; M. Prestwich, *Cranfield: Politics and Profits under the Early Stuarts* (Oxford, 1966) pp. 69–70, 401–3.
48. K.R. Andrews, *Elizabethan Privateering* (Cambridge, 1964) pp. 53–70; W. L. Rutton, *Three Branches of the Family of Wentworth* (1841) pp. 168–74.
49. *Royalist's Notebook*, pp. 6–7, 41, 164–9, 196.
50. R. Lockyer, *Buckingham* (1981) chaps 1, 2; p. 155.
51. *Guise Memoirs*, pp. 108–9; E. A. B. Barnard, 'The Pakingtons of Westwood', *Trans. Worcs. Arch. Soc.*, new ser., 13 (1936) pp. 36–8; M.K. McIntosh, 'The Fall of a Tudor Gentle Family: the Cookes of Gidea Hall, Essex, 1579–1629', *HLQ*, 41 (1977–8) pp. 279–97.
52. *Reresby*, p. xxxii; K. Bedingfield, *The Bedingfields of Oxburgh* (n. p., 1912) pp. 79–80; Prestwich, *Cranfield*, pp. 218, 221, 386, 392–406; LAO, Monson 19/7/1/1–7; H. A. Wyndham, *A Family History, 1410–1688* (Oxford, 1939) pp. 175–83, 223–4.
53. W. Knowler (ed.) *The Earl of Strafforde's Letters and Dispatches*, 2 vols (1739) i, p. 170; Simpson, *Wealth of the Gentry*, pp. 142–78; M. F. Keeler, *The Long Parliament, 1640–1641* (Philadelphia, 1954) pp. 402–3.
54. I. Grimble, *The Harington Family* (London, 1957) pp. 65–74, 143–64.
55. Ibid., pp. 86–142; R. Hughey, *John Harington of Stepney* (Columbus, Ohio, 1971) pp. 55–9; T. Park (ed.) *Nugae Antiquae*, 2 vols (1804) i, p. 168; Holles, p. 162.
56. Grimble, *Harington Family*, pp. 187ff.
57. IOW RO, OG/CC/23; W.R. Prest, *The Rise of the Barristers* (Oxford, 1986) pp. 106, 180–1; Holmes, *Lincolnshire*, p. 67; IOW RO, OG/CC/23; Larminie, *The Newdigates* (forthcoming) Ch. 12.
58. Cliffe, *Yorkshire*, pp. 82–3, 94; R. Spalding, *The Improbable Puritan. A Life of Bulstrode Whitelocke* (1975) pp. 32, 38; NRO, IC 25; W.R. Prest, *The Inns of Court under Elizabeth and the Early Stuarts* (1972) p. 40.
59. Prest, *Rise of the Barristers*, pp. 11, 41; *Lowther Family*, pp. 17, 27, 202, 212–14.

## Chapter 4 Wealth: Spending

1. NRO, IC 528; M.E. Finch, *Five Northamptonshire Families, 1540–1640*, Northants. Rec. Soc., 19 (1956) pp. 74–6.
2. PRO, STAC 8/17/24: for Tresham's expenditure on building, household and display, see Finch, *Northamptonshire Families*, pp. 80–3; Holles, p. 229; W. Knowler (ed.) *The Earl of Strafforde's Letters and Speeches*, 2 vols (1739) i, p. 169; Cliffe, *Yorkshire*, pp. 106–7; Alice T. Friedman, *House and Household in Elizabethan England* (Chicago, 1989) pp. 12, 165. For further discussion of the motives for and expenses of building, see Stone, *Crisis*, pp. 549–55.

3. Holles, pp. 201, 203.
4. Ibid., pp. 121–7, 215–25; Finch, *Northamptonshire Families*, p. 82.
5. *Reresby*, p. xxxiii; Stone, *Crisis*, pp. 211–14, 572–81.
6. Finch, *Northamptonshire Families*, pp. 82–3, 92–3; A.M. Mimardiere, 'The Finances of a Warwickshire Gentry Family, 1693–1726', *Univ. of Birmingham Hist. J.*, 9 (1963–4) pp. 137–43; *The History of Parliament: The House of Commons, 1715–1754*, ed. Romney Sedgwick, 2 vols (1970) i, p. 3; Thomas Habington, *A Survey of Worcestershire*, ed. J. Amphlett, 2 vols (Oxford, 1895) i, p. 49; ii, pp. 28–9.
7. *Royalist's Notebook*, p. 229; NRO, IC 38 (for examples of similar warnings, see A. G. Dickens (ed.) 'Estate and Household Management in Bedfordshire, *c.*1540' *Bedfords. Hist. Rec. Soc.*, 36 (1956) p. 38; YAS, DD56 M2 unfol., 1632, 6 Sept. letter from Sir Henry to Henry Slingsby). H. A. Lloyd, *The Gentry of South-West Wales, 1540–1640* (Cardiff, 1968) p. 45; WRO, CR 136 A20; Jenkins, *Glamorgan*, pp. 199, 241–4.
8. H. S. Scott (ed.) 'The Journal of Sir Roger Wilbraham', p. 22 in *Camden Miscellany 10*, Camden Soc., 3rd ser., 4 (1902); *Letters of John Holles* ii, p. 310; Finch, *Northamptonshire Families*, pp. 78–80; J. P. Cooper, 'Patterns of Inheritance and Settlement by Great Landowners from the Fifteenth to the Eighteenth Centuries', pp. 221–3, and the appendix, reworking and expanding Stone's figures, pp. 306–12, in J. Goody, J. Thirsk and E. P. Thompson (eds) *Family and Inheritance* (Cambridge, 1976); E. F. Gay, 'The Temples of Stowe and their Debts', *HLQ*, 2 (1938–9) pp. 399–438.
9. *Collectanea Topographica & Genealogica*, 2 (1835) pp. 68–90 [Foljambe]; *Reresby*, pp. xli, 1–2; R. E. C. Walters, *Genealogical Memoirs of the Extinct Family of Chester of Chicheley* (1878) p. 344; P. Roebuck, *Yorkshire Baronets, 1640–1760: Families, Estates, and Fortunes* (Hull, 1980) pp. 222–38 [Liddell-Bright].
10. A. Simpson, *The Wealth of the Gentry* (Cambridge, 1961), pp. 91–102 [Bacon]; Holmes, *Lincolnshire*, pp. 67, 187 [Brownlow]; Gay, 'Temples and their Debts,' pp. 408, 412–16; C. Markham, *Markham Memorials*, 2 vols (1913) i, pp. 49, 53, 72.
11. Cliffe, *Yorkshire*, pp. 129–35, 161; M. J. Hawkins, 'Wardship, Royalist Delinquency and Too Many Children: the Portmans in the Seventeenth Century', *Southern History*, 4 (1982) pp. 56–64; M. J. Hawkins (ed.) *Sales of Wards in Somerset, 1603–1641*, Somers. Rec. Soc., 57 (1965) pp. xxi-xxxi; C. B. Phillips, 'The Royalist North: the Cumberland and Westmorland Gentry, 1642–1660', *Northern History*, 14 (1978) pp. 183–84; *Collectanea Topographica & Genealogica*, 2 (1835) pp. 76–81.
12. Roebuck, *Yorkshire Baronets*, pp. 118–19, 257–60.
13. Finch, *Northamptonshire Families*, pp. 76–8, 179–81; H. Bowler (ed.) *The Recusant Roll, 1593–1594*, Catholic Rec. Soc., 57 (1965) pp. xxx, xliii; Simpson, *Wealth of the Gentry*, pp. 162–4, 175–6 [Cornwallis]: PRO, STAC 8/291/12 [Parham]: Cliffe, *Yorkshire*, p. 213 [Pudsey]; H. Aveling (ed.) 'The Recusancy Papers of the Meynell Family of North Kilvington . . . . 1596–1676' in *Miscellanea*, Catholic Rec. Soc., 56 (1964) pp. 47–9; PRO, STAC 8/175/4 [Pocklington sessions] – the protection of recusants was one of the major issues that divided the Yorkshire JPs

in the early seventeenth century; see G.C.F. Forster, 'Faction and County Government in Early Stuart Yorkshire', *Northern History*, 11 (1975) pp. 70–86: PRO, STAC 8/21/15; G.H. Ryan and L.J. Redstone, *Timperley of Hintlesham* (1931) pp. 53–6: T.B. Trappes-Lomax, 'The Owners of Irnham Hall', *Lincs. Architectural and Arch. Soc.: Reports*, 9 (1962) pp. 164–77 [Thimbleby].

14. This section relies on M. Havran, *The Catholics in Caroline England* (Oxford, 1962) pp. 90–7; H. Aveling, *Northern Catholics: the Catholic Recusants in the North Riding of Yorkshire, 1585–1790* (1966) pp. 212–20, 225–35; Cliffe, *Yorkshire*, pp. 210–30.
15. PRO, SP 23/122 pp. 391, 407, 409 [Thimbleby]; Hughes, *Warwickshire*, p. 268 [Throckmorton]; Aveling, *Northern Catholics*, pp. 302–3, 313–15; Aveling (ed.) 'Recusancy Papers of the Meynell Family', p. 93.
16. Ibid., pp. 323–7, 336–8, 365–7, 372; J.A. Williams, *Catholic Recusancy in Wiltshire*, Catholic Rec. Soc., monograph series, 1 (1968) Ch. 1.
17. J.A. Mousely, 'The Fortunes of some Gentry Families of Elizabethan Sussex', *EcHR*, 2nd ser., 11 (1958–9) pp. 476–8; G.H. Glanville, 'Aspects of the History of the County of Surrey, 1580–1620', Univ. of London, PhD thesis, 1972, pp. 398–9; Cliffe, *Yorkshire*, pp. 228–30; Aveling, *Northern Catholics*, pp. 217–18, 353–4.
18. There is an excellent survey of the extensive literature on this subject in C. Clay, 'Landlords and Management,' *AHEW*, 5 sect. 2, pp. 119–54.
19. Holmes, *Lincolnshire*, pp. 177–8; J. Eales, *Puritans and Roundheads: the Harleys of Brampton Bryan and the Outbreak of the English Civil War* (Cambridge, 1990) pp. 177–8, n. 47; M. Blundell, *Cavalier: Letters of William Blundell to his Friends* (1933) p. 13; Clay, 'Landlords and Management', p. 140; PRO, SP 23/194 pp. 113–29.
20. A. Everitt, *The Community of Kent and the Great Rebellion* (Leicester, 1966) pp. 141, 142; B. Schofield (ed.) *The Knyvett Letters* (1949) pp. 38–41, 144; C. Holmes, *The Eastern Association in the English Civil War* (Cambridge, 1974) pp. 130–1; Hughes, *Warwickshire*, p. 193; J.P.F. Broad, 'Sir Ralph Verney and his Estates 1630–1696', Univ. of Oxford, D.Phil thesis, 1973, pp. 31, 60, 64.
21. H.J. Habakkuk, 'Landowners and the Civil War', *EcHR*, 2nd ser., 18 (1965) p. 131, 134–5; P.G. Holiday, 'Land Sales and Repurchases in Yorkshire after the Civil Wars, 1650–1670', *Northern History* 5 (1970) pp. 67–92; Blackwood, *Lancashire*, pp. 120–30; C.B. Phillips, 'The Royalist Composition Papers and the Landed Income of the Gentry: a Note of Warning from Cumbria', *Northern History*, 13 (1977) pp. 161–74; J.T. Cliffe, 'A Rejoinder', ibid., 14 (1978) pp. 164–8.
22. Habakkuk 'Landowners and the Civil War', pp. 136, 139; Phillips, 'Royalist North', p. 190; Blackwood, *Lancashire*, p. 125; Hughes, *Warwickshire*, p. 268.
23. R. Meredith, 'A Derbyshire Family in the Seventeenth Century: the Eyres of Hassop and their Forfeited Estates', *Recusant History*, 8 (1965–6) pp. 51–2: Roebuck, *Yorkshire Baronets*, pp. 157–61; Habakkuk, 'Landowners and the Civil War', p. 138; C.B. Phillips, 'Landlord–Tenant Relationships, 1642–1660' in R.C. Richardson (ed.) *Town and Countryside in the English Revolution* (Manchester, 1992) pp. 242–5;

J. Broad, 'Gentry Finances and the Civil War: the Case of the Buckinghamshire Verneys', *EcHR*, 2nd ser., 32 (1979) pp. 195–200; and 'The Verneys as Enclosing Landlords, 1600–1800', pp. 34–9, in J. Chartres and D. Hey (eds) *English Rural Society, 1500–1800: Essays in Honour of Joan Thirsk* (Cambridge, 1990); Everitt, *Community of Kent*, pp. 276–8, 280.

24. *Sir George Sondes his Plain Narrative* (1655) in Thomas Park (ed.) *The Harleian Miscellany*, 12 vols (1805–15) x, p. 50; Phillips, 'Royalist North', p. 189; Schofield (ed.) *Knyvett Letters*, p. 156; IOW RO, OG/CC/53; Meredith, 'Derbyshire Family', pp. 16–17, 24–6, 55–6; M. Slater, *Family Life in the Seventeenth Century* (1984) pp. 86–104.
25. Clay, in 'Landlords and Management', pp. 119–54, emphasises that family survival had financial, social and psychological costs; Holiday, 'Land sales', pp. 82–3.
26. *CSPD 1697*, p. 170.
27. P. Williams, *The Tudor Regime* (Oxford, 1979) pp. 60–80; J. Guy, *Tudor England* (Oxford, 1988) pp. 93, 98–102, 383–4; Fletcher, *Sussex*, pp. 203–6; P. Clark, *English Provincial Society from the Reformation to the Revolution* (Hassocks, 1977) pp. 225, 227, 245, 256; C. Russell, *Parliaments and English Politics, 1621–1629* (Oxford, 1979) p. 73; H. J. Habakkuk, 'English Landownership, 1680–1740', *EcHR*, 1st ser., 10 (1939–40) p. 8.
28. Holmes, *Eastern Association*, pp. 136–7; Habakkuk, 'English Landownership', pp. 8–9.
29. Anchitell Grey, *Debates of the House of Commons*, 10 vols (1763) 1, pp. 274, 321; C. D. Chandaman, *The English Public Revenue* (Oxford, 1975) pp. 138–95.
30. J. V. Beckett, 'English Landownership in the Late Seventeenth and Eighteenth Centuries: the Debate and the Problems', *EcHR*, 2nd ser., 30 (1977) pp. 574, 579; W. Ward, *The English Land Tax in the Eighteenth Century* (Oxford, 1953) pp. 8–10, 18–20, 22–5; G. E. Mingay, *English Landed Society in the Eighteenth Century* (1963) pp. 81–3, 85; *HMC Portland*, viii, p. 96.
31. Finch, *Northamptonshire Families*, pp. 168–9; Roebuck, *Yorkshire Baronets*, pp. 161–78.
32. Cliffe, *Puritan Gentry*, pp. 114–17; V. Larminie, *Wealth, Kinship and Culture: the Newdigates of Arbury, c.1585–c.1685* (forthcoming) Ch. 2; N. Jones, *God and the Moneylenders* (Oxford, 1989) p. 88.
33. On credit mechanisms in general, see Stone, *Crisis*, pp. 513–28; for Tresham, see Finch, *Northamptonshire Families*, pp. 83–4; for Isham, ibid, p. 27, and NRO, IC 129, 140; for Slingsby, YAS, DD56 M2, bundle of letters 1600–20, no. 28; L. Stone (ed.) 'Sir Edward Montagu's Directions to his Son', *Northamptonshire Past and Present* (1958) pp. 221–3; see also IOW RO, OG/SS/1 fo. 87.
34. Higford, p. 587; H. J. Habakkuk, 'The Rise and Fall of English Landed Families, 1600–1800: II', *TRHS*, 5th ser., 30 (1980) pp. 205–10.
35. R. W. Turner, *The Equity of Redemption* (Cambridge, 1931) esp. pp. 24–32; Stone, *Crisis*, pp. 527–8; Cliffe, *Yorkshire*, pp. 147–50; Lloyd, *Gentry of South-West Wales*, p. 46.
36. Jenkins, *Glamorgan*, p. 197; Holmes, *Lincolnshire*, p. 72.

37. *The Spectator*, no. 106 (July 1711); F. M. Heal, *Hospitality in Early Modern England* (Oxford, 1990) p. 168; Cooper, *Aynho*, p. 32; D. Underdown, *Somerset in the Civil War and Interregnum* (Newton Abbot, 1973) p. 39; J. S. Morrill, *Cheshire, 1630–1660: County Government and Society during the English Revolution* (Oxford, 1974) pp. 78–9; Sir F. Pollock (ed.) *Table Talk of John Selden* (1927) p. 67.

## Chapter 5 Administration

1. B. Schofield (ed.) *The Knyvett Letters* (1949) pp. 33–41, 116, 118, 121, 134, 137, 144, 151, 154; J. P. F. Broad, 'Sir Ralph Verney and his Estates, 1630–1696', Univ. of Oxford, D.Phil thesis, 1973, pp. 31, 60, 64.
2. William Lambarde, *Eirenarcha: or of the Office of the Justices of Peace* (1582) pp. 36–8.
3. FSL, V. a. 143, p. 65; Heywood Townshend, *Historical Collections* (1680) p. 355; for a general discussion of the attitudes of the Elizabethan government, see A. H. Smith, *County and Court: Government and Politics in Norfolk 1558–1603* (Oxford, 1974) pp. 76–80.
4. *The Merry Wives of Windsor*, Act 1, sc. 1.
5. m.i. to Thomas Heton, St Peter's Church, Wisbech. The 1636 figures are calculated from the commissions of the peace for six sample counties given in J. H. Gleason, *Justices of the Peace in England, 1558–1640* (Oxford, 1969) pp. 135–7, 156–7, 179–80, 198–9, 217–18, 236–7; for the post-1660 developments, see L. K. J. Glassey, *Politics and the Appointment of the Justices of the Peace, 1675–1720* (Oxford, 1979) pp. 20–1.
6. The Gawdy–Lovell rivalry is analysed in Smith, *County and Court*, pp. 181–92; for Philip Gawdy's networking at the court, see ibid., pp. 67–8; I. H. Jeayes (ed.) *The Letters of Philip Gawdy* (Roxburghe Club, 1906) pp. 78, 82, 104–5, 131, 156.
7. PRO, STAC 8/30/6, 175/4 fo. 15; J. B. Calnan, 'County Society and Local Government in the County of Hertford *c*.1580–*c*.1630', Univ. of Cambridge, PhD thesis, 1979, p. 150; W. J. Tighe, 'Courtiers and Politics in Elizabethan Herefordshire: Sir James Croft, his Friends and his Foes', *HJ*, 32 (1989) pp. 271–2; A. Wall, 'Faction in Local Politics, 1580–1620', *Wilts. Arch. Magazine* 72–73 (1980) p. 132.
8. C. V. Wedgewood, *Thomas Wentworth, First Earl of Strafford* (1961) p. 56; for the feud between Wentworth and Sir John Savile which forms the background to this incident, see S. P. Salt, 'Sir Thomas Wentworth and the Parliamentary Representation of Yorkshire, 1614–1628' *Northern History* 16 (1980) pp. 130–68; Holmes, *Lincolnshire*, p. 81.
9. William Cavendish, Duke of Newcastle, *The Country Captain* (The Hague, 1649): this was acted at Blackfriars in 1639 or 1640; LAO, Monson 7/12/7, 7/14/9; Calnan, 'County Society and Local Government', p. 139; NLW, Wynn, no. 1469; PRO, STAC 8/156/18.
10. The best accounts of the duties and burdens of the shrievalty are Smith, *County and Court*, pp. 139–46; T. G. Barnes, *Somerset 1625–1640: a County's Government During the 'Personal Rule'* (Oxford, 1961) pp. 124–42, and J. S. Cockburn, *A History of the English Assizes 1558–1714* (Cambridge, 1972) pp. 54–5, 65, 105; Cliffe, *Puritan Gentry*, p. 212;

*Wentworth*, pp. 12–13, 37–8; CRO, R(S) 1/542, 861; C. B. Phillips, 'The Gentry of Cumberland and Westmorland, 1600–1665', Univ. of Lancaster, PhD thesis, 1973, pp. 255–6; S. M. ffarington (ed.) *The Farington Papers*, Chetham Soc., old ser., 39 (1856) pp. 28–9; *HMC Portland*, ix, pp. 141–2; *Letters of John Holles* i, pp. 139–40; ii, p. 310.

11. N. E. McClure (ed.) *The Letters of John Chamberlain* 2 vols, Memoirs of the American Philosophical Soc., XII (Philadelphia, 1939) i, p. 131; T. Birch (ed.) *A Collection of State Papers of John Thurloe*, 7 vols (1742) iv, p. 215; NLW, Wynn, nos. 365, 392, 548, 550, 616, 923, 1043.
12. NLW, Wynn, nos. 942, 1000, 1441; Phillips, 'Cumberland and Westmorland', p. 253; Smith, *County and Court*, pp. 146–54.
13. J. E. Neale, *Elizabeth I and her Parliaments, 1584–1601* (1957) pp. 399–400; Calnan, 'County Society and Local Government', p. 152; FSL, L. a. 570; John Hawarde, *Les reportes del cases in camera stellata, 1593–1609*, ed. W. P. Baildon (1894) pp. 134–9, 334–6; PRO, STAC 8/172/10; 217/4.
14. For good general discussion of this theme, see A. Wall, 'Patterns of Politics in England 1558–1625', *HJ*, 31 (1988) pp. 947–63; Wall, 'Faction in Local Politics', pp. 119–33; G. C. F. Forster, 'Faction and County Government in Early Stuart Yorkshire', *Northern History*, 11 (1976) pp. 70–86; A. J. Fletcher, 'Honour, Reputation and Local Office Holding in Elizabethan and Stuart England' in A. Fletcher and J. Stevenson (eds) *Order and Disorder in Early Modern England* (Cambridge, 1985) pp. 92–115. Holmes, *Lincolnshire*, pp. 98–99; Hawarde, *Reportes*, pp. 68, 108, 265–67, 368.
15. J. A. Guy, *The Cardinal's Court* (Hassocks, 1977) pp. 33, 121, 137; J. Bruce (ed.) *Liber Famelicus of Sir James Whitelocke* Camden Soc., old ser., 70 (1858) pp. 22–23; Fletcher, 'Honour, Reputation and Local Office Holding', p. 105; Hawarde, *Reportes*, pp. 134–9, 234.
16. Guy, *Cardinal's Court*, pp. 120, 137; for general discussion of the later charges, see Cockburn, *Assizes*, pp. 57–9, 67–9, 181–6; A.Fletcher, *Reform in the Provinces* (1986) pp. 47–9; the quotations are from Hawarde, *Reportes*, p. 21 and BL, Add. 32,518 fo. 129.
17. STAC 8/259/1; Clive Holmes, 'Women: Witnesses and Witches', *PP*, 140 (1993) pp. 70–2; Michael Dalton, *The Countrey Justice* (1635) p. 22 – the discussion of this topic is even fuller in this edition than in the first edition of 1618 [p. 20]. For a general discussion of the later manuals and the 'models of the model justice', see N. Landau, *The Justices of the Peace, 1679–1760* (Berkeley, 1984) pp. 333–62.
18. Samuel Ward, *Jethro's Justice of Peace* (1618) p. 65; Thomas Scot, *The High-waies of God and the King* (1623) p. 80; Holmes, *Lincolnshire*, pp. 81, 83. M. Walzer, *The Revolution of the Saints* (1966) pp. 228–9, 233–5, 246–7, 257–67, is excellent on magistracy as the religious 'calling' of the gentry but he is wrong – as the example of Sanderson, a conformist and apologist for the established church, shows – to see this as a peculiarly Puritan position. For the bards, see J. G. Jones, *Concepts of Order and Gentility in Wales, 1540–1640* (Llandysul, 1992) pp. 149–96.
19. V. M. Larminie, *The Godly Magistrate*, Dugdale Soc., Occasional Papers, no. 28 (1982) pp. 15–19; WRO, CR 136 B632, 718; R. D. Hunt (ed.) 'Henry Townshend's "Notes of the Office of a Justice of the Peace"

1661–1663' *Worcs. Hist. Soc.*, new ser., 5 (1967) pp. 68–137, especially pp. 88, 93, 101. And, generally, see Fletcher, *Reform*, pp. 149–58.

20. WRO, CR 136 B711; Lord Ashcombe (ed.) 'A Charge Given by Hugh Hare', *Surrey Arch. Coll.*, 12 (1895) p. 128; for an excellent discussion of the learning and rhetoric of the charges, see the introduction, by E. M. Halcrow, to *Charges to the Grand Jury at Quarter Sessions 1660–1677 by Sir Peter Leicester*, Chetham Soc., 3rd ser., 5 (1953) esp. p. xxx.
21. PRO, STAC 8/31/13; J. Samaha, *Law and Order in Historical Perspective* (New York, 1974) pp. 67–8; Essex RO, D/DHt M49 fos 1–4.
22. Ben Jonson, *Bartholemew Fair*, Act 2, sc. 1.
23. Robert Bolton, *Two Sermons Preached at Northampton at Two Severall Assizes* (1639) particularly pp. 32–6, 63–4; P. Seaver, 'Community Control and Puritan Politics in Elizabethan Suffolk', *Albion*, 9 (1977) p. 300; P. Collinson, 'Magistracy and Ministry: A Suffolk Miniature' in his *Godly People* (1983) pp. 445–66; Hughes, *Warwickshire*, pp. 49–50, 71; Holmes, *Lincolnshire*, pp. 81, 83.
24. *Barrington Letters*, p. 91: Smith, *County and Court*, p. 203; BL, Lansdowne 27/70; MacCulloch, *Suffolk*, pp. 198–208; E. Rose, *Cases of Conscience* (Cambridge, 1975) pp. 160–8.
25. J. S. Morrill, 'Sir William Brereton and England's Wars of Religion', *JBS* 24 (1985) pp. 312–14; Calnan, 'Hertford', pp. 49–51, 83–4, 103; B. W. Quintrell, 'The Government of the County of Essex, 1603–1642' Univ. of London, PhD thesis, 1965, pp. 44–51; Hughes, *Warwickshire*, p. 352.
26. NRO, IC 18, 25; Cholmley, p. 38; Fletcher, *Sussex*, p. 222. The development of local administrative agencies is best covered in Fletcher, *Reform*, particularly Part II; for petty sessions, see pp. 122–35, and P. Slack, 'Books of Orders: the Making of English Social Policy, 1577–1631', *TRHS*, 4th ser., 30 (1980) p. 15.
27. For accusations against individual commissioners, see PRO STAC 8/145/25; 235/18. J. Guy, *Tudor England* (Oxford, 1988), pp. 383, 384; C. Russell, *Parliaments and English Politics, 1621–1629* (Oxford, 1979), pp. 45n, 49–53, 375–6, 398; IOW RO OG/BB/37/76; Fletcher, *Sussex*, p. 203.
28. C. D. Chandaman, *The English Public Revenue* (Oxford, 1975), pp. 55, 60, 65, 86, 91, 93, 95, 99–100, 102, 145, 149–50, 176, 185; *Reresby*, pp. 104–105, 119, 125, 270, 348; Anchitell Grey, *Debates of the House of Commons* 10 vols (1763), iii, pp. 236–45.
29. Chandaman, *English Public Revenue*, p. 86; H. Horwitz, *Parliament, Policy and Politics in the Reign of William III* (Manchester, 1977), pp. 28, 39, 63, 93, 137, 145, 321; J. V. Beckett, 'English Landownership in the Late Seventeenth and Eighteenth Centuries: the Debate and the Problems', *EcHR*, 2nd ser., 30 (1977) pp. 574, 579; W. R. Ward, *The English Land Tax in the Eighteenth Century* (Oxford, 1953) pp. 1–59, 66–85; C. Brooks, 'Public Finance and Political Stability: the Administration of the Land Tax, 1688–1720', *HJ*, 17 (1974) pp. 281–300.
30. Ibid., pp. 292–94.
31. L. Stone & J. C. Fawtier Stone, *An Open Elite? England 1540–1880* (Oxford, 1984) pp. 270–1; Jenkins, *Glamorgan*, pp. 88–9; Holmes, *Lincolnshire*, p. 83; J. M. Rosenheim, 'County Governance and Elite

Withdrawal in Norfolk, 1660–1720' in A. L. Beier, D. Cannadine, J. M. Rosenheim (eds) *The First Modern Society: Essays in English History presented to Lawrence Stone* (Cambridge, 1989) pp. 95–125. Discussion of the increased number of JPs, and the growing reluctance of nominees to take the oaths is drawn from Landau, *Justices of the Peace*, pp. 138, 140 and appendix A; *The Spectator*, no. 122 (July 1711). It should be noted that Professor Landau argues, in her detailed analysis of Kent, that the traditional ruling élite were not, as in Glamorgan, those likely to seek to avoid responsibility (pp. 318–28). Similarly detailed work on other counties may modify our general conclusion, which is based on more impressionistic evidence from other localities.

32. Stone and Stone, *Open Elite?*, p. 270.
33. Smith, *County and Court*, pp. 78–9; Landau, *Justices of the Peace*, Ch. 5; Richard Brome, *A Jovial Crew* (1641); James Shirley, *The Witty Fair One* (1628), Act 2, sc. 2; Stone, *Crisis*, p. 391; Henry Fielding, *Tom Jones*, bk. 7 Ch. 9.
34. For 1640–60, see Fletcher, *Reform*, pp. 32–3; a number of local studies argue the basic efficiency of county government in this period, see, for example, J. S. Morrill, *Cheshire 1630–1660: County Government and Society during the English Revolution* (Oxford, 1974) Ch. 6; Hughes, *Warwickshire*, pp. 280–90; S. K. Roberts, *Recovery and Restoration in an English County: Devon Local Administration, 1646–1670* (Exeter, 1985) p. 26–33; G. C. F. Forster, 'County Government in Yorkshire during the Interregnum', *Northern History*, 12 (1976) pp. 84–104.

**Chapter 6 Politics**

1. N. Pevsner, *The Buildings of England: Herefordshire* (1963) p. 228; R. Tittler, *Architecture and Power: the Town Hall and the English Urban Community, c.1500–1640* (Oxford, 1991) pp. 44–5.
2. T. P. Slaughter (ed.) *Ideology and Politics on the Eve of Restoration: Newcastle's Advice to Charles II*, Memoirs of the American Philosophical Soc., 159 (Philadelphia, 1984) p. 47; Gilbert Talbot held the Shrewsbury title, as seventh earl, from 1590 to 1616.
3. *Wentworth*, pp. 11–12, 37–46.
4. Slaughter (ed.) *Newcastle's Advice*, pp. 48–49. An excellent general discussion of this theme is K. Sharpe, 'Crown, Parliament and Locality: Government and Communication in Early Stuart England', *EHR*, 101 (1986) pp. 321–50.
5. Stone, *Crisis*, pp. 117, 751; K. Sharpe, *The Personal Rule of Charles I* (New Haven, 1992) pp. 414–22: J. F. Larkin (ed.) *Stuart Royal Proclamations: . . . Charles I* (Oxford, 1983) pp. 350–3; Sheffield City Library, Wentworth Woodhouse papers, Strafford 12/151, 219. See also 12/165, 195.
6. H. A. Lloyd, *The Gentry of South-West Wales* (Cardiff, 1968) pp. 112–18; M. James, 'At a Crossroads of the Political Culture: the Essex Revolt, 1601' in his *Society, Politics and Culture* (Cambridge, 1986) pp. 416–65.
7. For Northumberland, see M. James, 'A Tudor Magnate and the Tudor State', pp. 56–62 in his *Society, Politics and Culture*, pp. 48–90; for

Norfolk, A.H. Smith, *County and Court: Government and Politics in Norfolk, 1558–1603* (Oxford, 1974) pp. 21–44, 148, 157, 181.

8. G.W. Bernard, *The Power of the Early Tudor Nobility* (Brighton, 1985) p. 180, and Ch. 6 *passim*; D. Willen, *John Russell, First Earl of Bedford: One of the King's Men* (1981) pp. 62–6; Stone, *Crisis*, pp. 201–7, 220–1.
9. James, 'Tudor Magnate', pp. 58–59.
10. James, 'Tudor Magnate', pp. 66–70, and 'Change and Continuity in the Tudor North', pp. 100–2, 122, in his *Society, Politics and Culture*, pp. 91–148; J. Guy, *The Cardinal's Court* (Hassocks, 1977) pp. 72–4.
11. James, 'Crossroads of the Political Culture', p. 424; W.T. MacCaffrey, 'Talbot and Stanhope: an Episode in Elizabethan Politics', *BIHR*, 33 (1960) pp. 73–85; quotation is p. 79.
12. For Bacon, see C. Holmes, 'Parliament, Liberty, Taxation, and Property', pp. 146–8 in J.H. Hexter (ed.) *Parliament and Liberty from the Reign of Elizabeth to the English Civil War* (Stanford, 1992) pp. 122–54.
13. *Wandesford*, p. 10; F.J. Levy, 'How Information Spread Among the Gentry, 1550–1640', *JBS*, 21 (1982) pp. 11–34; for Kent, see P. Laslett, 'The Gentry of Kent in 1640', *Cambridge HJ*, 9 (1947–9) pp. 155–6; K. Fincham, 'The Judges' Decision on Ship Money in February 1637: the Reaction of Kent', *BIHR*, 57 (1984) pp. 230–7.
14. C. Read (ed.) *William Lambarde and Local Government* (Ithaca, 1962) pp. 79, 164; *Wentworth*, pp. 152–5; R. Cust and P.G. Lake, 'Sir Richard Grovesnor and the Rhetoric of Magistracy', *BIHR*, 54 (1981) pp. 40–53; we are grateful to Richard Cust for transcripts of Sir Richard Grovesnor's speech to the freeholders in February 1624 and his charges to sessions of January 1625 and 1626 from the Eaton Hall manuscripts.
15. D. Starkey, 'Which Age of Reform?', pp. 16–25, in C. Coleman and D. Starkey, *Revolution Reassessed* (Oxford, 1986); J. Guy, 'The King's Council and Political Participation', pp. 124–6, in A. Fox and J. Guy, *Reassessing the Henrician Age* (Oxford, 1986); Holmes, 'Liberty, Taxation, and Property', p. 147; J.E. Neale, *Elizabeth I and her Parliaments, 1584–1601* (1957) pp. 376–83. For complaints against purveyors, see A. Woodworth, 'Purveyance for the Royal Household in the Reign of Queen Elizabeth', *Trans. of the American Philosophical Soc.*, new ser., 35 (1945) pp. 37–8.
16. P. Croft, 'Parliament, Purveyance and the City of London 1589–1608', *Parliamentary History* 4 (1985) pp. 9–11; Neale, *Parliaments 1584–1601*, pp. 388–93.
17. P. Zagorin, *The Court and the Country* (1969) pp. 33–9, 44–51; L. Stone, *The Causes of the English Revolution* (1972) pp. 105–8.
18. Slaughter (ed.) *Newcastle's Advice*, p. 56.
19. The argument here depends heavily on Richard Cust's analysis: see his 'News and Politics in Early Seventeenth-Century England', *PP*, 112 (1986) pp. 60–90. See also FSL, L. a. 235, 237, 243–4, 253–4, 264–5, 268–9, 277 (Bagot); PRO, SP 12/275/146 (Percy); J.S. Morrill, 'William Davenport and the 'Silent Majority' of Early Stuart England', *J. of the Chester Arch. Soc.*, 58 (1975) pp. 115–129.
20. J.E. Neale, *The Elizabethan House of Commons* (1949) pp. 21–55, 140–61.

21. Ibid., p. 150; S. P. Salt, 'Sir Thomas Wentworth and the Parliamentary Representation of Yorkshire, 1614–1628', *Northern History*, 16 (1980) p. 130; M. A. Kishlansky, *Parliamentary Selection* (Cambridge, 1986) p. 69; R. Cust, 'Politics and the Electorate in the 1620s' in R. Cust and A. Hughes (eds) *Conflict in Early Stuart England* (1989) pp. 143–6, 157–8; G. W. Robinson (ed.) *The Winthrop Papers*, 5 vols (Boston, Mass., 1929–47) i, pp. 324, 326; J. H. Plumb, 'The Growth of the Electorate in England from 1600 to 1715', *PP*, 45 (1969) pp. 105–6.
22. D. Hirst, *The Representative of the People?* (Cambridge, 1975) pp. 157–84; Holmes, 'Liberty, Taxation and Property', pp. 145–6; *Wentworth*, pp. 152–7.
23. A. Hughes, 'Local History and the Origins of the Civil War' in Cust and Hughes (eds) *Conflict in Early Stuart England*, pp. 235–7; M. Jansson (ed.) *Proceedings in Parliament, 1614* (Philadelphia, 1988) p. 64.
24. NLW, Wynn, nos. 1242, 1243, 1365; *Norfolk Arch.*, 24 (1930–32) pp. 15–16; W. Hamper (ed.) *The Life, Diary and Correspondence of Sir William Dugdale* (1827) pp. 156–7, 165, 287.
25. PRO, SP 12/132/9: Smith, *County and Court*, pp. 99–102, 110–11, 253–65; MacCulloch, *Suffolk*, pp. 262–6; BL, Lansdowne 74/1–9.
26. For the Essex 1627 presentment, see Bod. L., MS Firth c.4 pp. 322–4: for earlier use of the grand jury, see Essex RO, Q/SR 174/63–70; 194/33; 237/13. Religious grievances: PRO, ASSI 31/71/5 fos 10, 11; Bedfordshire RO, J 1323. Ship-money: T. G. Barnes (ed.) *Somerset Assize Orders*, Somerset Record Soc., 65 (1959) pp. 60–1; PRO, SP 16/345/76, 466/42; Notts. RO, DD4P 68/12; Essex RO, Q/CP 3 p. 115.
27. For general discussion, see C. Holmes, 'The County Community in Stuart Historiography', *JBS*, 19 (1980) pp. 54–73; Cockburn, *English Assizes*, pp. 188–237; Fincham, 'The Judges' Decision on Ship Money', p. 232.
28. NLW, Wynn, no. 1257; *Wentworth*, pp. 5, 314; Cliffe, *Yorkshire*, pp. 282–306; Cust, 'Politics and the Electorate', pp. 143–51; Salt, 'Sir Thomas Wentworth', pp. 130–68.
29. T. G. Barnes, *Somerset 1625–1640: A County's Government During the 'Personal Rule'* (Oxford, 1961) pp. 281–98; Phelips's 'Discourse' is SomsRO, DD/PH227/16.
30. R. Cust, *The Forced Loan and English Politics 1626–1628* (Oxford, 1987) pp. 195–97, 201–5, 217, 248, 249, 263; for Sir Reginald Mohun, see also CRO, R(S) 1/870–5; Holmes, *Lincolnshire*, pp. 98, 99, 107.
31. Cust, *Forced Loan*, pp. 138–9, 142, 163–4, 209–13, 286, 289; Holmes, 'County Community', pp. 68–9; Sir Robert Filmer, *Patriarcha and Other Writings* ed. J. P. Sommerville (Cambridge, 1991) pp. x–xi, xv–xx, xxxii–xxxiv: for Rodney, see CUL, Dd 3, 84B, sect. 9, pp. 114–16, 149–50.
32. Cust, *Forced Loan*, pp. 107–8, 218–23; Barnes, *Somerset*, pp. 216–23; PRO, SP 16/424/25; 426/39; 427/21; 454/49; Bod. L., MS Topog. Lincs. c.3 fos 68–299: NLW, Wynn, no. 1673; Sharpe, *Personal Rule*, pp. 899–901: Barnes, *Somerset*, pp. 277–8.
33. B. Schofield (ed.) *The Knyvett Letters, 1620–1644* (1949) p. 102.
34. C. Russell, *The Causes of the English Civil War* (Oxford, 1990) pp. 131–60; A. Fletcher, *The Outbreak of the English Civil War* (1981) pp. 302–7.

35. Ibid, pp. 91–124, 150, 284–90; J.S. Morrill, *Cheshire 1630–1660: County Government and Society during the English Revolution* (Oxford, 1974) pp. 45–53; K. Feiling, *A History of the Tory Party, 1640–1714* (Oxford, 1924) pp. 38–41.
36. J.S. Morrill, 'The Religious Context of the English Civil War', *TRHS*, 5th ser., 34 (1984) pp. 155–78; Holmes, *Eastern Association*, pp. 34–55; J.S. Morrill, 'Sir William Brereton and England's Wars of Religion', *JBS*, 24 (1985) pp. 311–32; J. Eales, *Puritans and Roundheads: the Harleys of Brampton Bryan and the Outbreak of the English Civil War* (Cambridge, 1990) pp. 149–77.
37. R. Hutton, *The Royalist War Effort* (1982) pp. 15–17; J.G. Marston, 'Gentry Honor and Royalism in Early Stuart England', *JBS*, 13 (1973–4) pp. 21–43; Feiling, *Tory Party*, pp. 54–58; B. Manning, *The English People and the English Revolution* (1976) pp. 231–3.
38. Hutton, *Royalist War Effort*, pp. 23–4, 39–40; Fletcher, *Outbreak*, p. 384; Holmes, *Lincolnshire*, pp. 145–50, 156–7; Holmes, *Eastern Association*, pp. 41–7, 55–62; Hughes, *Warwickshire*, pp. 164–5.
39. Holmes, *Eastern Association*, pp. 33, 41, 248 n.39; A. Everitt, *The Community of Kent and the Great Rebellion, 1640–1660* (Leicester, 1966) pp. 107–25.
40. Blackwood, *Lancashire*, pp. 10, 38; P. Roebuck, *Yorkshire Baronets, 1640–1760: Families, Estates, and Fortunes* (Hull, 1980) p. 43; J.T. Cliffe, *Puritans in Conflict* (1988) pp. 51, 135–7; Holmes, *Lincolnshire*, p. 205.
41. G.E. Aylmer, 'Who was Ruling in Herefordshire from 1645 to 1661?', *Trans. Woolhope Naturalists' Field Club*, 40 (1972) pp. 373–87; A.H. Dodd, 'Nerth y Committee' in his *Studies in Stuart Wales* (Cardiff, 1952) pp. 110–43; C.B. Phillips, 'County Committees and Local Government in Cumberland and Westmorland, 1642–1660', *Northern History*, 5 (1970) pp. 34–66; G.C.F. Forster, 'County Government in Yorkshire during the Interregnum', *Northern History*, 12 (1976) pp. 100–4.
42. *Royalist's Notebook*, pp. 110–11. The best discussion of the transformation of local committees is D. Underdown, *Pride's Purge* (Oxford, 1971) pp. 24–39; for Holland, see Holmes, *Eastern Association*, pp. 191–2.
43. Ibid., pp. 191–2; Everitt, *Community of Kent*, pp. 143–52, 218, 220–1; C. Holmes (ed.) *The Suffolk Committees for Scandalous Ministers, 1644–1646*, Suffolk Rec. Soc., 13 (1970) pp. 108, 111, 112.
44. *Royalist's Notebook*, pp. 105–6; Underdown, *Pride's Purge*, pp. 32, 33, 35, 36; Hughes, *Warwickshire*, pp. 234, 246.
45. Cliffe, *Puritans in Conflict*, pp. 61, 122–3, 178; Alan Everitt, *Suffolk and the Great Rebellion*, Suffolk Rec. Soc., 3 (1960) p. 19; Hughes, *Warwickshire*, pp. 228–9, 239, 241–2.
46. D. Underdown, 'Settlement in the Counties, 1653–1658' in G.E. Aylmer (ed.) *The Interregnum: the Quest for Settlement 1646–1660* (1972) pp. 165–82; D. Underdown, *Somerset in the Civil War and Interregnum* (Newton Abbot, 1973) pp. 185–6; Phillips, 'County Committees', p. 58; *A Narrative of the Late Parliament (so called)* (1657) and *A Second Narrative* (1658) in R. Oldys (ed.) *The Harleian Miscellany*, 12 vols (1805–15) vi, pp. 474, 503, 507.

47. R.H. Tawney, 'Harrington's Interpretation of his Age', *Procs. of the British Academy*, 24 (1941) pp. 199–223; J.T. Rutt (ed.) *The Diary of Thomas Burton*, 4 vols (1828) iii, p. 133; P. Zagorin, *A History of Political Thought in the English Revolution* (1954) pp. 132–41; J.G.A. Pocock, *The Machiavellian Moment* (Princeton, 1975) p. 395.
48. *Reresby*, pp. 21–2; *Verney Memoirs*, ii, pp. 7, 8, 23, 41–3; J. Isham (ed.) *The correspondence of Bishop Brian Duppa and Sir Justinian Isham, 1650–1660*, Northants. Rec. Soc., 17 (1951) pp. 8, 10, 35, 41, 71, 135; SBT, DR37/Box 88, Elizabeth Peyto to Sir Simon Archer. For the economic difficulties faced by the gentry, see above pp. 150–6.
49. D. Underdown, *Royalist Conspiracy in England, 1649–1660* (New Haven, 1960) p. 151; Everitt, *Community of Kent*, pp. 119, 277–81; Underdown, *Somerset*, pp. 190–1; *Burton's Diary*, i, p. 240.
50. *Verney Memoirs*, i, pp. 320, 322; J. Spurr, *The Restoration Church of England, 1646–1689* (1991) pp. 1–28; R.S. Bosher, *The Making of the Restoration Settlement* (1957) pp. 10–14, 30–1, 37, 43–4; E.P. Shirley, *Stemmata Shirleiana* (Westminster, 1873) pp. 150–6.
51. R. Hutton, *The Restoration* (Oxford, 1985) pp. 89, 95; Hughes, *Warwickshire*, pp. 331–2.
52. A. Grey, *Debates in the House of Commons from the year 1667 to the year 1694*, 10 vols (1763) i, p. 398; Lord Braybrook (ed.) *The Autobiography of Sir John Bramston*, Camden Soc., old ser., 32 (1844) p. 117: Hutton, *Restoration*, pp. 181–4; A. Fletcher, *Reform in the Provinces* (1986) pp. 351–73.
53. The best general discussion is P. Seaward, *The Cavalier Parliament and the Reconstruction of the Ancien Regime, 1661–1667* (Cambridge, 1989) pp. 40–1, 196–214; *Bramston's Autobiography*, pp. 116–17; H.A. Wyndham, *A Family History, 1410–1688* (Oxford, 1939) pp. 188–9, 262–4. For a similar mythic history, still retailed in 1691, of a Cumberland family, Phillippson of Thwatterden, see Jane M. Ewbank (ed.) *Antiquary on Horseback: the Collection of the Rev. Thos. Machell* (Kendal, 1963) pp. 88, 113, 122. For the 1661 elections, see Kishlansky, *Parliamentary Selection*, pp. 128–30.
55. Seaward, *Cavalier Parliament*, pp. 43, 103; C.D. Chandaman, *The English Public Revenue* (Oxford, 1975) pp. 37–9, 200–2; J. Thirsk, 'Agrarian Problems and the English Revolution' in R.C. Richardson (ed.) *Town and Countryside in the English Revolution* (Manchester, 1992) p. 191; M.L. Bush, *The English Aristocracy: a Comparative Synthesis* (Manchester, 1984) p. 127; P.B. Munsche, *Gentlemen and Poachers: the English Game Laws, 1671–1831* (Cambridge, 1981) pp. 8–27, 180–1.
55. Grey, *Debates*, i, pp. 272–5, 395–9.
56. I. Green, *The Re-Establishment of the Church of England, 1660–1663* (Oxford, 1977) pp. 181–5; Hutton, *Restoration*, pp. 152–4, 159–61. For the purges of the corporations in the 1680s, see J.R. Jones, *The Revolution of 1688 in England* (1972) pp. 43–7, 141–3; Holmes, *Lincolnshire*, pp. 247–8; Jenkins, *Glamorgan*, p. 130. For Land Qualification legislation, see G. Holmes, *British Politics in the Age of Anne* (1967) pp. 163, 178–83; J.H. Plumb, *The Growth of Political Stability in England* (1967) pp. 142–3.

57. Hutton, *Restoration*, pp. 151–2, 199, 206–7; B. Reay, *The Quakers and the English Revolution* (1985) pp. 105–6; Bosher, *Restoration Settlement*, pp. 200–4; Green, *Re-Establishment*, pp. 187–96; *HMC, Third Report*, pp. 92–3; A. M. Coleby, *Central Government and the Localities: Hampshire 1649–1689* (Cambridge, 1987) p. 139; CUL, MS Dd 9, 43, pp. 60, 61; Holmes, *Lincolnshire*, pp. 86, 222; Spurr, *Restoration Church of England*, pp. 61–5; Samuel Petto, *A Faithful Narrative of the Wonderful and Extraordinary Fits* (1693) p. 20; Grey, *Debates*, ii, pp. 23, 25, 35.
58. Ibid., pp. 13–14; Spurr, *Restoration Church of England*, pp. 188–90, 209–19; Holmes, *Lincolnshire*, pp. 229–30, 247; Coleby, *Hampshire*, pp. 200–5.
59. J. R. Jones, *The First Whigs* (Oxford, 1961) pp. 162–3; *History of Parliament: The House of Commons 1660–1690*, ed. B. D. Henning 3 vols (1983) i, pp. 321–2; Coleby, *Hampshire*, pp. 213–18; Holmes, *Lincolnshire*, pp. 244–8.
60. L. K.J. Glassey, *Politics and the Appointment of Justices of the Peace, 1675–1720* (Oxford, 1979) pp. 63–91; *Bramston's Autobiography*, pp. 120–60, 172–8, 304; *Reresby*, pp. 494, 496, 584: see also *HMC Le Fleming*, p. 210; *HMC Hastings*, 2, pp. 182–3.
61. Henning (ed.) *The Commons, 1660–1690*, ii, pp. 411–12; iii, pp. 411–19; *Bramston's Autobiography*, pp. 326, 338; Zagorin, *History of Political Thought*, p. 132; Seaward, *Cavalier Parliament*, pp. 39–40.
62. Ibid, pp. 42–51; J. P. Kenyon, *Revolution Principles: the Politics of Party, 1689–1720* (Cambridge, 1977) Chs 4, 7, 8.
63. Seaward, *Cavalier Parliament*, pp. 48, 130–40; H. Horwitz (ed.) *The Parliamentary Diary of Narcissus Luttrell, 1691–1693* (Oxford, 1972) p. 398; H. Horwitz, *Parliament, Policy and Politics in the Reign of William III* (Manchester, 1977) pp. 138, 265, 292; Glassey, *Politics and the Appointment of Justices of the Peace*, Chs 4–9; for gentry response in parliament, see especially pp. 17, 131–2, 142–7, 164, 209.
64. Seaward, *Cavalier Parliament*, pp. 276–301; Grey, *Debates*, ii, pp. 200, 226; D. C. Whitcombe, *Charles II and the Cavalier House of Commons, 1663–1674* (Manchester, 1966) pp. 141–65.
65. Henning (ed.) *The Commons, 1660–1690*, ii, pp. 574–6; 3, p. 477; Grey, *Debates*, iii, p. 48; Holmes, *Lincolnshire*, p. 257.
66. Ibid., p. 238; Plumb, *Political Stability*, pp. 48, 133–4, 142–6; Holmes, *British Politics in the Age of Anne*, pp. 130–6.
67. Holmes, *Lincolnshire*, pp. 256–7; Kishlansky, *Parliamentary Selection*, pp. 201–23; Plumb, *Political Stability*, pp. 73–97.
68. Holmes, *British Politics in the Age of Anne*, p. 182; Grey, *Debates*, ix, pp. 423–4.
69. Ewbank (ed.) *Antiquary on Horseback*, p. 134; *The Freeholder*, 22, 5 March 1716. This paragraph owes much to the arguments of Plumb, *Political Stability*, Chs 3–6; Holmes, *British Politics in the Age of Anne*, Ch. 5; I. Kramnick, *Bolingbroke and his Circle: the Politics of Nostalgia in the Age of Walpole* (Cambridge, Mass., 1968) pp. 56–83.

**Chapter 7 Education**

1. *Wandesford*, pp. 6–18.

2. *Thornton*, pp. 8–9, 40, 105, 161.
3. *Clenennau Letters*, pp. 126–7.
4. J. Thirsk and J. P. Cooper (eds) *Seventeenth-Century Economic Documents* (Oxford, 1972) pp. 752, 755; J. Youings, *Sixteenth-Century England* (1984) pp. 117–18; *Royalist's Notebook*, p. 249.
5. Cliffe, *Yorkshire*, p. 68; Thomas Fuller, *The History of the Worthies of England*, 2 vols (1811) ii, p. 523; PROB, 11/F54 Noodes; 21 Wrastley; 9 More; V. Larminie, *Wealth, Kinship and Culture: the Newdigates of Arbury, c.1585–c.1685* (forthcoming) Ch. 7; R. Brathwait, *The English Gentleman* (1630) p. 458.
6. The state of debate on the educational revolution is well summed up in R. O'Day, *Education and Society, 1500–1800* (1982). C. D'Evelyn (ed.) *Peter Idley's Instructions to his Son* (London, 1935); *The Advice of a Father, or Counsel to a Child* (London, 1688).
7. Lawrence Humphrey, *The Nobles or Of Nobility* (1563) sig. rii; *A Memorial of Walter Mildmay to his Son, Anthony* (Apethorpe, 1893); BL, Harl. 227, fo. 14; *The Glasse for Housholders* (1542) sig. evii; FSL, W. b. 484, p. 5; D. Disney, *Some Remarkable Passages in the Holy Life and Death of Gervase Disney, Esq.* (1692) pp. 24–5.
8. *D'Ewes*, i, p. 29; L. Pollock (ed.) *With Faith and Physic: the Life of a Tudor Gentlewoman* (1993) p. 26; J. E. Stephens (ed.) *Aubrey on Education* (1975) p. 19; J. T. Cliffe, *The Puritan Gentry Besieged, 1650–1700* (1993) pp. 150–1.
9. FSL, W. b. 484, p. 5; *Royalist's Notebook*, p. 249; FSL, V. a. 180; *The Glasse for Householders*, sig. eix; Dorothy Leigh, *The Mother's Blessing* (1616) pp. 16–24; N. Orme, *From Childhood to Chivalry: the Education of English Kings and Aristocracy, 1066–1530* (1984) p. 33; *Guise Memoirs*, p. 113; Cliffe, *Puritan Gentry*, p. 73.
10. *Whitelocke*, pp. 44–5; Slingsby, pp. 53–4; *The Letters of John Holles* i, pp. 29–36; KAO, U350, C2/62, 71, 78, 93.
11. E. S. De Beer (ed.) *The Diary of John Evelyn*, 6 vols (Oxford, 1955) iii, pp. 206–7; Holles, p. 227; Samuel Clark, *The Lives of Sundry Eminent Persons* (1683) pt.ii, p. 110; Orme, *From Childhood to Chivalry*, p. 158.
12. L. Pollock, '"Teach her to Live under Obedience": the Making of Women in the Upper Ranks of Early Modern England', *Continuity and Change*, 4 (1989) pp. 231–58; Pollock, *With Faith and Physic*, p. 28.
13. D. Gardiner, *English Girlhood at School* (1929) p. 119; NLW, Wynn, no. 967; M. Blundell (ed.) *Cavalier: Letters of William Blundell to his Friends, 1620–96* (1933) pp. 55–7 and App. VI: Blundell was proud of the literacy of his female relatives: of a letter from his sister Winifred he noted that another sister could produce pieces 'at least as well writ'; Cholmley, pp. 8–9; J. M. Osborn (ed.) *The Autobiography of Thomas Whytehorne* (1962).
14. M. Slater, *Family Life in the Seventeenth Century: the Verneys of Claydon House* (1984) p. 137; *Verney Memoirs*, i, pp. 501–2; J. Cornwallis, *The Private Correspondence of Jane Lady Cornwallis, 1613–44* (1842) p. 277.
15. Orme, *From Childhood to Chivalry*, pp. 58–60, 64–5; O'Day, *Education and Society*, p. 187.

16. D. M. Meads (ed.) *Diary of Lady Margaret Hoby* (1930) pp. 7–9, 167, 182; Cholmley, pp. 49–51; *Royalist's Notebook*, pp. 162–3.
17. Pollock, '"Teach her to Live Under Obedience"', p. 243
18. Cholmley, p. 87; Bod. L., Rawl. D 859, fo. 12; Cliffe, *Puritan Gentry*, p. 33; PROB, 11/22 Bennett, F17 Tashe; Pollock, '"Teach her to Live Under Obedience"', p. 239; SRO, D1057/O/1 A & B, fo. 82v; FSL, X. d. 446, p. 58.
19. *Royalist's Notebook*, p. 249; J. Johnson, *The Gloucestershire Gentry* (Gloucester, 1989), p. 109.
20. C. E. Whiting, 'Sir Patience Ward of Tanshelf', *YAJ*, 34 (1939) p. 245.
21. William Perkins, 'A Treatise of the Vocations or Callings of Men' in *Works* (1612) iii, p. 759; FSL, W. b. 484, p. 6; CRO, R(S) 1/72; P. Millican, 'The Gawdys of Suffolk and Norfolk', *NA*, 26 (1936–8) p. 383; *Verney Memoirs*, ii, pp. 95–6; M. H. Burnett, 'Authority and Obedience: Masters and Servants in English Literature and Society, ca. 1580–1642', Univ. of Oxford, D.Phil thesis, 1989, pp. 110–11.
22. Fletcher, *Sussex*, p. 37; Bod. L., Rawl. D 923, fo. 334; L. Campbell, 'Sir Roger Townshend and His Family: a Study in Gentry Life in Early Seventeenth Century Norfolk', Univ. of East Anglia, PhD thesis, 1990, p. 16; NLW, Wynn, no.238.
23. W. J. Craig (ed.) 'The Letters of James Ryther of Harewood', *YAJ*, 56 (1984) p. 105; Sir James Perrott, *The History of Sir John Perrott* (1728) p. 19; Stone, *Crisis*, p. 675–6; *Reresby* pp. xxxvi-ii; Holles, p. 215.
24. Cliffe, *Yorkshire*, pp. 68–9; M. James, *Family, Lineage and Civil Society* (Oxford, 1974) pp. 103–6; Johnson, *Gloucestershire Gentry*, pp. 17–31; W. P. Griffith, 'Schooling and Society' in J. G. Jones (ed.) *Class, Community and Culture in Tudor Wales* (Cardiff, 1989) pp. 100–2; J. and S. C. Venn (eds) *The Matriculation Books of Gonville and Caius College* (1887); O'Day, *Education and Society*, pp. 36–7.
25. Johnson, *Gloucestershire Gentry*, p. 36; MacCulloch, *Suffolk*, pp. 146–7; J. McConica 'Scholars and Commoners in Renaissance Oxford' in L. Stone (ed.) *The University in Society*, 2 vols (Princeton, 1974) i, pp. 177–9; Larminie, *The Newdigates*, Ch. 7.
26. *Guise Memoirs*, p. 115; *Aubrey on Education*, pp. 19–20; LAO, Monson 7/14/61; Stone, *Crisis*, p. 686.
27. NLW, Wynn, nos. 180, 266, 267, 348, 360, 429, 438, 440, 443, 449, 473, 696, 706, 877.
28. 'The Letters of President Gwynne', *The Eagle*, 19 (1897) p. 2; T. Hodges, *Two Consolatory Letters written to . . . the Countess of Westmorland* (1669) p. 7; CRO, R(S) 1/26; *Wandesford*, p. 16; *Letters of John Holles*, i, p. 63; *D'Ewes*, i, p. 121; *Guise Memoirs*, p. 116; Whiting, 'Sir Patience Ward of Tanshelf', p. 146. On the problems of discipline within the university see J. K. McConica 'The Collegiate Society' in J. K. McConica, (ed.) *History of the University of Oxford: vol. iii: The Collegiate University*, (Oxford, 1986) pp. 659–65.
29. William Shakespeare, *Henry IV: Part II*, Act 3, sc.2; J. M. J. Tonks, 'The Lyttletons of Frankley and their Estates, 1540–1640', Univ. of Oxford, B. Litt. thesis, 1978, p. 144; L. Stone, 'The Size and Composition of the

Oxford Student Body' in Stone (ed.) *The University in Society*, i, p. 43; Cliffe, *Yorkshire*, pp. 75–6; FSL, X. d. 446, p. 58; E.K. Bennet, 'Notes from a Norfolk Squire's Note-book', *Cambridge Antiq. Soc.*, 43 (1883) p. 217.

30. YAS, DD56 M2, unfol. (July 1619); NRO, IC 14; *D'Ewes*, i, p. 141; FSL, L. a. 49–62; NLW, Wynn, no. 572; B. Schofield (ed.) *The Knyvett Letters, 1620–44* (1949) p. 19; *Oxinden Letters*, i, p. 104.
31. For summaries of the debate on undergraduate numbers see O'Day, *Education and Society*, pp. 81ff; J. Looney, 'Undergraduate Education at Early Stuart Cambridge', *History of Education*, 10/1 (1981) pp. 9–19; McConica, 'The Collegiate Society', pp. 666ff; Stone, 'The Size of the Oxford Student Body', pp. 27–8.
32. Johnson, *Gloucestershire Gentry*, p. 110; V. Morgan, 'Cambridge University and "the Country"', in Stone (ed.) *The University in Society*, i, p. 236; Cliffe, *Yorkshire*, pp. 73–4; M. McIntosh, *A Community Transformed: the Manor and Liberty of Havering 1500–1620* (Cambridge, 1991) p. 264; Jenkins, *Glamorgan*, pp. 49, 226.
33. R. Hughey (ed.) *The Correspondence of Dame Katherine Paston*, Norfolk Rec. Soc., 14 (1941) p. 83; *Wentworth*, p. 18; *Wandesford*, p. 18; NRO, IC 19; BL, Add. 34,161, fo. 7; NLW, Wynn, no. 464.
34. V. Larminie, 'The Undergraduate Account Book of John and Richard Newdigate, 1618–21', *Camden Miscellany* 30, Camden Soc., 4th ser., 39 (1988) pp. 156–7; McConica, 'The Collegiate Society', pp. 666ff; Looney, 'Undergraduate Education at Early Stuart Cambridge', p. 17.
35. Ibid, pp. 12–16; PRO, SP 46/15; Larminie, 'Account Book of the Newdigates', pp. 161–216; *Whitelocke*, p. 48; S.C. Lomas (ed.) 'The Memoirs of Sir George Courthop', *Camden Miscellany* 11, Camden Soc., 3rd ser., 13 (1907) p. 104; McConica, 'The Collegiate Society', p. 710; even Edward, Lord Herbert of Cherbury, whose rejection of the university curriculum is often cited as paradigmatic, advocated a year of logic and 'the ground of the Platonic and Aristotelian philosophy' as part of the training for a gentleman, S. Lee (ed.) *The Autobiography of Edward, Lord Herbert of Cherbury* (2nd edn, 1906) pp. 24–5.
36. C. Holmes, 'The County Community in Stuart Historiography', *JBS*, 19 (1980) pp. 59–60; G.E. Mingay, *The Gentry* (1976) pp. 156–7; Morgan, 'Cambridge and "the Country"', p. 183; Henry Glapthorne, *Wit in a Constable* (1639) Act 1, sc. 1; *D'Ewes*, i, pp. 120–2.
37. *The Eagle*, 27 (1906) p. 330; J.H. Bettey (ed.) *Calendar of the Correspondence of the Smyth Family of Ashton Court*, Bristol Rec. Soc., 35 (1982) p. 63; A.L. Rowse, *Simon Forman: Sex and Society in Shakespeare's Age* (1974) pp. 277–8; M. Curtis, *Oxford and Cambridge in Transition, 1558–1642* (Oxford, 1959), p. 276; CRO, R(S) 1/26; J.G. Nichols (ed.) *Narratives of the Reformation*, Camden Soc., old ser., 77 (1859) p. 239; *Whitelocke*, p. 48.
38. Sir Hamon Le Strange (ed.) 'Sir Nicholas Le Strange to his son Hamon', *Norfolk and Norwich Archaeological Soc.*, 9 (1880–4) p. 330; *Wandesford*, p. 16; Morgan, 'Cambridge University and "The Country"', pp. 214–24; W.D. Christie (ed.) *Memoirs, Letters and Speeches of Anthony Ashley Cooper, First Earl of Shaftesbury* (1859) p. 16; Larminie, 'Account Book of

the Newdigates', pp. 189ff; H.C. Porter, *Reformation and Reaction in Tudor Cambridge*, (Cambridge, 1958) p. 271; R.G. Marsden, *College Life in the Time of James I* (1851) pp. 40–2; A. Fairfax-Lucy, *The Lucys of Charlecote* (1958) pp. 109–12. Edward Herbert was at University College, Thomas Lucy at Magdalen.

39. Slingsby, pp. 303–6; 318; Cliffe, *Puritan Gentry*, p. 128; Bettey, *Correspondence of the Smyth Family*, p. 67; *Aubrey on Education*, p. 28.
40. Cliffe, *Yorkshire*, p. 73; T.G. Barnes, *Somerset 1625–1640: a County's Government During the 'Personal Rule'* (Oxford, 1961) p. 31; Jenkins, *Glamorgan*, p. 226; W. Prest, *The Inns of Court under Elizabeth and the Early Stuarts, 1590–1640* (1972) p. 9; YAS, DD56/0/7; Lomas (ed.) 'Memoirs of Sir George Courthop', p. 104.
41. Orme, *From Childhood to Chivalry*, pp. 76–9; Prest, *The Inns of Court*, pp. 29–32.
42. *HMC Portland*, ix, p. 15; Cholmley, p. 38; IOW RO, OG/CC/23; *Reresby*, pp. 4–5; W.P. Baildon (ed.) *Les Reportes del Cases in Camera Stellata 1593–1609* (1894) p. 315; William Shakespeare, *Henry IV: Pt.ii*, Act 3, sc.2.
43. J.W. Clay and J. Lister (eds) 'The Autobiography of Sir John Savile, of Methley, knt, Baron of the Exchequer, 1546–1607', *YAJ*, 15 (1900) p. 423; Prest, *The Inns of Court*, pp. 137–73; R.L. Edgworth, *Essays on Professional Education* (1809) p. 313; V.F. Stern, *Sir Stephen Powle of Court and Country* (1992) pp. 25–6.
44. W.H. Long (ed.) The Oglander Memoirs (1888) p. 165; NRO, IC/25; *Wentworth*, p. 18; IOW RO OG/SS/1, fo. 83; Cholmley, p. 38.
45. Prest, *The Inns of Court*, pp. 33–40; *Whitelocke*, pp. 49–50; L.A. Knafla, *Law and Politics in Jacobean England* (Cambridge, 1977) pp. 48–9; Larminie 'Account Book of the Newdigates', pp. 217–68; such evaluation must have reinforced the prestige of the legal profession itself see J.P. Dawson, *The Oracles of the Law* (Ann Arbor, 1968) p. 45; NLW, Wynn, no. 836.
46. Edward Waterhouse, *A Discourse and Defence of Arms and Armory* (1660) p. 134; Higford, p. 58; Stone, 'Size and Composition of Oxford Student Body', pp. 48–50.
47. Stone, *Crisis*, pp. 693–4; IOW RO, OG/SS/1, fo. 87, Strode headed this section of his advice 'Travayle not'; R. Clutterbuck, *The History and Antiquities of the County of Hertford*, 3 vols (1815–27) i, p. 238; Jenkins, *Glamorgan*, pp. 227–8.
48. *Letters of John Holles*, i, pp. 52–3; Cliffe, *Yorkshire*, p. 80; *Reresby*, pp. 6–18; J. Stoye, *English Travellers Abroad, 1604–1667* (revised ed., New Haven, 1989), pp. 143ff; *Aubrey on Education*, p. 135.
49. G.C. Brauer, *The Education of a Gentleman: Theories of in England 1660–1725* (New York, 1959).

## Chapter 8 Civility, Sociability and the Maintenance of Hegemony

1. J.E. Stephens (ed.) *Aubrey on Education* (1975) p. 29; YAS, MS. 178, pp. 1–2; W. Vaughan, *The Golden Grove* (1600) sig. S6v; R. Brathwait, *The English Gentleman* (1630) p. 457.

2. W. C. Hazlitt (ed.) *Inedited Tracts*, Roxburghe Soc. (1868) p. 43; R. A. Rebholz (ed.) *The Poems of Sir Thomas Wyatt* (1978) pp. 188–9; Sir John Harington, 'The Prayse of a Private Life' in N. G. McClure (ed.) *The Letters and Epigrams of Sir John Harington*, (New York, 1972) p. 333; William Cornwallis, *Essays* (1600) sig F8.
3. J. Nicolas (ed.) *The Memoirs of Lady Fanshawe* (1829) p. 3; Harington, 'The Prayse', p. 339.
4. W. Clark-Maxwell, 'An Inventory of the Contents of Markeaton Hall', *J. of Derbys. Arch. and Nat. Hist. Soc.*, 51 (1930) p. 132; NLW, Wynn, no. 185; WYRO, TN/C/1/323; M. Girouard, *Life in the English Country House* (New Haven, 1979) pp. 166–70; Henry Peacham, *The Compleat Gentleman*, ed. V. B. Heltzel (Ithaca, 1962) p. 67; N. Wright, 'The Gentry and their Houses in Norfolk and Suffolk from ca.1550–1850', Univ. of East Anglia, PhD thesis, 1990, p. 450.
5. S. Jayne, *Library Catalogues of the English Renaissance* (Godalming, 1983); Bod. L., Eng. Hist. b.159, fos 118v–20v; see also the lists of Sir Valentine Pell's books in CUL, Ch(H), Pell Papers; J. Gage, *A History of Hengrave in Suffolk* (1822) pp. 23–35; N. Ker, 'Sir John Prise', *The Library*, 5th ser., 10 (1955), pp. 1–24; D. J. McKitterick, *The Library of Sir Thomas Knyvet of Ashwellthorpe, ca. 1539–1618* (Cambridge, 1978); a good example of the steadier purchase of books in the early seventeenth century is the listing of Sir Thomas Barrington's purchases from 1635 to 1639: M. E. Bohannon, 'A London Bookseller's Bill', *The Library*, 4th ser., 18 (1938) pp. 417–46.
6. O. L. Dick (ed.) *Aubrey's Brief Lives* (1949) pp. 26–7; E. M. Halcrow (ed.) *Charges to the Grand Jury at Quarter Sessions, 1660–67 by Sir Peter Leicester*, Chetham Soc., 3rd ser., 5 (1953) p. 152; McKitterick, *Sir Thomas Knyvett*, pp. 9–14; Jenkins, *Glamorgan*, p. 231; UCW Bangor, Mostyn 9066; P. Morgan, 'Frances Wolfreston and "Hor Boaks"', *The Library*, 6th ser., 11 (1989) pp. 197–219.
7. Higford, p. 592; IOW RO, OG/AA/27, fo. 31; OG/AA/29, fo. 62; *Thornton*, p. 190; Henry Peacham, *The Art of Living in London* in R. Oldys (ed.) *The Harleian Miscellany*, 12 vols (1805–15) ix, p. 87.
8. J. Thirsk and J. P. Cooper (eds) *Seventeenth-Century Economic Documents* (Oxford, 1972) p. 24.
9. *The Advice of a Father or Counsel to a Child* (1688) p. 17; Cassandra, Duchess of Chandos, *The Continuation of the History of the Willoughby Family*, ed. A. C. Wood (Eton, 1958) pp. 103–8; Samuel Garey, *Ientaculum Iudicum, or a Breake-fast for the Bench* (1623) sig. A3v–4; Bartholemew Parsons, *A Christians Remembrance or Felicity by Hope: a Sermon Preached at the Burial of Sir Francis Pile, Bt.* (Oxford, 1635) p. 35.
10. On honour and the household see M. James, 'English Politics and the Concept of Honour' in his *Society, Politics and Culture* (Cambridge, 1986) pp. 308–415; Henry Wotton, *The Elements of Architecture* (1624) p. 82; S. Greenblatt, *Renaissance Self-Fashioning* (Chicago, 1980).
11. F. Heal, *Hospitality in Early Modern England* (Oxford, 1990), pp. 36–48, 153–68; *The Institucion of a Gentleman* (1555) sig. G2; Holles, p. 45; *The Genealogist*, 17 (1900–1) p. 12; T. Manningham, *A Sermon at the Funeral of Sir John Norton, Bt., preached at East Tistead, Hampshire* (1687) p. 17.

12. M. Howard, *The Early Tudor Country House* (1987) pp. 72–8; Parsons, *A Christians Remembrance*, p. 35; Willoughby Household Ordinances, 1572 [?] in *HMC Middleton*, p. 539.
13. Girouard, *English Country House*, pp. 119ff; Wotton, *Elements of Architecture*, p. 71.
14. For a full discussion of these duties and of changing attitudes see Heal, *Hospitality in Early Modern England*, pp. 91–141; Bezaleel Carter, *The Wise King and the Learned Judge* (Cambridge, 1618) p. 62.
15. Heal, *Hospitality in Early Modern England*, pp. 74–7; WYRO, Ingleby 3272; NLW, Wynn, no. 2492; PRO, SP 16/282/26; James Shirley, *The Witty Fair One* (1628), Act 2 sc. 1.
16. T. D. Whitaker (ed.) *The History and Antiquities of Craven*, 2 vols (1878) ii, p. 379; T. Fuller, *The Holy State and the Prophane State* (1642) p. 153; J. Nichols, *The Progresses of Queen Elizabeth*, 3 vols (1823).
17. *Archaeologia* 25 (1834) pp. 419–512; NorfRO, Bradfer-Lawrence VIIb/5; Raynham MS, Bacon Household Book, 1620–8; IOW RO, OG/SS/1, fo. 85v; H. H. E. Craster (ed.) *History of Northumberland*, 10 vols (1909), ix, p. 158; R. Carew, *A Survey of Cornwall* (1602) p. 65.
18. Holles, p. 42; N. J. G. Pounds (ed.) 'William Carnsew of Bokelly and his Diary, 1576–7', *Journ. of the Royal Inst. of Cornwall*, new ser., 8, pt.1 (1978) pp. 33, 40, 44, 49; Hazlitt, *Inedited Tracts*, p. 64; many gentlemen here followed William Cecil's advice to his son 'Certain Precepts for Well-Ordering of a Man's Life' in F. Peck (ed.) *Desiderata Curiosa*, 2 vols (1732–5) i, p. 65; NorfRO, Le Strange NE2, p. 9.
19. PRO, SP 12/11/14, 13/14; WYRO, Ingleby 3272.
20. For general background see R. Carr, *A History of Fox-hunting* (1976); D. H. Madden, *The Diary of Master William Silence* (1897); R. Blome, *The Gentlemans Recreation* (1686); Ben Jonson, *The Complete Poems*, ed. G. Parfit (1975) p. 189; Robert Burton, *The Anatomy of Melancholy*, ed. T. C. Faulkner, N. K. Kiessling and R. L. Blair, 2 vols (Oxford, 1989), i, p. 289; F. R. Raines (ed.) *The Journal of Nicholas Assheton, Esq*. Chetham Soc., old ser., 14 (1848); J. Eames, 'The Poems of Sir William Kingsmill', Univ. of Birmingham, PhD thesis, 1981, pp. 288–94; Holles, pp. 215–6, 219; T. H. Brooke, 'The Memoirs of Sir Hugh Cholmley', Univ. of Oxford, B. Litt. thesis, 1937, pp. 38, 48, 52.
21. *CSPD 1627–8*, p. 193; for an important new analysis of gentry attitudes to hunting see R. B. Manning, *Hunters and Poachers: a Cultural and Social History of Unlawful Hunting in England 1485–1640* (Oxford, 1993): the Nimrod comment, from Sir William Blackstone's observation on the Game Law, is cited at p. 57.
22. James Cleland, *The Institution of a Young Nobleman* (New York, 1948) p. 134; Madden, *Diary of Master William Silence*, pp. 363–4; Sir William Davenant, *The Wits* (1634), Act 3, sc. 1; Timothy Oldmayne, *God's Rebuke in Taking from us that Worthy and Honourable Gentleman, Sir Edward Lewkenor* (1619) pp. 32–3; John Gerard, *The Autobiography of an Elizabethan*, ed. P. Caraman (1951) pp. 15, 37.
23. Carr, *A History of Fox-hunting*, pp. 24–8; Carew, *Survey of Cornwall*, p. 23; J. V. Beckett, *The Aristocracy in England, 1660–1914* (Oxford, 1986) p. 342; M. Vale, *The Gentleman's Recreations: the Accomplishments and*

*Pastimes of the English Gentleman, 1580–1630* (Cambridge, 1977) p. 41; *Oxinden Letters*, i, pp. 106–7.

24. H. Owen (ed.) *George Owen's Pembrokeshire*, 4 vols, Society of Cymroddhorion Rec. Ser. (1892–1936), i, p. 269; D. Brailsford, *Sport and Society: Elizabeth to Anne* (1969) p. 31; H. Chauncy, *The Historical Antiquities of Hertfordshire* (1700) p. 178; WYRO, TN/C/2/278; Fletcher, *Sussex* p. 29; L. Stone and J. C. Stone, *An Open Elite? England 1540–1880* (Oxford, 1984) pp. 314–15; L. Campbell, 'Sir Roger Townshend and His Family: a Study in Gentry Life in Early Seventeenth Century Norfolk', Univ. of East Anglia, PhD thesis, 1990, p. 64; *Royalist's Notebook* p. 84; D. M. Meads (ed.) *The Diary of Lady Margaret Hoby* (1930) p. 120.
25. Vale, *Gentleman's Recreations*, pp. 98, 94; W. L. Woodfill, *Musicians in English Society, from Elizabeth to Charles I* (Princeton, 1953) pp. 252–79; J. Raine (ed.) *Wills and Inventories of the Northern Counties of England*, Surtees Soc., 2 (1835) p. 430; *HMC App. to 7th Rep.*, p. 525.
26. D. Price, *Patrons and Musicians of the English Renaissance* (Cambridge, 1981) pp. 61, 71–96, 143–47; J. Nicholas (ed.) *The Memoirs of Lady Fanshawe* (1829) p. 14; *Whitelocke*, pp. 64–6, 71.
27. Thomas Elyot, *The Boke named the Governor*, ed. S. E. Lehmberg (1962) p. 22; the children of the Earl of Bridgewater were major performers in Milton's masque; E. A. Parry (ed.) *The Letters from Dorothy Osborne to Sir William Temple* (1914) p. 255; D. G. Greene (ed.) *The Meditations of Lady Elizabeth Delaval*, Surtees Soc., 190 (1978), p. 40; during 1570–1 the Constable household was visited by four different groups of players, WYRO, Ingleby 3272; Holmes, *Lincolnshire* pp. 102–3; C. Howard, *Sir John Yorke of Nidderdale* (1939) pp. 24–7; H. Aveling, *Northern Catholics: the Catholic Recusants of the North Riding, 1585–1790* (1966) pp. 290–1.
28. Anthony Fitzherbert, *The Book of Husbandry* (?1534), fos. 68v–9; FSL, V. a. 180; W. Knowler (ed.) *The Earl of Strafforde's Letters and Despatches*, 2 vols (1739) i, p. 170; IOW RO, OG/SS/1, fo. 88v; PRO, STAC 5/H22/21; William Hinde, *A Faithfull Remonstrance of the Holy Life and Happy Death of John Bruen* (1641) p. 114; Cliffe, *Yorkshire*, p. 272; *Wentworth* p. 22; E. M. Hakrow (ed.) 'Sir Peter Leicester's Precepts to his Son', *Trans. of the Lancs. and Ches. Antiq. Soc.*, 66 (1950–1) p. 71.
29. *Wandesford*, p. 26; Gerard (ed.) *Autobiography of an Elizabethan*, pp. 165, 170; Stone, *Crisis*, pp. 567–72; for a comparable example see T. Breen, 'Horses and Gentlemen: the Cultural Significance of Gambling among the Gentry of Virginia', *William and Mary Quarterly* 3rd ser., 34 (1977) pp. 239–57; G. Williams (ed.) *Glamorgan County History* (Cardiff, 1974) iv, p. 96.
30. H. Colvin and J. Newman (eds) *Of Building: Roger North's Writings on Architecture* (Oxford, 1981) p. 4; Sir W. Dugdale, *The Antiquities of Warwickshire* (1730) p. 1121; W. G. Hoskins, 'The Great Rebuilding', *PP*, 4 (1953) pp. 44–59; Stone, *Crisis*, pp. 550–1; Stone and Stone, *Open Elite?* Table 11.1.
31. J. A. Gotch, *A Complete Account of the Buildings Erected in Northamptonshire by Sir Thomas Tresham* (Northampton, 1883) pp. 21–30;

N. Pevsner *The Buildings of England: Worcestershire* (London, 1968) p. 157; Colvin and Newman (eds) *Of Building* p. 7.

32. J. Summerson, 'John Thorpe and the Thorpes of Kingscliffe', *The Architectural Review*, 106 (Nov. 1949) p. 293; F. Bacon 'Of Buildings' in *Works*, ed. J. Spedding, 14 vols (1857–74), xii, p. 230; Wotton, *The Elements of Architecture*, p. 82; Slingsby, p. 52; Colvin and Newman (eds) *Of Building*, p. 22
33. Campbell, 'Sir Roger Townshend', pp. 32–57; Colvin and Newman (eds) *Of Building*, pp. 77–87; Wright, 'The Gentry and their Houses', p. 14; NRO, IC 312.
34. Girouard, *English Country House*, pp. 122–44; R.T. Gunther (ed.) *Sir Roger Pratt on Architecture* (Oxford, 1928); Colvin and Newman (eds) *Of Building*, p. 68; on Belton see G. Jackson-Stops, 'Belton House', *Country Life*, (29 August 1991) pp. 66-9.
35. Howard, *Early Tudor Country House*, pp. 69–72; Stone, *Open Elite?*, pp. 329–30, though this exaggerates the transition from urban to isolated sites.
36. E.S. Rohde (ed.) *The Garden Book of Sir Thomas Hanmer, Bart* (1933) p. xviii; J. Harris, *The Artist and the Country House* (1979); R. Strong, *The Renaissance Garden in England* (1979) pp. 73ff; E.S. De Beer (ed.) *The Diary of John Evelyn*, 6 vols (Oxford, 1955) i, p. 9; K.V. Thomas, *Man and the Natural World* (Oxford, 1983) p. 228; William Harrison, *Description of England*, ed. G. Edelen (Ithaca, 1968) p. 265; Campbell, 'Sir Roger Townshend', pp. 62–5; *Royalist's Notebook*, p. 94–5; BL, Add. 38,599, fo. 54v; De Beer (ed.) *Diary of John Evelyn*, i, p. 5; Bacon, 'Of Gardens' in *Works*, xii, pp. 485–92.
37. Heal, *Hospitality in Early Modern England*, pp. 308–9; A. Raine (ed.) *York Civic Records*, 8 vols, Yorks. Arch. Soc. Rec. Ser., 98–119, (1939–53) viii, p. 70; P. Borsay, '"All the Town's a Stage": Urban Ritual and Ceremony, 1660–1800' in P. Clark (ed.) *The Transformation of English Provincial Towns* (1984) p. 247; Ralph Knevet, *Rhodon and Iris* (1631) preface; W.H. Hudson and J.C. Tingey (eds) *Selected Records of the City of Norwich*, 2 vols (Norwich, 1906–10), ii, pp. 401–3.
38. Thomas Heywood, *The Dramatic Works*, 6 vols (1874), iv, p. 54; PRO, STAC 8/23/5; IOW RO, OG/AA/29, fo. 9v.
39. Pounds, 'William Carnsew', pp. 35, 40, 45; Brailsford, *Sport and Society*, pp. 106, 116; W.D. Christie (ed.) *Memoirs, Letters and Speeches of Anthony Ashley Cooper* (1859), p. 21; IOW RO, OG/AA/27, fo. 62v.
40. Oliver Heywood, *Autobiography and Diaries*, ed. J.H. Turner, 4 vols (Brighouse and Bingley, 1881–5), ii, pp. 271–2; W.A. Leighton (ed.) 'Early Chronicles of Shrewsbury', *Trans. of Shrops. Arch. Soc.* 1st ser., 3 (1880) p. 338; J.P. Hore, *The History of Newmarket and Annals of the Turf*, 3 vols (Newmarket, 1885) i, p. 333; H.E. Lippincott (ed.) *Merry Passages and Jeasts* (Salzburg, 1974) p. 102; NRA, Kingsmill MS. 1291.
41. Borsay has traced 12 race meetings in the sixteenth century, but a further 21 in the first quarter of the seventeenth century: P. Borsay, *The English Urban Renaissance: Culture and Society in the Provincial Town, 1660–1770* (Oxford, 1989) p. 181.

42. Hore, *History of Newmarket*, i, pp. 328, 347; PRO, C8/89/160; Burton, *Anatomy of Melancholy*, i, p. 288; Blome, *The Gentlemans Recreation*, p. 8; Stone, *Crisis*, p. 570; Gervase Markham, *Cavelarice, or the English Horseman* (1615) iii, p. 56; Bod. L., Rawl. D 859, fo. 163; Holles, pp. 196–7; on the same process of gambling as conflict displacement in seventeenth-century Virginia see Breen, 'Horses and Gentlemen', pp. 249–57.
43. J. M. J. Tonks, 'The Lyttletons of Frankley and their Estates, 1540–1640', Univ. of Oxford, B. Litt thesis, 1978, pp. 67–8; G. P. V. Akrigg, *Jacobean Pageant* (1962) p. 70. See above pp. 224–5.
44. R. W. Malcolmson, *Popular Recreations in English Society, 1700–1850* (Cambridge, 1973) pp. 68–72; Jenkins, *Glamorgan*, pp. 268–71; C. Whitfield (ed.) *Robert Dover and the Cotswold Games: Annalia Dubrensia* (1962); D. Underdown, *Revel,Riot and Rebellion* (Oxford, 1985) p. 64.
45. Francis Bacon, *Apophthegms* in *Works*, vii, p. 175; James I, *Workes*, ed. J. Montagu (1616) p. 567
46. On the growth of London see N. Brett-James, *The Growth of Stuart London*, London and Middx. Arch. Soc. (1935); L. Stone, 'The Residential Development of the West End of London in the Seventeenth-Century' in B. Malament (ed.) *After the Reformation: Essays in Honour of Jack Hexter* (Manchester, 1980) pp. 167–213; F. J. Fisher, 'The Development of London as a Centre of Conspicuous Consumption in the Sixteenth and Seventeenth Centuries' *TRHS*, 4th ser., 30 (1948) pp. 37–50; F. Heal, 'The Crown, the Gentry and London: the Enforcement of Proclamation, 1596–1640', in C. Cross *et al* (eds) *Law and Government under the Tudors* (Cambridge, 1988) pp. 211–26.
47. A. G.Dickens (ed.) 'Estate and Household Management in Bedfordshire *c*.1540' *Beds. Rec. Soc.* 36 (1956) p. 38; Heal, *Hospitality in Early Modern England*, pp. 106–70; BL, Add. 27,447, fo. 86; PCC wills of gentry with surname initials B and T.
48. J. Harington, *Horae Consecratae or Spiritual Pastime* (1682) p. 367; *Clenennau Letters*, pp. 113–14; James I, *Poems*, ed. J. Craigie, 2 vols, Scot. Text. Soc, 3rd ser., 12, 26, 1955–8, ii, p. 178; FSL, L. a. 21; Anne Aston was a Lucy by birth, and her restlessness was apparently seconded by her formidable mother Joyce: A. Fairfax-Lucy, *The Lucys of Charlecote* (1958) pp. 87–9; KAO, U350 C2/105.
49. *Letters of John Holles*, ii, p. 271; Meads (ed.) *Diary of Lady Margaret Hoby*, pp. 149–65; Cholmley, pp. 20–1; *HMC De Lisle and Dudley*, ii, p. 176.
50. R. F. Williams (ed.) *The Court and Times of James I*, 2 vols (1849) ii, p. 353; John Taylor, *Works* (1630) p. 238; Slingsby, pp. 44–5; K. Frost, 'Prescription and Devotion: the Reverend Dr. Donne and the learned Dr. Mayerne', *Medical History*, 22 (1978) p. 409; PRO, SP 16/219/60; NLW, Wynn, no. 348; M. E. Finch, *Five Northamptonshire Families, 1540–1640*, Northants. Rec. Soc., 19 (1956) p. 26.
51. Stone, *Crisis*, p. 396; P. Clark, *English Provincial Society from the Reformation to the Revolution* (Hassocks, 1977) p. 209; C. G. Durston, 'London and the Provinces: the Association between the Capital and the Berkshire County Gentry of the Early Seventeenth Century', *Southern History*, 3 (1981) p. 52; Heal, 'The Crown, the Gentry and

London', pp. 221–3; Inner Temple Library, Petyt MS 538/43, fo. 181v; Bod. L., Bankes Papers, Calendar; SBT, DR 37/87, unfol.; Fletcher, *Sussex*, pp. 42–5; P.E. Ralph (ed.) *Sir Humphrey Mildmay, Royalist Gentleman* (New Brunswick, 1947) pp. 32–3; Jenkins, *Glamorgan*, pp. 243–4.

52. Fisher, 'Conspicuous Consumption', p. 50; J.H. Bettey (ed.) *Correspondence of the Smyth Family of Ashton Court*, Bristol Rec. Soc., 35 (1982), pp. 54–5; Edward Waterhouse, *The Gentleman's Monitor* (1665) p. 295.
53. An important early defence of the values of the city is in W.C. Hazlitt (ed.) *Cyvile and Uncyvile Life* (1586), *Inedited Tracts* Roxburghe Soc. (1868) pp. 33–80; William Yonger, *The Unrighteous Judge* (1621); on the construction of civility see A. Bryson, 'Concepts of Civility in England, *c.*1560–1685', Univ. of Oxford, D.Phil thesis, 1984; De Beer (ed.) *Diary of John Evelyn*, iii, pp. 397–8.
54. PRO, SP 12/275/146; quoted in Stone and Stone, *An Open Elite?*, pp. 253–4.

**Chapter 9 The Gentry and the Church**

1. Sir Henry Spelman, *The History and Fate of Sacrilege* (1698) pp. 258–9; *DNB*: Spelman. The 1698 edition of *Sacrilege* was the first: it depends on a late MS. found in Bodley after the first was destroyed in the Fire of London. It was rumoured that printing was delayed for fear of offending 'the Nobility and Gentry'.
2. Spelman, *History of Sacrilege*, pp. 252, 267–8; L. Campbell, 'Sir Roger Townshend and His Family: a Study in Gentry Life in Early Seventeenth Century Norfolk', Univ. of East Anglia, PhD thesis, 1990, pp. 42ff.
3. Spelman, *History of Sacrilege*, p. 269.
4. J.E. Neale, *Elizabeth I and Her Parliaments 1584–1601* (1957) ii, pp. 148–64; there are various versions of the speech including Bod. L., Tanner 79, fos. 133–8.
5. M. Howard, *The Early Tudor Country House: Architecture and Politics 1490–1550* (1987) gazetteer; A.L. Rowse, *Tudor Cornwall* (1941) pp. 219–22.
6. Thomas More, *A Dialogue Concerning Heresies*, ed. T.M.C. Lawler, G. Marc'hadour and R.C. Marius (New Haven, 1981) p. 301, and Christopher St German, *A Treatise Conernynge the Division between the Spiritualytye and Temporaltye* (?1540), p. 14, both cited by Peter Marshall, 'Attitudes of the English People to Priests and Priesthood: 1500–53', Univ. of Oxford, D.Phil thesis, 1990, pp. 267–8; see, for example, John Coverdale, accused of coming to an affray in a military tunic, Marshall, 'Attitudes of the English People', pp. 185–6; PRO STAC 2/C2/28/105; Req. 2/3/293; M. Knight, *Piety and Devotion among the Warwickshire Gentry, 1485–1547*, Dugdale Soc. Occas. Paper, 32 (1989) p. 31.
7. M. Bowker, *The Henrician Reformation: the Diocese of Lincoln under John Longland, 1521–47* (Cambridge, 1981) p. 123; J. Youings, *Sixteenth-Century England* (1984) p. 191; R. O'Day, 'Ecclesiastical Patronage: Who

Controlled the Church?' in F. Heal and R. O'Day (eds) *Church and Society in England: Henry VIII to James I* (1977) pp. 152–3; N. Davis (ed.) *Paston Letters and Papers of the Fifteenth Century*, 2 vols (Oxford, 1971) i, p. 178; PROB 11/15 Bennett; 38/Noodes; A.J. Pollard, 'Richard Clervaux of Croft: a North Riding Squire in the Fifteenth Century', *YAJ*, 1 (1978) p. 162; IOW RO, OG/AA/27, fo. 9v; C. Richmond, 'Religion and the Fifteenth-Century Gentleman', in R.B. Dobson (ed.) *The Church, Politics and Patronage in the Fifteenth Century* (Gloucester, 1984) pp. 198–9; C. Carpenter, 'The Religion of the Gentry in the Fifteenth Century' in D. Williams (ed.) *England in the Fifteenth Century* (Woodbridge, 1987) pp. 53–74. For an argument against too strong an emphasis on 'privatisation' see E. Duffy, *The Stripping of the Altars: Traditional Religion in England, 1400–1580* (New Haven, 1992) pp. 121–4, 131–3.

8. D. Knowles, *The Religious Orders in England*, 3 vols (Cambridge, 1959) iii, pp. 266–7; Rowse, *Tudor Cornwall*, pp. 169–72; M. Gray, 'Change and Continuity: the Gentry and the Property of the Church in South-East Wales and the Marches' in J. Gwynfor Jones (ed.) *Class, Community and Culture in Tudor Wales* (Cardiff, 1989) p. 5.
9. S. Jack, 'Monastic Lands in Leicestershire and their Administration on the Eve of the Dissolution', *Leics. Arch. and Hist. Soc.*, 41 (1965) p. 15; G.A.J. Hodgett, *Tudor Lincolnshire* (Lincoln, 1975) pp. 61–2; M. Gray, 'Change and Continuity', p. 7; P. Clark, *English Provincial Society from the Reformation to the Revolution* (Hassocks, 1977) p. 29.
10. On acceptance of the clergy see C. Haigh, *English Reformations: Religion, Politics and Society under the Tudors* (Oxford, 1993), pp. 40–9; Marshall, 'Attitudes of the English People', pp. 68ff. Specific information on the gentry drawn from a Prerogative Court of Canterbury will sample of 389 wills with B and T surnames, 1500–58; F. Heal, *Hospitality in Early Modern England* (Oxford, 1990) pp. 62–3; S. Brigden, *The Reformation in London* (Oxford, 1989) pp. 96ff.
11. G.R. Elton, *Policy and Police: The Enforcement of the Reformation in the Age of Thomas Cromwell* (Cambridge, 1972) pp. 125–7, 152–5; Jack, 'Monastic Lands in Leicestershire', pp. 13–14; Haigh, *English Reformations*, pp. 47–9.
12. There is a massive literature on the dispersal of estates after the Dissolution. Particularly relevant surveys are: J. Youings, *The Dissolution of the Monasteries* (1971); C. Kitching, 'The Disposal of Monastic and Chantry Lands' in Heal and O'Day (eds) *Church and Society* (1977) pp. 119–36.
13. T.H. Swales, 'The Redistribution of the Monastic Lands in Norfolk', *NA*, 24 (1966) pp. 14–44; J.A. Youings 'The Terms of the Disposal of the Devon Monastic Lands 1536–58', *EHR*, 69 (1954) pp. 18–38; *LP*, xiv, i, 1338, cited in Youings, *The Dissolution of the Monasteries*, p. 229.
14. *LP*, xiii, i, 19.
15. G.W. Copeland, 'Some Problems of Buckland Abbey', *Trans. of the Devonshire Assoc.*, 85 (1953) pp. 41–3; Howard, *Early Tudor Country House*, pp. 136–62; Knowles, *Religious Orders*, iii, p. 386; J. Nichols, *The History and Antiquities of Leicestershire*, 4 vols in 8 (1799–1811) 3, i,

p. 326; Tregonwell was a noted conservative: Gregory apparently followed the views of his father.

16. C. Hill, *Economic problems of the Church from Archbishop Whitgift to the Long Parliament* (Oxford, 1956) p. 133ff; D. M. Barratt, 'The Condition of the Parish Clergy between the Reformation and 1660, with Special Reference to the Dioceses of Oxford, Worcester and Gloucester', Univ. of Oxford, D.Phil thesis, 1949, pp. 353, 361; C. W. Foster (ed.) *The State of the Church: Documents relating to the Diocese of Lincoln*, Lincoln Rec. Soc., 23 (1926) p. lvi; H. Owen (ed.) *George Owen's Pembrokeshire*, 4 vols, Cymroddorion Record Society (1892–1936) ii, pp. 298–305; R. A. Marchant, *The Church under the Law: Justice, Administration and Discipline in the Diocese of York, 1560–1640* (Cambridge, 1969) p. 125; Thomas Habington, *A Survey of Worcestershire*, ed. J. Amphlett, 2 vols (Oxford, 1895) i, p. 434.
17. Cliffe, *Puritan Gentry*, pp. 182–3; R. O'Day, *The English Clergy: the Emergence and Consolidation of a Profession, 1558–1642* (Leicester, 1979) pp. 86–7; William Hinde, *A Faithfull Remonstrance of the Holy Life and Happy Death of John Bruen* (1641) p. 87; R. Hughey, *John Harington of Stepney* (Columbus, 1971) p. 63; Hill, *Economic Problems*, pp. 212–14; R. Houlbrooke, *Church Courts and People during the English Reformation, 1520–1579* (Oxford, 1979) p. 194; *Lowther Family*, p. 213; m.i. Iwerne Courtney Church, Dorset.
18. A major source of confusion was leases made by the monastic houses in the few years before Dissolution: see, for example, the case of Westwood Rectory, Worcestershire, in Youings, *Dissolution of the Monasteries*, pp. 251–3.
19. The Monins correspondence is collected in Bod. L., North c.6 and b.12, 19 and 20. Among the general material is a narrative of the affair of Waldershare, North b.12, fo. 258; b.19, fo. 40ff; E. Hasted, *The History and Topographical Survey of the County of Kent*, 12 vols (Canterbury, 1800) x, p. 53
20. P. Clark, *English Provincial Society*, p. 179; H. Bowler (ed.) *Recusant Rolls nos. 3 and 4, 1594–96*, Catholic Rec. Soc., 61 (1970) p. 159; A. Everitt, *The Community of Kent and the Great Rebellion, 1640–1660* (Leicester, 1966) pp. 90, 181; Bod. L., North b.20, fo. 226; fo. 161; c.6, fo. 32.
21. *HMC Portland*, ix, pp. 66–7; *Clenennau Letters*, p. xvii; IOW RO, OG/AA/27, fo. 37v; J. Gwnfor Jones, 'Bishop William Morgan's Dispute with John Wynn of Gwydir', *Jnl. Hist. Soc. Church in Wales*, 22 (1972) pp. 49–78 and 'Bishop Lewis Bayly and the Wynns of Gwydir, 1616–27', *Welsh Hist. Rev.*, 6 (1973) pp. 404–23.
22. J. Oswald, *Some Memorandums of Matters of Fact* (1702) p. 55; S. G. Doree (ed.) *The Parish Register and Tithing Book of Thomas Hassall of Amwell*, Herts. Rec. Soc. Publ., 5 (1989) p. 182; Fletcher, *Sussex*, p. 57
23. Bod. L., North c.6, fo. 78; NRA, Kingsmill MSS no. 1383; BL, Eg. 2713, fo. 222; NUL, Clifton c.84.
24. NRO, IC 119; NRA, Kingsmill MSS no. 1338; *D'Ewes*, ii, pp. 26–7, 31, 99, 103–7, 217; C. Howard, *Sir John Yorke of Nidderdale* (1939) p. 18; PRO, STAC 5/H50/4.

25. For a summary of the tithe litigation of this period see Houlbrooke, *Church Courts and People*, pp. 117–50; B. Anderton (ed.) 'Selections from the Delaval Papers in the Newcastle upon Tyne Public Library', *Public. of the Newcastle upon Tyne Record Comm.*, 9 (1929) pp. 153–4, 156–7, 159; NUL, Clifton c.30–2; Holmes, *Lincolnshire*, p. 58.
26. KAO, U350 Q1/7; PRO, SP 16/347/27, 1; KAO U133 L3/2; U350 Q1/6, Q1/2, Q1/1; part of the dispute is summarised in S. P. Salt, 'The Origins of Sir Edward Dering's attack on the Ecclesiastical Hierarchy *c*.1625–1640', *HJ*, 30 (1987) pp. 24–5.
27. W. Dugdale, *The Antiquities of Warwickshire* (1730) p. 113; IOW RO, OG/AA/28, fo. 35; Spelman, *The History of Sacrilege*, p. 252; Foster, *The State of the Church*, pp. 221–32.
28. YAS, MS 178, p. 6ff; J. Simmons, 'Brooke Church, Rutland, with notes on Elizabethan Church-Building', *Leics. Arch. and Hist. Soc.*, 35 (1958–9) pp. 36–55; N. Pevsner, *The Buildings of England: South and West Somerset* (1958) pp. 223–4; N. Pevsner, *The Buildings of England: Dorset* (1972) pp. 236–7; Foster, *State of the Church*, pp. 219–36. The church-building in the later Tudor and Stuart period is still inadequately researched, largely because of a reluctance to attempt the difficult problem of stylistic dating, but see A. Woodger, 'Post-Reformation Mixed Gothic in Huntingdonshire Churches', *Archaeological J.*, 141 (1984) pp. 296–308.
29. KAO, U350 Q1/8; Bod. L., Tanner 68, fo. 212v; R. W. Ketton-Cremer, *Norfolk in the Civil War* (1969) p. 72. On the law of pewing and its development in England after the Reformation see K. Dillow, 'The Social and Eccesiastical Significance of Church Seating Arrangements and Pew Disputes, 1500–1740', Univ. of Oxford, D.Phil thesis, 1990; YAS, MS 178 pp. 7–8; *Archaeologia Cambrensis*, 9 (1878) p. 142. M. Wynn-Catto, *Old Blood of Merioneth: a Short History of the Nanney-Wynn Family* (private pub., 1989) p. 13; N. Pevsner, *The Buildings of England: Leicestershire and Rutland* (2nd ed., 1989) p. 110.
30. K. A. Esdaile, *English Church Monuments, 1510–1840* (1946) pp. 44–54; N. Llewellyn, *The Art of Death* (1991) pp. 46–9, 101–21; Webster, *The Duchess of Malfi*, quoted in C. Gittings, *Death, Burial and the Individual in Early Modern England* (Beckenham, 1984) p. 202; PROB 11/38 Noodes.
31. J. Weever, *Ancient Funeral Monuments Within the United Monarchy of Great Britain* (1631) p. 2: the Hackness tombs of the Hoby family are good examples of the non-figural tradition, which was adopted as official policy during the Commonwealth; Cliffe, *Puritan Gentry*, p. 133; E. S. De Beer (ed.) *The Diary of Sir John Evelyn*, 6 vols (Oxford, 1955) iv, p. 304; on the problems of Catholic burial see J. Bossy, *The English Catholic Community 1570–1850* (1975) pp. 140–4; H. Aveling, *The Catholic Recusants of the West Riding of Yorkshire, 1558–1790*, Proc. of Leeds Phil. and Lit. Soc. (1963) p. 252.
32. PROB 11/25 Hogen; Duffy, *Stripping of the Altars*, p. 489; PROB 11/36 Bodfelde; 40 wills out of 250 leave clothing bequests before 1547, only 19 leave plate; on value expressed through intimacy in gift-giving see I. Kopytoff, 'The Cultural Biography of Things' in A. Appadurai (ed.) *The Social Life of Things: Commodities in Cultural Perspective* (Cambridge, 1986) pp. 64–94.

33. In Kent, Yorkshire, Sussex, Warwickshire and Suffolk, 99 parishes have surviving examples of plate which can confidently be attributed to gentry donation before 1690. Of these, only eight parishes have pieces that were clearly given in the Jacobean period, and there are two possible donations for the late Elizabethan period, plus a fine cup and paten in Sussex which have no inscription, but were almost certainly purchased under the will of Thomas Lewkenor in 1598. C. E. Woodruff, 'Kent Church Plate', *Archaeologia Cantiana* 25–27 (1902–5); T. M. Fallow and H. B. McCall, *Yorkshire Church Plate*, 2 vols, YAS Record ser. (1912); S. A. Jeavons, 'Church Plate of Warwickshire', *Birmingham Arch. Soc.* (Cheltenham, 1963); J. E. Crouchman, 'Sussex Church Plate', *SAC*, 53–5 (1910–12); E. C. Hopper *et al.* 'Church Plate in Suffolk', *PSIA*, 8–9 (1894–97).
34. Slingsby, pp. 9–10; IOW RO, OG/SS/1, fo. 81; NRO, IC 3415; George Herbert, *The Temple and The Priest to the Temple* (1908) pp. 268–9; Sir John Wynn, *History of the Gwydir Family*, ed. A. Roberts (1878), pp. xi-xii.
35. V. Larminie, *Wealth, Kinship and Culture: the Newdigates of Arbury, c.1585–c.1685*, (forthcoming), Ch. 7; *HMC Var. Coll.*, ii, p. 391; J. T. Cliffe, *The Puritan Gentry Besieged, 1650–1700* (1993) p. 103.
36. FSL, V. a. 459; N. J. G. Pounds, 'William Carnsew of Bokelly and his Diary, 1576–77', *Journ. of the Royal Institution of Cornwall*, new ser., 8, pt. 1 (1978) p. 38.
37. F. Heal, *Of Prelates and Princes* (Cambridge, 1980) pp. 162–79, 247–55; P. Collinson, *Archbishop Grindal* (1979) pp. 268–9; R. B. Manning, *Religion and Society in Elizabethan Sussex* (Leicester, 1979) pp. 91–128; Hamon L'Estrange, *The Reign of King Charles, an History* (2nd edn, 1656) p. 144.
38. F. Heal 'The Archbishops of Canterbury and the Practice of Hospitality', *JEH*, 32 (1982) pp. 558–60; K. Fincham, *Prelate as Pastor: the Episcopate of James I* (Oxford, 1990) pp. 73–5; PRO, STAC 8/14/7, fo. 30.
39. Cliffe, *Puritan Gentry*, pp. 180–3; Cliffe, *Yorkshire*, p. 269; C. E. Welch, 'An Ecclesiastical Dispute at Woodhouse', *Leics. Arch. and Hist. Soc.*, 35 (1958) pp. 56–61.
40. Sir Henry Spelman, *De non temerandis ecclesiae*, 4th edn (Oxford, 1668) intro; Hill, *Economic Problems of the Church*, pp. 303, 293; E. P. Shirley, *Stemmata Shirleiana* (Westminister, 1873) p. 150.
41. C. Jackson (ed.) *The Diary of Abraham de la Pryme*, Surtees Soc., 54 (1870) pp. 53, 150; J. Spurr, *The Restoration Church of England, 1646–1689* (New Haven, 1991) p. 219: Spurr stresses the continuing weakness of the Church in the post-Restoration period.

## Chapter 10 Piety and Belief

1. Slingsby, pp. 7–8, 55.
2. Ibid, pp. 3–4, 9–10, 18–20, 21, 302–8; HHL, HM 43,213.

3. See M. Todd, 'Seneca and the Protestant Mind: the Influence of Stoicism on Puritan Ethics', *Archiv für Reformationsgeschichte,* 12 (1983) pp. 182–199.
4. N. Davies (ed.) *The Paston Letters and Papers of the Fifteenth Century,* 2 vols (Oxford, 1971–6) i, p. 39; W. A. Pantin, 'Instructions for a Devout and Learned Layman' in J. J. G. Alexander and M. T. Gibson (eds) *Medieval Learning and Literature* (Oxford, 1967) pp. 389–422; A. J. Pollard, *North-Eastern England during the Wars of the Roses* (Oxford, 1990) p. 185; Richard Whitford, *A Werke for Housholders* (1530); P. Tudor, 'Changing Private Belief and Practice in England: Devotional Literature 1475–1550', Univ. of Oxford, D.Phil thesis, 1984, pp. 124ff; see above all the important new study of these sources in E. Duffy, *The Stripping of the Altars* (New Haven, 1992) pp. 209–65. Social differentiation in books of devotions and prayers only began to become common from the mid-sixteenth century; H. C. White, *The Tudor Books of Private Devotion* (Madison, 1951) pp. 166–7.
5. On the general need for caution in employing will preambles as indicators of belief see M. Zell, 'The Use of Religious Preambles as a Measure of Belief in the Sixteenth Century', *BIHR,* 50 (1977) pp. 246–9; J. D. Alsop, 'Religious Preambles in Early Modern English Wills as Formulae', *JEH,* 40 (1989) pp. 19–27; the following remarks on wills are drawn from the PCC sample already discussed; see above p. 424 n.10 On Christocentric devotion see Tudor, 'Changing Private Belief', pp. 91–5; PROB 11/40 Holgrave.
6. PROB 11/ 32 Adeane, 17 Ayloffe: only 13 wills among our sample make any request of this kind before 1540. For the 'puritanical' strain in late medieval religion see C. Richmond, 'Religion and the Fifteenth Century Gentleman' in R. B. Dobson (ed.) *The Church, Politics and Patronage* (Gloucester, 1984) pp. 202–3.
7. PROB 11/2 Maynwaryng; M. Knight, *Piety and Devotion among the Warwickshire Gentry, 1485–1547,* Dugdale Soc. Occas. Paper, 32 (1989) p. 7; the devotional guide referred to above could have been prepared for one of Throckmorton's ancestors, since it survives among the Throckmorton MSS; *VCH Gloucester,* vii, p. 83; J. Polsue, *Parochial History of the County of Cornwall,* 4 vols (Truro, 1867–73) iii, p. 74.
8. For similar evidence on benefactions see J. J. Scarisbrick, *The Reformation and the English People* (Oxford, 1984) pp. 2ff; MacCulloch, *Suffolk,* p. 135; PROB 11/15 Porch, 17 Hogen, 22 Fetiplace; Knight, *Piety and Devotion,* p. 21; PROB 11/13 Holgrave, 7 Holgrave.
9. C. Carpenter, *Locality and Polity: a Study of Warwickshire Society, 1401–1499* (Cambridge, 1992) p. 225.
10. Ibid, p. 242; see also Pollard, *North-Eastern England,* pp. 182–3; K. Mertes, 'The Household as a Religious Community' in J. T. Rosenthal and C. Richmond (eds) *People, Politics and Community in the Later Middle Ages* (Gloucester, 1987) pp. 124–6.
11. R. Lockyer (ed.) *Thomas Wolsey, Late Cardinal; his Life and Death written by George Cavendish* (1962) p. 141; Pantin, 'Instructions for a Learned Layman', pp. 399–400.

12. C. Garrett, *The Marian Exiles, 1553–1559* (Cambridge, 1938); W.S. Hudson, *The Cambridge Connection and the Elizabethan Settlement of 1559* (Durham, NC, 1980) pp. 48–60; M. Dowling, *Humanism in the Age of Henry VIII* (Beckenham, 1986) pp. 62–8.
13. Nicholas Harpsfield, *The Life and Death of Sir Thomas More*, ed. E.E. Reynolds (1963) pp. 100–01; T. Stapleton (ed.) *The Plumpton Correspondence* (Gloucester, 1990) pp. 231–4; MacCulloch, *Suffolk*, p. 189; Bod. L., Rawl. D 1345.
14. P. Collinson, *The Birthpangs of Protestant England* (1988), p. 77; S. Brigden (ed.) 'The Letters of Richard Scudamore to Sir Philip Hoby September 1549-March 1555' *Camden Miscellany 30*, Camden Soc., 4th ser., 39 (1990), pp. 75–6, 100; PROB/11, 35 Populwell; J. Wake, *The Brudenells of Deene* (1954) pp. 48–9.
15. John Foxe, *The Acts and Monuments*, ed. J. Pratt, 8 vols (1877) v, 31–2, appendix iii; *DNB*, Richard Tracy; J. Eales, *Puritans and Roundheads: the Harleys of Brampton Bryan and the Outbreak of the English Civil War* (Cambridge, 1990) p. 22. For another example of this Protestant family identity see R.H. Fritze, '"A Rare Example of Godlyness Amongst Gentlemen": the Role of the Kingsmill and Gifford Families in Promoting the Reformation in Hampshire', in P. Lake and M. Dowling (eds) *Protestantism and the National Church in Sixteenth-Century England* (1987) pp. 144–61; A. Fairfax-Lucy, *Charlecote and the Lucys* (1958) pp. 61–2. Latimer was cousin to William Lucy's wife.
16. Foxe, *Acts and Monuments*, vi, 632–4; vii, 227–35, 454, 517; Garrett, *The Marian Exiles*, p. 41 and *passim*; D. MacCulloch (ed.) 'Vita Mariae Angliae Reginae', *Camden Miscellany 28*, Camden Soc., 4th ser., 29 (1984) pp. 253–7.
17. On the wide diversity of devotional manuals and spiritual advice coming from the presses under Edward VI see Tudor, 'Changing Private Belief', pp. 188ff; H. Aveling, *Northern Catholics: the Catholic Recusants in the North Riding of Yorkshire, 1585–1790* (1966) p. 75, uses the vivid term 'hard neutralism' to characterise much gentry behaviour in these years; PROB 11/1 Spert, 32 Tashe, 10 Coode.
18. See Ascham's dedication of *The Scholemaster* to Queen Elizabeth in *The Whole Works*, ed. Dr. Giles, 3 vols (1865) iii, pp. 65–75; R. Hughey, *John Harington of Stepney* (Columbus, 1971) p. 59; C. Cross (ed.) *The Letters of Sir Francis Hastings, 1574–1609*, Somerset Rec. Soc., 69 (1969) pp. 4–5.
19. E. Cameron, *The European Reformation* (Oxford, 1991) pp. 311–13.
20. Of particular importance for the Catholics was Stephen Brinkley's translation of Loarte's *The Exercise of a Christian Life* (1579); Southwell aimed more obviously than any other at the religious susceptibilities of the gentry community.
21. Lewis Bayly, *The Practice of Piety* (1612). Even the revised STC finds it somewhat difficult to count the precise number of editions because of pirating, etc.; NLW, Wynn, no. 896; NRO, IL 4046; CRO, R(S), 1/462; H.C. Maxwell-Lyte, *A History of Dunster*, 2 vols (1909) i, p. 178.
22. Bayly, *Practice of Piety*, pp. 293–4, 540–660.

23. C. Aspinall-Oglander, *Nunwell Symphony* (1945) p. 49; *Wandesford*, p. 12; FSL, V. a. 459; Bod. L., Rawl. D 676. V. Larminie, *Wealth, Kinship and Culture: the Newdigates of Arbury, c.1585–c.1685* (forthcoming), Ch. 2; E. A. Parry (ed.) *The Letters from Dorothy Osborne to Sir William Temple* (1914) p. 259; FSL, V. a. 180 [Mildmay/Fane]; NRO, Montagu of Boughton, vol. 3 fos. 235ff [Montagu]; YAS, DD94/Box 4 [Frankland of Great Thirkelby]; see, for example, *Clenennau Letters*, p. 126; CRO, R(S) 1/26 [Jonathan Rashleigh's advice to son]; BL, Add. 34,161, fo. 7 [Sir Roger Twysden to son Charles].
24. D. Mead (ed.) *The Diary of Lady Margaret Hoby* (1930); NRO, Montagu of Boughton, vol. 3, fos. 235ff; *Clenennau Letters*, p. 134; Cliffe, *Puritan Gentry*, p. 35; John Gerard, *The Autobiography of an Elizabethan*, trans. and ed. P. Caraman (1951) pp. 30–1, 52; M. Rowlands, 'Recusant Women, 1560–1640', in M. Prior (ed.) *Women in English Society, 1500–1800* (1985) p. 163; *Thornton*, p. 103; KAO, U1655 F8.
25. John Barlow, *The True Guide to Glory: A Funeral Sermon Preached at the Burial of Lady Strode* (1614) p. 48; we are grateful to Jeri McIntosh Cobb for this reference. Collections of private prayers survive for a number of women including Lady Anne Twysden and Lady Elizabeth Delaval: KAO, U1655 F8; D. G. Greene (ed.) *The Meditations of Lady Elizabeth Delaval*, Surtees Soc., 190 (1975); NRO, IC 3415; IL 3365; L. Pollock (ed.) *With Faith and Physic: The Life of a Tudor Gentlewoman* (1993) p. 28; E. S. De Beer (ed.) *The Diary of John Evelyn*, 6 vols (Oxford, 1969) iv, p. 431; Rowlands, 'Recusant Women', pp. 163–4; Gerard, *Autobiography*, pp. 191–3.
26. Richard Brathwait, *The English Gentleman* (1630) pp. 161–4; *The English Gentlewoman* (1631) pp. 69–70; John Chadwick, *A Sermon preached at Snarford . . . at the Funerals of Sir George Saint-Paule* (1613) p. 24; J. A. Gotch, *A Complete Account . . . of the Buildings Erected in Northamptonshire by Sir Thomas Tresham* (1883) p. 30; Sir John Conway, *The Poesie of Floured Prayers* (?1569) sig. Ai-ii.
27. Cliffe, *Puritan Gentry*, p. 35; Larminie, *The Newdigates*, Ch. 8; N. J. G. Pounds (ed.) 'William Carnsew of Bokelly and his Diary, 1576–77', *Journ. of the Royal Institution of Cornwall*, new ser., 8, pt. i (1978) pp. 48, 53.
28. M. F. Stieg (ed.) *The Diary of John Harington, MP*, Somerset Rec. Soc., 74 (1977) p. 7; *Thornton*, p. 11. Much the same set of attitudes, shorn of the language of special providences, can be found in devout Catholic writings of the period.
29. H. E. Lippincott (ed.) *Merry Passages and Jeasts: a MS Jestbook of Sir Nicholas Le Strange (1603–55)* (Salzburg, 1974) p. 71; PRO, STAC 8/138/18; H. Dixon (ed.) 'An Original Account of the Springett Family', *The Gentleman's Magazine*, 36 (1851) p. 367.
30. Samuel Clark, *The Lives of Thirty-Two English Divines* (1677) p. 158; William Hinde, *A Faithfull Remonstrance of the Holy Life and Happy Death of John Bruen* (1641) pp. 68–76; Robert Harris, *Samuel's Funerall* (1622) sig. A4v. For other examples see Cliffe, *Puritan Gentry*, pp. 34–6; J. Morris (ed.) *Troubles of our Catholic Forefathers Related by Themselves*, ser. iii (1872) pp. 467–9.

31. Bod. L., Rawl. D 676; C 868; DRO, D/BUL/M4, fo. 23 [this last is partly printed in J. Hutchins, *The History and Antiquities of the County of Dorset*, 4 vols (1861–74) iv, pp. 5–6]; *Whitelocke*, pp. 64–5; J. Davies, *The Caroline Captivity of the Church* (Oxford, 1992) pp. 162–3; Slingsby, p. 20; J. Nicholls, *History and Antiquities of Leicestershire*, 8 vols in 4 (1795–1811) 3, ii, p. 592.
32. Carpenter, *Locality and Polity*, pp. 242–3; Lippincott (ed.) *Merry Passages and Jeasts*, p. 126.
33. BL, Add. 33,572, fo. 8; IOW RO, OG/SS/1; F. R. Raines (ed.) *The Journal of Nicholas Assheton, Esq., of Downham in the County of Lancaster*, Chetham Soc., old ser., 14 (1848) pp. 3, 13, 15, 19, 25: Assheton at least noted the text on a couple of occasions; YAS, MS. 178, p. 9.
34. Slingsby, p. 303; NRO, Montagu of Boughton, vol. 3, fo. 239; *D'Ewes*, ii, p. 21; Hinde, *A Faithful Remonstrance*, p. 194; *Thornton*, pp. 117–18; Pollock, *With Faith and Physic*, p. 64; *Diary of John Evelyn*, iii, p. 203.
35. Bayly, *Practice of Piety*, p. 509; S. McGee, *The Godly Man in Stuart England* (New Haven, 1976); FSL, W. b. 483, fo. 23.
36. W. K. Jordan, *The Charities of Rural England* (1961) pp. 41–9; NLW, Wynn, no. 647.
37. SBT, DR 10/2076; *Wandesford*, p. 19; L. Stone (ed.) 'Sir Edward Montagu's Directions to his Son', *Northants Past and Present* (1958) p. 223; Bod. L., Rawl. C 929; Larminie, *The Newdigates*, Ch. 8; Todd, 'Seneca and the Protestant Mind', pp. 196–9.
38. IOW RO, OG/SS/1, fo. 2; Barnaby Potter, *The Baronet's Buriall* (1613) p. 36; Sir Edward Dering, *The Foure Cardinall-Vertues of a Carmelite-Fryar* (1641); *A Discourse of Proper Sacrifice* (Cambridge, 1644); for a discussion of Dering's ideology see S. P. Salt, 'The Origins of Sir Edward Dering's Attack on the Ecclesiastical Hierarchy, *c.*1625–40', *HJ*, 30 (1987) pp. 21–52; Rowlands, 'Recusant Women', pp. 160–6; Steig (ed.) *Diary of John Harington*, p. 5; Hinde, *A Faithfull Remonstrance*, p. 161.
39. J. Spurr, *The Restoration Church of England, 1646–1689* (New Haven, 1991) has a valuable chapter on the nature of post-Restoration piety, pp. 331–75; Matthew Hale, *The Counsels of a Father* (1817); J. T. Cliffe, *The Puritan Gentry Besieged, 1650–1700* (1993) pp. 90–1.
40. Ibid., pp.123–35; E. M. Halcrow (ed.) *The Charges to the Grand Jury at Quarter Sessions 1660–67 by Sir Peter Leicester*, Chetham Soc., 3rd ser., 5 (1953) pp. 159–64.
41. UCW Bangor, Mostyn 183; Spurr, *Restoration Church*, pp. 230–1; among those with whom Fell corresponded was Richard Newdigate.
42. WYRO, MX 238; Francis Osborne, *Advice to a Son* (1656) p. 143.

## Conclusion

1. Robert Dallington, *A Method for Travell. Shewed by Taking the View of France as it Stoode in the Yeare of Our Lord, 1598*, (1604) sig. S3–4; Sir John Reresby, *Memoirs and Travels*, ed. A. Ivatt (1904) p. 37; Fynes Moryson, *An Itinerary* (1617) bk.iii, p. 221.

2. John Evelyn, *Miscellaneous Writings*, ed. W. Upcott (1825) p. 81; Reresby, *Memoirs and Travels*, p. 14; B. Muralt, *Letters Describing the Character and Customs of the French and English Nations*, (1726) pp. 6, 53–4: the letters were the product of a visit to England in 1694, though he did not publish them for more than a quarter of a century.
3. Evelyn, *Miscellaneous Writings*, p. 79; John Northleigh, *Topographical Descriptions, with Historico-Political and Medico-Physical Observations made in Two . . . Voyages through . . . Europe*, (1702) pp. 102–3; quoted in J. Lough, *France Observed in the Seventeenth Century by British Travellers* (Stockfield, 1984) p. 92; Moryson, *An Itinerary*, bk.iii, p. 151; Evelyn, *Miscellaneous Writings*, p. 72; Thomas Fuller, *The Holy State and the Profane State* (1841) p. 106.
4. Muralt, *The French and English Nations*, p. 4; W. D. Robson-Scott, *German Travellers in England, 1400–1800* (Oxford, 1953) p. 70.
5. *The Genealogist*, 16–17 (1899–1901) pp. 106, 207–14.
6. Hart died in 1738. For the rest of his memorial see above pp. 236–7 and illustration 20.

# Bibliography

*For abbreviations, see list at the beginning of Notes* (p. 384).

The modern study of the gentry began with the controversy concerning the 'rise' of the class in the century before the Civil War, inaugurated by R. H. Tawney in two seminal articles published in 1941:

R. H. Tawney, 'Harrington's Interpretation of his Age', *Proceedings of the British Academy*, 27 (1941) pp. 199–223.

R. H. Tawney, 'The Rise of the Gentry, 1558–1640' *EcHR*, old ser., 11 (1941) pp. 1–38.

Tawney argued that the Civil War was to be understood as the attempt by the gentry to seize political power commensurate with the substantial advances in wealth and social importance that they had made in the preceding century. Tawney's argument provoked a scintillating debate, including a bold attempt to invert his thesis totally. The war was fought by the gentry, certainly, but they as a class were the victims, not the beneficiaries, of economic change

H. R. Trevor-Roper, *The Gentry 1540–1640, EcHR*, supplement i (1953).

The debate, now largely moribund, generated not only polemic, but a series of studies designed to test the hypotheses concerning the economic situation of the gentry canvassed by the major protagonists. However, one contribution to the debate inspired by Tawney's hypothesis succeeded in transforming future studies radically. This was

L. Stone, *The Crisis of the Aristocracy, 1558-1641* (Oxford, 1965).

Stone's study was rooted in an examination of the economic experience of the peerage, but broadened out to discuss a far wider range of topics: family life; the nature of their political authority; their education and religious beliefs; their cultural interests. This work encouraged historiographical development in two directions in the further study of the upper classes: first, studies of particular areas or individual families that, with Stone, sought to raise questions beyond the narrowly economic that had been the focus of the earlier works inspired by Tawney; second, further examination of the topics the potential of which Stone's analysis had revealed.

In the period since the publication of Stone's seminal study, scholarly works, both of areas and families, and of particular topics, have been informed by other historiographical developments. So discussion of family life among the gentry has been informed by debate around the argument that early modern England saw a major transformation in attitude in all social groups to the form and function of the family, and in the quality of emotional relations – between parents and children and husbands and wives – within it. Equally, discussion of the gentry's political assumptions and culture has been modified by the arguments of the 'revisionists', who have sought to challenge the traditional 'Whig' account of national political development, in which a liberty-loving House of Commons criticised, challenged, and ultimately destroyed the attempts of the Stuart kings to establish a more absolutist state.

This bibliography lists those works that have been influential in the formation of our thinking, and which might be useful to readers seeking more information on particular families, areas, or topics. We have included primary sources only in those cases where the edition has a significant substantive introduction.

We begin by listing, first, local studies, then family studies. Then we list works on particular topics, organised broadly to follow the structure of the book. Each chapter list begins with a reference to the works, referred to by the number assigned them, from the catalogues of local and family studies where these have particularly useful discussions of the topic in question. Works from the first two lists marked ** contain important contributions to a number of the specific topics and, to avoid repetition, are not referred to again in the chapter listings.

## GENERAL STUDIES


1. C. G. A. Clay, *Economic Expansion and Social Change: England 1500–1700*, 2 vols (Cambridge, 1984).
2. J. T. Cliffe, *The Puritan Gentry: The Great Puritan Families of Early Stuart England* (1984).
3. M. James, *Society, Politics and Culture: Studies in Early Modern England* (Cambridge, 1986).
4. G. E. Mingay, *The Gentry: the Rise and Fall of a Ruling Class* (1976).
5. J. S. Morrill, 'The Northern Gentry and the Great Rebellion', *Northern History*, 15 (1979) pp. 66–87.
6. D. Palliser, *The Age of Elizabeth: England under the Later Tudors 1547–1603* 2nd ed. (1992).
7. L. Stone, *Social Change and Revolution in England* (1965).
8. L. Stone and J. C. Stone, *An Open Elite? England 1540–1880* (Oxford, 1984).


## STUDIES OF PARTICULAR AREAS

The older works of this genre, while not limiting themselves solely to economic analysis, tend to be most concerned with the issues raised by Tawney. The field was transformed in 1966 by the seminal study of Kent by Alan Everitt, and by his two pamphlets produced in 1969. Everitt argued that the enduring character of the gentry's engagement in the government and the culture of their respective localities, not their economic fortunes, was the key to the understanding of the Civil War. Each county formed a 'community', dominated by a circle of gentlemen, 'with its own ethos and loyalty'. The gentry's concern to insulate their localities from the demands of the central government, to guarantee their effective autonomy, explained the apparently chaotic political history of the seventeenth century. The viability of Everitt's model has been questioned by some scholars, but the analysis derived from it has vastly increased our understanding of the social and political worlds of the gentry. For general discussion, see


**9.** A. Everitt, *The Local Community and the Great Rebellion*, Historical Association pamphlet G.70 (1969).
**10.** A. Everitt, *Change in the Provinces: the Seventeenth Century* (Leicester, 1969)**
**11.** C. Holmes, 'The County Community in Stuart Historiography', *JBS* 19 (1980) pp. 54–73**


Studies of particular localities


**12.** B.G. Blackwood, *The Lancashire Gentry and the Great Rebellion, 1640–1660*, Chetham Soc., 3rd ser., 25 (1978).
**13.** P. Clark, *English Provincial Society from the Reformation to the Revolution* (Hassocks, 1977).
**14.** J.T. Cliffe, *The Yorkshire Gentry from the Reformation to the Civil War* (1969) **
**15.** A.M. Coleby, *Central Government and the Localities: Hampshire 1649–1689* (Cambridge, 1987).
**16.** A. Everitt, *The Community of Kent and the Great Rebellion* (Leicester, 1966).
**17.** A. Fletcher, *A County Community in Peace and War. Sussex, 1600–1660* (1975)**
**18.** J.E. Hollinshead, 'The Gentry of South-West Lancashire in the Later Sixteenth Century', *Northern History*, 26 (1990) pp. 82–102.
**19.** C. Holmes, *Seventeenth-Century Lincolnshire* (Lincoln, 1980)**
**20.** C. Holmes, *The Eastern Association in the English Civil War* (Cambridge, 1974).
**21.** A. Hughes, *Politics, Society and Civil War in Warwickshire, 1620–60* (Cambridge, 1987)**
**22.** M.E. James, *Family Lineage and Civil Society: a Study of Society, Politics and Mentality in the Durham Region, 1500–1640* (Oxford, 1974).
**23.** P. Jenkins, *The Making of a Ruling Class: the Glamorgan Gentry 1640–1790* (Cambridge, 1983)**
**24.** J. Johnson, *The Gloucestershire Gentry* (Gloucester, 1989).
**25.** H.A. Lloyd, *The Gentry of South-West Wales* (Cardiff, 1968).
**26.** D. MacCulloch, *Suffolk and the Tudors: Politics and Religion in an English County, 1500–1600* (Oxford, 1986).
**27.** R.B. Manning, *Religion and Society in Elizabethan Sussex* (Leicester, 1979).
**28.** J.S. Morrill, *Cheshire 1630–1660: County Government and Society during the English Revolution* (Oxford, 1974).
**29.** C.B. Phillips, 'The Gentry of Cumberland and Westmorland, 1600–1665', Univ. of Lancaster, PhD thesis, 1973.

**30.** J. T. Rosenheim, 'An Examination of Oligarchy: the Gentry of Restoration Norfolk', Univ. of Princeton, PhD thesis, 1981.
**31.** A. L. Rowse, *Tudor Cornwall* (1941).
**32.** A. H. Smith, *County and Court: Government and Politics in Norfolk 1558–1603* (Oxford, 1974).
**33.** R. B. Smith, *Land and Politics in the England of Henry VIII: the West Riding of Yorkshire, 1530–1546* (Oxford, 1970).
**34.** D. Underdown, *Somerset in the Civil War and Interregnum* (Newton Abbot, 1973).
**35.** M. G. D. Wanklyn, 'Landed Society and Allegiance in Cheshire and Shropshire in the First Civil War', Univ. of Manchester, PhD thesis, 1976.

STUDIES OF INDIVIDUAL FAMILIES

Such studies have a long pedigree. Most of those written before the mid-twentieth century, while they may contain useful information, are works of familial piety, nicely caught in Lawrence Stone's acid phrase 'history of the upper classes by the upper classes for the upper classes'. Some of the earlier works are, however, more sophisticated, and are cited here with recent studies that are keenly aware of recent historiographical trends.

**36.** M. Blundell (ed.), *Cavalier: Letters of William Blundell to his Friends* (1933).
**37.** T. H. Brooke, 'The Memoirs of Sir Hugh Cholmley', Univ. of Oxford, B. Litt. thesis, 1937.
**38.** L. Campbell, 'Sir Roger Townshend and His Family: a Study in Gentry Life in Early Seventeenth Century Norfolk', Univ. of East Anglia, PhD thesis, 1990.
**39.** B. G. Charles, *George Owen of Henllys* (Aberystwyth, 1973).
**40.** E. Cope, *The Life of a Public Man*, Proc. of the American Phil. Soc., 142 (1981).
**41.** J. Eales, *Puritans and Roundheads: the Harleys of Brampton Bryan and the Outbreak of the English Civil War* (Cambridge, 1990).
**42.** A. Fairfax-Lucy, *The Lucys of Charlecote* (1958).
**43.** I. Grimble, *The Harington Family* (London, 1957).
**44.** V. Larminie, *Wealth, Kinship and Culture: the Newdigates of Arbury, c.1585-c.1685* (forthcoming) **
**45.** C. Markham, *Markham Memorials*, 2 vols (1913).
**46.** D. M. Meads (ed.) *The Diary of Lady Hoby* (1930).
**47.** C. E. Moreton, *The Townshends and their World: Gentry, Law and Land in Norfolk, c.1450–1551* (Oxford, 1992).
**48.** C. B. Phillips (ed.) *The Lowther Family Estate Books*, Surtees Soc., 191 (1979).
**49.** N. J. G. Pounds (ed.) 'William Carnsew of Bokelly and his Diary, 1576–7', *Journ. of the Royal Inst. of Cornwall*, new ser., 8 (1978) 1 pp. 14–60.
**50.** B. Schofield (ed.) *The Knyvett Letters* (1949).
**51.** A. Searle (ed.) *The Barrington Letters*, Camden Soc., 4th ser., 28 (1983).

52. J. M. J. Tonks,'The Lyttletons of Frankley and their Estates, 1540–1640', Univ. of Oxford, B. Litt. thesis, 1978.
53. J. Wake, *The Brudenells of Deene* (1954).
54. H. A. Wyndham, *A Family History, 1410–1688* (Oxford, 1939).

**Chapter 1: Lineage**

Number **3** [ch.8]; **5**; **18**.

55. J. P. Cooper, 'Ideas of Gentility in Early-Modern England', in the volume of his essays, *Land, Men and Beliefs: Studies in Early-Modern History*, ed. G. E.Aylmer and J. S.Morrill (1983) pp. 43–77.
56. A. J. Fletcher, 'Honour, Reputation and Local Office Holding in Elizabethan and Stuart England' in A. Fletcher and J. Stevenson (eds) *Order and Disorder in Early Modern England* (Cambridge, 1985) pp. 92–115.
57. J. G. Jones, *Concepts of Order and Gentility in Wales, 1540–1640* (Llandysul, 1992).
58. A. Sharp, 'Edward Waterhouse's View of Social Change in Seventeenth-Century England', *PP*, 62 (1974) pp. 27–46.
59. P. J. Styles, 'The Heralds' Visitation of Warwickshire 1682–3' in his *Studies in Seventeenth Century West Midlands History* (Kineton, 1978) pp. 108–49.
60. J. Thirsk, 'The Fashioning of the Tudor-Stuart Gentry', *Bulletin of the John Rylands Lib.*, 72 (1990) pp. 69–85.
61. A. R. Wagner, *English Genealogy* (Oxford, 1960).

**Chapter 2: Family**

Numbers **24, 36, 38, 39, 40, 41, 42, 48, 49, 50, 51, 52, 53, 161**.

62. L. Bonfield, 'Marriage, Property and the "Affective Family"', *Law & History Review*, 1 (1983) pp. 297–312.
63. J. P. Cooper, 'Patterns of Inheritance and Settlement by Great Landowners from the Fifteenth to the Eighteenth Century' in J. Goody, J. Thirsk and E. P. Thompson (eds) *Family and Inheritance* (Cambridge, 1976) pp. 192–327.
64. K. M. Davies, 'Continuity and Change in Literary Advice on Marriage' in R. Outhwaite (ed.) *Marriage and Society: Studies in the Social History of Marriage* (1981) pp. 58–80.
65. C. Durston, *The Family in the English Revolution* (Oxford, 1989).
66. K. A. Esdaile, *English Church Monuments, 1510–1840* (1946).
67. R. A. Houlbrooke, *The English Family, 1450–1700* (1984).
68. A. MacFarlane, *Marriage and Love in England, 1300–1840* (Oxford, 1986).
69. L. Pollock, 'Younger Sons in Tudor and Stuart England', *History Today* (June, 1989) pp.23–9.
70. L. Pollock (ed.) *With Faith and Physic: The Life of a Tudor Gentlewoman* (1993).
71. R. Priestley, 'Marriage and Family Life in the Seventeenth Century', Univ. of Sydney, PhD thesis, 1988.

72. M. Slater, *Family Life in the Seventeenth Century* (1984).
73. M. Slater, 'The Weightiest Business: Marriage in an Upper-Gentry Family in Seventeenth-Century England', *PP*, 72 (1976) pp. 25–54.
74. L. Stone, *The Family, Sex and Marriage in England, 1500–1800* (1977).
75. L. Stone, *Road to Divorce: England 1530–1987* (Oxford, 1990).
76. J. Thirsk, 'Younger Sons in the Seventeenth Century', *History*, 54 (1969) pp. 358–77.
77. A. Wall, 'Elizabethan Precept and Feminine Practice', *History*, 75 (1990) pp. 23–38.
78. J. Wilson, 'Icons of Unity', *History Today* (June 1993) pp. 14–20.

## Chapters 3 and 4: Wealth

*Pre-Civil War*

Numbers **12, 26, 30, 31, 33, 35, 47, 43, 52, 60**.

79. *The Agrarian History of England and Wales*, ed. J. Thirsk vol. 4 (Cambridge, 1967) [*this provides a convenient summary of much of the work undertaken by the date of its publication*].
80. J. Cornwall, *Wealth and Society in Early Sixteenth Century England* (1988).
81. M. E. Finch, *Five Northamptonshire Families, 1540–1640*, Northants. Rec. Soc., 19 (1956).
82. E. F. Gay, 'The Rise of an English Country Family: Peter and John Temple to 1603' and 'The Temples of Stowe and their Debts', *HLQ*, 1 (1937–8) pp. 367–91; 2 (1938–9) pp. 399–438.
83. M. J. Hawkins, 'Wardship, Royalist Delinquency and Too Many Children: the Portmans in the Seventeenth Century', *Southern History*, 4 (1982) pp. 55–89.
84. M. K. McIntosh, 'The Fall of a Tudor Gentle Family: the Cookes of Gidea Hall, Essex, 1579–1629', *HLQ*, 41 (1977–8) pp. 279–97.
85. R. Meredith, 'The Eyres of Hassop, 1470–1640', *Derbys. Arch. J.*, 85 (1965) pp. 44–91.
86. C. B. Phillips, 'Landlord–Tenant Relationships, 1642–1660' in R. C. Richardson (ed.) *Town and Countryside in the English Revolution* (Manchester, 1992) pp. 224–50.
87. A. Simpson, *The Wealth of the Gentry* (Cambridge, 1961).
88. J. Thirsk, 'Agrarian Problems and the English Revolution' in R. C. Richardson (ed.) *Town and Countryside in the English Revolution* (Manchester, 1992) pp. 169–97.
89. P. Rutledge, 'Sir Thomas Knyvett and his Norfolk manors, 1577–1591', *Norfolk Archaeology*, 32 (1961) pp. 343–52.

*Post–1660*

Numbers **12, 30, 48**.

90. *The Agrarian History of England and Wales*, J. Thirsk (ed.) vol. 5, part 2 (Cambridge, 1985) [*again, an excellent survey*].

**91.** J. V. Beckett, *Coal and Tobacco: the Lowthers and the Economic Development of West Cumberland, 1660–1760* (Cambridge, 1981).
**92.** J. V. Beckett, 'English Landownership in the late Seventeenth and Eighteenth Centuries: the Debate and the Problems', *EcHR*, 2nd ser., 30 (1977) pp. 567–81.
**93.** L. Bonfield, *Marriage Settlements, 1601–1740* (Cambridge, 1983).
**94.** J. P. F. Broad, 'Sir Ralph Verney and his Estates 1630–1696', Univ. of Oxford, D.Phil thesis, 1973.
**95.** M. G. Davies, 'Country Gentry and Falling Rents in the 1660s and 1670s', *Midland History*, 4 (1977–8) pp. 86–96.
**96.** H. J. Habakkuk, 'The Rise and Fall of English Landed Families, 1600–1800', *TRHS*, 5th ser., 29 (1979) pp. 187–207; 30 (1980) pp. 199–221; 31 (1981) pp. 195–217.
**97.** A. M. Mimardiere, 'The Finances of a Warwickshire Gentry Family, 1693–1726', *Univ. of Birmingham Hist. J.*, 9 (1963–4) pp. 130–43.
**98.** G. E. Mingay, *English Landed Society in the Eighteenth Century* (1963).
**99.** P. Roebuck, *Yorkshire Baronets, 1640–1760: Families, Estates, and Fortunes* (Hull, 1980).

### Chapter 5: Administration

Numbers **8, 9, 12, 13, 15, 16, 20, 26, 28, 29, 30, 32, 34, 35, 50, 57, 184**.

**100.** T. G. Barnes, *Somerset 1625–1640: A County's Government During the 'Personal Rule'* (Oxford, 1961).
**101.** J. B. Calnan, 'County Society and Local Government in the County of Hertford *c*.1580–*c*.1630', Univ. of Cambridge, PhD thesis, 1979.
**102.** A. Fletcher, *Reform in the Provinces* (1986).
**103.** G. C. F. Forster, 'County Government in Yorkshire during the Interregnum', *Northern History*, 12 (1976) pp. 84–104.
**104.** L. K. J. Glassey, *Politics and the Appointment of the Justices of the Peace, 1675–1720* (Oxford, 1979).
**105.** J. H.Gleason, *The Justices of the Peace in England, 1558–1640* (Oxford, 1969).
**106.** E. M. Halcrow (ed.) *Charges to the Grand Jury at Quarter Sessions 1660–1677 by Sir Peter Leicester*, Chetham Soc., 3rd ser., 5 (1953).
**107.** G. Jones, *The Gentry and the Elizabethan State* (Llandybie, Dyfed, 1984).
**108.** N. Landau, *The Justices of the Peace, 1679–1760* (Berkeley, 1984).
**109.** C. B. Phillips, 'County Committees and Local Government in Cumberland and Westmorland, 1642–1660', *Northern History*, 5 (1970) pp. 34–66.
**110.** B. W. Quintrell, 'The Government of the County of Essex, 1603–1642', Univ. of London, PhD thesis, 1965.
**111.** S. K. Roberts, *Recovery and Restoration in an English County: Devon Local Administration, 1646–1670* (Exeter, 1985).
**112.** J. M. Rosenheim, 'County Governance and Elite Withdrawal in Norfolk, 1660–1720' in A. L.Beier, D. Cannadine, J. M. Rosenheim (eds) *The First Modern Society: Essays in English History presented to Lawrence Stone* (Cambridge, 1989) pp. 95–125.

## Chapter 6: Politics

*Tudor*

Numbers **3** [chaps. 2–4, 7, 9], **13, 22, 25, 27, 31, 32, 33, 47, 108**.

**113.** G. W. Bernard, *The Power of the Early Tudor Nobility* (Brighton, 1985).
**114.** F. J. Levy, 'How Information Spread Among the Gentry, 1550–1640', *JBS*, 21 (1982) pp. 11–34.
**115.** W. T. MacCaffrey, 'Talbot and Stanhope: an Episode in Elizabethan Politics', *BIHR*, 33 (1960) pp. 73–85.
**116.** A. Wall, 'Patterns of Politics in England 1558–1625', *HJ*, 31 (1988) pp. 947–63.

*1603–1660*

Numbers **9, 12, 16, 20, 28, 29, 34, 35, 36, 37, 40, 41, 50, 51, 54, 100, 102**.

**117.** R. Cust, *The Forced Loan and English Politics 1626–1628* (Oxford, 1987).
**118.** R. Cust, 'News and Politics in early Seventeenth-Century England', *PP*, 112 (1986) pp. 60–90.
**119.** R. Cust, 'Politics and the Electorate in the 1620s' in R. Cust and A. Hughes, *Conflict in Early Stuart England* (1989) pp. 134–67.
**120.** R. Cust and P. G. Lake, 'Sir Richard Grovesnor and the Rhetoric of Magistracy', *BIHR*, 54 (1981) pp. 40–53.
**121.** G. C. F. Forster, 'Faction and County Government in Early Stuart Yorkshire', *Northern History*, 11 (1976) pp. 70–86.
**122.** D. Hirst, *The Representative of the People?* (Cambridge, 1975).
**123.** R. Hutton, *The Royalist War Effort* (1982).
**124.** M. A. Kishlansky, *Parliamentary Selection* (Cambridge, 1986).
**125.** J. G. Marston, 'Gentry Honor and Royalism in Early Stuart England', *JBS*, 13 (1973–4) pp. 21–43.
**126.** J. S. Morrill, 'The Religious Context of the English Civil War', *TRHS*, 5th ser., 34 (1984) pp. 155–78.
**127.** J. S. Morrill, 'Sir William Brereton and England's Wars of Religion', *JBS*, 24 (1985) pp. 311–32.
**128.** J. S. Morrill, 'William Davenport and the 'Silent Majority' of Early Stuart England', *J. of the Chester Arch. Soc.*, 58 (1975) pp. 115–29.
**129.** C. Russell, *Parliaments and English Politics* (Oxford, 1979).
**130.** K. Sharpe, 'Crown, Parliament and Locality: Government and Communication in Early Stuart England', *EHR*, 101 (1986) pp. 321–50.
**131.** D. Underdown, *Pride's Purge* (Oxford, 1971).
**132.** D. Underdown, 'Settlement in the Counties, 1653–1658' in G. E. Aylmer (ed.) *The Interregnum: the Quest for Settlement 1646–1660* (1972) pp. 165–82.

*Post–1660*

Numbers **15, 30, 192, 104, 108, 111, 178**.

**133.** C. Brooks, 'Public Finance and Political Stability: the Administration of the Land Tax, 1688–1720', *HJ*, 17 (1974) pp. 281–300.

**134.** C. D. Chandaman, *The English Public Revenue* (Oxford, 1975).
**135.** K. Feiling, *A History of the Tory Party, 1640–1714* (Oxford, 1924).
**136.** G. Holmes, *British Politics in the Age of Anne* (1967).
**137.** H. Horwitz, *Parliament, Policy and Politics in the Reign of William III* (Manchester, 1977).
**138.** R. Hutton, *The Restoration* (Oxford, 1985).
**139.** J. R. Jones, *The Revolution of 1688 in England* (1972).
**140.** I. Kramnick, *Bolingbroke and his Circle: the Politics of Nostalgia in the Age of Walpole* (Cambridge, Mass., 1968).
**141.** P. B. Munsche, *Gentlemen and Poachers: the English Game Laws, 1671–1831* (Cambridge, 1981).
**142.** J. H. Plumb, *The Growth of Political Stability in England* (1967).
**143.** P. Seaward, *The Cavalier Parliament and the Reconstruction of the Ancien Regime, 1661–1667* (Cambridge, 1989).

### Chapter 7: Education

Numbers **2, 7, 10, 36, 38, 39, 52, 55, 57, 60, 67, 70, 77, 158, 178**.

**144.** V. Larminie, 'The Undergraduate Account Book of John and Richard Newdigate, 1618–21', *Camden Miscellany 30*, Camden Soc., 4th ser., 39 (1988).
**145.** P. Laslett, 'The Gentry of Kent in 1640', *Cambridge HJ*, 9 (1947–9) pp. 148–64.
**146.** J. Looney, 'Undergraduate Education at Early Stuart Cambridge', *History of Education*, 10/1 (1981) pp. 9–19.
**147.** J. K. McConica (ed.) *History of the University of Oxford: vol. iii: The Collegiate University* (Oxford,1986).
**148.** J. McConica 'Scholars and Commoners in Renaissance Oxford' in L. Stone (ed.) *The University in Society*, 2 vols (Princeton, 1974) i, pp. 151–82.
**149.** V. Morgan, 'Cambridge University and "the Country"' in L. Stone (ed.) *The University in Society*, 2 vols (Princeton, 1974) i, pp. 183–245.
**150.** R. O'Day, *Education and Society, 1500–1800* (1982) [*an excellent survey of recent debates*].
**151.** N. Orme, *From Childhood to Chivalry: The Education of English Kings and Aristocracy, 1066–1530* (1984).
**152.** L. Pollock, ' "Teach her to Live Under Obedience": the Making of Women in the Upper Ranks of Early Modern England', *Continuity and Change*, 4 (1989) pp. 231–58.
**153.** W. R. Prest, *The Inns of Court under Elizabeth and the Early Stuarts* (1972).
**154.** J. E. Stephens (ed.) *Aubrey on Education* (1975).
**155.** L. Stone, 'The Size and Composition of the Oxford Student Body' in L. Stone (ed.) *The University in Society*, 2 vols (Princeton, 1974), i, pp. 3–110.
**156.** L. Stone, 'The Educational Revolution, 1560–1640', *PP*, 28 (1964) pp. 41–80.
**157.** J. Stoye, *English Travellers Abroad, 1604–1667* (New Haven, 1989).

## Chapter 8: Society and sociability

Numbers **2, 4, 8, 22, 37, 38, 49, 55, 57, 60, 141, 154**.

**158.** A. Bryson, 'Concepts of Civility in England, c.1560–1685', Univ. of Oxford, D.Phil thesis, 1984.
**159.** F. Heal, *Hospitality in Early Modern England* (Oxford, 1990).

**160.** H. Colvin and J. Newman (eds), *Of Building: Roger North's Writings on Architecture* (Oxford, 1981).
**161.** Alice T. Friedman, *House and Household in Elizabethan England* (Chicago, 1989).
**162.** M. Girouard, *Life in the English Country House* (New Haven, 1979).
**163.** R. T. Gunther (ed.) *Sir Roger Pratt on Architecture* (Oxford, 1928).
**164.** M. Howard, *The Early Tudor Country House* (1987).
**165.** N. Wright, 'The Gentry and their Houses in Norfolk and Suffolk from *ca.*1550–1850', Univ. of East Anglia, PhD thesis, 1990.

**166.** M. Vale, *The Gentleman's Recreations: the Accomplishments and Pastimes of the English Gentleman, 1580–1630* (Cambridge, 1977).
**167.** R. Carr, *A History of Fox-hunting* (1976).
**168.** S. Jayne, *Library Catalogues of the English Renaissance* (Godalming, 1983).
**169.** R. B. Manning, *Hunters and Poachers: a Cultural and Social History of Unlawful Hunting in England, 1485–1640* (Oxford, 1993).
**170.** D. Price, *Patrons and Musicians of the English Renaissance* (Cambridge, 1981).
**171.** R. Strong, *The Renaissance Garden in England* (1979).

**172.** C. G. Durston, 'London and the Provinces: the Association between the Capital and the Berkshire County Gentry of the Early Seventeenth Century', *Southern History*, 3 (1981) pp. 39–53.
**173.** F. Heal, 'The Crown, the Gentry and London: the Enforcement of Proclamation, 1596–1640' in C. Cross, D. Loades and J. J. Scarisbrick (eds) *Law and Government under the Tudors* (Cambridge, 1988) pp. 211–26.
**174.** L. Stone, 'The Residential Development of the West End of London in the Seventeenth Century' in B. Malament (ed.) *After the Reformation: Essays in Honour of Jack Hexter* (Manchester, 1980) pp. 167–212.

## Chapters 9 and 10: The Church and Belief

Number: **2, 13, 26, 27, 31, 36, 40, 41, 42, 46, 49, 51, 52, 53, 65, 66, 70, 107, 120, 126, 127**.

**175.** H. Aveling, *Northern Catholics: the Catholic Recusants in the North Riding of Yorkshire, 1585–1790* (1966).
**176.** J. Bossy, *The English Catholic Community 1570–1850* (1975).
**177.** C. Carpenter, 'The Religion of the Gentry in the Fifteenth Century' in D. Williams (ed.) *England in the Fifteenth Century* (Woodbridge, 1987) pp. 53–74.

**178.** J. T. Cliffe, *The Puritan Gentry Besieged, 1650–1700* (1993).

**179.** P. Collinson, 'Magistracy and Ministry: A Suffolk Minature' in his *Godly People* (1983) pp. 445–66.

**180.** P. Collinson, *The Birthpangs of Protestant England* (1988).

**181.** E. Duffy, *The Stripping of the Altars: Traditional Religion in England, 1400–1580* (New Haven, 1992).

**182.** R. H. Fritze, '"A Rare Example of Godlyness amongst Gentlemen": the Role of the Kingsmill and Gifford Families in Promoting the Reformation in Hampshire' in P. Lake and M. Dowling (eds) *Protestantism and the National Church in Sixteenth-Century England* (1987) pp. 144–61.

**183.** C. Haigh, *English Reformations: Religion, Politics and Society under the Tudors* (Oxford, 1993).

**184.** C. Hill, *Economic Problems of the Church from Archbishop Whitgift to the Long Parliament* (Oxford, 1956).

**185.** M. Knight, *Piety and Devotion among the Warwickshire Gentry, 1485–1547*, Dugdale Soc., Occasional Papers, 32 (1989).

**186.** V. M. Larminie, *The Godly Magistrate*, Dugdale Soc., Occasional Papers, 28 (1982).

**187.** S. McGee, *The Godly Man in Stuart England* (New Haven, 1976).

**188.** P. Marshall, 'Attitudes of the English People to Priests and Priesthood: 1500–53', Univ. of Oxford, D.Phil thesis, 1990.

**189.** R. O'Day, *The English Clergy: the Emergence and Consolidation of a Profession, 1558–1642* (Leicester, 1979).

**190.** C. Richmond, 'Religion and the Fifteenth-Century Gentleman' in R. B. Dobson (ed.) *The Church, Politics and Patronage in the Fifteenth Century* (Gloucester, 1984) pp. 193–208.

**191.** M. Rowlands, 'Recusant Women, 1560–1640' in M. Prior (ed.) *Women in English Society, 1500–1800* (1985) pp. 149–80.

**192.** J. Spurr, *The Restoration Church of England, 1646–1689* (New Haven, 1991).

**193.** P. Tudor, 'Changing Private Belief and Practice in England: Devotional Literature 1475–1550', Univ. of Oxford, D.Phil thesis, 1984.

**194.** J. Youings, *The Dissolution of the Monasteries* (1971).

# Index

*Notes*: ** following a name indicates a modern scholar whose views are cited in the text; bt = baronet.